D0935015

The Ministers Manual for 1987

SIXTY-SECOND ANNUAL ISSUE

MINISTERS MANUAL

(Doran's)

1987 EDITION

Edited by

JAMES W. COX

1817

HARPER & ROW, PUBLISHERS, SAN FRANCISCO

Cambridge, Hagerstown, New York, Philadelphia, Washington
London, Mexico City, São Paulo, Singapore, Sydney

Editors of THE MINISTERS MANUAL

G.B.F. Hallock, D.D., 1926–1958
M.K.W. Heicher, Ph.D., 1943–1968
Charles L. Wallis, M.A., M.Div., 1969–1983
James W. Cox, M.Div., Ph.D.

Acknowledgments are on page 385

THE MINISTERS MANUAL FOR 1987

Copyright © 1986 by James W. Cox. All rights reserved. Printed in the United States of America. For information address Harper & Row, Publishers, Inc., 10 East 53rd Street, New York, NY 10022. Published simultaneously in Canada by Fitzhenry & Whiteside Limited, Toronto.

FIRST EDITION

The Library of Congress has cataloged the first printing of this serial as follows:

The ministers manual: a study and pulpit guide, 1926–. New York, Harper.

V. 21–23 cm. annual.

Title varies: 1926–46, Doran's ministers manual (cover title, 1947: The Doran's ministers manual)

Editor: 1926– G. B. F. Hallock (with M. K. W. Heicher, 1942–)

1. Sermons—Outlines. 2. Homiletical illustrations. I. Hallock, Gerard Benjamin Fleet, 1856– , ed.

| BV4223.M5 | 251.058 | 25–21658 rev* |
| | [r48n2] | |

ISBN 0-06-061599-0

86 87 88 89 90 HC 10 9 8 7 6 5 4 3 2 1

PREFACE

Planning has helped worshipers through the ages to give the best account of their devotion to God. The Jewish people, from ancient times to the present, have observed special festivals that represent the work of God among them. Christians began their special observances with weekly celebrations of the Lord's Day, the first day of the week, commemorating the resurrection of Christ. Later Christian worship was expanded to include Advent and Christmas, Lent and Easter, Ascension and Pentecost, and other special days and seasons.

While many communions use great latitude in conducting their services of worship, others find it helpful to focus attention systematically on the significant events of the Christian year and to use the Lectionary as a guide for the selection of sermon texts, or at least as a check-list to determine if any important scriptures or doctrines are being overlooked. The materials in *The Ministers Manual* should be equally useful to ministers who freely choose and order their texts and to those who are committed to following the Lectionary.

A different feature this year is the series of expanded sermonic sketches based on the Gospel lessons from the Common Lectionary (Section II). Also, brief Sermon Suggestions based on the Old Testament and Epistle lessons accompany the Worship Aids for Fifty-Two Weeks (Section XI).

Once more in *The Ministers Manual* are rich resources for pastors, lay workers, Sunday school teachers, seminary students, missionaries, youth leaders, chaplains, and others.

I am grateful to many individuals and publishers for permission to quote from their material. I continue to be grateful to the trustees of The Southern Baptist Theological Seminary and to President Roy Honeycutt for their practical encouragement; to Alicia Gardner, office services supervisor; to Gaylyn Bishop, who typed the manuscript, and to Clara McCartt and Dr. Lee R. McGlone for valuable editorial assistance. I am also appreciative of the careful work of the editorial staff at Harper & Row, San Francisco.

James W. Cox
The Southern Baptist Theological Seminary
2825 Lexington Road
Louisville, Kentucky 40280

CONTENTS

SECTION I: *General Aids and Resources*

Civil Year Calendars

1987

JANUARY

S	M	T	W	T	F	S
				1	2	3
4	5	6	7	8	9	10
11	12	13	14	15	16	17
18	19	20	21	22	23	24
25	26	27	28	29	30	31

FEBRUARY

S	M	T	W	T	F	S
1	2	3	4	5	6	7
8	9	10	11	12	13	14
15	16	17	18	19	20	21
22	23	24	25	26	27	28

MARCH

S	M	T	W	T	F	S
1	2	3	4	5	6	7
8	9	10	11	12	13	14
15	16	17	18	19	20	21
22	23	24	25	26	27	28
29	30	31				

APRIL

S	M	T	W	T	F	S
			1	2	3	4
5	6	7	8	9	10	11
12	13	14	15	16	17	18
19	20	21	22	23	24	25
26	27	28	29	30		

MAY

S	M	T	W	T	F	S
					1	2
3	4	5	6	7	8	9
10	11	12	13	14	15	16
17	18	19	20	21	22	23
24	25	26	27	28	29	30
31						

JUNE

S	M	T	W	T	F	S
	1	2	3	4	5	6
7	8	9	10	11	12	13
14	15	16	17	18	19	20
21	22	23	24	25	26	27
28	29	30				

JULY

S	M	T	W	T	F	S
			1	2	3	4
5	6	7	8	9	10	11
12	13	14	15	16	17	18
19	20	21	22	23	24	25
26	27	28	29	30	31	

AUGUST

S	M	T	W	T	F	S
						1
2	3	4	5	6	7	8
9	10	11	12	13	14	15
16	17	18	19	20	21	22
23	24	25	26	27	28	29
30	31					

SEPTEMBER

S	M	T	W	T	F	S
		1	2	3	4	5
6	7	8	9	10	11	12
13	14	15	16	17	18	19
20	21	22	23	24	25	26
27	28	29	30			

OCTOBER

S	M	T	W	T	F	S
				1	2	3
4	5	6	7	8	9	10
11	12	13	14	15	16	17
18	19	20	21	22	23	24
25	26	27	28	29	30	31

NOVEMBER

S	M	T	W	T	F	S
1	2	3	4	5	6	7
8	9	10	11	12	13	14
15	16	17	18	19	20	21
22	23	24	25	26	27	28
29	30					

DECEMBER

S	M	T	W	T	F	S
		1	2	3	4	5
6	7	8	9	10	11	12
13	14	15	16	17	18	19
20	21	22	23	24	25	26
27	28	29	30	31		

1988

JANUARY

S	M	T	W	T	F	S
					1	2
3	4	5	6	7	8	9
10	11	12	13	14	15	16
17	18	19	20	21	22	23
24	25	26	27	28	29	30
31						

FEBRUARY

S	M	T	W	T	F	S
	1	2	3	4	5	6
7	8	9	10	11	12	13
14	15	16	17	18	19	20
21	22	23	24	25	26	27
28	29					

MARCH

S	M	T	W	T	F	S
		1	2	3	4	5
6	7	8	9	10	11	12
13	14	15	16	17	18	19
20	21	22	23	24	25	26
27	28	29	30	31		

APRIL

S	M	T	W	T	F	S
					1	2
3	4	5	6	7	8	9
10	11	12	13	14	15	16
17	18	19	20	21	22	23
24	25	26	27	28	29	30

MAY

S	M	T	W	T	F	S
1	2	3	4	5	6	7
8	9	10	11	12	13	14
15	16	17	18	19	20	21
22	23	24	25	26	27	28
29	30	31				

JUNE

S	M	T	W	T	F	S
			1	2	3	4
5	6	7	8	9	10	11
12	13	14	15	16	17	18
19	20	21	22	23	24	25
26	27	28	29	30		

JULY

S	M	T	W	T	F	S
					1	2
3	4	5	6	7	8	9
10	11	12	13	14	15	16
17	18	19	20	21	22	23
24	25	26	27	28	29	30
31						

AUGUST

S	M	T	W	T	F	S
	1	2	3	4	5	6
7	8	9	10	11	12	13
14	15	16	17	18	19	20
21	22	23	24	25	26	27
28	29	30	31			

SEPTEMBER

S	M	T	W	T	F	S
				1	2	3
4	5	6	7	8	9	10
11	12	13	14	15	16	17
18	19	20	21	22	23	24
25	26	27	28	29	30	

OCTOBER

S	M	T	W	T	F	S
						1
2	3	4	5	6	7	8
9	10	11	12	13	14	15
16	17	18	19	20	21	22
23	24	25	26	27	28	29
30	31					

NOVEMBER

S	M	T	W	T	F	S
		1	2	3	4	5
6	7	8	9	10	11	12
13	14	15	16	17	18	19
20	21	22	23	24	25	26
27	28	29	30			

DECEMBER

S	M	T	W	T	F	S
				1	2	3
4	5	6	7	8	9	10
11	12	13	14	15	16	17
18	19	20	21	22	23	24
25	26	27	28	29	30	31

Church and Civic Calendar for 1987

JANUARY

1 New Year's Day
  The Name of Jesus
5 Twelfth Night
6 Epiphany
15 Martin Luther King, Jr.'s Birthday
18-25 Week of Prayer for Christian Unity
18 Confession of St. Peter
19 Robert E. Lee's Birthday
25 Conversion of St. Paul
28 St. Thomas Aquinas

FEBRUARY

1 National Freedom Day
  Boy Scout Sunday
2 Presentation of Jesus in the Temple
  Groundhog Day
3 Four Chaplains Memorial Day
8 Race Relations Sunday
12 Lincoln's Birthday
14 St. Valentine's Day
15-22 Brotherhood Week
16 Washington's Birthday Observed
17 Day of Prayer for Students
22 Washington's Birthday

MARCH

3 Shrove Tuesday
4 Ash Wednesday
6 World Day of Prayer
8 First Sunday in Lent
  Girl Scout Sunday
15 Second Sunday in Lent
  Purim (Feast of Lots)
17 St. Patrick's Day
22 Third Sunday in Lent
25 The Annunciation
29 Fourth Sunday in Lent

APRIL

5 Fifth Sunday in Lent
12 Passion/Palm Sunday
12-18 Holy Week
14 Passover Begins
16 Maundy Thursday
17 Good Friday
18 Easter Eve
19 Easter
25 St. Mark, Evangelist

27-May 3 National Farm Worker Week

MAY

1 May Day
  Loyalty Day
  St. Philip and St. James, Apostles
3-10 National Family Week
10 Festival of the Christian Home
  Mother's Day
18 Victoria Day (Canada)
22 National Maritime Day
25 Memorial Day Observed
28 Ascension Day
30 Memorial Day

JUNE

3 Shavuot
7 Pentecost (Whitsunday)
  Children's Day
11 St. Barnabas, Apostle
14 Trinity Sunday
  Flag Day
21 Father's Day
29 St. Peter and St. Paul, Apostles

JULY

1 Dominion Day (Canada)
4 Independence Day
25 St. James, Apostle

AUGUST

6 The Transfiguration
15 Mary, the Mother of Jesus
24 St. Bartholomew, Apostle

SEPTEMBER

6 Labor Day Sunday
7 Labor Day
8 Birth of the Virgin Mary
21 St. Matthew, Apostle and Evangelist
24 First Day of Rosh Hashanah
27 Christian Education Sunday
  Rally Day
28 Frances Willard Day
29 St. Michael and All Angels

OCTOBER

3 Yom Kippur (Day of Atonement)
4 World Communion Sunday
  St. Francis of Assisi

7 Child Health Day
8 First Day of Sukkoth
11 Laity Sunday
12 Columbus Day
15 Shmini Atzeret
World Poetry Day
18 St. Luke, Evangelist
World Order Sunday
24 United Nations Day
25 Reformation Sunday
28 St. Simon and St. Jude, Apostles
31 Reformation Day
Halloween

NOVEMBER

1 All Saints' Day
2 All Souls' Day
3 Election Day
6 World Community Day
8 Grandparents' Day
Stewardship Day
World Peace Sunday
11 Veterans Day
Armistice Day
Remembrance Day (Canada)

22 Thanksgiving Sunday
Bible Sunday, American Bible
Society
Christ the King
26 Thanksgiving Day
29 First Sunday of Advent
30 St. Andrew, Apostle

DECEMBER

6 Second Sunday of Advent
Universal Bible Sunday
13 Third Sunday of Advent
15 Bill of Rights Day
16 First Day of Hanukkah
17 Wright Brothers Day
20 Fourth Sunday of Advent
21 St. Thomas, Apostle
24 Christmas Eve
25 Christmas Day
26 St. Stephen, Deacon and Martyr
27 St. John, Apostle and Evangelist
28 The Holy Innocents, Martyrs
31 New Year's Eve
Watch Night

Common Lectionary for 1987

The following Scripture lessons are commended for use in public worship by various Protestant churches and the Roman
Catholic church and include first, second,
Gospel readings, and Psalms according to
Cycle A from January 4 to November 26
and according to Cycle B from November
29 to December 31.

CHRISTMAS SEASON

January 4: Jer. 31:7–14 or Ecclus. 24:1–4,
12–16; Ps. 147:12–20; Eph. 1:3–6,
15–18; John 1:1–18

EPIPHANY SEASON

January 6 (Epiphany): Isa. 60:1–6; Ps.
72:1–14; Eph. 3:1–12; Matt. 2:1–12
January 11: Isa. 42:1–9; Ps. 29; Acts 10:
34–43; Matt. 3:13–17
January 18: Isa. 49:1–7; Ps. 40:1–11; 1
Cor. 1:1–9; John 1:29–34
January 25: Isa. 9:1–4; Ps. 27:1–6; 1 Cor.
1:1–17; Matt. 4:12–23

February 1: Mic. 6:1–8; Ps. 37:1–11; 1
Cor. 1:18–31; Matt. 5:1–12
February 8: Isa. 58:3–9a; Ps. 112:4–9; 1
Cor. 2:1–11; Matt. 5:13–16
February 15: Deut. 30:15–20 or Ecclus.
15:15–20; Ps. 119:1–8; 1 Cor. 3:1–9;
Matt. 5:17–26
February 22: Isa. 49:8–13; Ps. 62:5–12; 1
Cor. 3:10–11, 16–23; Matt. 5:27–37
March 1: Lev. 19:1–2, 9–18; Ps. 119:33–
40; 1 Cor. 4:1–5; Matt. 5:38–48 or
Exod. 24:12–18; Ps. 2:6–11; 2 Pet. 1:
16–21; Matt. 17:1–9

LENT

March 4 (Ash Wednesday): Joel 2:1–2;
12–17a; Ps. 51:1–12; 2 Cor. 5:20b–6:2
(3–10); Matt. 6:1–6, 16–21
March 8: Gen. 2:4b–9, 15–17, 25–3:7; Ps.
130; Rom. 5:12–19; Matt. 4:1–11
March 15: Gen. 12:1–4a (4b–8); Ps. 33:
18–22; Rom. 4:1–5 (6–12), 13–17;
John 3:1–17 or Matt. 17:1–9

March 22: Exod. 17:3–7; Ps. 95; Rom. 5:
1–11; John 4:5–26 (27–42)
March 29: 1 Sam. 16:1–13; Ps. 23; Eph.
5:8–14; John 9:1–41
April 5: Ezek. 37:1–14; Ps. 116:1–9; Rom.
8:6–11; John 11:(1–16), 17–45

HOLY WEEK

April 12 (Palm Sunday): Isa. 50:4–9a; Ps.
118:19–29; Phil. 2:5–11; Matt. 21:1–11
or (Passion Sunday) Isa. 50:4–9a; Ps.
31:9–16; Phil. 2:5–11; Matt. 26:14–
27:66 or Matt. 27:11–54
April 13 (Monday): Isa. 42:1–9; Ps. 36:5–
10; Heb. 9:11–15; John 12:1–11
April 14 (Tuesday): Isa. 49:1–7; Ps. 71:1–
12; 1 Cor. 1:18–31; John 12:20–36
April 15 (Wednesday): Isa. 50:4–9a; Ps.
70; Heb. 12:1–3; John 13:21–30
April 16 (Holy Thursday): Exod. 12:1–14;
Ps. 116:12–19; 1 Cor. 11:23–26; John
13:21–30
April 17 (Good Friday): Isa. 52:13–53:12;
Ps. 22:1–18; Heb. 4:14–16; 5:7–9; John
18:1–19:42 or John 19:17–30
April 18 (Easter Vigil): Gen. 1:1–2:2; Ps.
33; Gen. 7:1–5, 11–18; 8:6–18; 9:8–13;
Ps. 46; Gen. 22:1–18; Ps. 16; Exod.
14:10–15:1; Exod. 15:1–6, 11–13, 17–
18; Isa. 54:5–14; Ps. 30; Isa. 55:1–11;
Isa. 12:2–6; Bar. 3:9–15, 32–4:4; Ps.
19; Ezek. 36:24–28; Ps. 42; Ezek. 37:1–
14; Ps. 143; Zeph. 3:14–20; Ps. 98;
Rom. 6:3–11; Ps. 114; Mark 16:1–8

SEASON OF EASTER

April 19 (Easter): Acts 10:34–43 or Jer.
31:1–6; Ps. 118:1–14; Col. 3:1–4 or
Acts 10:34–43; John 20:1–18 or Matt.
28:1–10 (Easter Evening): Acts 5:29–
32 or Dan. 12:1–3; Ps. 150; 1 Cor. 5:6–
8 or Acts 5:29–32; Luke 24:13–49
April 26: Acts 2:14a, 22–32; Ps. 16:5–11;
1 Pet. 1:3–9; John 20:19–31
May 3: Acts 2:14a, 36–41; Ps. 116:12–19;
1 Pet. 1:17–23; Luke 24:13–35
May 10: Acts 2:42–47; Ps. 23; 1 Pet. 2:19–
25; John 10:1–10
May 17: Acts 7:55–60; Ps. 31:1–8; 1 Pet.
2:2–10; John 14:1–14
May 24: Acts 17:22–31; Ps. 66:8–20; 1
Pet. 3:13–22; John 14:15–21 (Ascension): Acts 1:1–11; Ps. 47; Eph. 1:15–

23; Luke 24:46–53 or Mark 16:9–16,
19–20
May 31: Acts 1:6–14; Ps. 68:1–10; 1 Pet.
4:12–14; 5:6–11; John 17:1–11

SEASON OF PENTECOST

June 7 (Pentecost): Acts 2:1–21 or Isa.
44:1–8; Ps. 104:24–34; 1 Cor. 12:3b–
13 or Acts 2:1–21; John 20:19–23 or
John 7:37–39
June 14 (Trinity Sunday): Deut. 4:32–40;
Ps. 33:1–12; 2 Cor. 13:5–14; Matt.
28:16–20
June 21: Gen. 28:10–17; Ps. 91:1–10;
Rom. 5:12–19; Matt. 10:24–33
June 28: Gen. 32:22–32; Ps. 17:1–7, 15;
Rom. 6:3–11; Matt. 10:34–42
July 5: Exod. 1:6–14, 22–2:10; Ps. 124;
Rom. 7:14–25a; Matt. 11:25–30
July 12: Exod. 2:11–22; Ps. 69:6–15;
Rom. 8:9–17; Matt. 13:1–9, 18–23
July 19: Exod. 3:1–12; Ps. 103:1–13;
Rom. 8:18–25; Matt. 13:24–30, 36–
43
July 26: Exod. 3:13–20; Ps. 105:1–11;
Rom. 8:26–30; Matt. 13:44–52
August 2: Exod. 12:1–14; Ps. 143:1–10;
Rom. 8:31–39; Matt. 14:13–21
August 9: Exod. 14:19–31; Ps. 106:4–12;
Rom. 9:1–5; Matt. 14:22–33
August 16: Exod. 16:2–15; Ps. 78:1–3, 10–
20; Rom. 11:13–16, 29–32; Matt. 15:
21–28
August 23: Exod. 17:1–7; Ps. 95; Rom.
11:33–36; Matt. 16:13–20
August 30: Exod. 19:1–9; Ps. 114; Rom.
12:1–13; Matt. 16:21–28
September 6: Exod. 19:16–24; Ps. 115:1–
11; Rom. 13:1–10; Matt. 18:15–20
September 13: Exod. 20:1–20; Ps. 19:7–
14; Rom. 14:5–12; Matt. 18:21–35
September 20: Exod. 32:1–14; Ps. 106:7–
8, 19–23; Phil. 1:21–27; Matt. 20:1–16
September 27: Exod. 33:12–23; Ps. 99;
Phil. 2:1–13; Matt. 21:28–32
October 4: Num. 27:12–23; Ps. 81:1–10;
Phil. 3:12–21; Matt. 21:33–43
October 11: Deut. 34:1–12; Ps. 135:1–14;
Phil. 4:1–9; Matt. 22:1–14
October 18: Ruth 1:1–19a; Ps. 146; 1
Thess. 1:1–10; Matt. 22:15–22
October 25: Ruth 2:1–13; Ps. 128; 1
Thess. 2:1–8; Matt. 22:34–46

November 1: Ruth 4:7-17; Ps. 127; 1 Thess. 2:9-13, 17-20; Matt. 23:1-12, or (All Saints' Day): Rev. 7:9-17; Ps. 34:1-10; 1 John 3:1-3; Matt. 5:1-12
November 8: Amos 5:18-24; Ps. 50:7-15; 1 Thess. 4:13-18; Matt. 25:1-13
November 15: Zeph. 1:7, 12-18; Ps. 76; 1 Thess. 5:1-11; Matt. 25:14-30
November 22: Ezek. 34:11-16, 20-24; Ps. 23; 1 Cor. 15:20-28; Matt. 25:31-46
November 26 (Thanksgiving): Deut. 8:7; Ps. 65; 2 Cor. 9:6-15; Luke 17:11-19

ADVENT

November 29: Isa. 63:16-64:8; Ps. 80:1-7; 1 Cor. 1:3-9; Mark 13:32-37
December 6: Isa. 40:1-11; Ps. 85:8-13; 2 Pet. 3:8-15a; Mark 1:1-8

December 13: Isa. 61:1-4, 8-11; Luke 1:46b-55; 1 Thess. 5:16-24; John 1:6-8, 19-28
December 20: 2 Sam. 7:8-16; Ps. 89:1-4, 19-24; Rom. 16:25-27; Luke 1:26-38

CHRISTMAS SEASON

December 24/25 (Christmas Eve/Day): Isa. 9:2-7; Ps. 96; Titus 2:11-14; Luke 2:1-20; (Additional Lessons for Christmas): Isa. 62:6-7, 10-12; Ps. 97; Isa. 52:7-10; Ps. 98; Titus 3:4-7; Heb. 1:1-12; Luke 2:8-20; John 1:1-14
December 27: Isa. 61:10-62:3; Ps. 111; Gal. 4:4-7; Luke 2:22-40
December 31 (New Year's Eve): Eccles. 3:1-13; Ps. 8; Col. 2:1-7; Matt. 9:14-17

Four-Year Church Calendar

	1987	1988	1989	1990
Ash Wednesday	March 4	February 17	February 8	February 28
Palm Sunday	April 12	March 27	March 19	April 8
Good Friday	April 17	April 1	March 24	April 13
Easter	April 19	April 3	March 26	April 15
Ascension Day	May 28	May 12	May 4	May 24
Pentecost	June 7	May 22	May 14	June 3
Trinity Sunday	June 14	May 29	May 21	June 10
Thanksgiving	November 26	November 24	November 23	November 22
Advent Sunday	November 29	November 27	December 3	December 2

Forty-Year Easter Calendar

1987 April 19	1997 March 30	2007 April 8	2017 April 16
1988 April 3	1998 April 12	2008 March 23	2018 April 1
1989 March 26	1999 April 4	2009 April 12	2019 April 21
1990 April 15	2000 April 23	2010 April 4	2020 April 12
1991 March 31	2001 April 15	2011 April 24	2021 April 4
1992 April 19	2002 March 31	2012 April 8	2022 April 17
1993 April 11	2003 April 20	2013 March 31	2023 April 9
1994 April 3	2004 April 11	2014 April 20	2024 March 31
1995 April 16	2005 March 27	2015 April 5	2025 April 20
1996 April 7	2006 April 16	2016 March 27	2026 April 5

Traditional Wedding Anniversary Identifications

1 Paper	7 Wool	13 Lace	35 Coral
2 Cotton	8 Bronze	14 Ivory	40 Ruby
3 Leather	9 Pottery	15 Crystal	45 Sapphire
4 Linen	10 Tin	20 China	50 Gold
5 Wood	11 Steel	25 Silver	55 Emerald
6 Iron	12 Silk	30 Pearl	60 Diamond

Colors Appropriate for Days and Seasons

White. Symbolizes purity, perfection, and joy and identifies festivals marking events, except Good Friday, in the life of Jesus: Christmas, Epiphany, Easter, Eastertide, Ascension Day, Trinity Sunday, All Saints' Day; weddings, funerals. Gold may also be used.

Red. Symbolizes the Holy Spirit, martyrdom, and the love of God: Good Friday, Pentecost and Sundays following.
Violet. Symbolizes penitence: Advent, Lent.
Green. Symbolizes mission to the world, hope, regeneration, nurture, and growth: Epiphany season, Kingdomtide, Rural Life Sunday, Labor Sunday, Thanksgiving Sunday.
Blue. Advent, in some churches.

Flowers in Season Appropriate for Church Use

January. Carnation or snowdrop.
February. Violet or primrose.
March. Jonquil or daffodil.
April. Lily, sweet pea, or daisy.
May. Lily of the valley or hawthorn.
June. Rose or honeysuckle.
July. Larkspur or water lily.

August. Gladiolus or poppy.
September. Aster or morning glory.
October. Calendula or cosmos.
November. Chrysanthemum.
December. Narcissus, holly, or poinsettia.

Historical, Cultural, and Religious Anniversaries in 1987

Compiled by Kenneth M. Cox

10 Years (1977). *January 1:* The Episcopal Church ordains the first woman priest since sanctioning their ordination the year before. *June 20:* Trans-Alaska pipeline opens, as oil begins 800-mile journey from Prudhoe Bay to Valdez. *August 16:* Elvis Presley dies in Memphis (b. 1935). *August 19:* Julius Henry (Groucho) Marx dies in Los Angeles (b. 1890). *December 25:* Charlie Chaplin dies in Switzerland (b. 1889).

20 Years (1967). *June 5:* The Six-Day Arab-Israeli War begins, renewing violence and unrest in the Middle East. *October 2:* Thurgood Marshall is sworn in as the nation's first black Supreme Court justice. *December 2:* First human heart transplanted at Groote Schuur Hospital, Cape Town, South Africa, by Dr. Christiaan Barnard.

25 Years (1962). *February 7:* Astronaut John Glenn makes the first U.S. orbits of Earth in a Mercury capsule 160 miles above the planet surface. *April 1:* Pope John XXIII orders retention of Latin as the language of the Roman Catholic Church. *June 25:* U.S. Supreme Court rules mandatory reading of prayers in public schools unconstitutional. *October:* Cuban missile crisis brings United States and Soviet Union close to war. *October 11:* Pope John XXIII convenes the Second Vatican Council in Rome. *November 7:* Eleanor Roosevelt dies in New York City (b. 1884).

30 Years (1957). *March 25:* Treaty of Rome is signed by six European nations, establishing a European Economic Community (the Common Market) to promote competition with the United States and Great Britain. *September 9:* President Eisenhower signs into law the first U.S. civil rights act enacted since Civil War reconstruction days. *October 4:* Soviet Union launches the unmanned spacecraft Sputnik I, spurring a space race with the United States.

40 Years (1947). Dead Sea Scrolls discovered at Khirbet Qumran. Brooklyn Dodger Jackie Robinson breaks the color barrier by becoming baseball's first black major-leaguer. Norwegian anthropologist and explorer Thor Heyerdahl crosses the open Pacific Ocean in 101 days aboard his balsa raft Kon-Tiki.

45 Years (1942). Adolf Hitler and his Gestapo chief Heinrich Himmler begin their methodical annihilation of European Jews. *February 19:* President Roosevelt issues an executive order under which 110,000 Japanese-Americans living in coastal Pacific areas are placed in concentration camps.

50 Years (1937). Diabetics are treated

for the first time with zinc promatine insulin. President Roosevelt's court-packing scheme to reform the U.S. Supreme Court is defeated. *May 6:* The hydrogen-filled dirigible *Hindenburg* explodes at Lakehurst, N.J., ending the brief era of transatlantic dirigible travel. *May 27:* San Francisco's Golden Gate Bridge opens, then the world's longest suspension bridge. *June 4:* An Oklahoma City grocer introduces the supermarket shopping cart, beginning a revolution in food buying. *June 11:* George Gershwin dies (b. 1898).

60 Years (1927). Protestant World Conference on Faith and Order is held at Lausanne, Switzerland. *May 21:* Aviator Charles Lindbergh lands his single-engine monoplane *Spirit of St. Louis* in Paris, completing the first nonstop transatlantic flight. *August 23:* Nicola Sacco and Bartolomeo Vanzetti die in an electric chair at Dedham Prison in Massachusetts, despite nationwide efforts to have authorities drop charges for lack of evidence.

75 Years (1912). The *Book of Common Prayer* of the Episcopal Church of Scotland is revised. *March 1:* Captain Albert Louis makes the first parachute drop from an aircraft. *March 12:* The Girl Scouts of America begins in Savannah, Ga. *April 15:* The "unsinkable" S. S. *Titanic* scrapes an iceberg and sinks in the icy North Atlantic, as 1,513 people die.

100 Years (1887). *March 8:* Congregational minister Henry Ward Beecher dies in Brooklyn, N.Y. (b. 1813). *June 21:* Britain's Queen Victoria celebrates her Golden Jubilee. *November 13:* The Irish "Bloody Sunday" takes place in London.

125 Years (1862). *February:* Julia Ward Howe's "The Battle Hymn of the Republic" appears in *The Atlantic Monthly*. *May 6:* Henry David Thoreau dies in Concord, Mass. (b. 1817). *September 11:* O. Henry (William Sidney Porter) born in Greensboro, N.C. (d. 1910). *September 22:* President Lincoln issues the Emancipation Proclamation, declaring all slaves free effective the next year.

150 Years (1837). *March 3:* President Jackson officially recognizes the Republic of Texas, after approval by Congress. *June 20:* Queen Victoria begins a sixty-four-year reign over the British Empire. Samuel Morse invents the telegraph in New York.

175 Years (1812). *February 7:* Charles Dickens born in Portsmouth, Hampshire, England (d. 1870). *February 23:* Napolean annuls the Concordat. *May 7:* Poet Robert Browning born in London (d. 1889). *June:* Pope Pius VII is brought to Fontainebleau as a prisoner. *June 18:* President Madison declares war on Britain, beginning the War of 1812.

200 Years (1787). *September 17:* America's Constitutional Convention passes the federal Constitution. *October 27:* First of the "Federalist Papers" appears under the name "Publius" in the New York *Independent Journal*, explaining the new Constitution. Right Reverend Charles Inglis is made Bishop of Nova Scotia, becoming the first Anglican bishop in Canada.

250 Years (1737). University of Gottingen founded. *January 29:* Political writer Thomas Paine born in England (d. 1809).

300 Years (1687). Unconverted Huguenots are banished from France. Sir Isaac Newton publishes his *Principia Mathematica*. *April 2:* James II issues the Declaration of Indulgence, suspending all penal laws against Catholics and nonconformists.

325 Years (1662). *May 19:* The Act of Uniformity requires use of the *Book of Common Prayer* and consent of Anglican clergy to the *Thirty-Nine Articles*. Connecticut is granted a charter.

375 Years (1612). Two Unitarians are burned at the stake, the last heretics to be burned in England. Japanese edict forbids Christianity.

400 Years (1587). Vatican Press is established. *February 8:* Mary, Queen of Scots, is beheaded at Fotheringay Castle by order of her cousin Elizabeth.

425 Years (1562). Huguenots are formally recognized in France by the Edict of St. Germain, which permits them to worship outside towns.

450 Years (1537). Pope Paul III excommunicates all Catholics engaging in slave trade, voiding all contracts made by Catholics who have deprived Africans of liberty or goods.

525 Years (1462). Pope Pius II annuls the *Compactate* of Iihlava, forbidding the chalice to the laity.

575 Years (1412). St. Joan of Arc born (d. 1431).
600 Years (1387). Geoffrey Chaucer begins *The Canterbury Tales* (completed 1400).
650 Years (1337). Edward III of England claims the French throne, and the Hundred Years' War begins.
825 Years (1162). Thomas Becket begins his tenure as Archbishop of Canterbury (d. 1170).

Anniversaries of Hymns, Hymn Writers and Hymn-Tune Composers in 1987

Compiled by Hugh T. McElrath

25 Years (1962). Death of Clifford Bax (b. 1886), author of "Turn back, O man, forswear thy foolish ways"; Alfred S. Loizeaux (b. 1877), author of stanza 3 of "God our Father, we adore Thee"; B. E. Hardy (b. 1897), composer of WHEELER ("Behold, a little child").

50 Years (1937). Birth of Peter Cutts, composer of SHILLINGFORD, WYLDE GREEN, and many tunes set mostly to hymns of his contemporary, Brian Wren; Broadman Ware, author of "Teach me, O Lord, to care"; Philip M. Young, composer of ACCLAMATION ("O gracious Lord, accept our praise"); John Ylvisaker, arranger of BABYLONIAN RIVERS ("By the Babylonian rivers"). Death of George Currie Martin (b. 1865), author of "Thy words to me are life and health"; William Rowlands (1860), composer of BLAENWERN ("Love divine all loves excelling"); Hampton H. Sewell (b. 1874), composer of SEWELL ("He included me"); Arthur Somervell (b. 1863), composer of WINDERMERE ("We give Thee but Thine own"), CHORUS ANGELORUM ("Praise to the Holiest in the height") and others; Su Yin-Lan (b. 1915), composer of SHENG EN ("The bread of life for all men broken"); Clara T. Williams (b. 1858), author of "Satisfied."

75 Years (1912). Birth of Graham George (b. 1912), composer of THE KING'S MAJESTY ("Ride on, ride on in majesty"); Eva B. Lloyd, author of "Come, all Christians, be committed"; J. Edwin Orr, author of "Search me, O God"; Lloyd Stone, author of "This is my song." Death of William G. Fischer, (b. 1835), composer of FISCHER ("Whiter than snow") and HANKEY ("I love to tell the story"); George W. Kitchin (b. 1827), author of "Lift high the cross"; Albert L. Peace, composer of ST. MARGARET ("O love that wilt not let me go").

100 Years (1887). Birth of Alfred H. Ackley (d. 1960), author and composer of "He lives" (ACKLEY); G. F. Brockless (d. 1957), composer of FRITWELL ("Forget them not, O Christ, who stand"); C. Edgar Knowles (d. 1973), composer of MAHON ("Thou has made us for Thy glory"); Vera E. Walker, author of "Forth rode the knights of old"; Death of Jessie Seymour Irvine (b. 1836), composer of CRIMOND ("The Lord's my shepherd"); Richard Massie (b. 1800), translator of "Christ Jesus lay in death's strong bands" (Luther); Ludwig M. Lindeman (b. 1812), author of "Built on the rock the church doth stand"; William H. Monk (b. 1823), composer of EVENTIDE ("Abide with me") and arranger of DIX ("For the beauty of the earth" and others); George A. Macfarren (b. 1813), composer of DEDICATION ("Father, let me dedicate"); Ray Palmer (b. 1808), author of "My faith looks up to Thee" and "Jesus, these eyes have never seen" and translator of "Jesus, thou joy of loving hearts"; Rowland H. Prichard (b. 1811), composer of HYFRYDOL ("Praise the Lord, ye heavens, adore him" and many others); Joseph Tritton (b. 1819), author of "Head of the church and Lord of all"; George J. Webb (b. 1803), composer of WEBB ("Stand up, stand up for Jesus" and others).

125 Years (1862). Birth of Alfred E. Alston (d. 1927), translator of "Father most holy, merciful, loving"; Francis Duckworth (d. 1941), composer of RIMINGTON ("Give to our God immortal praise"); W. Stillman Martin (d. 1935), composer of GOD CARES ("God will take care of you"); Leila N. Morris (d. 1929), "What if it were

today?" (SECOND COMING) and "Let Jesus come into your heart" (MCCONNELSVILLE); Henry Newbolt (d. 1938), author of "O Lord almighty, thou whose hands"; H. Ernest Nichol (d. 1926), author and composer of "We've a story to tell to the nations" (MESSAGE); Adelaide A. Pollard (d. 1934), author of "Have thine own way, Lord"; Anna B. Russell (d. 1954), author of "Wonderful, wonderful Jesus"; Ernest W. Shurtleff (d. 1917), author of "Lead on, O King eternal"; Robert George Thompson (d. 1934), composer of BLAIR-GOWRIE ("Away with gloom, away with doubt").

125 Years (1862). Death of Harriet Auber (b. 1773), author of "Our blest Redeemer, ere he breathed"; George W. Bethune (b. 1805), author of "There is no name so sweet"; Neil Dougall (b. 1776), composer of KILMARNOCK ("Come, let us to the Lord our God" and others); Robert Edwards (b. 1796), composer of CAER-SALEM ("O'er the gloomy hills of darkness"); Bernard S. Ingemann (b. 1787), author of "Through the night of doubt and sorrow"; Andrew Reed (b. 1787), author of "Holy Spirit, light divine"; John H. Gurney (b. 1802), author of "Lord, as to thy dear cross we flee."

150 Years (1837). Birth of E. W. Bullinger (d. 1913), composer of WELLINGHAM ("From the north and south and east and west") and BULLINGER ("God, who touchest earth with beauty"); Oscar Clute (d. 1902), author of "O love of God most full"; William C. Dix (d. 1898), author of "As with gladness men of old," "Alleluia! Sing to Jesus," and "What child is this?"; O. M. Feilden (d. 1924), composer of ENON (ST. JOHN BAPTIST) ("O my Savior, lifted"); Alfred R. Gaul (d. 1913), composer of DEDICATION ("What can I give to Jesus"); Henry L. Gilmore (d. 1920), author of "The haven of rest"; William B. Hays (d. 1885), author of "Revive us again"; John R. Sweney (d. 1899), composer of SWENEY ("More about Jesus"), SUNSHINE ("Sunshine in my soul") and STORY OF JESUS ("Tell me the story of Jesus"); A. C. Swinburne (d. 1909), author of "Thou whose birth on earth"; James Walch (d. 1901), composer of SAWLEY ("God, make my life a shining light") and

TIDINGS ("We've a story to tell to the nations"); John H. Yates (d. 1900), author of "Faith is the victory." Death of Samuel Wesley (b. 1766), composer of BETHLEHEM ("And let our bodies part") and DON-CASTER ("Put thou thy trust in God").

175 Years (1812). Birth of George N. Allen (d. 1877), author of "Must Jesus bear the cross alone"; John Hullah (d. 1887), composer of BENTLEY ("O word of God incarnate"); Ludwig M. Lindeman (d. 1887), author of "Built on the rock the church doth stand."

200 Years (1787). Birth of Franz Gruber (d. 1863), composer of STILLE NACHT ("Silent Night"); Henri A. Madan (d. 1864), composer of HENDON ("Take me life and let it be consecrated," "Ask ye what great thing I know"); Andrew Reed (d. 1862), author of "Holy Spirit, light divine." Rippon's *Selection of Hymns*, source of the anonymous "How firm a foundation."

250 Years (1737). Birth of Johann Michael Haydn (d. 1809), composer of LYONS ("O worship the King"). Death of John Bishop (b. ca. 1665), composer of ILLSLEY ("He wants not friends that hath not love"); Benjamin Schmolk (b. 1672), author of "My Jesus, as thou wilt," "Blessed Savior, we are here," and "Open now the gates of beauty."

275 Years (1712). Birth of Joseph Hart (d. 1768), author of "Come, ye sinners, poor and needy."

325 Years (1662). Birth of Samuel Wesley (d. 1735), author of "Behold the Savior of mankind." Death of Johann Crueger (b. 1596), composer of NUN DANKET ALLE GOTT ("Now thank we all our God"), GRAEFEN-BURG ("We walk by faith and not by sight"), HERZLIEBSTER JESU ("Ah, holy Jesus, how hast thou offended?"), JESU MEINE FREUDE ("Jesus, priceless treasure") and others; Henry Lawes (b. 1598), composer of LAWE'S PSALM 47 ("Son of the Lord most high"), WHITEHALL (PSALM VIII) ("None lacks a friend who hath thy love").

350 Years (1637). Birth of Johann C. Ebeling (d. 1676), composer of BONN (FROEHLICH SOLL) ("All my heart this night rejoices") and DU MEINE SEELE SINGEN ("O happy band of pilgrims"); Thomas Ken (d. 1711), author of "Praise God from all blessings flow," "All praise to thee, my

God this night," and "Awake, my soul, and with the sun." Death of Ben Jonson (b. 1573), author of "I sing the birth was born tonight."

375 Years (1612). Death of Hans Leo Hassler (b. 1564), composer of PASSION CHORALE ("O sacred head now wounded"). Original publication of the Ainsworth Psalter, the psalter brought to America by the Pilgrim founders of Plymouth Colony in 1620. Tunes surviving from this psalter: OLD HUNDREDTH ("All people that on earth do dwell"); OLD 124TH ("Turn back, O man, forswear thy foolish ways") and PSALM 68 ("Great God, arise and with thy might").

Quotable Quotations

1. God's opposition to evil is in reality the opposition of love whereby love maintains its purity.—Gustaf Aulen.

2. Christ changes all our sunsets into dawns.—Clement of Alexandria.

3. You can be idle for him, if so he wills, with the same joy with which you once labored for him.—Phillips Brooks.

4. The heart has its reasons which reason knows nothing of.—Blaise Pascal.

5. The one aim and end of all we have inherited, all we have been taught, in our Christian homes and in the Church of Christ, is that we should, each one, and all in fellowship, come to have Jesus Christ as our own Lord and Master, the eternal God as our Father and our Friend, in the communion of the Holy Spirit.—D. M. Baillie.

6. Religion always appears under two contrasted guises. . . . It is first an austere and disturbing challenge, and then it is a glorious and happy feast.—John Baillie.

7. Man finds it hard to get what he wants, because he does not want the best; God finds it hard to give, because he would give the best, and man will not take it.—George Macdonald.

8. The tendency to claim God as an ally for our partisan values and ends is . . . the source of all religious fanaticism.—Reinhold Niebuhr.

9. There is only one way that self can ever be healthily denied or taken away, and that is by letting God love it off our hands.—John Claypool.

10. When you see a man with a great deal of religion displayed in his shop window, you may depend upon it he keeps a very small stock of it within.—Charles Haddon Spurgeon.

11. Hating people is like burning down your own house to get rid of a rat.—Harry Emerson Fosdick.

12. Many might go to heaven with half the labor they go to hell, if they would venture their industry the right way.—Ben Jonson.

13. God will not look you over for medals, degrees, or diplomas, but for scars.—Elbert Hubbard.

14. Religion is the best armor in the world, but the worst cloak.—John Newton.

15. God tempers the wind to the shorn lamb.—Laurence Sterne.

16. In giving freedom to the slave, we assure freedom to the free—honorable alike in what we give and what we preserve.—Abraham Lincoln.

17. The fear of death is worse than death.—Robert Burton.

18. Truth is truth, whether from the lips of Jesus or Balaam.—George Macdonald.

19. Habit, which is the power by which evil rules us, is only strong in a vacant life.—Phillips Brooks.

20. What keeps the wild hope of Christmas alive year after year in a world notorious for dashing all hopes is the haunting dream that the child who was born that day may yet be born again even in us and our own snowbound, snowblind longing for him.—Frederick Buechner.

21. Many have puzzled themselves about the origin of evil; I observe that there is evil, and that there is a way to escape it, and with this I begin and end.—John Newton.

22. Deeper than the daily news is the providence of God.—John P. Newport.

23. Integrity has no need of rules.—Albert Camus.

24. I do not know what I may appear to the world; but to myself I seem to have been only like a boy playing on the seashore, and diverting myself by now and

then finding a smooth pebble or a prettier shell than ordinary, while the great ocean of truth lay all undiscovered before me. —Sir Isaac Newton.

25. The soul is dyed the color of its leisure thought.—Marcus Aurelius.

26. A secular life tends to narrow our outlook because it induces us to close the book after reading the first chapter. A Christian life compels us to leave the book open to the end.—Emile Cammaerts.

27. Be ready at all times for the gifts of God, and always for new ones.—Meister Eckhart.

28. It takes a first-class preacher and a first-class hearer to get up a first-class sermon.—Sam P. Jones.

29. It is an old paradox: independent people who regularly separate themselves from the crowd will often be the ones whom the crowd most wants to follow. —Alan Loy McGinnis.

30. Habit if not resisted soon becomes necessity.—St. Augustine.

31. There are two types of churches in the world today: churches on maintenance and churches on mission.—D. Wade Armstrong.

32. The Providence that watches over the affairs of men works out of their mistakes, at times, a healthier issue than could have been accomplished by their wisest forethought.—J. A. Froude.

33. There is just as much religion in laughing as in crying.—Sam P. Jones.

34. A man takes a drink; then the drink takes a drink; and next the drink takes the man.—Japanese proverb.

35. Only Christian hope is hope, for it is hope that is grounded in God.—Raymond Bryan Brown.

36. A man lives by believing something, not by debating and arguing about many things.—Thomas Carlyle.

37. Let your religion be less of a theory and more of a love affair.—G. K. Chesterton.

38. Anyone can carry his burden, however hard, until nightfall. Anyone can do his work, however hard, for one day. Anyone can live sweetly, patiently, lovingly, purely, till the sun goes down.—Robert Louis Stevenson.

39. Strange to see how a good dinner and feasting reconciles everybody.—Samuel Pepys.

40. He will never know the height of true joy who has not the capacity for deepest grief. Music cannot come from a violin while the strings are loose.—Leslie R. Smith.

41. Do you wish to find out a person's weak points? Note the failings he has the quickest eye for in others.—J. C. and A. W. Hare.

42. There can be no faith so feeble that Christ does not respond to it.—Alexander Maclaren.

43. Your Won't power ought to be equal to your Will power.—Sam P. Jones.

44. I could not say I believe. I know! I have had the experience of being gripped by something that is stronger than myself, something that people call God.—Carl G. Jung.

45. No man is useless while he has a friend.—Robert Louis Stevenson.

46. Pray often; for prayer is a shield to the soul, a sacrifice to God, and a scourge for Satan.—John Bunyan.

47. The one principle of hell is—"I am my own!"—George Macdonald.

48. Riches enlarge, rather than satisfy appetites.—Thomas Fuller.

49. There is little we touch, but we leave the print of our fingers behind.—Richard Baxter.

50. Die when I may, I want it said of me by those who knew me best, that I always plucked a thistle and planted a flower where I thought a flower would grow. —Abraham Lincoln.

51. Doubt comes in at the window when inquiry is denied at the door.—Benjamin Jowett.

52. Faith is saying amen to God.—Merv Rosell.

53. If one wants to see genuine beauty, he will find it in the tender lines which sacrificial love has drawn upon a mother's face.—Leslie R. Smith.

54. If thou bear the cross cheerfully, it will bear thee.—Thomas à Kempis.

55. Men never do evil so completely and cheerfully as when they do it from religious conviction.—Blaise Pascal.

56. We have within us, each one, so much more of his power than we ever

spend—such misers of miracles we are, such pinchpenny guardians of grace.—Frederick Buechner.

57. When someone tells me that he has never had a moment of probing religious doubt I find myself wondering whether he had ever known a moment of vital religious conviction.—Harold A. Bosley.

58. Unholy tempers are always unhappy tempers.—John Wesley.

59. A man stands revealed both by the things he strives to gain and by those he seeks to avoid.—Everett Dean Martin.

60. Every great and commanding movement in the annals of the world is the triumph of enthusiasm.—Ralph Waldo Emerson.

61. Satisfaction comes from the process and the attainment of the goal, not possession of it.—Ari Kiev.

62. There is no way of photographing the future. But we may all blueprint it, and do our best to make the resultant structure correspond to our hopeful blueprints.—Clement Wood.

63. What a man believes may be ascertained not from his creed, but from the assumptions on which he habitually acts.—George Bernard Shaw.

64. The word of cheap grace has been the ruin of more Christians than any commandment of works.—Dietrich Bonhoeffer.

65. God respects me when I work, but he loves me when I sing.—Rabindranath Tagore.

66. From God there is no flight, but unto him.—*The Koran.*

67. It is more important to do than to do well.—Albert Ellis.

68. Faith in immortality is not the child of human feebleness seeking an opiate; it springs from human strength pounding against the too narrow bars of our mortality.—Harry Emerson Fosdick.

69. The saints have been more acutely aware of sin precisely because they are saints; their convex, more rounded out towards God, has implied a deeper concave.—George A. Buttrick.

70. Welcome, welcome, cross of Christ, if Christ be with it.—Samuel Rutherford.

71. God's heart is big enough to encompass the universe and near enough to feel our sorrow.—James W. Cox.

72. Be willing to have it so. Acceptance of what has happened is the first step to overcoming the consequences of any misfortune.—William James.

73. He who waits to do a great deal of good at once, will never do any thing.—Samuel Johnson.

74. The Lord gets his best soldiers out of the highlands of affliction.—Charles Haddon Spurgeon.

75. Do what you can, with what you have, where you are.—Theodore Roosevelt.

76. Scenery is fine—but human nature is finer.—John Keats.

77. The lot assigned to every man is suited to him, and suits him to itself.—Marcus Aurelius.

78. You can become wise by noticing what happens when you aren't.—Laurence J. Peter.

79. Nowadays people know the price of everything and the value of nothing.—Oscar Wilde.

80. I can hardly think there was ever any scared into heaven.—Sir Thomas Browne.

81. Who rises from prayer a better man, his prayer is answered.—George Meredith.

82. "Do the duty which lies nearest thee," which thou knowest to be a duty! Thy second duty will already have become clearer.—Thomas Carlyle.

83. When any duty is to be done, it is fortunate for you if you feel like doing it; but, if you do not feel like it, that is no reason for not doing it.—Washington Gladden.

84. The time to relax is when you don't have time for it.—Sydney J. Harris.

85. Some persons grumble because God places thorns among roses. Why not thank God he placed roses among thorns?—Anonymous.

86. Home is where the heart is.—Pliny.

87. Fear is the father of courage and the mother of safety.—Henry H. Tweedy.

88. The greatest happiness you can have is knowing that you do not necessarily require happiness.—William Saroyan.

89. Laws are never as effective as habits.—Adlai Stevenson.

90. Example is the most powerful rhetoric.—Thomas Brooks.

91. When God, who sees all and who wishes to save us, upsets our designs, we stupidly complain against him, we accuse his providence. We do not comprehend that in punishing us, in overturning our plans and causing us suffering, he is doing all this to deliver us, to open the Infinite to us.—Victor Hugo.

92. Many are deceived in the end who at first seemed to be led by the Holy Spirit. —Thomas à Kempis.

93. There is no beautifier of complexion, or form, or behavior, like the wish to scatter joy and not pain around us. —Ralph Waldo Emerson.

94. He that voluntarily continues ignorant is guilty of all the crimes which ignorance produces.—Samuel Johnson.

95. The sin that ruins the world roots back into the sins we personally consent to.—Harry Emerson Fosdick.

96. The fact that we do not always "feel" the answer to prayer should not discourage us. A sailor measures his progress by the stars, not by the temperature in the cabin.—George A. Buttrick.

97. You cannot find, I believe, a case in the Bible where a man is converted without God's calling in some human agency— using some human instrument.—D. L. Moody.

98. Fortunately, analysis is not the only way to resolve inner conflicts. Life itself remains a very effective therapist.—Karen Horney.

99. People ask you for criticism, but they only want praise.—Somerset Maugham.

100. The Scripture is to be its own interpreter, or rather the Spirit speaking in it; nothing can cut the diamond but the diamond; nothing can interpret Scripture but Scripture.—Richard Watson.

Questions of Life and Religion

These questions may be useful to prime homiletic pumps, as discussion starters, or for study and youth groups.

1. Are religion and psychiatry friends or enemies?

2. How can we reconcile suffering and death with the love of God?

3. Is tithing a practical way of fulfilling our Christian stewardship?

4. Does the New Testament do away with the need for the Old Testament?

5. What are constructive ways of expressing anger?

6. What can we do about the common uneasy feeling of being "found out"?

7. What should be the attitude of Christians toward scientific knowledge?

8. Does "positive thinking" contribute to physical health?

9. How does the historical Jesus help our understanding of God?

10. Do parents and children ever have to be adversaries?

11. What does it mean to pray "in Jesus' name"?

12. How can we effectively share our Christian faith with our friends?

13. Did God quit speaking when the New Testament canon was completed?

14. How does one handle a series of personal or family misfortunes?

15. What should be our attitude toward people whose way of life offends our moral sensibilities?

16. Can we ever call suffering the will of God?

17. How can a criminal make a spiritual comeback?

18. Is the Bible outmoded?

19. What is the meaning of baptism?

20. What is the meaning of the Lord's Supper or Holy Communion?

21. How important is a public confession of faith in Jesus Christ as Lord and Savior?

22. Why is preaching necessary?

23. What causes religious doubt?

24. What is "cheap grace"?

25. How sure can we be of God and the promises in the Bible?

26. What should be our attitude toward other religions?

27. Is it ever right to compromise our convictions?

28. Did Jesus Christ abolish the Ten Commandments?

29. In what sense is the cross the means of our salvation?

30. Do we need creeds?

31. What must we do to be saved?

32. Is divorce ever right?

33. Why is the resurrection of Jesus Christ important?

34. What should we do about our enemies?

35. What is the meaning of "freedom in Christ"?

36. How can one recognize and test a call to a special Christian vocation?

37. Why doesn't God stop war?

38. How can parents bring out the best in their children?

39. How can Jesus be our example today?

40. What guidelines can help us interpret the Bible for inquiring minds?

41. What authority should the pastor have in the local church?

42. What should we pray for?

43. How can we explain or justify the inequities of life?

44. When is a person truly successful?

45. Can work become a harmful compulsion?

46. What evidence do we have for the truth of Christianity?

47. What is the relationship of faith and reason?

48. What can nature tell us of God?

49. Are our decisions and actions planned by God?

50. What is implied by our being "the body of Christ"?

51. Can we expect miracles to happen today?

52. What can we do to make Christianity more attractive to unbelievers?

53. Should we enjoy life while others cannot enjoy it?

54. What results can we expect from prayer?

55. How can we set up a continuing practice of family worship?

56. Is there value in confessing our sins?

57. How can we make good decisions?

58. How can we prepare for old age?

59. Is it right to "toot your own horn"?

60. What can we do to deepen our ap-preciation of people we think very different from ourselves?

61. Should the world of business have ethical standards different from other aspects of life?

62. Is voting a moral issue?

63. What is love?

64. Can conscience be a bad guide?

65. How does one learn patience?

66. What is the evidence for genuine conversion?

67. Should a good person expect to be criticized?

68. Is fear of death a normal attitude?

69. How can we learn what God wants us to do in particular cases?

70. What can we do to encourage downhearted and defeated people?

71. What should we do when people reject our efforts to do them good?

72. What can we do when we are afraid?

73. Can we worship just as well outside the church?

74. How can we gain and keep friends?

75. Does goal setting have value for Christian service?

76. What harm is there in gossip?

77. What steps can we take to grow in our Christian life?

78. Are handicaps ever helpful?

79. What is true happiness?

80. When is humility appropriate?

81. Is laughter a Christian virtue?

82. What does the Bible teach about the future life?

83. What qualities should we find in Christian leaders?

84. How can we keep a marriage alive?

85. What is a miracle?

86. Is the making of money dangerous?

87. When does proper zeal become improper fanaticism?

88. How can we prepare to serve the world outside the church?

89. What guidelines will help us to tell right from wrong?

90. Is it possible for Christians to serve idols?

91. Is work a curse or a blessing?

92. What is the difference between knowledge and wisdom?

93. Is war ever Christian?

94. Should we think of trouble as God's punishment?

95. How can we apply the Ten Commandments to life today?
96. Is drinking alcoholic beverages a religious problem?
97. What is success?

98. Is self-fulfillment a worthy goal?
99. Should we sacrifice ourselves for others?
100. Who is a saint?

Biblical Benedictions and Blessings

The Lord watch between me and thee, when we are absent from one another. —Gen. 31:49.

The Lord bless thee, and keep thee; the Lord make his face to shine upon thee, and be gracious unto thee; the Lord lift up his countenance upon thee, and give thee peace.—Num. 6:24–26.

The Lord our God be with us, as he was with our fathers; let him not leave us, nor forsake us; that he may incline our hearts unto him, to walk in all his ways, and to keep his commandments, and his statutes, and his judgments, which he commanded our fathers.—1 Kings 8:57–58.

Let the words of my mouth, and the meditation of my heart, be acceptable in thy sight, O Lord, my strength, and my redeemer.—Ps. 19:14.

Now the God of patience and consolation grant you to be likeminded one toward another according to Christ Jesus; that ye may with one mind and one mouth glorify God, even the Father of our Lord Jesus Christ. Now the God of hope fill you with all joy and peace in believing, that ye may abound in hope, through the power of the Holy Ghost. Now the God of peace be with you all.—Rom. 15:5–6, 13, 33.

Now to him that is of power to establish you according to my gospel, and the preaching of Jesus Christ, according to the revelation of the mystery, which was kept secret since the world began, but now is manifest, and by the scriptures of the prophets, according to the commandment of the everlasting God, made known to all nations for the obedience of faith: to God only wise, be glory through Jesus Christ for ever.—Rom. 16:25–27.

Grace be unto you, and peace, from God our Father, and from the Lord Jesus Christ.—1 Cor. 1:3.

The grace of the Lord Jesus Christ and the love of God, and the communion of the Holy Ghost, be with you all.—2 Cor. 13:14.

Peace be to the brethren, and love with faith, from God the Father and the Lord Jesus Christ. Grace be with all them that love our Lord Jesus Christ in sincerity. —Eph. 6:23–24.

And the peace of God, which passeth all understanding, shall keep your hearts and minds through Christ Jesus. Finally, brethren, whatsoever things are true, whatsoever things are honest, whatsoever things are just, whatsoever things are pure, whatsoever things are lovely, whatsoever things are of good report; if there be any virtue, and if there by any praise, think on these things. Those things, which ye have both learned, and received, and heard, and seen in me, do; and the God of peace shall be with you. —Phil. 4:7–9.

Wherefore also we pray always for you, that our God would count you worthy of this calling, and fulfill all the good pleasure of his goodness, and the work of faith with power; that the name of our Lord Jesus Christ may be glorified in you, and ye in him, according to the grace of our God and the Lord Jesus Christ.—2 Thess. 1:11–12.

Now the Lord of peace himself give you peace always by all means. The Lord be with you all. The grace of our Lord Jesus Christ be with you all.—2 Thess. 3:16–18.

Grace, mercy, and peace, from God our Father and Jesus Christ our Lord.—1 Tim. 1:2.

Now the God of peace, that brought again from the dead our Lord Jesus, that great shepherd of the sheep, through the blood of the everlasting covenant, make you perfect in every good work to do his will, working in you that which is well-pleasing in his sight, through Jesus Christ, to whom be glory for ever and ever.—Heb. 13:20-21.

The God of all grace, who hath called us unto his eternal glory by Christ Jesus, after that ye have suffered a while, make you perfect, establish, strengthen, settle you. To him be glory and dominion for ever and ever. Greet ye one another with a kiss of charity. Peace be with you all that are in Christ Jesus.—1 Pet. 5:10-11, 14.

Grace be with you, mercy, and peace, from God the Father, and from the Lord Jesus Christ, the Son of the Father, in truth and love.—2 John 3.

Now unto him that is able to keep you from falling, and to present you faultless before the presence of his glory with exceeding joy, to the only wise God our Savior, be glory and majesty, dominion and power, both now and ever.—Jude 24-25.

Grace be unto you, and peace, from him which was, and which is to come; and from the seven Spirits which are before his throne; and from Jesus Christ, who is the faithful witness, and the first begotten of the dead, and the prince of the kings of the earth. Unto him that loved us, and washed us from our sins in his own blood, and hath made us kings and priests unto God and his Father; to him be glory and dominion for ever and ever.—Rev. 1:4-6.

SECTION II.
Vital Messages from the Lectionary
(Gospel Texts)

January 4. (Epiphany Sunday). Wisdom for All the World

TEXT: Matt. 2:1–12.

Wise men came from the East seeking a special person—the king of the Jews. Perhaps they were scholars from Persia. In any case, they were steeped in ancient lore. All signs from their studies and discussions pointed in one direction. A star became their guide, and they followed its leading. To them it was the quest of a lifetime. It was even more: it represented what the ages had yearned for. Therefore, nothing was too costly to celebrate that magnificent event. Inconveniences and hazards of travel were trivial. Gold, frankincense, and myrrh were proper gifts to bring. So they came across the miles, bearing their precious gifts, to do homage to him who was to be not only the king of the Jews, but of worlds upon worlds, King of kings and Lord of lords.

Behind the drama of the wise men was a larger story that reached into the dim past, outward to the farthest reaches of humanity, and inward to the individual hearts of the wise men themselves. What were the significant factors in the coming of the wise men?

I. *The coming of the wise men signaled universal need.* The hearts of people everywhere in all times have sought God. They have not always sought him by name. Every restless longing for something or someone better, more powerful, more just, more loving, someone ultimate, every such longing has been in truth a reaching

out for God. Every pagan or heathen ritual, every idol of wood or stone or metal, has indicated this longing for God. Even the most cruel and reprehensible forms of worship are grotesque but significant forms of this yearning. How would any hand reach upward seeking God if God had not already extended a hand in quest of his creatures? So, as the Apostle Paul says, they "seek God, in the hope that they might feel after him and find him. Yet he is not far from each one of us" (Acts 17:27 RSV).

II. *The coming of the wise men signaled the fulfillment of ancient prophecy.* We do not know whose prophecies they consulted. No doubt they had access to the prophecies of the Jews. Matthew definitely emphasizes that the coming of Jesus was the fulfillment of what the inspired ancients saw in the future and of the deepest and finest yearnings of the generations past. Therefore, events celestial and events terrestrial coincided to bring to pass the unveiling of the mystery of the ages.

III. *The coming of the wise men signaled personal faith.* They were bold enough to break away from whatever traditions of their own culture might have kept them from finding the most complete fulfillment of their personal spiritual pilgrimage. At the same time, they blazed trails for others to follow. Indirectly, they became perhaps the first Christian missionaries. That is why, when we tell this story, we call the occasion Epiphany—the manifestation of Christ to the Gentiles. There-

17

fore, God has put Christ before all of us and each of us—our King and our Lord. As with the wise men, we bring our first and best gift—our gift of faith, and then whatever tokens, however costly, that represent the finest treasures of our hearts. —James W. Cox.

January 11. To Fulfill All Righteousness
TEXT: Matt. 3:13–17.

I. From the beginning Christians have struggled to explain Jesus' baptism at the hands of John the Baptist. It could imply, as a John the Baptist sect claimed, that Jesus was John's follower and thus the lesser of the two. Or, since John baptized on the basis of "repentance for forgiveness of sins" (Matt. 3:2,11), it could mean that Jesus was confessing sin. If he was "without sin" (Heb. 4:15) or "knew no sin" (2 Cor. 5:21), as his followers claimed, he should not need John's baptism. John himself responded to the first issue. The one who came *after* him would be greater than he, so much so that John wouldn't be worthy of being his servant (3:11). When Jesus came, therefore, John protested. "I need to be baptized by you, and do you come to me?"

II. Jesus insisted anyway. He did not come because he had to repent *his* sins. Rather, two other purposes compelled him. First, he came because of the need of the people. Note the plural, "for us." The one stood in for the many who needed repentance and transformation of life. In him God was doing what the people could not do for themselves. Second, he came "to fulfill all righteousness." Righteousness is a big word in Matthew. It is central to his understanding of the kingdom of heaven, which Jesus was announcing and bringing to pass. In the last judgment only the righteous will enter this kingdom. The righteous are those who do good instinctively, without even thinking about it. They have to protest, when the king invites them to enter, "Lord, when did we see thee hungry and feed thee, or thirsty and give thee drink?" They had simply acted out of the goodness of their hearts. They had not thought of reward. Who can attain to such character as that? No one, surely, by *human* striving! That is why

Jesus comes for baptism. He does for all humankind what we cannot do for ourselves. He submits obediently. He abandons himself totally and unreservedly to God for us.

III. Who was this one who came when he did not have to in order to take upon himself the sins of others? A voice from heaven gives us a clue. The clue lies in a combination of two texts from the Old Testament—one a messianic text from Ps. 2:7, the other a servant text from Isa. 42:1. Jesus is the Messiah of Jewish hope, but he is not a Messiah like David. He does not come in order to conquer the enemies of Israel or restore the nation to its Davidic glory. He is, rather, a servant of God who will give his life for the salvation of the people. Baptism at John's hands, therefore, merely prefigures a greater baptism, the baptism of death, the baptism of the cross. In receiving John's baptism Jesus announced his calling and mission as the Messiah of the Remnant—Servant of God. In a context where most persons expected a Messiah like David the choice was not an easy one, and Jesus' resolve was tested again and again. Human beings always find it easier to take the road of pride and glory than to take the one of humility and suffering.—E. Glenn Hinson.

January 18. A Witness for Christ
TEXT: John 1:29–34.

The greatness of many lies in their superior achievements. The greatness of John the Baptist lay in his recognition of the superiority of Jesus. John did many outstanding things and showed remarkable courage even before he baptized Jesus, but his real importance is that he pointed people to Jesus. And upon his witness others followed the Christ.

I. *He spoke clearly of Christ.*

(a) "Behold the Lamb of God." The Christ whom John announced had a humanly impossible task—to take away the sin of the world. "Who can forgive sins but God?"

Only the Lamb of God, Jesus Christ, could take away the sin of the world. Jesus proved his ability to do this by forgiving the sin of individuals who took him seriously, who believed that he came from

God and spoke and acted for God. As long as Jesus Christ demonstrates that he is able to take away the sin of an individual, we need never doubt that he can take away the sin of the world.

(b) "A man . . . preferred before me." John would never have attained his unique place in history and could not have done the will of God, if he had not been willing to be a servant of the truth. John was so strongly convinced that Jesus was the Christ that he was willing to do anything to advance Jesus before the world (John 1:8).

II. *He reported an authentic experience.*

(a) "I saw the Spirit descending." The other Gospels tell us of Jesus' baptism, but not the Gospel of John. Perhaps John omitted this because it might lead some readers to think that John was superior to Jesus because John baptized him. We rightly assume Jesus' baptism. It was at Jesus' baptism that John recognized Jesus as the Christ, the Son of God.

This is the explanation of John's later behavior toward Jesus, of his willingness to move to the shadows in order that Jesus might stand in the light. John did this because he was convinced that something greater than his own ministry and popularity was at stake.

(b) "Descending, and remaining on him." John was given opportunity to verify his faith in Jesus as the Son of God and as the Messiah.

Jesus gave evidence by what he did as well as by what he said that the Spirit was continuously on him. He sounded no false note at any time. Sometimes his actions and words baffled and offended those who saw and heard him, but at no point did he betray his Father or his followers. Nevertheless, so the record tells us, even John doubted (Matt. 11:3–5).

(c) "I saw, and bare record." These words summarize the ministry of John the Baptist. John knew certain facts, and his sure knowledge gave him his courage. God grants to true believers in Jesus Christ today an experience to which they, too, can give witness. God often works in a hidden way, but he works—and he gives an inner assurance of truth.

Every day we are faced with situations where we can act out of our own desires and do no one any good, or we can say, "He must become more important, while I become less important" (John 3:30 TEV). In saying and acting on this we can do everybody good. God's witnesses get the job done more surely when their rule is this: "Love one another warmly as brothers in Christ, and be eager to show respect for one another" (Rom. 12:10 TEV).—James W. Cox.

January 25. Answering the Call

TEXT: Matt. 4:12–23.

I. *They heard his call.* Many rabbis had disciples in Jesus' day, as did prophets such as John the Baptist. It is not unusual that Jesus would also have disciples. When he began to preach of the kingdom at hand he would quite naturally draw a following comprised of those anxiously looking for any signs of God's light beginning to peek through the surrounding darkness of their world, as well as the usual quota of curiosity seekers. What was unusual was the way Jesus chose his disciples. The disciples of the rabbis chose the one with whom they wished to study the Law. Their devotion was to the Law and not to the teacher. If they thought that they could learn more from another teacher, they would switch allegiance. Jesus, however, is shown to have chosen his own disciples. They did not choose him; he chose them. He chose them to be devoted to him as the one who was embodying God's kingdom.

Jesus came to them in the midst of life when they had made no particular preparations for him, and he caught them by surprise with his unusual demand, "Come after me." To that point their lives had centered around making a living from the sea. Jesus offered them a new vision as well as a new life.

The text does not tell us what it was that went through the minds of those fishermen when they heard that summons. Nor do we know what it was that possessed them to leave everything behind to follow him. We can only guess. For we too have heard that same voice calling at different times in our lives, and our hearts have been strangely warmed, even possessed, by its authority. It has a convincing ring because it comes from the one who made our hearts in the first place and who knows them inside and out.

II. *They left immediately.* Jesus said, "Come," and the text says they went immediately. They left their nets, boats, and families to follow Jesus to unknown destinations. If they had known then what Jesus' end would be, they might have had second thoughts about following him. But the kingdom of God was at hand, Jesus said, and there was no time for second thoughts. One person later was interested in the prospect of joining Jesus' enterprise, but he asked if he might not first be allowed to bury his father (Matt. 8:21–22). Jesus said no. He called like Elijah (see 1 Kings 19:19–21), but he was more than Elijah. His task was far greater, and time was short. The fishermen somehow knew that and seized the opportunity to respond while there was still time to respond.

III. *They left everything.* Discipleship was not periodic volunteer work that could be offered at one's own convenience and on one's own terms. Jesus did not offer them a benefits package or a golden parachute clause and said nothing about a retirement plan. They would soon discover that they left everything to become the hated of the world (Matt. 24:9). It would cost them everything, but it would be worth the cost.

IV. *They came after him.* Jesus is in motion and invites the disciples to join him on his way. Sometimes they got in his way and had to be reminded to "get *behind* me" (Matt. 16:23). Sometimes they tried to strike out on their own, only to sink in the sea of their doubts (Matt. 14:28–33). Sometimes they wanted to anchor Jesus' feet on some glorious mountain so that they could then relax and bask in the glory (Matt. 17:4). At the end of the road they abandoned him altogether, running for their lives and trying to save their own skins (Matt. 26:56).

It was not easy following *after* Jesus. But when they realized that he had saved their lives by his death, they were able to do a little better. They knew then that when so many others had fallen by the wayside, they had made the right choice when they traded their nets in for a cross. The retirement plan really turned out to be much better than they had ever dreamed. —David E. Garland.

February 1. Merciful Blessings
TEXT: Matt. 5:7 (5:1–12).

I. *I desire mercy.* Jesus twice quoted Hosea 6:6 to his opponents: "I desire mercy and not sacrifice" (Matt. 9:13, 12: 7), because they failed to comprehend what God really wanted from his people. There are two ways of approaching religion. One places emphasis on ethical-spiritual matters; the other on ceremonial matters. Concern with the latter can lead to a cold formalism, smugness, and indifference or scorn for those who are religiously less successful. The opponents of Jesus embodied this approach. Jesus, on the other hand, embodied mercy, which is marked by grace and love for both God and fellow humans. For Jesus, mercy—reconciliation—outweighs all cultic considerations (see 5:23–24). One cannot force one's way to God's altar and expect forgiveness and mercy while leaving a trail of bodies in one's wake.

II. *Forgive us our trespasses.* We pray to God in the Lord's prayer to forgive us but only as we have forgiven others. The Lord's prayer in Matthew is followed by the statement that unless we are forgiving, we cannot be forgiven. Our forgiveness is not based on our having forgiven others first, but it does suggest that whatever in us renders us incapable of showing mercy also renders us incapable of receiving mercy.

If we shut off mercy to others, we shut ourselves off from God's mercy. This is illustrated in the parable of the unmerciful servant (Matt. 18:23–35). We cannot expect to receive from God what we are not prepared to give to our fellow human beings. Therefore, we need to see others as God sees them and "mercy" them as he has already mercied us (see Matt. 18:33). Otherwise, we place ourselves in the grave danger of being exactly like the opponents of Jesus who scorned others as unworthy of forgiveness.

III. *Blessed are the merciful.* The reward of compassion is to receive compassion, not only from other humans, but more importantly from God. Two parables in Matthew that depict the final judgment (Matt. 18: 23–35, 25:31–46) single out mercy as the criterion that will determine one's ultimate destiny. The blessed inherit the kingdom prepared for them from the foundation of the world (Matt. 25:34). The blessed are those who showed mercy to the disadvantaged and unwanted. They did what God wants from us—mercy. —David E. Garland.

February 8. Salting the Earth
TEXT: Matt. 5:13–16.

I. *You are somebody.* Think of who Jesus was addressing when he told them that they were the salt of the earth. They were not the great religious leaders with a worldwide power base. So far they were nothing but a collection of exfishermen and nobodies. In comparison to the earth, the world, and the power brokers, who were they? They were the poor, the mourners, the meek, the hungering, and the persecuted. They had no denominational network and no great budget. Yet, Jesus said, they would salt the earth, light the world, and bring glory to God through their works simply because God had called them and they had responded.

II. *You are necessary.* Salt was a necessity that was utilized for many functions in first-century life. Christians as salt of the earth are necessary to life.

(a) It was used to flavor food. A little boy defined salt as what makes food taste bad when it is not on it. You are necessary to make life taste better (see Job 6:6).

(b) It was used as a preservative. You are necessary to fight against spiritual decay in the world.

(c) It was used as a fertilizer that killed weeds and improved soil at a deeper level. You are necessary to improve the soils (see Matt. 13:3–9, 18–23) so that they may be more receptive to the seed of God's word.

(d) It was used as an antiseptic for wounds. It stings. Jesus did not say, "You are the sugar of the world." You are not here to sweeten the world; you are necessary to purify it even if it stings.

(e) It was used as a fire catalyst. You are necessary to start spiritual fires in the lives of others.

III. *You had better be worth your salt.* In Palestine, much salt was gathered by evaporation from the Dead Sea. The water contained other saltlike substances, and it was possible for the sodium chloride crystals to dissolve away leaving only a bitter tasting substance that only looked like salt. Salt could lose its taste. With this in mind, Jesus does not congratulate his disciples for their high privilege. What they are is not for their own benefit but for the benefit of the world. Be warned if the salt loses its savor. Everyone hates an insipid religion; and savorless Christianity is as worthless as savorless salt. It is not even worth putting on the dung pile (Luke 14: 35) but is destined to be thrown out on the path and trodden under foot.—David E. Garland.

February 15. A Case of Murder in the Heart
TEXT: Matt. 5:17–26.

Many of us feel safely righteous, because, like the rich ruler, we have obeyed the Ten Commandments from our youth (Matt. 19:16–20). When we thought we could at least congratulate ourselves for not being murderers, Jesus identifies anger with murder. Jesus pulls the rug out from under our complacency with his demands for a righteousness that exceeds even that of the proverbially righteous (Matt. 5:20).

I. *Anger is dangerous.* The Bible recognizes anger as a natural human emotion, but it also recognizes that it is very dangerous. God warned Cain that because of his anger sin was crouching at the door (Gen. 4:6–7). Paul warned us that unchecked anger gives opportunity for the devil (Eph. 4:27). It is the first step toward murder. Jesus was concerned about getting at the root of sin; and in this case, murder begins in the heart. It is given life in the murderous look and the contemptuous slur. When you treat someone as if he or she were a nothing, in effect, you have already destroyed them.

II. *Mishandling our anger.* To get angry is to be human. The issue for Jesus, however, is how we handle our anger. The New English Bible is correct in translating Matthew 5:22, "Everyone who nurses anger." Problems come when we feed it and justify it so that it continues to grow like a cancer. Problems come when we deal with our anger inappropriately.

Some people attempt to deny their anger. They will go into withdrawal and try to pretend that nothing is wrong. They engage in cold warfare. It is difficult to deal with someone's anger when they refuse to talk. Others handle their anger through guerilla warfare. They use hit-and-run tactics; and the victim frequently has no idea who or what hit them. Others ventilate their anger. They are like nuclear warheads. They explode, and everyone around is wiped out by the fallout.

III. *Be reconciled.* Anger is like pain; it gives us a warning. It serves the function of alerting us to a disruption in our relationships with others or our environment. We need to pay attention to it so that we can make changes in our lives to correct the problem. Jesus would have us use our anger creatively. We should deal with annoying differences honestly so they do not destroy our relationship with another. We need to go to our brother or sister quickly to resolve the problems before they become impossible to resolve.—David E. Garland.

February 22. How Do I Look?

Text: Matt. 5:27–30 (5:27–37).

I. *The setting.* In the Old Testament adultery was defined as intercourse between a man and a woman married to or betrothed to an Israelite (Deut. 22:22; Lev. 20:10). It was the violation of the marriage of another Israelite. A husband did not commit adultery against his wife, only against another husband, because wives were the property of husbands (see Exod. 20:17). He was the one offended since his property had been violated.

Unconditional fidelity, while encouraged for all, was demanded only of the woman. One can see the double standard in the story of Judah and Tamar (Gen. 38:1–30) and in the ceremony of the bitter water for the suspected adultress (Num. 5:11–31). There was no ceremony for the suspected adulterer.

II. *Adultery redefined.* Jesus did not tolerate inequities or hypocrisy. He was always tightening up the loopholes that humans attempt to squirm through to evade God's will. Here he redefines adultery. It does not just involve the married man or woman but any man who looks upon any woman in order to lust after her. It is not simply the physical act but the lustful leer.

III. *Women are not objects.* Jesus bestowed on the women of his day the same dignity as men. He treated them as persons on the same level as men. They were not objects. When the woman is subjected to the lustful look, she is reduced to an object of sexual gratification for the male. In our English idiom we must translate it, "He commits adultery with her." In Greek, the verb takes a direct object without a preposition: "He adulterizes her." This is what the lustful look does; it turns persons into objects. One can see this reflected in the slang used for the opposite sex; they are inevitably described in terms of objects.

IV. *Solving the problem.* Jesus was not alone in his concern about adultery. Other teachers warned of the problem: women were considered an occasion for sin, a danger to any devout man. The prescription was to segregate women, to keep them from view. The devout men do not look at them or talk with them (see John 4:27). In this approach, the problem does not reside in a person's lust but in women as an occasion for lust. Those men wanted to avoid lust not because women had rights, but because women were dangerous.

Jesus does not say do not look; rather, do not look with lust. This could be interpreted to mean, Do not nurture the thoughts that looking brings. The problem resides in the looker and not in the lookee. In our day it is a problem for both men and women. Jesus knew that adultery begins in the heart (Matt. 15:19), and it may require rigorous discipline to heal (see 1 Cor. 9:27). The goal is to be able to look at a person of the opposite sex and see a person, not an object for our personal sexual gratification.—David E. Garland.

March 1. Radical Discipleship: The Macho Need Not Apply

Text: Matt. 5:38–48.

In Luke 14:25–33 Jesus warned would-be disciples to count the cost before signing on with him in a burst of enthusiasm. Do they know what it means to follow Jesus? Will they be able to finish what they start? Have they heard what Jesus taught?

I. *Being able to endure injury.* An eye for an eye is what most have heard and what most believe. For Jesus, this was not good enough. The disciple is not to return force for force, evil for evil. Jesus gave three illustrations of what he was talking about.

(a) When one is struck on the right cheek, one is to overcome the initial impulse to strike back. This is even harder than it seems. When one is struck on the *right* cheek it is from a backhanded slap. It is not just when we are slugged we are not to slug back, but when we are subjected to insulting violence we are to turn the other cheek.

(b) When one is sued, let them have the shirt off your back (incidentally, something forbidden them in Exod. 22:26–27). As Paul said, "Why not suffer wrong?" (1 Cor. 6:7). Love is able to endure all things (1 Cor. 13:4).

(c) When one is compelled by the enemy to go one mile, meet oppression with kindness. This refers to a hated form of exploitation that gave Romans the right to impress whomever or whatever they wanted for one mile (see Matt. 27:42). "Going the extra mile" has been domesticated to mean giving 110 percent or working especially hard. Jesus meant that we are to do this for the enemy. The enemy is not only to be prayed for but served.

II. *Living out God's way.* It is no wonder that with teaching like this many would-be followers decided it would be smarter to return home (see John 6:66–69). Jesus' way was too hard, but he was teaching his disciples the way of God. He shines his sun and rains his rain on both the good and the evil. While we were still enemies with God he sent his son to die for us (Rom. 5:8, 10). If we are to be God's children, that is, those who demonstrate in their way of life the character of the Father, we must love as he loved.

III. *What more do you do?* Jesus warned his disciples at the beginning of the sermon that unless their righteousness exceed that of the Pharisees they will have no part in the kingdom of heaven (Matt. 5:20). The righteousness of the Pharisees was proverbial. One former Pharisee claimed that when it came to righteousness he was blameless (Phil. 3:6). The rightousness of the toll collectors did not compare. Yet many Christians would like to get by with toll collector righteousness. They would greet with the pronouncement of peace only those who greeted them. They would love only those who loved them in return. What is good enough for the everyday world, however, is not good enough for Christians. If you love only those who will love you back, it is simply a business deal, tit for tat. God expects that we will love even those who would gladly nail us to a cross if they could—just as he did. He expects perfection in this; and there is no such thing as being only a little perfect. —David E. Garland.

March 8. Coming Face to Face with the Enemy

TEXT: Matt. 4:1–11.

John had proclaimed that Jesus was the mightier one who was coming. When Jesus was baptized, the heavens opened and a voice declared that this was indeed the beloved Son. What kind of Son would he be? How would he live out his Sonship? How would he accomplish his mission? How would he use his power as the mightier one? We see the devil stepping in, desperately trying to preempt the Spirit. The devil had his own plans along with some attractive offers that no son of this world would turn down. Jesus came face to face with the enemy who would distort God's word with lies. Jesus, however, was not a son of this world; and the devil failed but did not give up the fight. The tempter still lurks, biding his time to snare more unsuspecting prey. While we do not face temptations of messianic proportions as Jesus did, we still must come face to face with the enemy and his lying words.

I. *The word of self-indulgence.* After a long sojourn in the desert, Jesus was quite naturally hungry. The devil coaxed him. "You have to eat, and you have the power right at your finger tips. Just say the word and presto, bread aplenty! Why not? You have to survive." He would have Jesus profane his power to satisfy earthly appetites.

We can see the devil's point of view because we think along the very same lines. You have to survive. Our needs need to be gratified—preferably instantly. More than once we have desired magical powers to serve our purposes rather than God's. We would love to withdraw from the human condition in order to banish hunger and pain from our lives. We are tempted like Simon Magus to ask for power that we might do with it as we please to please ourselves (Acts 8:19). But when our worldly appetites are sated, we still have a gnawing emptiness in our lives. God has to remind us again and again that life is not just bread. What looked so wonderful to us turns out to be little more than cotton candy that melts away into nothingness in our mouths and leaves us hungrier than before. Only then do we learn what real life is. It is something that comes only from God and his word. That word says, If you would save your life, what have you saved? If you have gained the whole world what have you gained? (Matt. 16:24–26) Paul understood this when he wrote that he counted all his earthly gain as loss so that he might gain what was truly worthwhile—life in Christ.

II. *The word of self-conceit.* The devil attempted to flatter Jesus by reminding him that he was someone special. Had he not heard that voice at the baptism? Since you are Son of God, test him to see if he keeps his promises. Use your status to your own advantage. God has to be at your disposal; that is part of his job description.

Jesus did not put God to the test, but all too often we would. We hear the promises to us and deceive ourselves into thinking that God has set up this world just for us. As a result, we treat God as if his only purpose is to do our bidding. We would dictate to God, who will follow through for us because we are so special! We face the temptation to claim the promises not to bring glory to God but to bring glory to ourselves.

III. *The word of cynicism.* The devil showed his final card in a last desperate effort to win Jesus to his way of doing things. He showed him the world. You can have it all on easy terms. Do obeisance to me, and do things my way. If it is the world you want, I have it all in my back pocket and can show how to make it all yours.

The world is full of lures. We are fooled sometimes into thinking that, the world being what it is, you have to deal with it on its terms. If you want earthly kingdoms, or for that matter, just to get by, you have to use earthly means. You have to dominate and exploit. You have to learn how to win with intimidation through power ploys. To step up in this world you have to step on somebody. God's ways of loving enemies and giving of your life do not work. We are tempted to desert God for the tried and true ways of Satan. If you will fall down and worship the devil and his ways, you are destined to fall farther than you bargained; and you will make life a hell on earth. His ways have indeed been tried, but they are not true.—David E. Garland.

March 15. Finding Christ in the Ordinary

Text: John 3:1–17.

A small gallery in Houston, Texas, displays the works of the artist Rothko. At first the dark canvases appear to have nothing on them, but if visitors take time to sit on one of the benches their eyes will gradually discern faint shapes and colors on the canvas. The outlines of the figure of Christ begin to appear. He was there all along, but only the person who waits will see him. That, of course, is precisely the effect the artist intended.

I. *Conversation in the dark: Jesus and Nicodemus.* Jesus' conversation with Nicodemus illustrates how a person can be in the presence of Jesus and not find life in him. Nicodemus illustrates the struggle of one individual to see and hear and find life through Jesus.

John deliberately uses references to light and darkness because for him Jesus is the light of the world. When John says that Nicodemus came to Jesus at night, we can guess that he is nodding at us as if to say, "And you know what that means." Nicodemus was still trapped in unbelief. In the darkness of unbelief, in an ordinary courtyard, Nicodemus meets Jesus, the light of the world.

II. *The mystery of water and spirit: birth from above.* Jesus is the redeemer who has come "from above" (3:31), and Nicodemus finds him completely incomprehensible. Those whose vision and understanding is limited to the physical, material realities of this world cannot grasp the reality or the life of the world above.

Jesus' words are ambiguous. Did he mean that a person had to be born again or born from above in order to see the kingdom of God? Nicodemus assumes that Jesus meant he had to be born again and wonders aloud how in the world anyone could be born again.

III. *War between the worlds: above and below.* In the conversation between Jesus and Nicodemus we see one from the realm above meeting one from this world, the heavenly meeting the earthly. At the end of John 1, Jesus promised his followers that they would see the heavens opened and the angels of God ascending and descending upon the Son of Man (1:51). Jesus is now the new Bethel (see Gen. 28: 12), the one in whom heaven and earth meet.

He is therefore supremely able to reveal the Father (John 1:18) and to make known the ultimate truths of the world in which we live. The revelation he brings has the power to heal, to make the broken whole, and to give life (John 3:16).

At some point each of us stands as did Nicodemus, addressed by Jesus, called to faith, yet struggling to understand and accept his call. Perhaps some will hear echoes "from above" in the words of this conversation.—R. Alan Culpepper.

March 22. Love for the Excluded

TEXT: John 4:5–26.

The gospel can be preached in many ways, but it is often not heard until it is seen in the life of another person. Letting Christ's love be seen in our lives means that we will go out of our way to accept those who are being excluded. Jesus was a master at sensing when a person was excluded. His conversation with the Samaritan woman is a beautiful example of how love can overcome barriers.

I. *An outcast people.* Jews avoided contact with Samaritans, but Jesus had to travel through Samaria. It was part of his divine mission. Redemption requires breaking down walls of hostility.

Jesus stopped at the well at the sixth hour. Most interpreters understand this reference to mean noon, the heat of the day, an unusual time to make the daily trip to the well. Did the woman deliberately go to the well at this time to avoid contact with the other women of the village? People who have been rejected and excluded often go out of their way to avoid contact with others.

II. *Crossing the racial barrier.* Jesus took the initiative. Profound spiritual conversations may begin simply at the level of shared need. Jesus' request for a drink from a Samaritan was shocking. His real concern was not a drink of water but revealing God's love to this rejected woman from a despised people.

When Jesus offered her living water, she replied ironically, "Are you greater than our father Jacob?" He was, of course, but to her he was still just a thirsty stranger. John repeatedly emphasizes that Jesus was greater than Moses or the Patriarchs (1: 17; 5:46; 8:56–58).

III. *A new twist to an old story.* When Jesus told her to go and bring her husband, she responded that she had no husband. The conversation took an intriguing turn. Repeatedly in the Old Testament one of the patriarchs traveled to a foreign country and met his wife at a well. Each encounter reflects something about the hero's life and character (cf. Gen. 24; 29; Exod. 2: 15–22). Jesus' encounter with the Samaritan woman fits the pattern up to a point. Yet, while the patriarchs and Moses met their wives at a well, the Samaritan woman met her Lord.

IV. *Crossing the religious barrier* (see John 4:20). Religious differences all too often are the barriers that separate persons. An excluded person may be defensive toward a well-meaning Christian. There is no basis here, however, for saying that we should help only those who deserve our help.

Jesus was not concerned about where the Jews or the Samaritans worshiped: "Worship the Father in Spirit and in truth" (4:24 RSV).

While the woman ironically wanted to wait until the Messiah came (4:25) before inquiring about spiritual matters, Jesus insisted that the present was the time for decision and commitment. She had been accepted. Now was the time for her to respond to his love. Sometimes the wrong decision is the decision to let the right moment pass.—R. Alan Culpepper.

March 29. Sight for the Blind
Text: John 9:1–41.
The story unfolds as a drama in seven scenes. Jesus gives sight to a man born blind; in the process the blind man receives faith as well as sight. In a sense we are all born blind. We must all have our eyes opened to the light by faith. John 9, therefore, tells the story of everyone.

I. *The healing* (9:1–7). In popular theology, suffering was viewed as a consequence of sin. When people suffered it had to be because they had sinned. Why was the man born blind? Jesus would not stand before a man who had never seen the light of day and debate the cause of his illness. He set about to give the man sight so that the disciples would see that God had not caused the man's blindness.

John affirmed that the Word was the creator of life and that he was the "light of men" (1:3–4). Now Jesus stoops to spit and make clay. The blind beggar no doubt knew all too well what spit was, but this spit would bless rather than curse. Jesus' action recalls the creative act of God: He formed humanity from the dust of the ground (Gen. 2:7). Because the man was born blind his sight could not be restored. It took no less than a new creation.

Jesus anointed the blind man and sent him to wash in the Pool of Siloam. With the greatest brevity possible, John tells of the miracle itself: he went, he washed, and he came away seeing.

II. *Neighbors question the man* (9:8–12). Even he did not understand how he had been healed. He could only tell his neighbors who made it happen—"the man called Jesus" (9:11 rsv).

III. *The Pharisees question the man* (9:13–17). The Pharisees found no joy in the fact that a man who had never seen the light of day could now see. The man himself was beginning to see more clearly, for he said, "He is a prophet" (9:17 rsv).

IV. *The Pharisees question the parents* (9:18–23). The Pharisees continued to investigate whether the Sabbath had been violated. The parents confirmed that their son had been born blind, but they did not know how he had been healed.

V. *The Pharisees question the man again* (9:24–34). The irony of the situation becomes absolutely delightful. The Pharisees are in a real predicament. How could they deny that the man had been healed? On the other hand, how could a man sent from God violate the Sabbath? In contrast to the Pharisees' confident "we know," the man professed ignorance. He only knew that once he was blind but now he could see. Their "blindness" was their own choosing.

VI. *Jesus questions the man* (9:35–38). Jesus comes to the man who had been cast out by the Pharisees. He was concerned to test the man's vision. Fourteen questions are asked in this chapter, but this is the most important: "Do you believe in the Son of Man?" The man had come a long way but did not yet fully realize who Jesus was: "Who is he, sir?" With delightful wit Jesus answered, "You have *seen* him!" The man's vision was now complete and clear: "Lord, I believe."

VII. *The Pharisees question Jesus* (9:39–41). Finally, the Pharisees meet Jesus, who had come into the world to bring light. In the process he brought sight to the blind and exposed the blindness of those who claimed knowledge but did not know him. The Pharisees responded in unbelief, "We are not blind, are we?" But they had already pronounced judgment on themselves. Jesus answered: "If you were blind, you would have no guilt; but now you say, 'We can see,' your guilt remains" (9:41 rsv). The reversal is complete: The man born blind has received his sight, and those who were confident they could see have had their blindness exposed. Such is the mercy and judgment of God.

What is your last word in this story, "Lord, I believe!" or "We are not blind, are we?"—R. Alan Culpepper.

April 5. The Raising of Lazarus, Martha, and Mary

TEXT: John 11:17–45.

Death and grief are not pleasant subjects, but dealing with them before they are thrust upon us will give us added spiritual resources when we need them. Jesus' ministry to Mary and Martha shows us how he comforted the bereaved, and his raising of Lazarus pointed to his power over death.

I. *Lazarus: one whom Jesus loved.* Lazarus is introduced as the one Jesus loved (11:3, 36). Lazarus was Jesus' "friend" (11:11), one of "his own." These terms are important in John. Remember, "Greater love has no man than this, that a man lay down his life for his friends" (15:13 RSV). In John the raising of Lazarus provoked Jesus' arrest and crucifixion (11:45–53). Giving life to Lazarus cost Jesus his own life. He laid down his life for his own. Lazarus, therefore, represents all whom Jesus loves.

Jesus had said that the hour was coming when all of those in the tombs would hear the voice of the Son of God and live (5:25, 28–29; cf. 10:3–4). Jesus approaches Lazarus' tomb, calls him by name, and leads him out. Lazarus, therefore, is a dramatic example of Jesus' power over death and a sign of the resurrection of all believers. But more, Lazarus shows that all who believe in Jesus' name have already received eternal life (5:24; 1 John 3:14).

II. *Martha: Jesus is the resurrection.* Martha's greeting reflects bitterness: "Lord, if you had been here, my brother would not have died" (11:21 RSV). Anger toward God is a natural reaction when someone we love has died. It is natural for us to recall the events that led to a loved one's death and say "if only" or "what if," but we don't know what the future holds and we can't relive our lives with the benefit of hindsight.

Martha needed to understand that the power of the resurrection was already present in Jesus. She represents many Christians whose hope for life lies only in the future, as though eternal life were something that will not begin until after death. But Jesus meant that our fellowship with him and the Father now is already "eternal life" (see John 17:3). Eternal life, therefore, refers to a quality of life, not just the length of life.

Martha is John's model for the courageous faith that confesses that Jesus is the giver of life, even in the midst of grief (see 11:27).

III. *Mary: devoted to Jesus.* When Mary approached Jesus, she fell at his feet. That posture characterizes her devotion to Jesus every time she appears in the gospels (see John 11:2; 12:3; Luke 10:38–42). Mary, therefore, does not distinguish herself by her confession of faith but by her love for Jesus.

Lazarus embodies *hope* for life beyond death, Martha is characterized by her confession of *faith*, and Mary is distinguished by her *love* for Jesus. At the center of the Gospel of John we meet three people who portray the virtues so dear to Paul: faith, hope, and love (1 Cor. 13:13).

IV. *Conclusion.* The raising of Lazarus from death, and the raising of Martha and Mary from grief to faith was a sign, not a proof. Jesus is the resurrection and the life. Do you believe this?—R. Alan Culpepper.

April 12 (Palm Sunday). God's Perplexing Way of Winning

TEXT: Luke 19:28–40.

This is a day of joy for us who believe in Jesus Christ. We can wave palm branches if we wish. We can shout, "Hosanna!" All the triumphs of truth are ours. God has given to us many fabulous treasures, the heritage of the centuries: his promise to Abraham, the deliverance of Israel from slavery in Egypt, the coming of Jesus Christ to redeem humankind, and the opportunity to know the good news of Christ today.

We rejoice not only because we are Christians, but also because we are human beings. We rejoice in the happiness of a young man and a young woman when they stand at the marriage altar. We rejoice when a child is born. We rejoice when a good harvest is gathered and when some stroke of good fortune comes to ourselves or to our friends.

But isn't it amazing that this day is still a day of rejoicing? Much has happened to spoil the joy of this day. Less than a week after Jesus made his triumphal entry into Jerusalem, he was dead—crucified. Yet that was not the end of joy.

The apostolic command from a jail cell is this: "Rejoice in the Lord always; again I will say, Rejoice" (Phil. 4:4 RSV). God's way of victory and rejoicing is not the simple matter that we might wish.

I. Out of the Palm Sunday experience of Jesus come four observations. We never experience pure happiness on this earth. There may come an ecstatic, lucid moment that gives life a reference point or a goal, a place to leave from or a place to set out toward. It is these special times that give meaning to all the rest of life.

However, every sunlit hour casts its shadow. The temple in Jerusalem, so full of history and memories, where Jesus delighted to be at the age of twelve, was marked for destruction and fell in A.D. 70. The exalted experience of baptism was followed by temptation in the wilderness. Peter's confession was followed by the announcement, "The Son of man must suffer many things, and be rejected by the elders and chief priests and scribes, and be killed, and on the third day be raised" (Luke 9:22 RSV). After the glory of the Mount of Transfiguration came the sight of a pitiful epileptic boy waiting to be healed. And after the palm branches and hosannas of the pilgrims, Jesus looked toward unbelieving Jerusalem and wept (Luke 19:42–43 RSV). Happiness is always pursued by its shadow.

No one ever saw life more clearly than Jesus did. He saw every shadow and every menacing cloud. But he saw more than that. He saw the light, the inner beauty and the joy that rise above everything evil in human experience. He rejoiced in the triumph of the moment because of what it stood for—the final victory of God. So when the Pharisees complained because his admirers cried out in praise to God, Jesus replied, "I tell you, if these were silent, the very stones would cry out" (Luke 19:40 RSV).

If we find real happiness here, it will be because we keep going in spite of a thousand things that would cast us down. Now if this is true, how can we gain the courage to laugh in the face of trouble?

II. The courage to rejoice comes from our faith in the overruling purpose of God. We must make a distinction between happiness and joy. So far we have used the words almost interchangeably, but in fact their meanings are different. Happiness depends largely on how things go around and about you, what happens to you on the job, at home, and among your friends. Joy, on the other hand, may be practically independent of outward circumstances. It depends on God. Why were the pilgrims rejoicing on Palm Sunday? Because they believed in God and his salvation. They believed that Jesus had brought this salvation. What a remarkable fulfillment of ancient prophecy was unfolding before their eyes! (Zech. 9:9) Deliverance from their oppressors! No wonder there was rejoicing when Jesus approached Jerusalem!

III. None of us should think that this triumphant faith is easy to acquire (Rom. 5:3–4).

You cannot take these steps of faith without growing. Joy will come in spite of everything. The person who has wept has learned best how to rejoice. The person who has looked into the depths of the deepest despairs can most clearly the heights of hope. The person who has bowed to God's will actually reigns with him.

If you and I cannot rejoice today, perhaps we have no right to rejoice. Have we believed that God is Lord, that he is the rightful ruler of this world? Have we believed that God can make even the wrath of man to praise him? Have we committed our lives to his way? If not, perhaps the only fitting thing, then, would be to weep for ourselves, knowing that the tears of Christ over Jerusalem were for us, for us who have rejected him, for us who have chosen our own way.

IV. What we have considered up to this point has taken us close to the mystery of the cross. Jesus' coming into Jerusalem on Palm Sunday was under the shadow of the city's impending doom and his own crucifixion. But he rode on to die, sustained by an invincible joy. This is what Paul said was a stumbling block to the Jews and foolishness to the Greeks. "But to those who are called, both Jews and Greeks, Christ the power of God and the wisdom of God" (1 Cor. 1:24 RSV).

He died in order that the unworthy might have the right to rejoice. How could he do it? Hebrews tells us: "(He) for the joy that was set before him endured the cross, despising the shame, and is seated at the right hand of the throne of God" (12:2 RSV).—James W. Cox.

April 19 (Easter). A Witness of the Living Lord

TEXT: John 20:1–18.

Perhaps the first witness to the resurrection was Mary Magdalene. She was not an apostle. An old ending to Mark's Gospel identifies her as a person out of whom Jesus had cast seven demons (Mark 16:9). Nothing about her qualified her especially for being a witness. Like other disciples, she was simply one whom the Lord had helped, a changed and grateful person.

I. *An alarming discovery.*

(a) Hasty resignation. When Mary Magdalene came to Jesus' tomb early on Sunday morning, she and the other women with her came to do an act of human devotion (Mark 16.1). They were resigned to the idea that Jesus was dead, really dead.

Mary's very human devotion to a very human Jesus made it possible for her to come to know him in a way in which she had not known him before. Human gratitude and affection took her to the place where something wonderful was about to happen.

(b) Unfounded alarm. When Mary arrived at the tomb, she discovered that the stone covering the entrance had been taken away. This meant one thing: Someone had come and had stolen Jesus' body. This was a human act of desecration. Jesus' enemies had got what they asked for. Jesus was dead. Was that not enough?

Mary was mistaken. Jesus' body was indeed gone. But it did not mean that Jesus' enemies had stolen it. This was no human act, but an act of God. The worst had happened to Jesus when he died on the cross; she believed that the worst had happened again. But Jesus had been raised from the dead. How quickly we misread the meaning of events!

When we make hasty judgments of God and the events that transpire about us we may miss the truth. Whoever thinks of Jesus' life as ending on the cross has definitely missed the truth.

II. *The birth of faith.*

(a) Slowness to believe. Through blinding tears Mary saw Jesus standing near the tomb but thought he was the gardener. We live every day of our lives on "resurrection ground" but nothing seems different to us. Why are we so slow to believe, to take into our lives the meaning of God's mighty and gracious acts?

God is under compulsion to explain nothing he has done in the world, miraculous or otherwise. Amazingly, God permits us to explain away his most wonderful works. He leaves us free to believe or not to believe, for God will not force our faith. Even good church people may become so enchanted with scientific explanations for everything that they miss the religious dimension altogether. Mary Magdalene had to be bowled over with proof before she could believe anything but that someone had stolen Jesus' body from the tomb.

(b) Halfway faith. Mary discovered that the figure she had mistaken for the gardener was none other than her Lord. So thankful was she to have her grief dispelled that she would not let him go (v. 17).

What Mary needed was not proof that Jesus had arisen—though she was given such proof. She needed a deep experience of the meaning of her Lord's resurrection. We can surrender the physical body of Jesus in order that we may know his glorified presence among us and within us (John 20:29).

III. *A significant testimony.*

(a) A deeper faith. It is clear that Mary accepted and acted on the word of Jesus. Faith went deeper than sight and touch.

(b) A shared faith. Truth so wonderful has to be shared. It changes the appearance of everything. When we realize that God has raised Jesus from the dead, we have the assurance that no situation is too difficult for God and that the living Christ will never leave us or forsake us. One can dare to take up his cross and follow after him who loved us and gave himself for us.

In his service, every threat of death is at the same time a promise of life.

It was given to Mary Magdalene to announce good news, the best news. We, too, have the privilege today of telling by word and life that "the most wonderful thing has happened."—James W. Cox.

April 26. Christ Alive—Then and Now

TEXT: John 20:19–31.

What happened on the third day after Jesus' death on the cross? John gives many helpful details that indicate something of the nature of the resurrection.

Strong evidence was put forward to show that the human body was raised. Jesus showed his disciples his wounded hands and side (v. 20). But his was a glorified body that could pass through locked doors (v. 19). The facts gave proof that there was an empty tomb, that what the disciples and more than five hundred other eyewitnesses saw was not merely a hallucination or even a vision from God, but was Jesus Christ himself.

I. *Doubt removed.*

(a) Thomas could not believe that Jesus had risen from the dead (v. 25). Thomas was no cynical skeptic. He shared the same confusion that plagued the other disciples. Only after the resurrection itself and the coming of the Holy Spirit did the full meaning of Jesus' words dawn on them. When confronted with the risen Christ, Thomas gladly believed, saying, "My Lord and my God!" (John 20:28).

(b) Ponder these questions for the strengthening of your faith: Apart from the resurrection of Jesus Christ, how can you explain the transformed lives of the disciples who went out to die for their Lord? Or the phenomenal growth of the church on and after Pentecost? Or the conversion of some of the priests in Jerusalem? How can you explain the disciples' belief in the deity of Jesus? Or the conversion of Saul of Tarsus? How can you explain what happens in the lives of those who really trust Jesus Christ today?

II. *Disillusion overcome.*

(a) What some people need in this connection is not more proof of the fact of a risen Christ. They, like Simon Peter, need to know what the living Lord means in personal experience.

(b) Peter, the outspoken disciple, had promised much but had delivered little, in spite of his good intentions. He made his way back to his boat and his nets, followed by the other disciples. Even after his profane denial of his Lord, Peter still led his friends by his magnetic personality.

(c) The risen Christ appeared, then, to the disciples at the Sea of Tiberias (John 21:1ff). There he restored Simon Peter to confidence and usefulness. Only a Christ who really lived could have pulled Simon out of his pit of despair and set him once more at the tasks of Christian leadership and the preaching of the gospel.

III. *Apostles all.*

(a) The reassurances of the risen Christ to his disciples were not merely for their private comfort. Since Christ is risen, there is work to do—work for all of us. This is the gospel: the Christ who died is risen indeed! The Christian's task is to live by this truth and to make it known to the world. Paul put it this way: "God was in Christ, reconciling the world unto himself" (2 Cor. 5:19); also, he "hath given to us the ministry of reconciliation" (2 Cor. 5:18).

(b) Some Christians stand trembling and inadequate before their task because they depend on their own puny resources rather than on the unlimited power of God. Therefore, the words "Tarry ye . . . until ye be endued with power from on high" (Luke 24:49) belong with the words "Go ye therefore, and teach all nations" (Matt. 28:19).—James W. Cox.

May 3. The "Aha!" Sign

TEXT: Luke 24:13–35.

I. How strange that these two disciples, neither of them one of the twelve, failed to recognize Jesus the entire journey to Emmaus, approximately seven miles. Walking, the trip must have taken at least two hours. Yet a whole array of signs failed to pierce a thick cloud of incognition that surrounded their minds and hearts. Should persons who had spent so much time with Jesus not have recognized his walk? Or his voice? But no, they seemed a bit impatient with his impertinent and uninformed questions. Was he the only resident of Jerusalem who didn't know about Jesus of Nazareth and how his death had dashed their hopes? We can't even excuse them on the grounds that they had no earlier clues, for they themselves related the story of an empty tomb. If they were not ready to believe the women who had first discovered it, they had a confirmation from others. Yet not even a Bible study led by the Master himself succeeded in breaking through. They weren't ready to believe and to see.

II. One familiar sign did what all the other evidences failed to do. Jesus took bread, blessed it, broke it, and gave it to them. Suddenly the cloud vanished. Unseeing gave way to seeing. Incognition yielded to cognition. The uncomprehended became comprehensible. The disciples recognized him. Why did this action do what a long journey, discussion, and Bible study could not do? Would it not have been the power of a familiar action? Doing something often done with Jesus triggered inward perceptions that the other things had left untouched. How many times had Jesus done what he did here? Was it only at the Last Supper? Surely not. These two disciples hadn't been there. No, Jesus must have shared meals dozens of times with a larger circle of disciples in which he had gone through this familiar routine of breaking bread. The breaking of bread became an "Aha!" sign, one that his followers would associate with no other person. When they joined him in this acted parable, therefore, they had to exclaim, "Aha! It is Jesus!" So has this same sign done through the centuries for generation after generation of those who have been "slow of heart to believe."

III. Cognition ignited by a familiar sign set off two other reactions. These two now recalled how their hearts had burned within them as Jesus spoke to them and opened the Scriptures as they journeyed from Jerusalem to Emmaus. That road looked different in their rearview mirrors. One "Aha!" now caused some other "Aha!s." The flame that had burned in their hearts on the road had not risen high enough or become hot enough to burn away the cloud of incomprehension and

grief. But when the familiar sign of breaking bread burned away the cloud, they remembered. They also felt compelled to go and tell others. Discovery demanded disclosure. Once skeptics, unconvinced by a whole range of evidences, they could not wait to share the news. That very hour, Luke says, they got up and returned to Jerusalem to tell the Eleven and others gathered with them how the risen Lord had become known to them in the breaking of bread. So also do we hasten to tell.
—E. Glenn Hinson.

May 10. An Open Door
Text: John 10:1–10.
The closed door is all too common today. It is a symbol of the plight of the impoverished and unemployed.

I. John 10 presents Jesus as both a shepherd and a door for the excluded. Like the blind man in John 9 (see John 9:34 and 10:4), the outcast are not alone in strange surroundings. They have a friend and guide who can lead them, and—better—he can give abundant life.

(a) The image of sheep and shepherds is used frequently in the Old Testament (Pss. 23, 80, 100; Isa. 40:11; Jer. 31:10). Ezekiel 34 contains many of the themes developed in Jesus' parables: the Lord will shepherd his sheep; he will judge among the sheep; and he will punish the shepherds who do not care for the sheep. This chapter provides the background against which the people could understand what Jesus said about sheep and shepherds in John 10.

(b) We seize the image of Jesus as shepherd; he also said, "I am the door." The implication is that all those who come to the sheep by other means are thieves and robbers. Jesus may well have had in mind earlier political and religious leaders, but the people of God are always vulnerable to false leadership.

II. Two tests distinguish true Christian leadership: (1) whether the person gives evidence of having come to the church through the leadership of the Lord, and (2) whether the leader stays to defend the flock when it is attacked. False leaders, the hirelings, do not come in by the door; and because they care nothing for the sheep, they flee in time of adversity.

(a) As the door for the sheep, Jesus is the way to truth and life (see John 14:6). No one can come to the Father except through him. As the door, Jesus is the way by which the sheep may enter the security of the sheepfold and go out to find pasture. Either way, his design is the same—that they may have life and have it abundantly (John 10:10). John emphasizes that Jesus is the giver of new life, eternal life, life from another aeon, which begins now when the believer is born from above. This life is sustained by the revelation and word of Jesus, living water and living bread—in other words, by his sustaining power.

(b) Whereas Jesus' mission is to give life, the thief comes to kill and destroy. That is the fundamental nature of evil: it kills and destroys. Jesus, on the other hand, gives life and seeks to give to all the quality of life which John describes as eternal and abundant.

III. Being the church of the open door (see Rev. 3:8, 20) means not only being receptive to outsiders, it means being Christ to others, the door through which they may find eternal life.—R. Alan Culpepper.

May 17. Finding Your Way Home

TEXT: John 14:1–14.

The Wizard of Oz was a spectacular, memorable film, one of the first in color. Judy Garland played the little girl who met the tin man without a heart and the lion who lacked courage. All she wanted was to find her way home.

I. Confused? Don't despair. Jesus was leaving them. One of them would betray him, and Peter would deny him three times. Still, he said, "Let not your hearts be troubled" (John 14:1).

Jesus assured the disturbed disciples that their separation would be temporary. Most important, regardless of how terrible things seemed to be, regardless of how complete their loss appeared to be, "Keep on believing in God, and also in me" (14:1). Sometimes belief is all a person has to hold on to, but it can be enough. Jesus assured them that they would be together again. He was going to prepare a place for them.

II. Tired of waiting? A room now. William Tyndale, the sixteenth-century translator who influenced the wording of English translations of the Bible more than any other single person, translated the Greek word monai as "mansions," which in Old English meant "dwelling places." "Dwelling places" is the exact meaning of the Greek term, but the more picturesque "mansions" calls to mind vivid images of "pie in the sky by and by." John leaves no uncertainty about eternal life: life that begins here and now will continue in his fellowship forever. But the disciples were not worried about where they would be after death; they were concerned about how their relationship with the Lord could continue if he were leaving them. Jesus assured them that there would be many abiding places, many other occasions for upper room experiences. He had replaced the temple as his Father's house (see John 2:17–22), and now he was going to make it possible for believers everywhere to experience fellowship with him through the Spirit. And he would come to take them to be with him (14:3).

III. Confused? Jesus shows the way. The disciples did not understand.

First Thomas confessed that they did not know where Jesus was going (14:5). Thomas understood that Jesus was going to die (11:6), but he did not understand that Jesus' death would also be the means of his exaltation and his return to the Father. Philip did not yet understand that Jesus was himself the revelation of the Father (14:8–9). Jesus was the way (the process), the truth (the means), and the life (the goal). In him the disciples had seen the Father.

Are you tired, despairing, or confused? Jesus has prepared a place just for you—a room with a view.—R. Alan Culpepper.

May 24. A Place in the Heart

TEXT: John 14:15–21.

The search for God has led religious seekers on exotic quests, to faraway temples, to rigorous disciplines of self-denial, prayer, and fasting. Yet in looking far and wide and in trying the exotic many have failed to find fulfillment.

The first disciples were religious seekers, followers of John the Baptist. Jesus' first words in the Gospel of John are, "What do you seek?" Their response to Jesus was, "Where are you staying?" (John 1:38).

I. *Love as the condition of communion.* At the end of his ministry, Jesus promised to send "another counselor," the "Spirit of Truth" to those who would love him and keep his commandments. Love would be expressed in obedience, and the Lord's response would be to give those who love him what they want most, a fuller experience of his presence.

II. *The mysterious coming.* Jesus assured the disciples that in "a little while" the world would not see him, but they would see him (14:19), and he would show himself to them (14:21). Still the disciples were puzzled. Judas (not Judas Iscariot but another Judas) asked the obvious question, how would he reveal himself to them but not to "the world." Here "the world" means unbelievers. Jesus then explained what he meant by "dwelling places." He and the Father would come and make their dwelling place in all who love Jesus and keep his teachings (14:23). That was the great mystery Jesus was trying to reveal to them. They would not be left orphaned (14:18); Jesus would come again to be with them in the Spirit. This coming is not the second coming at the end of time, for the world will not recognize it. Neither was Jesus referring to the resurrection appearances or the experience of a few spiritually elite Christians, for this promise was to all who love him. Following the resurrection, the presence of God would not be confined just to the temple in Jerusalem or to the incarnate Son of God but would reside in the life of every believer.

III. *The Lord's abiding place.* The disciples' first question to Jesus in the Gospel of John is, "Where are you staying?" or, Where do you dwell, or abide (1:38). Now they knew the answer: Jesus would make his dwelling place in them and in all who love him.—R. Alan Culpepper.

May 31. Glory

TEXT: John 17:1–11.

What Jesus came to do, what he did during his days on earth, and why he did it— these are all put forward in his high priestly prayer.

I. *Jesus prayed for himself.*

(a) This was not a selfish prayer. He always pointed people past himself to the Father.

(b) Jesus' work was the work of the Father. Their objective was and is to give eternal life (cf. John 3:16).

(c) This eternal life is a quality of existence that we shared in joyous fellowship with the Father and the Son. It begins for the believer in this life. The Son's joy and glorification consist in this relationship signaled at different points in his ministry (see John 1:14, 2:11; 11:4, 40; 12:28, esp. 12:23–26). As William Temple said, "If a man knows the Spirit within him, the source of all his aspiration after holiness, as indeed the Spirit of Jesus Christ, and if he knows this Spirit of Jesus Christ within himself as none other than the Spirit of the Eternal and Almighty God, what more can he want? *This is the eternal life.*"

II. *Jesus prayed for his disciples.*

(a) He had revealed the name of God in his acts and in his words. This was the Yahweh of the Old Testament (see John 14:9b).

(b) Jesus' prayer was that his disciples be instruments and reflectors of what came from the Father through him.

(c) Jesus prayed that his disciples might enjoy the unity that he, the Son, had with the Father. This was not uniformity, but unity. "Though he was in the form of God, [he] did not count equality with God a thing to be grasped, but emptied himself, taking the form of a servant, being born in the likeness of men (Phil. 2:6–7 RSV). The relation of Father and Son as distinct persons was and is the model for the unity of Christ's people (see Phil. 2:3–4). To quote William Temple again: "[This unity is] something much more than a means to any end—even though that end be the evangelization of the world; it is itself the one worthy end of all human aspiration." —James W. Cox.

June 7 (Pentecost). Living Water

TEXT: John 7:37–39.

I. Jesus chose a climactic occasion, the final (probably the eighth) day of the Feast of Tabernacles, for this disclosure of himself as the water of life. This feast entailed a special water ritual. Each day for seven days of the feast a golden flagon was filled with water from the pool of Siloam (which itself means "sent") and was used for libations in the Temple. Although this custom probably originated as a ritual for making rain, in Jesus' day it initiated prayers for rain during the Feast of Tabernacles. In a land where rain is a rare and precious gift it would have special importance. The second of the eighteen benedictions linked rain inseparably to God as the one "mighty to save." With special care, therefore, Jesus chose the last, the eighth, day of the feast when the water ritual was not performed to make his dramatic declaration.

II. Jesus, not the pool of Siloam, is the fountain of living water. "Siloam" meant "sent." But here was a greater one whom God had "sent." The Siloam ritual recalled the water that flowed from the rock in the desert when Moses struck it (Num. 20:2–13). It symbolized too the hope for a coming Messiah (Isa. 12:3). The Apostle Paul used this typology to encourage the Corinthians. The desert wanderers had drunk from "the supernatural Rock which followed them," that is, Christ (1 Cor. 10:1–5). Believers, therefore, also become in a secondary way sources of this same living water. Joined to Christ, the spring, they are the stream through which courses the water that wells up to eternal life (4:15). Those who receive this water will not thirst again; they will have God himself.

III. John proceeds to put this in perspective for his own contemporaries. Living water means the Spirit, which believers of his day knew. Looking backwards from the vantage point of Pentecost, we understand what John meant, for we have immediate, firsthand experience through the Spirit. Jesus' hearers, however, could not comprehend what he was saying, for the Father had not yet sent the Paraclete (14:26). The Spirit was to be sent only when Jesus had completed his work, when he had been glorified. In John, remember, Jesus' glorification takes place through his lifting up on the cross where he could draw all people to himself. Just as Moses installed a serpent on a pole so that the people would lift their eyes heavenward

and live (Num. 21:9), so Jesus would be lifted up in order that whoever should believe in him would look up and live (John 3:14–15). Jesus is thus glorified in and through death. Glorification through death will seem strange to many persons in our day. How can one win by dying? How can one triumph by surrender? Such persons forget the transcendent power of God, which brings life out of death, and with which human beings can get in touch only by submission to God.—E. Glenn Hinson.

June 14. Marching Orders
Text: Matt. 28:16–20.
Jesus had a plan to win the world. Its success depended primarily on eleven men. They were ordinary, yet extraordinary men. They had been with Jesus for many months, watching him, hearing him, enjoying his presence.

He had made an appointment with them (Matt. 26:32; 28:7) and they kept the appointment—at a mountain in Galilee. This act of obedience fitted them to hear and accept his marching orders. They had enlisted in his forces—now what?

I. *A Christian imperative.* We speak of the Great Commission frequently with the emphasis on the word *go.* So the commission appears to be confined to the foreign missionary. But the word we translate "go" is not an imperative in the original Greek. It is a participle, "going." The imperative is "make disciples." The sentence then reads, "Going therefore, make disciples."

Understood this way, the Great Commission is clearly directed to every modern disciple. We are not required to go anywhere. We are charged simply to make disciples. This relationship between Jesus and his disciples is to be duplicated by those disciples and their disciples until we come into the picture ourselves. An imperative is a direct command. You and I cannot evade it: "Make disciples." Tell men and women and boys and girls about God's love for them—about God's gift to them. It's imperative.

II. *A wide horizon.* There are no limits to these marching orders. God made and loves the whole world. Although it is a participle, the word *going* is a part of the marching orders. As a matter of fact, it is wider than a simple imperative "go" would be.

Wherever you go, make disciples. Whenever you go, make disciples. However you go, make disciples. This is your business, all over the world.

Another participle that appears in the text is *baptizing*. It follows logically on the imperative "Make disciples." Christian baptism is an outward manifestation of the Christian commitment. Indeed, baptism itself is a commitment—into the death, burial, and resurrection of Jesus (Rom. 6:3ff.).

A third participle is *teaching*. It is a necessary part of the imperative "Make disciples." There is more involved than the initial response of the believer. A lifelong commitment to learning is described in the participle *teaching*. All truth is included and obedience is presupposed. Our marching orders are for a lifetime.

III. *A reassuring affirmation.* Not even the eleven disciples who had been with Jesus personally could have accepted the challenge without the firm promise, "I am with you always." Certainly we treasure it.

There is a quality in the "with you"—a quality of unlimited fellowship. It does not matter what the situation, what the peril, what the opportunity, what the responsibility, "I am with you!"

There is a quantity in the "always to the end of the age." Just as danger will not sever the relationship, neither will the passage of time. One does not grow too old for the promise. Time exercises no control over the affirmation.

Can you believe it? Will you obey it? All of this involves the triune God: Father, Son, and Holy Spirit. Here are marching orders for the Christian disciple—then and now!—J. Estill Jones.

June 21. Voice of Authority
TEXT: Matt. 7:21–29.

Many voices are being heard today discussing authority. There are discussions of governmental authority, of economic authority, of social authority, as well as of spiritual authority. Sometimes the voice of spiritual authority is identified with the

Bible. Sometimes it is composed of both the Bible and churchly traditions. Sometimes it is recognized in the pastor or some other spiritual leader. The passage in the Gospel according to Matthew clearly identifies the voice of authority in the words of Jesus.

I. *Saying and doing.* The last paragraphs of the recorded Sermon on the Mount deal with the subject of authority. Jesus is described as a teacher "having authority, and not as their scribes."

Many are impressed by those who regularly speak religious language. It is not enough to intersperse our conversations with frequent allusions to God. Indeed, this approaches profanity unless matched by godly living. Can you not imagine that a person who says "Lord, Lord" all of the time would be disqualified as truly religious?

Name dropping is a current practice which appeals to some people. Many times it is deceptive; it suggests that the person whose name is dropped approves the behavior or words of the person using their name. Jesus would have none of it. Even doing mighty works in the name of the Lord is subject to the clear understanding of and obedience to the will of God.

II. *Hearing and doing.* The parable of the foundations was designed to sum up the Sermon on the Mount. It is a parable challenging people to obedience. Perhaps two verses in the Epistle of James serve as a commentary: "Be ye doers of the Word and not hearers only" (James 1:22–23).

The contrast is between wisdom and folly. James contrasts the two throughout the letter. The wise man builds his house or his life on a firm foundation, the foolish man on an insecure foundation. One man hears the truth and bases his life on it. The other man hears the truth and decides it is not important.

The storms come upon all—both the wise and the foolish. The most genuinely godly families have tragedies as terrible as families that ignore God and his truth.

What makes the difference? The foundation! Construction of the houses to all outward appearances is the same. The storms are the same. Only the foundations are different.

The voice of authority summarized the issues: The one who hears and does the will of God will be secure. The one who hears and considers or talks about—without doing—or ignores the will of God knows no security.

III. *Teaching with authority.* Little wonder that the people recognized the authority in Jesus' voice. He was speaking about life-and-death issues.

Jesus taught with an authority that was independent of tradition and free of prejudice. His authority was based on his relation with God and his loyalty to the truth. He spoke with the authority of God himself.

And his hearers recognized his authority. Indeed they contrasted it with the teaching of the scribes who did not have authority. It was not and is not a matter of speaking profound words with many syllables—even about mighty works performed. It was and is a matter of relating oneself to God and consciously doing his will.

So the voice of authority speaks in our own day!—J. Estill Jones.

June 28. Eating with the Wrong Crowd
TEXT: Matt. 9:9–13.

"A person is known by the company he keeps." "One bad apple can spoil the barrel." I've heard it all my life. For Jesus, then, to be accused of eating with the wrong crowd is not an unusual reaction. What possessed him to ignore the niceties of respectable society?

I. *He invited a tax collector to follow him.* This was his first offense. Of course he had already invited four fishermen to be his followers. So perhaps this was not his "first" offense. Fishermen did not exactly belong to Galilee's Four Hundred in high society!

Matthew was his name. Beyond the commonness of the fishermen, Matthew probably enjoyed a good income. He had purchased the right to collect taxes from his fellow Jews and he intended to make a profit. This was a position that compromised his Jewish loyalties. Indeed, Matthew the publican was marked as a traitor or at least one who was sympathetic with the Roman government. He was probably accused of cheating other Jews. Hardly a likely candidate for discipleship!

II. *The tax collector invited others to meet him.* A meal in the ancient world was a time of close fellowship. When Matthew entertained many tax collectors and "sinners" with Jesus the implication was that Jesus belonged to that crowd—traitorous tax collectors, adulterers, too-sharp business men, those who drank too much wine, and many other offenders. Was the name and person of Jesus to be dragged into the dirt of commonness?

The Pharisees were judgmental. How would Matthew and Jesus fare in your community? Does the church have a ministry to this crowd beyond making harsh judgments? There is no indication there that Jesus condemned them.

Congratulations to Matthew! He not only entertained Jesus but introduced him to his friends. Pharisees must have compromised their hypocrisy to even get within earshot of such a gathering.

III. *Jesus justified his action by Scripture.* Jesus had accepted the invitation. He knew what sort of crowd was eating with him. He knew that by Pharisaical standards he was violating the law. Three statements sum up his response:

(a) "They that are whole have no need of a physician, but they that are sick." Not a quotation from the Old Testament, the statement is yet true to the spirit of the prophets. Had not Elijah gone to a Syrian woman to minister to her need? The love of God conquers personal prejudice.

(b) "I desire mercy and not sacrifice." This is a quotation from Hosea (6:6) and suggests that mercy rules over rules. This is the spirit of Old Testament prophecy. Jesus fit into the same tradition. The Lord God grieved over the restlessness of his people. Their spiritual life was unpredictable.

(c) "I came not to call the righteous, but sinners." Neither is this a direct quotation from the Old Testament, but it is a clear description of Jesus' ministry. Whom does he call? Publicans and sinners—and Pharisees.

The church continued to have a problem with table fellowship. Even in liberal Antioch Paul found the Antioch Jewish

Christians susceptible to pressure from Jerusalem Jewish Christians. Peter was convicted of eating with the wrong crowd. Even Barnabas ceased eating with Gentile Christians. Paul rebuked them all (Gal. 2:11–21).

Wrong crowd indeed.—J. Estill Jones.

July 5. Sheep—No Shepherd

TEXT: Matt. 9:35–10:8.

It's a tragedy to behold: great numbers of sheep gathered for shearing or for slaughter. The somewhat romanticized, certainly intimate relationship between sheep and a good shepherd is no longer visible.

Jesus belonged to a culture much more familiar with sheep. We may not see the great crowds of milling persons at a state fair as sheep. He probably would.

I. *Multitudes!* He saw them. They were everywhere, much like the children playing in the neighborhood at Sunday school time. It is clear that he moved in their midst, not waiting for them to come to him as counselor. Through the cities and the villages he walked, teaching and healing.

Of course the multitudes gathered about him. And of course he was moved with compassion for them. Much as the shepherd was moved with compassion for his sheep, Jesus looked on men and women, boys and girls. They were both distressed and scattered—no shepherd.

The crowd at a ball game, at a political rally—does it move you to compassion, or do you envision that crowd in the Sunday morning service?

II. *Harvest time!* It is strange that he should change the figure from sheep to harvest. The harvest is ready, as ready as in Jesus' glance. When you calculate the brevity of human life, you understand how critical the timing is. It's ready.

It's great—this harvest. We deal with large numbers, not great numbers whom we may have won, but great numbers of the unreached. So far as you can see there are people made in the image of God, able to respond to God.

It's beyond us—this harvest. We shall have to pray that the Lord will send forth laborers.

III. *Chosen!* As if in response to their prayer for laborers he called them unto himself, preparing to send them forth. We probably ought to be cautious in our praying for laborers! He called twelve, representing symbolically the twelve tribes of Israel.

His choice involved his authority, transferable to them. His choice always involves authority and power, authority over evil and power to heal. The twelve were about to assume the role of shepherd.

We remember them—Simon, Andrew, James, John, Philip, and all the rest. It makes you wonder how much we might have remembered about them if they had not followed Jesus. We remember their names, but we do not know the name of the rich young ruler who refused to follow him.

IV. *Sent!* Jesus sent them out into the fields—the crowds. As they went he charged them to go to the lost sheep. The sheep wandering aimlessly about were to have a shepherd after all—a dozen of them were to represent Jesus.

They were to preach the kingdom. It was and is at hand. In the ability of the twelve to share Jesus' power there lies the recognition of the kingdom's presence.

But sheep are never satisfied simply to be called by name, to be "preached at." The clearest indication of the kingdom's presence was the ability of these dozen shepherds: "Heal the sick, raise the dead." The shepherds were to minister to the needs of the sheep.

And so the Good Shepherd looks after the sheep.—J. Estill Jones.

July 12. Fear Not!

TEXT: Matt. 10:24–33.

The admonition is familiar in the New Testament. The angels spoke reassuringly to the shepherds in announcing the birth of Jesus: Fear not! (Luke 2:10). The Son spoke encouragingly to the prophet of Patmos: Fear not! (Rev. 1:17). We need the message.

I. *The truth will be revealed.*

Fear not! You may be wallowing around in false rumors, untrue propositions, and illogical deductions. The truth will be revealed, and you are a disciple of the truth. Jesus reminded his followers that they were his disciples and that they could expect no kinder treatment than he experienced. This is the truth. Discipleship involves ministry and the truth makes servants of us all. He had begun to receive opposition and his disciples could expect to share in it.

Among the false accusations was one identifying Jesus with Beelzebub, prince of demons. Of course it was not true, but in their loyalty to him they shared the accusation. Although for a time they might dwell under that shadow, the time would come when the truth would be apparent.

Fear not! You can afford to rely on the truth. Truth will out! The resurrection replaced the fear of the crucifixion.

II. *Death is not the worst enemy.*

Fear not! You come to understand this in visitation and conversation. We are tempted to dread death as the final defeat, but we know that there are conditions worse than death—at least we Christians know.

Do not be afraid then of those who merely have power to inflict physical death. Have you witnessed a death that you consider a blessing? The fear of death plagues us, but we know better. Is this not the real power of death? The writer of Hebrews describes this fear as being the power that holds us in bondage (Heb. 2: 14–15). We need to hear the word of Jesus: Fear not!

To be sure, there is a place for honest, honorable fear. There is an enemy whom we would do well to fear. Temptation is powerful, partly because it so often appeals to our motive for self-preservation. Our yielding to temptation repeatedly and rebelliously suggests that our loyalties may be in question. Be more afraid of spiritual death—of spiritual failure.

Beyond the sufferings of the crucifixion lay the joys of the resurrection.

III. *You're on the right side.* Fear not! After a strong affirmation of your worth to God, there is the third clear imperative: Fear not. Sparrows are plentiful. To think that the heavenly Father keeps count of those that fall is amazing. And the hairs of your head are numbered: God keeps count.

You are on the side of the concerned heavenly Father. The experience of Israel as the nation crossed into the land of promise featured a choice between Mt. Gerizim and Mt. Ebal—the one a confession of God, the other a rejection of God (Deut. 27:11ff.).

Every person confronts the same choice. The promise is as clear as the warning. You don't have to fear the indecision of God. If we confess Christ, he will confess us. If we deny Christ, he will deny us. It's that simple. The entire paragraph is phrased in the positive.

You're on the right side. Fear not! Three times the admonition: Fear not— the truth will be revealed; Fear not—death is not the worst enemy; Fear not—you're on the right side.—J. Estill Jones.

July 19. Priorities

Text: Matt. 10:34–42.

You can't do everything. You can't be everywhere. So you choose the most important task and the most important place. We have become accustomed to establishing certain priorities. These determine our action. These direct our ministry.

I. *Worth fighting for.* The words are sharp and straightforward: "Don't begin to suppose. . . ." They come from the Prince of Peace. Is it not surprising that Jesus should speak in these terms? Is he simply a realist?

If we are dealing with priorities, is this his method of establishing them? The passage begins with a call to arms and concludes (v. 42) with a disarming kindness.

Of course there are some things worth fighting for. These are not in terms of self-preservation, but the protection of certain principles. What priorities—family, self— are worth the sacrifice? Or is there another?

II. *Family vs. God.* Everyone knows that the family is of primary concern. The family takes first place—almost. Let us suppose that the family is at cross-purposes with God. We are not talking about the government or even the church. The family takes precedence over either. But God? Is it possible for the family to be divided over spiritual priorities?

The family is a priority second only to God himself. A person's first loyalty is to the family. We may suppose that the reference in Matthew is to a family divided over spiritual matters—over loyalty to God. Under these circumstances loyalty to God is the priority (Mic. 7:6).

The family takes its ranking with respect to its relations with God. The supreme loyalty is to God and to his purpose. Any loyalty threatening that one is out of line: "He that loveth father, mother, son, or daughter more than me. . . ." There is every encouragement elsewhere to love the family, but love to God is the first priority.

III. *Self vs. God.* In establishing a ranking of priorities the family outranks self. It is probable, however, that the conflict of self with God is more apparent. For the first time in the Gospel according to Matthew there is a reference to the cross.

The emphasis on the negative is interesting: "Who is not worthy of me?" Taking the cross designed for self and following after Jesus is the denial of self and the assertion of loyalty to God. This loyalty expresses itself in following—day by day.

Another way of expressing it is in terms of lost and found. When self becomes the priority, the self is saved—but what a self!

IV. *Contagious.* With the cross now in the foreground the identity of Master and disciples becomes clearer. There is a close relationship between Father, Son, and disciple. The right priorities make it possible.

Then there is the matter of rewards, a subject that Jesus discussed freely. He knew that we were interested. What's in it for me, other than a cross? There is the reward of a righteous man, Job perhaps. Observe that the principle of sacrifice is yet around.

It is contagious. Receiving and giving characterize the disciple's life. Following Jesus involves us in the ministry of giving. This is a priority—a cup of cold water to the thirsty. This insures a disciple's reward.

You see, we began with conflict; we conclude with ministry. That's life—establishing priorities.—J. Estill Jones.

July 26. Come Unto Me
TEXT: Matt. 11:25–30.

Is this not characteristic of Jesus? He called the fishermen, the tax collector, the others of the Twelve, the rich young ruler, and many others (Luke 9:57–60). Some followed. Many refused the invitation. The pattern still persists.

I. *I represent the Father: "Come!"* The paragraph preceding our text is a denunciation of those who rejected Jesus' ministry. To the tragedy of such rejection Jesus spoke words of thanksgiving: at least some had observed God's revelation in himself. The high and mighty had rejected him, but the babes had accepted him. This was the Father's work.

The Son is the Father's revelation and the Father's invitation. Jesus always appealed to men and women to do the Father's will. The invitation here reminds us of the prophet's word (Isa. 55:1).

The Son is the Father's final revelation. God had spoken many times in many ways through many people, but in Jesus he spoke most clearly, most lovingly, most appealingly (Heb. 1:1–3). The word of the Father, spoken through Jesus, is "Come."

II. *You are weary.* All of us are. Ask your friends, your family, your associates. From dawn to dark they worked—and many before dawn on the Sea of Galilee, and many after dark. They probably welcomed the relief of following Jesus about the countryside.

On the other hand, some must have been tired of not working. Many of our contemporaries are. Perhaps this is even more difficult to endure. Few things are more wearying than sitting around with nothing to do.

Aren't you tired of warmongering? The front page of every newspaper tells of a new threat.

Aren't you tired of terrorism? It doesn't seem safe to fly, to drive, or even to walk.

Aren't you tired of hunger? Perhaps you've never experienced it yourself. But you have seen the bloated bodies of little children, the thin, emaciated bodies of hungry adults.

Aren't you tired of oppression? Tyrants rule half the world and their subjects can only endure. Can you do more?

Aren't you tired of it all? The Apostle Paul even cautioned the Thessalonians about being "weary in well-doing"! (2 Thess. 3:13)

III. *I will give you rest.* This is his promise, and it makes the invitation most attractive. You see, he knew what it was to be tired and hungry (John 4:6). He understands the plight of most of the world.

He relieves weariness by offering rest. He relieves anxiety by offering calm. He relieves frustration by offering satisfaction.

His promise is clear: "I will give you rest!" It is extended to all the weary in the world, to all the heavy laden. If you have thought about the world's suffering enough to be burdened by it, he will give you rest.

IV. *You become my disciple.* This is giving rest? He spoke of yokes and learning. Oxen wear yokes at work. Students sweat when learning.

The yoke helped the oxen to pull more easily. Believe it: his yoke is satisfying and easy. His learners knew him to be gentle, "meek and lowly in heart."

Millions can attest, his yoke is easy and his burden is light. And this while busying themselves as disciples of Jesus. His word is yet appealing: "Come unto me."—J. Estill Jones.

August 2. Harvest of Surprise

TEXT: Matt. 13:1–9, 18–23.

I. Every parable related by Jesus had a hook in it (as in fish hook). There was always something so unusual or different that the audience would be caught or "hooked." Once Jesus had the audience's attention, he moved them on to some spiritual truth. In the famous parable of the sower, the emphasis should be upon the unusual fact of a hundredfold harvest at the end. In biblical Palestine such a harvest was unheard of. Farmers threw their seeds upon the field and then plowed them under. In such haphazard farming, many seeds never germinated, let alone produced fruit. The point of the parable is the surprise harvest at the end of the growing season.

II. The point should be made that in spite of all the hazards, the farmer reaped a hundredfold. In spite of the fact that some seeds fell along the paths and were eaten by the birds, there was a hundredfold harvest. In spite of the fact that some seed fell on rocky soil and wilted in the scorching sun, there was a hundredfold harvest. In spite of the fact that some seed fell among the thorns and were choked, there was a hundredfold harvest. Great confidence is thus given to the proclaimer that a victorious harvest will be attained. Sometimes Christians tend to dwell on the negatives—worship attendance down, giving on a disastrous curve, no new members in a year. Yet the parable tells us to expect victory. It is always easier to preach about the people who are not at church on Sunday morning than to address the needs of those who are there. We can dwell on missed opportunities rather than the real live possibilities before us. The proverbial fisherman usually spends more time talking about the one that got away rather than the actual catch. It always seems to be larger and more exotic than any real catch. We can dwell on the seed that was lost or look forward expectantly to the hundredfold harvest from what we have.

III. The parable of the sower belongs to a category of seed parables that teach the truth "from small beginnings expect great results." In Mark's account (4:1–8) of the same parable, the context broadens to include two other seed parables. Jesus had just called his disciples and here began to teach them that the small beginnings of his ministry would expand into a great harvest. In the parable of the sower the small seed thrown out upon the land might seem insignificant. Yet within a few months, the heads of grain would crisscross the fields. Who would have thought that from twelve disciples would spring forth a spiritual kingdom that would encircle the globe? Quite a harvest of surprise! —James L. Blevins.

August 9. Patiently Waiting

TEXT: Matt. 13:24–30, 36–43.

I. The parable of the tares among the wheat calls for the virtue of patience on the part of believers. The cost involves patience beyond the normal limits. Like the biblical farmer one might be tempted to rush out and pull out the weeds (darnel) from the wheat. Yet the hundreds of weeds had roots that were intertwined with the wheat. The best approach was to wait for the harvest when the plants could be safely separated. Waiting is sometimes the most difficult part of the kingdom. Fools rush in where often the better approach would be to wait upon the Lord to work out the problem. In haste, we often make snap judgments about people rather than waiting to get to know them better. Sometimes, snap decisions are made rather than waiting upon knowing the will of God.

II. Waiting, however, should not be viewed as passive living but rather expectant openness to the future. The believer knows that God has control of the world and will bring it to an end according to his purposes. The Christian is not called upon to take a stoic attitude toward the world. He or she knows that the righteousness of God will one day prevail. Yet the kingdom has broken into the world. God's mercy and love are already with us. Waiting involves actual service in his name. Perhaps waiting implies that not all of the victories are going to be won in our lifetime. Perhaps it is knowing that the kingdom is larger than any one of us or any one church. We are but small drops in the large sea of God's kingdom. Yet God's rule does include us in the present as we wait patiently for God's day of fulfillment. Believers thus cannot be passive members of the kingdom. Waiting involves laying hold of present opportunities and participating in the kingdom.

III. Waiting also includes casting an eye toward the future. At the end of the long road is the ultimate victory. We live in the certainty that God's kingdom will be realized in the future. God's rule does include justice and righteousness. The Christian cannot view the present world with its injustice and evil without the fervent hope that one day all that will be eradicated. Waiting involves the fervent hope that evil will be rooted out and good will be victorious. The righteous will one day "shine like the sun in the kingdom of their Father" (Matt. 13:42 RSV). An eye cast toward the future does not mean an otherworldly spirit. Expectant waiting emphasizes that one's present experience with God is just a foretaste of the kingdom's fullness. One

day the tares will be separated from the wheat and the harvest will be complete. —James L. Blevins.

August 16. Counting the Cost
TEXT: Matt. 13:44–52.

I. The kingdom does involve a cost—it is worth all that one has. It is like the man who sold all his possessions to obtain the treasure buried in the field. Sometimes the most worthwhile things in life have a high price attached to them. A college education has a very high price tag attached to it. Yet college graduates earn thousands more dollars over a lifetime than those who do not graduate. The grace of God is free—salvation is a gift. Yet the kingdom offers a challenge that demands all. Any less is not worthy of the kingdom. When one is confronted by the good news of the gospel, one will do everything to possess it.

II. Sometimes it is difficult to know when you have found the treasure or the pearl of great price that you have been looking for. Some people search for years to find meaning and purpose in their lives. They seek the latest thrill and excitement or the most recent fad. We all have heard of the jet set. They travel from place to place all over the world seeking that which is stimulating and exciting. Many young people are searching for that treasure to which they can give their lives. The gospel is that pearl of great price. Often we come to the end of the road before we ever find it.

III. What you devote your life to is of the highest importance. Someone has said that you always have time for what is important to you. Where you spend most of your life says volumes about the priorities of your being. From the Christian point of view such decisions have eschatological implications. The day is coming when our Lord will ask us concerning the treasures of our lives. What issues have demanded our time and energy? Those who have put the kingdom first—have counted the cost—will see their Lord face to face.

IV. Kingdom members will know how to sort through life and make the vital decision among the old things in their lives as well as the new. The cost of the kingdom demands an assessment of life. The call of Christ causes me to evaluate life. Some of the old things are worth taking along on the pilgrimage. Yet other new things are needed as well. God's kingdom places new demands and priorities on believers. At times it is painful to assess your life. The question "What is really important to me?" is a difficult one to confront. Even more stressful is the question "What is really worth all my life?" Yet sacrifice and pain are always a part of worthwhile accomplishments. Assessment of one's life is never an easy thing. The cost is high, yet very worthwhile. The Master challenges us to give our all and in so doing to really discover life. We cannot put our hand to the plow and look back. The kingdom demands all that we have.—James L. Blevins.

August 23. Christ, the Compassionate Helper

TEXT: Matt. 14:13–21.

In the midst of our ofttimes incompassionate world, consider our compassionate Christ. His feelings ever went out to the suffering and needy. He not only empathized with them, he also sought to share with them and to meet their needs.

I. *Compassion in the death of others.* The text reminds us of the compassion of Christ in the face of death. The news of the tragic, uncalled-for, and obscene death of John the Baptist struck deep sorrow into Jesus' breast: "When Jesus heard this, he withdrew . . . to a lonely place apart." Never an unmoved stoic at the death of others, he was instead moved with sympathy and compassion. Here, as is so poignantly displayed in his weeping at Lazarus' death (John 11:35), we see the deep compassion of Jesus in the wake of death.

II. *Compassion on the multitudes.* Often when feeling the press of the masses, the pain of overcrowding, and the suffering of overpopulation, we attempt to shut the multitude out of our mind and seek escape in various ways. The great Christ, though suffering his own inward emotional pain, displayed a different attitude to the masses. Christ was moved to love and deep feeling for the great throng of humanity and its many needs.

III. *Compassion for the sick.* In a world of competition and survival of the fittest, we can easily ignore the sick, the injured, and the infirm. That was never the way of the Christ. His feelings always went out to the blind, the lame, the paralyzed, the deaf, the mute, and the ill. It was not, however, enough for him to empathize with them. The compassion of Christ led him to action—to a ministry of reaching out to them, to lifting them up and healing them (14b).

IV. *Compassion for the hungry.* Christ was never content to care only for the spiritual and religious needs of others. He was too much of a realist, one who cared for the whole of life, to make that mistake. Neither did he make the mistake of allowing the overwhelming magnitude of the problem (notice the number of five thousand men besides women and children) to immobilize him. Nor did he let the scanty resources (five loaves and two fish) frustrate him. He was not content with mere compassion, empathy, and feelings for the hungry; he acted to meet the needs.

True Christian compassion avoids the callousness of closed hearts. It feels deep concern for the needy of the world and reaches out to them with hands to work for meeting all their needs.—Ronald F. Deering.

August 30. Devotion and Faith Overcoming Fear and Failing

TEXT: Matt. 14:22–33.

I. *Prayer and devotion.* Too often we sail into the unknown, the storms, and the darkness of life, relying only on our own strength and skill.

Jesus did not make this common mistake. He strengthened himself with devotion and prayer "as he went up into the hills by himself to pray." The Gospel accounts of the life of Jesus are replete with examples of his gathering up of spiritual resources through his times alone with the Father and time spent in meditation and prayer.

While Jesus was always compassionate toward the crowds and anxious to help them, he always remembered the need for private, personal renewal. He modeled that in his own life and taught his disciples its absolute necessity in their lives as well.

II. Victory over waves, wind, and night.
People in the boat of life, alone and relying only on their own resources, are soon threatened and overwhelmed by the storms, the waves, the winds, and the darkness of life's seas. The mighty Jesus, strengthened by prayer and devotion, walked on the sea, over the rampaging waves, and through the stormy night to come to his frightened and perishing disciples. He triumphs over the storms of lives as surely as he does over the natural elements as the Christ of the universe.

III. Fear and terror. Still fear and terror fill the lives of those living on their own resources. Even the coming of their Lord in the midst of their trials can be misunderstood. They mistake even him for a ghost. Terrified, they cry out in fear.

When his people hear him speak, hear his voice, understand his message in the storm, however, they take heart, are encouraged, and fear is banished.

IV. Faltering faith and sinking fear. It is not just for once that the Lord of the storm must be recognized, if the Christian is to remain free of fear able to overcome the storms of life. Faith must remain constant, the vision must be riveted on the Lord and not distracted by the faithless preoccupation with what would make us fail.

Faith centered in the Christ made possible Peter's walk over the stormy sea and he felt the joy of victory. But when he moved his attention from the Christ to the waves, the storm, the dark, and their threats against him, his faith faltered, and he began to fall.

True to Christ's everlasting love, he immediately extended his hand to his falling disciple. We have but to take the hand of the Master, place our faith in him, and we win again over fear and terror, the waves, the storms, and the darkness, for we reach out to the one who is "truly . . . the Son of God."—Ronald F. Deering.

September 6. Jesus and a Foreigner
TEXT: Matt. 15:21–28.
The story of Jesus and the Canaanite woman of Tyre and Sidon reflects the prejudice and animosity that the Jews of Jesus' time felt toward Gentiles. It can also be a powerful corrective for our own hostilities to strangers and lack of concern for foreigners.

I. Mercy for foreigners. Despite the attitude of exclusivism and disdain for foreigners of his own people, Jesus did not reply harshly to the pleading request of the alien woman. Nor did he allow the prompting, even the begging, of his prejudiced disciples to turn away his mercy, as they pleaded with him to send away this strange woman. He realized that the deep, tender, and human feelings of this Gentile woman were just as precious as those of any Jewish mother.

Perhaps Jesus in retiring to this area of Tyre and Sidon, outside of the land of the Jews, was seeking rest and release from the anguished needs of the throngs about him. But even on "vacation" Jesus could not deny or relinquish the spirit of mercy that consistently characterized his life and ministry.

Mercy is what the woman asked for. Jesus knew that true mercy—the unmerited favor of God—was a blessing that no Jew was any more worthy of than any Gentile foreigner. Its availability was more in the quality of the giver (God) than in the recipients (human beings).

Here in this place and incident in the life of Jesus, even in the Gospels, it is clear that God's mercy, his saving grace, and indeed his salvation was not to be limited to the Jews but was meant to extend to all humankind.

II. Help for the demon possessed. Probably it was not only to show the universal availability of the grace of God that Jesus helped this woman. It must also have been, at least in part, because of the suffering of the daughter. Whether a little child, an older girl, or a woman, Jesus recognized and honored that special relationship between parent and child, mother and daughter.

The Master must have been especially touched by her affliction—"severely possessed by a demon." The power of evil spirits to ravage God's creatures must have grieved his heart, and moreover the severity of what demons had done to her life and the grief that it had brought to a mother's heart.

Jesus would not allow the prejudices, the exclusivism, and provincialism of his time to prevent him from acting to free victims of the work of the Evil One.

III. *Rewards for faith and persistence.* Most of all, the Master must have been moved to give his miraculous gift of healing by the reality and depth of the woman's faith. He tested that faith with the assertion that he was "sent only to the lost sheep of Israel." But that did not deter her. She went even further and knelt, calling him Lord and confidently requesting his help.

Further, he tested her faith with the saying about the unfairness of giving children's bread to the dogs. But she replied plaintively, "Yes, Master, but the crumbs for the puppies!" Her faith was genuine and deep, but we should note also that it was persistent.

Jesus recognized her faith and its persistence and gave her the reward that follows faith so naturally in the grace of God, even for strangers.—Ronald F. Deering.

September 13. Knowing Jesus

TEXT: Matt. 16:13–20.

Of all the knowledge that we can ever attain, the Bible affirms that knowing Jesus is the most important of all. Even Jesus in his own lifetime emphasized the importance of knowing him.

I. *What others think of him.* Jesus begins the quest, as well we might, by asking what other people say of him. The answers of the ordinary people of his day suggest the world's understanding of him in our own time. He is seen as a man of God, as a miracle worker, as a great prophet and teacher. Indeed, the greatness of Jesus is apparent not only to the ordinary people of his own day, but also in the testimony of persons of twenty centuries since. Even today millions of people, though not his disciples, understand his greatness historically, ethically, and culturally.

II. *A personal understanding of Jesus.* It was not enough for Jesus, however, for his disciples to know or even accept what others thought or said about him. He wanted even more to know what his disciples personally thought of him. The question "Who do you say that I am?" (v. 15) caught them, and catches us, with the inescapable personal nature of the claims of Jesus upon our lives. It is not enough to know him in history, in theology, in religion. Jesus insists upon a personal, intimate, experiential knowledge of him. It is a knowledge not just of the mind, but of faith, of acceptance, of fellowship and commitment that he demands. It bespeaks a relationship to him that each one of us must have individually, independently of all others, personally, and intimately.

III. *The son of the living God.* This knowing of Jesus is most accurately put both in his day and in our own in knowing Jesus as "the Christ, the Son of the Living God" (v. 16). The phrase witnesses to Jesus as the fulfillment of all of God's promises to the Jews for a Messiah, a Savior, a priestly King. It acknowledges in Jesus the fulfillment of God's plan for humanity, from beginning to end, from creation to eternity. It acknowledges the incarnation of God, the breaking of God into time, human life, and history in the flesh and blood of his son, Jesus of Nazareth. Further, it acknowledges him as Son of a *living* God, a God who is vital, active, working, and purposeful—the eternal God.

IV. *The blessedness of knowing him.* Jesus declares the blessedness of knowing him in this way. It is the greatest knowledge of life. It is a knowledge that brings joy, peace, and security. This blessed knowledge comes not from "flesh and blood," that is humanly; it comes as a gift of the grace of God himself (v. 17b). This most intimate knowledge of him can never be just intellectual, the result of human work; it is God's gift, his grace.

V. *Foundational knowledge.* It is this kind of personal, intimate, experiential knowledge of Jesus as "the Christ, the Son of the Living God" that is the rock upon which he builds his church. It is the foundation of the church. Death itself cannot prevail against this knowledge. This knowledge offers the keys of the kingdom of heaven, and it has the power of both binding and setting free both on earth and in heaven.—Ronald F. Deering.

September 20. Cross and Crown

TEXT: Matt. 16:21–28.

In God's plan for Christ, the cross of his suffering was to lead to the crown of his resurrection. As his teachings show, this is also the way for his followers. God rewards undeserved, righteous suffering with his ultimate reversal, giving the crown rather than cross.

I. *The suffering way of Christ.* Immediately following his disciples' recognition of who he really was, Jesus began to teach his disciples the way that had been divinely ordained for him. He was to walk the way of perfect obedience to the will of the Father. This way was bound to bring him opposition and animosity from the misguided religious leaders of his day. It would cause him to suffer not only rejection, but spiritual and physical persecution. He revealed that his righteous and total obedience would lead even to his death.

The word *must* in verse 21 should not be overlooked. By this word Jesus seeks to show that this course is a necessity. It is a part of the divine plan to bring salvation to a lost world—to bring all people to God, and to reveal his plan for the way his people also should live their lives.

II. *The natural rejection of the suffering way.* In the quick and forceful objections of Peter we see immediately the natural human rebellion against the way of God for both Christ and his followers. Peter will have nothing to do with this way; he rebukes Jesus. Reflecting the selfishness and resistance of human nature against such total obedience and self-sacrificing, innocent suffering for others, he cries out against this divinely ordained way for Jesus. He says, "God forbid." He would replace divine wisdom with human self-centeredness, selfishness, and cowardice.

Jesus turns back upon his disciple in his error. He calls Peter "Satan," meaning that he has allowed himself in his flawed thinking to become the instrument of the evil one. Peter had become an adversary of Jesus in this regard. He was tempting Jesus to reject the way of total obedience to God, to flee from his will in order to escape suffering. He sees in Peter's attitude and words a real hindrance to life and work of the Christ.

III. *The disciple must follow the way of the Master.* Difficult as it may have been for Peter to learn of righteous and innocent suffering as the way for Christ, how much more difficult it must have been for him to learn that this, too, is the way for the disciples of Christ. For Jesus now teaches that it is not only true that he must live this way, but also his disciples. Those who come after him must deny themselves; they must share the cross of his sufferings and pattern their lives after him. The disciples, too, are called upon to live a life of self-sacrifice, of losing their lives for his sake.

The disciples are promised, though, that just as the cross was the path to resurrection and the crown in Jesus' own life, so it is with the disciples. Those who walk after him in this way will find their lives. He warns them just as sternly that if they reject this way—the way of God, both for Christ and the disciple—they will surely ultimately forfeit their lives, even though they may have gained the whole world. And he asks the haunting but powerful question, "What would that profit a man?"—Ronald F. Deering.

September 27. Life in the Church
TEXT: Matt. 18:15–20.

Life in the church and dealings between Christians are to be determined not by their own ideas of rights and privileges, or even of political democracy, but by the teachings of its Lord—Jesus Christ.

I. *Disagreements between brothers and sisters.* Given the inescapable difference in people —their backgrounds, emotional predispositions, experiences in life, and intellectual levels—it is inevitable that there will be disagreements between people. Further, given the fact that all people are sinful by human nature, it is inevitable that they will on occasion be unkind, wrong, and hurtful to their fellows. This is true especially as people are closely related to each other, even in the church.

Jesus instructs his disciples on how they are to deal with differences among Christians. There may be a disagreement, hurtful words, wrong acts, or disruptive attitudes and feelings. Jesus' first instruction is that we are to go immediately, directly, and personally to the individual with whom we have a difference. We are not to hide, ignore, or cover up our differences. We are to accept, acknowledge, and confront each other over our differences. It is taken for granted, in the fellowship of the church, that we will do this in the spirit of goodwill and with positive goals. If this brings reconciliations, this is the best solution to the problem and should be the end of the matter.

If the problem is not resolved between the two persons together, Jesus says that the two having problems should reach out to one or two others to work together with them to resolve the dispute. This should be a sort of Christian arbitration, whereby a few mutually loved and loving, respected brothers or sisters would help to restore broken relationships.

II. *Submission to the church.* It is only when direct personal dealings with each other and the helpful efforts of a few others have failed to bring reconciliation, that Jesus tells us that we should refer the problem to other processes. He gives no instructions to us to go to court with each other, or to try to resolve our disputes by human law. He requires us to bring our disputes before the church—the corporate, shared fellowship of other disciples. It is then required by Jesus that we listen to the judgment of the church, accept its corporate wisdom, and be reconciled to one another. If either, or both, will not listen to the church, that is, accept its wisdom and judgment, and be reconciled to each other, then one or both by this refusal mark themselves off as outsiders to the fellowship of the church.

III. *The power of agreement.* Jesus moves now to instruct his disciples about the great power of agreeing together. He shows them how this kind of agreement has power to bind and stop evil, and how it has the power to liberate and set free the good upon earth and in heaven. When we are agreed, united, and work together, we can bind and hold back the destructive forces at work in the world. In that same harmony, together we can set people and things free to accomplish good upon the earth.

IV. *The ever-present Christ.* At last Jesus brings his disciples to understand that in gathering in his name, in resolving their differences in his fellowship, and in binding the evil and loosing the good in this world, they may be sure that he himself is there with them, indeed in the midst of them. In fact, it is his presence, truly acknowledged, felt, and accepted in our lives that enables us to resolve differences. It is his power in the church that enables it to bind and set free; and it is the agreement of his disciples with the will of Christ that brings the promise that anything asked in this spirit "will be done for them by my Father in heaven" (v. 20).—Ronald F. Deering.

October 4. Forgiving As We Have Been Forgiven

TEXT: Matt. 18:21–35.

Of all the Christian graces, perhaps the most difficult to incorporate fully into one's life is the spirit of forgiveness. Yet Jesus insisted that we let forgiving one another have a prominent place in the Christian life.

I. *How often shall we forgive another?* The very question that Peter asked of Jesus reveals the natural, sinful, human inclination to limit forgiving of one's fellows. Surely every good man or woman would say a person should be forgiven once. A religious person would go further and say one should be forgiven twice. Everyone deserves a second chance. Catching a gleam of Jesus' spirit of forgiveness, Peter adds to his question, "As many as seven times?" Jesus however will not limit forgiveness to seven times but insists on seventy times seven. That quantity is large in itself, but we must note that the number seven in the Bible already symbolizes wholeness and completeness. Then note that Jesus is represented here as multiplying it by ten to seventy, and then multiplying it again by seven, the number again of wholeness and completeness. The inescapable conclusion is that a Christian must forgive without limit, just as it is with God and Christ.

So often we see revealed in the life and work of Jesus the reality of his teaching and his words. It is no less true in the matter of forgiving others. This is seen poignantly and powerfully in his prayer for those who evilly mistreated him in his crucifixion when he cried out, "Father, forgive them, for they know not what they do" (Luke 23:34).

II. *The mercy of being forgiven.* Jesus now tells his disciples the touching story of a servant's great debts to his lord, the lord's calling him to account, and the pronouncement of just punishment. Then comes the cry for mercy and forgiveness from the servant, who is then freely released from deserved punishment, set free, and forgiven. Surely Jesus means for his disciples and for us to see in the story to this point the great joy, release, and freedom that forgiveness brings to the heavily burdened recipient of mercy.

III. *The sin of the unforgiving heart.* Jesus' story progresses, however, to reveal the great sin of the unforgiving heart. Having experienced the great and free forgivingness of his lord, the wicked servant could not or would not display that spirit of forgiveness in his own life toward others indebted to him. Indeed, we see this man deal harshly with his fellow in the same matter for which he himself had been forgiven. The situation seems even worse when we remember that this man had been forgiven a debt of "ten thousand talents" and would not forgive his servant an infinitely smaller debt of "a hundred denarii" (vv. 24, 28). Not only does he not forgive, he also goes deeper in sin and wreaks vengeance on the debtor.

In the story the lord hears of the unforgiving spirit of his forgiven servant and brings deserved judgment upon him. Just so, says Jesus, will the Father do to every one who will not forgive a brother from the heart.—Ronald F. Deering.

October 11. Is There Any Justice?
TEXT: Matt. 20:1–16.
I. *The problem of injustice.* Every one of us knows how it feels to be treated unfairly. In actual fact, we may not in a particular case be treated unfairly at all, but we may feel like a victim of injustice if we expected something different from what we got.

So it is not hard to sympathize with the disappointed laborers in Jesus' parable. The saying of Jesus, therefore, may hit us hard: "So the last will be first and the first last."

Does this mean that we live in a world where the unexpected is the rule, where even wrong is forever on the throne? This puts the issue of justice and injustice before us.

II. *The sources of the sense of injustice.*
(a) Puzzling things do happen to us. Two children grow up in the same community. Both marry, and the home of one is fulfilling, while the home of the other is a nightmare. One college roommate goes on to success in a profession, but the other is killed in an accident on the day of graduation. Even the Bible adds to our puzzlement (see Matt. 24:40–41; Rom. 9:13).

(b) Is it any wonder, then, that we sometimes feel that no one cares, or that we have been dealt with arbitrarily? In Archibald MacLeish's *J.B.,* J.B.'s wife says, "Cry for justice and the stars / Will stare until your eyes sting."

III. *Possible solutions.* What can we possibly do about the riddle of inequality, our feeling of often being the victims of injustice?

(a) We can accept injustice as a necessary part of life and ignore it. But we are not Stoics; we are Christians, and we care. We have to try to root out injustice, if we can, from our own behavior and from society.

(b) Though we cannot completely accept injustice or completely eliminate it, we can trust God with the problem. Abraham put the question sharply when he asked, "Shall not the Judge of all the earth do right?" (Gen. 18:25 RSV).

IV. *Working out the best solution.*
(a) Then what does and will God do?
(1) He participates in what is going on in our lives. Nothing human is alien to his loving concern and involvement. So Jesus Christ came in the flesh, the very embodiment of God's concern and love. Like the servant in Isaiah, "he has borne our griefs and carried our sorrows" (Isa. 53:4a RSV).

(2) Not only does he participate with us in what is going on in our lives, he also pronounces the final judgment on the whole situation. He knows—and he alone —whether it is just and fair. And here is where the words of Jesus begin to make great, good sense. God in his love is full of gracious surprises: "So the last will be first and the first last" (v. 16 RSV).

(b) But is there anything that we can do about our sometimes bitter feeling that life—including God—is unjust? We can do what Habakkuk did. After our complaining we can listen to God as he says, "The righteous man shall live by his faithfulness—his faith, such as it is, that produces a dogged clinging to God in spite of everything" (Hab. 2:4; cf. 3:17–18).

(c) Is there really any other possibility of fulfillment, life being what it is? Some come off better in the end than they ever dared hope, but no one will be at last short-changed.—James W. Cox.

October 18. Sinners Over Saints?
TEXT: Matt. 21:28–32.

I. The kingdom of God is for all people —good and bad. The gospel is directed to all who have need. The universal appeal of the good news echoes across our world. The Christian mission has always been directed to all people in the world, no matter their social status. In the Jewish temple of the first century A.D., walls kept various classes of people separate from God. There was a court of the women, a court of the Gentiles, and a court of Israel. In Jesus' teaching, these walls came tumbling down. Sinners were invited to sit down with the righteous keeper of the Law. Women were allowed to be active in the kingdom as well as the men.

II. In fact, according to Jesus, the repentant sinner entered the kingdom ahead of the self-righteous keeper of the Law. The son who rejected his father's demands but later repented and carried them out, Jesus praised. Yet the son who said yes to his father's demands but never carried out his wishes was condemned. The kingdom of God has different standards than many institutions in our world. For many modern people, lip service is all that is needed. A premium is placed upon saying the right thing at the right time. It is difficult to find anyone to carry through with assigned duties and obligations. Workers that one hires to do repair jobs in the home often do not live up to their contracts. Even workers in the church will take on an office or a Sunday school class and never carry the project through to completion. We have become a society of words and more words—often empty words. The kingdom is made up of those who let their "yes be yes" and their "no be no." There is nothing to be gained in the kingdom by an empty yes to the Lord. Pretense cannot be abided in the work of God. The church cannot be a stage in which we play our parts on Sunday, only to return to normal living on Monday. Throughout the centuries, Christianity has been rightly charged at times with hypocrisy.

III. How will the sinner enter the kingdom ahead of the righteous one? How will the repentant son enter ahead of the self-righteous one? Jesus looked upon the hearts of individuals. Today, we classify people with labels—drunkard, harlot, divorcée. We fail to see the possibilities in a fellow human being's character. The church has lost its mission to be the spiritual hospital of the world—mending up broken lives. Jesus taught that salvation is available to those who recognize the sin of their lives and turn to him in an attitude of repentance. The self-righteous person never recognizes that kind of need. The sinner who truly repents and turns to God has a much better chance of seeing what the kingdom of God is all about. This world's walls are broken by the power of the gospel.—James L. Blevins.

October 25. Majoring in the Minors
TEXT: Matt. 21:33–43.

I. From those who have received much, much is expected. Israel had received the promises of the covenant. As workers in the vineyard, they should have received the landowner's son, but they rejected him instead. God's servants, the prophets, had spoken to Israel preparing them for the arrival of the Son. Sometimes in life, those best prepared are the very ones who miss out on the opportunities. People who are really blessed with talents are at times the ones who are least aware of it. The promises of God surround us all, yet there are those who never lay hold of them. The truth is evident that we shall be held responsible for these missed opportunities. In Christ, abundant living stands before each of us. Yet each individual must step forward to grasp life and make the most of it.

II. The best gifts are the unexpected ones. In our parable, the vineyard was let out to other tenants. The Gentiles least expected to be heirs of the kingdom. They were often called dogs by the Jews. It often comes as a surprise to the outsiders that they are included in the kingdom. God never seems to work in human channels of logic and reason. The surprise element is always present in the plans of God. Humans often think in terms of getting even or revenge. God works through the medium of love and mercy. The woman taken in adultery expected to be condemned, but Jesus spoke words of forgiveness to her. The prodigal son expected to be turned out by his father; he did not expect a feast in his honor and his father's signet ring. The thief on the cross might have expected to be tormented by the crowd but instead he heard words of hope spoken from Jesus. When you are at the bottom of the rope of despair, mercy and grace seem least expected. At the darkest moment of life, the appearance of light is a surprise. Yet the message comes that those caught in the miry clay of life have become heirs—heirs of the promises of God.

III. Matthew tells us that the son was cast out of the vineyard and then slain. The cross of Christ stands as a symbol of hope to the outcasts and rejects of the world. Jesus himself was born in a stable, not the inn of Bethlehem. He had no place to call his own. He worked in a carpenter's shop as a construction worker, not as a teacher in some high class rabbinical school. When he did teach, he had no classroom, only the fields and hillsides of Galilee. Even his death was by crucifixion, a penalty reserved for robbers and extremists. His place of burial was a borrowed tomb. One with such a strong tradition of being an outsider can speak relevant words to the outcasts of the world. The focus of the gospel is always upon the outsiders of our world. Those invited to God's kingdom include everyone who will receive the invitation. The vineyard has been given to other tenants —the least expected ones.—James L. Blevins.

November 1. Abounding Joy
TEXT: Matt. 22:1–14.

I. Jesus often compared the kingdom to a wedding feast. The major reason he did this was that such feasts were occasions for joy. If there is anything that should typify Christian living it is the quality of joy. It is never a momentary joy that comes from hearing something funny. Rather, it is a joy that comes deep from within. There is a little chorus that young people sing in their retreats called "Down in My Heart." The first line goes, "I've got the joy, joy, joy, joy down in my heart." This is the kind of joy that Jesus spoke about. It is a joy that starts deep in the heart and wells up to fill your whole soul. Strangely, it is a joy that often stems from struggle and suffering from within. In ancient Palestine, very few people got enough to eat or drink. An invitation to a wedding feast was an occasion for great joy. It meant one week of feasting and drinking. The kingdom in like manner opens the door to abundant living.

II. The kingdom also demands a radical decision from those invited. The invitations to the wedding feast were sent out, but many excuses were given for not attending. God grants to each of us the freedom to say yes or no to the invitation. The invitation, however, demands some kind of decision. One must accept or reject the invitation to joy and abundant living. One can live a life surrounded by legitimate excuses and miss some of the greatest opportunities of life. Mundane affairs always make their claims upon our time. Yet we always seem to find time for those things that are important to us. The kingdom cannot take a back seat to other endeavors. It has the unique ability to lay claim on all that we are. It can really be nothing else. The joy of the kingdom is involved in throwing off the tired old excuses and giving a resounding yes to the kingdom.

III. The call to the marriage supper is a universal one. Yet there is a note that repentance is demanded. In the parable at hand, the guests show up but some are not properly dressed for the occasion—they have no wedding garments. Sometimes we turn faith into a carnival religion. We emphasize the joy, excitement, and emotion but never underline the demands. Faith is more than walking down the aisle in some tent crusade or revival. It must include a radical change of living. The power of Christ can effect that. The true joy of the wedding feast stems from the change of heart that has come about on the inside.

The proper wedding garment is the resulting righteousness bestowed upon us by our Lord. We dare not take God's grace and mercy for granted. We must always view his call to us as sacred and serious. —James L. Blevins.

November 8. God And/Or Caesar?
TEXT: Matt. 22:15–22.

I. The Pharisees put Jesus in a very delicate position. Were he openly to affirm payment of taxes to hated Roman captors, he would appear to be a traitor to his people. Were he openly to oppose, the Romans would immediately pounce on him as a potential troublemaker—an ardent and dangerous Jewish nationalist. He got himself off of the horns of this dilemma by putting us on another one. Caesar should get what he deserves. God should get what he deserves. Jesus didn't say what should happen when what belongs to Caesar would clash with what belongs to God. A number of people today feel the tension. Should one pay the portion of taxes that will build more powerful nuclear weapons, construct more sophisticated guidance systems, buy longer range missiles, or add to military hardware that threatens the survival of humankind? Sometimes it can't be God and Caesar; it must be God or Caesar. Does Jesus' paradox take that into account?

II. "Render to Caesar the things that are Caesar's" is sometimes taken to mean, "Caesar should get whatever Caesar wants!" States do make such absolutist claims. They monopolize power. Controlling both military and police forces, they sometimes operate above law. Once totalitarian rulers control the law, they tolerate no opposition. Is that what Jesus proposed? Far from it! We must not miss the point of his action in calling for a coin and asking whose image it bore. Caesar, in this case Tiberius, could claim what he could put his image on—the coin of the empire. He could not demand also what only God had put his image on—humankind. Paying Caesar what is due does not imply servitude of body, mind, and soul. As one early Christian perceived, we "honor" the ruler, but we "fear" God (1 Pet. 2:17). Resistance to the powers that be is sometimes justified, necessitated, when Caesar steps beyond his due to claim what belongs to God alone. The major question is not whether citizens can oppose but what means they employ when they do so. Should they resort to physical violence? Or does Jesus' way permit only nonviolence? Since even the latter involves risk of violence, how much should we risk? There are no simple answers, as El Salvador, South Africa, the Middle East, or the Philippines testify powerfully today.

III. Major stress must always fall on what we render to God. Coins of the realm belong to Caesar, but absolute obedience belongs to God alone. God has stamped his image and likeness upon us. He has bought us back when we have fallen under control of others. So we are not our own (1 Cor. 6:19–20). From the beginning, Christians have found themselves in the position of the apostles before the Sanhedrin, having to judge "whether it is right in the sight of God to listen to you rather than to God" (Acts 4:19). For this they have paid a high price—harassment, imprisonment, torture, and death. Caesar often confuses his claims with God. Jesus himself soon learned that.—E. Glenn Hinson.

November 15. Love Says It All
TEXT: Matt. 22:34–46.

I. Christians have always struggled to decide how Old and New Testaments relate to one another. In the second century Marcion of Pontus solved the problem by rejecting the Old Testament altogether. God the Father of Jesus Christ, he insisted, is a God of love and forgiveness, whereas the God of the Old Testament is a God of anger and judgment. Marcion proceeded from there to put together his own canon—an edited version of the Gospel according to Luke and ten of Paul's letters. Some Gnostic teachers dealt with the difficulty by picking and choosing among parts. Ptolemaeus decided some parts were demonic, others human, and still others divine. Here Jesus shows that the Old Testament will turn out better if we view it in its essence rather than in its particulars. In its essence, it too, just as Jesus himself, teaches love—love of God and love of neighbor. This is the frame from which both Law and Prophets hang.

Whatever their particulars, all of them seek to achieve this goal. The Law contains many ways to apply love.

II. Jesus may have surprised his hearers momentarily when he answered the lawyer's question about the great commandment, for he did not cite one of the ten; he quoted, rather, part of the Shema recited three times daily by devout Jews. Was this due merely to familiarity? Or was it content? Surely the latter. The decalogue mentions God's love for those who love him, but it does not drive to the heart of the matter as Deut. 6:4–5 does. With our whole being we are to love God, nothing held back. Notice that Matthew's version reflects a bit of accommodation to culture. The passage in Deuteronomy says we are to love with all our heart, soul, and might Mark 12:30 says heart, soul, mind, and might; Matthew says heart, soul, and mind. Either way the point is clear: "Love with all you've got!"

III. Jesus here speaks of love of neighbor as a second commandment. Some early Christians, however, thought it could stand by itself as a statement of the whole. Whoever loves the neighbor has fulfilled the whole law, the Apostle Paul observes, for the commandments are summed up in love for neighbor (Rom. 13:9–10; Gal. 5:14). Is there some contradiction in thought here? Surely not. The commandment is really a single commandment: to love. For human beings love takes on visible and tangible form in what we do to neighbor. Love, true love, loves in particular. Its testing comes in specific applications. To exclaim "Oh, how I love everybody" is easy. Actually to love the unlovely, the enemy, is impossible, save when we know God's love in us. As John reminds us, "No person has ever seen God. Yet if we love one another, [people will know that] God abides in us and his love is perfected in us" (1 John 4:14). We can't claim we love God if we hate brothers and sisters.—E. Glenn Hinson.

November 22 (Thanksgiving). Giving as a Way of Thanksgiving

Text: Matt. 23:1–12.

I. Jesus did not fault the scribes and Pharisees for what they thought or said. Quite the contrary, he complimented them. We should do what they say. They urged others to obey the Law, the revealed will of God. They obviously knew what that Law demanded—compassion, uprightness, goodness, care for others. As one former rabbi observed, they had a zeal for God (Rom. 10:2). On a scale of intentional piety ranging from one to ten the scribes and Pharisees would have scored nine or ten. Why, then, did Jesus indict them? For the same reason he could indict us. Deeds did not match words and intentions. Like Talkative in Bunyan's *Pilgrim's Progress,* they made piety a matter of words and religious acts rather than practice. Too much they did was "to make a noise therewith." Lengthened phylacteries, wider tassles, prominence in the synagogues, and being hailed in the marketplace ranked higher than downright goodness such as those invited to enter the kingdom in Matt. 25:31–46 displayed. They acted so selflessly, the invitation came as a surprise! They had to ask, "When did we do that?"

II. Where does piety go wrong? Certainly not in intention. The scribes and Pharisees surpassed all others in intention. The breakdown occurs, rather, somewhere between intention and action. The good we would do, we don't do. The evil we don't want to do, we do (Rom. 7:15). Something interferes with the power to do what we intend. What got in the way of a high level of commitment by scribes and Pharisees? Jesus gave a clue in the parable of the Pharisee and the tax collector (Luke 18:9–14). The Pharisee trusted so much in his own good intentions and religious scruples he didn't open himself to God's power. The tax collector, on the other hand, had no confidence whatever in his own goodness. Indeed, he could do nothing but hang his head, beat his breast, and cry, "God, be merciful to me a sinner!" Yielding, surrender, abandonment to God was the critical step. God's power could flow in and begin to work. This one who had absolutely no claim was okayed by God.

III. The way of Christ is the way of the servant. It is the way of humility. It is the way of abandonment to God. Jesus echoes many Old Testament refrains when he says that those who exalt themselves will be humbled and those who humble themselves exalted. "God resists the proud," says Proverbs, "but gives grace to the humble." Jesus' insistence on singleminded devotion to God sounds a little harsh. "Don't follow an earthly teacher and don't name any earthly person father," he demands. "Trust only the heavenly Father." What we must realize is that other human beings—even rabbis and fathers—cannot supply the kind of righteousness that will fit us for the kingdom. Only God can supply that. He does so absolutely without charge. To receive it, however, we must give everything. We must surrender ourselves and become servants.—E. Glenn Hinson.

November 29 (Advent 1). Semper Paratus

TEXT: Mark 13:32–37.

I. Advent is a summons to constant readiness, *Semper Paratus* of the Christian. Readiness is required, first, precisely because no one except the Father knows the time. The angels do not know it. The Son does not know it. Why does the Father keep counsel only with himself on this? Why doesn't he at least share the secret with the Son? Does the Father want to heighten suspense and anticipation to the point we can't stand any more? Jesus doesn't say. He simply accepts the reality. Constant readiness for Advent is required, second, because it may happen suddenly and unexpectedly. It may occur like the return of an owner who has gone away and left his house in charge of his servants. He may come back when least expected.

II. The key word is *watch.* The Christian life is lived as a constant watch. In early centuries devout Christians would get up at midnight to pray in the belief Christ might return then. They maintained round-the-clock vigils. They did not want to be caught off guard. In the view of the Apostle Paul our present time has been lifted to a new level of meaning because it is bounded by the Advent that has already occurred and an Advent that is yet to occur. We live, as it were, between D-day and V-day. Thus it becomes our earnest endeavor to "make the most of the time" (Col. 4:5). Such a perspective carries significant implications for Christian behavior. Early Christianity, like its parent Judaism, based moral principles on its expectations of Advent and Judgment. Although they attracted people largely from the lower socioeconomic levels, Christians astonished their contemporaries by getting common persons to "live like philosophers." Life lived under the searchlight of eternity also invites a concern for better stewardship. Living in this *kairos*, one cannot take time or talent lightly.

III. Constant readiness is difficult for human beings. We don't like waiting and watching. From Jesus' day on people have tried to trigger the second coming so they wouldn't have to wait any longer. The writers of the Gospels knew some who were doing so in their day. That is why they included these words of Jesus. During the second century, the Montanists predicted that the millennial kingdom would headquarter in Pepuza in Phrygia, hometown of Montanus, founder of the sect. About A.D. 1200 a flurry of millenarian activity arose around predictions of Joachim of Flora. One of the persecuted sects of the Protestant Reformation attempted to set up a capital for the millennial kingdom first at Strassburg and then at Münster. In the United States William Miller predicted Christ would return in 1843, and then, when that date failed to materialize, he postponed it. His followers, the Seventh Day Adventists, have had to make further adjustments. The apocalyptic circumstances of recent decades have generated frequent efforts to anticipate the Coming. —E. Glenn Hinson.

December 6 (Advent 2). Good News for Those Who Finish Second

TEXT: Mark 1:1–8.

God's saving grace has come to many "First-Place Finishers," people who are the publicized leaders in their fields. These are the people or groups of people whose names are recognized instantly, the headline makers of our daily newspapers. Because of their popularity and accomplishments, these individuals often give testimonies at church banquets and rallies and on religious TV programs. We can be grateful to God for redeeming many people who always finish first.

I. But what about the rest of the multitude—those who finish third, or eighth, or 200th—the ordinary folk who do not share the limelight with the first-place finishers or get much attention at all? John the Baptist, as our text reminds us, always finished second, for he was always pointing beyond himself to the perfect one. In Christ's presence, John did not feel worthy to do what a slave would ordinarily do—untie the sandals of his master. John's message, symbolized by water baptism, stressed repentance; the coming of the Holy Spirit provided the dynamic power for continued right living. His role was that of messenger, preparer, the one who would decrease as the Lord increased (John 3: 30). John would exclaim, "Look, over there. He's the one I told you about!" Mark makes it crystal clear in the first verse of his Gospel that the gospel is the story of Jesus Christ, not of John.

II. This does not mean, however, that those who finish second or third are of no value or importance, for the good news of Advent is for all. All are invited—the superstars, those whose lights flicker and almost go out, and everyone between the two extremes. In any athletic event, one person or team finishes first; the others are the also-rans. But in God's sight, everyone is someone. In fact, the Bible tells of God's special care and concern for people who are often neglected—children, the poor, widows, those who have been overlooked or discarded by society. In God's good time a reversal of roles occurs. People from everywhere come into God's kingdom, and those who might have been last by some standards are now first (Luke 13:30). In God's sight, then, the place of finishing becomes secondary to his acceptance, and his love is given to all.

III. There is one further word. What about those who seem in danger of not finishing at all, those who faint and fall by the wayside, those who can never quite get it all together? These individuals may make noble resolves, dream big dreams of finishing at or near the top, but somehow it never works out. These people, too, need to receive John's message and look to the lamb of God who is able to take away all the sins of all the world (John 1:36). Mark saw John as the one who fulfilled the prophecy of Isaiah concerning the messenger, and it was Isaiah who pictured God as the one who gives power to the faint and strength to those who are weak (Isa. 40:29). To this power John gave witness; the power of God demonstrated perfectly in the life, death, and resurrection of Jesus and continued in the lives of believers through the Holy Spirit (Acts 1: 8). This is John's witness—John, the one who always came in second.—Paul M. Debusman.

December 13 (Advent 3). Good News for a Dark World

TEXT: John 1:6–8, 19–28.

I. The world to which Jesus came was a dark world. In personal and social ethics, darkness prevailed. Entire groups of people such as slaves and women were either ignored or treated as at best second-class objects. Killing of deformed or unwanted infants was acceptable. Racial differences were magnified. There was religious darkness because the worship of pagan gods was common. Even the Jewish religion had been corrupted by the heavy burdens of centuries of traditions, and righteousness was often defined as outward observance of ceremonies.

II. We live in a dark world. We have made many improvements in the quality of life since the time of Jesus. We can travel faster and farther, communicate quicker, build taller buildings, and manufacture more items than people in Jesus' day could have imagined. Yet, darkness rules many areas of private and public life, and for all of our progress in technology, the darkness is as great in many ways as it was in Jesus' day. We still assign groups of people to inferior places because of their skin color, sex, or place of birth. We are afraid to walk the streets of many cities after dark, and crime now reaches its tentacles into formerly safe rural areas. We bow down before the gods of drug dependency and compulsive gambling. We cheat in just about every area of life, from income tax reports, to marriage, even to reports of church statistics. There is a general permissiveness that blurs the distinctions between right and wrong. Above and probably behind much of this darkness looms the fragile nature of peace, the fear of nuclear destruction, and the outbreak of all sorts of conflicts and wars.

III. In Jesus' day, and in our time, there is one true light. Our Scripture passage reminds us that John carefully pointed beyond himself to the true light of the world. John was not the light. When the representatives of the Jewish leaders asked John about his credentials, John again gave witness to Jesus. Our world is full of pretenders who promise light but can finally deliver only ultimate darkness. Religious cults abound, as do all sorts of self-help programs that encourage people to lift themselves up by their own bootstraps. Many of these programs promise quick cures for all our problems and instant success for all endeavors. John baptized people who had recognized sin and turned from it by God's power, but still the world longed for the true light. John refused the titles "Christ," "Elijah," and "prophet." Resisting the temptation to start a "John the Baptist Cult," he made it clear that Jesus was the true light so desperately needed by the dark world.—Paul M. Debusman.

December 20 (Advent 4). Receiving Unexpected News

TEXT: Luke 1:26–38.

While the angel's news to Mary is unlike the news any of us will ever receive, our responses may parallel hers when we experience God's presence in our lives.

I. Mary was first deeply troubled and confused. She knew that she was a virgin and could not imagine how she could give birth to a child. Her response was like that of Zechariah when an angel of the Lord told him that Elizabeth in her old age would give birth to a son. The Apostle Peter similarly was confused when God spoke to him in a vision near Joppa, giving him the unexpected and troubling news that he was not to consider anything ritually unclean that God had declared clean. We also are often not prepared to receive the word of God when it comes to us, and so we do not know how to respond. In his *Confessions* (bk. 8, chap. 12), St. Augustine tells of his confusion when he experienced God's call to salvation and holy living. Like Moses and Jeremiah, we wonder if God knows what he is doing when he calls us to certain tasks of ministry; we may even wonder if God has called us or entrusted us with a special task or if we are only imagining it. Are we capable of responding to God's unexpected news? Like Mary, we wonder, "How can this be?"

II. Mary's final response was one of humble acceptance and obedience. She was reminded that God had made it possible for her relative Elizabeth to become pregnant and that there is nothing that God cannot do. The Apostle Peter had demonstrated a similar response when Jesus called him to be his disciple. Peter had fished all night long with no luck. For him to put his nets out again seemed futile, yet he obeyed the Lord's command with humble acceptance: "But if you say so, I will let down the nets" (Luke 5:1–11). Uncertainty and confusion may be our initial reaction when God breaks into our lives with unexpected news. This news may be that we hear for the first time that he loves us and forgives us even though we feel unlovable and too guilty to be forgiven. This news may be that God is calling us to accept people as brothers and sisters who we think are not worthy of being in our family. Or this news may be that God is calling us to serve him in a different way or in a different place than we now do. When we recognize that this is God's news to us, humble acceptance and obedience should follow.

III. Mary's response was not based on what she could accomplish, for she was a virgin, but on what God could accomplish through her. Mary was a virgin; Elizabeth was old and past the child-bearing years. Peter had fished all night. Moses was a poor speaker, and Jeremiah was too young. The apostles were ordinary men with no education. The Apostle Paul, as Mary, knew that it was not what he could do but what the Lord could do through him. When God gives us unexpected news of what he will do for us and through us, we should remember with Mary that we are his servants and that it will be according to *his* word and *his* power.—Roger L. Omanson.

December 27. Three Reasons for Giving Thanks

TEXT: Luke 2:22–40.

According to the teachings of the Law, Mary and Joseph traveled from Bethlehem to Jerusalem in order to fulfill two traditional Jewish practices. Mary offered a sacrifice of birds for her purification (Lev. 12:6, 8), and Jesus' parents presented him to the Lord (Exod. 13:2, 12, 15). There in the temple in Jerusalem two pious old Jews, a man and a woman, saw the baby Jesus and gave thanks to God. We can learn from them reasons to be thankful to God.

I. Simeon thanked God that God had kept his promise. Simeon could now die in peace since God had kept his promise that Simeon would not die before he saw the Lord's Messiah. The promise of a human being is all too often broken or forgotten. But the Bible is filled with statements that God keeps his promises (Gen. 21:1; 28:15; Neh. 9:8; Josh. 13:33; 21:45; 1 Kings 8:20). The Bible is also filled with the many promises of what God will do for his people (2 Cor. 7:1; Gal. 3:14; 2 Tim. 1:1; Heb. 9:15; 2 Pet. 3:13; Jas. 1:12; 2:5).

II. Simeon thanked God that God's salvation was available for all peoples of the world, both Jews and Gentiles. Our vision too easily becomes narrow and restricted to serving people and sharing the good news of salvation with people who look like us, or who think and live as we do. The book of Acts tells the story of the unhindered gospel. Barriers of race, nationality, sex, and social status were all crossed and broken down by the gospel of salvation for all people. St. Augustine wrote that God's love is a circle whose center is nowhere and whose circumference is everywhere. Let us, with Simeon, be thankful that God's salvation is for *all* people, even for us.

III. Anna was a model of piety as she worshiped God continually and spoke about Jesus to all in Jerusalem who were expecting redemption. We ought to be thankful for faithful people such as Anna. Hearing the good news of the gospel is like discovering the world's largest buried treasure. If we knew that the treasure was life, and love, and joy, could we possibly keep it all a secret? Anna gave thanks to God for providing the Savior, but she did not keep this good news a secret. If we are truly thankful for what God has done for us in Jesus Christ, then we must tell others. Peter and John were brought before the Sanhedrin and ordered not to speak or teach any more in the name of Jesus. But they refused to be silenced, for they could not help speaking about what they had seen and heard (Acts 4). Unknown Christians throughout the history of the church have, like Anna, testified to others about having met Jesus Christ in their lives. Because of their witness, the love of God revealed in his Son now reaches to all parts of the world.—Roger L. Omanson.

SECTION III. Resources for Communion Services

SERMON SUGGESTIONS

Topic: A Meal to Remember
TEXT: 1 Cor. 11:23–26.

I. My wife and I had a memorable dinner in Florida. I ordered something called "O Sole Mio Trio." It consisted of three filets of sole wrapped around bits of shrimp, crab, and scallops, and all smothered in a piquant wine and cheese sauce. The satisfaction of the dinner prompted me to reflect on other memorable meals in my life.

What are your favorite memories of meals? Try thinking about them sometime. They provide a wonderful recapping of experiences.

II. Then think about the disciples of Jesus and this meal in the Upper Room. The disciples must have had favorite memories too. Perhaps Philip recalled the dinner he had eaten with a dark-eyed young woman from Capernaum, of sweet, tender fish and light, fluffy wheat cakes served with honey on them. James and John surely remembered the last meal they ate with their father in the boat before they left to follow Jesus in his itinerant ministry: cheese and bread and new wine, and melons afterwards. And maybe Matthew liked to think of the time he and another disciple were in a little village, when Jesus had sent them out to declare the coming of the kingdom, and a family had invited them in for roast lamb and all the trimmings.

But, of all their memories, which do you imagine were the best?

For some, surely it was hard to forget that time in the wilderness when Jesus said the blessing over a few loaves and fishes and fed five thousand people. What bread or fish ever tasted better?

For others, it was even harder to top that beautiful breakfast by the sea, when they had fished all night and were tired and hungry and Jesus called to them from the shore, "Let down your nets on the right side"; and they did, and the nets became unbelievably heavy and alive with fish; and when they rowed to shore, there was Jesus with a fire already going, ready to cook the fish and eat with them. That was a magnificent breakfast!

Yet, for all of them, the very best memory, better even than dinner in the wilderness and breakfast by the sea, was the meal they ate with Jesus in the Upper Room the evening before he was crucified.

It was probably a Passover meal. If it was, they had a lamb and bread and wine and herbs, and probably some cheese and fruits and nuts. But it was the bread and wine they remembered most vividly. Judas, the traitor, had already left. And Jesus, in a winsome mood, perhaps a touch of sadness in his voice, said the blessing over the bread, and then, as he passed it to them, said, "Here, this is my body, which is broken for you." He could see ahead into the night, what Judas would do, and into the events to follow. He would indeed be broken. Then he did the same with the wine. "This is the blood of the new covenant," he said. "Multitudinous seas incarnadine," said Milton; his

56

blood would stain them forever, the Creator dying for the whole creation. And then, almost whimsically, he added: "Whenever you do this, do it in remembrance of me."

III. Memory, to the Hebrew mind, had strange powers: it reinvoked the experience, set it in motion again, brought it into being once more. When they remembered, as they did every time they gathered, he was there. The bread and the wine brought him back to them.

The strangest part is, it does the same for us. We were not there, but when we contemplate it and receive the bread and cup, we relive it as if we had been there, and Christ is here in our midst, offering himself to us all over again. There are people here who will tell you they have felt it. I have felt it.

When I was a boy, the church I belonged to had a large oak communion table. On the front side of it, carved in deep letters like the letters on a tombstone, were the words "In Remembrance of Me." Sometimes, when no one was around, I would trace the letters with my finger. It was a very special table, and I knew that something special happened when the church gathered around it.

The same something special happens here when we gather around this table. Christ breaks bread with us and shares the cup with us. And, mysteriously, we feed on him as he does. It is a miracle as great as any he ever performed in his ministry—as great as feeding five thousand people in the wilderness. It was his last meal with the disciples, but it never ends.

Most last meals must end. I remember the last time I ever ate with my mother. I shall always treasure the memory of that meal and the talk we had together as we ate it. But that meal is over, and I cannot bring it back except in memory.

This meal with Christ comes back every time we gather around the table and remember. It is never finished. It goes on and on. And one day it will be taken up into the great heavenly banquet, when we shall eat and drink with him in the kingdom.

This is a meal to remember!—John Killinger.

Topic: You Must Test Yourself

TEXT: 1 Cor. 11:28.

I. If we take the New Testament teaching seriously we cannot avoid thinking that the Lord's Supper is "for sinners," indeed, only for sinners. We must not think of the sacrament as being in some way a symbol of our goodness, assuming that we have the right to participate in it as a sort of reward for our high standing in a difficult spiritual and moral examination. "Come as you are": that is always implicit in the invitation to the Lord's Supper. But this is not to suggest that you can come to it carelessly or casually.

II. Paul, in his first letter to the Corinthian church, gave this rule for a worshiper's preparation for Communion: "A man must test himself before eating his share of the bread and drinking from the cup." I think that the word "test" found in the New English Bible is a better translation of the Greek word than is "examine," which is given in both the King James and Revised Standard Versions. The word was used not only of persons but also referred to the testing or proving of metals, and it has to do with the careful inspection and evaluation of basic qualities and an estimation of present condition and of future performance. He is not demanding the kind of testing for which marks or grades are given. Rather, he is demanding the kind of testing that reveals the real nature of that which is being tested.

III. Perhaps at times you feel that you really aren't good enough to take Communion. I sometimes feel that way. Such feelings may be commendable and honest, but generally they are a matter of distorted sensitivity, and they show a serious misunderstanding of the nature and purpose of the Lord's Supper. This whole "good enough" business in religion insists that one ought not participate in certain Christian practices until one has attained a high degree of spiritual and moral excellence. But if a standard of near perfection is to be demanded, who among us, really, is good enough to take Communion?

IV. We are not called to perfection or near perfection; we are called to confession, called to look into our hearts and be honest with God and with ourselves about what we see there. Confession, Paul declares, must precede Communion. Richard Hooker, a great English churchman of the sixteenth century, wrote that a congregational prayer of confession should be applied by each worshiper to his or her "own particulars." We must not let the words of the prayer or confession simply roll off our tongues and then through our conscience without disturbing a thing. We must let those words remind us of our own acts of unfaithfulness and lovelessness, our own tendencies towards arrogance and self-centeredness, our own malice and envy—our own sin.

V. John Calvin put the matter very realistically in this way: "If we allege as a pretext for not coming to the Supper, that we are still weak in faith or in integrity of life, it is as if a man excuse himself from taking medicine because he is sick." It is only the imperfect, the needy, the anxious, the uncertain, only the sinful, who should come to the Lord's Supper. If, as you come to the Supper, you can say, as the publican in the parable said, "O God, have mercy on me, sinner that I am," then you will meet there the merciful, forgiving Lord, and there you will receive healing for your heart's hurt and strength and guidance for your life's journey. In the First Letter of John this assurance is given: "If we confess our sins, he (God) is just, and may be trusted to forgive our sins and cleanse us from every kind of wrong."

You must test yourself before eating your share of the bread and drinking from the cup. This testing, this confessing, is not a negative thing, not a wallowing in self-condemnation, not a bleak pessimism about yourself. It is a matter of honesty about your self and with yourself and before God, and a trusting that God forgives you and accepts you and helps you to the life of meaning and purpose, of peace and fulfillment.

It is one of the great creative paradoxes of the Christian faith that you qualify yourself to take Communion only by acknowledging that you are unworthy to do so. Take it! It's for sinners—sinners who are shown the way to redemption and fulfillment through their faith in Jesus Christ, the living Lord.—J. A. Davidson.

Topic: A New Covenant Is Risky Indeed
TEXT: Jer. 31:31–34; 1 Pet. 2:4–10; Luke 22:14–20.

I. Let's think for a few minutes about covenant—in the biblical sense—and see what this means to us.

A covenanting relationship with God is one in which you and I are free to enter; we are free to remain; we are free to withdraw. Covenant, in the biblical sense, shows God is the one who takes the initiative—God is the initiator, the primary actor, the motivator, the mover, the one who comes to us. Covenant with God means two things: (1) We are privileged to receive and benefit from God's acts. (2) We are invited to join with God in caring for others and for the world. Covenant, then, is God's act and our response.

The call for us to participate in covenant with God goes all the way back to creation itself: "In the image of God, God created them. . . . male and female God created them. . . ."—*imago dei.* This call is seen in the life and experiences of Noah, Moses, Abraham, Isaiah, Jeremiah, Jesus, the disciples, and the early church. In covenant, God takes the initiative; God makes promises to us; God assumes responsibility; God provides for us on the way of our pilgrimage; God gives us signs along the way.

II. God's call to us to enter into covenant does not always lead to success or victory or coming out on top; it does not always take us immediately into the promised land. It is high risk to wait upon the Lord, to listen to the Word of the Lord, to respond to the voice of God, to enter into covenant with God!

III. As I read in the Old Testament and in the New Testament about the covenanting experiences of God, I read of no experiences at all where the people of God move immediately from covenant to the promised land!

Always, between covenant and the promised land there is wilderness. Always.

We have the notion that covenant with God is ours to control. Not at all. God is in control. The call and the claim and the covenant often come when we are not ready. Someone has said there are three images in the New Testament that are covenanting or are receiving images: baptism, the Lord's Supper, the Holy Spirit. We often feel instead that we are in control. It's seen very simply in the way we express ourselves: we think baptism is something we do. We think the Lord's Supper is something we take. We think the Holy Spirit is something we have. Three very possessive, controlling verbs—to do, to take, to have. It's easy to see why some of us think we are in charge. Baptism is not something we do; it is something we receive. The Lord's Supper is not something we take; it is something we receive. The Holy Spirit is not something we have; it is something we receive! Covenant means "I will be your God; you shall be my people."

IV. But that is risky business. Covenant often comes when we are not ready! Covenant often comes where and when we do not want it! Covenant often means responsibility we don't care to take! It did for Moses, Jeremiah, Isaiah, and Jesus! We may end up working with people we don't want to work with, fighting for causes that are not popular, that we'd rather leave alone, dealing with issues we're not quite ready to face.

V. If, therefore, the next few weeks, the next year, or even the rest of your life—as was the case for Moses—seem like a wilderness as you chart a new life, begin a new way, search for new truth, live out a new covenant, just remember: it's okay to be in the wilderness! Some pretty good folks have been there—and are still there with us—folk like Moses, Abraham, Jesus! Right there in the wilderness, there is the certainty and the reality of God's presence for the journey, and there are symbols for us on our pilgrimage. The manna for the children of Israel, the pillar of cloud by day, and the pillar of fire by night. We still have signs like that; we still have a rainbow that comes in the day. We still have bread, wine, a towel, and a basin. We still have a cross. "This cup which is poured out for you and for many is the new covenant in my blood." "Are you willing to drink of the same cup of which I must drink?" Yes, my friends, covenant with God is risky business. Risky business, indeed!—Robert T. Young.

Topic: On Putting People in Their Place
TEXT: Luke 14:7–11.

At some fancy dinner parties in our nation's capital, where and with whom you are seated is of great concern. They say that if you want to know who is on the way up and who is on the way out, all you have to do is look to see where the guests are seated.

In some first-century circles there was a similar obsession with seating. Everyone wanted a place among the celebrities. Jesus was invited once to one of these fancy parties in the home of an influential Pharisee. He arrived and watched with amusement as some of the guests, convinced of their own high status, seated themselves in the places of honor. Jesus smiled inwardly. He knew that when the host arrived some quick reshuffling would occur, much to the embarrassment of these early arrivals. He saw a lesson in all this. He had himself the makings for another parable. What was that lesson?

I. *Guests should wait to be seated.*

(a) At first glance, this parable appears to be nothing more than a lesson in etiquette for party-goers. It certainly is that. Do not presume. Wait to be seated. And if you cannot wait, take an inconspicuous seat until you know the wishes of the host. That way you will avoid embarrassment for one and all.

(b) Good manners are not everything—they do not guarantee success, they will not solve our personal or the world's problems—but they can eliminate some of the stress from life and make our personal relations more pleasant. But having said this I hasten to add that I do not think Jesus came to teach us the social graces. The Lord of Lords was sent to redeem the world, not to instruct us in etiquette. Indeed, one of the things for which he was criticized was his willingness to sit at a table with anyone.

II. *Humility is a commendable virtue.* "He who exalts himself will be humbled and he who humbles himself will be exalted."

(a) No one likes a pushy person. Go-getters get only so far because, while we openly applaud their aggressive self-assertion, inwardly we resent it and secretly we resist it. Pushy people eventually get put in their place. Humble people quietly move up.

(b) Throughout history, humility has been a commended virtue. The writer of Proverbs said, "With pride comes disgrace; with humility wisdom" (Prov. 11:2). St. Augustine wrote, "It is humility that makes men angels." And Emerson said, "None shall rule but the humble."

(c) Jesus himself had humility. He was not too proud to wash his disciples' feet, not too proud to minister to the lowest and the least. He taught, "If you would be great, you must be servant of all," and he commended a childlike humility and innocence. No wonder Paul wrote of him, "He did not count equality with God a thing to be grasped, but emptied himself . . . and humbled himself" (Phil. 2:6, 8).

(d) But there is danger in regarding this parable as nothing more than good advice. If we set out to cultivate humility, if we become self-effacing to ingratiate ourselves with others, if we pretend modesty when really we are quite pleased with ourselves, we end up with a calculated kind of humility that is not a virtue but a sin, and a sin of the worst kind, because it is a sin that deceives. To get at the real meaning of this parable, we have to go deeper still.

III. *God is the one who puts people in their place.*

(a) As is true of all Jesus' parables, this one has to do with God, the kingdom of God, and our relationship with him. God is the host. This is his party. God is the one who puts people in their place. The lesson of this parable is that we do not humble or exalt ourselves. Only God can do that.

(b) He will humble us by showing us the world and life as he sees it and by showing us our place in the scheme of things. A popular but inaccurate expression is "the patience of Job." Job really wasn't all that patient. He griped and complained. God does not answer his complaints. Rather, God shows him the world from his viewpoint and what he is trying to accomplish. That puts Job in his place and reduces him to silence. When we come into the presence of the Almighty and see ourselves and life as he sees it, we too will be humbled. As Tyron Edwards put it, "True humility is not a groveling, self-despising spirit; it is seeing ourselves as God sees us." When we measure ourselves against the greatness of God, pride dies and humility grows.

(c) But God in whose presence we are humbled has acted in Christ to exalt us and to bring us to his kingdom. A. M. Hunter is right: "The best places are not man's choice but God's gift." The same God who puts us in our place when we think more of ourselves than we should has set aside a place of honor at his banquet table for you and for me. That is a humbling thought, too. There are two kinds of humility: the humility of the servant who bows his head, and the humility of the child who lifts his head to see the smile on his parent's face. The humility that makes us bow and the humility that lets us soar. God gives both kinds.—H. Alden Welch.

ILLUSTRATIONS

A LIVING PRESENCE WITNESSED IN THE BIBLE. As I walk on down through the Highway of the Book, I find myself suddenly surrounded by new things, new traditions, new faces, new forms, new ideals, new hopes, new life, a new approach to God the Father, a new estimate of goodness, a new standard of religion and life, a new hope. I feel as one who has walked suddenly from an old cathedral of Europe into the sunlight of God's outdoors. I have suddenly walked from the Old Testament into the New and my "heart burns within me" because of what I meet. Everywhere in the pages of the New Testament, I feel the vital living presence of the Christ. As I walk through the New Testament he walks beside me. I hear his voice on mountainsides at night in prayer. I hear his voice along the streams, in the meadows, and beside the Sea of Galilee. I know as I walk though the New Testament that he is walking by my side.

And if I were so blind as not to know that he was present; if my soul was so dead as not to feel his presence beside me, his voice speaking to me would awaken me from my stupor to his divine presence. I would hear him speaking, "I am with you always; even unto the end." I could not forget that and my spirit would burn within me at that voice.—William Stidger.

LOOKING AND FINDING. There is a considerable difference between looking for God and finding him. You and I are always tempted to think God is to be found by way of kings and protocol, that he ought to act the way we would act if we were God, instead of taking him at his word. Naaman found out and so can we. Naaman, like the prodigal in the far country, came to himself and accepted himself for what he was in the eyes of God—no captain of the host or man of distinction, but simply a man in need of health. It's all God asks, you know. Just that you come to him without pretensions or gifts, simply as a soul in need of his health. And he will cleanse you, too. —Edmund A. Steimle.

ACCEPTANCE. We cannot move by an analogy from our acceptance of one another to what the New Testament means in saying that we are accepted by God. Our acceptance of God does not imply mutuality. It is a word spoken to us, and it is incredible. Our acceptance of each other, and even our acceptance of God, are always conditional acceptances. What marks the word acceptance by God is the unconditional fact that God accepts precisely the unacceptable. The holy accepts, goes after, and loves the sinner.—Joseph A. Sittler.

FRIEND OF SINNERS. Don't lose heart because you are tempted. You will be more conscious of temptation now you have given yourself to God and are trying to do right. The devil is now your bitter enemy; he will seek to trip you at every step. He would delight in overthrowing you; your fall would be a great victory for him. But, remember, you are not alone. Jesus is not only for you, he is within you and all about you as a wall of fire; you have nothing to fear; the Mighty One lives to

bring you through the temptation. You do not fight alone, or you would fail. The lamb slain before the throne is also the lion of the tribe of Judah, and he lives to give victory again and again. Be not afraid! But you say, "Suppose I am overtaken and fall into sin, what am I to do then?" Go back to God instantly for pardon and cleansing. The command is "Sin not"; "but if any man sin we have an advocate with the Father" (1 John 2). If a little boy should go out, just after being washed and dressed and made beautifully clean, and fall down into the mud and spoil the clean clothes and cut his hands and face, you know what that child would do, do you not? He would get up crying, all dirty and bleeding, and would run back to mother—his best friend—and tell her all about the fall, the cut hands and face, and she, like the mother she is, would wash and cleanse, heal and kiss him; she could do no less. God is better than a mother. Try him. Do not lie there; get up and go to him for pardon and healing, and he will say to thee, "As one whom his mother comforteth, so will I comfort thee" (Isa. 56:13).—Gipsy Smith.

COMMUNION.
God of grape and God of grain
God of sun and God of rain
God of laughter, God of pain
God who let his Son be slain.
God of mercy, God of grace
God of time, and God of space
God of cross and hidden face
God who has not left this place.
God of life and God of light
God of peace yet God of might
God who rose from death's dark night
God who reigns beyond our sight.
In this bread and in this wine
here we join with Thee to dine
at this table let us find
strength to let thy light to shine.
—Richard C. Brand, Jr.

SECTION IV.
Resources for Funeral Services

SERMON SUGGESTIONS

Topic: Because He Is My Shepherd
TEXT: Ps. 23.

Jesus is our good shepherd. It is the identity of the shepherd that urges us to think of ourselves as his sheep.

Today we have again come to the valley of the shadow. Death is the darkest valley of life that we must travel. The Twenty-third Psalm assures us that God is our shepherd, and because of that we have abundant assurances.

I. *Because the Lord is my shepherd, I shall not want.* (Read 23:1–3a.) Jesus promised that we would never want for food, shelter, clothing, and life's necessities while we put him first. But at this moment you want more than physical items. You want what no store can sell, no merchant can provide. You want confidence, comfort, and cheer.

(a) He provides comfort. He has been where we are and he knows how we feel.

(b) He provides confidence, even in this crisis of life when we have feelings that we feel we cannot bear.

(c) He provides good cheer. Jesus turned the tears of more than one funeral into shouts of joy. On the day that Jesus came back to life the sounds coming from the cemetery were those of a festival: laughter, delight, excitement, and hope.

II. *Because the Lord is my shepherd, I am led in righteousness.* (Read 23:3b.) Any other shepherd might lead me into sin. The very mention of sin at a funeral is enough to dismay us, but not if Jesus is our shepherd.

(a) He leads us in the way of forgiveness, goodness, and purity.

(b) I may die as a sinner, but I am a sinner who is saved by his grace. That is an old Christian promise, but it deserves to be retold at the funeral of any Christian.

(c) "For his name's sake," he is righteous, and so are his followers. We share in his righteousness.

III. *Because he is my shepherd, I am not afraid.* (Read 23:4–5.) The shepherd's staff is used for both correction and comfort of the sheep. He can use its crook to retrieve a lost lamb from trouble. That same staff becomes a deadly weapon to drive away a hungry wolf or sneaky thief.

(a) His staff is our comfort. It is curious that our faith has come to be symbolized by a cross when a staff would be much more appropriate. Perhaps we should put a shepherd's staff upon our church steeples and into our stained glass windows instead of the cross.

(b) With Christ as our shepherd we are not afraid. He defends us from our enemies. The staff frightens them, but the sight of that staff is a comfort to us.

(c) The good shepherd wants to comfort you today, in your own time of grief and loss.

IV. *Because the Lord is my shepherd, I shall dwell with him.* (Read 23:6.) The analogy of the psalm changes here. We no longer think of ourselves as sheep following a shepherd, but as house guests of a generous host. We are accorded all the pleasures of Middle Eastern hospitality.

(a) We dwell in the Lord's house in this life. We will exist in his own presence. There is comfort in that.

(b) We shall dwell in the Lord's house in the next life. Jesus spoke of his Father's house and its many rooms, a place for everyone in the family. There is a place there for you.

"And I shall dwell in the house of the Lord forever." This last line of the psalm is as perfect as the first line, "The Lord is my shepherd." I needed for those words to be said, especially today.

I need to know that life goes on, beyond the valley of the shadow of death. I need to know that life is good there. I need to know that life is infinite there. But most of all, I need to know that my good shepherd, my good host, is there. Without Jesus being there heaven would not be heaven. But Jesus is there and he makes heaven heavenly.

The Lord is my shepherd. Because of that truth this day is not one of tragedy, but of comfort, assurance, and victory. —David Beavers.

Topic: "To Depart and Be with Christ
Text: Phil. 1:23.

I. *Christ calls death "falling asleep."* He is using one of the phrases that daring and trustful men had coined, and he is giving it proof and reality. When he stands beside the bed of Jairus' little daughter he softly says, "Talitha cumi," "My little lambie, arise." He is awaking a child from sleep. When he stops the bier of the widow of Nain's son he calls, "Young man, I say unto thee, arise." He is calling one who is at rest back to active life again. When he stands at the tomb of Lazarus, dead four days ago, he cries, "Lazarus, come forth." He is calling one who is lying in the rest chamber to the light of the day and its duties. As a little child will come in from its play when the shadows fall; as workers seek rest when their day's toil is done; so, said Jesus, when we die, we sleep. But we sleep to wake.

II. *He calls it "going to the Father."* This is the word that remained unspoken until the end, but it was his most cherished thought. When he gathers his disciples together in the upper room, and he is upon the eve of his dying, then the word is like a refrain in a song, a recurring note of music in his addresses. Again and again he repeats, "I go to my Father." He is like an emigrant who has been for years in another hemisphere and in the land of strangers. He has been busy with its life and its industries. He has endured its hardships and isolation. Now the time of his sojourn is over and the hour of his return is come. He is going to the Father. He is going home.

III. *He calls it an "exodus."* "They spake of his decease." In the literal and significant meaning of the word it was his "exodus." We cannot doubt why the word was chosen. It is the thought of death from the point of view of one who is about to go out by it as by a door. How full of light is this word! Death is an exodus, a going out from the land of the stranger, from the house of bondage, from affliction and thankless toil, from the state of the slave. Death is a deliverance and a boon. It is a going through a wilderness, with its loneliness and its pain and privation, but it is a going through a wilderness upon a journey which is to end in the promised land. —J. H. Clough.

Topic: The Sun Also Rises
Text: Ps. 30:1–5; Mark 16:1–6.

Clovis Chappell's paraphrased words are appropriate for this time: one day ill-mannered death, boots muddied, with a sickle in his hand, a dark robe upon his back, stalked forth from a newly made grave. He came to meet Christ on the cross, and even for the Son of God, death could not be persuaded to come another day. We, likewise, have prayed for our beloved that death would not take her; we took her to the finest doctors, and she put up a courageous fight. But death could not be persuaded to come another day.

I. Everyone faces at some time the darkness when the robed messenger of death comes knocking at your door to take a loved one away. He is no respecter of persons.

To be sure, life sometimes lays crises in our laps that we do not ask for, we do not want, and we pray would never have happened; but they happen. Death often comes unexpectedly. It brings darkness, not for the one dead, but for the ones left behind. The loved one is gone, never to return upon this earth as he or she was. Left behind are tears, sadness, faded flowers, and memories of one we would give anything to have returned.

The disciples of Jesus felt the same way when they saw their Master, the Savior of the world, hanging on the cross. Despair was represented by the sky as the sun went dark and night approached in midday: "There was darkness over the whole land until the ninth hour" (Mark 15:33). Jesus Christ's darkest moment was on Golgotha's hill as he hung upon the cursed cross and said, "It is finished." I am certain that to Jesus' family and friends it was all over for him.

Added to that, despair and darkness increased when Jesus died and was laid in a tomb. Imagine how Mary and Mary Magdalene felt when they went to the tomb at early dawn of the third day.

In times of grief, the psalmist offers comfort: "Even when we walk through the valley of the shadow of death, God is with us." That shadow may be long and that valley deep, but God's light can overtake the darkness and his strength can help you walk through the low times of life.

The two women at the tomb of Jesus had not realized yet that the sun's rising above the horizon, with its picture of the new day's light breaking into the darkness of night, pointed to a deeper spiritual truth. The angel in white said it best: "Do not be amazed; you seek Jesus of Nazareth who was crucified. He has risen, he is not here" (Mark 16:6).

II. We come, then, to the hope that only Jesus Christ can lead us from the darkness of night to the joy of the morning. Grief is like being lost in a tropical jungle, dark as midnight. The rain beats down as you stumble blindly trying to find a way out. The briars tear at your body as you stumble and fall. You are frightened; you feel like screaming, "Help! Help me out of this darkness!" You may feel like just sitting down and crying. But early in the morning the sun rises to drive away the clouds and the darkness of night. You find a road leading out of the jungle and safely home.

The psalmist said, "Weeping may endure for the night, but joy comes in the morning" (Ps. 30:5b). Just as the sun awakens us to a new day, God's radiant grace can give life a fresh start and the promise of eternal life through resurrection.

Jesus Christ, the Son of God, can shine in your darkness. He promises, "As I live, ye shall live also." The sun does go down, but the sun also rises.—Ronnie R. Blankenship.

Topic: "The Power of His Resurrection"
TEXT: Phil. 3:10.

There is no sublimer fact in the spiritual history of man than his steady, unwavering belief in his own immortality. Encompassed on every side by darkness, he yet proclaims in every age his unalterable conviction that there is light beyond. Tossed always by storm, and often lost in blinding mists, he yet believes that he is steering straight for that haven which eye has never seen. Faced by the spectre of death, he still perseveres in the certainty that life is all and that death is naught; and when the soul seems to perish he holds that it does but pass, with the wings of the dove, to life and spring and heaven's bloom and the bosom of his God.

I. We may loose the silver cord and break the golden bowl: man will still believe that God is for him. Take him into the churchyard, wrinkled with its green mounds, and ask with scorn, "Are all these who lie here immortal?" and he will say, "They are." Stoop in the sepulcher and take a handful of dust, and ask, "Was this immortal?" and he will answer with his indomitable "Yes." This Faith is all the more sublime because of the obtrusive violence and tremendous volume of the facts by which it is confronted. Nature and experience and the oblivion of the grace seem to laugh it to scorn. Man lives amid a universe of death. The very ground we tread on is full of the dust of death, of the material particles which have been used by living organisms since the time of Adam: dead genera, dead species, dead generations, dead empires, dead races. As far as outward facts are concerned, as we walk by sight only and not by faith, death seems to be the sole universal despot, and the prodigy of life to be ended with the greater worm. The great and the small, the rich and the poor, are there; servant and master are mingled in undistinguishing death. We know very well that the same fate awaits us, and awaits us soon. The dead are the more in number, and long before another Easter has come round many of us who now sit here will have joined that greater number. Day by day brings us nearer on the downward slope to the rolling waters of the prodigious tide which has swallowed up our fathers. Thinner that curtain of darkness than a spider's web through which day by day, year by year, one by one, we all shall pass, and each one of us shall pass alone. And how strange, how oppressive, how awful, how unbroken is the silence of all these unnumbered dead! From the other side of the curtain not one gleam of light, not one syllable of sound, from all these millions has ever come. The wise man enters the darkness, but out of it he cannot speak even the words to us which we would barter for all his wisdom. Dante has nothing more henceforth to tell us, nor Shakespeare, nor Milton; childhood and innocence can whisper from it no syllable of consolation to the breaking hearts of father or mother. Yet generation after generation the children of men, wise and unwise, innocent and guilty, believe in their immortality with a faith insensibly sublime.

II. How is this? It is partly because there is something in man far above the evidence of his senses. What the lips of silent death cannot or will not reveal to him, that God whispers into his soul; and therefore he believes insensibly that death is the semblance, and that life is the reality, even if the mind sinks into dotage and the body into dust. Among nations unenlightened by special revelation this belief has faded into vague hope, and a life of sin does more by far than anything else to weaken and destroy it; but to us who are Christians, to all who are the true children of the kingdom, God hath in these last days spoken by his Son, and given to us in him, not a fond expectation, but a sure and certain hope of the resurrection to eternal life. It is Christ alone who in the highest sense has brought life and immortality to light. The tomb is dark no longer; the

message of Easter has made it luminous; it is bright henceforth with angel presences; we have learned by fellowship with his suffering to know Christ and the power of his resurrection.

That resurrection is the central fact of all Christianity. To the Christian it needs no further proof; as certainly as we live, as certainly as we shall die, so certainly we believe that Christ rose and that with him we too shall rise.

III. But we must never forget that as the resurrection is not an isolated, so it is not a secondary, fact. The apostles, the early witnesses of the church of God, put it in the very forefront of their testimony. By the stupendous importance of its meaning, it stands side by side with the creation. That was the victory of omnipotence over nothingness; this is the victory of omnipotence over dissolution. Both are parts of the same divine universal work of love, the redemption of mankind. There are some, there are many, in these days who would fain persuade us that Christianity would still be Christianity if we gave up altogether the supernatural. It is a delusion, as St. Paul told us nearly nineteen centuries ago. If no living Christ issued forth from the garden-sepulcher, that becomes the grave not of man only, but of a religion, with all the hopes based upon it, and all the splendid enthusiasms which it has inspired. "If Christ be not risen, then is our preaching vain, and your faith is also vain. Yea, and we are found false witnesses of God"—how clearly St. Paul confronts the full force of the issue—"we are found false witnesses of God because we have testified of God that he raised up Christ." If the dead are not raised, if Christ be not raised, then your faith is vain; ye are yet in your sins, ye have not then been redeemed; "then they also who have fallen asleep in Christ have perished. If in this life only we have hope, we are of all men most miserable." St. Paul confesses that if we give up the resurrection we give up everything with it.—F. W. Farrar.

Topic: Our Resurrection.

TEXT: Ps. 88:10.

The great question of the human heart is, "Shall the dead rise and praise thee?" or, as Job puts it, "If a man dies, shall he live again?" So every child of humanity ofttimes finds himself thinking on this question. After life here, what then? After death, what? Shall I pass into earth, into unconsciousness and unrecognition forever? Is death the end; or shall I rise again? Shall I live hereafter, shall I know and be known?

I. *Our resurrection is desirable.* Man, everywhere and at all times, has desired to live after death. There is that in our nature that is not satisfied with the things of this life, but looks beyond to greater joys and happiness. This desire among all men has been given expression to, in the various views and creeds held by the different nations. We desire to live hereafter because of friendships formed and love enkindled here. These features of life that bring to the soul its chief joys, we would have continued forever. If in this life only we have hope in Christ, we are of all men most miserable.

II. *Our resurrection is possible.* If we are the result of certain forces in nature, we must be closely allied to nature and capable of its changes and phenomena. Our observation of nature's growth convinces us that its growth is made by certain kinds of deaths and resurrections. The harvest is the result of the dying grain. The natural law of life is death and renewal of life. Our resurrection is possible in God. He who created the body from nothing can renew the body in death. It is possible in Jesus Christ who conquered death and is able to give us the same conquering power. (See 1 Cor. 15:12–16.)

III. *Our resurrection is certain.* We desire it. God is able to raise us from the dead, and God will give us the desire of our hearts. It is certain because God's greatest glory is in man's resurrection. The effect of sin is death. Christ came to destroy the power of sin and death. This can be fully accomplished only in man's resurrection; therefore if there be no resurrection then Christ and God have failed. It is certain because Christ has promised it. "I will come again and receive you unto myself that where I am there ye may be also." So Paul is confident in proclaiming our resurrection in Christ. (See 1 Cor. 15:20–22).—T. P. Revell.

Topic: The Mayfly Life

TEXT: Matt. 6:27–30.

One hot summer day we were inundated by mayflies, which are insects with tiny bodies and great, flimsy, gossamer wings. They live their entire life in just a few hours. In the morning a mayfly is young and frisky, by noon it is middle-aged, and by evening it is old, frail, and dying. We pity the little creature because of its short life span.

But the Old Testament speaks of Adam who lived to be 930 years old and Seth who was 912; Jared was 962, and Methuselah lived to be 969! They would pity us with our puny life span of a mere seven or eight decades.

Today we mark the passing of a little person who lived the life of a mayfly. His was a brief life, totally lacking in what we call the quality of life. He never walked to school. He never learned to talk. He will never go to a party nor bring home a report card. He will never ride in a wagon. He will never find a quarter under his pillow where he left a baby tooth the night before. But those who knew him and cared for him say that he enjoyed his life, as ephemeral as it was.

He gave pleasure to those who loved him. He gave pleasure to God. He knew pleasure. So before we mourn the brevity of his life we might remember that a complete life can be lived in what is a very condensed time span.

Jesus said in our text that even the grass and flowers enjoy the blessings of God, but their life span is no longer than a single day. Explore that idea with me.

I. *Life, however brief, is still life, and it should be celebrated.* Life is the miracle of God. It is the gift of God's own breath to a human being. This little one shared life with us. He was one of us as much as was Albert Einstein or Babe Ruth or Beethoven or Ronald Reagan. He touched us and changed us.

One of my best friends and his wife were parents of a severely retarded baby boy. People tried to be kind but they said the most unkind words to them after their son died. "He is better off now," they said, when they really believed that his parents' life would now be better. Or they said,

"He is now a little angel," when his parents thought he was angelic as he was. Or they said, "You can have another baby," but they could never have that baby again.

My friends said of their son, "We loved him as he was. He was perfect." Life, however brief, or different, is still life, and it is to be celebrated.

II. *Life, however brief, is not limited to this world.* King David mourned the death of his newborn son with the words, "He cannot come to me but I can go to him." We are tempted to believe that in order to have eternal life one must have a long life upon earth. The Bible teaches us that any human life that begins here can continue with God after death.

This little person that we mourn today had one great advantage over us—he never sinned. He was, and shall forever be, innocent. He now lives in the land of innocence. And he does live there, in the presence of God.

Jesus said, "Suffer the little children to come unto me." He also said, "Except you become as a little child you cannot enter the kingdom." It is their innocence that is to be admired. Their innocence continues with the Lord, even now after death.

III. *Life, however brief, is to be mourned when past.* Years from now you will still mourn this child. It is not required that he live long to be missed. Just because he lived so short a life, and such a different life from us, does not mean that he is not to be mourned.

The Golden Rule appears in this: if we do not mark the passing of others, who will notice when our own life ends? Those of us who are mature and feel ourselves to be informed have come to have a deep respect for life in all its forms. So we do grieve the end of even the briefest life.

The passing of one we love is not just an excuse to cry, but it is an honest reason to mourn, and for straightforward sorrow. The wisest man in the Old Testament wrote, "There is a season for everything . . . a time to be born and a time to die . . . and . . . a sad face is good for the heart."

This little one lived the briefest of lives. But before we mourn it we must remember that life is splendid and unique and is to be celebrated. Then we can go on to reflect that life that begins here continues with God, and finally we can take time to mourn, which is honest and even healthy. —David Beavers.

ILLUSTRATIONS

CHRIST'S LOYAL LOVE. Where Christ is, there is infinite hope. And, for my part, I mean to trust him even on the great white throne. I have no plea except just this— that he said, "Him that cometh to me, I will in nowise, for no conceivable reason, for no statable case, cast out." And here is a poor failure coming to give in his account. As Christ decides, so may it be. So it will be. But where Christ is, there is a wild, a wonderful, an infinite hope. And Christ is still Christ even on the judgment seat. And those who saw him face to face for years have set down this as one of his most certain characteristics—that, having loved his own that were in the world, he loved them unto the end. And to us also he clings in that same unbelievably loyal way; loves on whatever we may do; will not be turned from it.—Arthur John Gossip.

THE BEYOND. Dr. Frank Boreham of Australia once wrote a book with the title *The Other Side of the Hill.* He said that was the oldest question in the world: What's on the other side of the hill? Wherever you find a man you will find him looking toward horizons. In the cool of the evening —that is, in his highest moments—he is looking to where the hilltops break the skyline, muttering to himself, "I wonder, I wonder what is on the other side of that hill?" Dr. Boreham went on to say that this is how history and geography came to be. The first man looked out to the distant hills and wondered, just wondered, but his sons and his grandsons climbed them. They went beyond them, east and west and north and south they went. Losing touch with the old home, they climbed one range, then another; settled in this valley, and then in that valley, and so tribes and races and nations and empires came to be. The other side of the hill, that's what did it—the charm of the unknown, the everlasting whisper in man's soul.—J. Wallace Hamilton.

ETERNAL LIFE.   Whatever else Jesus believed, he believed that he came from God and went to God; that God is the God of the living and not of the dead; that it is life which matters, life more abundant; that he has pioneered for us all and that where he is, there shall we be also.

The whole idea of our immortality is not primarily a matter of the indefinite prolongation of our life in time. As has been, so is—this is the Buddhist idea of hell and not of heaven. Our meditations on the matter must always be translated into the terms of what St. John's Gospel calls "eternal life." Eternal life is not merely life in time, it is a quality of life, a different kind of life from that we know only too well. It is this prospect and this faith that touches the human heart and stirs the human mind. As the old woman in Synge's play says, "I have put away sorrow like a shoe that is muddy and worn out."—Willard L. Sperry.

A TRIUMPHANT PATH.   At the close of the last century the notorious agnostic Robert Ingersoll died after a life spent in fierce attacks on Christian beliefs. I am not attacking the man or his methods of unsettling a vast number of people. But it was significant that when notices were sent out announcing a form of funeral service, they carried the brief sentence: "There will be no singing." The plain truth was that there was nothing to sing about. If Ingersoll's contentions were true, then there would be nothing facing humanity but blank, naked despair. But Christianity is a religion of singing—a triumphant faith in which the undertone is confident hope and everlasting joy in the knowledge that goodness shall prevail over evil, light over darkness.—Archer Wallace.

MANY ABIDING PLACES.   Before I was old enough to go to school, I delighted in visiting the elderly couple in the big old house across the road. Downstairs were large spacious rooms that were fun to explore. I do not remember the furnishings of these rooms, but I still recall the graciousness of the small gray-haired lady whose cookie jar seemed to be always full.

Sometimes I was allowed to go up the broad stairs, through a large bedroom, and into a world of mystery and beauty—the studio of the artist daughter. The many sizes of brushes, the tubes of paint, and what the artist did with them were endlessly fascinating.

I recapture that long-ago feeling of happiness and expectancy as I consider the many rooms that Jesus told us are in his Father's house.—Mary Louise Williams.

THE ENEMY DEFEATED.   We would like to believe that life is invincible and death a defeated foe. Even Bernard Shaw, no friend of orthodox belief, rebelled against the allotted span of threescore years and ten. Man, he said, needs at least three hundred years to do justice to his accumulated experience and to understand his world. John Keats, in his early twenties, was aware of his own genius. He also knew that he was doomed to die young. "I have fears," he said, "that I may cease to be before my pen has gleaned my teeming brain."

Easter is the great affirmation of life's invincibility. God is not the most unscrupulous waster in the universe, making this marvelous thing called human personality only to throw it away, cast as rubbish to the void, after a few years; only to have his creation destroyed by a germ, a virus, a heart attack, or just physical decay. God raised up Jesus from the dead, shattering the myth of death's invincibility, drawing its sting, defeating its power. If at one point in history the enemy's grip has been broken, then its reign is done.—John N. Gladstone.

A FUNERAL PRAYER FOR A CHRISTIAN WHO DIED SUDDENLY

A few days ago, Lord, we could talk face to face with Charlie, just as we can still do to each other on this day. We could do all those good, natural things that enrich life on this earth, make it worthwhile and happy and challenging. We could shake hands, share memories, express concerns, sing songs and anthems, look each other straight in the eye, solve problems, laugh at things that were truly funny, pray. Charlie's death brings all those good and natural things to a sudden close in our relationship to him.

So his death and departure from this earth prompts us to grip and not let go many wonderful lessons taught by the life he lived on this earth. We know for sure, Lord, that he loved you. You were not a stranger to Charlie, not an impersonal God, distant and far away and unconcerned. Charlie prayed to you—often—as friend to friend, as student to teacher, as patient to physician, as child to father. The quality of his life as a Christian disciple, as a dedicated churchman, is known by us to be the result of a person who walks and talks with you, who prays often, and who leans upon your word.

You have called Charlie to his eternal home, to the house of many mansions, to the place that you have prepared for him. We trust that time as we know it, weaknesses and frailties as we know them, sicknesses and sorrows as we know them, heartaches and fears and mysteries as we know them—all such things are over for Charlie. And he is in the midst of an eternal reunion with those that have gone on before, with those who will come later, and with you, our God and Father, whom now he can see beyond the darkness and beyond the shadows, all hindrances cast aside, as face to face. Praise be to you, our Father God, for the eternal hope and love that come to us, through the work of salvation you have accomplished for us in the

person of Jesus Christ, our crucified, risen, and ruling Lord and Savior.

Look down with favor upon us who are attending this memorial service. For much we need your tender care. Charlie has gone home, but we continue our pilgrimage upon this earth. We need the support that you alone can provide. We need your rich promises. We need your healing touch on the wounds and griefs that are too heavy for us to bear until in faith we put those things, and ourselves, in the palm of your hand. Thank you, Lord, for being with us in this present life, as well as in the life that is sure to come. Thank you for inviting us to come to you with all the trust and expectation and confidence a little child has when he comes to a mother or father who loves him.

Give a very special kind of support and help to Charlie's family. Be their strength and stay in the midst of their sorrow and loss. Provide them with that direction and purpose that will give them hope and health and happiness. Surround them with your living presence, and make them know that all the rest of us stand ready to serve you by serving them according to their particular needs and desires. Yes, Lord, even cause us to go on our way rejoicing, knowing in faith that: beyond sorrow is salvation, beyond loneliness is your presence, beyond grief is goodness in the land of the living, beyond unwanted surprises is the love that will never let us go, beyond this life on earth is life eternal.—Gordon H. Reif.

SECTION V. Resources for Lenten and Easter Preaching

SERMON SUGGESTIONS

Topic: Christ and the Church

TEXT: Rev. 2:1; 3:20.

The book of Revelation is a drama in which the author uses pictures to convey his meaning. In chapters two and three he sets before us three pictures of Christ which, taken together, point to the relationship Christ has with his Church.

I. In the first picture we see Christ holding the Church in his hand.

(a) Thus in Rev. 2:1 John, the author of Revelation, portrays Christ as one who "holds the seven stars in his right hand." There are four things that I would ask you to note. (1) Stars are not literal stars such as we see in the heavens but are identified by John with the angels of the seven churches (1:20). Jesus Christ holds the seven churches of which he writes in his hand. (2) Seven was regarded by the people of that day as a symbol of completeness. John is saying that Jesus Christ is holding the whole Church in his hand. (3) When the word John uses for hold (*kratein*) has a direct object after it, it means that the whole object is gripped and held. Jesus Christ has the whole Church completely in his hand. (4) Finally, in speaking of that Church being in Christ's right hand—the right hand was the hand that held the sword—John is saying that Jesus Christ has absolute power and control over that Church (Ps. 118:15–16).

(b) What does this picture mean? That the Church is under the protection of Christ and that nothing can happen to it which Christ does not allow!

That was something which those first-century Christians needed desperately to hear, for in the background of these opening chapters of the Revelation there lurks the threatening figure of the Roman emperor Domitian. There is no overt reference to him but in phrase after phrase his presence is implied. From the very beginning the power of the emperor is set over against the power of the Galilean. Christ is pitted against Caesar, Rome against the Redeemer. That contrast between Christ and Caesar is not only heightened but is actually brought into the open in chapter 4 where Christ is referred to as Lord and God. That was the official title of Domitian, the Roman emperor, so what John is saying is twofold. He is saying, first of all, that their one true Lord is Christ not Caesar and that therefore they must worship only him. And secondly he is saying that since Christ is Lord and God, he is on the throne, he is in the place of authority and power. And being there enthroned, he will watch over them; he will protect them from the emperor.

II. The second picture shows us Christ standing in the midst of the churches, "walking among the seven golden lampstands," which are the seven churches.

(a) What is he standing there for? What is he doing? He is there as the Lord of the Church. He is there as the One to whom the Church is responsible and the One who is responsible for the Church. He is there to counsel the Church and he is there to comfort the Church, not in the modern sense of soothing its feelings but in the original sense of that great word—strengthening its life by offering encouragement and empowering it with his Spirit!

(b) Is that not what you see in the letters to the seven churches? There is counsel there. Thus Ephesus is commended for its patient endurance and criticized for its loss of love (2:4). Smyrna is consoled for its suffering but at the same time exhorted "to be faithful even unto death" (2:10). In the case of Pergamum we see that Christ rebukes it for its lack of orthodoxy even as he calls upon it to defend the faith (2:16). For Thyatira there is a warning against conformity and a plea that they "hold fast what they have" (2:25). In like manner Philadelphia is urged to make the most of its opportunity (3:8) and Laodicea is told to "buy from me gold refined by fire," that is, to beware of material values and to seek those things which are above (3:18). There is counsel and there is comfort. There are promises of victory—and there is the pledge of God's help in time of need (3:10).

(c) In these letters to the seven churches we see Christ standing in the midst of the churches; we see him walking among the seven golden lampstands. Is that not what the Spirit of Christ is still doing today? He is speaking to us in the events of our time —rebuking, warning, and exhorting. "He that hath ears to hear let him hear" (2:7, 11, 17, 29; 3:6, 13, 22).

III. John's third portrayal is the picture of Christ standing at the door of his Church seeking admission. "Behold I stand at the door and knock; if any one hears my voice and opens the door, I will come in to him and eat with him and he with me" (Rev. 3:20).

In our interpretation of that verse we have been influenced by Holman Hunt's great picture "The Light of the World." He has painted Christ standing before the door of the human heart, garbed as prophet, priest, and king. He comes claiming the right of admission and in his coming he brings a twofold light. The lantern in his hand represents the light of the law

—"the entrance of thy word giveth light" —and it makes clear both our willfulness and our failure. The other light is the light of his countenance, and it proclaims the wonder of his love and the greatness of his provision. So standing there he knocks, seeking admission.

All that is true, gloriously true. But having said that we need to note that John's message is not addressed primarily to the individual but rather to the Church—to those who have already accepted him as Savior and acknowledge him as Lord. Jesus Christ is standing not only at the door of our individual hearts but also at the door of the Church—his Church—our Church—seeking admission. He wants us to be done with every appearance of evil. He wants us to be done with our self-centeredness and disobedience. He wants us to be done with our sectarianism and party strife! And he wants us to be done with our selfish reservations and our limited commitment. "O shame, thrice shame upon us, to keep him standing there."—S. Robert Weaver.

Topic: Do You Know Who You Are?
TEXT: 1 Sam. 17.19–51.

Do you know who you are? I know that sounds like a funny question. You would probably say, "Of course, I do," and respond with your name. But that is not what I am asking for. In most cases we really do not know who we are. We don't know what makes us act the way we do or what makes us mad or glad. In other words, we do not know what really makes us tick. Many of us have lost our identity. We have to wear the right clothes or be in the right organizations to be somebody. We have forgotten how to preserve our own identity. In doing God's work, however, there is no room for being anybody else except who God created. God wants you to be who you are, and in David we have a prime example of someone who knew what made himself tick and knew who he was in God's plan.

I. *David was a defender of his faith in God.* David was incensed that anyone could insult his God and get away with it. He asked the question, "Who is this uncircumcised Philistine, that he should defy the armies of the living God?" (v. 26). If you listen closely you can see that David was angry. What about us? What do we do when we hear someone downgrading the Lord? Do we speak out or do we in silence deny who we are? Israel was supposed to be God's chosen people. God had done so much for them; but now that the shoe was on the other foot, what was Israel doing for God? David was angry. He defended his God.

II. *David had faith that he would be victorious over Goliath (vv. 34–37).* When David was taken to Saul, he said that he would kill Goliath. Although David was a man of small stature, he was determined to face this giant-sized man. In verse 33, you can identify Saul's contempt for David's gesture. David, however, had faith that God would deliver him from Goliath's hand. He pointed to the many times he had faced wild animals in caring for his father's flock and was delivered. In his mind, this would be no different. We meet many giants today whom we may be afraid to face for fear of failure, but we have to be like David and let God's power protect us and guide us and we, too, shall be victorious. David had faith.

III. *In facing Goliath, David had to be himself (vv. 38–40).* Saul finally agreed to let David face Goliath, but he wanted David to wear his armor. This was almost a comical scene. David put on Saul's armor, but one problem arose. Since David was a small man and Saul was a big man, Saul's armor was too big and heavy for David. Not only was David unable to move in Saul's heavy armor, but he also rejected it because he wanted to be himself. How many times today do we try to be like someone else? We may want to emulate certain qualities of a person's character, but we need to be careful that we do not put on the whole armor of that person. For example, many preachers would like to have the abilities of a Billy Graham, but I could promise you failure if you tried to be exactly like him. People are impressed, not by the person you try to be, but by the person you are. You will reach more people for Christ by being yourself than by trying to be someone else. We need to learn from David that only by being ourselves will we be victorious over the Goliaths we face.

David showed that you do not have to be a mighty warrior to overcome a mighty foe. Be yourself and let God take the person you are and make your life victorious. —David M. Jones.

Topic: Suffered Under Pontius Pilate

No one can deny that the symbol of Christianity is a cross. And the reason is that Jesus Christ, founder of the Christian religion, died on a cross.

I. *His death.* The death of Jesus Christ is central to the Christian faith. The Apostles' Creed itself implies this. It says of Jesus that he was "born of the virgin Mary, suffered under Pontius Pilate." The creed tells us nothing about his example, his teaching, or his mighty works. It jumps straight from his birth to his death.

In this emphasis the creed faithfully reflects the teaching of Scripture. Jesus clearly taught the centrality of his death. Not only did he repeatedly predict it, saying, "the Son of man must suffer," but he referred to it as his "hour," the hour for which he had come into the world. And it is of the greatest significance that during his last evening on earth, when instituting the Holy Communion by which he wanted his followers to remember him, he gave them broken bread to eat and wine to drink. And the bread and wine speak of his death, of his body broken and his blood shed in death on the cross.

The apostles echoed the teaching of Jesus. "I decided to know nothing among you except Jesus Christ and him crucified," wrote the Apostle Paul. I can safely say to you, without fear of contradiction, that if the cross is not central in your religion, then your religion is not biblical Christianity.

II. *Fact not myth.* The death of Jesus Christ is historical. It is to stress this that the Apostles' Creed says he "suffered under Pontius Pilate." We know from historical sources outside the Bible that Pontius Pilate was appointed procurator of Judaea by the Emperor Tiberius in the year A.D. 26. At the heart of our religion is a person who "suffered under Pontius Pilate."

Exactly what happened to Jesus under Pontius Pilate is described in the creed by four verbs: He "suffered, . . . was crucified, dead, and buried." He suffered before he was crucified. Then he was crucified. To be crucified was, in the eyes of the Roman world, to be disgraced as well as tortured. Having suffered and been crucified, Jesus died. And having died, his body was buried, while his soul (separated from his body by death) went to Hades, as the abode of the dead is called in the New Testament. This is the meaning of the phrase in the creed, "He descended into hell."

Now all these words emphasize the reality of the sufferings and death of Jesus Christ. His pain was real and terrible. He did actually die; his burial proves it.

III. *For our sins.* The third truth about the death of Jesus Christ is that it was sacrificial. He died as a sacrifice for sin. I know very well that his death has other meanings. But although these explanations of the death of Jesus are true, they do not exhaust its meaning. Nor are they the explanations on which the New Testament writers lay their emphasis. No. They tell us again and again that "Christ died for our sins." What is the relation between our sins and his death? Both Peter and Paul tell us. Peter wrote, "He bore our sins in his own body on the tree." Paul said, "Christ redeemed us from the curse of the law, having become a curse for us, for it is written, 'Cursed be everyone who hangs on a tree.'" He bore our curse. It was transferred to him. Voluntarily, deliberately, in his immeasurable love for us, he took upon himself the penalty due to us from our sins. And as a sign and symbol of it, he was hanged on a tree, of which it is written in Scripture, "a hanged man is accursed by God."

This is unfashionable theology in the church today. It is rejected by many. And we must be cautious, in our statement of it, not to go beyond Scripture, and never to represent God as a pitiless ogre from whom Jesus rescued us. God loved us and himself came after us in his Son, and bore in our place the curse of the law. The cross originated in the love and mercy and grace of God.

IV. There are three final lessons that I learn from the cross.

(a) First, that my sin is foul beyond words. If there were no way for our sins to

be cleansed and forgiven but that the Son of God should die for them, then our sins must be sinful indeed.

(b) Second, I learn that God's love is great beyond all understanding. He could have abandoned us to our just fate and left us to perish in our sins. But he didn't. He loved us, and he pursued us even to the desolate agony of the cross.

(c) Third, I learn that salvation is a free gift. I do not deserve it. I cannot earn it. I do not need to attempt to procure it by my own merit or effort. Jesus Christ on the cross has done everything that is necessary for us to be forgiven. He has borne our sin and curse. What then must we do? Nothing! Nothing but fall on our knees in penitence and faith, and stretch out an open, empty hand to receive salvation as a gift that is entirely free.—John R. W. Stott.

Topic: Why Jesus Died

Text: 1 Cor. 15:3.

There are certain dates enshrined in our memory. The day Jesus died is one of them. It was a day of great drama, the time of a significant deed, and no other day seems as high or holy as the day Jesus died. The annual season of Lent helps us to remember and renew our vows to God and to rejoice in his mercy toward us in Jesus. This week in his life began with high clamor from palm-waving admirers. It ended with Jesus crucified, dead, and buried as a supposed political enemy of Rome.

What made the joyful clamor of that Day of Palms change to such hateful jeering on that Day of Pain? Why did Jesus die? Yes, we know when Jesus died, but let us remind ourselves about why he died. My text speaks to that issue: "Christ died for our sins" (1 Cor. 15:3). Christian faith and experience are based upon a divine happening in his death.

I. *Tragic human circumstances.* Why did Jesus die? The answer is in two parts. The first part has to do with some tragic human circumstances.

(a) There was the crafty work of Joseph Caiaphas, high priest, who instigated the death of Jesus. Caiaphas and other members of the Sanhedrin helped Judas map the plan to trap and betray Jesus. Caiaphas headed the court that judged Jesus and condemned him to death. As the spiritual leader of Israel, Caiaphas should have been confirming the truth Jesus was speaking; instead, Caiaphas passed judgment upon him with all the others. Caiaphas held a position of which he was not worthy. He schemed, with full knowledge of his doings. He was determined to have Jesus killed, and he succeeded.

Having made its decision, the Sanhedrin then convinced Pilate to impose the death sentence. As procurator of Judea he had the civil power to impose that sentence.

(b) The Jews were under Roman law, which limited their self-government at many points—the death penalty being one of them. Had Jewish power not been so curbed, Jesus might have died at the hands of a stoning mob. But he was crucified. We Christians remind ourselves of this whenever we repeat that awesome sentence from the Apostles' Creed: ". . . suffered under Pontius Pilate."

Falsely accused of being an agitator, a threat to the authority of Rome, Jesus was crucified as a political criminal. Pilate knew that he was not. Pilate did not want to condemn Jesus to death. But those crafty religious leaders had so fixed the case that Pilate's governorship would have been in jeopardy had he not gone along with them. Pilate felt trapped—and he was. He literally washed his hands of the matter, which shows that he considered the whole case a dirty business. Mark tells us, "So Pilate, wishing to satisfy the crowd, released for them Barabbas; and having scourged Jesus, he delivered him to be crucified" (15:15).

(c) Mark's report shows us a third circumstance: the bloodthirstiness of a fickle populace. Jesus had become sport for a cruel-minded crowd that insisted he must be crucified. Pilate asked the crowd, " 'Why, what evil has he done?' But they shouted all the more, 'Crucify him' " (Mark 15:14).

The problems of mob psychology are too familiar to need elaboration at this point. Jesus was crucified as a result of a calculated scheme, political pressure tactics, and thoughtless feelings of an excited crowd. Jesus was the victim of a secret plot, a scared politician, and silly people obeying misguided authorities. Had they been more sensible, the populace could have had Jesus released. Pilate gave them this choice. But the people chose Barabbas instead.

These were the human circumstances behind why Jesus died.

II. *Death as a volunteer.* But the text insists that more was at work in the death of Jesus than human schemes. "Christ died for our sins in accordance with the scriptures." His death was not purely circumstantial; it was providential. Jesus did not die merely as a victim; he died as a volunteer. Jesus Christ died for our sins: to remove sin from us and to remove us from sin. He died in our place. He died for our peace. God sent Jesus to let him die for our sins, and he announced the plan through the prophets of old.

So we remind ourselves again: Jesus died to effect our deliverance from sin. Something was at stake in his death. God was at work in his death. This does not minimize the part sinful people played in killing Jesus. But it does highlight the commitment Jesus made to reconcile us to God. He died in the will of God, showing the love of God for us. Thus his death uncovered our human guilt and at the same time showed the aggressive goodwill of God. God was in the death of Jesus. But the Sanhedrin, Judas, Pilate, and the people were no less involved. God used the circumstances of their sins and brought blessing out of a cruel deed.

The death of Jesus is therefore no isolated fact merely listed on the records of Rome and Palestine. His death makes us see our sins and confront God in the process. In responding to the cross, we are responding to God.

What does his death mean to you? He volunteered himself to save you. In the light of his deed, what will you do across the rest of your life for him?—James Earl Massey.

Topic: The Silence Is Broken
TEXT: Acts 2:36–47.
Scientists have set up various listening stations with electronic ears listening twenty-four hours a day hoping for some

message from beyond the stars that would indicate there is life somewhere in the universe beyond us. So far there has been no word of any worlds beyond us. But the resurrection of Christ has broken that silence. The first indication of a sound from beyond came from the prophets through the centuries and increased with the coming of John the Baptist. Then Christ appeared with his ministry that drew great crowds of people, but he was suddenly cut off by the cross. He arose from the tomb, was seen by his disciples over forty days, and then once more disappeared from them. The disciples somehow knew that they had now come to be in touch with life beyond, with a whole world and kingdom from beyond. But there would be two things that would affirm the reality that the silence from beyond had been broken. There would be the presence of the Holy Spirit of Christ in the world. There would be the transformation of those who found new life in Christ by means of the Holy Spirit.

I. *Affirmed by the presence of the Holy Spirit of Christ.*

(a) Christ born at Bethlehem was God present in the flesh and blood of our own existence. But that same Christ told his disciples to wait until they were empowered by his holy, unseen presence on the day of Pentecost. Up until then the reality that the silence from beyond had been broken was the word of a few who had seen an empty tomb, and a few appearances of the risen Christ. But the coming of the Holy Spirit of Christ into the world at Pentecost would affirm his living presence to all.

The followers of Christ, empowered by the Holy Spirit, were blown out into the street to tell the story of this Christ, and what he had done to change their life. And since that time wherever this simple gospel story has been preached, that same Holy Spirit of Christ has applied it to the human heart, and for those who would hear, it has transformed lives. God's story is the story of all stories.

(b) The simple story preached that day at Pentecost is the most concise statement of the gospel of Christ to be found anywhere. That's the message the early church preached again and again. It is the story of God present in Christ, doing many miraculous works. This Christ was then handed over to the powers of darkness and lawlessness who crucified him and buried him. Then God raised him from the dead so that he now sits on the throne in heaven, King of Kings and Lord of Lords. This same Christ will someday return to judge all people. In the meantime we are called upon to repent and to be baptized in his name.

(c) That's the simple story that the Holy Spirit applies to every human heart that will hear it. And with the application there comes forgiveness, salvation, and hope. And it all comes because at the moment one believes this unseen Spirit of Christ enters his life. Since that moment in time, everyone who has heard the story of Christ has also felt the convicting power of that Holy Spirit of Christ that says in a very determined way, "This is God's truth for you, and you must accept it as your only hope!"

II. *Affirmed by resurrected living.*

(a) Christ was tangible in flesh and blood during his earthly ministry. But when he ascended into the heavens, he told his disciples they would become his body of flesh and blood in the world. Since that time God has chosen to work through the church, his flesh-and-blood presence in the world, empowered by the Holy Spirit of Christ.

(b) To live the resurrected life is to dare to live in this world without becoming merely one with it. It is often to stand against culture, to stand against custom, and to stand against power. The early followers found that they were called upon to stand against the same power that had crucified Christ. When King Henry II schemed to make his friend Thomas Becket Archbishop of Canterbury so that he could control all branches of power, he had no idea that once Becket was invested as archbishop, something transforming might happen to him. Suddenly he took the office seriously, so seriously that he defied the king who had placed him there, to the king's surprise and outrage. There was no way to account for the sudden change in Becket apart from the Spirit of

Christ. He suddenly began to live a resurrected life. And in the end, he was assassinated for it. But he chose bravely to die rather than to give up the new life which he had found. A few years ago I stood in the great cathedral at Canterbury and saw the place where Becket, though warned he was about to be killed, chose to kneel in prayer until the assassins had come to do their work. Such resurrected living is a constant affirmation in our world that the silence from beyond has been broken. The Apostle Paul wrote to the church at Colossae, "Now are we risen with Christ." He then challenged them to live the risen life.

(c) We have some characteristics of the risen life that were found in that early church.

(1) It is said they "continued steadfastly in the apostles' doctrine and fellowship, in the breaking of bread, and in prayers" (Acts 2:42). In other words, they had a hunger for growth, for a knowledge of the Scriptures, for an intimate relationship with Christ, for a real partnership with him. That's why they came together to pray and to break bread in the observance of the Lord's Supper. Above all else they wanted to know him better.

(2) Another characteristic is found in the statement: "Now all who believed were together, and had all things in common, and sold their possessions and goods, and divided them among all, as everyone had need" (Acts 2:44–45). To put it simply, their compassion for the needs of one another was so great that they were willing to sell whatever they had to help their friends in Christ have food on their table. Such love puts to shame the selfishness of the world and affirms that one greater than all the world is residing in such lives.

(3) In addition to this, there is a sense of awe that encompassed all that those early believers did: "Then fear came upon every soul, and many wonders and signs were done through the apostles" (Acts 2:43). The fear spoken of is a word that speaks of awe. The risen life lives in awe of God, contemplating the tremendous gift of life that he has given, and the limitless power of the Holy Spirit of Christ that dwells within each believer, and encompasses the church as a whole. They saw no limit to what God could do in their lives.

(d) We live this risen life out of hope, and that hope comes to us from the risen Christ in our midst as the Holy Spirit. We still have trials and tribulations as do all. But the resurrection gives us the hope by which to live the risen life, and the power as well. We still know something of silence when we stand at a graveside, or by a hospital bed, or in a divorce court. But we have hope.—Bob Woods.

ILLUSTRATIONS

CONFESSION.   Confession is primarily to God; however, honest confessions to one's fellows also are good for the soul. Jane has carelessly said unkind things about her neighbor, Mary. Mary is understandably upset, and her resentment shows. If Jane lets the matter continue a permanent barrier may go up between the neighbors. But Jane values Mary's friendship, and she remembers Jesus' teaching that we should love one another. She goes to Mary, acknowledges what both of them know she has said and done, and asks Mary's forgiveness. So the channels of communication are cleaned out, and a good relationship is restored. It is like that between us and God. Unless we want a barrier to come up between us and God— and remember, the walls are built from our side!—we must confess our sins to God and receive his forgiveness.—James W. Cox.

FIGHTING AGAINST DEATH.   Of all men, we hope most of death; yet nothing will reconcile us to—well, its *unnaturalness*. We know that we were not made for it; we know how it crept into our destiny as an intruder; and we know who has defeated it. Because our Lord is risen we know that at one level it is an enemy already disarmed; but because we know that the natural level also is God's creation we cannot cease to fight against the death which mars it, as against all those other blemishes upon it, against pain and poverty, barbarism and ignorance. Because we love something else more than this world, we love even this world better than those who know no other.—C. S. Lewis.

GOD'S HIDDENNESS.   As lyrical poets of sickness, harassment, doubt, and guilt, a few became channels of divine revelation. Some of the psalmodic theologians labored under the plight of their spiritual isolation. They sang the hidden God. Others were tortured by an obsession for God. They sang the hauntingness of presence. A few reached a plateau of confident serenity. They sang the sufficient grace.

When the prophet Isaiah of Jerusalem observed that "Yahweh concealed his face" (Isa. 8:17) or the Second Isaiah in Exile mourned the absence of Yahweh from the fate of his own people, saying, "Verily, verily, thou art a God that hidest thyself" (Isa. 45:15), their complaint amounted in effect to a confession of faith. To be aware of divine hiddenness is to remember a presence and to yearn for its return.—Samuel Terrien.

THE EXTENDED CROSS.   Jesus died once for all, it is true. But the cross goes on, both as a continuing and as a recurring experience. The Apostle Paul said that he made up what was lacking of the sufferings of Christ for his church, meaning that there was more suffering necessary and that he was going to do his part. But Paul did not exhaust the need. You and I, whenever we give up something for Christ and his church or for anyone on earth that Christ loves, we are being crucified with Christ and helping in his redemptive work. —James W. Cox.

GOD'S WISDOM.   The basic plan of life cannot be finally defeated. The will of God prevails even when the Son of God is crucified. In that very crucifixion God has absorbed the contradictions of historic existence into himself. Thus Christianity transmutes the tragedy of history into something which is not tragedy. God is revealed as not only the ground but as the goal of human existence and man's rebellion against God is proved to be an abortive effort which cannot finally prevail. —Reinhold Niebuhr.

GOD'S REDEEMING PRESENCE.   The discovery of Christ implies the discovery of the redeeming presence of God within the anguish of human experience. Now God is perceived not only in terrible confrontation with the world of man, but present within it as suffering love. This presence makes possible the ultimate vindication of the creation, and thus the reconciliation between the power and the goodness of the creator. By the same token, it vindicates the hope that human suffering has redeeming significance.—Peter L. Berger.

EASTER'S BRIGHT JOY.   A wife and mother, whose young husband dies unexpectedly, amazes many of the people who know her, though her close friends are not too surprised. Her cross of grief and pain is not a dead end, and she carries on without self-pity and with incredible courage. Of course she cries, like anyone else. She often feels the pain of loneliness and yearning for the one she has loved and lost for a while. Yet her life radiates something different. Easter, resurrection, and all the hope that Easter inspires has made the difference.—James W. Cox.

PILATE'S CASE.   In this connection, you can't help thinking about that other famous hand-washer, Lady Macbeth. Unlike Pilate, Lady Macbeth had committed murder herself, and what she kept trying to wash away in her sleep, long after her hands themselves were clean as a whistle, was her tormenting sense of guilt over the terrible thing she had done. She never succeeded, of course, but God is merciful, and one can hope that in the long run he did the job for her.

Pilate's case is different and worse. For him, it was not so much the terrible thing he'd done as the wonderful thing he'd proved incapable of doing. He could have stuck to his guns and resisted the pressure and told the chief priests to go to hell, where they were obviously heading anyway. He could have spared the man's life. Or if that is asking too much, he could have spared him at least the scourging and catcalls and have spoken some word of comfort when there was nobody else in the world with either the chance or the courage to speak it. He could have shaken his hand. He could have said goodbye. He could have made some two-bit gesture which, even though it would have made no ultimate difference, to him would have made all the difference.

But he didn't do it, and on that basis alone you can almost believe the sad old legend is true that again and again his body rises to the surface of a mountain lake and goes through the motion of washing its hands as he tries to cleanse himself not of something he'd done, for which God could forgive him, but of something he might have done but hadn't, for which he could never forgive himself.—Frederick Buechner.

PRAYERS OF CONFESSION

Lord, you have given us a world full of rich resources to feed us all and to provide us with all that body and mind could need; yet the poor are still with us, deprived of food, of homes, of education and dignity; deprived of healing and of hope. Forgive our inhumanity; forgive our politics and commerce; forgive our selfishness and greed; forgive us for leaving Christ unfed, unhoused, without healing and hope.

God of compassion, have mercy upon us as we make our confession. What we ought to have done still awaits action, while we commit acts not in accord with your will. We think of ourselves before others; we serve our own needs. We keep for ourselves the gifts of your graciousness. The new life you offer is not yet proclaimed in the land. Forgive us our sins and make us more faithful. Help us to use our time wisely as we follow Christ's way.

Almighty God: you love us, but we have not loved you; you call, but we have not listened. We walk away from neighbors in need, wrapped up in our own concerns. We have gone along with evil, prejudice, warfare, and greed. Loving God, help us to face up to ourselves, so that, as you move toward us in mercy, we may repent, turn to you, and receive forgiveness.

O God, spirit of peace and grace, whose salvation is never far from truly penitent hearts, we confess the sins that have alienated us from you and brought us trouble and sorrow. We are sorry for the duties forgotten and the absence at times of our faith in you. O merciful Lord, grant us to humble ourselves before you and to receive the remission of all our sins.—E. Paul Hovey.

SECTION VI. *Resources for Advent and Christmas Preaching*

SERMON SUGGESTIONS

Topic: Your Light Has Come

TEXT: Isa. 60:1 NEB.

I. "Arise, Jerusalem, rise clothed in light; your light has come and the glory of the Lord shines over you. For, though darkness covers the earth and dark night the nations, the Lord shall shine upon you and over you shall his glory appear." Those words from the beginning of the sixtieth chapter of the book of Isaiah were spoken to the people of Jerusalem who had recently returned from long exile in Babylon. As they begin the difficult tasks of reconstruction, their joy goes sour and their hope evaporates. It is to these despairing people that the prophet shouts, "Arise, Jerusalem, rise clothed in light; your light has come and the glory of the Lord shines over you."

II. I now tell you about another prophet, a twentieth-century secular prophet, who spoke in a time of great confusion, of shattering crisis.

H. G. Wells was in a quite remarkable way a symbol of the human adventure in the first half of our century, and the moods he expressed and stimulated are still widespread in our civilization. For most of his life he was an apostle of hope—hope in science and technology, hope in education, hope in our capacity to develop a paradise on earth.

During the Second World War he struggled valiantly to keep alive his hope for humankind. In 1942 he published a little book, *The Conquest of Time*. In his last chap-ter he propounded what he called "The Religion of the New Man." This was to be a new faith, a faith to provide the dynamic for our redemption of ourselves by ourselves for ourselves. And this is a faith that, in one form or another, still commends itself to many people.

This new faith begins by disposing of God as God is understood in the Judeo-Christian biblical heritage. It rules out everything beyond that which can be examined and tested and measured by scientific methods. It repudiates the biblical understanding of human nature and human existence under God, and it refuses to acknowledge the hard fact of human sin. It scoffs at the notion of life eternal. This new religion will have a simple trust in our inherent capacity to solve all the problems of our lives. This is a religion, Wells declared, that can carry us from the murky dawn in which we now live into a bright day of glorious achievement.

But H. G. Wells was not able to maintain his optimistic trust in human capacities. Not long before his death in 1946 he issued another personal manifesto, a little book to which he gave the ominous title *Mind at the End of Its Tether*. He summed up with these words: "The world is at the end of its tether. The end of everything we call life is at hand, and cannot be evaded." Sparkling hope had been transformed into the bleakest despair.

III. "Arise, Jerusalem, rise clothed in light; your light has come and the glory of the Lord shines over you." That was the

79

challenge of Isaiah to his countrymen as they wandered about aimlessly in the deepening twilight, waiting for the darkness that seemed to them inevitable.

This image of the light from God challenging the darkness of the world recurs throughout the Bible. In the evocative poetry with which John's Gospel begins we find this declaration: "The light shines in the dark, and the darkness has never quenched it."

But we must not be presumptuous about this. We must never think that God is bound, by his very nature, always to pull humankind's chestnuts out of the fire. No such guarantees are given either in the Bible or in human experience. The Bible teaches consistently that God's light for the world must be made effective in the world through people who, in faith and obedience, strive to serve his purposes of justice and mercy and love.

We Christians are called to reflect the light of God on all the structures and processes of society. Apathy toward the great issues and concerns of our time is a denial of God, a repudiation of Jesus Christ—no matter how good and pure and holy a person may be in his or her private life. —J. A. Davidson.

Topic: Directions to Bethlehem
TEXT: Isa. 40:1–11; Mark 1:1–8.

You ask anyone in the New Testament how you get to Bethlehem, they will say the same thing. You go out to the desert, keep on going until you get to the River Jordan. You'll see a man out there, standing waist deep in the water, baptizing people. That's John the Baptist. If you want to go to Bethlehem, you start there.

They all say the same thing—Matthew, Mark, Luke, John—all four Gospels. They all say, if you want to go to Bethlehem, see what's happened, understand what it means, then go see John.

You go to the Bible to find out what Christmas means and you run into John the Baptist. You can't get away from it. You ask, how do we get to Bethlehem from here, from where we are now? Go out to the desert, keep going until you get to the River Jordan. There you will find a man standing waist deep in the water baptizing. That'll be John. Ask him. Ask John

how you get to Bethlehem. That's what he's out there for.

I don't know about you, but I don't want to ask him. I don't want to ask him, because I know what John is going to say to me.

John is a prophet. And somewhere we got the idea that prophets are concerned only with the future. We use the word that way in English. We think a prophet is somebody who predicts what is going to happen in the future, and that's partly right. That's the part of the prophet that we think is all right. We don't mind that. What is hard to take about prophets is what they say about the present. They say things like, "Why don't you practice what you preach?" They remind you of what you know and don't want to be reminded of. They never say the right thing. The right thing is what the right people want to hear. Prophets are always going to the right people and saying the wrong things, saying what the right people don't want to hear. They all did that. All the biblical prophets did that. And they all paid the consequences for doing it.

John the Baptist is no exception. He goes to Herod—not the one who is ruling at the beginning of this story; he was Herod the Great. He goes to Herod Antipas, Herod the Great's son. Herod Antipas, like his father before him, felt himself to be liberated from the morality that other people have to live by. In fact, all the Herods felt that they were liberated even from common decency. Herod Antipas, guilty of murder, incest, and God knows what else. He was now married to his niece, who was also his sister-in-law.

Now the Jews had this crazy idea that morality is serious business, and what's more, it's corporate. They knew nothing about this "what I do is my own business as long as it doesn't hurt anybody else" kind of morality. They believed that everything you and I do either hurts or helps somebody else. They believed that society is not made up of autonomous atoms. They believed that society is corporate like we are. That is, having a body. So if you got an abscess anywhere the whole body would get sick. And if you are the king, that's sort of like being the head or the heart of the body politic. The king might not be any better or worse than anybody else in the society, but his sin or his virtue has greater effect on the society than anybody else's. That's true not only of kings but of all leaders, so the prophets are always going to the leaders. It was sort of a shortcut way of reforming the whole society. You go to the head and tell them what they know but don't want to hear. Nobody dependent on the king for salary or status, or even life, will tell him what he doesn't want to hear. So prophets got that job. They didn't volunteer, either. God sent them out there.

John went to Herod, told him, "You are an embarrassment to this nation and an affront to God." And Herod said to John, "You are under arrest." He locked him up in the castle at Machareus, till one night Herod's stepdaughter, who was also his grandniece, said she wanted John's head on a platter—and she got it.

You know what happened when Jesus heard about John? You know what he said? He said, "There is no man born of woman greater than John." There's no higher praise than that, unless it's what John said of Jesus. He said, "He who is coming after me is mightier than I, the thong of whose sandals I am not worthy to stoop down and untie."

There's a strong affinity between John the Baptist and Jesus of Nazareth. They're like cousins. That's why all the Gospel writers say, John knows who Jesus is. So if you want to know how to get to Bethlehem from where you are now, go see John. He knows who Jesus is. Go see John. And I don't want to, because I know what John is going to say.

This is the second Sunday in the season of Advent, the season of preparation for Christmas. We are two weeks' journey now away from Bethlehem. We're almost there, we might as well get it over with, go out there and see John. He says to us exactly what you would expect him to say. He says what he has been saying for two thousand years. He says, "Repent." Practice what you preach. Live up to the ideals and the standards that you believe in. That's what repent means. Repent doesn't mean to go through some sort of period of remorse for being so bad; repent means start doing something good. Repent

means start practicing what you preach. And that's what John says every Advent. Every year, the second Sunday in Advent, we come up to it. Repent!

I've been preaching about John for twenty-five years now, and in preparing this sermon I decided, I'm going to ask John a question. "John, how come you keep talking about repentance at Christmas time? Can't you get into the spirit? No wonder you're not on any Christmas cards. You're in danger of becoming the Grinch that stole Christmas. This is a happy time, this isn't a gloomy time."

And old John then comes out of the water. He has been in there so long his legs are blue. He says, "You fixin' to go to Bethlehem?" "Yes, that's where we're headed. In two weeks we'll be there." "Well, maybe you don't understand what happened there. I'll admit, it wasn't as I expected either. I expected the Messiah to come in glory with a sword, separate the righteous from the sinners, but that didn't happen. Instead he came in humility as a baby. He didn't come with a bang, but with a whimper. Not in force to defeat the kingdom of Herod, but in love to win the hearts of believers. So what you are faced with is what people have been faced with ever since I came out here and started baptizing. You are faced with a choice. Which king are you going to give your loyalty to, Herod or Jesus? To the kingdoms of this world or to the kingdom of God?"

Then he asked me, "Why are you going to Bethlehem? Are you going to Bethlehem to get Jesus to bless your world the way it is, or are you going to Bethlehem to let him change you so you can change the world?"

You see, that's why I didn't want to see John. I knew what he was going to say, and I didn't want to hear it. I wanted to hear that because God came into this world the way it is, the way it is, is all right with God. And John won't let me believe that.

If I'm going to survive, if I'm going to make it in this world, then I've got to be realistic. And Herod may be wrong, but Herod rules. Not Jesus.

But John the Baptist won't let us get away with that. He won't do it. He says, the kingdom of God is here; Jesus brought it. Not as I expected, but it's here. "The one who follows me is greater than I am, whose thongs I am not worthy to untie." He's the Messiah, all right. "So the kingdom is here."

With that he shuffles back to the river. "It's here, all right," he says as he turns his head and looks back over his shoulder. "You know it's here. The problem is, if it's here the only way you're going to know for sure is to choose it. And when you're ready, I'll be here." And with that he braces his bony feet against the river bottom and cries again, "Repent! For the kingdom of God is here!"

John is there to remind us that Advent is a time of repentance. John is there to remind us that the proper preparation for Christmas is doing what Jesus taught. If we are alienated from somebody this is the season of reconciliation. If we have been self-righteous now is the time for us to be understanding of other people. If we have been dispassionate toward the poor, now is the time for us to get some feeling in our life for something other than ourselves and see the conditions of other people. If we have assumed that war and violence are the only ways to solve the problems of this world now is the time to try something else. If we have put our trust in material things to save us now is the time for us to put our trust in God. If we have assumed that we are going to be judged by our avoidance of evil, now is the time for us to see that we're going to be judged by our doing of the good.

John is there to remind us of that. He is there to remind us that there are moral consequences to Christmas. It wasn't a fairy tale. It wasn't make-believe. The Messiah was born at Christmas. That means a beachhead was established in this world. And the kingdom of God is now here. There are now two kingdoms here. Which one has your loyalty?—Mark Trotter.

Topic: The Angels of God
Text: Luke 2:1–14.
I. "The angel of the Lord came upon them and they were sore afraid." One of the characteristics that Americans share is a reputation for being a very pragmatic people, a people who, at least in our own self-concept, honestly believe that given the facts, we can wrestle with reality no matter how complex it may be. We are a people who believe of ourselves that we are friends of reality, and we hear in our Gospel that the angel of the Lord comes with the bright light of God, with the truth of God, to demonstrate the complexity of reality.

You and I need not be reminded that we are surrounded on this troubled planet with difficulties on every quarter. And the question that we ask ourselves in such a season as this is, do we have the power, the courage as individuals, to face this world of reality? Do we have the courage to face these messengers of God, these angels, not beatific creatures as pictured in High Middle Ages' painting, but these messengers of God who come to us and remind us of the realities of God? When they do so, all of us, in some region of our lives and souls, are struck with fear, with anxiety, because this is a fearful world. We see the problems of our species and our relative inability to do anything about them as individuals. And so in the first instance, the messenger of God who comes to us brings us the awesome reality of our world.

II. Another angel says, "I bring you good tidings of great joy which shall be to all people."

(a) If I were to ask you to list what you deem to be the most critical social problems of our day, I am sure that many of you would list drugs, or alcohol, or divorce. In reality, the most difficult problem of our society is the growing tendency for all men and women to be separated from one another—to suffer a protracted, however dignified, loneliness, to suffer a separation from other people on the intimate levels of life. There is a growing tendency to say in our heart of hearts that our lives do not count. This gnawing fear abides with so many people in our society that bold would be the man or woman here who could or would say that he or she has not suffered the ravages of such depression, such separation from themselves and from those around them, who has not had anxieties of soul that would suggest perhaps our lives do not count.

(b) And God sent to you, to me, and to the human family, that which we celebrate in this festival of Christmas. God sent to us a companion; he did not send to us an answer. He sent to us a companion to walk through time and eternity with us. It is common to human nature to ask God questions. Why do the good suffer? God does not answer our question. He sends to us a companion who also suffers.

(c) We are surrounded with difficult and burdensome circumstances on every hemisphere, virtually in every nation of the world. People were starving one hundred years ago when Phillips Brooks stood in this pulpit. They were starving in Africa. There were economic and political privation on every hemisphere of the world but men and women did not know of it instantaneously as you and I do. The angel of truth has visited our generation and the angel of truth will not depart. These are the realities of our world. You and I come to this condition of duty and responsibility, we the choice-makers, with an almost desperate frenzy to know our God, to know this companion who walks with us amid these many difficulties.

III. "Glory to God in the highest and on earth peace, goodwill toward men." Where do we find this peace? Where do we find this peace in our souls that gives us the possibility of slumber that surmounts these visitations of reality? It is on the road of life that we meet the Christ. It is on the road to Emmaus where we meet the Christ, as did his disciples. It is on the road to Emmaus in our depressions, in our loneliness, in our befuddlement. It is on the road of life, working, believing, struggling. There is the Christ. With reality in one hand and hope in the other hand, we are led by this companion of ours, this Christ, to a new world.—Spencer Morgan Rice.

Topic: We're All Step-Parents
TEXT: Luke 2:39–52.

You don't have to know very much about human development to know that children's lives are shaped profoundly by their parents or surrogate parents—both

biologically and environmentally. When Luke says "Jesus increased in wisdom and in stature and in favor with God and man," I think that's his first-century Greek way of saying that Jesus developed as human being just like every other little boy and girl who ever walked the face of this earth, that Jesus was fully human. If we look at the life and ministry of our Lord from this perspective it suggests a lot to us about the home and family into which he was born and in which he was reared.

I want to suggest three important areas of our Lord's life and ministry I contend were influenced by Joseph and his relationship with Mary.

I. The first I call Jesus' earthiness, or if you want me to be less crude, his humanness. Jesus lived among an exceedingly religious group of people. They tried so hard to appeal to the holiness of God that they lost sight of God's humanity—his love and kindness and generosity and patience and forgiveness and grace.

And there it was walking among them— the humanity of God, revealed in the face of Jesus. The Gospels describe this quality of our Lord in various ways: threshing grain on the Sabbath when people were hungry, befriending Samaritans going home to dinner with a publican, a tax collector.

So they ran him out of town and hung him on a cross. Jesus was an embarrassment to the pious Jews of his generation, and to those of us invested in shallow legalisms and self-righteous do-gooderism in our age.

II. A second revolutionary idea Jesus revealed was his attitude toward women. The rabbis wouldn't speak to women in public. They prayed three times a day thanking God they had not been born Gentile or female. And Jesus utterly shattered this sort of shallow chauvinism. It's been 2000 years and Western civilization hasn't caught up with his ideal yet.

This son of a carpenter dared to see women differently than they had ever been seen before. If you don't believe me, ask that woman about to be stoned to death in John 8 or the Samaritan woman who encountered Jesus at Jacob's well. No one— certainly no man—had ever respected them so graciously or confronted them so profoundly. Jesus saw in both of these women more than either had ever believed about herself before. And Jesus called each of these women to respond at a level of responsibility both had carelessly avoided up to this point in their lives.

Where do you suppose Jesus got his attitude towards women? I submit that he got a lot from having a strong, capable mother and a dad who was secure enough he didn't need to compete with her or try to keep her down to feed his own weak ego. Jesus had a mother who refused to patronize her husband by playing dumb or weak in order to try to make him look smart or strong.

God chose a spunky Jewish girl and her shy boyfriend, the carpenter Joseph, to parent his son, Jesus. And from what I can tell, they did a pretty good job.

III. Most important was Jesus' idea about God. What we believe about God will ultimately determine how we live out every other facet of our lives. As I said earlier, Jesus was born into the life of an exceedingly religious group of people. And their idea of God was that he was primarily tyrant and taskmaster, judge and lawgiver. And Jesus said, "No, folks. You've missed it. God isn't like that at all. God isn't a judge and a lawgiver, a tyrant and a taskmaster primarily to be feared and obeyed. No, God wants us to be his children, to relate to him, to know him and experience him in a warm, close, personal, and gracious way." Jesus called God "Father," "Abba," "Daddy."

Now that is utterly revolutionary. That's what got Jesus killed—his personal relationship with God as loving Father. Jesus' idea of God was simply unacceptable to the most religious people of his day. The idea of God coming so close to us, touching our lives, knowing us and living intimately with us in such a personal way—that was utter blasphemy to the pious Jew of Jesus' day.

Again, where do you think Jesus got his concept of God? Certainly some of it came from Mary and Joseph who were themselves good stewards, good sharers with God of an important responsibility, the

rearing of God's own Son. The ministry of our Lord suggests that amidst the legalism characteristic of that home, given its cultural setting, a spirit of God as "Loving Parent," "Abba," "Daddy," must have dwelt there too.

In a very real sense we are all step-parents, foster parents, surrogate moms and dads. All those children whose lives we touch and who touch us in all sorts of ways, whether they carry our genes or not —our children's friends, the kids in our neighborhood and here at church, those we teach in school and work with in Scout troops or coach on Little League teams, they're all God's children, and he's entrusted us with their parenting.

Perhaps the most important vocation in our lives is to relate to our children in such a way that they'll see the spirit of Jesus, their elder brother, in our lives so that they will want to give their lives to him and trust him personally as their Lord and Savior.

Like Mary and Joseph, God has chosen us, as well, to parent his children in such a way that someday they too will know him as "Daddy," "Abba," "Loving Father."—Monty Knight.

Topic: Zechariah's Story

TEXT: Luke 1:5–25, 57–80.

I. The first character whom Luke brought onstage was Zechariah. Zechariah was probably close to fifty years old, maybe a little older. He had a wife named Elizabeth. Very early in the story we are told that Zechariah was a priest. We are also told that Zechariah and Elizabeth were good people. Their problem, however, was that they had no child because Elizabeth was barren and they were both advanced in years (Luke 1:7). They were God-fearing people, yet they could not have children. This was a serious problem. The ancient Jews believed that if you had no children you were cursed of God. And a childless marriage was grounds for divorce.

Zechariah was one priest out of twenty thousand priests in the Holy Land. But these priests did not serve all year. Except for the special holy days, these priests served only one week, twice a year. Every priest looked forward to serving twice a year. But Luke says that Zechariah was selected "to enter the temple of the Lord and burn incense" (v. 9 NASB). This was a great privilege, for a priest could live all his life and never be asked to burn incense on the altar.

As Zechariah served, conscious of what a high honor it was to burn the incense, he was moved to pray. And, like us, he prayed for those things closest to his heart. He prayed for Elizabeth, who wanted a child she could never have. He prayed for himself and their marriage and all the grief of their barrenness.

As Zechariah served and prayed, an angel appeared and said, "You're going to have a baby." Zechariah, who believed in prayer, thought he was hearing things. "Here I am in middle age with a wife who's nearly too old to bear children, and we're going to have a baby!"

But the angel continued, "This will be a special child, and many people will find the way because of him." Zechariah didn't know what to think. However, we know that he was struck completely dumb and couldn't say another word. And, as foretold, Elizabeth became pregnant. She probably experienced some of the same physical and emotional responses to pregnancy that women experience today, such as excitement, anticipation, nausea, and perhaps cravings for particular foods.

Finally the baby was born. Everyone was happy. They rejoiced and celebrated the birth of the child. But no one was more happy than Elizabeth and Zechariah. Luke said the parents took the baby to the temple on the eighth day for his circumcision. The priest said, "We'll call him Zechariah." However, Elizabeth firmly said, "No, his name is John." All the people in the temple must have been surprised because boy babies were supposed to be named after their fathers or grandfathers. So the priest looked at Elizabeth and saw that she was determined about the baby's name. And since Zechariah still could not speak, he wrote "His name is John" on a writing tablet. Luke said that at once Zechariah's voice came back, and he began to sing a doxology. Luke does not say but I can almost see Elizabeth, head held high,

marching out of the temple with her baby in her arms.

This baby, this John the Baptist, cousin of the Lord Jesus, would one day be a voice in the wilderness much like Isaiah had written about years and years before. He would prepare the way. He would sway many with his words. Even after Jesus was known to be the Son of God and John had been killed, he would still have his followers.

II. What does this story tell us about our own stories?

(a) God really does come to the faithful. Both Zechariah and Elizabeth were God-fearing people (Luke 1:6). They lived as best they could. God really does come to his children. Look closely. Zechariah and Elizabeth were as human as the rest of us. I'm sure they had their spats and there were days when Elizabeth didn't want to get out of bed. The heartbreak of having no children was very real to them both.

At Christmas we sing "O Come All Ye Faithful." And what it means is that God, despite our meanness and our sinning and our littleness and all the things of which we are ashamed, comes to us as he came to Zechariah and Elizabeth. And despite it all, we really do want to adore him and let him change our lives.

(b) God really does listen to his children. The great grief was that this couple had no children. This story assures us that God deals with our griefs as he did with theirs.

Their great grief was childlessness, and to their barrenness new life came. Does not this story mean that he comes to our barrenness and our hopelessness as well? Years before Isaiah had prophesied: "Surely he hath borne our griefs and carried our sorrows" (5:4). That is the Advent story. There is one who comes to us where we are in what we face.

So the apostle is right: nothing can separate us from the love of God—not a barren womb, not a divorce, not a grief that keeps us wondering if we can make it through the weeks to come, not even cancer or whatever we bring to the altar that harms or disturbs us. As he heard the longings of Zechariah and Elizabeth, he listens to us, too.

(c) The way of peace will come. The story did not end as they thought it would. The boy, John, was always a little strange. He wasn't a perfect child. Some blamed his behavior on his living with old folk. Some said they spoiled him too much. John kept to himself. He loved nature. He wore strange clothing and didn't even drink when he got older. He ate natural food and was a preparer. People listened to John and their lives were changed.

What is the point? Peace comes, but not as we expect it—not like Roy Rogers or Gene Autry riding off into the sunset singing, "I'm back in the saddle again." No, it doesn't happen like that. But even where they were Zechariah and Elizabeth discovered the Old Testament prophecy coming true: "The day shall dawn upon us from on high to give light to those who sit in darkness and in the shadow of death, to guide our feet into the way of peace" (Luke 178b-79 RSV).

People today need light. Some are afraid of the shadows of death. Some of us have feet that stray. Yet here we discover that God came to men and women like us, and life was different—not easy, but different and special. Peace comes, even here.

So we do simple things, wonderful things. We tell stories; we sing songs; we light candles; we send money to faraway places. Isn't that what Christmas is all about?—Roger Lovette.

ILLUSTRATIONS

WHAT HOLDS US TOGETHER.   I received a very interesting Christmas present. It was an electric glue gun. I thought of so many practical things I could do with it. For one thing, I have a pair of house slippers with a sole that is very floppy. I tried to glue it down. It stayed for a while. It wasn't as good as the commercials indicated. Then I started thinking of all the practical uses for that glue gun. I thought I could really use it in my ministry. I imagined some very difficult counseling situations in which families are having a lot of trouble. In my imagination I could hear myself saying to them, "Now let's just join hands and have a prayer together." Then when everyone's eyes were closed, I would reach back and grab my new present—my electric glue gun—and just zap them with it as their hands were joined together and say to them, "Now go and work things out together." Then I thought it would be a great idea to use it in weddings. I imagined myself performing a wedding saying, "Now will you join hands." When they joined hands and their eyes were closed, I would reach back for my electric glue gun and give them a good shot of that glue; I would say, "This is for life! You all stay together for better or worse!" The more I thought about it the more ideas I got for the use of that glue gun. Then, of course, I knew that no glue gun could really solve the brokenness of life. The mystery and wonder of Christmas is this: that the one who came to visit our planet is the one "in whom all things hold together," who is the source of healing for our brokenness and our fragmentation.—Joe A. Harding.

WAITING IN HOPE.   Archibald Rutledge wrote about sailing with Sam Singleton on the Santee River in South Carolina. They were going to a place called Tranquillity, which had been appropriately named, where they would shoot duck for a few days. They left home about one o'clock one winter night. They had planned to drop down for ten miles on the ebb tide, reaching their destination around daybreak.

The stars were out when they left home, but they were soon lost behind a fog so dense that they could hardly see the bow of their little boat. As they were going with the tide, they felt secure, but they began to wonder when they passed looming shores that were unfamiliar to them. Then for an hour there was no visible land. Waves, which were suspiciously like sea waves, began to rock the boat. The roar of the surf became almost clamorous. Attempts to reach either shore were in vain. The tide seemed to be turning, and the boat was shipping water. Gallons of it. Rutledge was seized by great fear when Sam Singleton said, "Never mind, Cap'n; it will be daybreak soon." It became one of the great moments of his life to which he often returned for hope and encouragement. He wrote of it: "And even now, after all these years, whenever the shadows are deepest and most impenetrable, I seem to hear, out of that dim celestial past, the quiet voice of Sam Singleton saying to my doubting heart, 'Never mind, Cap'n; it will be daybreak soon.' "

Advent is like Sam Singleton saying "Never mind, Cap'n; it will be daybreak soon."—Chevis F. Horne.

THE NETWORK OF PROVIDENCE.   About ninety years ago a family journeyed from England to Scotland for a summer vacation. The young son of that family was swimming one day and suddenly was seized with cramps. He shouted for help; from a nearby field a farm boy heard his cry and successfully dragged the English lad from the water. The father of the afflicted swimmer was deeply grateful. He asked the young hero, "What do you plan to do with your life?" "Oh, I suppose I will be a farmer like my father," the boy replied. "Isn't there something else you would rather do?" "Oh yes, sir; I've always wanted to be a doctor but we're poor people and we could never afford to pay for my education." "Well, you never mind that," said the English gentleman; "You shall have your heart's desire and study medicine. You make your plans and I will take care of the cost." And that is exactly what happened.

There is more to the story. That farm boy did become a doctor. Much later, in December 1943, Winston Churchill was dangerously ill with pneumonia somewhere in North Africa. His doctor asked Sir Alexander Fleming, the discoverer of penicillin, to fly to Africa to attend the sick statesman. Fleming arrived within a few hours, administered the drug and saved Churchill's life—for the second time. It was this same person, Alexander Fleming, who had pulled Winston Churchill out of the swimming hole many years before.

Do you see in that account the working of God? I do! From an unexpected childhood circumstance, a future evolved leading to the medical achievements of Sir Alexander Fleming and the World War II triumph of Britain under the indomitable leadership of Sir Winston Churchill. Churchill's father was the instrument God used to provide Fleming's education; Fleming's skill as a physician was used by God to spare Churchill, and on the story goes. The human network, when open to God's purposes, is a vital and awesome thing. You and I are a part of that network! —John H. Townsend.

WHEN GOD IS PRESENT.   We cry out against the absence of God, when actually he is so present that we miss him. We feel quite safe from a God floating around on a cloud someplace, but we are threatened by the God who invades our home, our job, our relationships. The fleshliness and bloodiness of God is an offense to humans. This is what the incarnation is about. Religious people and the politicians in Jesus' day did not want a God so present as to threaten their vested interests.—John Thompson.

SOMEBODY TO LOVE ME.   In England during the second World War, some soldiers were on furlough in London. They walked around the city and witnessed all its devastation after the bombing from German planes. As it happened, they passed by a children's home on Christmas Day, and they wondered what kind of Christmas these children had had in this difficult time. They went into the building and saw that there were no Christmas decorations, no tree, and no presents because there had been no money at all to buy anything for these children. As the soldiers walked among the children, they reached in their pockets to see if they had anything to give them. They gave them a piece of string, a coin, a stick of chewing gum, a pocketknife, or whatever they had in their pockets. They wanted to give something to the children to say "Merry Christmas." One soldier went up to a young boy who reminded him so much of his nephew back home. As he looked at that boy he said, "Son, what would you like for Christmas?" The boy answered, "Mister, I just want somebody to love me."—William Powell Tuck.

WHAT CHRIST HAS ACCOMPLISHED.   Such and so many are the Savior's achievements that follow from his incarnation, that to try to number them is like gazing at the open sea and trying to count the waves. One cannot see all the waves with one's eyes, for when one tries to do so those that are following on baffle one's senses. Even so, when one wants to take in all the achievements of Christ in the body, one cannot do so, even by reckoning them up, for the things that transcend one's thought are always more than those one thinks that one has grasped.—St. Athanasius.

VALUING OTHER LIVES. Mighty and loving Father, in the midst of these days of love and good cheer for friends and family, grant to us a growing sense of the worth of every human life. Let us not forget the sufferings and sacrifice of motherhood, the cares and cost of fatherhood, the protection and help of society, without which human life would not endure. Forgive us for the light estimate we have put on the father and mother of somebody else, the careless regard for the other person's son and daughter, the wicked indifference to other people's little ones. Give us the grace and strength, Almighty God, to do collectively for the unfavored and unprivileged members of the human family what our hearts prompt us to do for our own flesh and blood who need our protection and help.—George W. Coleman.

SECTION VII. Evangelism and World Missions

SERMON SUGGESTIONS

Topic: Inescapable Summons

TEXT: Luke 16:1–8

(a) The branch office manager played fast and loose with his company's money. His department went in the red. His boss was aware of the situation, cornered him, and gave him a thirty-day notice. The manager was shaken. He had been drifting along, making some bad deals, wasting money on expense accounts; but he figured that his company was so large that no one would notice. After all, the company could not make profit in every area, and it would be able to write off his division as a tax deduction. Now suddenly the branch office manager's future was in jeopardy. His pipe dreams were shattered. All his ambitions for promotion were scuttled. He faced the great crisis of his business career. So he sat down in his swivel chair, stunned. He made a swift assessment of his alternatives: he could accept failure, close the books, pack up the office. And so he contemplated construction work, checked on his biceps, and decided that would not do. Then he thought of selling pencils on the sidewalk, and his pride overtook him. Then another alternative that was not obvious in the situation broke into his awareness. He could act boldly and quickly in the face of impending ruin. He could choose to act with dispatch. And so he became a one-man collection agency, singled out the big accounts, reduced them sharply, and turned dead accounts into cash. His hope was that the customers would be so pleased with his action on their part that they would either give him a job or at least a place to sleep.

Then the boss showed up a second time, found out what the branch office manager had been up to, and applauded his actions! He did not commend him for his previous mismanagement but for his bold wheeling and dealing.

(b) It is very likely that Jesus refashioned a story gossiped in the streets, a secular story that he used for religious purposes. It is not that Jesus wants us to go and mismanage. It is not that he wants us to copy this man's slippery morals. And yet in a daring fashion Jesus was willing to use an ambiguous situation about a dishonest character because there was one thing about this man's actions that was right. When he faced a crisis, when he was in a jam, and when he assessed the alternatives, he saw the necessity of bold action while there was time. There was right action while there was time (Riggenbach). It is bold action which Jesus wished to commend in our story.

I. As we first find this branch office manager, this steward, he is indeed in a desperate plight. He has been caught red-handed, either in poor business tactics or in dishonest business activities. This happens when Christ invades our lives today. When Christ invades our daily routines, our flimsy excuses and moral standards do not meet his expectations. When God comes in Jesus Christ, threatening our way of living and calling our lives into question, he will not allow us that luxury of a sidelong glance at some obvious sin-

89

ner to bolster our personal pride.

II. In our parable we see how Christ brings us in a moment of truth to a desperate plight and allows us to see reality as it really is. Not only is there a desperate plight portrayed in the parable, but there is an inescapable summons implied throughout. For Christ tosses a challenge into our laps. Like the dishonest businessman, we must decide.

And indeed, as is the case with him, so it is with us. Evasion of decision is not possible. There is a great feeling of urgency surging through the parable. This sense of urgency coursing through the story demands some kind of resolution to the crisis.

And is there not need among Christians today to have some sense of urgency about the gospel? For some of us were drawn into the church by a sense of urgency. Is it not true in many instances that people have been drawn into the preaching ministry, into missions, into concern for social problems, through a burning sense of urgency that the gospel really matters enough to become concerned and to care?

And is there not in this Christian sense of urgency a creative spinoff? If indeed there is a sense of urgency that Christ brings to life, and the gospel places upon our lives, there is also then some meaning to human existence. Then indeed there is a quality of living and of life that is worth living and worth having. There are so many in our times, and surely within our congregation, who on occasion in honesty do not recall any good motive why they ought to stay alive or why they ought to be engaged in any significant purpose in life. It is helpful for us, in the light of that, to be recalled by this unusual parable to the reality that there is meaning given us in the gospel of Christ, that life itself has a pulsating quality about it. We have a God who cares about the salesman struggling to make a living, and about the teenager who may be disappointed, and about a diplomat looking for life.

Our parable dramatizes an inescapable summons to say yes, to say no, to make some kind of response.—Peter Rhea Jones.

Topic: The Rewards of Returning: The Parable of the Prodigal Son

TEXT: Luke 15:11–24.

The well-known parable told by the Lord Jesus Christ is considered by literary critics—even those of the secular world— as perhaps the greatest story human ears have ever heard. It has all the drama, pathos, and tension that go into the making of a great short story. We know it commonly as the parable of the prodigal son.

There was a significant Bible scholar of a past generation, however, who said to name it so is actually to misname it. He argued that the real impact and emphasis that Jesus desired those first hearers to grasp from the story—hence, that which the Spirit of God would impress upon our lives today—was *not* upon a young man who took all the good things of the father's house and selfishly hoarded them to himself. There was nothing more unusual about that sort of experience in Jesus' day than in ours. Rather, said the scholar, the prime emphasis is upon the father. That was the unusual part of Jesus' parable, because the offended father received the son not with rejection or recrimination, but with understanding, forgiveness, and compassion. Therefore, said the scholar, the parable should more correctly be called "The Parable of the Father's Heart." This will become increasingly clear as we delve into the impact of what Christ was trying to communicate in this beautiful short story.

In the light of this basic principle of the parable, verse 22 of Luke 15 takes on pronounced significance. From that verse one sees what this compassionate, understanding father gave as gifts to his young son when he returned home. Remember his words? The father said to the servant, "Bring quickly the best robe and put it on him and put a ring on his hand and shoes on his feet." The *robe,* the *ring,* the *shoes;* the rewards of returning, love gifts that the compassionate father lavished upon his son as he stood at the household gate.

I am quite confident that Jesus did not interject that twenty-second verse merely to enhance the human interest of the story or to stimulate the imagination. Surely the verse contains something of significant spiritual reality for us to grasp. Never did a word fall from the lips of our Lord that was not intended to have an impact upon our lives.

But obviously, before we can understand what Jesus was trying to say with the symbolic language of the robe, the ring, and the shoes, we need to understand who the two principal personalities in the parable are. The father? Clearly, our Lord was speaking of God, the Father. No one but God the Father could have the compassion of the father in the parable. The son? That is not difficult to discern either. You and I are the prodigal. The reasoning is simple. Every one of us has taken the good things of the father's house: food, clothing, shelter, the necessities of life—life itself. Then we tend to hoard these things or spend them on our desires, thus developing self-centered lives. That inevitably cuts us off from the father's house, thrusts us into a "foreign country," and makes us prodigal children.

But the point of the entire parable is this: whenever we are willing to turn from that kind of a self-oriented life and give ourselves to God, thus putting our faith and trust in Jesus Christ as Lord and Savior, in that moment the loving compassionate Father will give to all of us a robe, a ring, and shoes for our feet. Let's plunge into the drama of the parable and see if we can discover what our Lord was saying to us in this beautiful pictorial language.

Put yourself imaginatively back into the first century, right into the dramatic scene that took place when that young man stood before the father. It becomes immediately apparent why the first words the father spoke were "Bring quickly the best robe and put it on him." Remember where the young man was prior to his return to the father's house? Jesus described it in quite cultured language, as we would have expected. He said the young man was "in the field feeding swine." Not everyone would express it in quite so dignified a manner.

In the setting of this job the young man was reduced to absolute poverty. Thus he had no resources to clean himself up, no money to buy new clothes and present himself in an acceptable manner before the father. Can you catch the pathos of the scene? There the prodigal stood, dejected, head bowed, as he nervously shifted about in the old tattered, filthy garments of the pigpen. When the compassionate father saw his son in that condition, little wonder he turned to the servants and said, "Quickly, bring the best robe and put it on him."

Notice further, our Lord injected a little adjective in that statement: "Bring quickly the best robe and put it on him." This conjures up in one's imagination a scene something like this: In the days when the young man was still in the far country and the loving heart of his father yearned for his son, the father would perhaps take one of the servants into what we would call today a wardrobe room. From the shelf he would take a costly garment, unfurl it, and say perhaps something like this to his servant: "You see this robe? Look at all the beautiful artwork by the artisans who designed it. That magnificent embroidery is done with gold and silver thread. The semiprecious stones encrusted therein were most expensive. Why, this garment cost a small fortune. It's the best robe money can buy. No one is to touch it, even get near it. It's reserved for my son if he will ever come home." When that glad reunion hour actually arrived and there stood that young man in his pitiable condition and the father said, "Bring quickly the *best robe,*" I am sure those servants knew just the one of which he was speaking.

A beautiful picture! But what was the Savior trying to say? There is a verse of Scripture in the Old Testament that may afford an answer. Perhaps our Lord even had it in mind. In the book often called the Gospel of the Old Testament, the book of the prophet Isaiah, in chapter 61 and verse 10 the prophet stated, "I will greatly rejoice in the Lord. My soul shall exalt in my God, for he has clothed me in the garment of salvation; he has covered me in the robe of righteousness." Catch that last phrase, "He has clothed me in the *robe of righteousness.*"

The same prophet Isaiah said three chapters later, "*Our* righteousness"—our attempt to be good, to live a decent life, thinking that somehow that kind of "righteousness" may curry favor with God—"*is as filthy rags.*" We stand before God, even at our human best, in the torn, tattered, filthy garments of the pigpen. Our righteousness is as filthy rags. But if we can understand the poverty of our soul, and say with the young man in the parable, "I will arise and go to the father," God in his great mercy and forgiveness will strip off the old garments of the far country, cleanse us completely, and clothe us in the righteousness of Jesus Christ.

That garment, Jesus' robe of righteousness, is best, for it was purchased at a terrible cost. Its price was the cross. Jesus Christ bought it for us all when he died and shed his blood. And what a thrill, what a joy, is found when it is put on. To be cleansed and permit God to clothe one in the righteousness of Christ, thus knowing God's acceptance, is life's greatest experience. The guilt goes, the remorse flees, the emptiness disappears, and floods of peace and joy in the knowledge of forgiveness roll into life's deepest recesses. Moreover, Christ's robe of righteousness is not only the best robe, it is the *only* robe. God accepts no one who is not so clothed. Are you wearing that garment?

Now as if all that were not enough, the gifts of God's grace merely begin there. Our Lord went on to say, "Put a ring on his hand." Rings are many times a symbol of important earthly relationships. The band of gold many of us wear on the third finger, left hand, is a symbol of a very important earthly relationship. It symbolizes the ideal marital state. Many pastors have illustrated it when they said to a young couple, "From time immemorial the ring has been used to seal important covenants. When the race was young and parliaments unknown the great seal of the state was often fixed upon a ring worn by the reigning monarch and its stamp was the sole sign of imperial authority. Friends often exchange this simple band of gold. . . ."

But what about the ring in the parable? Was the young man receiving a wedding ring? Hardly! Yet it was most important. The ring was what we would call today a signet ring. That is, it was a ring into which was engraved the family crest, the family

mark. It was used in the sealing of important documents. For example, when contracting parties entered into an agreement, the actual covenant was not binding even after it was signed. It had to be sealed with sealing wax, and while the wax was warm and impressionable, the signet ring bearing the family mark would be pressed down in it. That bound the parties to the agreement. Now note: only the father and sons had the privilege of wearing such a ring. That is significant. What is being implied?

With the ring, our Lord has injected a most beautiful little twist into this parable. It will aid our understanding of the point. Reflect back on verses 18 and 19. In those verses we see the young man premeditating a three-point prayer. He said, "I will arise and go to my father, and I will say to him, (1) 'Father, I have sinned against heaven and before you; (2) I am no longer worthy to be called your son; (3) treat me as one of your hired servants.' "

After planning his prayer, the young man wisely went home—good resolves are never sufficient, one must *act* on them. There he stood before his father and began. One, "Father, I have sinned against heaven and before you." The father wanted to hear that, because it was true. The Bible says, "All have sinned and come short of the glory of God" (Rom. 3:23). One must acknowledge personal sin. Two, "I am no longer worthy to be called your son." The father wished to hear that also. None is worthy. None has a claim on God. "There is none righteous, no not one" (Rom. 3:10). Remember, we are *all* prodigals. The young man was just about to utter his third request: "Treat me as a hired servant," but breaking in, the father interrupted him and said, "Put a ring on his hand." And the young prodigal got the message immediately. He knew only sons received the signet ring. He was not going to be welcomed as a hired servant, but as a son. He never prayed his third request—he was to be a son. Here was the ring of sonship to prove it. What a thrill must have shot through his very soul.

That is why the Scriptures state, "As many as received him (the Lord Jesus

Christ) to them does God give the privilege to become children of God" (John 1:12). What a joy to receive that status! The identity crisis goes; we know who we really are; we become children of God. You join the family of God. You are home. Life takes on meaning and reality. Emptiness and futility vanish and the days are filled with song. You belong. "Put a ring on his hand." And yet there is more.

The father said, "Put shoes on his feet." Again we must project ourselves imaginatively into the drama of the scene. It is the first century in a wealthy farm family. In that situation we tend to picture the sons of the family as sitting under the swaying palms of a desert oasis. One group of servants fans them with ostrich-plume fans. Others drop figs and grapes in their mouths while they conjure up enough energy to chew and swallow. Beautiful, exotic music wafts over the sand dunes as they loll the hours away. Nothing could be further from reality. We have probably seen too many TV programs. The sons worked all day just as did the hired servants. However, there was a difference. The hired servants were required to work bare footed. That was a sign of servitude. The sons wore sandals as they undertook their chores. So the principle of sonship again emerges.

But another picture begins to surface. We sometimes imagine that being a Christian is to be at ease at some spiritual desert oasis (usually called the church). Servants make it comfortable for us (the caretakers). Then that other servant crams spiritual grapes and figs down us pleading, "Chew and swallow." We call him the preacher. All the time the beautiful exotic message filters out of the sand dune we know as the choir loft. So we just loll away a few hours a week—or month—and say, "Doesn't it make you feel good to go to church?"

Is that Christianity? Never! When you come to God through Jesus Christ, you not only receive the robe of righteousness and the ring of sonship, you also put on the sandals of service. You come to God to serve faithfully. Actually, you cannot have the robe and ring without the shoes.

Yet, it is right there that life takes on real purpose and goal. You have something to do that genuinely counts.

The service of Christ is a great joy, never a burden. Jesus said, "My yoke is easy and my burden is light" (Matt. 11:30). What a thrill to serve the living God.

So the story ends—in a party. That is correct, a party. "They killed the fatted calf and made merry." That is a first-century, mideastern party. God does not invite you to a dreary, drab life. He invites you to his party and he prepares you for it by giving you a robe of righteousness, a ring of sonship, and sandals of service. What gifts! Won't you come home and receive them—now.—Lewis A. Drummond.

Topic: There's a Storm Warning Out!
TEXT: Matt. 7:21–29.

Our Scripture speaks about a long-term storm warning, and a storm that makes rushing to a cellar futile, or looking for a closet in the middle of the house a wasted effort. The storm spoken of by the Scripture is one that you cannot escape. It comes to all. So it is not a storm you can evade; it is one for which you must prepare. To help prepare us for that certainty, Christ told a parable about two men, each of whom built a house. One is called a wise man, the other is called a fool. We can learn something from looking carefully at this parable.

I. *The similarities of the builders.* One thing I have discovered through the years is that by and large, everyone wants basically the same things. Each of these men recognized the need of a house. They each set out to build one. They recognized their families had needs. And they had certain goals to provide those needs.

II. *The differences between the two builders.* Although there were many similarities, the differences between the two become apparent only in light of the storm warnings. The differences appear with regard to how seriously each one takes that warning. Isn't it strange that we so quickly jump into the business of marriage and family and children, as though we needed no advice from anyone?

Since the storm warning is long-term and has no prescribed dates or hours, it is easy to put it in the background of our thinking. That's what one man did. He was anxious to get on with his life. So he didn't worry about such matters as digging down through the sand until he came to the solid rock on which he could build for the storm. He just found a nice dry place on the flood plain and began to build. He was in a hurry. He knew what he wanted. Why ask anyone?

The other builder, the wise man, recognized he was a beginner. He apparently got some good advice. He dug until he found solid rock. And there he built his home. He took more time. He could not rush on with it as the other man. And although both houses looked the same to the passerby, there was a world of difference between them. And someday that difference would be quite evident.

III. *The inescapable storm.* The storms are the same for everyone, and we cannot escape them. We live our life in the path of the storm. Everything we do must stand the test of the storm.

There is a sense in which there are preliminary storms that precede the final one. They come in all shapes and sizes. They come in financial trials; they come in tragedies and car wrecks; they come in cancer cells and tidal waves; they come in divorces and divided families. But perhaps the worst storm of all is time itself and the ravages it takes.

There was a time when it seemed the power of the Roman eagle would never cease. There was a time when it seemed as though Napoleon would never be defeated. There was a time when Hitler's Third Reich seemed destined to subjugate all people under its power. Yet each movement carried within it the silent seed of destruction that came with greed and power and ugliness. Each was doomed to self-destruct with the passing of time.

Each of the builders built a home. One survived the final storm. But one fell, and our Lord said, "Great was the fall of it!" All the building had been for naught. And the final storm destroyed it all!

IV. *Facing the storm.* The wise man built a life on the solid rock, and what he built survived the storm. The difference was the foundation. And it does not take very much imagination to recognize that Christ is talking about basing your life on the only solid rock there is in this universe—Jesus Christ.

Jesus gives some very practical insight on how we can determine if our own faith is real, and therefore whether or not we are building on the rock. Jesus said real faith is evidenced by those who hear what he has to say and then act upon it—those who hear and do.

Jesus talked of "hearing and doing his words." This is a kind of summary of the whole Sermon on the Mount (Matt. 5–7). Christ said that there is only one way, the narrow way to him. And he said there is only one gate. And he said true faith is exhibited by those who take his words seriously and then act upon them. Those who heard him were astonished because he spoke with such authority. He said there are not many ways. He said there is one way! And he said that way involves hearing his words and doing them.

It was our Lord himself who asked: "Why call ye me Lord, Lord, and do not the things which I say?" (Luke 6:46). James had a word at this point also. He said, "Faith without works is dead, being alone!" (James 2:17) Just as the proof of the pudding is in the eating, so proof of faith is in the doing. Jesus was not saying that works are the same as faith. But he was saying that real faith hears and does. It acts! It gives! It follows without knowing where! It gives without counting the cost!

V. *Taking the storm seriously.* St. Augustine suggested that we ask the very simple question, "With whom am I in love?" It has much to do with whom we will follow. The Christian must look toward the end of time and accept the reality of the final storm, of death and judgment. When you have really seen that, then who you really are and what you are going to do in this world has been settled.

Those who heard Christ were amazed at the way he spoke with such authority. What he was really saying was simple. He said either you live life my way, or ahead of you awaits total ruin, even hell itself.

Psychologists tell us it is dangerous to feel an emotion and then not to translate that into action. To do it repeatedly is to destroy something very sensitive in the soul. God troubles our heart in an effort to get us to take the long look, and therefore to take the storm seriously, and then to live in light of it.—Bob Woods.

Topic: Who Speaks for Jesus? The Importance of Every-Member Evangelism
TEXT: Luke 19:28–40.
I. *Evangelism ought to be a vital part of our life.* We tend to take a lot for granted, especially in secure older churches, and forget that no church was ever built on mere spit and tradition, that somewhere, sometime, someone had to go out into the highways and byways and bring people together in Christ. We are like the lifesavers in one of Merrill Abbey's books, rescuers on a rockribbed seacoast who had done such a tremendous job of saving storm-wrecked sailors that the citizens of their region bought them a splendid house and provided for their every comfort; and then they grew so languid and comfortable that they stopped going out to rescue people! We belong to a big church and assume that our work is done. Jesus' command to go into all the world and preach the gospel falls on deaf ears—or strikes us as words to ministers and missionaries, not to average Christians.

Part of our trouble is a psychological block. It doesn't take us long, especially in a church with a beautiful sanctuary, to dissociate ourselves from coarser forms of Christianity in which congregations engage in every-member evangelism, knocking on doors, handing out pamphlets, and badgering people about their souls and the end of the world. We are "First Church"—noses atilt—and we don't *do* things like that! We don't, do we? And I will be the first to say I am glad we don't. Not like that. I wouldn't for a minute put down the churches that do; somebody probably needs to do it. But I am glad it is not our style.

I have always liked a little story I heard years ago from Kenneth Chafin, who was at that time a professor of evangelism in Fort Worth, Texas. It was about a veteran old soul-winner who spent most of his time going around after the unconverted and winning them into the kingdom. His Bible was as marked up as a novice's travel guide, and there was nobody, but nobody, he couldn't quote and cross-reference into salvation. One day he was out making his rounds with a beginning soul-winner, a young man who was thinking about entering the ministry. The young man was impressed and amazed as, one after another, various persons targeted for conversion surrendered to the Lord. The two had been at it all day when late in the afternoon they pulled up at the curb outside an expensive ranch house in an exclusive subdivision and walked up the flagstone walkway that wound through a carpet of lush, green grass. As the walk wound past a picture window, they saw the man of the house sitting inside. He was in his shorts, lying back in a great reclining chair, watching a football game on TV. He had a can of beer in one hand, and the other hand was idly stroking the head of a beautiful great dane lying beside the chair. As the old soul-winner reached for the doorbell, the young man stopped his arm a moment. "Before we go in there," he said, "I need to know something." "What's that, son?" asked the older man. "What kind of good news do we have for him?"

There is a lot of truth about evangelism in that little story. Good news begins at the point of our realization of need. And, because our needs vary, the way the good news is presented must vary. The method of winning a soul to Christ that worked for a down-and-out gas station attendant in one section of the city would not work for the up-and-out business executive relaxing in front of the TV set. The man in the ranch house probably had as much need for Christ as the man in the gas station; but his way of perceiving himself and his need was different, and the evangelists should have taken that into account.

II. *Jesus expects his followers to acclaim him to other people.* If they don't, the very stones in the ground will cry out to acclaim him, Jesus once said. There ought never to be any shyness in us about confessing the lordship of Christ and what it means in the structuring of our lives and hopes. In fact, there is probably some correlation between such shyness and our failure to lead mature Christian lives. But we are also expected, if our imaginations are converted as well as our mouths, to be able to transcend mere abecedarian approaches to spiritual matters and witness to Christ in an idiom that other people can understand and relate to. Let me give you two or three pictures to show you what I mean.

(a) Picture number one: Here is a teenager named Mike who has been in and out of detention several times in the past three years. He comes from a well-to-do home but is constantly in trouble. He is a known user of alcohol and drugs. His parents are at their wits' end with him. A traditional evangelistic approach to Mike—someone going into the detention hall, sitting next to him, and showing him in the Bible that he is lost and damned without Christ, and then asking him to become a Christian— might work, within limits, because Mike is in an extreme situation and will grab at anything. But suppose an interested Christian goes to Mike with love and gifts and says, "Mike, I care about you and I hate to see you screwing up your life this way. I know everything looks bleak from where you sit. I suppose it would be that way with me if I had had to live in your shoes. But thank God I've had some spiritual experiences that have turned me around and set me on a pretty productive path in my life. Let me tell you about them, and then you see if you think something similar to them might occur in your own life." The Bible might come later, as part of Mike's rehabilitation course, but it wouldn't be thrown at him as a magic book without reference to a specific human situation.

(b) Picture number two: Here is a young woman named Jill. She is twenty-seven years old, a college graduate, unemployed, mother of two small children, and her husband has just left her for another woman. Jill's life is more in pieces than it has ever been before, but she is managing to keep a stiff upper lip. You can see the hurt in her eyes and in the slow way she moves around the living room, but she is a tough woman and she will hold things together. You know she used to go to church and still attends occasionally, but she has never shown any signs of being strongly committed to Christ. You would like to witness to her about your faith but don't want to offend her. You don't begin by quoting Scripture. Maybe you start by inviting her to lunch day after tomorrow. She needs the new perspective of getting away from the house once in a while. And maybe you say, "Jill, I don't mean to pry, but I wonder if any of what we learned in Sunday School as girls is having a special meaning for you these days." Perhaps she will say, "Why, what do you mean?" And you say, "Well, I mean about Christ and how he sustains us if our faith in him is strong." And, before you know it, you are deep into a heart-to-heart talk about faith, in which you can make your own personal witness to the significance of Christ.

(c) Picture number three: Here is a fifty-three-year-old naval officer named Jim who lives in your neighborhood. He seems to have plenty of money, plays golf at the club, takes nice trips to Nassau and Bermuda in the wintertime, and drives a luxury automobile. His wife attends church but he doesn't. As far as you know, he has no faith commitment at all. He is a little like the man in the picture window. How do you witness to him? Perhaps you begin by inviting him into your golf game. You get to know him and what some of his experiences in life have been. You try to discern whether Christ has ever been part of them in any way. Maybe you learn that his parents were avid churchgoers and forced him to attend when he didn't want to; he didn't like the brand of perfervid Christianity forced upon him. When he was old enough to join the navy, he rebelled against church and never had any more to do with it. He can tell you about all the hypocrisies of those who do attend church. And perhaps at this point you say, "Yes, it's true; we don't live up to what we profess to believe. But, Jim, I don't know what I would do without Christ in my life. My soul would be an absolute desert without him. I couldn't face growing older and watching the dissolution of everything if I didn't have an eternal hope in my heart. I wonder that you can." And the wedge is driven, the goal is in sight.

(d) Note: In every one of these pictures, the church and Christian fellowship are important. We do not go out to evangelize in a vacuum. We do it in the context of a world where people are hurt and lonely and a church where those who are in

Christ come together for healing and fellowship. That's always part of the wider background of a picture. Conversion may begin when people decide to trust Jesus with their lives, but it continues in the shared life of Christians in the church, and it never ends until we are finally converted into the kingdom beyond death. This is one of the problems with television evangelism. It makes cut-flower Christians, Christians who will fade away in a few days because they lack the nourishing soil of a loving fellowship in which to grow and make mistakes and grow some more. All true evangelism begins and ends in the fellowship of the church.

III. *Your life and your church's life are both incomplete without the witnessing process.* You and your church need to be doing evangelism in order to stay alive in Christ. The minute you receive the good news of Christ and fail to pass it on in the course of daily living, you become like the Dead Sea, that remarkable body of water that is dead precisely because it receives life-giving water and doesn't pass it on. And your church is the same way. Its only life comes through sharing what it has received.

In Guy Eden's book *Portrait of Churchill*, Eden tells the story of the heroic evacuation of Dunkirk during the bleak early days of World War II. Every ferry boat, every trawler, every pleasure craft the English people had was pressed into service to sail across the channel and bring back the remnants of the Allied army that had been forced onto the beaches of Dunkirk. Eden reports that one man, a government servant, rowed his canoe back and forth to Dunkirk three times, under heavy shelling, to rescue people. Imagine that: three times in a canoe! Talk about individual responsibility! And that's precisely what we're talking about when we talk evangelism—every member's responsibility to be a faithful witness to Jesus Christ. If we don't do it, the very stones will cry out to own his lordship.—John Killinger.

Topic: Christian Duplication
TEXT: 1 Kings 20:23–30; 2 Cor. 5:17–19.

I recently received a catalog in the mail from a company known as Christian Duplications International. The catalog advertised equipment for reproducing cassettes and other such material.

What struck me was the name, "Christian Duplications." I allowed my imagination to roam for a while and finally settled on the conviction that this name precisely spells out the job of the church. We are to be about the task of calling people to faith in Christ—the task of "duplicating" Christians.

People have often attempted to domesticate God, just as the Syrians did in the passage from 1 Kings. To work in missions is not to try to limit God's activity to the boundaries of our nation. Instead, mission involves accepting the task of calling those closest to us to the claims of Christ. There are several reasons to work for and support missions.

I. *The Word of God commands it.* 1 Tim. 5:8 reads, "But if anyone does not take care of his relatives, especially the members of his own family, he has denied the faith and worse than an unbeliever" (TEV). Paul was speaking to Christians in their relations to other Christians. However, I am not stretching the intent of the passage to point out that we are under divine mandate to take care of all people in the sense of telling them about the Lord of life. God's Word is clear in its instruction, both explicit and implicit, about the responsibility the Christian community has to evangelize those outside that community.

II. *The condition of humankind warrants it.* Those who have reflected upon their own spiritual condition will not be surprised to learn that in the biblical sense they are sinners. Such is the condition of all persons without Christ. This condition is reason enough to reach out to these people with the Word of life.

Jesus once asked his disciples if they would leave him, as many of his other followers were doing. They answered, "To whom would we go? You have the words that give eternal life" (TEV). Jesus has entrusted those words to his present-day followers in the church. Our task is to give those quickening words to people who have not heard them.

III. *The love of God inspires it.* Why go to all the trouble and expense of spreading the gospel? The best answer I have is that the love of God inspires this work and sacrifice. As one who has been forgiven his sins, I can empathize with those who have not had this experience. I want them to know the love of God as I do. This love is what motivates the entire Christian community to engage in missions action.

IV. *The gifts of Christians channel it.* The church could talk abstractly about missions all day long and still accomplish nothing if individuals do not respond to the challenge of providing monetary support. God has entrusted us with the entire earth and expects us to use it responsibly. Part of that responsibility is to give our money toward the staffing and support of missions.—Don M. Aycock.

ILLUSTRATIONS

CONVERSION.   On Monday evening, November 23, 1654, a brilliant French mathematician and philosopher was reading his Bible. Suddenly the whole room was illuminated. Blaise Pascal could only think of this tremendous encounter with God in terms of fire. He wrote down these words: "God of Abraham, God of Isaac, God of Jacob, not of philosophers and scholars. Certitude, certitude, feeling, joy, peace, God of Jesus Christ!" He wrote out two copies of this experience, one on parchment and one on paper, and sewed them into the lining of his coat so that he could remember the luminous moment of his conversion, the moment that transformed his life and shaped the balance of his years. "He went on his way rejoicing." —John N. Gladstone.

MEASURING AND WEIGHING.   Dr. F. Townley Lord once described an American woman who floated down the aisle to greet him after morning service in Bloomsbury Chapel, London, as having a condescending air. "Oh, Dr. Lord," she tittered, "how many members do you have here in your *little* English Baptist Church? Why, back home in Texas, our Baptist church has *three thousand!*" Dr. Lord smiled his sweetest and murmured, "Why, madam, here in England we never *count* our members; we *weigh* them!" That was his quaint way of protesting that quantity is a fine thing, but quality a finer thing.— Craig Skinner.

WONDERFUL DISCOVERIES.   There is a magnificent saying of St. Brendan to the pagan King Brude. The king had listened to an exposition of the gospel, the story of what Jesus Christ has done for our salvation. He asked St. Brendan the question: "What shall I find if I accept your gospel and become Christ's man?" The saint replied: "If you accept this gospel and become Christ's man, you will stumble on wonder upon wonder and every wonder true."—John N. Gladstone.

SECTION VIII.
Resources for Preaching on Ethical Issues

BY ALLAN M. PARRENT

Topic: Faith and Justice, Faith and Work
TEXT: Hab. 1:1–6, 12–13; 2:1–4; 2 Tim. 1:6–14; Luke 17:5–10.

It would be difficult to find Old Testament and New Testament passages that together carry more of the essence of the Reformation than do these lessons. First, from the Old Testament lesson, "Behold, he whose soul is not upright in him shall fail, but the righteous shall live by his faith." These words from Habakkuk came to be central to Paul's doctrine of justification. The same words became the rallying cry of the Reformation, the basis of Luther's doctrine of justification on which, according to him, the whole church stands or falls.

Second, there are the words of Christ to his disciples recorded in the Gospel lesson from Luke: "When you have done all that is commanded of you, say, 'We are unworthy servants; we have only done what was our duty.'" These words speak directly to that central religious issue of the Reformation, the relationship of faith and works.

Faith and righteousness (or justice), faith and works—both themes are as central to the Christian moral life today as they were for Luther five hundred years ago, or for Paul and Jesus two thousand years ago. And both themes have to do with the fundamental religious question of trust. In whom or what do we put our ultimate trust, and what does that mean for the way we live our lives?

I. *From justice to faith.* One of the high-

lights of a 1983 trip to East Germany was, in addition to visiting the major Luther sites, attending a kirchentag, or church assembly. This one was held in the rebuilt and again beautiful city of Dresden. On a warm Sunday afternoon, in the heart of a communist state, where it is not to one's advantage to be a professing Christian, I stood with 90,000 East German Christians and sang *"Ein Feste Burg,"* that great Reformation hymn of trust that we know as "A Mighty Fortress Is Our God": "And though this world, with devils filled, should threaten to undo us, we will not fear, for God hast willed his truth to triumph through us." It is a hymn that Habakkuk might have found congenial.

(a) The prophet Habakkuk is concerned about the absence of justice in Judah. He describes his society as one in which justice never goes forth except in perverted form. He asks the age-old question of why a just God allows the unjust to flourish. But instead of trying to provide his own answer, he decides to wait for God's answer. The answer, however, seems at first to have little relationship to the question: "Write the vision; make it plain upon tablets, so he may run who reads it. For still the vision awaits its time; it hastens to the end—it will not lie. If it seem slow, wait for it; it will surely come, it will not delay. Behold, he whose soul is not upright in him shall fail, but the righteous shall live by his faith."

Write the vision? What does that have to do with correcting injustice or creating a

99

just society? Ultimately, everything. It has everything to do with the moral life of both individuals and societies, with the direction in which they walk, and with the goal toward which they aim. It is our vision that causes us to see things in a particular way, to walk in a particular way, and to seek to shape the world in a particular way. And it is the writing of our vision, our proclamation of it and witnessing to it, that assists others to see the way they are to walk through this life.

God's people are called to make the Christian vision public, to make it plain, so that even those in a hurry can read it. It is only as men and women have a proper vision of justice that they can recognize perverted justice as perverted. It is only as they have a clear vision of what a just society should be that they understand what might be done to shape their social environment to be more in keeping with that vision. When a society's vision is unclear, prophetic calls to justice fall on uncomprehending ears. Thus a prophet like Habakkuk must go back to the prior job of writing or clarifying the vision, witnessing again to fundamental but ignored truths.

(b) And what was that fundamental and abiding vision revealed to Habakkuk? It was in two parts, short, seemingly meager, but in truth profound. First, "He whose soul is not upright in him shall fail." The nation or individual that proceeds upon a policy that is not upright or just, will fail. A just God will not allow evil to triumph ultimately. That is the way God made the world, and we live in a moral universe. Second, "The righteous (nation or individual) shall live by faith." Trust in God is the only sure basis of strength and security in this world where evil has not yet been fully overcome. The truly just are those who dare to trust in God regardless of current circumstances. They will be sustained ultimately by their faithfulness to the vision and to the promise that it will become a reality.

It may be slow in coming. Some may wish to bring it to fruition before its time. But we are not to anticipate God or try to force his hand. History is filled with examples showing that the utopian fanaticism of impatient visionaries is at least as destructive as the inaction and despair of those devoid of vision. A persevering faith that continues to be sensitive to injustice, but continues to act to alleviate injustice in spite of the fact that injustice continues to persist, that kind of faith must be based on something more than visible good results. The only faith by which the righteous can live for very long is faith based not on results but on trust in the author and revealer of the vision itself, and on his promise that it will come. Habakkuk's own response to the vision affirms exactly that kind of trust: "Though the fig trees do not blossom, nor fruit be on the vines, . . . yet I will rejoice in the Lord, I will joy in the God of my salvation." Concern for justice, if it is to endure, will eventually drive us to fundamental questions about the object of our basic trust. In short, justice questions drive us to faith questions.

II. *From faith to justice.* But the reverse is equally true. Faith questions drive us to justice questions. We cannot as Christians sever faith from doing all that is commanded of us by a just God.

(a) In the Gospel lesson the disciples say to Jesus, "Increase our faith." But Jesus, in responding to their plea, tells them a story about servants doing their duty, that is, about works not faith. The immediate point is that servants are expected to do all that they are commanded to do by their master. They have no reason for expecting any special reward simply for doing their duty, even if they do it all and do it well. The same is true of those who are servants of God. In other words, in God's sight we cannot be better than necessary. Leslie Newbigin has made this point well: "For if we suppose that we can make up for past failure by extra effort in the future, we are acting on the assumption that it is possible to have a sort of credit balance in goodness, i.e., that it is possible to do more than our duty. If I suppose that my goodness today is going to compensate for my failure yesterday, I am really supposing, as far as today is concerned, that I can be better than necessary."

(b) There are two important points here. The first is that works are integrally related to faith. People of faith, we who seek to be faithful servants, we who dare to trust, are expected to do our duty. We are expected to do justice, to do good works, to order our lives in accordance with God's commandments. The second point, however, is that works are not a substitute for faith. We are justified and made righteous by faith alone, totally apart from any reliance on our good works.

(c) But if the proper response to the word of God is faith toward God, the proper result of that faith is good works toward our neighbors. If it is by faith alone that we are justified, it is by good works that such faith is expressed, works that are the free and grateful response to the fact that we have already been justified. Luther, like Paul, never rejected good works, except as a basis for justification. In fact he stressed as much as possible the importance of good works in the life of faith. Christ does not free us from good works. Rather, he frees us from false views concerning good works. Christians do not perform good works in order to be justified, but because we already are.

III. *Daring to trust.* God works in mysterious ways through those who dare to trust in him. Habakkuk's concern for social justice led him to a crucial insight about faith. The disciples' concern for increased faith led them to a crucial insight about works, about doing what was commanded. Each of these unexpected results can speak to the Christian community today.

(a) First, there is a word here for those of us who, like Habakkuk, seek to bring greater justice to an unjust world. Our proper concern for justice must be rooted in a biblical vision if it is to endure the persistence of injustice. It must be rooted in a daring trust of the one who promises shalom, but who promises it only at its own appointed time. Otherwise our concern for justice will be in danger of evolving into despair on the one hand or utopian fanaticism on the other.

Identification with the weak and the powerless is fundamental to the Christian tradition. Still, as Luther knew, there is a freedom that no oppression can take away, just as there is a liberation that no change in social and political circumstances can ever bring about by itself. This is certainly not meant to belittle the struggle for jus-

tice. It is meant, however, to keep that struggle in proper perspective, and to keep it attached to the roots of faith that nourish it.

(b) Second, there is a word here for those of us who, like the disciples, are concerned to increase our faith. Our proper concern for our faith will be expressed best in just actions, actions by obedient servants who seek to be faithful to the commandments of the One we dare to trust. Otherwise, our relationship with God will be severed from our relationship with God's creatures, and that is a theological if not a logical impossibility. Luther taught us that our vertical relationship to God and our horizontal relationship to our neighbors are so inseparably joined in faith that one is unthinkable without the other. Freedom in faith and freedom to love are separated only at the expense of both.

The gospel, then, enables justice seekers to dare to trust in God, even in the midst of persistent injustice. The gospel also enables faith seekers to dare to trust in God, and to express that trust freely, as servants, in works of love.

Topic: Where Faith and Politics Meet
TEXT: Isa. 1:10–20; Luke 19:1–10.

It is very easy, and sometimes quite tempting, to speak disparagingly about politics, politicians, and political institutions. This is especially true near election time, with its mindless ads, simplistic rhetoric, and political posturing.

But perhaps we should not engage too easily, or with unseemly relish, in the popular pastime of denigrating our politics, our politicians, and our political institutions. The fact that we take for granted our political liberties and the orderly transfer of power should not diminish the fact that historically they are rather infrequent occurrences among the nations of the earth. For present liberties we can give thanks to God who is Lord of all things, including that realm of life we call politics.

Political authority is, after all, instituted by God, we are told in Scripture. Rulers who rule properly, that is, those who use their delegated power responsibly for the attainment of beneficial secular goals, are even called "servants of God" and "ministers of God," irrespective of their faith. While Scripture and tradition warn us of the idolatrous tendencies of *all* political power, there is nevertheless a fundamental Christian affirmation of the political realm, the political task, and political leadership that we cannot ignore.

It is certainly dangerous for our soul's health to identify our faith with a particular political program, policy, or structure. But it is equally dangerous to see our faith as irrelevant to such programs, policies, and structures. Our politics, like our religion, can be fairly subjected to criticism, but it cannot legitimately be dismissed by, or hermetically sealed off from, a vital Christian faith. The question for Christians, then, is not whether but in what way God would have us to understand the relation between our faith and our politics, not whether but how we are called to relate these two aspects of human existence, each of which touches every part of our lives. Our two Scripture lessons can help us in our search for an answer.

I. *Worship and the social order.* The Old Testament lesson tells us of a nation that tried to seal off its religion from its politics, that is, a nation that tried to sever its worship from the quality of its public and social life and its use of political and economic power. "Hear the word of the Lord you rulers of Sodom! Give ear to the teaching of our God you people of Gomorrah!" It is of course the rulers and people of Israel who are being addressed and likened to the rulers and people of the sin cities of Sodom and Gomorrah. And why was this? Not evidently because of any flagrant sexual licentiousness. Surely it was not because of secularism. There were evidently, according to Isaiah, enough sacrifices, burnt offerings, solemn assemblies, and prayers to satisfy even the most insatiable appetites for religious ceremonial.

No, in a fundamental sense the controversy that God has here with his people is political, in the fullest meaning of that word. The covenant involves more than formal worship; it also involves, as an integral part of that worship, justice and righteousness in the social order. The idea that there is no legitimate separation between worship and social justice is a constant scriptural theme, repeated almost *ad nauseum* by the prophets. Far from being some radical new teaching of naive political activists, the integral relation of worship and social justice was a fundamental tenet of Israel's faith that the prophets saw was being seriously eroded. The immorality they saw stemmed in a real sense from Israel's failure to continue to mix religion and politics. "What to me is the multitude of your sacrifices, says the Lord. . . . Bring no more vain offerings; incense is an abomination to me. . . . When you spread forth your hands I will hide my eyes from you; even though you make many prayers, I will not listen; your hands are full of blood."

And why does God reject their worship? Why does he refuse to see their hands outstretched in prayer but to see instead blood on their hands? Because worship that chooses to ignore its own this-worldly implications, especially toward the victims of social ills, is not worship; it is an abomination. Worship that takes place complacently in the midst of the serious maldistribution of God's material blessings is offensive to God. Celebrations of God's goodness that do not lead to efforts to reflect God's goodness in the structures of communal life are objects of God's hatred. Through Isaiah God calls upon his people to reestablish those connections: "Cease to do evil, learn to do good." And what does that mean in concrete terms? It means, says Isaiah, to "seek justice," and to spell it out a little more clearly for the obtuse, he says that it means to "correct oppression, defend the fatherless, plead for the widow."

To seek justice, of course, is the quintessential political task, along with the order-maintaining task of justice. And God is here saying, if you would truly worship me, concern yourselves with matters of justice and injustice in the social order; if you would truly praise me, order your communal life in ways that reveal my righteous will for *mishpat* (justice) and *sedeqah* (righteousness). The Father of our Lord Jesus Christ is a loving and compassionate God who therefore is not indifferent to those cries. And he is not indifferent to the questions of justice to which such cries summon those who hear them. He calls those who worship him to a life in which love of God and love of neighbor are integrally and inseparably related. And when love of neighbor excludes attention to the relative justice of those political institutions that in large part shape the neighbor's life, it is something less than the love of neighbor that worshipers seek to live out.

II. *Faith and political vocation.* If God is concerned with political structures and their effect on human beings, God is also concerned with those who make political structures function justly or unjustly, that is, with the powerful. There is a deep concern both in Scripture and in many Christian prayer books for those who bear the authority of government, for how they understand the source of their authority, and for the purposes for which they use their power.

Zacchaeus in the New Testament lesson was one of these governmental authorities. He was not emperor or tetrarch, but he was chief tax collector, a not insignificant position. And he was also rich, a fact evidently not unrelated to his use of his official capacity. Of course, Zacchaeus was also a collaborator, but when the crowd murmured that Jesus had "gone in to be the guest of a sinner," the sin seems to be more his known dishonesty than his official position. At least dishonesty is the sin of which he repented.

Zacchaeus, we are told, sought to see Jesus, and he succeeded in a way he probably had not intended. He had a transforming personal encounter with Jesus, addressed him as Lord, and heard Jesus declare, "Today salvation has come to this house." We are not told much about what really took place between them, but we are told about the manifestation of that salvation. We are told about the response of this born-again politician. The chief tax collector acknowledged his unjust practices and his abuse of his political power. He undertook restitution to the exploited, even beyond the requirement of the law. He promised similar restitution to others he may have cheated by the betrayal of his public trust. But so far as we know, he did not give up his official position. He did not become one of the Twelve. He evidently did not conclude, and neither did Jesus, that tax-collecting was an intrinsically evil vocation.

No, Zacchaeus's transforming encounter with the one he called Lord transformed, among other things, his perception of his vocation and his way of carrying it out. Instead of becoming a *former* tax collector he became a *just* tax collector. That did not mean, however, coercing taxpayers to adhere to certain personal behavior standards advocated by the tax collector's religion. It meant being a just and honest tax collector administering a just and equitable tax structure. Bringing justice to the social order is the *raison d'être* of every public position, tax collectors included.

III. *The plumbline for good politics.* The mixing of faith and politics has been an issue of increasing interest and debate in our national life. While some see such mixing as inappropriate, embarrassing, illegal, or, even worse, unsophisticated, classical Christianity has always refused to exclude the political arena from God's care and concern or from the Christian's area of responsibility. The real question, at least among those who have refused to confine God to a religious ghetto, has always been not whether but how to relate faith to politics.

There is no blueprint for it. And there are dangers in the effort, whoever undertakes it—the danger of self-righteousness; the danger of equating group interest with God's will; the danger of a too narrow and personalistic vision of political morality; the danger of making the state more than a good state by using it to coerce the Christianizing of society; the danger of making the state less than a good state by making it subservient to special interests, economic or otherwise, in the name of religion.

But there is at least one guideline that is clear, according to Isaiah, Luke, and a great cloud of other biblical witnesses. That guideline is justice. Certainly we are called to love, and certainly the person who is in Christ knows a higher obligation that transcends justice. But love is no substitute for justice. Undue emphasis on the higher possibilities of love in personal relations may tempt Christians to let individual acts of charity become a substitute for seeking justice. To the worshipers of Israel, Isaiah of Jerusalem said, "Seek justice" in your social order. And the response of the born-again tax collector was to do justice in his particular function in the social order.

There are many moral visions of politics. We have seen several on the national scene in recent years. How do we distinguish among them? How do we tell the true from the false prophets? Through Scripture we have heard the witness of the prophet Isaiah and the politician Zacchaeus. Now listen to a modern prophet and politician, the Reverend John Danforth, Republican Senator from Missouri and an ordained clergyman:

Nothing requires that religions remain neutral toward politics. . . . However, it does not follow that any old political position deserves to be called religious. . . . The job of the religious commentator on the political scene is to reflect on contemporary events in the light of scriptural tradition. . . . What is found in scripture, over and over again, is a boundless concern that justice be done to the needy—the poor, the fatherless, the widow. . . . Like it or not, this message of social justice is at the heart of the biblical standard for political commentary. A political position that does not include serious concern for the plight of the needy may have many interesting aspects, but it simply does not meet the biblical norms, and it should not be labeled religious.

That is the guideline, that is the plumbline, that is the central core of the biblical message about politics. We who would respond faithfully to God in Christ and relate our faith to all of life, including political life, can give thanks for that guiding lamp unto our feet as we tred across that busy but dimly lit intersection where faith and politics meet.

Topic: The Other Side of the Gospel
TEXT: Amos 5:18–24; Matt. 25:1–13.
One of the dangers for those so bold as to preach the gospel is that what is said or done publicly may be heard or seen to mean something other than what was intended. For example, "Blessed are the poor in spirit" might be misinterpreted so as to spiritualize all the concrete biblical references to the physically poor and hungry. Paul's admonition that "those who don't work don't eat" might be misapplied so as to heap scorn even on those weary from looking unsuccessfully for jobs in a depressed economy. The danger of such misuses is of course enhanced when part of the gospel is soft-pedaled, assumed, or omitted entirely, that is, when the other side of the gospel is not clearly proclaimed.

That phrase is meant to carry a double meaning. The other side means the neglected emphasis, the flip side that doesn't get played very often. The other side also means what comes next, beyond the telling of the basic gospel story. The readings from Amos and Matthew can help to illuminate this other side in both senses.

William Muehl, professor of preaching at Yale and Christian layman, recently gave an address entitled "The Problem of Taking It All Seriously." Three of his illustrations are useful for showing the results of a truncated gospel that neglects the other side, and each cries out for a fuller apprehension of that gospel.

I. *Mercy and justice.* First, Prof. Muehl quoted a statement of a college student made to a conference of theologians: "I've heard a lot of talk about God's mercy and his eagerness to forgive us no matter how badly we foul up, but I've heard very little about how God may be at work in history to keep us from fouling up in the first place. I almost get the feeling that Christians have a duty to foul up, so that God has a chance to do his thing." Christianity is apparently seen by many to be inordinately preoccupied with cleaning up messes after the fact and too little concerned for the practical business of structuring justice and maintaining the social fabric of human life and human institutions so as to have fewer messes to clean up in the first place. The problem is that the God of mercy, preached alone, can become the enemy of the God whom to know is to do justice.

But from the other side of the gospel

comes the good news that God who is merciful is also just. He is concerned greatly about the practical business of structuring justice. He is a God of both mercy and justice, both love and judgment, despite our best efforts at times to limit him. And just as he has not left us comfortless, he has also not left us without guidance about how to live the Christian life. He has shown us what is good; to do justice, to love mercy, and to walk humbly with God, the three linked inextricably together. The Church cannot faithfully preach only one or two.

In Martin Luther King's famous "I Have a Dream" speech, he addressed those who were asking when the blacks would be satisfied:

> We can never be satisfied as long as our bodies, heavy with the fatigue of travel, cannot gain lodging in the motels of the highways and the hotels of the cities. We cannot be satisfied as long as our children are stripped of their selfhood and robbed of their dignity by signs stating: "For Whites Only."—No, we are not satisfied and we will not be satisfied until justice rolls down like waters and righteousness like a mighty stream.

Those familiar words of Amos, at that historical moment in our nation's history, help to illuminate the integral relationship between God's judgment and God's mercy, between God's justice and God's love. The God of love and mercy is not paradoxically but inevitably the God who is not indifferent to human suffering and oppression. God is merciful and is therefore just. This is good news not only to the victims. It is also good news to those with power and responsibility who would prefer to prevent messes when possible, and who seek guidance from their faith about how to translate love into justice in a world not yet conformed to the will of God.

II. *Forgiveness and responsibility in history.* A second of Prof. Muehl's illustrations was a statement made to him by a leading Christian layman and businessman:

> I realize that every decision I make every day at my desk has ethical implications. And I often ask ministers for advice. But they never have anything helpful to say.

I have begun to suspect that they would rather wait until I make a mistake and then assure me of God's forgiveness.

Muehl noted that even assuring the man of God's judgment would have suggested at least that his decisions had some significance. But by talking only about forgiveness, proclaimers of the gospel can be understood to say that what people such as this actually do at their desks has no importance in God's eyes, that God doesn't really care what happens in history but is concerned only to redeem us from it. The problem is that the God of forgiveness, preached alone, can become the enemy of the God who is Lord of history.

But from the other side of the gospel comes the good news that the God who forgives is also the God of history. And that gives significance to history. It affirms the importance of our own daily decisions and actions that help to make up history. Like the business executive, what we do at our desks matters, both to God and to a variety of neighbors. It is important what kind of tenants in God's vineyard we are, and how we use whatever number of talents he has given us. No one else has been called by God to your and my particular roles, relationships, offices, and responsibilities, in this time and place in history. And what we do in them and with them is important because God has expectations of each of us.

Now Amos tells us about Israel's expectations of God. The Day of the Lord was to be a great day of joy, a final victory over all that was opposed to God. And Matthew tells us that the foolish maidens of the parable also had expectations of participating in the coming marriage feast, the symbol of the kingdom of God. But they both forgot about God's expectations of them in their historical situations. In short, they ignored the other side of the gospel.

In the Gospel lesson, Matthew tells us that we can know neither the day nor the hour of the bridegroom's coming. The admonition to watch, to be prepared, would seem to mean, therefore, *not* a calculated change in one's pattern of life at the right time, so as to comply outwardly with the bridegroom's expectations. Rather it would seem to mean doing gladly, freely, regularly, naturally, and as competently as possible the work God has given us to do "at our desks"—in our particular and unique roles and vocations.

This points to the real wisdom of the minister who was asked what he would preach on if he could preach only one more sermon before the Lord's return. "I would preach," he said, "on the lesson for the day." He would do what he had been given to do and thus would be doing anyway. With that perspective, such acts as maintaining or improving human institutions, or simply doing our jobs well, then become the natural fruit of our worship, not unnatural acts calculated with an eye toward spiritual advancement.

The Christian gospel has as much to say about how we use the power and responsibility God has given us as it does about being forgiven. And using our allotment of power or talents to do the work God has given us to do is not only natural for the sheep of his fold; it is also a witness to the fact that what happens in everyday human history matters, and that our part in it is significant.

III. *Grace and connectedness of life.* Prof. Muehl's third illustration was that phenomenon of revival crusades which sociologists of religion call "the repeaters," those who seem almost to make an avocation of accepting Christ. Night after night the repeaters walk down the aisles when the invitation is given. Now those who engage in such repetitive rebirth rituals could be just very ingenious sinners who manage to fall from grace every twenty-four hours. But it is more likely, Muehl notes, that for the repeaters the attraction of the ritual lies in its being the only way they know to act out a rewarding relationship with God. Their faith says so much about grace, and so little about how one might relate to God and his world beyond the moment of conversion, that they simply go through that conversion experience again and again. The problem is that the God of grace, preached alone, can become the enemy of the God who would be Lord of all facets of our lives.

But from the other side of the gospel comes the good news that the God who is gracious is also the God who provides us with a center to which we can connect all of life. The God who saves us is also the God who would grant us wisdom and courage for the living of these days, after conversion. He desires lives that are integrated in Christ, not disintegrated lives in which religious experience is sealed off from the rest of human experience, compartmentalized, and disconnected from the public arena where so much of human history takes place.

It was precisely against the unconnectedness of the Hebrew religion of his day that Amos railed so vehemently. It was precisely in that spiritually debilitating separation of worship from the quality of corporate and institutional life that he saw the secularization of his time. Only that unbiblical division would allow a spiritualized religion to flourish in Israel in the midst of the blatant economic injustices that were so obviously at variance with their covenant with God.

The response to Amos, of course, was that what he had to say was inappropriate in Bethel, because there religion dealt with spiritual matters. That is merely an ancient example of the constant temptation to put asunder what God has joined together, to secularize all of life by pushing religion off to one side, and to do it ironically in the name of spirituality. This false separation, so foreign to the biblical tradition, is in fact what leads to such things as the repeaters—because of it they often don't have a clue about how to live the Christian life in the world.

We are by nature worshiping or spiritual beings. We are also by nature social or political beings. The gospel is addressed to both. The gospel is spiritual, though it is not to be spiritualized. It concerns mercy, forgiveness, and grace. The gospel is also political, though it is not to be politicized. It concerns justice, human responsibility in history, and the connectedness of all facets of our lives in God's world. Let us proclaim and give thanks to God for the good news of both sides of his gospel.

SECTION IX. *Resources for Preaching on the Miracles of the Gospels*

BY JOHN B. POLHILL

Topic: A New Teaching? An Introductory Sermon

TEXT: Mark 1:22–28.

This is the first miracle story recorded in Mark's Gospel, and it contains one unique feature that makes it particularly suitable for an introductory sermon on the Gospel miracles.

I. The feature that distinguishes this from other exorcisms is the response of the crowd when Jesus casts out the demon: "What is this? A new teaching!" (v. 27). Their referring to the successful exorcism as a "teaching" comes as a surprise.

II. The key is to note that before the demoniac came upon the scene Jesus had been teaching in the synagogue and had already evoked astonishment at his presence and authority (v. 22). The exorcism serves to verify that impression.

III. This authoritative teaching of Jesus must have involved his message of the presence of God's kingdom, a note that Mark has recorded a few verses earlier in his account (v. 15). The exorcism illustrates this presence of the divine rule in the ministry of Jesus. A saying of Jesus recorded by Matthew makes the same point: "But if it is by the finger of God that I cast out demons, then the kingdom of God has come upon you" (Matt. 12:28).

IV. From a wider perspective, the unique feature of this exorcism makes a point applicable to all the miracle stories. They are modes of teaching—about the kingdom of God, about Jesus, about faith and discipleship.

Topic: The Greater Miracle

TEXT: Mark 2:1–12.

In the broad biblical concept of the miraculous, a miracle is any special evidence of divine providence. This particular miracle story illustrates that, for it shows God's presence in two types of healing, both physical and spiritual. Two miracles take place: a paralytic is healed, and his sins are forgiven.

I. The story departs from the usual pattern of healing narratives at the outset. After the man has been lowered by his friends into Jesus' presence, one would expect the healing to proceed straightway. It doesn't. Instead, Jesus assures the man that his sins are forgiven. One should not be sidetracked at this point in wondering whether Jesus shared the view often debated by his contemporaries whether physical maladies were to be seen as a punishment for previous sin. That issue is not raised in the text. The only place where Jesus directly addresses that question is in John 9:1–3, and there he rejects that sort of speculation as irrelevant. The point in our text is that Jesus is concerned with the our total being, our spiritual as well as our physical needs.

II. It is this which provokes the negative response of the scribes. When Jesus does move to heal the paralytic, the response is one of wonder and glory to God (v. 12). The stumbling block for the scribes are the words of forgiveness, "This is blasphemy. . . . Only God can do that" (v. 7).

III. But this is precisely the point of the

107

whole narrative. It is highly christological: Jesus has in himself the divine authority to forgive sins (v. 10). The subsequent healing serves to confirm that authority, but the real offense for the scribes and the real focus of the story is the forgiveness of sins. No physical sickness is as debilitating as the burden of a guilty conscience, no human need as great as the right relationship to God. Jesus concerned himself with the total being of the man. He healed his paralysis, but he ministered to his spiritual needs as well. And in a real sense, the latter was the greater miracle.

Topic: Three Sermons from the Gerasene Demoniac

Text: Mark 5:1–20.

Some of the more detailed miracle stories offer a number of points subsidiary to the actual miracle itself, each of which may be developed into a sermon. The following outlines from the story of the Gerasene demoniac will illustrate this.

I. *Home from the tombs.* The advantage of this sermon is that it covers the entire narrative and holds the story together rather than focusing on a single motif.

(a) The demoniac represents a completely alienated person.

(1) He was alienated from himself. He was self-destructive, "bruising himself with stones" (v. 5).

(2) He was alienated from God. Demon possession is itself symbolic of an extreme sense of the absence of divine presence in one's life.

(3) He was alienated from his community. His madness endangered the community, and they had relegated him to the first-century equivalent of the isolation ward, binding him to tombstones.

(b) Jesus brought him complete reconciliation:

(1) To himself. He was completely restored, "clothed and in his right mind" (v. 15).

(2) With God. He even begged to become a follower of Jesus, joining the train of disciples (v. 18).

(3) With his community. Jesus would not let him join his entourage but commanded that he return to his own people (v. 19). That would be his place of greatest witness. That would also be his most difficult place of witness, for that is where they had known him in his days of madness. Only by returning and witnessing there would he have full assurance that the madness had really gone for good.

II. *"So he gave them leave."* The motif of the demons and the pigs can be developed by itself into a sermon.

(a) The demons wanted to determine their own destiny—"send us into the swine" (v. 12). At its deepest level, sin is self-centered, self-assertive, with no concern for any divine direction in one's life. This is true on the individual as well as the corporate level.

(b) Jesus granted their request. "So he gave them leave" (v. 13). God is not coercive. He honors freedom. Paul expressed the same thought in describing the perversion of the Gentiles in the first chapter of Romans. His phrase was: "God gave them up" (Rom. 1:24, 26, 28). Jesus likewise gave the demons up to their own designs.

(c) The demons enter the herd, which rushes into the sea, and all are drowned. Who was drowned? Just the pigs, or the demons as well? In the ancient belief about demons the idea prevailed that drowning was one means of destroying them. This seems to be the point of the Markan narrative. The demons chose their own destiny and became masters of their own destruction. The demonic, left to its own devices, often leads to its own destruction.

III. *Jesus, upsetter of the status quo.* The reaction of the demoniac's neighbors provides another teaching from this exorcism story.

(a) The townsfolk handled their mad citizen as best they knew, binding him outside town to the tombstones. That way, he no longer threatened their lives or property. It was their solution to a bad situation, and they had learned to live with it.

(b) Jesus' therapy was far more effective. He restored the demoniac to his right mind. He transformed him from the mad man of the cemetery back to a responsible citizen.

(c) The response of the townsfolk was

fear. They begged Jesus to leave (v. 17). Why? Was it not that he was a threat to their way of life? Surely they were concerned about the loss of the pigs, but the text connects their fear with finding the man restored to his senses (v. 15). They preferred their own solutions at the expense of one man tied to the tombs to the disturbing presence of one who could do the impossible, who could transform madness to sanity. It was simply easier to live with their own compromises than to risk the uncertainties that Jesus' presence presented.

Topic: "Help My Unbelief"
TEXT: Mark 9:14–29.
This story revolves around the theme of faith.
I. It begins and ends on the note of the disciples' lack of faith. Jesus had earlier given them authority to heal and to exorcise (Mark 6:7, 13), but while he was absent on the Mount of Transfiguration, they had failed in their attempts to heal the epileptic boy (Mark 9:18). The account ends on the same note, as the disciples ask Jesus why they had failed. He responds, "This kind cannot be driven out by anything but prayer (and fasting)" (v. 29).
II. In between is the father's entreaty of Jesus. He becomes the example of the praying faith the disciples lacked.
(a) The father is often criticized for his lack of faith. Jesus' abrupt response, "If you can!" seems to invite that criticism. But that is to miss the point. The father is a model of faith. "I believe; help thou my unbelief."
(b) His is not a heroic, self-sufficient faith. It is a struggling faith, aware of its own inadequacy, a faith that feels insufficient even to express itself. It is a dependent, trusting faith, not easily discouraged, but drawing its strength from the Master. It is praying faith, and to that sort of faith, the Master responds.

Topic: "Even the Puppies"
TEXT: Mark 7:24–30 (Matt. 15:21–28).
I. One is taken aback by Jesus' use of the term *dog*, which reflected the worst Jewish prejudice toward Gentiles. Even Matthew had problems with it, for he does not include the reference to dogs. It does not completely alleviate the problem to note that the Greek text has "little dogs," a term used for household pets. The real source of the difficulty, however, may be that one's focus is wrong. The focus of the story is on the faith of the Syrophonecian woman, not the attitude of Jesus.
II. When one concentrates on the woman, Jesus' words become a test. They say in the most direct way possible: "What right do you, a Gentile, have to request mercy from a Jewish miracle worker. There are Jews enough to occupy all his time and effort."
III. When viewed from this perspective, the woman's faith becomes transparent. She has reason to believe *this* miracle worker does not share such prejudices. She is undaunted and cleverly responds to Jesus' rebuff. And, her faith triumphs. It is the only time in the Gospels that someone bests Jesus at repartee, and he responds by granting her request.

Topic: "Like Walking Trees"
TEXT: Mark 8:22–26.
I. Why a two-staged miracle? The Gospel miracle stories usually stress the immediacy with which Jesus heals. Only occasionally is any healing technique mentioned; characteristically he only gives a healing word. Why, then, the difficulty in this story?
II. The solution is to be found in the Markan context. This story immediately precedes the incident at Caesarea Philippi where Peter first professes his conviction that Jesus is Messiah. But he does not fully understand the nature of Jesus' messianic role. When Jesus refers to the necessity of his suffering, Peter rebukes him (v. 32). The two-staged healing of the blind man becomes a lesson applicable to Peter. Peter saw Jesus as Messiah; he had come to that first stage of vision. The second yet remained. He could not yet see the need for a cross. He would not fully "see" Jesus until he did.
III. There is a general lesson in faith here. The "sight" of faith is a growing, developing thing. It does not come all at

once, neither for Peter, nor for any Christian.

Topic: "Though I Was Blind, Now I See"
TEXT: John 9:1–41.

In his own unique way, John develops a story of Jesus' healing a blind man into a sermon on coming to the sight of faith. In Johannine language, the physical recovery of sight becomes a "sign," a pointer to the man's whole pilgrimage to faith in Jesus.

I. The story begins with Jesus giving sight to a man who had been born blind (vv. 6f). At this initial stage, the man can testify that Jesus healed him, but he does not even know where Jesus is (vv. 11–12). When the Pharisees press him, he is a bit more committed in his profession of Jesus: "He is a prophet" (v. 17). Pressed a second time, he becomes bolder and responds with sarcasm (v. 27) and with deepened confession: "If this man were not from God, he could do nothing" (v. 33). Rejected by the Jewish authorities and approached by Jesus, the man makes his final confession: "Lord, I believe" (v. 38). He has now come all the way from physical to spiritual vision.

II. The man's pilgrimage to faith illustrates the development of faith. It begins with an initial encounter. Jesus did something for him, and he can testify to that. It is, however, in his bearing testimony to that initial encounter, often under hostile circumstances, that his real faith grows and leads to a full understanding of and commitment to Jesus.

Topic: What Is Lawful?
TEXT: Mark 3:1–6.

This story belongs to those miracle accounts that are set within a controversy of Jesus with the Pharisees over their oral tradition. As with this story, the issue often involves the proper observance of the Sabbath. Jesus' healing is in violation of the tradition and directly challenges that sort of legalism. Jesus does not challenge the validity of the Torah, only the "traditions of men" that sought to elaborate upon it. He does not reject the law, he rejects legalism. This raises the question, When does law become legalism?

I. Law becomes legalism when it loses sight of its purpose and becomes a set of rigid rules. The oral tradition had developed so many rules to curtail labor on the Sabbath that it ruled out even the possibility of healings. The good purpose of the Sabbath law now became an instrument of harm (v. 4).

II. The law becomes legalism when it becomes a thing in itself. Its intentions and purposes are forgotten. It exists for itself.

III. The law becomes legalism when it becomes an instrument of inhumanity. Jesus pointed out that the law was given to serve humanity, not enslave it (v. 27). When understood and used as the divine purpose designed to serve humanity, the law liberates. For example, the Sabbath provides humans needed rest from labor. When law becomes legalism and exists for itself, it loses sight of human values and is an instrument of slavery.

Topic: Cooperating with God
TEXT: John 5:1–9.

The clue to interpreting this miracle story is the rather unusual conversation between Jesus and the lame man.

I. "Do you want to be healed?" (v. 6). It would seem superfluous to ask a lame man if he wanted to be healed, but perhaps he had never really faced the possibility. He had been totally dependent on others for thirty-eight years and had learned to live with the situation—and the sympathy. Healing would mean he would now be responsible for himself; it would involve a total reorientation of his life. Not everyone wants to be healed.

II. "But, sir, I have no one to put me into the pool. . . ." (v. 7). The man replies with excuses, actually, with despair. "It isn't that I don't seek healing, it's that I can't be healed. . . . I'm paralyzed and helpless." The man needed to overcome his sense of helplessness, to recognize the possibilities that stood before him in the person of Jesus.

III. "Rise, take up your pallet, and walk" (v. 8). The man could have protested: "Don't you think I've tried many times before? These muscles in my legs, they haven't moved for thirty-eight years." He didn't. He responded in faith. He made the effort, and in his effort Jesus worked the miracle. Isn't that the way God often works in lives—working in and through the best of human effort?

Topic: One Came Back
TEXT: Luke 17:11–19.

I. The man had something to be grateful for. He was a leper, unclean, a social outcast. He was a Samaritan, hated by Jews, but Jesus the Jew had healed him.

II. He knew how to express his gratitude. All ten lepers were healed; surely all had a measure of gratitude. Only he returned to express it. He knew that the priest's certification of his cleanness was necessary before he could return home, but he was willing to delay that a while to thank the one who made it possible.

III. He received something for his gratitude. Jesus responded, "Your faith has made you well [saved you]" (v. 19). The greek word *sozo* is ambiguous. It can refer to either physical or spiritual deliverance. The latter seems to be the meaning intended by Luke. After all, the ten had been cleansed of their leprosy. This man seems to have received something more. He experienced not only the healing but the grace of the Master. His response indicates the depth of his experience, for gratitude is the most natural reaction to grace.

Topic: Touching the Untouchable
TEXT: Mark 5:25–34.

I. The woman was an untouchable. Her particular malady rendered her perpetually unclean by the Jewish ritual law and as untouchable as a leper. The crowd was not a hindrance. It was her opportunity. She hoped to hide in the anonymity of the crowd and catch one healing grasp at Jesus.

II. Jesus accepted her touch. He never shrank from leper or harlot, from the ritually or socially unclean. He rejected the artificial barriers between the sacred and profane that the ritual law represented. He freely reached out to touch all untouchables.

III. Jesus would not, however, settle for just her touch. He made her come forth from the crowd, tell her story, and take responsibility for her actions. There is an obvious example here for the ministry of the church. Meeting human need is imperative, but the ultimate goal is to develop whole persons, responsible disciples.

Topic: What Money Can't Buy
TEXT: Mark 5:21–43.

The details of the narrative point to Jairus' being a man of means with servants and status in his community. His money was unable to secure his daughter's health, but Jairus had other resources that prevailed when his money failed.

I. *Money can't buy the faith of Jairus.* He trusted that Jesus could heal his daughter and risked his standing in his community by approaching one so controversial with his fellow synagogue leaders.

II. *Money can't buy the love that Jairus showed for his daughter.* It was love that led him to take the risks in approaching Jesus. Love is not strong when it stops at the pocketbook. Love is likewise not profound when it fails to reach beyond the pocketbook. Jairus' love did. When his money failed, he put himself on the line for his daughter.

III. *Money can't buy the gift of life that Jairus received.* The text refers to the daughter "sleeping," but this was a common early Christian designation for death. As with the other stories of Jesus raising the dead, the restoration of Jairus' daughter is a pointer to the resurrection and the abiding life that all have who trust and love the Master.

Topic: The Wine of Life
TEXT: John 2:1–11.

The miracle at Cana can be approached in many ways. It shows Jesus enhancing the celebration of life. It is an enacted form of Jesus' saying about putting new wine in old skins. It also builds on a common Old Testament theme. There wine has the following associations:

I. *With joy* (Hos. 14:7; Jer. 31:12). Think of the joy that this Near Eastern bride's father must have felt. Wedding feasts often lasted several days. To run out of wine meant serious loss of face in the community. Jesus solved the shortage and allowed the celebration to continue.

II. *With abundance* (Joel 3:18; Amos 9: 13–14). Just as the Old Testament prophets foresaw a coming age of blessing when the mountains would drip with new wine, so Jesus brings wine in abundance. In Johannine language, the miracle is a "sign": "I came that they might have life and might have it more abundantly" (John 10:10).

III. *With suffering and death* (Ps. 60:3; 75: 8). Whether or not one sees eucharistic overtones in the miracle of Cana, the Johannine text connects it with Jesus' "hour" (John 2:4), and in John the word "hour" refers primarily to Jesus' death. The wine of Cana is in a real sense a sign of this cup of death by which Jesus draws humankind to the Father.

Topic: Feeding the Multitudes

TEXT: Mark 6:31–44, 8:1–10 (parallels); John 6:1–13.

All four Gospels include the miraculous feeding of 5,000, and Matthew and Mark contain an additional story of the feeding of 4,000. These may be approached in a number of ways.

I. *Divine providence.* This interpretation of the feeding of the multitudes goes back to the church fathers. Augustine, for instance, saw the miracle as illustrating the divine providence that provides the needs of life day by day. Jesus used his creative power to work the same sort of miracle that regularly happens when nature provides a rich harvest from a small supply of grain.

II. *The messianic banquet.* All the miracle stories have a christological dimension, and this is particularly true of the nature miracles. The feeding of the multitudes can be seen against the Jewish expectation of a future banquet to be shared with the Messiah in his kingdom. The Lord's Supper itself is an anticipation of the time of the messianic kingdom when the community will join its Lord in drinking anew from the fruit of the vine (Mark 14:25). Indeed there are details in the feeding narratives themselves that evoke the eucharist, such as the reference to "blessing" and "breaking" the loaves (Mark 6: 41).

III. *The universal motif.* Mark and Matthew have two feeding stories, one involving 5,000, which is set in Jewish territory, and one involving 4,000 in a primarily Gentile context. The doublet is a reminder that Christ is the Messiah who provides for all his people, Jew and Gentile alike.

IV. *The bread of life.* Characteristically, the Gospel of John provides its own commentary on the significance of the feeding miracle. The loaves provided the multitude are a "sign," a pointer to Jesus as the bread of life (John 6:35–40). This is Johannine "sacramentalism" at its profoundest—the bread that is necessary for physical existence points to that spiritual bread in Jesus that brings eternal life.

Topic: Catchers of Men

TEXT: Luke 5:1–11.

A miraculous catch of fish also appears in John 21:1–14 in the context of a postresurrection appearance. Though both accounts emphasize the disciples' role in mission, this motif is more pronounced in Luke where the context is that of the call of the disciples.

I. *True discipleship begins with a sense of unworthiness.* "Depart from me, for I am a sinful man. . . ." (v. 8) One is reminded of Isaiah's similar protest when he was called (Isa. 6:5). Actually, this is an expression of faith, the sense of personal unworthiness and dependence upon God necessary to being a fit vessel for service.

II. *The next step in discipleship is to receive the Lord's invitation, his call.* "Henceforth you will be catching men" (v. 10). In Isaiah's call, this took the form of a question: "Whom shall I send . . . ?" (Isa. 6:8a).

III. *The final stage is the response.* "Here am I, send me!" (Isa. 6:8b); "they left everything and followed him" (Luke 5:11). The response is immediate and unqualified. It is a commitment to the radical no-strings-attached discipleship that Jesus demanded.

Topic: The Master's Calm

TEXT: Mark 4:35–41.

I. The miracles that occur at sea should be viewed from the perspective of the ancient Jew's fear of the sea. The Jews were an inland mountain people. Their fear of the sea is reflected in the many Old Testament passages that represent the sea as Leviathan, a mythical creature of doom and dread. For them, the sea was "the deep," the primeval watery chaos that forever threatens to return and is held back only by the divinely created and maintained firmament. The miracles at sea thus involve human dread at its deepest level.

II. In contrast to the genuine fear of the disciples is Jesus' calm. Far from being perturbed by the storm, he is asleep in the stern, head comfortably resting on a cushion. His word bringing peace to the seas is only an extension of the calm in his own demeanor. It is, of course, a miracle that affirms divine providence. From early times, Christians have interpreted this text as illustrating the Master's bringing peace to the little ship of the church tossed about on the seas of life. And so it does. Sometimes the storms do not so quickly abate, but the calming presence of the Master is there, assuring his disciples of his ultimate providence, causing their fears to abate and giving courage to weather the storm.

Topic: Faith Inundated
TEXT: Matt. 14:28–33.

Matthew alone recounts the incident of Peter seeking to join Jesus in walking on the water. It is a lesson about faith.

I. *Peter's faith lacked firm footing.* It was self-initiated. At his own invitation he sought to walk to Jesus on the water (v. 28). Jesus did not prevent him—he never does—but Peter was on his own.

II. *Self-initiated faith can lead to doubt.* So it was with Peter—striking out on the water, having second thoughts, sinking, his enthusiasm suddenly inundated

III. *Solid faith is grounded in the Master.* It trusts in him and finds its footing there. "Lord, save me" (v. 30). Those are words of faith, words of trust and dependence. Peter had the wrong focus. He fixed on the wind and on his feet. Had he kept his gaze on Jesus, he would never have foundered.

SECTION X. Children's Stories and Sermons

January 4. Now We Can See

Text: John 1:1–18. "In him was life, and the life was the light of men. And the light shines in the darkness, and the darkness did not comprehend it" (vv. 4–5).

Object: Photo illustrations of candles burning in the darkness.

Boys and girls, did any of you go to a candlelight service at Christmas time? (Let them answer.) It's fun to go to those kinds of services, isn't it! When you get to have your own light and see how it cuts right through the darkness, that's exciting.

Here's a picture of some candles. You see the words surrounding the flames? Can anybody here read the words? Let me read them to you. They say, "The life was the light of men." Those words come from the Gospel story for today. Do you know who those words are talking about? (Let them answer.) Those words are talking about Jesus. Jesus is like light in our darkness. That's why we light candles in church, like the ones on the altar, or like the ones in this picture. They remind us that Jesus is the light of the world.

Have you ever been in a room where there was no light at all? (Talk about it.) You can stumble over the furniture, can't you! Or even stub your toe or break a bone. Sometimes when there's a storm outside, the lights will all go out. And then we look for a flashlight, or a candle. When that tiny light starts burning, we can see, because it only takes a little light to chase darkness away.

Did you know that Jesus gives some of his light to you and me? He wants us to be lights in the darkness, just like he is. This picture can remind us of that. You see, some candles are tall and some are short. Some burn more brightly than others. That's the way it is with us. Jesus is a bright light. We may not shine as brightly, but every extra candle that burns in the night helps people see the way to God. When we live with Jesus and do what he asks us to, we become like candles burning in the night. And Jesus gives us light to fill our lives.—*Children's Sermon Service Plus!*

January 11. Never Alone

How would you like to spend the winter at the North Pole—alone? It doesn't sound like much fun, does it? Richard E. Byrd, a famous aviator, navigator, and explorer, did something like that—only it was near the South Pole, where it is just as cold.

In 1934 Byrd took a group of fifty-six men to Antarctica to spend the winter in what was called Little America. The reason they went was to learn more about that almost unknown part of the world. For five months—think of it!—for five months Admiral Byrd lived 123 miles farther on toward the south pole. And he lived there in a tiny hut by himself. Nobody had ever done what he did before, and nobody did it again for twenty-one years. But it was wonderful experience to study that part of God's world. One thing

114

he saw was almost too beautiful to describe—the aurora australis, the southern lights. Above and beyond the ice and snow he saw the many-colored lights hanging like gorgeous curtains and draperies from the sky, wave after wave of sheer beauty. After such experiences, he sat down in his hut and wrote these words, "Though I am cut off from human beings, I am not alone."

You and I can know that wherever we are, we are never alone—never really alone—for God is there. God made everything there is, and he is our heavenly Father. We know that he loves us and cares for us. The psalmist said it beautifully when he wrote: "I can *never* be lost to your Spirit! I can *never* get away from my God! If I go up to heaven, you are there; if I go down to the place of the dead, you are there. If I ride the morning winds to the farthest oceans, even there your hand will guide me, your strength will support me" (Ps 139:7-10, *The Living Bible*).—James W. Cox

January 18. Are You Special?

Sometimes girls and boys don't know how important they are to the lives of the grown-ups. The Bible tells us about a boy who shared his lunch of bread and fish with Jesus, and somehow, by a miracle, five thousand people were fed. One of the greatest leaders in the history of the church was Augustine. He was also a very good man and is called *Saint* Augustine. One day, before he was a Christian, he heard some children playing on the other side of a garden wall. It sounded like they were saying, "Take it up and read it. . . . Take it up and read it." He thought God might be saying something to him through those words. So he took up a copy of the Scriptures, opened it, and read some words that went right to his heart. His mother, Monica, had been praying for a long time that he would become a Christian, and her prayer was being answered through the words of the children. Augustine soon was baptized and became one of the greatest preachers and teachers of all time. The children had a part in it all. The grown-ups do a lot of good things for boys

and girls, but don't forget—you can do a lot of things for grown-ups too.—James W. Cox.

January 25. Keeping Promises

When Lendy was four years old she stayed at a day care center while her parents went to work. All morning she played with her friends and listened to her teacher tell stories and sing songs. She liked playing with the dolls in the house living area, so she and her friend, Lisa, played school with all the dolls. After lunch all the children listened to music while they rested on their cots. This gave Lendy time to think about being away from home, and she missed her mom and dad very much. She would think and think about them and some days she would wonder if they would really come back for her. She remembered her daddy's words, "I'll be back at five o'clock. Have a happy day with your friends!" It was scary to think that they might forget where they had left her. What if my daddy forgets to keep his promise, she worried.

Sometimes Lendy would worry so much that it would make her stomach hurt and then she would cry. Her teacher would comfort her and say, "Your daddy will be back. Remember what he said this morning? He promised you that he would come back for you. Lendy, your daddy will keep his promise!" Every day when Lendy would wonder and worry, the teacher would remind her that her daddy would come at the end of the day, as he had promised.

One afternoon Lendy came home to Grandma's house with her daddy. She ran into the kitchen where Grandma was cooking supper. "He came back. He came back. Grandma, Daddy kept his promise. He came back!"

Lendy had learned that her daddy did what he had said he would do. He had kept his promise. The Bible is full of God's promises. When we are afraid, he promises to be with us and to comfort us. When we are lonely, he is a friend we can count on. He keeps on loving us no matter what we do. Lendy's daddy kept his promise

to Lendy. God keeps his promises to us.
—Kathryn Chapman.

February 1. Children Can Make a Difference

A few years ago a little girl made front-page news. Samantha Smith wrote a letter to the leader of the Soviet Union. She told him about how she wanted the Soviet Union and the United States to make peace with each other. She hoped that the leaders of both countries could help keep our world from war. Samantha received an invitation to the Soviet Union because of her letter. The leader asked her to come and get to know his country. She and her parents did just that. Samantha Smith's letter proved to be an important gesture in working towards a better understanding and relationship between the United States and the Soviet Union.

Many times problems seem so big to us that we doubt whether we can make any difference at all. We don't believe that our efforts will amount to much. Some people use this excuse to keep from trying to help.

When the church was just getting started many years ago Paul wrote a letter to a young man named Timothy. He told him not to let anyone look down on him just because he was young. Instead, Paul told him, be an example to them by the way you live. Try to make whatever difference you can. The Bible is full of stories about children who made a big difference. A small boy helped Jesus feed a crowd of 5,000 just by giving him his lunch. Miriam helped save the baby Moses from death. David killed the giant Goliath with only five smooth stones and a sling.

All our gifts, whether great or small, mean something to God. He can use each one of them to bring about good.—Carol Younger.

February 8. God's Valentine

In our country and in some other countries of the world, we have a beautiful custom. We have a special day that we call Valentine's Day. Boys and girls give pretty cards to one another to show that they are friends. Sometimes at school they put all their valentines into a big box and draw out one or more for each person.

Also, they may make special valentines for their teachers or their parents to show that they appreciate what their teachers and parents mean to them. Grown-ups have their own ways of observing Valentine's Day. They may give gifts to people they especially love.

To many people, particularly boys and girls, the giving of a valentine means only, "You are my friend." But to older boys and girls and grown-ups, it may mean, "I love you!" God has sent us his valentine, and it is his way of saying to all of us, whether we are young or old, "I love you." This is what we read in God's valentine to us: "For God so loved the world that he gave his only begotten Son, that whosoever believeth in him should not perish, but have everlasting life." We give our valentines on the fourteenth day of February, that is, on only one day of the year. God gives his valentines every day. He keeps telling us that he loves us. How do we get the message every day? By reading the Bible—that's where he tells us that he loves us. Of course, we don't read on every page those special words, "For God so loved the world." But everything in the Bible is meant to tell us that, even if it uses different words. And how do we feel about God? The Bible tells us, "We love him, because he first loved us." So we have a valentine for God too. When we obey him, when we do what he wants us to do, that is our way of saying to God, "I love you." —James W. Cox.

February 15. "White" Water and Racial Understanding

When I was a boy in Texas, black people and white people were not allowed to use the same public buildings. They were segregated from one another in schools, theaters, restaurants, and other public places. Restrooms and buses, lunchrooms and even water fountains were marked "white" or "colored," words that described the separation of the races.

Once, at a large department store, I took my eleven-year-old self to one of the "colored" water fountains. When no one was looking, I pushed the button and took a big drink of the water. Then I hurried away, only to realize it tasted the same as our "white water." Perhaps it seems silly now, but it was the beginning of my understanding about people, black and white, in my very segregated world. Fortunately we no longer have official segregation in America. But we can still have a lot of wrong ideas about people of other races or religions.

When Jesus says, "Do unto others the way you would have them do unto you," he is talking about all people, races and nationalities. If we practiced that, who knows what good things we might learn? —Bill J. Leonard.

February 22. Telling the Truth

According to an old story, there was once an emperor who ruled over all the people in his country. He thought that because he was such a special person he should look like a special person also. He wanted to wear the finest clothes ever made, so he searched for someone to make them. Finally, he met a tailor who said that he would make the emperor a wonderful outfit. The clothes would be so beautiful that the only people who could see them were those who were extremely wise. Of course, the tailor was just pretending to make clothes. Actually, he wasn't making a suit for the emperor at all. But because the great ruler didn't want to appear stupid, he raved about how extraordinary the clothes were. All the people around the emperor said that they were special clothes too, for no one wanted to look dumb. Finally, when the whole outfit was finished, there was a parade. The emperor rode in the streets with his new clothes on. No one knew what to say. Then, a little boy suddenly yelled out that the Emperor had no clothes on. The emperor realized that the boy was right. It took this little one, who didn't worry about impressing anyone, to tell the truth.

Sometimes it is easy to avoid saying what we believe to be true, because no one else seems to tell the truth. We might be afraid of being different, or not being liked very much. When we don't tell the truth we may get tangled up in lies. We might lose our ability to know what is true and what is not.

Jesus said, "You shall know the truth, and the truth shall make you free." When we decide to live like Jesus did, we make the decision to tell the truth, no matter how hard that might be. When we live this way, we don't have to get tangled up in lies.—Carol Younger.

March 1. Ever Get Hungry?

Object: a candy bar.

Everyone here knows what I have in my hand. I am sure that nobody here really likes candy. I am sure that everybody here is allergic to candy. Right?

What I want to do today is to give this candy bar to "Jimmy" and ask him to eat it. Jimmy, come right on up here and let me give you this candy bar. I want you to pull the paper off and eat the candy bar. (Jimmy comes forward, unwraps the candy bar and eats.)

Boys and girls, isn't it nice that Jimmy could have our candy bar? I am sure that nobody else here wanted the candy, did you? Of course you wanted the candy bar. We all did.

I wonder how you felt while Jimmy was eating the candy? Weren't you just a little envious? Didn't you wish that you could have a bite? Couldn't you just taste the delicious chocolate as Jimmy ate?

None of us here has really been hungry, really. Sometimes we say we are starving—but we get plenty to eat, don't we? But there are a lot of people in the world who don't have enough to eat. They are not like us. And they sort of feel about us like we felt about Jimmy when he ate all the candy bar and we just stood here looking, with our mouths watering.

Jesus said that when we feed the hungry we are serving him. It isn't much fun just to watch somebody else eat candy. It may even make us mad. And it isn't good religion to eat and eat and never think about helping those children around the world that are hungry. Let's think of ways we can help feed the hungry.—Roger Lovette.

March 8 (Lent). Grace Greater Than Our Sin

We used to play a funny game at youth fellowship meetings. The object of the game was to see who could remain standing the longest. The tricky part was that someone would read a long list of conditions that a person had to meet in order to keep standing. For example, the reader might say, "Sit down if you forgot to brush your teeth this morning." If we played that game this morning, we could see which of us never made any mistakes. We could find which of us is a perfect person. We all start standing. Now, you must sit down if you have ever broken into a bank. We are probably doing just fine at this point. You must sit if you have ever broken a window. Sit if you have ever broken a rule, or hurt someone's feelings, or told somebody else's secret. Probably all of us find some condition on this list that we need to sit down on.

Long ago there were people Jesus talked to who thought they were perfect. They worked hard to keep all the rules and not make any mistakes. Jesus made them angry because he showed them that no one keeps all the rules—no one is perfect. The Bible says *all* have sinned and fallen short. This sounds like bad news. But the good news is that God loves us even with all the mistakes we make. When we make errors, God does not stop loving us. He did not wait until we were perfect before he loved us. While we were still sinners, Christ died for us.—Carol Younger.

March 15. What's on the Inside?

Central Concept: Humankind is in no position to ultimately judge itself; judgment is the province of God, who holds, along with the power of judgment, the ultimate power of redemption.

Children's Concept: It is easy for people to criticize (judge) one another from what they see on the outside, but only God knows each person's thoughts, feelings, and reasons for being as they are.

Object: The best object for this lesson is a geode that has been sliced in half. Since this may not be readily available to you, you may use a coconut, a walnut, a pineapple—any object whose unattractive outside covers a valuable inside. Whatever the object, the conversation will probably go much the same.

What is this I have? (A rock, a stone.) Would you say that it is pretty? (No, it is ugly.) What do you think the inside is like? (Ugly too?) This is a special rock that has been cut in two in a special way. Would you like to see what the inside is like? (Yes . . . Show them what the inside looks like. Oooooohhhh!) You wouldn't have guessed that from just looking at the outside, would you? (No.) Well, sometimes people are like that. We may think they are not attractive, or maybe they do something that we don't like and we assume that they are ugly or unkind people, but we really don't know what they are like on the inside. Only God knows what people are like on the inside. The next time you think someone isn't a very nice person because of what you see on the outside or what you see them doing, I would like you to remember this special rock, which is called a geode, how its outside fools us, and how beautiful it turns out to be on the inside.—Marilyn P. Haney, *Word and Witness.*

March 22. Exit Signs

Did you ever notice the exit signs in a theater or in some other public building? What does the word exit mean? It means *the way out.* It is always good to know a way out when you are in a place that is closed in. When you stay in a hotel, you may see on the door of your room a diagram or picture that shows you the way to get out of the hotel in case of a fire. In an emergency the usual way out may not be the best or safest way. "Don't use the elevators in case of fire, use the stairways." So, exits are very important. They can save your life. The Apostle Paul said that God has a special exit for us when we are tempted to do something wrong or bad. Have you ever been tempted to do something wrong and wondered how you could keep from doing wrong? One exit, one way of escape is just to walk away from the temptation and think about something good. Another way of escape is simply to say no. When Satan tempted Jesus, Jesus said no three times. Then Satan left him alone. You see, an exit is very important, and God will give you a way of escape if you will only look for it.—James W. Cox.

March 29. When to Say No

Text: Luke 4:1–13. "Jesus, full of the Spirit, was led about by the Spirit in the wilderness for forty days, being tempted by the devil" (v. 1).

Object: Something that would be tempting to, but harmful to, children.

Boys and girls, what have I in my hand today? (Hold up the object.) Have you ever wanted to use one of these? (Let them answer.) Sometimes it seems as though it would be fun to do certain things even though they might be hurtful to us. How do you think this could hurt us? (Talk about it.)

Sometimes one of our big problems is finding ways to say no when we want to say yes. What makes it even harder is that God's enemy, the devil, tries to get us to say yes when God wants us to say no. Don't you think it would have been easier —and a lot safer—for God just to take all the temptation away from us so we wouldn't ever get into trouble? (Talk about it.) It might have been easier for God, but life would not have been very interesting that way, would it! There would be no surprises, and we wouldn't learn very much. Maybe that's why God lets us struggle with trouble and temptations all the time: he doesn't want our lives to get so boring that we lose interest in everything.

But still, we need help saying no at the right time, don't we! In today's Gospel story Jesus had that problem too. The devil tried to tempt Jesus with all kinds of attractive things. What helped Jesus say no? (Talk about it.) One thing that helped was that Jesus had already learned what was good and bad. That helped him. Another thing was that God stayed with Jesus the whole time, making him strong enough to stand up to the devil. The Bible tells us that Spirit of God was with him in the wilderness, protecting him. Did you know that God's Spirit is with us all the time too? That's right. Sometimes the Spirit talks to us through our conscience. Sometimes he uses the things we've learned from our parents and in church and in the Bible to keep us out of trouble.

Never be afraid to say No when God wants you to!—*Children's Sermon Service Plus!*

April 5. Being Happy When Others Are Blessed

There is an old, old story told by Aesop, a famous storyteller who is thought to have lived a long time before Christ was born. He said that a dog crossing a river with a piece of meat in its mouth saw its own reflection in the water, as in a mirror. The dog thought it saw another dog with a bigger piece of meat and tried to take the meat away from it, but lost its own meat when it snatched at the other. The current swept the meat down the river, and the dog was left with nothing.

This is what happens many times to selfish people. They fret and sulk and pout when somebody else seems to have more than they have. When they do that, they can't enjoy what they have. The Bible tells us to "rejoice with those that rejoice," to find happiness in their happiness. Whenever we are pleased by the good things that happen to others our own life is richer.—James W. Cox.

April 12. Learning to Give

A young boy named Marshal had a choice to make. His mom gave him two coins one Sunday morning—a dime and a quarter. She told him to put one in the offering plate and keep the other. He thought long and hard about this decision. His older brother gave him a list of everything he could do with a quarter. His mother just waited to see what he would do at the offering time. Finally in the service someone passed Marshal the plate. He put the quarter in first. His mother smiled. After a moment he slipped the dime in also.

To give all we have is a tough decision for us to make. Jesus taught us that giving all we have is what makes a difference in this world. He said this when the poor widow put her two copper coins in the offering. He showed how a little boy's lunch could feed a hungry crowd. He told us to give a sweater as well as a coat to someone who wants a jacket. Learning to give is not easy, but it is the way we learn about loving Jesus.—Carol Younger.

April 19. Christ Is Alive!—Everywhere!

All of us know that our Lord Jesus Christ died on the cross. Many things remind us of that. Many churches have a cross on the steeple. Many churches have a cross inside the sanctuary. Some churches are even built in the shape of a cross lying down. The cross is used also as an ornament worn on a chain around the neck or on the lapel of a coat. But we sometimes forget that God raised our crucified Lord from the dead. On the third day after Jesus died on the cross, God brought him to life again, in a glorified body.

John Masefield, a famous poet, imagined a conversation between the wife of Pontius Pilate, the man who gave Jesus up to be killed, and a Roman officer who was at the cross when Jesus was crucified. She asks: "Is he dead?" "No," answers the officer, "He is not dead." "Where is he then?" she asks. The officer answers, "Let loose in the world, lady, where neither Roman nor Jew can stop his truth."—James W. Cox.

April 26. The Trees that Prayed

In a legend about three trees in a forest, each of the trees had a prayer. The first one asked that the woodsman make it into a majestic palace where kings could dwell. It wanted to become a place of beauty. The second tree asked that it might be made into a big ship. It wanted to be the mightiest of all ships that sailed the seas. The third tree wanted to be made into polished wood so that it could become a church. It wanted to be made into the tallest and most important building in the land.

The woodsman came along and cut down the trees. The first tree was cut into rough boards that were used to make a stable and a manger. It was not a palace but it became the birthplace of the King of kings. The second tree was cut down thirty years later. Once again the boards were rough and they were made into a fishing boat. It was not the greatest of all ships but it sailed on the Sea of Galilee and on its

planks stood the Master who gave us the message of the ages. Three years later the third tree was cut down. Instead of a steeple and a beautiful church the tree was used to make a cross. And from that cross hung the Savior who gave us the promise of new life and life for evermore. So the prayers of the trees were answered but not in the way they expected. God understands our hearts. He knows our needs, he hears our prayers. He always answers them but not always in the way we hope or expect. He answers them not because of what we want but because of what we need.—John Bishop.

May 3. No Need for Words

When silent actors show us with their bodies how they are feeling and what they are thinking it is called mime. Have you ever seen a mime on television or on a street corner? People can tell what they are thinking and feeling without using words.

There are several ways in which we can talk to God without using words. One way is through our attitudes. Attitudes are the way we act because of what we have been thinking and feeling. For instance, if I have been thinking about how angry I am with my brother when he comes up to me, I may show my anger by hitting him. My attitude is negative. It means no! And I have shown my negative attitude through my actions. Attitudes can be positive, too. They mean yes! When I am happy and am smiling, I might feel like hugging my friend. Where warm feelings for my friend are showing, people know that my attitude is one of love. We talk to God through our choices, too. Boys and girls can make decisions. They can choose about things that are good for boys and girls to choose. When I make wise choices that honor persons and take care of God's world I am answering God in a wise way without using words. Sometimes I may make bad choices that hurt other people and myself. Taking someone else's money or telling lies about a friend are poor choices. The plans we make are a way of talking to God without words. Deciding to love Jesus and live in a way that would please him is a good plan to make. Living in a hateful way that hurts people who love you is not a good plan. God planned for families to live together and to learn how to get along. Our plans show how we talk to God.

God too talks to us without words. One of the most meaningful ways in which God says things to us is through the beauty and order in his creation. Every spring God talks to us through spring flowers and blue skies and the green grass. One way he tells us of his love is through an orderly world where we see summer follow spring and winter follow fall. People who love us, families and friends, are another way of God talking to us. A parent who hugs us at bedtime and a grandparent who listens to our adventures at school remind us of how God puts his loving arms around us by way of our family. Smiles and hugs and gifts and a house to come home to after school are everyday reminders of how God speaks through people who love us. God's most important way of talking to us without words is through his wise plan for the world. He sent Jesus into the world so that we could see for ourselves what God is like. God has planned for us to accept Jesus and to love him and to live for him. The Bible tells us of this great love, and has shown much of it through his great love for the world he created.

Sometimes there is no need for words. We communicate when we speak and we communicate when we don't speak. Listening to God with our heart when there are no words to hear may be one of the most important things we need to do. Listen today in worship and try to hear what God is saying to you.—Kathryn Chapman.

May 10. Life Is Special
Object: A flower.

Boys and girls, I have a flower in my hand. Isn't it a pretty flower? I am going to hand it to several of you. And when I hand it to you I want you to take one petal or leaf off the flower. (Hand it from child to child until the flower and the leaves are gone.) Now I am going to ask you to do something very hard. I am going to ask those of you that took a flower or a petal to put them back together so that the flower looked like it did before. (The children might try, they might laugh.)

I am surprised that you couldn't put the flower back together. But we know that it just cannot be done. Once you have destroyed the flower—torn it apart—it cannot be beautiful anymore.

Jesus said many times that life is precious and life is special. We have to handle flowers with care or we can crush the petals and hurt the flowers. We can hurt each other, too. And we can get hurt. Life is precious and life is special. Remember the flower. Once you have hurt something you may not be able to put it back like it once was. Remember that with your friends and even your parents. Handle with care. —Roger Lovette.

May 17. Goodness and Mercy
Text: "Surely goodness and mercy shall follow me all the days of my life: and I will dwell in the house of the Lord for ever" (Ps. 23:6).

The old ghost town lies in a deep canyon in the desert mountains of Arizona. It was once a rip-roaring settlement where murders were commonplace. The remains of dugouts with iron roofs dot the hillsides. One house is different. It is an above-ground structure, laid up by a mason of rare competence. The roof has rotted away.

Two large sandstone rocks stand at the front corners of the foundation. On one of them is chiseled the word "goodness," and on the other, "mercy." No one knows who cut the inscriptions, but anyone familiar with the beautiful Twenty-third Psalm knows where the words came from. They raise interesting questions that can be answered only by the unquoted part of the sentence: "and I will dwell in the house of the Lord for ever."

Since the ghost town is more than one hundred years old, we can assume that its former occupant is now in the place that Jesus prepared for him and all others who believe in the Son of God. The Father's house will never be left in ruins and no resident will ever be evicted by death.— Harold E. Dye.

May 24. Walls
Let's talk about walls. What is a wall for? A wall is to keep something or someone

out or to help someone on the inside feel safe and secure. Some cities along rivers have floodwalls to keep the water out of the streets and houses when the river rises after heavy rain. Long before Jesus was born the Chinese built what is called the Great Wall of China, a wall that was 1500 miles long when the work stopped. The Chinese built the wall to keep out their enemies, but it never really did what it was supposed to do. Their enemies got in anyway.

There are invisible walls—walls you can't see—that keep people away from each other. Hate, prejudice, anger, misunderstandings, lies, cheating, and things like that build invisible walls between people, so that they don't talk to each other and won't have anything to do with each other. Jesus came to tear down these invisible walls, by helping people to love each other and not hate, treat each other right and not lie and cheat, help each other and not hurt. The Jews and Gentiles who lived in the time of Jesus were kept apart by an invisible wall, but the Bible says that Christ "broke down the wall that separated them and kept them enemies" (Eph. 2:14 TEV). We can love and know and understand people different from us, people we don't like for some reason. Why? Because our Lord Jesus Christ has broken down the invisible wall that would keep us apart.—James W. Cox.

May 31. Not of This World

When Jesus was crucified, a sign was put on the top of his cross: The King of the Jews. It was meant as a kind of joke, for those who crucified him and others who wanted him crucified did not believe he was a king at all. But Jesus was and is a king, a special kind of king. He said, "My kingship is not of this world." Jesus did not come in the form of a human being to rule over nations. He came to rule over our hearts, and he does it by causing us to love him. Anyone who loves and obeys Jesus is treating him as if he were a true king, which he is. The Bible tells us that the time will come when every knee will bow and every tongue confess that Jesus Christ is Lord, to the glory of God the Father. Are you glad that Jesus is king? —James W. Cox.

June 7. Finding God

Object: Telephone book.

Anybody here know how to use a telephone? Now how many of you know how to look up numbers in the telephone book? The first part of the book has names and addresses and phone numbers. Johnny, let's see if you can find your father's name and address and number (look through the book). Here it is. Mr. James Smith, 200 Lakeshore Drive, 662–1100. Isn't that your telephone number, Johnny?

In the back of the book we find what we call yellow pages. Why are they different from the white pages? (Response.) You find business numbers in the yellow pages. It tells you where to buy toys and clothes and all kinds of things.

I need a volunteer right now. I want one of you to take this phone book and look up God's telephone number. (One child takes the book. They look through the book.) You can't find God's number in the telephone book. It isn't there. God doesn't have a telephone number. You don't need a telephone to talk to God. The Bible says that he hears us when we talk to him anytime, anyplace. And the Bible also says that even sometimes when we feel too sad to talk and don't know what to say his Spirit listens and understands. Isn't that wonderful? You don't have to use the telephone to talk to God. You don't have to be in a special place. He hears us and he loves us. Isn't that good news?—Roger Lovette.

June 14. A Little Child Will Lead Them

When you are the smallest and youngest one in the house, it is easy to believe that no one pays attention to you. You think to yourself that what you say does not really matter. Jesus tried to correct this idea that children are not important. He believed that children were good examples to people. Paul tells Timothy not to let anyone look down on him because of his age. Rather, he must be an example to everyone with what he says and does.

Children really do influence older people. One summer day a very tired youth minister was taking a group of children to the zoo. This minister was a little down in the dumps. She felt that nobody really cared too much about learning to live as

Jesus did. Suddenly she looked at Kristy, age six and Jeff, one seat in front of Kristy, age seven. Kristy had a peanut butter snack, and Jeff was eyeing it hungrily. "Do you like peanut butter, Jeff?" As he nodded yes she reached into her brown bag and gave him a package of snacks. They both grinned. Then Kristy turned to her bus seat friend and offered her some of her treat. Jeff watched carefully, thought a moment, and put his bag in front of *his* bus seat buddy. A smile grew on the young minister's face. Thank you God, for small signs of hope, for the things that children teach us.—Carol Younger.

June 21. Let's Take a Trip

(Boys and girls love movement and they love surprises. This children's message includes both.)

How many of you like to take trips? Tell me about some of the trips that you have made. Some special places that you have enjoyed. (Wait for their participation.)

This morning we are going to get up and take a trip. (The boys and girls get up and the pastor begins to walk up the aisle.) Let's see, we are going to stop right here (Stop before a person in the church who is celebrating their fiftieth wedding anniversary, a staff member who is celebrating a special occasion. One Sunday we stopped by a member who was celebrating her ninetieth birthday that week and led the congregation in singing "Happy Birthday.")

Sarah, why don't you ask Mr. and Mrs. ——— the year they got married. I wonder what was the day of the week—and what time did they get married. Fifty years is a long, long time to be married.

Let's all bow our heads and thank God for Mr. and Mrs. ——— and for their marriage of fifty years. And let us pray for every marriage in this church.—Roger Lovette.

June 28. Peter's Sandals

Text: Acts 12:1–10.

Simon Peter knew his friends were praying for him. He knew because they were that kind of friends. They loved him. They believed in prayer. They knew he was in trouble. So of course they would be praying for him.

Simon Peter's courage had led him into difficulties before, but never as bad as this. He was locked in prison, bound by chains between two soldiers, with other soldiers guarding the prison door. He was not locked up for doing anything wrong. He had been arrested because he insisted on talking about Jesus—in the temple or wherever men would listen—even though the rulers at Jerusalem had told him to stop his preaching. As it is told in the Bible: "Peter was kept in prison, but prayer was made without ceasing of the church unto God for him."

Simon Peter was praying too. He could not see how God could free him from prison, but he was sure he could not get himself out. Those two soldiers to whom he was chained might fall asleep but they would wake up fast enough if he started trying to unfasten the chains. Then there was the great lock on the prison door with the jailers standing outside of it. Peter was the sort of person who usually worked with God to make his prayers come true. He was not the kind who sat back and asked God to do the things he could do for himself. But this time there did not seem to be a single thing he could do to help God make his prayers come true. There was nothing for Peter to do but to pray and to trust God to answer his prayers and the prayers of his friends of the church. The feeling that his friends were gathered together somewhere, in one of their homes, gave him courage as he prayed.

Suddenly, as Peter prayed, someone appeared. The Greek word for Peter's helper is given in the Bible story as *angelos*. That can be translated "messenger" or "angel." Peter knew this messenger was sent by God in answer to his prayers and to the prayers of his friends. This messenger was in some way able to do the things that Peter could not possibly do for himself. Somehow the messenger had been able to get by the guards and unlock the prison door. Somehow he was able to unfasten the chains that bound Peter to the two soldiers. Peter was free to go out into the street and to join the friends who were praying for him in the house of Mary, the mother of John Mark.

God's messenger had done all the things that Peter could not do for himself.

There was one thing, however, that Peter could do to make ready to go out into the night. Apparently Peter was so excited by all that was happening that he forgot to do something that he would ordinarily have done without thinking. According to the custom of the East, he had left his sandals by the door. Naturally he would, without giving it a thought, slip his feet into his sandals and stoop down to bind up their lacings. But tonight, when so many things had happened to him, he forgot the ordinary little things. It seems from the Bible story that Peter started to walk out into the night barefooted.

And did the messenger of God stoop down and put on Peter's sandals for him? Not at all. He was there to do the things that were too hard for Peter to do alone.

"Peter," the messenger of God reminded him, "put on your sandals!" So Peter bound his own sandals on his feet and followed—past the first guard, past the second guard, through the heavy iron gate that opened for them, through the street nearest the prison, and on into the streets where Peter would be safe to go alone and join his Christian friends who were praying for him in the house of Mary, the mother of John Mark. Those prayers had been answered, but, in the answering, Peter had done the things which he could do.—Alice Geer Kelsey, *Pulpit Digest.*

July 5. Who Needs Rules?

Central Concept: Freedom, as understood by the Christian, is not anarchy, but freedom within the boundaries of commitment and responsibility.

Children's Concept: Freedom does not mean "without rules."

Story: It was near the Fourth of July. Kathy knew that the Fourth of July was a celebration of freedom, and she didn't feel much like celebrating freedom, because she didn't think she had much. It seemed to her that her life was full of rules that didn't give her much freedom at all, and she told her mother that that was how she felt. So on the evening of the third of July she was surprised—and pleased—when her mom said, "Your father and I have decided to give you your wish to really

celebrate the Fourth of July, so you may do whatever you wish and just as you wish all day tomorrow—no rules all day long!"

One of the rules Kathy didn't like was the rule that she had to make her bed before she ate breakfast, so on this special Fourth of July she left her room without making her bed or straightening her room or picking up yesterday's dirty clothes and putting them in the clothes hamper. She headed straight for the kitchen where she had a big dish of vanilla ice cream just swimming in chocolate sauce for breakfast.

She then watched game shows on television all morning long—the usual rule was just two hours of television a day—and actually felt bored, but she didn't admit that to anybody.

When it was time for lunch, everybody else in the family had ham sandwiches and carrot sticks and peaches for dessert, but Kathy had another extra big dish of ice cream with marshmallow and peanuts on it in addition to the chocolate sauce.

By about two o'clock in the afternoon she was feeling really uncomfortable when she looked at her messy room and her unmade bed, and her tummy felt kind of funny, but she didn't say anything to anybody. She went swimming.

She was usually permitted to stay at the swimming pool for three hours at the most, but on this Fourth of July without rules she stayed all afternoon and into the evening. It was seven o'clock when she finally got out, and when she got home she realized she had missed the Fourth of July picnic and her back was hurting something awful from the sunburn she had gotten. She felt really tired from making decisions for herself all day, so she had another big dish of ice cream and marshmallow and nuts for supper.

Kathy was determined not to go to bed until midnight, and her parents did not say one word to her about getting to bed. But by nine o'clock her eyelids kept shutting, so she just crawled into her unmade bed, which really felt lumpy, and as she did she broke one of the pieces of her favorite game which had not been put away. She had to be careful how she lay because her sunburn hurt so much—and her tummy ached, too. As she fell asleep, she was thinking how good it would be tomorrow when she got back to having some rules! She decided that freedom was just fine—as long as she didn't have too much of it! —Marilyn P. Haney, *Word and Witness.*

July 12. On Getting Along

Have you ever considered locking your brother or sister in a closet for a while? Have you ever wanted to push his or her face into a plate of spaghetti? Sometimes we get irritated or upset with people to whom we are really pretty close. The problem with the spaghetti or locking someone in the closet is that the trouble only gets bigger.

Once two brothers were having just such a problem getting along. They decided to go to the park. The oldest told the youngest that they would seesaw. After all, that's what the oldest one wanted to do, so the younger one would have to do this. But the youngest one wanted to play Frisbee. After an argument the first decided that he would show that brother and go seesaw by himself. Fine, thought the youngest, I'll just throw my Frisbee alone. Of course, the two boys had a miserable time. They discovered that they needed each other if they wanted to have a good time. They decided that it was important to get along with each other, even if it meant taking turns sometimes.

Maybe that's why God thought up the idea of families and friends and churches. Maybe that's also why he says that by loving each other we're showing love for him. It takes some work, but it may be the best thing we ever do.—Carol Younger.

July 19. Writing Letters

Did you ever write a letter to someone you liked very much? Sometimes boys and girls write a letter to Santa Claus or have their daddy or mother to do it. Sometimes they send a letter to grandaddy and grandmother—a very nice thing to do. They may tell about a birthday party and the nice presents, the games, and the refreshments. Letter writing can be fun, and the people who get the letters may be made very happy that someone thought of them. A real nice thing to do is to write a letter

to someone who is sick. Why not draw a picture and drop it in the envelope, along with the letter, and you may help an unhappy person to smile again, maybe even laugh out loud.

Jesus was God's letter sent to us from heaven. Not really a letter, of course, but doing what a letter would do. Jesus told us something. He told us what God is like. He told us what God wants us to do in this world, and he told us what kind of people God wants us to be.

What can you do with a letter anyway? You can lay it aside and forget to read it. You may misunderstand what the letter says even after you have read it carefully. You may need someone to help you understand what the letter says. This is really true for all of us. None of us, regardless of how far along we are, ever gets too big to have someone tell us what the gospel story in the Bible means to us—that is God's way of telling us, first, that he loves us, and next, that he wants to share himself with us. If you want someone to know you better and understand you better, you can write that person a letter and tell him or her about yourself. We have a Bible, and it tells us a lot, but he has sent Jesus Christ, one letter, and the Holy Spirit, another letter. God knows all about us but he wants us to know about him too.—James W. Cox.

July 26. The Boy Named Laughter

Isaac was the second of the patriarchs or fathers in the Old Testament. His name came from a foreign word that means "laughter." How would you like to be named Laughter? Isaac's mother, Sarah, was old when she was promised a child, and we read in the Bible (Gen. 18:12–15) that she laughed when she found out that she was going to have a baby. This was probably the reason that her son was named Laughter.

The story about Isaac in the Bible is short. Some people might think that it is not an important story because the stories before and after it are much longer. These longer stories are about Isaac's father, Abraham, and Isaac's son, Jacob. Even though the Bible tells us more about Isaac's father and then later about his son, we can learn quite a bit about Isaac, the boy named Laughter.

First of all, this child of promise reminds us that God is faithful and gracious to us. God promised Abraham and Sarah a child even though they were old, and the promise came true when Isaac was born.

Also, since Isaac became an important person whom God used to work out his plan, we can be sure that God wants to work through us no matter how small or young we are. In many ways we are like Isaac.—Kenneth M. Craig, Jr.

August 2. God Works in Us

Once a mother duck laid many little duck eggs. As she looked around one day she found an egg that was apart from the others. That one must have rolled away from home, she decided. So, she hatched the egg right along with the others. Now when that egg finally cracked the little duck in it was not like the others. The duck was rather ugly and clumsy and did not enjoy the things the other ducks liked. The duck was so strange to the others that they called him the Ugly Duckling. Some time passed and the ducks got bigger and older. One day they gathered together, determined to have fun at the ugly duckling's expense. However, when they waddled down to the water they couldn't find the ugly one anywhere. Suddenly the brightest duck pointed to the one they were looking for. Instead of finding someone to tease they saw a beautiful swan gliding on the water. The ugly duckling had changed into what it was meant to be all along.

Sometimes you and I are like that ugly duckling. We waddle around feeling sorry for ourselves because we are not as clever or handsome or athletic as all the other ducks our age. You and I must remember that inside each of us is a special person God is helping us become. We should not be so surprised when people change. God is at work in us all the time, helping us grow into that person he knows we can be. Next time we feel sorry for ourselves and don't like ourselves very much let's remember that we are important to God.

—Carol Younger, adapted from Hans Christian Andersen.

August 9. Time to Be Quiet

Text: Mark 6:30–34. "And he said to them, 'Come away by yourselves to a lonely place, and rest awhile,' " (v. 30).

Objects: A pair of earmuffs and a blindfold.

Boys and girls, which would you rather be: busy or quiet? (Let them talk about it.) Sometimes it's great to be busy, with lots to do and lots of things happening. But sometimes it's good to slow down and be quiet, isn't it. What would happen if you were always so busy that you never got a time to stop and rest and think? Right. You'd get worn out.

Today's Bible story tells us that Jesus always needed to find times to slow down and get away to a quiet place by himself. It happened because sometimes he almost got worn out, helping people and healing and preaching the way he did.

Jesus wants you and me to take time to be quiet and think about God too, doesn't he? Let's try an experiment for a minute. I need a volunteer. (Select one.) Now, will you please put on these earmuffs and a blindfold? (Let the volunteer do it.) Now, how do you feel? A little silly? Of course you do. Because none of the rest of us are wearing earmuffs and a blindfold. But while you have them on, ask yourself, if I could close my eyes and ears for a whole hour—but not fall asleep—what would I think about? Would I think about myself? Other people? God?

Now take off the earmuffs and the blindfold. (Wait for them to take them off.) God wants us all to put on earmuffs and a blindfold sometimes. We don't really have to use real ones. But we need to stop sometimes and close our eyes and our ears to the world and think about God. God will talk to us when we are quiet and thinking about him and listening for him. Sometimes we can do it when we're sitting in church, waiting for the service to begin. Or at the end, waiting for the ushers or the pastor to let us go out the door. Or we can do it when we are lying in bed, waiting to go to sleep. Take some time this week to be quiet for God.—*Children's Sermon Service Plus!*

August 16. Modern Gideons

Did you ever hear of Gideon? He was a great warrior. With only three hundred men he defeated thousands of the Midianites who were trying to destroy his people, the Israelites. When we think of Gideon we think of someone who had only a little power but who was able to do great things through the strength that God gave him.

Sometime when you are spending the night in a hotel or motel, look around and you will probably find a Bible. Open it up and you will see a notice that tells you that this Bible was placed in the room by the Gideons. Almost eighty years ago a group of Christian men, members of Gideons International, placed their first Bible in a hotel room in Iron Mountain, Michigan. Since that time they have placed the Bible or parts of the Bible in hotels, motels, schools, nursing homes, hospitals, and prisons in more than one hundred countries. They believe that the word of God, the Bible, is powerful; that what it says can change the lives of people and make them better persons. They believe that even though they are few, God can do great things through them, just as he did through Gideon and his three hundred men.—James W. Cox.

August 23. The Great Supper

Text: "The Lord said unto the servant, Go out into the highways and hedges, and compel them to come in, that my house may be filled" (Luke 14:23).

Rick was fourteen years old. He had a shock of hair that wouldn't stay put. He had a smile that would.

Not long after Rick was baptized, his pastor was standing at the door of the church auditorium shaking hands with members of the congregation who had attended the service. A big, ruddy-faced man, his attractive wife, and two sons walked by.

"Your church missionary found us and invited us to come here this morning," said the woman.

"Church missionary?" said the pastor, wonderingly.

"I mean Rick." She turned quickly and indicated Rick, who stood behind her with a radiant face. "Rick is our neighbor. He simply made us come this morning and we are so glad that we did. You can expect us back."

Rick's wide grin covered his face.—Harold E. Dye.

August 30. Outside and Inside

Everyone at Gordan Elementary School knew Todd and even though he was different, in Mrs. Walker's class he was one of the gang. If you came to school feeling sad or angry, Todd had a way of making you smile. If you lost something, Todd would be right there to help you find it. On the playground Todd could think of the neatest games to play. But Todd did not look like all the other boys and girls. In fact some people said that he was ugly. You see, Todd's family had a fiery car accident when he was younger. The accident had left Todd's face badly burned and although his injuries had stopped hurting long ago, his face looked like a scary Halloween mask.

There were days when Todd would feel hurt and angry inside because some kids had made fun of him or someone had said unkind things to him or adults had stared at him with shocked looks on their faces. Then he would wonder why *he* had to look that way when all his friends looked normal.

One day Vickie came to school. She had pretty soft curls and big, brown eyes but Vickie had only short stubby arms, not like everyone else. Vickie looked scared and uncomfortable when she entered Mrs. Walker's classroom for the first time, but before recess was over that morning Todd had made her feel so welcomed that she wasn't scared any more.

The next week Ralph started Sunday School at Todd's church. Ralph was a big fellow for his age, but he couldn't talk normally. He would stutter and stammer even when he said his name. Other kids made fun of him but Todd listened patiently to everything Ralph had to say and even seemed to want to hear more about him.

That night when Todd went to bed he said to his mother, "I'm sure glad that God has helped me to see how other kids look on the inside and not just how they look or talk on the outside." Are you like Todd? Do you make friends with other boys and girls no matter how they look on the outside, or do you only make friends with people who look and act like you?—Doris Borchert.

September 6. Learn Your Lessons Well

I knew a little boy who could never admit he did not know how to do something. He would not ask questions in class because he wanted everyone to think he knew all the answers. One year he got a bright red bike for his birthday. He was so excited that he pulled his parents outside that very minute to watch him ride it. When they got to the sidewalk his Dad began to put the training wheels on for him. "I can ride without them," he insisted. After much stubbornness on his part, he persuaded his Dad to let go. In just a few seconds he fell down. Still insisting that he could ride without any help, he tried a few more times—once running into the brick fence. He finally said quietly, "Dad, why don't you put those training wheels on."

Everybody likes to know how to do things. Everybody also has many things he or she needs to learn. Knowing and learning go together. When we think we know all we need to know, we don't learn anymore. We aren't able to understand as much as we could, or do all the things God gives us to do. God teaches us through people like our parents and teachers and friends. We learn from books. The Bible helps our minds stretch and shows us how to live. God made us in such a way that there would always be something for us to learn, or some new way that we might grow.—Carol Younger.

September 13. A Time For Celebration

Pete Rose, the veteran Cincinnati Reds baseball player, made his 4,192d hit in big league baseball play on Wednesday night, September 11, 1985. He broke Ty Cobb's long standing record before a crowd of 47,237 in Riverfront Stadium. The anticipation of Rose's breaking Ty Cobb's record had been building all season.

When the ball was sliced to left center on a clean hit, the crowd jumped to its feet with wild applause and cheers. The Goodyear blimp flashed 4,192 in lights on its side. Rose stood before the crowd wiping his eyes and tugging at his red batting helmet. He said, "I was doing pretty good until I looked up in the air and saw my dad and Ty Cobb up there. That did it." President Reagan called on the phone and addressed Pete by one of the nicknames given to him years ago, "Pete Rose, alias Charlie Hustle."

It was a time of celebration in Cincinnati that night as Pete Rose was guaranteed a reservation in baseball's Hall of Fame at Cooperstown, New York.

Sports have a way of exciting people. Winning leads to celebration, losing leads to depression. But there is always another opportunity to try again. People like to celebrate.

Every Sunday should be a celebration. Coming together in church should excite us. We are all winners in God's book. It's easy to get discouraged and feel defeated. We dare not give in to defeat or depression. Pete Rose was called "Charlie Hustle" because he had the determination to continue to practice and play when others with lesser grit gave up.—Eugene I. Enlow.

September 20. Things Work Out

Do you know what a quilt is?

(Invite the boys and girls to answer your question.)

A long time ago a little girl named Nancy who lived in the country liked to spend her afternoons playing under the quilt frame while her mother and other ladies sewed on a beautiful quilt. The pattern of the quilt was called "Grandmother's Flower Garden." The colors of the threads were bright and beautiful and with each stitch the women made the quilt become more beautiful. While they talked Nancy pretended that her place underneath the frame was her play house. She pretended she was the mother and her dolls were her children. Every now and then she would stop playing and look up at the bottom of the quilt that was over her head. The threads were uneven and the colors were mixed up and it looked like someone had sewn the pieces together who didn't know how to sew very well. She wondered how it could be so pretty on the top and so ugly underneath.

One day as she walked to the barn with her daddy she was thinking about the time their house burned down. What a terrible day that was! Nancy still remembered how she cried when she lost all the things she loved to play with. Now they lived in another house and she was happy, but she still remembered the awful fire.

"Why do bad things happen to people, Daddy?" she asked.

"You know how you like to play under the quilt frame, Nancy? When you look at the underside of the quilt what do you see?"

"I see threads hanging down and rows of stitches that aren't even. Even the colors don't match," Nancy replied.

"What do you see when you stand beside Mama when she sews and you look at the top of the quilt?" he asked.

"I see threads that match and beautiful flowers all over the quilt. Soon it will be a finished quilt and they will give it to someone to keep warm," Nancy responded.

"That's how God's world is. Good things and bad things come together to make a beautiful life for people who love God and who follow his plan. He is making our life beautiful. Sometimes though we can only see our lives from underneath like the unfinished quilt. When we trust God with the good and the bad, the pattern of our life turns out to be beautiful."
—Kathryn Chapman.

September 27. This Is My Son!
Text: Mark 9:2–9. "This is my beloved Son" (v. 7).
Object: A wallet photo of a young man.

Good morning, boys and girls. Let's do some pretending. Let's pretend that you and I are walking down the street on a Saturday afternoon when all of a sudden a young man comes walking out of the alley, all scratched and dirty. He has black soot and ash all over him and his clothes look as if they should be given away to somebody. We're afraid he might smell worse than he looks, and he might do something to us we wouldn't like if we stick around there. So we just keep on walking.

Then on Sunday morning at church your father says to you, "I want you to meet somebody." He introduces you to the person he works for at his office, the person who pays your father's salary. This person says hello to you, and then pulls out his billfold, like this (pull yours out) and shows you this picture. (Show it to them.) Then he says, "This is my son. I'm really proud of him. Do you know what he did all day yesterday, while he could have been at home relaxing in front of television? He helped a poor family who had just had a fire get some of their things out of the house—or what was left of it."

As you look at the picture, you realize this is the same person you saw coming out of the alley the day before.

What would you say to the man who had the picture in his billfold? (Talk about it.)

God sent us his son, Jesus. Jesus sometimes got pretty dirty helping people in trouble. Other people, who didn't want Jesus' help, thought he was dangerous or disgusting, since he was always getting mixed up with dirty people. But Jesus' Father said, "That's my son, Jesus. I'm proud of him!" And if God was proud of Jesus, as our Bible story for today says he was, then we can certainly be proud of Jesus too. And we can live the way he does.
—*Children's Sermon Service Plus!*

October 4. St. Francis Loved People
St. Francis is one of the most beloved saints of Christian history. He lived during the thirteenth century in the little Italian town of Assisi. He founded a religious group known as the Franciscans. Perhaps St. Francis is best known for his love of God's creation including "all creatures great and small." His most famous sermon, the story goes, was to a flock of birds that he encouraged to praise God for everything.

But Francis did not merely love animals and birds, he loved human beings as well. In fact, he set out to care for the outcast members of his society, the people, like lepers, beggars, and thieves, whom nobody else wanted. No one was too sick or too sinful to receive his help. Every one who came to him was received and loved. Francis loved people—so should we.—Bill J. Leonard.

October 11. Look Around You

Boys and girls, what are eyes for? (Response.) That's right, eyes are for seeing. One of the wonderful things about being your age is that you can see everything clearly. Sometimes when people get a little older they don't see quite as well as they did when they were young. Sometimes they look at the same faces day after day and the same places and they don't really see everything that is around them.

I want you to use your eyes this morning to look around you at what you see. Let's step up to the pulpit. What is this big black book on the Pulpit? (Response.) Yes, it is a Bible. Feel how heavy it is. This Bible rests on the pulpit where the pastor preaches. It is a reminder that we listen to the words to hear God speak. The Bible is very important to us. The Bible talks about itself even. It says, "Thy word is a lamp unto my feet and a light unto my path." It gives us light and it leads us in the right direction.

But there are other things I want you to notice this morning. Let's step down a few steps and look at this table. Do you have a table in your house? Of course you do. What happens on the table in your kitchen or dining room? (Response.) Yes, we eat together at home, eat at church, too. Today is Communion Sunday. On the table is the food. We have bread and we have wine. Jesus said these were reminders of him and his love. We eat the bread as a reminder that he is the bread of life— we need him to live. He also said that the cup was a reminder of his blood that was shed for us when he died for us. He loved us that much. So when we come back here, before the table, we are reminded that Jesus feeds us and what he gives brings us eternal life.

(Go to the baptismal font or point to the baptistry. If you have neither of these in your church, have a glass of water nearby.) What happens here. We baptize. We use water. Why do you use water at home? (Response.) Yes, we use water to wash up with and to clean things. Sometimes we have to wash when we don't want to. But it is important. In the church water is a symbol. It stands for something important. It reminds us that when we take Jesus into our hearts and lives he forgives us. He cleanses us. He makes us clean all over. And baptism is a reminder that Jesus forgives us all.

We have one more thing I want you to see. I want you to look out into the congregation. What do you see? (Response.) Yes, people. There are all kinds of people here. Young and old and tall and short and bald-headed people and some with lots of hair. There are families here and single people and some of your friends. What we see when we look out is the real church. People just like us. With problems like ours. All kinds of people. And we are the fellowship, you and I and all of them. He takes people like us and builds a church.

Always use your eyes. Even in church. You never know what God will want you to see.—Roger Lovette.

October 18. Safe, Safer, Safest

A great Scottish preacher, James S. Stewart, told a story from the annals of the British Navy. One time a destroyer ship was in a harbor of the West Indies, and five other ships belonging to other nations were anchored there too. Suddenly a terrible storm came up, and the wind was wild and huge waves came sweeping into the harbor. The British captain took up his anchor and went out to sea, right into the teeth of the storm. Two days later he came back with his ship. His ship was battered but safe. The other five ships that stayed in the harbor were lying piled up and wrecked. They had tried to play it safe, and it was the most dangerous thing they could have done. It was only the ship that risked everything that came through.

Jesus said that if we want to be his disciples we must go wherever he leads us. That may seem very dangerous at times. But to be where Jesus is will always be the safest place. He said, "I am with you always."—James W. Cox.

October 25. When We Are Afraid

Sometimes we like to be scared. On Halloween we hunt down haunted houses, tell ghost stories, and watch scary movies. When we are scared by these things we know that someone will hold our hands, or hug us, or let us sleep in their room that night. There are times, though, when we get scared and it is not easy for us to feel better right away. Sometimes we are afraid of the first day at a new school. Maybe you don't like that time at night when all the lights are out and you have not fallen asleep yet. We are afraid we might not do something very well—like make the right decisions, or do the things that are best for us. In these times it is not always easy to get over our fears. What do you do when you are afraid then?

When King David was young, he had to face a huge man named Goliath. Young boys do not fight tremendously tall adults too often. Certainly David had every reason to be shaking in his shoes with fear. This same David said in the Psalms, "When I am afraid, I will put my trust in thee" (56:3). We need to remember those words of David. Whether we fear the dark, or making friends, or making the right choice, putting trust in God will strengthen us to face those fears.—Carol Younger.

November 1. Something's in the Way

Text: Mark 10:17–27 (28–30). "Go and sell all you possess, and give to the poor, and you shall have treasure in heaven" (v. 21).

Object: A television program guide.

Boys and girls, do you like to watch television? (Let them answer.) Which is better, watching television or doing things your parents want you to do? (Let them answer.) Actually that's not a very fair question, is it? Doing both things can be good. But it depends on which is more important at the time, doesn't it?

Let's suppose you have a television set in your bedroom. Now I don't really recommend this because it might encourage you to spend too much time watching television when you could be doing other more important things. But some boys and girls have TV sets in their rooms.

Now let's suppose your mother tells you she wants you to be sure to clean up your room, make your bed, take out the trash, and do the dishes. She says you can do these things any time you want to, just as long as they get done in the next three or four days. You agree to do them, but every time you go into your room you see a copy of the TV guide. And when you look inside, you remember there's a really neat program you wanted to watch. So you start watching TV while your mother waits for you to start doing your assignments. What will happen? (Discuss it.)

Right. Your mother is going to get very angry very quickly. Now, if you have good discipline, you'll do the work. But maybe what you should do is take the TV out of your room because it's in the way of doing more important things. God says we should try to find out what things in our life—like too much money, or a TV set in your room, or anything that might become too important to us—what things are stopping us from doing God's work. When we find out, we need to get them out of the way. Then we can do what God really wants from us. Is there anything in your life like that just now?—*Children's Sermon Service Plus!*

November 8. Hopeless Cases?

As a child, Helen Keller seemed to be a hopeless case. She was blind; she was deaf; and she could not speak. Also, she was a wild and uncontrollable child. She seemed a useless and violent cripple who would make no contribution to the world.

But one woman, Annie Mansfield Sullivan, saw what others did not—a glimmer of hope. Miss Sullivan became Helen Keller's teacher, and after months of struggle and disappointment Helen Keller "spoke" her first word—*water*—using sign language. She went on to become an accomplished writer and thinker—a leader in the movement for greater rights for the disabled.

In a sense, both Annie Sullivan and Helen Keller were miracle workers who gave hope to millions of disabled persons around the world. Before you ignore, criticize, or make fun of a disabled person, remember Helen Keller and her teacher,

Annie Sullivan. Give disabled people a chance and help them to have one.—Bill J. Leonard.

November 15. Trust Your Guide

Text: "Take therefore no thought for the morrow: for the morrow shall take thought for the things of itself. Sufficient unto the day is the evil thereof" (Matt. 6:34).

Some years ago a school bus was stranded in a Nebraska blizzard. The snow had covered the roads, and the driver could proceed no farther. In his charge was a busload of children. They could not possibly survive the night in the bus. To stay there meant death; to leave it, probably the same. He knew that in the blinding snowstorm, he soon would lose all sense of direction. A lad of fourteen said, "If you will trust me, I can get us out."

The bus driver had no choice. The children dropped down out of the bus and the youth started with them across the snow-blanketed prairie. Now and then he stopped, thrust his arm down deep into the snow, then corrected his direction. Finally the driver could contain his curiosity no longer and asked how he knew which way to go.

The boy said, "The wind blows from the northeast in the fall. When the snow began to fall, the wind had laid the grass down in its path. I simply felt the grass to see which way it lay under the snow, and I knew my directions."—Harold E. Dye.

November 22. Your Special Gift

When the teacher asked, "What special talents do you have?" Mark did not feel very special at all. Everyone he knew could do something well, but he was just plain Mark! Tim could hit a ball so hard he usually always made it to second base. Grady could run like the wind and Sandra was so smart that the teachers constantly asked her to do important things for them. Mark couldn't paint like Caroline or play soccer like Hank. He couldn't make everyone laugh like Brady or tell stories about faraway places like Thelma. In fact, Mark didn't feel that God had made him special in any way.

After school that day Mark ran into the house, threw his books down and went next door. Only a hedge divided Mark's yard from Mrs. Gardner's. Almost every day this white-haired lady who had to walk with a cane had cookies and milk ready for Mark and herself after school. As they ate he would tell Mrs. Gardner all the events that happened that day at school and then they'd play a game of Old Maid or Chinese checkers before Mark went out to play with his friends. Today Mark wasn't feeling like playing. After hearing Mark's story Mrs. Gardner said, "Why I'm surprised at you, Mark. God has given you a very special gift and I bet you haven't even thanked him for it. I have known many boys and girls," Mrs. Gardner continued, which was true because she had been a teacher for years and years, "but I have never met anyone who had the gift of giving friendship like you. Tell me who else you know that would spend play time after school to talk to an old lady and brighten her day? That takes someone with a gift of friendship to give, and you have this gift."

Mrs. Gardner was right. It does take someone with a special gift who is able to give that kind of love and care. What special gift has God given to you? Talk with your family or teacher today and discover your special gift and how you are using it. In fact you may have more than one.—Doris Borchert.

November 29. Advent: Getting Ready for Jesus

Advent means coming. The season of Advent is the four weeks before Christmas when Christians get ready to celebrate the birth of Christ. Each of the weeks has a special word that reminds the church what Jesus is like. The words are:

Hope—Jesus is the hope of the world.
Peace—Jesus is the Prince of Peace.
Joy—Jesus brings joy to the world.
Love—God loved the world so much that he sent Jesus.

Some families celebrate Advent with Advent calendars—special reminders for every day during the month before Christmas. Some churches have special services about Advent.

Advent helps us realize what Christmas is really about. It says, get ready. Something special is about to happen. Christ is born in Bethlehem. It is time to celebrate! How can you celebrate Advent this year? —Bill J. Leonard.

December 6. The Largest Gift

Text: "All they did cast in of their abundance; but she of her want did cast in all that she had, even all her living" (Mark 12:44).

The woman lived in an expensive home, wore exclusively fashioned clothes, and had everything she needed—including complete devotion to God. No one in the little church was surprised when her missionary Christmas offering was five hundred dollars.

In that same church was a family with meager financial resources. There were five children in the family. For weeks the children had saved their allowances, and on the last Sunday evening in December, after Christmas had come and gone, they brought five blue envelopes to the church. In each of the envelopes there were ten dimes.

Five hundred dollars on the one hand; five dollars on the other. A wealthy woman who gave from her abundance; five little children who gave from their scarcity; but all giving with the same motive—so that missionaries around the world could tell the story of Jesus.—Harold E. Dye.

December 13. John Baptizes Jesus

Text: "The Holy Ghost descended in a bodily shape like a dove upon him, and a voice came from heaven, which said, Thou art my beloved Son; in thee I am well pleased" (Luke 3:22).

During my first pastorate, a blind boy found Christ. Our country church had no baptistry; so we went out to an icy little stream that meandered through the fields and baptized after the fashion of John.

I waded out into the water and caught my breath sharply at its chill. I turned back toward the bank and reached up for the arm of the blind boy. He was being helped by loving friends.

Through my inexperience and clumsiness, I let the youth's arm slip; and he fell face downward into the cold water. I was horrified.

Of course the beautiful symbolism of the picture was broken for a moment, but for a moment only. As I lifted the boy to his feet, I whispered my apology into his ear. A sudden smile lighted his face, and in a voice which all could hear he said, "That is all right. I do not mind. I could not see the water, but I could see my Savior, and I want everybody else to see him."—Harold E. Dye.

December 20. The Gift of a Bigger Heart

One of my favorite Christmas stories is Dr. Seuss's "How the Grinch Stole Christmas." While all the Whos in Who-ville loved Christmas, the Grinch tried his best to take that special day away from them. He concocted a plan to steal all their toys and trees and food. Certainly, he decided, this will put an end to what was for him the absolutely worst part of Christmas—their singing carols in the town square.

No one quite knew why the Grinch wanted to steal Christmas. Some said his shoes were too tight, or his "head wasn't screwed on just right." Perhaps "the most likely reason of all was the fact that his heart was two sizes too small." However, in spite of his successful attempt to steal all the trimmings of the Whos' Christmas, the next day he heard them singing anyway. Suddenly, the Grinch learned something. Christmas doesn't "come from a store. . . . Christmas means a little bit more." He took everything back. He gave gifts to the Whos. In Who-ville they say "that the Grinch's small heart grew three sizes that day."

Why do we like this story so much? Hearing that someone as terrible as the Grinch can end up with a big heart makes a wonderful story. This story gives us hope too. There's something magic about Christmas that makes our hearts grow bigger. This is a gift that doesn't come from a store. God gives us such a gift of love at Christmas time that we want to give to others.

While we may not want to steal Christmas like the Grinch, we all have times we act rather "grinchy" or "grouchy." We may get mad because we don't get a certain present, or because something is too expensive for us to buy and give. We need to remember that Christmas doesn't come from a store. It is a time for our hearts to grow, when they might be a little too small. This is a time for us to remember the real gift of Christmas—and what that means.—Carol Younger.

December 27. The Boy with a Gift

What is your favorite song that we sing in church or Sunday School? We call these songs different things—choruses, hymns, psalms, or just songs. When we praise God in song, the song is called a hymn. Many of the songs we sing in church were written by ministers, but many of them were written also by men and women who were not ministers but just people who loved God and wanted to help other people praise God and sing to one another about God's goodness and love.

One of the best-known hymn writers of all time was Isaac Watts, who lived about three hundred years ago. When he was a small boy he made poems out of just about everything he said to people. His parents had tried many times to stop Isaac from

making everything he said sound like a poem. It got on their nerves so much that one time his father started to spank him, and Isaac cried and promised,

O father, do some pity take,
And I will no more verses make.

It was a good thing for us that he later felt that God wanted him to write verses for songs and hymns.

A hymn that we often sing at Communion was written by Isaac Watts: "When I Survey the Wondrous Cross."

He also wrote the great missionary hymn "Jesus Shall Reign Where'er the Sun." A hymn that we sing at Christmas was written by Watts: "Joy to the World, the Lord Is Come!" Can you believe it? He wrote more than six hundred hymns, and many of them are so good that we still sing them in our churches today. God gave Isaac Watts a wonderful gift, a great talent that he let grow from the time he was a small boy, and in the years to come that gift, that talent blessed the world.—James W. Cox.

SECTION XI. Sermon Outlines and Homiletic and Worship Aids for Fifty-two Weeks

SUNDAY: JANUARY FOURTH

MORNING SERVICE

Topic: A Perspective for the New Year
TEXT: Ps. 36:1–12; Phil. 3:13–14.

The Apostle Paul gives us a powerful passage that offers direction on how to live in the new year before us. There are at least two dimensions to his message. There are certain things that we need to forget and there are other things that we need to remember.

I. There are some things that we need to forget as we come into this new year.

(a) The first I would suggest is for you and for me to learn to forget our resentments. We need to let go of these resentments because they position our lives. They color our whole perspective on life. We need a way to cultivate the art of letting go our resentments. Let the new year provide us with an opportunity of forgiving them or seeking forgiveness and rise up as new men and women.

(b) Secondly, I would suggest that we forget our worries. That is not to say you should never have any concern about tomorrow. Intelligent concern and plans are necessary. But a lot of people have needless worry that nags at them, cripples them, and crushes them down to the ground. Constant worry as one's companionship is really a disguised kind of atheism, because it is an affirmation that we really do not believe in the providence, care, and presence of God to direct us and guide us.

(c) We could also learn to forget about our privileges. What is life going to do for me? If this is our perspective, we see ourselves as privileged persons who always want everybody and everything to give us the advantage or exemption. Instead of focusing on what life owes us we need to turn it around and see what you and I can do to care for the needs of other people. The higher, more Christian way is to seek to serve.

(d) We also need to learn to forget about our failures. Each of us in his or her experience has known some kind of failure. One sad thing is that so many people focus their lives only on their difficulties, failures, and lost opportunities and not on the newness of life which lies before them, and what they can be, do, and become.

(e) We also need to learn to forget our victories and our achievements. Sometimes we focus too much on thinking that we have arrived and forget the power, grace, and ministry of God and what we are because of his grace, love, and power. Forget where you are and be open to what God can call you to be.

II. There are some things that we need to remember. Forgetting those things behind us, press toward the mark for the prize of the high calling of God. What are

135

some of those things that we ought to try to remember?

(a) We need to remember the paradoxical nature that we have. We all have to confess that sometimes we do good and sometimes we do evil. Each of us is sinful. Sometimes we are sinners by rebellion, and we deliberately take that avenue. Sometimes we are sinners simply because we have taken a wrong path, and we may not know at that particular moment that it is the path that leads to destruction or difficulty. But we go that way anyway. You can't fool me or your wife or husband or parents or children that you are not a sinner. They know full well that you and I are. And so does each of us deep down inside. The Church does not say that we have no sin, but that we are sinners who come to experience the grace and forgiveness of God. We still need opportunities to begin again and again.

(b) I hope also that in this new year you and I will remember some of the difficult times we have experienced in the past. If we do not remember them, then we shall never learn any lessons from them. If you and I have gone through difficult times, then don't just focus on the difficulty but see what there was in this experience or difficulty that can enable you and me to live more creatively now.

(c) Remember also the available strength that each of us has. We do not face our difficulties, burdens, or problems alone. Paul tells us about the power and presence of God available to us as we move toward the high calling of God. Remember the available strength that comes to you from God in times of temptation, or when life is filled with burdens and problems. None of us faces them isolated or in our own resources or our own strength.

(d) I hope also that in this new year you and I will remember to be more tolerant. Paul tells us that he has not yet arrived. "I am still enroute. I am pressing toward the mark."

(e) I hope we shall also remember with Paul to persevere. Let's keep on pressing on. None of us has arrived spiritually. We are all small children still seeking to become more like Christ.—William Powell Tuck.

Illustrations

A SHIVER OF ANXIETY.   It is only natural that we ask ourselves at the beginning of a new year: What will it bring forth? While we ask this question, we are made aware that we can actually know nothing in a real sense about the future. It lies before us as an unexplored continent, mysterious, full of possibilities and experiences, full of uncertainty about the kinds of utterly unforeseen things that can take place.—Emil Brunner.

AN INSPIRING PRESENCE.   On a memorable evening Toscanini walked over to the podium for his final concert. He was over eighty, and they had built a slender railing for him. He touched it lightly with the fingers of one hand. Then he raised his baton. A student of mine was there and wrote of it, of how the orchestra seemed to steal softly as one man into the first quiet movement of the great symphony; and of how after a while, as the volume grew, first one and then another, the first violin, viola, cello, bass, lifted his eyes from the notes and fastened them on the maestro there, with the wistful little smile on his lips. And all the music they had in them swept up toward that face!—Paul Scherer.

Sermon Suggestions

THE RADIANT INFLUENCE OF GOD'S PEOPLE. Text: Isa. 60:1–6. (1) They reflect the glory of the Lord. (2) They shine in the midst of darkness. (3) They attract others to their light.

GOD'S OPEN SECRET.   Text: Eph. 3:1–12. (1) It was once hidden. (2) It is now revealed.

Worship Aids

CALL TO WORSHIP.   "I am Alpha and Omega, the beginning and the ending, saith the Lord, which is, and which was, and which is to come, the Almighty" (Rev. 1:8).

INVOCATION.   Eternal God, Lord of creation, everything around us points to you, telling of your wisdom and power, and we thank you for what we can know of you through nature. Yet you have given to us a Savior, Jesus Christ our Lord, who alone reveals your love in all its dimensions and splendor. We praise you for your handiwork in your universe and stand in awe of your majesty. We trust you and offer ourselves to you as we bow in penitence before the cross. Help us to render true worship as our voices blend with the music of the spheres and our lives serve your perfect will.

OFFERTORY SENTENCE. "Take ye from among you an offering unto the Lord: whosoever is of a willing heart, let him bring it" (Exod. 35:5).

OFFERTORY PRAYER. Lord, you have been gracious to us. You have given to us out of your riches. Now we return to you for your use a portion of what we have received. As you have willingly blessed us, may we in this way joyously bless your holy name.

PRAYER. Eternal God, before the mountains were brought forth or ever thou hadst formed the earth and the world, even from everlasting to everlasting thou are God. A thousand years in thy sight are but as yesterday when it is past and as a watch in the night. We, thy transient children on this earth, would set our lives against the background of thine everlastingness, there to learn humility, there to find inner stability and peace.

Grant us insight and vision that we may behold things seen as temporal and things unseen as eternal. Our lives are shallow; we need depth. Our lives are fretful and irritated; we need quietude and serenity. O God, throw thy greatness about us, and round our restlessness thy rest.

We come to thee at the year's passing with thankful hearts. For all that crowns life with beauty and blessedness we are grateful. Quicken our thanksgiving for the benedictions of family and friends, for books and music that inspire us, for our costly heritage in church and nation, for all the present blessings that gladden our hearts. If we came here careless or cynical, send us out rejoicing and grateful.

We come to thee with penitence for the sorry failures that spoil our recollections of the year gone by. We have been thoughtless and unkind when goodwill would have helped a friend. We have filled other lives with our smoke, darkening days that else might have been sun-clear. Surrendering to our worst, we have made it difficult for others to live at their best. We are sinners, Lord, and we confess it. O God, grant us such sincere penitence and such effectual desire for amendment, that through the gateway of another year we may pass forgiven and empowered.

We bring to thee our care for the new year and its manifold interests. We would build for our children a more decent, humane, and brotherly world. Grant us fresh faith and courage for the task. Often our hearts are cast down within us. Life is full of mystery. We look out across it as across a stormy ocean where clouds lie thick and billows rise high. If we have grown discouraged, undergird us with fresh confidence for life's high enterprise, and send us out into this new year with restored determination and devotion.—Harry Emerson Fosdick.

EVENING SERVICE

Topic: Discerning the Seasons
TEXT: Eccles. 3:1–14.

"What gain has the worker from his toil?" There is something in us that resists this question.

Let's look at this question and the whole notion of life's seasons. Some of us may be making resolutions today—and perhaps some of us are already breaking resolutions. What is the point of this toil, or this struggle to better our lives? Ecclesiastes suggests an answer. And our Gospel lesson provides an example of how one person—Joseph—found the point of his toil and struggles to safeguard the newborn Christ. So let's look at the poetry of Ecclesiastes and try to unpack this jarring, mysterious question.

First, Ecclesiastes says that the seasons of our lives are of God's creation. The seasons described in these lines are the deep, life-changing moments—moments when we acutely sense that our life is swept up in something bigger than ourselves, something that connects us to all things, living, dead, and even eternal. These are the sacred moments.

But then a question may arise within us. "Are we supposed to be resigned to the seasons of our lives, since God has ordained them, and you can't fight God?" Is Ecclesiastes really only weaving poetry around a philosophy of defeatism? Are these verses merely an expression of resignation to the rule of a tyrant God?

The answer is, emphatically, no. To believe that whatever comes our way must be God's will is to confuse God's will with our will. To believe that whatever is must be divine, is to destroy the distinction between the kingdom of heaven and the kingdom of earth. That is the crux—to see the seasons of our lives as God creates them, and not as we would pervert them. The point of life is to live in the seasons of God's creation—that is what Ecclesiastes means. The point is not our toil but our obedience. The point is not our achievements but our submission to God's will. The point is not what we effect in God's good season so much as it is faithfully living in that season of God's.

Life does not culminate when we reach our "high earnings" years, when our children marry, when we retire to the good life. Life has its apex in our death. Death certainly brushes away any notions of our effectiveness, our productivity, our wealth. All that matters here is a heart reconciled with the divine. All that matters here is obedience to God. That is the cul-mination of life. That is the point, the only possible point of our toil. To Ecclesiastes' question, "What gain has the worker from his toil?" we answer, "Obedience, faith—that is what we dare hope."

II. So how can we tell what God intends for our lives, what God's holy season for us is to be?

(a) First, it's a good idea not to second-guess God. My spiritual adviser reminded me that I shouldn't mix up my own, internal and very parental voice with the voice of our heavenly Parent, God. And, he advised, there is really only one way you can find out what the voice of the divine Parent is saying, and that is to pray and wait on God.

(b) Second, God doesn't ask us to do things we don't deeply want to do. We are God's, created in God's divine image, and however distorted and broken our relationship with the divine will is, we are ultimately intended to live aligned with the divine will. Redeemed and reconciled with God, our deepest yearnings are the yearnings of God, also, for us. God's will and God's seasons we yearn to reclaim and to fulfill.

(c) Third, God has given us a criterion for discerning God's will in the person of Jesus. Jesus' own example of the triumph of bold, self-giving love is the criterion against which we must weigh our own discernings of God's will. It is the criterion against which we can make sense of the courageous, obedient actions taken by many of the people the Scriptures describe.—Joanne M. Swenson.

SUNDAY: JANUARY ELEVENTH

MORNING SERVICE

Topic: The Conquest of Fear

Text: 1 John 4:18.

We may be sure that every one here, one way or another, faces the problem of fear. Fear runs so far back into the human heritage, takes such diverse forms, works its way out to such disguised results, that nobody, however normal, altogether escapes it.

No more can we in the modern world dispense with fear. It keeps us from being run over by automobiles, from being content with unsanitary conditions, from disobeying doctors' orders. The fear of ignorance is one reason why we get an education. The fear of war is one builder of the League of Nations. Fear runs through all of life—wholesome fear not only guarding us from danger but positively driving us to constructive enterprises of personal and public protection, so that if by "a fearless man" we mean one who thinks that there is nothing here to dread or from whose constitution the fear instinct has been left out, we are picturing not a wise man, but a defective mind.

Let no man, then, despise fear or call it wholly evil, for it has many meanings, and no good life is possible without its healthful presence. That, however, is not half the story. What ruin cannot fear work in a man's life when it gets loose!

Of course the Master talked about this subject. If, as the gospel says, he knew what was in man, how could he help it? Everywhere, all the time, men and women face fear—fear of others, fear of themselves, fear of change, fear of growing old, fear of disease and poverty—and at last many face what the psychiatrists call phobophobia, the fear of fear, being afraid of being afraid.

I. Well, then, how to conquer fear?

(a) For one thing, there is an area of fear not to be avoided or overcome without a clean and upright moral life.

The story of the garden of Eden goes back to so primitive an age that it pictures God taking an afternoon walk in the cool of the day, pictures a serpent talking, and a woman made out of a man's rib. It is a very ancient legend. All the more impressive is it to discover that even then human beings had found out at least one thing that human beings have been finding out ever since. For no sooner has Adam eaten of the forbidden fruit than we hear him saying to God, "I was afraid . . . and I hid myself." As every psychiatrist knows, that is as modern as this morning's newspaper —I was afraid.

We sin a little more and, beyond our power to foresee it, we face a growing habit. At first sin dressed itself in the garments of liberty and said to us, Be free! But now the inexorable laws of habit take charge and that illusory freedom turns out to be the bait to a trap of terrific tyranny. We were free to start. We are not free to stop. Then fear arrives. Yes, a whole troop of fears: fear of the consequence of what we have done to other people, fear of the gravitation by which a train of evil, once started, goes on and on to disasters we

could not guess, and always the dread of being found out. Fear—sleepless nights and haggard days filled by fear of being found—until one man kills himself, and another flees the country, and another resigns to save the credit of his institution.

(b) This, however, is not the whole story. Another wide area of fear is caused by trying to face the strain of life with inadequate interior resources. Did you ever spend a windy night in a tent when you were not sure how firm the stakes were and how stout the ropes might be, and when the gales rose with increasing fury? Nervous business! Multitudes of people are in that situation. Heavy gales, weak stakes—they are afraid.

(c) To be sure, some of the fears that people suffer from they are not responsible for, and their phobias cannot be cured by anything the victims alone can do. Their fears got a long head start on them in early childhood from unfortunate accidents or unwise parents. We parents have few duties more sacred than to see to it that our children do not catch from us unnecessary and abnormal fears.

(d) Much of our fearful living, however, moves in another realm, where the service of psychiatry is dubious unless the psychiatrist is a man of religious faith. For the trouble with us is simply that we are facing the heavy strain of life without adequate spiritual resources.

If a man's religious faith does not thus furnish him with adequate spiritual resources for life, there is something the matter with it. Out of the unseen, to one who has experienced the Christian gospel's practical effect, there comes a voice with all the resources of the Eternal Spirit, saying, You can. When fear whimpers, I cannot do what I ought to do, the voice says, You can. When fear complains, I cannot stand what I must endure, the voice says, You can.

II. I should like this morning to do something more than discuss the conquest of fear. I wish that the conquest could be achieved now by someone here who needs it.

(a) Fear is a hypnotist. It stares us out of countenance. It says to us again and again, You cannot, you cannot! So fear produces what it fears. It is a creative force. Listen to it long enough and its message turns out to be true: you cannot.

(b) "The only known cure for fear is faith," for faith also is creative. It produces what it has faith in. Live with it in the deep companionship of your soul, listen to its speaking out of the resources of the divine world, tap the infinite resources that it can release into your life, and at last you can.

(c) If fear and faith are so creative in the large, they are operating inside us, are they not? As your day is, so shall your strength be. And, however difficult the circumstances, you can have an inner victory, the conquest of panic and fear.

III. Even this, however, does not tell the whole story. There is one more field where fear grows rank and strong and where the only cure is goodwill, love.

(a) So the New Testament says, "Perfect love casteth out fear." When one stops merely repeating that text and sits down to think of it, it is a strange saying. What have love and fear to do with each other? They have so much to do with each other that one does not need to go down into the obscure and mystical depths of the human soul for an illustration. Our international relationships themselves are a perfect picture of the truth. Now, the old remedy for fear was great armaments. Armed to the teeth, a nation said, we shall not fear. But how futile is that old remedy in the new world! Great armaments are not now a remedy for fear. They are the major cause of fear.

(b) A fact that works thus in the large is probably operating inside our lives. What are some of us afraid of this morning? We are afraid of the superiority of other people, afraid that somebody is going to get ahead of us or be preferred before us, afraid of other people's disapproval if we do what we know is right. Jealousy, envy, bitterness, vindictiveness, a humiliating sense of inferiority in comparison with others—all such emotions are forms of fear.

(c) What is the cure, then, of this fear of people, jealous, envious, suspicious, sometimes bitter? We know the cure— God help us to achieve it! Love casteth out fear.—Harry Emerson Fosdick.

Illustrations

THE VALUE OF FEAR.   During World War II a radio commentator, when announcing the number of German fighter planes brought down, fell into the habit of terminating each announcement with the exclamation: "Who's afraid of the Focke-Wulf?" A member of the crew of a Flying Fortress, hearing about the commentator and his exclamation, sent him a picture of his plane and its crew and wrote at the bottom, " 'Who's afraid of the Focke-Wulf?' We are," and signed his name and the names of the entire crew. Were they cowards? On the contrary, they were brave men who realized full well that they were fighting against brave men. Had they known no fear, the wise fear that begets care, it is hardly likely that they would have survived a single encounter.—Robert J. McCracken.

IMPREGNABLE FAITH.   The child who finds his personal advantage not immediately and satisfactorily served by his prayers may discard his conceptions and terminate once and for all his religious quest. Sometimes the issue comes to a head only later in life, in conjunction with acute personal need. "Prayer does not stop bullets," was the refrain of many veterans; "they perforate both devout and infidel." "Religion has no survival value for me." A faith centered in self-advantage is bound to break up. To endure at all it must envisage a universe that extends beyond personal whim and is anchored in values that transcend the immediate interest of the individual as interpreted by himself. —Gordon W. Allport.

Sermon Suggestions

THE MISSION OF GOD'S PEOPLE.   Text: Isa. 42:1–9. (1) To bring justice to the world. (2) In the Spirit of God. (3) With liberating teaching of God's will.

IT ISN'T HOW YOU LOOK!   Text: Acts 10: 34–43. The gospel is for all the world. (1) From the beginning, the entire human family has needed the Christ. (2) Through the ages the prophets pointed toward a

Savior for all. (3) In the fullness of time, God's Spirit has made the blessing available to everyone.

Worship Aids

CALL TO WORSHIP. "I sought the Lord, and he heard me, and delivered me from all my fears" (Ps. 34:4).

INVOCATION. Lord, be thou in the singing and the prayers, the sermon and the offering, the silence and the words, in every soul that comes to worship, near to every burdened heart. Be thou all over again to us our mighty God.—E. Lee Phillips.

OFFERTORY SENTENCE. "And the King shall answer and say unto them, Verily I say unto you, Inasmuch as ye have done it unto one of the least of these my brethren, ye have done it unto me" (Matt. 25:40).

OFFERTORY PRAYER. Open our eyes, O Lord, and let us see the good that our gifts may do. Help us to minister to the hidden Christ in everyone. To that end, bless us with increasing awareness and openness of heart.

PRAYER. Oh God, who has ordained the seasons of the year and also the seasons of our lives, we praise you for the steadfastness of your love and mercy, which support us in every season and time of life. Help us now to open ourselves to the gift of your presence, which will transform our very existence. Where there is fear, give courage; where there is anxiety, give peace; where there is loneliness, give companionship. Let the mind of your Son Jesus become our mind as well, drawing us into fellowship and commitment and service. In a world that grows daily more difficult and complicated, lead us into simplicity of heart and soul. As others contend for place and possessions, make us joyful with relationships. Where the paths that we must walk become steep and narrow or overgrown with briers and weeds, hold our hands lest we stumble. Reveal yourself especially to those who suffer grief or illness, that they may be encouraged by a deeper knowledge of you. Help us to hear your Word for each of us as we wait before you in reverence and love.—John Killinger.

EVENING SERVICE

Topic: The Perils of Applause
TEXT: Rom. 1:32; Phil. 1:9, 10.

I ask you now to let your imaginations play over these words: "They actually applaud such practices." Here Paul is making the point that the applauding of evil is, in effect, participation in that evil. There is no suggestion here that all applause is evil, but some of it is, and there is peril in much of the rest of it.

I. Applause of evil can be, in effect, participation in that evil.

(a) Paul did not see morality as simply obeying laws and rules and conventions. Rather, he saw morality as founded in and motivated by love. Love, in the Bible, is not primarily an emotion but a matter of will—the active willing of the real and lasting good of other persons, a willing that sometimes entails sacrifice. Immoral behavior, then, is not essentially in the violation of laws and rules but in the violation of the sacred personhood of others, in the exploitation of others for one's own gain and satisfaction, in the breaking of good relations among persons and among groups of persons.

(b) So, you see, when Paul said, "They actually applaud such practices," he was not tut-tutting like a narrow-minded great-uncle. Rather, he was warning that when we applaud evil we are in reality involving ourselves in that evil, repudiating love as the primary motive in the moral life.

(c) There are subtleties here that we must not overlook. Our applause not only may encourage others in evil, but also may be a way in which we evade coming to honest terms with ourselves.

II. Applause often produces the kind of conformity that is morally uncreative.

(a) We are often manipulated into offering applause. When we are in groups we can be led into applauding things that very few of us as individuals would clap even one hand at.

(b) I do not suggest that artificially produced applause is really a matter of serious moral concern, but it does, nevertheless, illustrate how easily we can be stimulated to applaud the questionable and the shoddy. We often offer applause simply because we do not wish to be thought odd, insensitive, puritanical, for not applauding what everyone else is applauding.

III. Applause is sometimes the surrender by a person of his or her right and duty to exercise mature judgment.

(a) Today the mass media of communication seem to be producing conformities of response and attitude without people being aware of the extent to which they are being manipulated. We are all subjected to subtle coercion that can inhibit individual judgment.

(b) Perhaps we tend to applaud quickly because we feel that a willingness to applaud is a sign of broad-mindedness and tolerance. The heart of the matter here is not in either broad-mindedness or narrow-mindedness, for both can carry heavy loads of the bogus and the evasive. The heart of the matter is in independent-mindedness, in being your own man or your own woman, showing moral integrity in making your own judgments in things affecting the basic qualities and values of the good life.

IV. I now try to tie together all these loose ends with a text from another of Paul's letters. This one is from the beginning of his letter to the Philippians. "And this is my prayer, that your love may grow ever richer and richer in knowledge and insight of every kind, and may thus bring you the gift of true discrimination."

(a) Love, as the New Testament understands love, is the determination to serve the needs and the real good of others and to respect the full integrity of their personhood.

(b) In faith, through the disciplines and practices of faith, you can be helped to insight and power for that "true discrimination" which is indispensable in the full life under God, the life of meaning and purpose, the life of peace and joy. "For I am not ashamed of the Gospel. It is the saving power of God for everyone who has faith." There is no peril in applauding that.—J. A. Davidson

SUNDAY: JANUARY EIGHTEENTH

MORNING SERVICE

Topic: Blessed Are the Meek
TEXT: Matt. 5:5.
Behavior is often nothing more than a mirror of our internal attitudes toward life. So many people are unhappy with their lives that they are aggressively trying to steal some kind of happiness for themselves.

I. Jesus' plan for happiness has an attitude toward life that accepts powerlessness and finds power through it. "Blessed are the meek." In other words, blessed are those who face unpleasantness in life and do not become angry or embittered because of it. Blessed are those who are gentle, pleasant, and whose disposition is soothing.

II. The Bible presents contrasting pictures of what is meant by meekness.

A picture of the opposite of meekness is found in the parable that Jesus told of the wicked husbandmen in the twelfth chapter of Mark.

This parable demonstrates a sad picture of our world. Our society ignores transcendence and has no concept of accountability to God as creator and Lord of the world. Our society glories in a radical individualism that says, "If I do it, it is right." Our society tramples upon the concept of justice, fairness, and community because these concepts hold us responsible to others and make us a part of a community of rules and laws. Lastly, our society disdains authority and believes that the owner of the vineyard is too weak to punish wrongdoers and enforce what is right. This sad picture shows the human community destroying itself. This way of living makes peace impossible. No wonder so many people are unhappy.

III. However, the Bible also has a wonderful picture of the happiness that comes through meekness.

(a) Jesus is himself the perfect picture of what a meek person is like. The scene I have in mind is the so-called triumphant entry of Jesus into Jerusalem.

(b) Jesus came to Jerusalem as the promised saviour from God, yet he did not call attention to himself. He did not ride into the city with his hand raised and his finger pointing to the sky as if to say, "I'm number one." Jesus came as the Lord of a new kingdom; however, he did not come with weapons and threats, but with words of peace and with an offer of forgiveness. When others lost control of themselves and cried for his death, he remained in control of himself. When the cross became inevitable, Jesus did not become angry at the mob, or rebellious against God, but died in faithful duty as a servant of all humanity.

IV. One asks how this attitude can be attained. How can we be strong enough to move the world through love and not fear? How can we serve each other and perform our duties to God without becoming resentful and angry? How can we enjoy working quietly and not worry about those who are noisily promoting themselves?

(a) This is the answer: we must believe in our hearts and commit our lives to a promise from God that he can use our love to transform the world, and he can use our service to build a community of peace, and he will make our acts of simple kindness the building blocks of a new kingdom.

(b) We simply cannot reckon ourselves to be first in importance and first to be served, and first to have all our wants supplied and be happy. No one stays in first place forever. Rather, the attitude of meekness always sees our lives in relationship to God. In fact, we come to forget about ourselves, because God ranks first, service to others ranks second, and everything else seems to fall into a proper place. This is why Jesus said the meek shall inherit the earth. They would never think of taking it for themselves, but through the power of God working in their lives, the meek are changing the world and gradually building it into the new kingdom of God.

V. Jesus said, "Take my yoke upon you and learn of me; for I am gentle and lowly in heart, and you will find rest for your soul." Meekness is characterized as living with goodwill and friendly disposition toward fellow human beings and living with obedient faithful service in the presence of God. Happy are you when you can quit calling attention to yourself and give your attention to caring for others. Happy are you when you no longer need to make others afraid of you but can win them as friends through love. Happy are you when you outgrow the need for violence and can live in peace with others.—Kenneth E. Stout.

Illustrations

A SECRET OF SUCCESS.   Why was John Woolman's the first really effective voice in the Western world in denouncing human slavery? It was, as he has told us himself, because of his religious experience. The intensity of his devotion led directly to his social concern.

What Woolman's religion did for him was to develop in him an extraordinary tenderness toward all human beings, whether known or unknown. As he read that God had made all men in his image, Woolman really believed it, not merely with his head, but also with his heart. He opposed slavery forthwith, not because of some doctrinaire position arrived at by mere thought, but because he truly felt for all other creatures in the same essential predicament in which he found himself. He knew, then, that their similarities were more significant than their differences; he knew that pain and bereavement meant the same, and hurt the same, among black men as among white men, and among foreigners as among neighbors. Equality was transformed into solidarity.

Woolman's real secret, which truly accounts for his social sensitivity, lay in his sense of membership in what Albert Schweitzer has called "the fellowship of those who bear the mark of pain."—Elton Trueblood.

INCREDIBLE STRENGTH.   Think of the usurpers who have set themselves to build up empires on naked power, on sheer force. Think of Hitler, for a time almost like a Colossus bestriding the world. But only for a time. Such a tyranny over life and liberty could not in the nature of things, in God's world, last for long. It is history which makes it ridiculous to say, "Blessed are the Caesars, the Napoleons, the Stalins: for they shall inherit the earth."—Robert J. McCracken.

Sermon Suggestions

GOD'S SECRET WEAPON.   Text: Isa. 49: 1–7. (1) A people called by God for a special task. (2) A people sometimes discouraged and apparently defeated. (3) A people who find new strength in God.

HAVING OR WANTING.   Text: 1 Cor. 1: 1–9. As believers we should be thankful or prayerful for: (1) a rich understanding of the gospel; (2) ability to put our knowledge and faith into credible and persuasive words of witness; (3) spiritual gifts that will bless the people of God.

Worship Aids

CALL TO WORSHIP.   "Clothe yourselves, all of you, with humility toward one another, for 'God opposes the proud, but gives grace to the humble' " (1 Pet. 5:5b RSV).

INVOCATION.   Most worthy art thou, O good and gracious God, of all praises, even for thy own sake, who surpassest all things in holiness. By thee only we are made holy and sanctified. We praise thee for our glorious redemption, purchased for us in thy dearly beloved Son Christ Jesus, as our duty continually bids us: Give us therefore thy Holy Spirit to govern us. And grant that all things which breathe with life may praise thee, as the true life of all creatures, through the same Jesus Christ, our Lord, who reigneth with thee and the Holy Ghost, one God for ever and ever.—Ancient Scottish Prayer.

OFFERTORY SENTENCE.   "Praise the Lord, all people on earth; praise his glory and might. Praise the Lord's glorious name; bring an offering and come into his Temple" (Ps. 96:7–8 TEV).

OFFERTORY PRAYER.   Creator God, owner of the earth and all that is in it, make the offerings that we bring to your house praise you in this place and wherever your word is taught and proclaimed.

PRAYER.   To thee, our common Father, we lift up our hearts in gratitude for the blessings of the year, realizing that unearned good and unmerited protection have come to us, in addition to all that for which we have striven and that against which we have guarded. As we look out over the threshold of the new year, we pray thee, add to the common necessities of our daily life an overmastering desire to grow in moral and spiritual worth. Help us to see clearly that the physical and material, without the moral and spiritual, is death and destruction.

Help us to cultivate in our own natures those virtues which we think are lacking in our neighbors. Help us to rebuke injustice, selfishness, and bigotry by living the just, the generous, and the open-minded life. Let us not be content unless each day we have added some worth to our characters by some service done for our fellow men.—George W. Coleman.

EVENING SERVICE

Topic: That Perpetual Debt
TEXT: Rom. 13:8–10.

I. These are words of the Apostle Paul, reflecting the highest insights of Jewish faith and the clearest applications of Jesus' own teaching. Life is inseparable from obligation: a child learns that lesson soon. But obligations are not all the same; some are more important than others. Chief among them is the responsibility to love— to compassionately care for other people. Indeed, this duty is at the very top, according to St. Paul—and according to a vast accumulation of human experience.

II. That perpetual debt! It is the debt of love. That interaction between individuals which draws the best from each of them; which forgives and encourages and inspires their actions; which imparts courage and makes the days richer; which always is accepting and understanding, patient and sensitively aware; that is the love all of us need, the power equal to life's every demand. "Owe no one anything, except to love one another." Have no debts save this one, the debt to love.

III. We are talking about the world's greatest untapped resource. Worries are abroad about our too-rapid consumption of many of the earth's physical resources, but here is a spiritual resource of limitless potential, utilized all too modestly. What curious creatures we are! The world is starving for the blessings love can bestow, yet we struggle with scores of lesser remedies and continue with chronic maladies, taking two steps backward for every one that goes ahead. It is a case of knowing better than we do, of having a resource available that nonetheless is treated with benign neglect.

Without it, without love, we are nothing, as St. Paul so wisely said. Yet this greatest of all resources is left unappropriated and the shadows lengthen and the darkness descends. We seem to think we owe our enemies revenge, our allies and geographic neighbors condescension, our fellow citizens bland indifference. But the word of the Lord is, "Owe no one anything, except to love one another." This is life's real duty; that is what the world needs now. As incredible as it seems, we must owe everyone more than we can hope to pay. Largeness of spirit is called for; unrestrained goodwill should rule the day.

(a) Love does not permit the injury, hurt, or destruction of others. It holds the true interests of each person in scrupulous regard. Contrary to popular judgment, there is nothing soft or unrealistic about kindness and forgiveness. Nor is there anything threatening about honoring the light of God and the dignity of personhood in your neighbor, or even your enemy. There is everything right about that, and rewarding, and fulfilling for all parties concerned.

(b) Jesus' own message and example are the controlling meanings of love. He was not the first to teach and live by this norm, but he was the one who gave love its central and decisive place for the whole of life. Love, as Jesus showed is not an optional behavior among various possibilities; it is the comprehensive claim that is laid upon all, whatever a person's station in life. And it needs to be said that in the sight of God we all are accountable for how we pay.—John H. Townsend.

SUNDAY: JANUARY TWENTY-FIFTH

MORNING SERVICE

Topic: Little Things Are Important
Text: 1 Sam. 9–10.

An account of some donkeys getting lost hardly seems appropriate to be recorded in the pages of sacred Scriptures. A farmer sending his son and some servants to find the straying animals borders on trivia. But the pointless story gains great dimension as it reveals a link in the chain of circumstances God used to lead Saul to the throne and the subsequent events of history. The unfolding story, often unnoticed, gives us clues to some important truths of life.

I. Little things are important when God makes big issues out of our little actions.

(a) What began as a small event counted up finally to a supreme and glorious purpose. Important doors often swing on tiny hinges. Saul went to search for his father's donkeys and discovered a kingdom!

Each person in the story made independent choices. Yet through all these minor, little actions, Samuel was brought face to face with God's chosen king; and his will was fulfilled.

(b) Throughout the Bible its writers delight to tell us how intimately the secular actions of people interweave with the sublime and mighty issues of God. Two convicts met in an Egyptian prison, and Joseph found his destiny. The beauty of a dusky Jewish maiden so fascinated the king of Persia that she moved to the position where God used her to save his chosen people from massacre. A princess bathed in the Nile, rescued a floating child, and thus delivered a nation from slavery. An old man launched a giant killer when he sent some cakes and cheese by his youngest son to his soldier sons on the battlefield.

(c) In many instances the Bible illustrated the double action of God-directed purpose, finding fulfillment through human actions. No wonder David prayed, "Order my steps in thy word" (Ps. 119: 133). Every step, however small, is important; none are insignificant. Nothing is too small or too trivial to be shared with God. We need to take each step with his blessing, so that when he puts them all together, the plan will be clear and the destination right.

II. Little things are important when God hides big privileges behind little responsibilities.

This oft-forgotten story in the Old Testament reminds us of another important truth. Saul served well in the simple tasks assigned to him. He evidenced a wholesome attitude by treating a small responsibility as a big privilege. He was obedient (1 Sam. 9:1–5), patient (v. 4), and considerate (v. 5). Step by step his growth is charted. He was "a choice young man" (v. 2). Saul stands revealed as he treated his little responsibility as a big privilege and gave his best to it. We, too, can only make little things count when we recognize that God often hides his big privileges behind small responsibilities.

III. Little things are important when God sets big opportunities within our little experiences.

(a) Saul was searching for donkeys and found a kingdom. Donkeys were important to his farmer-father and essential to the harvest. Saul was faithfully carrying out his assigned task to find the lost animals. Instead he found God's divine purpose. Samuel, led of God, instructed Saul to shift his priorities from daily duties to divine destiny (1 Sam. 9:20). It was time to forget the lost donkeys and remember the desire of all Israel. The kingdom awaited his leadership. God awaited his commitment.

That's how to make the little things count! Look for God's purpose in them

all. See how each may be bent to his will.

(b) Saul's great tragedy was that he began so well but finished so badly (1 Sam. 15). He failed God in the Amalekite battle. Samuel reminded him (v. 17) of his lost opportunity. Still God used "all things" for the kingdom's good. God's eternal purpose marched on through the centuries, through David, to the babe of Bethlehem. God made the little things count for his kingdom, but they did not count for Saul. He was left a shipwreck on the shore beside the stream of God's purpose, a frustrated castaway who died by his own hand.

(c) Amid the routine duties of life in what may seem to be of little consequence, God often moves toward his divine destinies. Our task is to be obedient to his guiding Word and way lest we, too, become castaways in the ongoing purposes of God's kingdom.

The story of Saul's search teaches us to:
1. Remember God's providence
2. Recognize God's testing
3. Respond to God's guidance

God makes big issues out of little actions; he hides big responsibilities behind little privileges; he sets big opportunities within little experiences.—Craig Skinner.

Illustrations

DAILY REVELATIONS.   God is revealed to man daily in the humble thornbushes of fine men and women. It is legitimate to move from the perspective of goodness first reflected through the character of a wise father and a good mother to the view of the universe as God's field of operation. Such a view of God rooted first in the little society of the family in its best and most loving form and then extending its horizon to the Infinite is mature and indestructible.—Joshua Loth Liebman.

BIGNESS AND GREATNESS.   I am against bigness and greatness in all their forms, and with the invisible molecular moral forces that work from individual to individual, stealing in through the crannies of the world like so many soft rootlets, or like the capillary oozing of water, and yet rending the hardest monuments of man's pride, if you give them time.—William James.

Sermon Suggestions

WHEN GOD ACTS.   Text: Isa. 9:1-4. (1) Our fortunes change—from darkness to light. (2) Our attitude changes—from discouragement to joy.

HOW CHRISTIANS CAN HAVE UNITY. Text: 1 Cor. 1:10-17. (1) By seeing unity as God's will. (2) By avoiding personality cults. (3) By exalting the cross of Christ.

Worship Aids

CALL TO WORSHIP.   "I know thy works: behold, I have set before thee an open door, and no man can shut it: for thou hast a little strength, and hast kept my word, and hast not denied my name" (Rev. 3:8).

INVOCATION.

We come to worship, Father
We gather as thy children,
seeking
     to practice thy presence,
seeking
     to know thy will.
Thy Son, our Savior, promised
     "Seek and ye shall find. . . ."
We claim that promise,
     Father.—J. Estill Jones.

OFFERTORY SENTENCE.   "Speak to the people . . . that they take for me an offering; from every man whose heart makes him willing you shall receive the offering for me" (Exod. 25:2 RSV).

OFFERTORY PRAYER.   With thankful hearts we come to you, O Lord, to bring our offerings. May your name be praised through what we do in this very moment of dedication.

PRAYER.   We thank thee, O Lord, that every mountain height and every plain becomes a place of new privilege, and if we are thankful for the things that are past may we be more arduous about the things that are to be. May we, if we have risen to a point where we give these songs this morning, go still farther by thy grace, and may we to this end leave every unnecessary burden behind and so carry only what thy providence dost give us to carry. And by thine own Spirit, O Lord, wilt thou so influence us that we will cast our burden on the Lord, even though we know that every one shall bear his own burden and that we are commanded to bear one another's burden. Father, we pray thee in times of great concern that we may not be seeking to bear the burdens that thou must bear. Lord, let us know that this thing of civilization was from the beginning a divine adventure; that thou hast invested in it and that thou hast never withdrawn the capital of heaven. O Lord, may we not try to bear burdens that are thine and thine only and may we so take up the burdens of simple duty and the thing that is nearest to us that it shall be more easy for others to bear their burdens.—Frank W. Gunsaulus.

EVENING SERVICE

Topic: The Place of Patience
TEXT: Rom. 8:18-27.
Christians in the first century experienced a clear disappointment when their Lord did not immediately return, as many had anticipated. Other believers struggled to maintain their witness in a hostile society, never certain as to the outcome. It also was a world of commerce, movement, transition, and change. Not unlike our own day, it was difficult to step aside from the whirl of activity. Out of this context, perhaps because of it, the meaning and significance of patience as a Christian behavior came to be articulated.

I. *Clearly, patience means waiting.*

(a) But such waiting is not a passive mood or an inert, powerless behavior. In New Testament thought patience has substance and direction; it is not a vacuum; it "works."

(b) The book of Revelation speaks of "the patience of the saints" often translated "the endurance of the saints." The deeper meaning—beyond that of putting up with hardship or facing persecution—is that God's people possess a lively, outgoing power of faith. Theirs is an active energy, not defenseless resignation.

(c) What is signified by Paul's affirmation is that a person of patience is able to see in present adversity the light of a greater glory. Patient waiting has that understanding as its content. Trust in the ultimate goodness and purpose of God permits a calm and steady approach to present trials.

II. *Patience also describes human relationships.*

(a) That is to say, it is a quality of life that facilitates our interaction with one another. Its opposite, impatience, frequently destroys personal relationships. Christians are called to "bear with the failings of the weak." These admonitions suggest patience and thoughtful consideration. Where they are realized, there is found a beautiful experience, indeed.

(b) Without this virtue, each person toward the other, we risk misunderstanding. Even worse, we risk the total loss of human community. Patience, of course, is not an end in itself, but it creates a climate appropriate to achieving positive ends and goals.

III. *A vaster patience has been revealed in God's pursuit of you and me.* Through long chapters of history, through the honoring of personal freedom, through the calling of a chosen people, through the act of incarnation, God has nudged humanity toward his appointed goal. The divine patience continues yet.

In his patience is our hope; in God's timing is the perfect fulfillment of all that he has promised. Can we then do any less than give patience its deserved and rightful place in the ordering of our lives? —John H. Townsend.

SUNDAY: FEBRUARY FIRST

MORNING SERVICE

Topic: The Children and Their Games
Text: Luke 7:31–35.

Luke the physician included in his Gospel story a parable in which the Master accused his contemporaries of acting like children. I call it the parable of the children and their games.

In what way were the religious leaders of Israel acting like children? Jesus is alluding to the fickleness of children as they played their games in the marketplace. One of the children would say, "Let's play like we're having a funeral." "No," the others would reply, "that's too depressing," "OK," the first child would respond, "Let's play like we're having a wedding." "No," the others would say, "That's too exciting."

To what was Jesus referring? He was referring to their response to John the Baptist and to him. The religious leaders of the day rejected John the Baptist on the one hand because he was too solemn and austere. Then they rejected Jesus on the other hand because he was too joyful and alive.

What was the point? The point was that they were acting like spoiled little children who could not be satisfied. The characteristic that Jesus was condemning was their childishness.

What qualities did Jesus have in mind when he accused the Pharisees of childishness?

I. *First, he was condemning their shallowness.*

(a) One of the limitations of children is their difficulty in discerning the real value of things. They see everything around them but they are not always able to discern the relative value of things.

(b) Both John the Baptist and Jesus were a part of the unfolding drama of God's redemption, John with his call to repentance, and Jesus with his joyous proclamation of the good news. However, in the shallow estimate of the religious leaders, their value was overlooked. Like children in the marketplace, the religious leaders played their games, oblivious to the value of the ones who came into their midst.

(c) How often that fault is duplicated in our day. One of the most obvious shortcomings of our day is our failure to recognize just how important Jesus really is.

In the midst of the details and demands of your life, don't ever lose sight of the importance of Christ, or you will be like the children playing their games in the marketplace.

II. *Second, he was condemning their self-centeredness.*

(a) The "if-you-don't-play-it-my-way-I'll-take-my-toys-and-go-home" attitude is a very real part of childhood. Fickle in temperament, children are often difficult to please if everything does not go according to their wishes. Why? Because their world revolves around themselves. They are at the center of their world.

(b) So it was with the religious leaders of Jesus' day. John and Jesus with their consuming zeal did not play the tune which the Pharisees wanted to hear. Thus they were summarily rejected by the Pharisees.

(c) How often that is repeated in our churches today. One of the most detrimental deficiencies of our day is our failure to put Christ at the center of our lives.

(d) In John 15:5 Jesus said, "I am the vine and you are the branches; he who abides in me, and I in him, he bears much fruit; for apart from me you can do nothing." Putting Christ in the center of your life, making Christ the top priority of your life, abiding in Christ, that is the key. There will be no fellowship with God, there will be no discipleship, there will be no growth, there will be no life, without that.

III. *Third, he was condemning their shortsightedness.*

(a) Another quality of childishness is the overwhelming power of the immediate. A child's life is bracketed by the boundaries of the immediate. Everything is evaluated and judged on the basis of the immediate needs. It is extremely difficult for a child to take the long look.

(b) We indeed must live in today. But we must never forget that the actions and choices and relationships and habits that we initiate today will have repercussions tomorrow. Hearing the challenge of the world, "Eat, drink, and be merry, for tomorrow you may die," we must remember that tomorrow we may live. And if we do, we will have to live with the ill effects of our promiscuous living today.

(c) What is true in the earthly, temporal realm of our lives is also true of the spiritual, eternal realm of our lives. Some here this morning have been so caught up with the living of our days on earth that you have never prepared for eternity.

(d) Will you dare to take the long look this morning?

If you have no answer for that question, then you are like the children playing in the marketplace, for you have played the most fatal game of all. You have played the game of life without ever preparing for eternity. Every person here this morning can get ready for eternity before you leave this service. It is so easy that anyone can do it. It is so essential that everyone must do it. Take your life, and open it up, and invite Christ to come in and take control. Then, you will no longer be like the children playing their games in the marketplace. You will be one of God's children, adopted into his forever family.—Brian L. Harbour.

Illustrations

OPENNESS TO GOD.   To be open to God is to be open to the world and all its happenings. It is to be accessible to its invitations, its intimations, its incessant creation, its breaking and re-forming of patterns, its probes and provocations, its restless movement and its clusters of events, its overtones, and its ponderous throb and surging cacophony. To be open to God is to take the world in your heart, to bear its burdens and suffer its mystery, to ponder its endless meanings even in the midst of contradiction and absurdity; and to listen, not only to the thousand echoes which reverberate between the heavens and the earth, but also to the still, small voice—the voice of stillness itself, the very word out of which all words come and by which all things were made—and thus to know at last the exciting peace that passes understanding.—Samuel H. Miller.

THE SIDESHOWS OF LIFE.   The cult of the sideshow is evidence of a sense of defeat, as is the denial of the validity of life itself. The meaning of life is not to be found in the denial of life. Medals have never been struck for those who ran—no matter how well—from the battlefront; nor has anyone found the elusive quality of happiness in life's sideshows. The sideshows are the false goals of life, and those who pursue these false goals require special techniques to attain them. We call such false patterns the neuroses.—W. Beran Wolfe.

Sermon Suggestions

RECEIVING AND GIVING. Text: Mic. 6: 1–8. (1) What God has done for us. (2) What God requires of us.

GOD'S FOOLISHNESS. Text: 1 Cor. 1: 18–31. (1) In the means of salvation that he chose. (2) In the people that he accepts for salvation.

Worship Aids

CALL TO WORSHIP. "Blessed are they that do his commandments, that they may have right to the tree of life, and may enter in through the gates into the city" (Rev. 22:14).

INVOCATION. O God, how can we worship you unless you put your praise into our hearts? How can we obey you unless the love of Christ constrains us? We confess our coldness of heart and ask you to "kindle a flame of sacred love" within us, so that we may glorify your name.

OFFERTORY SENTENCE. "And he said to them all, If any man will come after me, let him deny himself, and take up his cross daily, and follow me" (Luke 9:23).

OFFERTORY PRAYER. Ever-living and ever-giving God, you have made us a part of what you are doing in the world and have given meaning to our life here on earth. May the offerings that we bring, extensions of our strength and labors, enter into your purpose and bring blessing wherever they are used.

PRAYER. Our heavenly Father, we praise you for your infinite wisdom, while we stand in awe of the mystery of your ways. Again and again in the history of the world and in our personal and private stories you have proven that your way is best. Still, we often reluctantly conclude and confess that you have been at work in all things to accomplish your good and gracious purpose.

We thank you for the wisdom of the cross by which you have purchased our salvation and in which you freely give us all things. We thank you for the wisdom of our own cross, which we often fail to understand and even rebel against. Yet grant to us the grace not to crucify Christ afresh to ourselves by any reckless thought of your power to overrule our sins. And grant to us the grace not to add to the burden of the crosses that others must bear in their brave and costly discipleship. —James W. Cox.

EVENING SERVICE

Topic: Your Name on It
TEXT: Rom. 5:1–11.

A gift awaits you, a gift with your name on it.

In the commercial world this approach must work since so many mailings of this nature are made. But there must also be a lot of disappointment. Leaving the commercial world to its advertising gimmicks, I still say as I began that a gift awaits you, a gift with your name on it.

If it is not a car or a trip or a bundle of cash, what could it possibly be? Better by far than these things is the gift of divine grace. That gift is personalized; it has your correct name attached to it; its value is both immediate and eternal.

Exactly what is this royal treasure, this gift of grace, and what does it mean to you and me?

I. Fundamentally, grace is unconditional love.

(a) "Unconditional" is an uncommon circumstance in everyday society. Most experiences we confront are organized around various sets of conditions and requirements. If you and I meet certain qualifications, we are accepted; if we measure up to previously established standards, we can do or be something we desire. But there is always a threshold that must be passed; we must have at least minimum abilities or assets to make the grade. Rare is the situation where absolutely no conditions are imposed.

(b) The grace of God, by contrast, from start to finish is love without stipulation. No person has to prove his or her worthiness; before God there are no eligibility requirements. We do not have to be certified, somehow, in advance. Grace surrounds us at the instant we say, "Just as I am . . . I come to Thee."

II. Such all-embracing love is not sloppy or sentimental, however. There is a cross behind it.

(a) Grace means acceptance, not necessarily approval. We tread the realm of mystery here; St. Paul helps us as he writes, "The proof of God's amazing love is this, that it was while we were sinners that Christ died for us." Paul goes on to say, "Nor, I am sure, is this a matter of bare salvation—we may hold our heads high in the light of God's love because of the reconciliation which Christ has made."

(b) Divine grace means that God has come to us where we are, that we might attain to where God is, at one in mutual fellowship and relationship. Herein lies the reconciliation that Christ has made. All of this is less a matter of intellectual analysis than of personal experience. So it is that we perceive the shadow of a cross and the offering of a life. Subsequent resurrection blessing intervenes, however, encompassing each one who is prone to say, "Just as I am, without one plea, But that Thy blood was shed for me. And that Thou bid'st me come to Thee, O Lamb of God, I come, I come!"

III. The gift of grace with your name on it, the unconditional love of God that accepts you in your personal need becomes for you a source of power, an energy for daily living.

(a) How right we are to say we live by grace! We move across the tides and currents of everyday affairs with strength greater than our own. None of these things is perfectly attained, for our willfulness sometimes intervenes. But with each relaxation of our lives into the divine Life, fresh energy is given; new power comes.

Grace is the explanation for it—and right we are to rejoice in it.

(b) If you hesitate or wonder about it, think of some time of crisis or special need, in your experience or in that of someone known to you. How did you fare? Were you at the limit of your resources, exhausted and unable to continue? And then did some fresh strength come, some new insight or capacity to cope? In retrospect, the problem became no less severe, but somehow you found your way. You were the recipient of grace, in modest or abundant measure. The love of God did not let you go. That is what it means to say that grace is power; it is the spiritual energy by which we live.

IV. And once again, this gift of grace has your name on it. I enjoy thinking of it in terms of the story of Zacchaeus.

(a) Zacchaeus was a small man; in his village of Jericho he was a hated man because he was a tax collector. His wealth was made by exacting monies from the poor. Suffice it to say, in the words of his enemies, Zacchaeus was a sinner. Of course, in that role, he stood with all his peers and with you and me.

(b) Sinner though he was, Zacchaeus was attracted to Jesus. Upon learning that his unusual person was passing through Jericho, Zacchaeus climbed a sycamore tree to see him. Once in the high branches, this tax collector was astounded to hear his name called—by Jesus, who declared before everyone, "Zacchaeus, make haste and come down; for I must stay at your house today." And it happened! Jesus entered the home of the man whose name he called; before that visit was over, Zacchaeus was pledging his good to the poor and his loyalty to Christ. Jesus responded, "Today salvation has come to this house."

(c) In that story, two things are plain. First, Jesus knew Zacchaeus by name, and that meant Jesus had something for him. Second, Zacchaeus was open and receptive; he was ready for salvation, for help and renewal from on high. Accordingly, God's grace was given! And this man's story can be every person's story. When your name is spoken it means the gift of grace is there. Love without condition— costly in character yet abundant with power—awaits you; it has your name on it.

With Zacchaeus, with history's legions, will you join in saying," Just as I am . . . I come."—John H. Townsend.

SUNDAY: FEBRUARY EIGHTH

MORNING SERVICE

Topic: God Shows No Partiality
TEXT: Acts 10:34–35.

I. Peter began life as a Jew. Jewish-born and Jewish-bred. Peter dressed like his people, believed in his people, and thought like them as well.

(a) Acts 10 pinpoints a time of breakthrough on Peter's part. He would no longer see Gentiles from the perspective of his background only but through the eyes of God. Peter was being opened by God to meet non-Jews on a new basis and with a different attitude.

(b) Peter was only one of the many Jewish Christians who had to undergo a change in their thinking about Gentiles. I will not dwell at length on their particular feelings and prejudices. Suffice it to say that the first Jewish converts seem to have believed that Jesus had come only to and for them, that salvation was for them alone —and any Gentiles who would join them must come as proselytes to Jewish life and ways.

(c) All of this was in the background when Peter visited Centurian Cornelius and his Gentile prayer group. Peter said, "You yourselves know how unlawful it is for a Jew to associate with or to visit any one of another nation, but God has shown me that I should not call any man common or unclean." Those terms *common* and *unclean* were loaded words. Used in some spirited situation they could be a verbal put-down of a Gentile. But Peter was now moving beyond all that, informed by a fresh perspective on how God sees people.

II. It is no small matter when persons of differing social, national, or racial backgrounds meet.

(a) Many of the common opinions held by one group about another are not always the truth about that group; in fact, many common and popular opinions are not always wise, nor kind, nor right.

(b) It is no small matter when any persons meet. Attitudes are expressed. Differences are seen and felt, and they must be handled in some way. A wrong move or statement can make one suspicious, untrusting, or even inflamed. Human relations become critical at just such points as these.

(c) God had worked in a vision to ready Peter for this forward move in thought and life. God wanted him to be prepared for his encounter with Cornelius and his friends. God was concerned that Peter be tolerant, yes, but also that Peter would sustain an attitude of openness and acceptance. The contact with Cornelius was crucial. God had ordained that it take place. That vision on the roof was preparatory for Peter. The meaning and import of it was to do something deep and lasting in Peter's mind and heart.

III. Prejudices still hinder our Christian mission. They block our necessary witnessing. We Christians must deal with them and dispel them in the interest of our common life and given work.

(a) Prejudices must be dealt with firmly and forthrightly. We are freed from imprisoning prejudices only as we open ourselves to God's view, sound information, worthy facts, and a ready love.

(b) Given the delicate task of witnessing for Christ, we must do so with his spirit of openness and regard. We are not ready to meet people in his name if we are still locked up behind unhealthy views about them or preoccupied with feelings about our own supposed betterness.

(c) When we Christians meet persons who are different, Jesus expects us to take the contact seriously and handle it from the perspective of love. Christians must seek always to understand persons and support them. Humanity is but one lump of life, worked over by the hand of God, and all variations among races and nations are not to be regarded as unsurmountable walls.

At a time when so many people are on the move, across our national lands, and all across our world, let us use the increasing contacts with appreciation, wisdom, and timeliness. The contacts are our opportunity.

(d) If you and I are too self-conscious about the differences between ourselves and the people we confront we can hardly hide this from their view. The same is true about the air of condescension: it will show itself in our posing, and it will undermine the needed ease that generates acceptance.

Class-consciousness, nation-consciousness, race- and self-consciousness all make the ones with whom we are dealing uneasy; they threaten them, because no regard is shown for the experiences other people bring with them. We must remember that no one chooses his or her past; that past is given by circumstance and history. But everyone can choose a future. And this is why we witness to persons about Jesus.

IV. We are called to witness for Jesus, so caring and sharing that those who meet us will experience love and become insiders. This is demanding work, to be sure, but it is God's way.

(a) All of us who truly value God's way will remove every obstacle in ourselves to it. We will go beyond what we have learned from people and live by what God is teaching us.

(b) Jesus instructs patiently, removing our wrong ideas, opening doors for contact. As we supply our willingness, we learn. As we continue with him, he makes us more and more effective. Jesus must remove our wrong ideas about people if we are to become effective in meeting them in his name.—James Earl Massey.

Illustrations

AN ANCIENT PRECEDENT.   Some of the foremost leaders of the Jewish people, even David and Akiba, were descendants of men and women who were not of the house of Israel. R. Jeremiah said: "A gentile who lives a Godly life is like a High Priest. Whence can you know that a gentile who practices the Law is equal to the High Priest? Because it says, 'Which if a man do, he shall live through them.' And it says, 'This is the Law of man.' It does not say: 'the Law of Priests, Levites, Israelites,' but 'This is the Law of man, O Lord God.' It does not say, 'Open the gates and let the Priests, Levites, and Israelites enter,' but 'Open the gates that a righteous people may enter,' and 'This is the gate of the Lord, the righteous shall enter it.' It does not say, 'The Priests and the Levites and Israel shall enter it,' but it says 'The righteous shall enter it.' And it does not say, 'Rejoice ye, Priests and Levites and Israelites,' but it says, 'Rejoice ye righteous.' And it does not say, 'Do good, O Lord, to the Priests and the Levites and the Israelites,' but 'Do good, O Lord, to the good.' So even a gentile, if he practices the Law, is equal to the High Priest." "I call heaven and earth to witness that whether it be gentile or Israelite, man or woman, slave or handmaid, according to the deeds which he does will the spirit of God rest on him." One world, one family, one moral law—Judaism was the first religion of humankind to preach the universal peace. —Abba Hillel Silver.

OPENNESS TO OTHERS.   As surely as a sailing ship is made to sail with the wind, so are you and I and everybody else in this wide world over made to live bound to each other as a brother is bound to a brother, giving and receiving mercy, binding up each other's wounds, taking care of each other. If we really look at our own lives, seeing not what we expect them to be but what they are, we cannot help seeing that. Nobody can. It need not have been so. It can be imagined otherwise. We might have been made to live on self-interest or solitude or pure reason. Yet it is so.

So either we get up and move away somewhere, anywhere, as though we had never seen this greatest of all miracles. Or we kiss the flower that bows its head to us, embrace the bright wind that seeks to fill our sails, open our arms, our lives, to the deepest miracle of reality itself and call it by its proper name, which is King of kings and Lord of lords, or call it by any name we want, or call it nothing, but live our lives open to the fierce and transforming joy of it.—Frederick Buechner.

Sermon Suggestions

SELF-DENIAL THAT ACCOMPLISHES SOMETHING.   Text: Isa. 58:3–9a. (1) Self-denial is an honorable and effective way to spiritual health. (2) Self-denial of a kind may be a substitute for a more important religious duty. (3) A lifestyle of total discipline not only does the will of God but also brings rewards.

GOD'S SAVING TRUTH.   Text: 1 Cor. 2: 1–11. (1) It bursts the bounds of human eloquence. (2) It transcends the subtleties of human philosophies. (3) Its power lies in the weakness of the cross.

Worship Aids

CALL TO WORSHIP.   "There is no difference between the Jew and the Greek: for the same Lord over all is rich unto all that call upon him. For whosoever shall call upon the name of the Lord shall be saved" (Rom. 10:12–13).

INVOCATION.   Creator God, Lord of the universe, our Redeemer, answer us out of your riches as we call to you. Especially today help us to see the wealth that lies hidden in the persons we often ignore, strenuously avoid, or even hate—persons in whom your love as a priceless treasure may be found.

OFFERTORY SENTENCE.   "God is able to make all grace abound toward you; that ye, always having all sufficiency in all things, may abound to every good work" (2 Cor. 9:8).

OFFERTORY PRAYER.   O God, use our gifts to remove walls of suspicion, prejudice, and hate, and build a sanctuary of understanding, fellowship, and love throughout the world, through the good news of our Lord Jesus Christ, who has made us all one in himself.

PRAYER.   Save us, O God, from both hypocrisy and sentimentality in our attitude toward one who is not of our race. May we treat the person as a brother or sister acknowledging rights, recognizing differences, and having regard to the welfare of the whole human family.

Help us to recognize the value of things that divide us as well as the worth of things that unite us. Let not selfishness, pride, or power betray us into aloofness from any persons. Neither let us ignore the great basic fact of diversity in unity which thou hast written all over the universe. Grant to us, each one, that grace of heart and poise of mind that will enable us to contribute our little share toward a just and happy solution of the great race problems that so vex the world.—George W. Coleman.

EVENING SERVICE

Topic: Toward Healthy Race Relations
TEXT: Acts 17:26–27.

To anyone who can remember fifteen years ago, the status of race relations today in our country seems miraculous. People of different racial origins get along much better than they did even one generation ago. Yet vestiges of prejudice linger, and the Christian response is not simply to ignore the fact.

Race Relations Sunday, observed today in many churches, is the perfect opportunity for the church to look at this issue, apply its biblical witness, and take a stand. Obviously, a special observance only one day out of the year cannot bridge the racial gaps if no other emphases are given. The church must be careful to do all it can throughout the year to improve race relations.

Why should any church devote a special day to observe this relationship? Why is it so special as to claim an entire worship emphasis?

I. *Healthy race relations are biblical.* The Word of God deals repeatedly with the human tendency to exclude people. The Jews wanted to exclude the non-Jews; the Greeks, the non-Greeks. Racial prejudice, although not new, is condemned in the Bible. Acts 17:26–27 clearly states the issue in a Christian perspective. God is the Father of all humans. Therefore we have the right to discriminate against no one, because they are our brothers and sisters in Christ.

II. *Healthy race relations are humane.* Whatever is noble to humankind is in perfect harmony with the Christian ideal. Wholesome relationships among people of differing racial origins are certainly in keeping with Jesus' command to love others as we love ourselves.

To reject someone on the basis of skin color is cruel and inhumane. The Chris-

tian has no right to do so. This prejudice is immoral as well as illegal.

III. *Healthy race relations are necessary.* Our world is too small to divide it up along racial lines. People simply have to live together. Since this is true, does it not make sense that people of differing races should get along?

IV. *Healthy race relations are mutually beneficial.* People of differing races can teach each other such matters as their histories, culture, and traditions. We can learn much about other people if we will listen. That learning will enrich our lives.—Don M. Aycock.

SUNDAY: FEBRUARY FIFTEENTH

MORNING SERVICE

Topic: Power in Prayer
TEXT: Mark 11:24–25.

I. Jesus said, "If ye have faith and you say to the mountain, 'Be rooted up and be thrown into the sea,' and if you do not have wavering doubt in your heart and if you believe, it will be."

(a) Careful scholars have sought to understand this passage, sometimes to domesticate it, but usually to seek to comprehend it. Most of them point out that a mountain stands for an obstacle, and here it refers to an obstacle in the way of the kingdom of God. And so when you pray for the mountain to be rooted up and to be cast into the sea, you are asking that a significant obstacle be taken out of the path. It is pointed out that intentional exaggeration is present here in order to call forth a reaction of genuine, unrehearsed astonishment.

(b) So let us see if this great promise, and the companion statements about forgiveness, can become an actual formula for power in prayer in our personal lives, and not merely a revered text in our Bibles.

Let us also allow the excitement, and indeed the risk, of daring prayer to be something we will struggle with in our lives. For if you are like me in this matter, you may be tempted into what may be

called middle-class prayer—the kind of prayer that risks nothing, the prayer that is prayed in such cautious ways that no matter how things turn out, it will be all right. The Jesus prayer promise will not allow us to cozy up to middle-class prayer, for his formula is far more adventuresome and risking and dangerous. It requires far more faith.

II. The prayer promise says that if we pray and do not have hesitating, wavering doubts, our prayers will be answered.

(a) Some of us have some doubts about prayer and about our own experiences of prayer. We have felt, among other things, that we live in a scientific world, in a world where there is natural law and where such natural law hems in or reduces realistic spiritual possibilities. But I would remind us that science has stumbled onto unpredictability and that quantum physics has discovered that those tiny little dancers cavort to an ever-changing tune, that not all within physics is predictable from natural laws.

(b) Sometimes we may incline to say that we will only accept or believe something that is humanly possible, our parameters and boundaries in which we are willing to work. If so, then we had best not accept the universe. We'd better not accept the cosmos and the planets and the stars, because they are not humanly possible! If we pray and pray without wavering doubts, says Jesus, then our prayers will be answered.

III. We recognize from our personal experience that sometimes our prayers are not answered or are refused.

(a) But bear in mind it's hardly possible for us to know God or to know ourselves if we do not know and accept God's no.

We learn about God and about who we are as we experience God's refusal. What if he never refused? What if none of our prayers were left unanswered in the form in which we gave them? We would simply conclude that we were magicians if all our petitions were accepted. We might imagine or confuse ourselves with God when we found no limits to our wills.

(b) I would hasten to add that without God's yes, we would not know who God is or who we are either, for it is also in the power and the presence of a prayer that is answered, of God's presence that does come, that we know who God is and who we are. If the only response we knew from God were no, our daily life in slavery would be a bleak silence under a steel gray sky.

IV. Have you ever prayed and felt it was useless? Or have you ever prayed and felt somehow that you were not even being forgiven, much less heard?

(a) It may have been because there was a blockage between you and God. Indeed, the prayer may not have gotten through. The truth may very well be that you are not forgiven. The spiritual reality is there is little use to prayer as long as you stubbornly refuse to forgive! If you insist on keeping the walls between yourself and others, if you are hanging on to hate, then do not imagine that God is forgiving you. He is not. He will not.

(b) If you want power in prayer, forgive. If you want to be in touch with God, not only to receive what he has to give, but to touch the hand, forgive. Jesus promised. "The heavenly Father will forgive you." You will feel forgiven because you have found the freedom to forgive, and that in itself has freed you up.

(c) We are facing prayer not as some kind of spiritual escape but as a kind of spiritual moment of truth, for when we are quiet and still in a worship service or in a quiet place and we pray, we may recall those relationships that are broken. We may remember hostility and anger and hatred that exists between spouses, between a brother and a sister, between associates in an office, between members in a church, and until and unless the hostility is broken down, there cannot be real power in prayer. For breakthrough we need tolerance in understanding others as generous as the tolerance we display toward our own errors.

V. Sometimes realistically we have a struggle because we don't want to forgive. That's the bottom line; we don't want to do it. The sad thing about hate is what hate can do to the hater. Hate doesn't just damage the object. It damages the subject. The dangerous thing about bitterness, slander, wrath, malice, and the whole cargo that Paul urges us to jettison is that these attitudes eat away like acids.

(a) Breaking through the struggle and the intention to keep those hostilities in place can make a difference and can allow prayer to happen. It helps to remember how generously we have been forgiven by God, to remember what we have done, and to remember what Christ has done for us. Whatever your theology, the essence of the faith comes down sooner or later to the cross of Jesus Christ, and for the great truth that he has done something for us that we could not do for ourselves, and that even as he forgave the soldiers who drove nails in his hands, through his cross he forgives us of anything we have done.

(b) If you want power in prayer, it's not just a matter of how often you pray or whether you say the right words or have the right posture or psychologize yourself in some fashion. It is whether you have allowed the wall to go down and have known God's forgiveness, and whether there is faith in your heart when you pray. Such prayer will have power, because he promised.—Peter Rhea Jones.

Illustrations

LATENT ENERGY.   The coal and oil in the earth lay there for untold centuries as a source of power, but the power was potential and did not become actual until people developed skills that could transform it from its crude form to the refined states that were necessary for its use. Nuclear energy has been sustaining life on the face of the earth since its beginning, for the sun runs its heating and lighting facilities from this power source. But we knew little about it and, even though our lives depended upon it, we did not even begin to understand it. Only within recent decades have we gained some knowledge of this endless source of energy. It took the bringing together of the refined skills of many great intellects in mathematics, physics, and applied engineering to release this newly discovered source of power. Now we can use it or abuse it. Which it is will depend upon yet another form of power we must learn to use.—Edgar N. Jackson.

WRESTLING WITH GOD. When God yields to prayer in the name of Christ, to the prayer of faith and love, he yields to himself who inspired it, as he sware by himself since none was greater. Christian prayer is the Spirit praying in us. It is prayer in the solidarity of the kingdom. It is a continuation of Christ's prayer, which in Gethsemane was a wrestle, an *agonia* with the Father. But if so, it is God pleading with God, God dealing with God—as the true atonement must be. And when God yields it is not to an outside influence he yields, but to himself.—P. T. Forsyth.

Sermon Suggestions

THE RIGHT WAY. Text: Deut. 30:15–20. (1) To love God continuously. (2) To obey God when moral choices appear. (3) To cling to God in times of desperation.

THE SECRET OF SUCCESS IN CHRISTIAN SERVICE. Text: 1 Cor. 3:1–9. (1) We are workers together under God. Different workers with different roles can be equally important. (2) In the last analysis, our best work amounts to nothing apart from the blessing of God, who makes our work truly succeed. (3) Therefore, there is no room for jealousy and strife in the Christian community, since it is "only God who gives the growth."

Worship Aids

CALL TO WORSHIP. "Seek the Lord and his strength, seek his face continually" (1 Chron. 16:11).

INVOCATION. O Lord, we know that you are mighty and we are weak, but we take heart, knowing also that your strength is not only the power to make the mountains tremble, but also and especially the power of love. We come to you with trust, relying on your strength to do in and through us what we could never do in our own power. So fill us with renewed faith, hope, and love.

OFFERTORY SENTENCE. "Upon the first day of the week let every one of you lay by him in store, as God hath prospered him" (1 Cor. 16:2).

OFFERTORY PRAYER. God of grace, you have prospered each of us with enough to give at least a token of that with which you have blessed us. Help us to measure out our gifts by what we have received and by our fitting gratitude.

PRAYER. Our Father, we know that you love us. No gift of yours could be greater than the gift of your Son, the revelation of your love and the means of our salvation. Yet some of us come before you perplexed. We have prayed for one thing and received another or nothing at all. We have expected abundant life, yet life has become for us pinched and frustrated. Nevertheless, you have promised your help to those who cry to you. Grant that we may not look so longingly at doors closed that we cannot see other doors opening before us. Give us the grace to accept, if it is your will, some lesser good that we may discover at last to be what is best of all. Let us not be afraid to struggle with you in our disappointments, assured that you sometimes inspire us to pray bold, believing prayers that may seem to be defiant even of you. Yet may we always be prepared to say, "Not my will, but yours be done."—James W. Cox.

EVENING SERVICE

Topic: Claiming Your Call
TEXTS: Isa. 6:1–8; 2 Cor. 15:3–8, 11; Luke 5:1–11.

The word *vocation* comes from the Latin *vocare*, "to call," and means the work a man or woman is called to by God. The problem for me and for you is that there are all different kinds of voices calling you to all different kinds of work. The problem is to find out which is the voice of God rather than of society or the superego or self-interest. Finding the voice of God and acting on it is finding your vocation.

I. How does one go about finding the voice of God in your life?

(a) Our Scripture lessons today reveal some possibilities. We see the young man Isaiah, who has been in grief over the death of his beloved king Uzziah. God's voice speaks to him in a temple setting. From his own worship experience, his own expression of thanksgiving and confession, a personal call comes. Isaiah is allowed to see his part in the future history of Israel and to know his life's meaning. Isaiah heard clearly the call, "Whom shall I send? And who will go for us?" The choice of vocation was made for Isaiah when he responded, "Here am I, Lord, send me." The call of Isaiah was focused in the decision and response he made. BUT I WONDER—how many of us are like Isaiah and hear the voice of God so clearly?

(b) It seems that Jesus had his own peculiar way of calling disciples—men and women who would choose to follow him as their way of life, their work. Each Gospel writer tells the story differently. Luke's version of Jesus' calling disciples had to do with a miraculous catch of fish. As Jesus is teaching the crowds from a boat by a lake, he talked in riddles. As the fishermen complained about a poor catch, Jesus consoled them, telling them not to bother: they would soon be catching people! As if to assure them, he urged them to cast their nets once more. The nets were dropped over the sides of the boats and hauled back in teeming with fish. The fishermen were convinced that this Jesus was from God— a miracle worker. They dropped their nets, gave up fishing for a living, and followed him. Other men and women also heard the voice of God in the miracles of God's divine action that surrounded them. BUT I WONDER—how many of us hear the voice of God concerning our vocation through miraculous action today?

II. Is it possible that God speaks to most of us today in a different way about our calling—our life's work? I believe it is not only possible, but probable.

(a) Frederick Buechner in his book *Wishing Thinking* has given us a good rule for finding the voice of God in our work. He shares: "The kind of work God usually calls you to is the kind of work (a) that you need most to do and (b) that the world most needs to have done."

(b) If we are to find and hear the voice of God in our vocational search, we must know what it is we want. We must have self-esteem and a sense of worth, which God intends for us. Without a basic sense of who we are, we cannot be stewards of the talents God gave us.

(c) Career and life planning deals with much more than what one does between nine and five on weekdays. Ideally, the search for vocation deals with one's whole life mission, one's life role, and one's lifelong identity. Vocation in our time means identifying one's goals, calling, values, and priorities—and yes, hearing the voice of God woven throughout the process.

III. A myriad of voices calls us to consider our place in the world of work. We will be advised and urged, cajoled and tempted to choose many options.

(a) Such a call might not come in a burst of recognition. It might not come through years of trying on life's experiences. But it will come. For we are chosen by God, called by God, named by God, and claimed by God. It is our lifelong task to choose God as our own, to call God into our lives, to name God as Creator, Redeemer, and Sustainer, and to claim our life as a gift to be shared with the world.

(b) I believe that finding our own calling will not be enough. To hear the voice of God in our lives is not enough. To claim the call of God, to act on it, to live with it, to rejoice in it, is our *vocation.* May it be so with all of us.—Charlene Kammerer.

SUNDAY: FEBRUARY TWENTY-SECOND

MORNING SERVICE

Topic: Life's Indispensable Portion
TEXT: 1 Cor. 13:1–13.

It is a commonly known fact that most of us confuse cultural possessions with religion. Not only do we confuse them, but we substitute them for religion on the assumption that they are more realistic, more sincere, and in this kind of world, more relevant.

The thirteenth chapter of 1 Corinthians shatters this illusion. This famous chapter is more than a romantic lyric on love. It is a rugged bit of philosophy with which the Apostle Paul does not hesitate to challenge our easy assumptions. He means to say that nothing in this world is worthwhile unless it has the spark of divine life. Without this spark of divine life, all else is incomplete.

I. Life is not worth living unless it possesses the spark of divine life. That is precisely what Paul says: "If I speak with the tongues of men and of angels, but have not love . . . it profiteth me nothing."

(a) There are people who believe that culture is a spiritual characteristic and performs spiritual functions. It has frequently been the self-apportioned prerogative of cultured people to think of themselves as having found a highway that leads straight to the city of God. And why not? Culture means much that religion also means. It is never provincial; it is always tolerant. It is never supercilious; it is always democratic. It invariably observes the amenities of life. And yet there is nothing more deceiving in this world than culture.

(b) A man tells me that he has no need of religion since he has many cultural interests. He reads much; he is a lover of good music. But what of it? Paul remarked rather ruthlessly, "Though I speak with the tongues of men and of angels, but have not love . . . it profiteth me nothing." Modern man is gullible. In trusting entirely to culture, he yields in fact entirely to his own vanity. We have need of culture; indeed, more culture than the world

has ever possessed. But culture left to itself is peculiarly sterile.

II. The Apostle Paul comes closer to our thinking when he says, "If I know all knowledge . . . but have not love, it profiteth me nothing."

(a) Here, many will say, is at last something that one can understand. A great many people do not know what to make of culture anyhow. But they do understand knowledge. It is practical; it has its tangible uses. As a matter of fact, all of us have staked our individual and national fortune upon knowledge. We have said, "Give people the facts and that will be enough for them. If people only understood, they would do this or they would not do that." Many of us have made education an instrument of social salvation.

(b) Never has there been more knowledge than there is today. It has been made available to more people than ever before. There are more books in our world than we can read. More information reaches us over the radio and through the public forum of the press than we can heed. Scientific knowledge is fabulous. Knowledge seems to be the key to every mystery and the open sesame to peace and every kind of economic security.

(c) Knowledge is indispensable, but it is not enough. We need to learn that there is no infallible knowledge, but there are infallible judgments, and that is exactly what the world needs. Beyond our technical understanding and erudition, we must now have a divine spark of wisdom wherein we learn what to do with the knowledge we possess. Once we learn that, hope will sit enthroned. Once we learn that, the road to social progress will be wide open. One does not learn that at universities; one learns that in the school of the spirit.

III. Now Paul leads us into deeper waters. He turns from culture and knowledge to religion. Can it be that we substitute religion for spiritual experience? That, at any rate, is what he intimates: "If I have all faith, so as to remove mountains, but have not love, it profiteth me nothing."

(a) That is disturbing, for here the apostle speaks of religion as ruthlessly as he has spoken of other matters. Religion is not enough. It also needs a divine fire. The world does not lack for religion. Probably because of that it has always resented the austerity of religion and its sheer formality.

(b) Religion is frequently absorbed within itself. It merely drives its own machinery. It propagates nothing; it creates nothing. That may be one reason why so many people rebel against it. To them it is all church, all ritual, all dogma, and all preachers; and all of them together do not add up to what religion ought to be. It takes more than that. Beyond intellectual satisfactions, it must have something to say to the heart. It must have this divine spark.

(c) After all, what is religion? It is the sharing with others of something that we have found. It floods our lives with quiet strength when we are frightened and can no longer hear anything in the world except the pounding of our own hearts. It is not long prayers. It is the other thing—the swift impulse. It is prayer that goes beyond petition. It is deeper than all words; it is sensing the hidden things of God. It is religion with a divine flame.

IV. The apostle has one more word to say: "You who substitute your generosity for religion, you, too, must hear me." "If I bestow my gifts upon the poor, but have not love, it profiteth me nothing."

(a) You see how tenaciously he clings to this one thought. He will not let us go. Here, indeed, we come to the most difficult portion of Paul's insistence. Many a good man has confused his generosity with his spiritual life or his religion. It is here where modern man is most likely to rebel, for he has long since believed that goodness and generosity and kindness and religion are merely different words for the same thing.

(b) People have given fortunes though they have little of the spirit of Christ. People have become martyrs and not made one soul better by their martyrdom. People have been generous and yet not lifted one person to a higher plane. Generosity that is not charged with compassion is an empty gesture. It may fill our stomachs; it will not put light in our eyes. It may warm our houses; it will not put a song in our hearts.

(c) After all, to receive and give the divine spark is the purpose of Christianity. The other day, I heard a little girl turn to her grandmother and say, "Granny, I know how to blow my trumpet without making a sound." I have thought a great deal about that young lady. Many of us are very much like her. We have learned to blow the trumpet without making it sound. That is what we have been doing with our Christianity. We have been Christians and nothing has come of it. Is it because we have lacked this divine spark? Is it because there is not divine fire in our faith? Is it because there is no wisdom in our knowledge and no tenderness in our generosity? Let us read Paul's great chapter once more. Love, the divine fire that God kindles within us and thereby makes bright all our possessions and talents, becomes life's indispensable portion. Without this fire, we are mere men and women walking through the dark and knowing only that life is a burden; but with it, culture, knowledge, religion, generosity become transformed and life takes on radiance.—Arnold H. Lowe.

Illustrations

A CRITICAL TURNING POINT. Psychologically and in principle, the precept *Love your enemies* is not self-contradictory. It is merely the extreme limit of a kind of magnanimity with which, in the shape of pitying tolerance of our oppressors, we are fairly familiar. Yet if radically followed, it would involve such a breach with our instinctive springs of action as a whole, and with the present world's arrangements, that a critical point would practically be passed, and we should be born into another kingdom of being. Religious emotion makes us feel that other kingdom to be close at hand, within our reach.—William James.

RETURNING GOD'S LOVE. Saint Catherine of Siena was asked by one of her nuns, "How can I pay God back for all of his goodness to me? How can I give back to God some glory for all his kindness, his love, his mercy, his generosity?" Saint Catherine answered, "It won't do you any good to do any more penances. It won't do you any good to build the great church, because God has the whole world as his sanctuary. It won't do you any good to add any more quiet time in prayer. But I tell you something which you can do to really pay God back for the love he gives you. Find someone as unloveable as you are, and give that person the kind of love that God has given you." When we try this prescription we grow spiritually.—Morton T. Kelsey.

Sermon Suggestions

OPEN YOUR HEARTS WIDE! Text: Isa. 49:8–13. (1) Because God has done great things for you. (2) Because you can do great things for others.

THE DUTY OF RELIGIOUS TEACHERS. Text: 1 Cor. 3:10–11, 16–23. (1) To build on the true and only foundation—Jesus Christ. (2) To be reverent in dealing with God's temple—the church. (3) To help Christians enjoy their freedom—in God.

Worship Aids

CALL TO WORSHIP. "By this shall all men know that ye are my disciples," said Jesus, "if ye have love one to another" (John 13:35).

INVOCATION. God of love, teach us anew the meaning of love. Help us to empty our minds of cheap, sordid imitations and give us a vision of the real thing, as we reflect on what your love for us is like.

OFFERTORY SENTENCE. "As we have therefore opportunity, let us do good unto all men, especially unto them who are of the household of faith" (Gal. 6:10).

OFFERTORY PRAYER. Lord, you have given us many opportunities to do good to others, and we thank you now for this op-

portunity. Bless these offerings, so that those whose lives are touched by what we do may bless your holy name.

PRAYER. Eternal God, whose purpose and whose laws pervade this vast universe, and make of it one world, we worship thee. We too in our personal lives need the wholeness and harmony which thou alone canst bring. From our confused and random living we would turn to thee to have our soul unified and made whole. Against all that divides our lives, scatters them, and makes them futile with confusion we pray to thee this day. Unite our hearts to serve thy will with single-minded devotion.

Grant us purposefulness, we beseech thee. Forgive us for our aimless living, for all the scattered devotion of our lives to things that matter little or not at all. Help us to discover a purpose in life so worth the soul's dedication that all our existence shall be drawn together about a central loyalty.

Give us faith, O God, faith in values so beautiful and good that our lives will be drawn into unity by our vision and love of them. Save us from cynicism, from skepticism, from all those maladies of the mind and moods of the spirit that spoil our lives, and help us this day to see thy will for us, excellent and august, beautiful and elevated, that we may believe in it and so be unified.

Give us love, O Lord. Bestow upon us the fine gift of friendliness. Forgive us for the way we tear our lives apart with our angers and hatreds. Teach us once more, Spirit of the Christ, that when we hate we do ourselves more harm than we do our enemies. Draw us together into unity because thou plantest good will at the center of our lives.

As thus we pray for those forces that draw our lives together and against those evils that scatter them in careless living, so we pray for those powers that draw our societies together. God forgive us for the prejudices and hatreds whereby we have cut asunder our humanity and have made of what might have been an earthly paradise a hard and bitter place.—Harry Emerson Fosdick.

EVENING SERVICE

Topic: Forgiveness of the Unworthy
TEXT: Mark 2:1–12.

I. Among the incidents of healing, some were more significant than others. One of the most significant concerned a paralyzed man who was healed in Capernaum. The significance lay in the fact that the condition of release was a sense of forgiveness, and this Christ gave the poor man in the most explicit terms. Sensing that the man was harassed by unresolved feelings of guilt, Christ began by telling him that his sins were already forgiven.

II. It is clear that the assertion of forgiveness was even more offensive to the Pharisees than was Christ's message of the kingdom or even his acts of healing. Forgiveness, especially when applied to the obviously unworthy, is a direct threat to any purely legal system. It plays havoc with any conception of the necessity of equality between deeds and punishment. The scribes, when they heard the assertion of forgiveness, faced only two alternatives; either they had to declare unending war on Christ or they had to learn to say humbly with the publican of the parable, "God be merciful to me a sinner." Their decision was to declare war, a war which led ultimately to the crucifixion, and their first warlike act was to accuse Jesus of blasphemy.

III. Christianity is meaningless apart from the centrality of forgiveness. The kingdom of Christ is not for the good and righteous people, though forms of goodness are a result of it, but rather for the people who know that they are not good. The gospel does not say, as we tend to say today, "Be good, and you will become worthy of meeting God." It says, instead, "Repent, and unacceptable as you may be, you are accepted." A religion that demands concrete evidence of goodness as a precondition of salvation is a religion of impossible burden. Consequently, Christ makes no such demand, but begins with sinners as they are. If forgiveness is real, each life can make a new redemptive start each day.

IV. There are people who say they do not need to make a vocal witness, because, as they express it, they "just let their lives speak." This appears to be humility, but is really self-righteousness. No person's life is good enough to speak with any adequacy. Christ himself indicated this when he put into his pattern prayer the phrase, "Forgive us our sins as we forgive those who sin against us." He expected this prayer to be endlessly necessary, so long as we are in this life. The entrance into Christ's kingdom is by the continual rebirth of the sinner into the fellowship of the forgiven. The redemptive fellowship, on which Christ necessarily depends, is made up of those whose first qualification for membership is the recognition that they are unworthy of membership.—Elton Trueblood.

SUNDAY: MARCH FIRST

MORNING SERVICE

Topic: A Glimpse of His Glory
TEXT: Mark 8:34–9:7.

At Caesarea Philippi, Jesus shocked his followers with two staggering blows. First, he confronted them with the indispensability of the cross for the achievement of his mission. Then, having introduced the disciples to the nature of his messiahship, Jesus proceeded to stagger them further by relating this messianic mission to the conditions of their discipleship. Since as disciples they were called to follow him, they, too, would share in the cross to which he went (Mark 8:34).

I. *The cross (Mark 8:34–9:1)*. The cross in a Christian's life is one of the most misunderstood realities in contemporary religion. This passage points us in the right direction by linking our cross to the cross of Christ.

The cross must mean to us precisely what it meant to him. The cross is often taken to refer to the defeats, failures, and frustrations of life. But such is the common lot of every person. There is nothing distinctively Christian in enduring such hardships. In the New Testament, the cross is a thing of victory, strength, and power. Thus the fundamental question is to inquire realistically into the meaning of the cross for Christ. At least three things begin to emerge from such a study of the Gospels.

(a) First is the fact that Jesus dies as a result of human sin. It was a monstrous eruption of unchecked iniquity that put him on the cross. The uncompromising character of his life had provoked a hornet's nest of sin, and in fury sin stung him until he was dead. He challenged their superficial hypocrisy, he rode roughshod through all their precious regulations, he left deep tracks in the smooth surfaces of their traditionalism and formalism, he laughed at their petty legalisms, he forgave their unforgivable harlots, he ate with their outcasts, he touched their untouchables, he hung out their hatreds on the line for all to see. Singed by the white flame of holiness that burned so brightly in his life, they determined to do him in. For he was a standing challenge to the prejudices, the bigotries, the strictures, and the cleavages of their culture.

In like manner, we participate in the true meaning of Christ's cross when we engage in a never-ending struggle with sin. Each of our lives needs to stand as an effrontery to evil. We must never turn aside, never dodge an issue, never compromise an inch. Rather, let us track sin to its lair and expose its rot and slime even when it festers beneath robes of respectability. In every situation we are called to confront the lowest levels of human degradation with the transcendent will of God.

(b) In the second place, Christ met a cross because he refused to compromise with sin. Thus he met sin at a deeper level of crisis than others could ever know. For no matter how passionately we oppose sin, finally we fall before its temptations. Sin never needs to go to the limit with us as it did with him. Yet, in such a showdown, he never turned aside, never compromised, never rationalized. Thus, his whole attitude made the cross inevitable. The plain fact is that he would die rather than sin.

So for us, the cross is not only the struggle in conflict with sin; it is also the sting of what sin will do when we refuse to turn aside.

(c) Finally, Jesus accepted the cross as an instrument of conquest over sin. It was the most purposeful thing he ever did. Setting his face steadfastly like a flint, nothing could deflect him from the showdown in Jerusalem (Luke 9:51). This would be God's great redemptive deed. For his cross would unleash that spiritual power that comes when sin had met its master.

For us, the cross is not a fate that we grimly accept. Rather, it is that fierce demonstration to all the world that when sin is at its ugly worst, God is at his redeeming best. The paradox of salvation is that sin is defeated by meeting its vicious, destructive power with the weakness of obedient love. The heart is changed only when someone is willing to endure shame—indeed, to lose life itself—for no reason than to be true to the spirit of the Son of Man.

II. *The crown.* But the picture was not one of unrelieved gloom. Just as Jesus would suffer and be killed, only to rise again (8:31), even so, despite their sufferings, some of the disciples would see the kingdom of God come with power in their day (9:1). The parallelism is unmistakable: through defeat to victory would be the paradox of his life and of theirs.

After Peter's confession, Jesus not only began, but continued to teach, that rejection, suffering, and death faced both himself and those who followed him. In the face of this shattering prospect, the disciples desperately needed courage, some unforgettable demonstration of God's approval of Jesus' plan, some assurance of victory in this apparently mad scheme.

(a) Thus, a few days later (9:2), as they were traveling south, Jesus took aside the leaders of the disciple band and permitted them to share with him an experience of glory.

Three details are recorded in describing the incident of the transfiguration, each of which makes clear that the disciples were permitted to share in a situation that was reminiscent of the glorious end of the world. The first was the transformation of Jesus into a shining figure of light (9:3). At once the disciples would be reminded of current Jewish hopes that pictured the expected Messiah as possessing such glorious attributes. Secondly, the appearance of Elijah and Moses (9:4) recalled the fact that these two figures, more than any others, were expected to return at the end of the world. Both had ended their earthly lives in a supernatural manner; thus it was easy to suppose that they would return as heralds of glory (2 Esd. 6:26). In the third place, the suggestion of Peter that three tabernacles be constructed (9:5) referred to the Jewish expectation that God would again pitch his tent with his people as he had done in the Exodus.

(1) However, the disciples misunderstood the meaning of such glory. In the very midst of his response to the situation (9:5), Peter was interrupted by the overshadowing presence of God out of which a voice came directing the disciples, not to perpetuate this ideal existence, but rather to go on listening to him who was the beloved Son (9:7). The unworthiness of Peter's foolish request moved Mark to add these words, "For he did not know what to say, for they were exceedingly afraid" (9:6).

(2) What was wrong with Peter's request? He had again failed to realize the price that must be paid before the glory of God could tabernacle among sinful humanity. Peter may have longed to return to the happiness of his early discipleship before the cross had been announced, or to escape from the conflict into a heavenly bliss, or to advance at once into the peace of the last days. God instead demanded that he and the other leaders of the disciple band go on listening to the Son.

(b) Two groups participated directly in this mountaintop experience: one was Jesus, the other was the three disciples. The incident must have had somewhat different meanings for each.

(1) For Jesus, the transfiguration was, like his baptism, a divine confirmation of his decision to walk the way of the cross. In the transfiguration experience, God ratified his act of faith and indicated once again that his approval rested on the one who walked such a way.

(2) The primary purpose of the transfig-

uration, however, was for the disciples. Here they were permitted to see an authentication of the announcements which Jesus had been making. He had said, despite rejection, suffering, and death, he was indeed the Son of Man who would rise from the dead. Here they were given a glimpse of that future glory. The multitudes had viewed Jesus as a prophet like unto Moses or as the new Elijah. Here, however, these two figures appeared to pay their homage to Jesus, and to indicate clearly that he was not the forerunner who would die a martyr's death, but that he was the Messiah who would die a death of glory. Thus, in the agonizing days that lay ahead, the disciples were able to find renewed strength in the memory that God had already vindicated the sacrifice of his Son. Even if but for a moment, they had been permitted to see the end from the beginning.

III. *No cross—no crown.* At first sight, it might appear that the transfiguration is totally irrelevant to our modern times. However, like the disciples, we are faced with the prospect of many a cross. Like them, we are tempted to wonder if God is really at work in his world, if righteousness is really stronger than evil, if it is really worth it to be faithful.

(a) But lest pessimism feed despair, God has not left himself without a witness. In more ways than one he permits his children to glimpse at least an intimation of the glory that is to be revealed. For those who have eyes to see, there is the light of heaven breaking behind the shadows of the cross. On the landscape of life there are just enough mountaintop experiences to give the strength to trudge the lonesome valley (cf. Isa. 40:31).

(b) Your mount of transfiguration may be a revival meeting, or a summer retreat at a conference center, or a crisis experience involving the death of a loved one. The place is not important, but it is crucial to experience those breakthroughs that anticipate the glory of the future and so confirm the sufferings of the past and present. Keep climbing the mountain until you behold Christ in all his radiance, then turn from that summit to walk with him to a cross in Jerusalem. As Christians, we are not exempt from the struggle with sin, but we are permitted to fight in the confidence that, no matter how dark the outcome may seem, a greater weight of glory awaits those who are faithful in the fray.—William Hull.

Illustrations

OUR CROSS.   The threefold condition of discipleship—deny self, take up one's cross, and follow Jesus—is a single condition, for the first two terms define and specify the third.

The call is not to deny oneself something, but to deny self. Asceticism can hand the victory to the self, for "self can ride as comfortably on a bicycle as in a limousine." Nor is the call to reject oneself. Self-hatred is not the way of Jesus, but a denial of the grasping self to liberate the greater one.

The cross Jesus invites his hearers to take up refers not to the burdens life imposes from without but rather to painful, redemptive action voluntarily undertaken for others. Lamar Williamson, Jr.

GLORY.   The present life of the Christians is lived in reference to the future glory. The thought of the apostles does not begin with the present and pass on to the eschatology as a kind of further stage. It begins with the eschatology, intent upon the coming parousia; and then it perceives that the eschatology is being anticipated in the here and now, and that the glory of the parousia seems to throw its light backwards upon the present life of the Church. We have seen how vividly the first epistle of Peter shows us the Church looking forward to the parousia and discovering that the glory already rests upon it in the midst of its suffering. So too Paul teaches that there is an anticipated glory wrought in the Christians by the Holy Spirit as an earnest or foretaste of the glory to come.—Arthur Michael Ramsey.

Sermon Suggestions

WHAT IT MEANS TO BE HOLY.   Text: Lev. 19:1–2, 9–18. (1) It means bearing a spe-

cial relationship to God. (2) It implies behaving in a special way toward God's people.

IN WHOSE COURT ARE WE TRIED?   Text: 1 Cor. 4:1–5. (1) Not in the court of public opinion. (2) Not in the court of private judgment. (3) But in the court of the all-wise God.

Worship Aids

CALL TO WORSHIP.   "We all, with open face beholding as in a glass the glory of the Lord, are changed into the same image from glory to glory, even as by the Spirit of the Lord" (2 Cor. 3:18).

INVOCATION.   Eternal God, thou who are able to relate eternity and time in a manner that we do not understand, bring to bear on our time this day thy eternal plan for thy world and help us to see how our lives, which are a gift from thee, may be best invested. They are all too brief, Father. Help us to use our time—even in this hour of worship—wisely.—J. Estill Jones.

OFFERTORY SENTENCE.   "The silver is mine, and the gold is mine, saith the Lord of hosts" (Hag. 2:8).

OFFERTORY PRAYER.   As we call thee Lord, help us to be aware of thy universal lordship and to know that because all things are thine, all things are ours also, for we are thy family. Grant that we may live and share as thy loving children.

PRAYER.   Dear Father in heaven, we come to you; and we want to come with thanksgiving; for you bless us again and again in many ways; again and again your light bursts forth, so that we can rejoice and say: Our life is in your hand. Watch over us especially, so necessary on this earth, so that here more and more the light of the true life may appear and that we may praise your name, as much as lies within us. Be with us and let your Spirit quiet our hearts.—Adapted from Christoph Blumhardt.

EVENING SERVICE

Topic: We Have No Bread

TEXT: Mark 8:14–21.

Since it was customary to take bread with them on a journey the disciples were quite concerned when they discovered they had forgotten to buy the bread they needed for the trip. All they had with them was a loaf of stale bread, which was the equivalent of a day's ration for a prisoner. They needed three loaves per person for the day and without it they faced serious hunger.

I. Human hunger isn't a modern phenomenon that first arose with the high unemployment of the past several years. It's an age-old problem. Hunger is no longer limited to the chronically unemployed. The new class of poor and hungry are the once well-off who have lost their jobs, and for whom unemployment benefits have been exhausted. It still exists in spite of the recent economic upturn, but as long as it doesn't touch us personally we seem to feel reasonably secure. But the fact is, we can get a pink slip at any time, and we can soon face the same words uttered by the disciples in the boat: "We have no bread" (Mk. 8:16b).

II. As the disciples discussed their precarious situation quietly among themselves, Jesus was well aware of it. Mark says he "asked them, 'Why do you discuss the fact that you have no bread?'" (Mk. 8:17a). It was natural to discuss their lack of bread. Even though they were in the boat with Jesus they were unaware of his awareness. He was letting them know by his question that he was aware of all their most pressing needs. He's always aware.

Jesus asks us to come to a distinct understanding of himself. When we're in need of bread and food, he nudges us to look beyond these to the one who made the bread. "Do you not yet understand?" Jesus asks. He wants our faith to rest in him instead of in the goods he uses to supply our needs. If our faith rests merely in the food he gives us instead of in him personally, it's shallow and unstable.

III. Jesus can supply our needs even when the material means seem severely limited. The one loaf of bread didn't offer the disciples any hope, especially when they needed a minimum of three loaves per person, but Jesus was waiting for them to present their problem to him. His heart goes out to hungry and hurting people, and he enables us to bring all of our problems and needs directly to himself. The personal testimony of Peter thirty years after this scene, during a time of severe persecution, confirms this: "Cast all your anxiety on him," he said, "for he cares about you" (I Pet. 5:7).

(a) His care reaches through us to the hungry and hurting people around us as we become his instruments in meeting their needs. He wants us to share our bread with people from the outside, but the problem with helping people is they sometimes, in severe deprivation, tend to isolate themselves. The disciples detached themselves inwardly from Jesus in the discussion of their lack of bread but he took the initiative in helping them to bring the problem to him. Hungry and deprived people need us to take the initiative sometimes in helping them to help themselves. And this offers the church one of its greatest opportunities.

(b) "Do you remember?" Jesus asked the disciples; bread wasn't the only thing they had forgotten. They had forgotten the meaning of his feeding both the five thousand and the four thousand. He was reminding them of the huge crowd of people present on both occasions when it came time to eat. Late one day they had only five loaves and two fish among the thronging crowd of five thousand people, but he blessed the bread, broke it, passed it around, and "they all ate and were satisfied" (Mk. 6:42c). "How many baskets full of broken pieces did you take up?" he asked. "Twelve," they said. He had fed another four thousand people in the same way. "How many baskets full of broken pieces did you take up?" "Seven," they said (Cf. Mark 8:19–21). They had forgotten that God has always supplied his people with meat, bread, and water (Cf. Exod. 16:12–22) just as they had forgotten to bring bread with them and failed to see and understand his providence among them.—James W. Fair.

SUNDAY: MARCH EIGHTH

MORNING SERVICE

Topic: When Judgment Comes

TEXT: Amos 2:4–8, 11–12.

Some of the most colorful characters in the Bible are those men known as prophets. The primary duty of a prophet was to speak forth the word of God to his own generation. Prophets were not so much foretellers as they were forth-tellers, proclaiming God's word to their own generation.

One of the prophets was the man known as Amos. His ministry was very brief. About him one commentator has suggested, "Never has so much momentous history been packed into such a brief space of time."

I. First of all, let's consider the man. What do we know about Amos?

(a) We know that his name Amos comes from the Hebrew word *amas*, which means to carry. Thus his name literally means "burden bearer." That is a fitting name, because this prophet bore on his heart a burden for the poor and mistreated of Israel.

(b) His father's name is not mentioned, which probably indicates that he was of very humble birth. He grew up in a town named Tekoa, about six miles south of Bethlehem.

Amos tells us that he was a herdsman of sheep and goats. His secondary occupation was a dresser of sycamore trees.

(c) When did Amos prophesy? The opening verse of the book associates him with the reigns of King Uzziah of Judah, the Southern Kingdom, and King Jeroboam in Israel, the Northern Kingdom. The precise date was probably around 760 B.C.

II. What was his message? His message was a message of judgment.

(a) Amos offered eight indictments in which the offender was first named, followed by specific charges, leading to a pronouncement of the penalty.

As Amos lambasted the first six nations with the message of judgment, those who were from Judah, the Southern Kingdom, and Israel, the Northern Kingdom applauded his message. In chapter 2:4, Amos turned the spotlight on Judah and Israel. In 2:4–5, Amos declared that God's judgment also will come upon Judah. The charge against Judah is that it has despised the law of God.

(b) All of this sets the stage for what is Amos's main point, which is the pronouncement of God's judgment upon Israel, the Northern Kingdom. It is this central message that we see in our text.

I want you to be aware of the context of this message of judgment. It was not a time of despair in Israel but a time of comfort and ease. The nation was prospering in every way: politically, economically, and even religiously. It was in that time that Amos brought the message of God's judgment, for lurking underneath the surface in Israel were some serious problems, which the prophet uncovered.

(c) The people of Israel believed that God was ready to bless them. The prophet declared that God was ready to judge them. Then he explained the reasons why.

(1) Amos pronounced judgment on Israel, first of all, for its social injustice.

Amos condemned his contemporaries in v. 7 "because they sell the righteous for money and the needy for a pair of sandals." The reference to selling the righteous for silver refers to bribing a judge to pronounce an innocent person guilty. They used their money to oppress those who had none.

The reference to a pair of sandals perhaps reflects the practice of passing a shoe from one party to another when a piece of property was sold (as in Ruth 4:7). If this was the case, they were probably using corrupt means and intimidation to take from the poor what land they had.

The prophet carried the indictment further in v. 7 where he accused them of trampling the head of the poor into the dust. God's people had become more concerned with things than they were with people. They loved money and used people to make more of it instead of loving people and using money to meet their needs.

(2) Second, Amos pronounced judgment on Israel for sexual immorality.

God had given Israel specific instructions concerning the proper use of the gift of sex. The regulations in God's law concerning sex were not given because the sexual drive is wrong but because it is strong and needs to be controlled. But God's people had become more concerned with pleasing themselves than they were with pleasing God. They were guided by the desires and dictates of their society instead of by the desires and dictates of their God.

When we allow the world to set our standards of morality and lose our sexual control, then we have become guilty of the same sin for which Amos condemned Israel.

(3) Third, Amos pronounced judgment on Israel for its spiritual insincerity.

Amos declared in verse 8, "They lie down beside every altar on garments taken in pledge. In the house of their god they drink wine taken as fine."

The garments taken in pledge were those which the rich had taken from the poor for collateral for loans. The law specified that such pledges were to be returned to the owners by sundown so that they might have covering during the night. The men of Israel, on the contrary, kept the garments for their own personal use. The wine that was used in worship was that which they had taken from the poor.

Here is the point of the prophet's indictment. The Israelites came to worship, but they smelled of their rebellion to God. Their bodies were at the place of worship, but their hearts were still in the world. They went through the motions of being religious, but they did not really mean it. They were insincere.

III. What does all of this mean?

(a) First, it is a warning. The fact that we are God's people does not exempt us from judgment. In fact, God's judgment begins with us. Every person here this morning needs to allow the spotlight of God's holiness to examine your life.

(b) The message of Amos means something else. It is a reminder that all sins are serious to God. We have a tendency to categorize sins into big sins and little sins, serious sins and trivial sins, and our sins are the little, trivial ones. In addition, sins of the flesh are the ones we usually consider the big sins. When we keep these out of our lives, we think we are okay. Not so, says the prophet of God. Social injustice and spiritual insincerity are just as serious, just as unacceptable to God as is the sin of sexual immorality. All sin is serious to God.

(c) The message of Amos carries yet another meaning. The prophet reminds us that when we sin against the Father and allow that sin to remain in our lives, we are hurting ourselves, for that sin will prevent God from pouring his blessings upon our lives. The point of the prophecy of Amos is that God's people had forfeited their right to God's blessings because of their sin.—Brian L. Harbour.

Illustrations

JUDGMENT NOW.   "The history of the world is the judgment of the world," says Schiller. The Bible not only does not contest this statement, but repeatedly confirms it. That the judgment of God prevails in history as well as in the life of the individual is the meaning of the stories of the flood and the tower of Babel, in which God judges in catastrophe the blasphemous deeds of men. They relate how God steps into history with his storms and upheavals to shatter those moments of human madness in which self-drunken men raise their towers to heaven. The Bible teaches us to observe how "he that soweth to the flesh shall of the flesh reap corruption." It shows us how "righteousness exalteth a nation, but sin is a reproach to any people," and that this is true of great and small, of the life of the nations as of individuals.—Emil Brunner.

JUDGMENT AND MERCY.   "Even if a sharp sword be laid upon a man's neck, let him not despair of [the divine] mercy." (Berakot 10). So even the individual Israelite need not despair. God is good and merciful. He is to be "accepted" and relied on always, whether he "judges" or "forgives." Even in his judgments mercy is close behind. David said, "If you judge me with the attribute of Judgment, I accept thee; and if you judge me with the attribute of Mercy, I accept thee" (Midrash on Ps. 56:10).—C. G. Montefiore and H. Loewe.

Sermon Suggestions

A MICROCOSM OF OUR HUMAN PLIGHT. Text: Gen. 2:4b–9, 15–17, 25–3:7. (1) God has created us with resources, freedom, and great potential. (2) All of these endowments are threatened by the misuses of freedom itself.

WHAT ONE PERSON CAN DO. Text: Rom. 5:12–19. (1) Adam set the stage for all human sin and guilt, bringing death. (2) Jesus Christ reversed the entire process, bringing life.

Worship Aids

CALL TO WORSHIP. "It is written, As I live, saith the Lord, every knee shall bow to me, and every tongue shall confess to God. So then every one of us shall give account of himself to God" (Rom. 14:11–12).

INVOCATION. O Lord, you know all about us, all of our unworthy thoughts and acts, and yet you invite us to meet together with you and with one another. Forgive us our sins, cleanse our thoughts, and make our presence here helpful to one another.

OFFERTORY SENTENCE. "Remember that the person who plants few seeds will have a small crop; the one who plants many seeds will have a large crop" (2 Cor. 9:6 TEV).

OFFERTORY PRAYER. O God, help us to visualize the harvest of good that we hope for and then to sow the seed of our giving accordingly. Grant us cheerful hearts and expectant love as we give.

PRAYER. We draw near to thee, O most blessed God! by all the memory of a past experience. Often called, and often coming, we have never been turned away; and we know that it is good to seek thee. In thee we have been made strong in the day of weakness. In thee we have found light in the day of darkness. In thee we have found remedy when sick and consolation when in distress and courage when in despondency. Thou has inspired us with every grace and virtue which we possess. Thou hast led us through a thousand scenes of experience, and never once hast betrayed us. All thy words, many as they are, and promising great things, transcending all other promises known among men, are yea and amen; and none can say that he has come unto thee, and been cast out; and none shall ever say it. Blessed be thy name, thou faithful God—thou loving Savior—thou teaching and comforting Spirit! We draw near to thee with confession of sin; yet, thou knowest it better than we. We know our unbelief; we know the hardness of our hearts; we know our vagrancy and pride; we know how easily we are tempted through the senses; we know how inert and self-indulgent we are prone to become; we know that we lie under thy hand of discipline to complain and to murmur, and in the midst of prosperity to forget thee, and to consider that prosperity as the work of our own wisdom and skill. We confess all the things in which we are imperfect and rude, or sinful. We confess the wrong that we do knowing that we do it, and the courses that we pursue though we are warned and admonished. If thou wert to treat us strictly according to our desert, we could not stand for a moment. It is because thy court is the royalty of love, it is because thou art a parent, it is because thou dost not sit as a judge, administering with inflexible law, it is because thou wilt have mercy on whom thou wilt have mercy, it is because thou hast liberty of heart to do the things which please thee, that we have hope.

O thou great Father of all! we draw near to thee as disobedient children, to confess our wrong and mourn over it and pray for deliverance from it. We beseech of thee that we may live worthy of our relationship to thee. We are thy sons. We are adopted into thy family. We are much loved and much forgiven. We are borne with, and helped, every day and on every side. Grant that every feeling of honor and gratitude and love may conspire to prevent our receiving all thy mercies, so many and so precious, and returning nothing but disobedience.

Forgive the past, and inspire the future. Grant that we may never be discouraged. If there be any that have begun to walk the royal way of life, and are perplexed and hindered, and see little of growth in themselves, still let them go forward. Grant that none may look back and count themselves unworthy of eternal life.—Henry Ward Beecher.

EVENING SERVICE

Topic: A Word of Warning to Israel—And to Us

TEXT: Amos 3:1–12.

Israel was the privileged nation of the world. God had revealed himself to them in a very unusual way. But instead of taking him seriously, they took his name in vain. Because of this God promised them that he would judge them and punish them for their sin.

I. To communicate this warning to Israel, God called on a sheep rancher by the name of Amos to deliver the warning to the nation.

Amos began his sermon by reminding the people of their privileged position. He called to their mind two events in Israel's history.

(a) First there was the Exodus. The Exodus is the watershed experience for Israel. It was in this event that the people were truly led by God in a marvelous way.

(b) But there is also the covenant that God had made with the people even before the Exodus. He reminded them that they are the only nation God has known intimately, to whom he has given the revelation of himself. The covenant was made with Abraham, and God had never broken it.

II. But just because of this great partiality, God expected the people to act a little differently. Instead of assuming an air of superiority and indifference, God expected them to show greater concern. But they had behaved just the opposite. They had come to feel that God would not punish them because they were his chosen people. But Amos declared what no other prophet before him had done. Amos warned that just because of this special relationship God was going to judge Israel with an even more exact demand.

(a) The sins he refers to are the ones mentioned in the second chapter. One peculiar aspect about them is that they are social sins rather than specifically religious sins. But Amos, in issuing his "Back to God" call, warned that in order to get back to God the people would have to come through their neighbors. They had to get right with their neighbors before they could get right with God. Their sins toward their neighbors have been grievous, and God was demanding payment. There was a very definite cause and effect relationship between Israel's sin and God's punishment of them.

(b) To punish them for their crime, God has chosen another nation to surround Israel and destroy them. He does not name the nation at this time, but in 721 B.C.—just slightly more than twenty-five years later—Babylon marched through and totally destroyed the nation and carried it into captivity. The picture that Amos paints is of an athletic event taking place in a great coliseum. Israel and its warring opponent are on the field. Egypt and Philistia are in the stands watching Israel be wiped out, destroyed by a foreign power. And one has to imagine that the stands were cheering the winner! Yet, even though this great tragedy is to come, there is still a very faint ray of hope.

(c) The coming destruction is going to be very severe. All that is going to be left are fragments.

III. There are a number of lessons here for us, as a church, as a nation, and as individuals.

(a) One sure word is that sin does not pay. For a while it may look as though we can get by without getting caught. We can point to others who seem to prosper so while living in sin. Sin does not pay—but God does!

Whether as a nation or as individuals, we will not escape God's wrath. We may think that we have gotten away, but at some point, sin must be paid for. This was true for the ancient Israelites, and it is true for us, too.

(b) But I think an even greater message from Amos for us is that privilege demands responsibility. Those to whom God has given much are required to respond accordingly.

If God has blessed you with a talent, intelligence, wealth, ability, he expects you to use it for him. Someday he is going to ask us for an accounting and we are going to have to give an answer.

(c) But even though God is demanding, he nonetheless holds out hope. As Amos spoke of the remnant, the little leftovers, as being used by God to begin again, we can point to the cross and declare that on that cross God has given all of us a second chance. There is forgiveness. There is escape from the day of judgment. But it will come as we confess our sin and stop trying to cover it up, it will come when we start letting our responsibilities be equal to our abilities.—James E. Taulman.

SUNDAY: MARCH FIFTEENTH

MORNING SERVICE

Topic: The Blessed Audacity of Struggling with God

TEXT: Gen. 32:24–32.

I. Israel, according to the Jahwist, was born on the night described in our text. This is the hour of the birth of the name that defines God's people for centuries to come. So, in a certain sense, this is the beginning of the people of God, the community of faith that has existed up to this very day.

(a) What a beginning! At the beginning of the history of Israel stands Jacob, the great fighter against God who because of his character received the name Israel. Therefore, Israel saw itself as a nation that from the time of its ancestor had continually fought against God, not for God. If you want to find God's people, the church, you will find them engaged in a struggle with God from the very beginning.

(b) In the Bible, people remonstrate and complain; they suffer every injustice and abysmal need of this world. Rebellious, remonstrating prophets fling it all into the face of God, for they do not like what is going on and do not find it easy to resign themselves to the will of God.

(1) In the book of Job, who is vindicated in the end as the true servant of God? It is not Job's pious, orthodox friends who can give all the right answers to the questions, declaring that God is absolutely right. No, it is the uppity Job himself, the one who remonstrates with God through thirty chapters.

(2) Because he can no longer stand for God to tell him what to do, the prophet Jeremiah curses the day of his birth and resigns from God's service. Yet this is the man who has pointed the way to God for millions of men for almost three thousand years.

(3) What do we find in the New Testament? The disciples of Jesus rebel against God's way, and in Gethsemane take to their heels and let Jesus go the rest of the way alone. And the most stirring cry of all came from Jesus just before he died: "My God, my God, why hast thou forsaken me?"

(c) In the midst of all of his confusion and rebellion, Jacob, this warrior against God, made a very striking statement: "I will not let you go unless you bless me." His demand makes this not merely the story of one of the many little rebels against God who are long since forgotten. Israel is no small-time rebel. Israel is a real rebel, a rebel who will not rest content with questions without answers, a rebel who persists in his rebellion until daybreak and then finds out for the first time that the one he has been wrestling with is actually God. God gives him no answer that he can easily take home and apply to every puzzle, by which he can know and explain everything. What kind of God would simply put himself in our hands and let us define him, name him, and explain him precisely and fully? That God would be an idol. But God does give him the blessing.

(d) What are we told about this blessing of God? It is a dislocated hip on which Jacob can only limp along. That—believe it or not—is God's blessing. If a person does not come back from an encounter with God limping on a dislocated limb, then we might question whether he or she has actually encountered God rather than just a homemade idol. Those Christians or, more particularly, those theologians who have a glib answer to every question and leave nothing unsaid, have not—whatever you may say—been at Jabbok or in Gethsemane. For where can you find the blessing of God apart from the dislocated hip?

II. At this point, Jacob receives the name Israel. With that, a history begins that comes down to the present time. It is the history of the people of God, the history of those who, like their ancestor Jacob-Israel, must always stand between the world and God. But repeatedly and continuously that must bring every need, every wrong, and every suffering of the world before God, and for his sake gain relief wherever God's love can reach mankind through them. As they do this, they are, of course, often rebellious, disobedient, and without understanding. It may be a long time before they are completely aware of the identity of the one with whom they wrestle. Nevertheless, they endure until they see God's face and experience his hard blessing.

III. But this is not all. The church of Jesus, out of whose tradition the Fourth Gospel comes, understood Jesus as the new Jacob-Israel. Just as heaven opened upon Jacob-Israel and the angels of God ascended and descended, in the same manner, according to John 1:51, heaven opened upon the Son of Man, Jesus. There the history of Jacob-Israel comes to fulfillment. There for the first time the struggle at Jabbok was fought through to the end. There Jesus has taken into the presence of God the tax collectors and the prostitutes, the sick and the dead, the hopeless poor and the callous rich. There he had to die as a rebel against God, not as a respected housefather of a home for converted sinners.

(a) There one has fought his way into the ultimate desperation where a man can do nothing more than cry out, "Why hast thou forsaken me?" There one has, in this ultimate desperation, refused to let God go and even in this situation has cried, "My God, my God." There one was not only struck on the hip, so that from then on he could only limp; there he died, wretched and crying aloud, under the derision of the very people he wanted to take with him to God. This was the end of all of his strength and his faith, because he took all of our doubts, all of our rebellion with him to his cross. Only the miracle of the grace of God could be counted on.

(b) Jacob-Israel limped away from his struggle with God, saying, "I have seen God face to face." The New Testament church says, "No one has ever seen God; the only Son, who is in the bosom of the Father, he made him known" (John 1:18). Between the struggle in temptation in which we can only hold fast to God in the faith of Jacob—"I will not let you go, unless you bless me"—and the sight into which, Paul tells us, faith will one day be changed, stands Easter and our forthcoming resurrection from the dead. Then we will at last see him as he is. "Beloved, we are God's children now; it does not appear what we shall be, but we know that when he appears we shall be like him, for we shall see him as he is" (1 John 3:2).

(c) My dear friends, this is the way we live between the Israel-struggle, fought through to the end in Gethsemane and at Golgotha, and the final consummation in which Peniel will be fulfilled and we shall see God as he is.—Eduard Schweizer.

Illustrations

GUILT TRANSFIGURED. But what precisely does deliverance from guilt mean and what concretely is the relation of the cross to this deliverance? The better phrasing of the situation would be "deliverance from the burden of guilt," for Christian salvation does not produce the guiltless man, if such a moral monster is really imaginable. It transforms guilt from its sheer negativity and its self-stultifying consequences into positive action flowing from forgiveness. If Christ has lifted this burden from our backs, as Bunyan so vividly portrays it in *Pilgrim's Progress,* it is not that we should henceforth have no responsibility about guilt. On the contrary, we are called to cross bearing and guilt carrying, a vocation which we should have shunned before or, if accepted, should have failed in because of concern with the self as a cross bearer. The invitation "Come to me, all who labor and are heavy laden, and I will give you rest" is followed in the Gospel by the command: "Take my yoke upon you, and learn from me. . . . For my yoke is easy and my burden is light." The lightness springs not from an empty pack but from a full pack correctly balanced and carried.—William J. Wolf.

FINDING NEW PURPOSE. The great griefs of life are often not the loss of someone by death. Death itself is definitive, unmistakably final, and easy to see as grief. Such a loss as divorce is haggle-hearted and undefined, remarkably indecisive, and hard to see as grief. Yet, some divorced persons I know have seen their temptations for what they were—to let their broken marriage become a stuttering, sputtering broken record that could play only one note. Therefore, they went on to a larger design and purpose in life and made God the center of their existence. Remarkably enough, they discovered that God loves and forgives and cares for divorced persons in some strangely wonderful and unexpected ways.—Wayne E. Oates.

Sermon Suggestions

WHEN FAITH COMES ALIVE. Text: Gen. 12:1–4a. (1) Faith's challenge. (2) Faith's reward. (3) Faith's mission.

WHAT CAN WE SAY FOR FAITH? Text: Rom. 4:1–5, 13–17. (1) With God, faith counts more than good works. (2) Faith opens up the promises of God to all humankind.

Worship Aids

CALL TO WORSHIP. "Cast thy burden upon the Lord, and he shall sustain thee" (Ps. 55:22).

INVOCATION. Today, our Father, we come into thy presence, as usual, from many walks of life, each of which has its peculiar burdens. Some of us may be near the breaking point. But thy word assures us that thou dost care for us and tells us that thou dost invite us to bring thee into our struggles. Take thy rightful place among us, gracious Father, and work with us even at the cost of pain and sacrifice on our part to make us what thou wouldst have us to become.

OFFERTORY SENTENCE. "Each one, as a good manager of God's different gifts, must use for the good of others the special gift he has received from God" (1 Pet. 4:10 TEV).

OFFERTORY PRAYER. Lord, we have nothing but what you have given us. We call these things ours, but in one way or another you have put them under our temporary control. Help us to surrender our all to you, so that when we receive it back we may use it to further your cause in the world, to bless those around us, and to bring us the kind of joy that builds us up and does not in any way blight your purpose for our lives.

PRAYER. Eternal God, rise with thy morning upon our souls, and call us to consecrate another day to thy service. We thank thee for rest and sleep, and for thy watchful care throughout the hours of darkness. Thou hast been as a wall of fire about our home, and thyself the glory in the midst. Thou dost care for each one of us, as if thou didst care for him only, and for all as if they were but one. We would commit our ways to thee afresh. Sustain us amid all our work, and solve the problems of our life that are too hard for us. May we be strong in the faith that all things work together for good to them that love thee. O God, our allotted time is as the passing of a shadow. Our life vanishes away even as a mist is scattered before the burning beams of the sun. Without thee we cannot live and dare not die. Draw us into fellowship with thy mind and will, that, renouncing the vain things which in times past have charmed, we may yield ourselves unreservedly to thee, that thou mayst use us to advance thy cause and kingdom in the world. Send forth thy Spirit into our hearts to quicken us with fresh zeal and devout aspiration, to rouse us to renewed struggle against the evil that is within and without us.—Samuel McComb.

EVENING SERVICE

Topic: A Portrait of God's Love

Text: Hosea 11:1–12.

The love of God is in fact so great a theme that the preacher who attempts to preach it is faced with the danger, in Kipling's words, of splashing at a ten-league canvas with brushes of comet's hair, resulting in an overwhelming impression of eternity and majesty and love.

I. We are confronted at the very start, in the very first verse, with the choosing, electing love of God.

(a) Why did God choose Israel? This is a question thoughtful people have been asking ever since God chose Israel! Why did God not call Egypt? Here lay Egypt basking by the Nile, wrapped in the jeweled web of centuries, the art of all the world gleaming in its eye. Or why did God not choose Assyria to the east, rising like a mighty young man flexing muscles, with the conquest of the world in his eye?

(b) We do not know. But this we do know: his was not a random choice. God did not choose Israel in a random fashion, just as he does not choose or elect us in a random fashion.

God doesn't operate that way. The basis of his selection of Israel is hidden from us, wrapped up in the mist of his counsel—but we do know that his choice of Israel was full of purpose. There was a vision and a destiny in the mind of the Eternal when he called Israel out of Egypt.

(c) It may well be that God called Israel out of Egypt for the very same reason that Paul said in effect (2 Cor. 4:7), "He did not

call in his time the noble and the rich, that this marvellous treasure of God might be found in pliable, earthly vessels." First Peter puts it like this: "But ye are a chosen generation; a royal priesthood, an holy nation, a peculiar people; that ye should shew forth the praises of him who hath called you out of darkness into his marvellous light."

The chief characteristic of this child-nation that God called as his own was their nobodyism, their need, their suffering, their lostness. And one is irresistibly led to bring the parallel home and realize that it is so with each of us when Jesus comes to us. We are full of need, lostness, nobodyism, and suffering; and then Jesus comes and says, "I have chosen you."

II. We see that God's love is not only a choosing love, but is a molding, shaping love that seeks to shape us into what God wants us to be.

(a) He cannot leave us the way we are: God takes care of, molds, teaches, and shapes his people. By a pillar of fire at night, and by a cloud in the day, God led his child-nation. God bent down and fed his nation from the water in the rock, the manna from the sky, the bird from the desert. God reached down and picked up his child in his arms at the gate of the promised land and said, "My child, see, it is for you!"

(b) God shaped and molded his people. And this is exactly the way I see God working in our lives. He has not only chosen and put his hand upon us, but he has also led us out of our spiritual bondage. He has taught us how to walk. He has enabled us to focus our lives that we might not be like a kaleidoscope, but that we might be focused—pure of heart, single of intent. The purpose—that God's mighty love through us might be reflected and others might see it. That's the kind of love God has—choosing love, shaping love, molding love—for beyond God's choosing there is a destiny.

III. Here is another aspect of God's love, a facet appearing almost to be inconsistent with what he has earlier said. How can a God who reaches down and picks up his child-nation now turn away and allow this nation to be swept off into captivity? Here we see the discipline of God's love.

(a) God's love is not weak and sentimental; his love is strong enough to stand aside and let us suffer the consequences of sins. God's love is strong enough to use even the evil that we bring upon ourselves and the punishment that it involves. There came a time, Hosea was saying—indeed, time after time—when this child-nation, whom God had taught to walk, lifted in his arms, and bent down to feed, turned its back upon God in rebellion and unrest. And God had the love to step back and let this child face the consequences of its own actions.

(b) God works this way in our own lives. He does not waste the consequences of our sin and our rebellion and our unrest. God uses the sword that devours, the yoke that galls, and the cross that shames—all

that we might become more like him through discipline.

(c) And so Hosea painted for us in this chapter a beautiful picture of God's love, specifically as a choosing, electing love, a love that will shape us and mold us, a love that will discipline and punish us when needed.

This image that Hosea used is a most touching one. There are perhaps few pictures more beautiful than that of a father, that of a mother, that of a parent teaching a child to walk; that of seeing a little child reach a small hand up for a parent's hand; that of seeing a parent choke up with emotion over his child.

That is God's love! Hosea's portrait of divine love was fashioned for a purpose inherent throughout the book: "Why would you turn away, O Israel?"—Earl C. Davis.

SUNDAY: MARCH TWENTY-SECOND

MORNING SERVICE

Topic: The Forks of the Road—Moses
TEXT: Heb. 11:24–26.

I. Moses is at the forks of the road. A very revealing place is this spot where the roads fork. Here every man shows himself for what he is. One man comes to the forks of the road and undertakes to stand perfectly still. Or he travels the road to the left for a season, then retraces his steps and for another season travels the road to the right. Such conduct indicates that he is afflicted with the fatal malady of indecision. When Moses comes to the forks of the road he refuses the one and sets himself steadfastly to travel the other. By so doing he shows himself a man of decision.

II. There were two elements in this decision of Moses, as there are in all decisions.

(a) There was a negative element. "Moses when he was come to years refused." That is, there was something to which Moses said no. Moses, when he stood at the forks of the road, looked at both roads, and to one of them he said a positive, vigorous, out-and-out no.

(b) But Moses did more than say no. He

did something more than refuse to take a certain road. He also said yes. He refused to travel one way, not that he might stand still, but that he might travel another way. When we hear the call of Christ almost the first thought that comes into our mind is not that to which we are to say yes, but that to which we are to say no. We think of the Christian life on its negative side rather than on its positive side. We think of what we are to quit being and doing rather than what we are to become and what we are to do.

(c) It is altogether right to remember that certain things must be given up in order for us to become followers of Jesus Christ. But we must also remember this: no amount of negatives will make us Christians. It is necessary to be able to say no. But to simply say no and stop there is to end in utter moral failure.

(d) The truth of the matter is that Christ is calling on you to say no not simply because he wants you to practice self-denial as an end. He is calling on you to say no to the lower because that is absolutely necessary in order for you to say yes to the highest. He is asking you to say no to the darkness because in no other way can you say yes to the light.

III. This decision of Moses was costly. There was much to be given up.

(a) This decision involved the giving up of the highest social position in all the land of Egypt. It was to pass in one step from this high position, not to a lower rank, but to the very lowest. It was to cease to be the son of the Egyptian princess in order to become the son of a Hebrew slave. When Moses said no to this high social position, he said no to something that makes a tremendous appeal to the average man and woman.

(b) When Moses made this decision, he said no to the pleasures of Egypt. The Egypt of that day was the New York of modern life. It was the playground of the world. When he said no he rejected all that could appeal to a man who was in love with worldly pleasure.

(c) His decision involved the giving up of the treasures of Egypt. The Egypt of that day was the granary of the world. Down from its unknown source every year came the Nile, giving to Egypt its fertility. To Egypt came the ships and caravans of many nations, carrying away its grain and leaving behind their silver and gold. When Moses, therefore, said no to the treasures of Egypt, he refused to grip and hold vast wealth that might have been his for the taking.

(d) For Moses to make this decision was to bring bitter disappointment to one who loved him, and to whom he was under very great obligations. I think we have never given sufficient credit to the Egyptian princess who was Moses' foster mother. The fact that she was a heathen did not prevent her from being a good woman. She took this little waif to her heart and protected him. It was to her that he owed his life. It was by no means easy, therefore, for a big-souled man like Moses to disappoint one who had thus helped him and who tenderly loved him.

IV. But the cost of this decision of Moses is not to be measured alone by what he gave up. What he chose in place of it all was also costly. When he refused all that Egypt had to offer, what did he accept in its stead? When he said no to the privileges that might have been his as the son of Pharaoh's daughter, to what did he say yes?

(a) He chose suffering. "Moses, when he was come to years, refused to be called the son of Pharaoh's daughter, choosing rather to suffer affliction with the people of God." Here is a man facing a road that he knows will lead him to suffering, to agony, to disappointment, to battle and conflict and tears.

(b) Yet, with his eyes wide open, he makes the choice. He does not dream for a moment that when he identifies himself with a horde of slaves he is going to have an easy time. He does not fool himself into believing that the course upon which he has decided will be all sunshine and all laughter. Yet, with his eyes wide open, and alive to all that is involved, he chooses to suffer affliction with the people of God.

V. How did Moses come to make this choice?

(a) He had a clear eye for distinguishing right from wrong. He saw that to cling to his rights would be to sin. He refused to blind himself to the fact that it was not simply sinful to choose the lowest, it was also sinful to choose the second best. He realized that God was calling him to choose the highest and to fail to so choose was to sin.

(b) He knew that the pleasures and gains of sin are only temporary. Sin is only charming in the present or in the immediate future. The sin of the future often seems as fair as an angel from heaven, but the sin of yesterday is as ugly as a fiend from hell.

(c) He had a keen eye for the things of real value. So clearly did he see, that he esteemed the reproach of Christ greater riches than the treasures of Egypt. It took a man deeply schooled in permanent values to reach that conclusion. The treasures of Egypt loomed large. They seemed very genuine and very weighty and very abiding. Yet Moses decided that the thing of real value was not the wealth of Egypt, but the reproach of Christ.

(d) Then Moses looked away from everything else to the coming reward. He believed that the future belongs not to sin but to righteousness. He believed it is the heritage, not of the holders of the treasures of Egypt, but of those who share the reproach of Christ. His faith gave him at once the far view and the true view.

VI. And what was the outcome of this decision?

(a) Moses received the reward of a Christlike character. Do you see that man coming down from the mountain with face that is strangely alight? Do you find your eyes dazzled in his presence as if you were looking upon a sunrise? Had Moses remained in Egypt he would have missed many a conflict and struggle. He would also have missed a face lighted with the light that shines in the face of Jesus Christ.

(b) Through this decision Moses was able to render a great service to his own nation and to the world.

But I am in doubt as to whether Moses' service in freeing his people has been greatly worth-while. They are such a peevish and fretful and whining lot. They are forever lusting for the fleshpots of Egypt. They are constantly complaining to Moses because he has not left them to die in the land of bondage. I cannot convince myself that his task has been worth the doing. So I speak my mind: "Pardon me, Moses. You have made a heroic fight. You have set your people free. But they are a cantankerous lot, and I fear your labor has been almost, if not quite, in vain."

But Moses does not seem to share my doubts. "Israel does not count for much now," he replies, "but remember that it is only a child. It has by no means arrived, but it is on the way. One day Israel is going to give to the world an Isaiah with his inspired eloquence and a Jeremiah with his broken heart and his streaming tears. One day Israel is going to give to the world a skylark named David and a flaming missionary named Paul. One day there is going forth from this little country the best of all good news: 'Behold, I bring you glad tidings of great joy, for there is born unto you this day a Savior, which is Christ the Lord.' Israel does not count for much yet. But it is on the way toward bringing the whole world into its debt."

(c) Then, incidentally, this decision enabled Moses to win heaven. The New Testament makes us sure of this. Read the story of the transfiguration. Christ has come. He is struggling under the burden of his coming cross. He needs help such as those deeply schooled in the mystery of suffering alone can give. Therefore, two men, passed from earth long years ago, come to talk with him of his coming crucifixion. Who are they? One of them is the man who esteemed the reproach of Christ greater riches than the treasures of Egypt.

(d) We must conclude, therefore, that the best day's work that Moses ever did was when he made possible the writing of this sentence: "By faith Moses, when he was come to years, refused to be called the son of Pharaoh's daughter; choosing rather to suffer affliction with the people of God than to enjoy the pleasures of sin for a season; esteeming the reproach of Christ greater riches than the treasures of Egypt: for he had respect unto the recompense of the reward." He won an inheritance among that elect company who "have washed their robes and made them white in the blood of the Lamb."—Clovis G. Chappell.

Illustrations

"RUTHLESS" GRACE.   The terrible and destructive aspect of the Godhead—the "tremendum" in theological language—originates as a subjective human experience, though an unavoidable one if our religious convictions and our rigid theology are smashed by the grace of God. We live in a jail that we call our castle; a foreign soldier breaks through the doors, come to free us by blasting the walls of our castle—and we fight him with the last might of our broken ego, calling him scoundrel, knave, and devil, until we are exhausted, overwhelmed, and disarmed. Then looking at the victor with disinterested objectivity we recognize him: St. Michael smilingly sheathes his sword.—Fritz Kunkel.

STEWARDSHIP OF DIFFICULTY.   When I was a student I had what in those days was regarded as a rather hopeless illness, which was not betrayed by my appearance. Because of this particular illness I was not able to submit a particular piece of academic work on time. When I tried to give an excuse for this to my professor he said, "Don't give sickness as an excuse and don't look for sympathy. Do you think fantastically healthy people are the only ones from whom we can expect anything? We ailing people [he himself was a sick man] have to give our all. We are the ones from whom God demands some accomplishment." At first I was furious with these remarks, but the memory of them has helped me many times. What I at first had perceived as an unjustified attack, the professor had meant as that exchange of values such as occurs in the message of Jesus. That is what we mean when we speak of the poor rich, the rich poor, and the healthy afflicted.—Helmut Thielicke, *Faith: The Great Adventure*

Sermon Suggestions

PUTTING GOD ON THE SPOT.   Text: Exod. 17:3–7. (1) Life inevitably brings us into unfavorable circumstances. (2) Our reaction may be bitter and complaining. (3) God often goes on blessing us despite our faithlessness and unworthiness.

WHEN GOD HAD PUT US RIGHT.   Text: Rom. 5:11. (1) We can expect to arrive at the destiny that God meant for us. (2) We can meet bravely and joyfully every trial as a stage on the way to that glorious destiny.

Worship Aids

CALL TO WORSHIP.   " 'I have set before you life and death, blessing and cursing,' saith the Lord, 'therefore choose life' " (Deut. 30:19b).

INVOCATION.   O God of peace, quiet the conflicts warring within our hearts, as both the flesh and the spirit struggle for ascendancy. Give us grace through this experience of worship, to the end that we can follow after the spirit and so reject the demands of the flesh.

OFFERTORY SENTENCE.   "Every one of us shall give account of himself to God" (Rom. 14:12).

OFFERTORY PRAYER.   Our Father, help us to realize that every day in our lives is a judgment day, that we are making decisions for which we are accountable to you. Give us the reverence and the wisdom to make every decision in the awareness of your saving presence.

PRAYER.   Almighty God, Lord of the universe, God of our salvation, we praise you for your mighty power, your steadfast love, and your redemptive presence among us. We lift our voices to you in song; we lift our hands to you in prayer; we bring our gifts to you in offering. We acknowledge that you are our creator; you are our redeemer; you have brought us through many trials; you have given us good things of this world to enjoy. We belong to you. Yet we confess that we have often failed to hearken to your voice. Sometimes we have been preoccupied with business, conflicts in our home, or trouble with a neighbor or business associate. Some of us may even have let our hearts gradually harden against you through accumulations of bitterness and envy. Forgive us, put us on right paths again, and restore to us the joy of your salvation.—James W. Cox.

EVENING SERVICE

Topic: Jesus and Anger
TEXT: John 2:13–17.
Anger is one of the most difficult areas of our lives. We are not quite sure what to do with it. Most of us really want to be like Jesus, and we just cannot see Jesus getting angry. So each time we get angry we feel some guilt about it. On the other hand, our anger is something that is very real. It is a permanent part of us. Even if we were to try we could not get rid of it.

I. Let us look to the life of Jesus Christ for our example. It comes as a shock to us to realize that Jesus knew what anger was. But he did! He was human!

(a) The events surrounding Jesus' anger are important. John describes the setting as the very first Passover in Jesus' ministry.

When Jesus entered the temple he encountered an unpleasant sight. There in the Court of the Gentiles the money changers had set up their stalls to make change for the Jews to pay the half-shekel temple tax. This tax could only be paid with temple coins. Any other currency had to be converted into the proper coinage. The tax itself was nearly two days' wages. If pilgrims from outside Palestine needed to exchange money, they were charged nearly a day's wages for the exchange.

In addition to this abuse, there were the traders who sold animals for the sacrifices. The law declared that the sacrificed animal had to be without blemish. It was very easy for the temple inspector—who owned the franchise for selling animals in the temple! —to find an imperfection in any animal that a worshiper might bring. And, as a matter of course, the animals sold by the inspector were much higher in price than an animal sold outside the temple.

(b) But when Jesus entered he saw that the very place where the people of other nations were to worship was filled with all of the noise, dishonesty, and stench of a slaughterhouse. How could anyone worship in an atmosphere like that?

This must have been the final straw that broke the camel's back. In anger he picked up some ropes that possibly had been used to tie the cattle and doubled these together, making a whip out of them. Then, with the whip in his hand and fire in his eyes, he began to drive out the cattle and merchants, to overturn the tables stacked with money, and to cleanse his Father's house.

(c) Does this incident in the life of Jesus bother you? Do you feel slightly uncomfortable in even talking about it? This picture of Jesus is certainly a long way from the picture of "gentle Jesus meek and mild." But Jesus is human, and anger is a human response.

If you feel uncomfortable with this anger in the life of Jesus, let me suggest that the reason is that you feel uncomfortable with your own anger. One important word that this experience would speak to us is that it is all right to be angry.

Both the Old Testament and the New Testament are filled with references to God's anger and wrath. If it is not right for us to be angry, then it is not right for God to be angry. If we do away with our anger,

we have to explain away God's anger as well.

II. Some anger is wrong. Some anger is destructive. Some anger can do more harm than good. How can we be angry like Jesus and not sin? Let me suggest three questions, three check points, three guidelines.

(a) The first question is, why was this anger aroused? This question also involves admitting that we are angry, that a certain event made us very angry. Is your anger completely personal or is it rooted in a cause, a principle beyond yourself? Jesus' anger in cleansing the temple is not one that stems from selfish reasons. His concern was that all people would be able to worship in the temple. His anger flamed white-hot when he saw Gentiles being shut out from his Father's house which was to be a "house of prayer for all nations."

(b) Second, look to see how your anger is expressed. Being angry over a just cause is not only excusable; it is greatly to be desired. But how can one express this anger in a legitimate way? Being angry and sinning not involves expressing our anger in an appropriate way. It means not pushing it under. It means admitting that you are angry. How you express your anger determines whether it will be a healthy or a diseased aspect of your life.

Expressing anger is a way of cleansing one's own personal temple. Openness in confronting people will make one's anger constructive instead of destructive.

(c) We have looked at the beginning point of anger. We have looked at the middle point. Let us now examine the end result of an anger that is not a sin.

The purpose of anger is to produce a change. We get angry when something is not right. But there is such a thing as producing a change that is so devastating it is destructive instead of constructive. Anger that does not lead to sin will work for one result: redemption. Anger is sin if it has the desire to destroy the person involved.

(d) When these guides to being angry and not sinning are all summed up together it would be this: one can be angry and not sin if the anger is not selfish, if it is expressed openly, and if it aims for redemption.—James E. Taulman.

SUNDAY: MARCH TWENTY-NINTH

MORNING SERVICE

Topic: God's Brutal Love

TEXT: 2 Chron. 36:14–23.

I. The history of civilization, in its darker aspect, is the record of the conquest and destruction of one nation by another. As certain as the proverbial death and taxes is the collapse of every mighty political order which men can assemble. That's life.

(a) This is not to say that nations should not struggle to arise and even to excel, for each plays a significant part during its prominence, some for better and some for worse. But in our universal human hunger to find something permanent, something to trust and believe in forever, nations simply do not qualify. God endures. That we believe, and history cannot claim to show otherwise until faith should suddenly disappear from human society. God is history's sole survivor.

(b) If ever there was to be an exception to this law of nations, should it not have been Israel, the gathered nation of God's own elect, his chosen people? It certainly appears that the Jews believed that the world's fate would never catch them. If there is a God, then how could he who led his people out of slavery, who delivered Canaan into their hands, prospered King David and suffered Solomon to erect a temple for his dwelling, how could that God ever stand by and see his Israel share the same gory end which comes to the godless nations? And why should anyone put his trust in a God, worship a Supreme Power, if God proves powerless when his worshipers need him most? When the enemy is banging down the gates, where is God then?

(c) Where is God when the enemy—with your blood in its eye—is banging down the gates? I give you the answer of Amos, of Isaiah, and of Jeremiah: God is outside the gates, out there with the enemy, making sure that their battering rams do the job. Is not God therefore the supreme traitor? "He that keepeth Israel," that "feedeth his flock like a shepherd," is out urging the wolves to devour the sheep.

(d) That is precisely what was read to us from 2 Chronicles. "The Lord . . . sent persistently to them by his messengers, because he had compassion on his people and on his dwelling place; but they kept mocking the messengers . . . despising his words . . . til the wrath of the Lord rose against his people, til there was no remedy. Therefore he brought up against them the king of the Chaldeans [or Babylon], who slew their young men with the sword . . . and had no compassion on young man or virgin, old man or aged; he gave them all into his hand."

II. Never before in the history of nations had such an interpretation been placed upon a national disaster. Whenever a city or a country fell anywhere in the world, its god fell too. The believers threw out his statue and went over to the winner's god. Their defeat was all the proof they needed that their religion had been false.

(a) But not Israel. Israel had managed to grow to real political prominence by the time of David, but right from the Exodus onward Moses and all the rest—though political leaders—had drummed righteousness into the mind of every Israelite. That was how their Lord God was different from all the world's graven images: he demanded justice for them, taking on Pharaoh for them; and then he demanded justice from them forever after. That was their covenant, their contract.

(b) That accountability was all that preserved Israel. She carried it into exile, which would have been the end of any other nation. By the foreign waters of Babylon she sat down and wept—not over her wounds but over her sins. She carried her conviction back with her when another foreigner had destroyed her destroyer, and those became her golden years. Israel never reached her incredible heights until after her utter and unwelcome devastation.

III. God's lordship over all history is a mysterious and sometimes a frightening thing. I cannot adequately explain it to you, because I do not expect ever to fully understand it. But I have seen it in history, in my own life, and in lives which I have observed at close range. God is indeed our heavenly Father, but he is by no means an indulgent parent. If you can accept a divine Lover who sides with forces even meaner than the Lover's own children, sides with them deliberately for the sake of his children, then perhaps you know what an awesome thing love really is. Those Chaldeans who ripped down the gates of Jerusalem were rotten barbarians. God did not favor their cause. He was recalling his own to their destiny. What a destiny it must have been for a Father to resort to such a brutal love! God let Jesus die on the cross. He allowed German Jews to be massacred. He let disease waste and kill my father. He tolerates cruelty between Christians, even sets the mean upon the meek. (a) For what purpose? That is not always clear, not right away, not usually for a long time afterward. The messengers seem to understand, but they are rare and are seldom the ones we supposed were the messengers. But no calamity is ever without a purpose. God remains Lord of history. (b) Paul remembered. That is how he could write these absurd words: "We know that all things work together for good"—for good!—"to those who love God. . . . Neither death nor life, nor principalities nor powers"—nor disease nor disasters nor explosions—"can separate us from . . . God." Out of every defeat there is a lesson, then a correction, a purification, and finally a reconciliation— and always beyond the ashes there is God. —Donald Stewart Miller.

Illustrations

THE SUFFERING OF THE RIGHTEOUS. We can understand why the evil may suffer, but what purpose is there to the suffering of the just and the innocent? Rabbi Jonathan, commenting on the text "the Lord trieth the righteous" (Ps. 11:5), said, "The potter does not test cracked vessels. It is useless to tap them even once, because they would break. He does, however, test the good ones, because no matter how many times he taps them they do not break. Even so God tests not the wicked but the righteous."—William B. Silverman, citing *The Midrash*.

YOUR GOD TOO SMALL. The malady of our time lies in its contracted thoughts of God. We think too narrowly and meanly of his power, his love, and his freedom to help men. That is what the "miracles" of Jesus and his teaching about faith mean— that God is more near, more real and mighty, more full of love, and more ready to help every one of us than any one of us realizes, that is their undying message. —D. S. Cairns.

Sermon Suggestions

WHAT COUNTS WITH GOD. Text: 1 Sam. 16:1–13. (1) First Scene: The failure of Saul as king. (2) Second Scene: Seeking a new king. (3) Third Scene: Weighing the prospects. (4) Fourth Scene: The choice and anointing of David.

HOW TO PLEASE THE LORD. Text: Eph. 5:8–14. (1) Know who you are—light in the Lord. (2) Live according to that light —avoid the works of darkness; practice what is good and right and true.

Worship Aids

CALL TO WORSHIP. "Let us be grateful and worship God in a way that will please him, with reverence and fear" (Heb. 12:28b TEV).

INVOCATION. God of power, God of love, almighty Father, today we ask you to help us to see beyond the events now being played out, dramas in which we win and lose, exult and suffer. Grant that we may see more deeply into your heart of mingled purpose and mystery and catch a new vision of your glorious eternal kingdom.

OFFERTORY SENTENCE. "I will freely sacrifice unto thee: I will praise thy name, O Lord; for it is good" (Ps. 54:6).

OFFERTORY PRAYER.   O God, every offering we bring is our act of faith in you, believing that the Christ we proclaim is the way, the truth, and the life; our act of faith in our brothers and sisters in Christ, believing that we all together will make good, responsible use of these gifts. Grant to us joy and generosity in this act of worship.

PRAYER.   Eternal God, source of all blessings and creator of all good, we pray for those who hunger and thirst after righteousness—those newly entered upon the pilgrimage of faith. Grant them strength not to fall, wisdom to know your truth, patience to discover your way to eternal life, and the joy of service in your kingdom. Provide them with the kindly strength and wise compassion of true friends to company with them on their journey toward the eternal city.

We pray for those who hunger and thirst for bread and water—who agonize over the emaciated faces and swollen bodies of children left unfed and dying. Grant us eyes to see the despair and anguish of hollow stares; give us ears to hear the cries of pain, the low moans of grief, the silent screams of desperation and lost hope; but more than this, grant us the grace to share the needed good. Save us from the selfishness that enslaves us to our desires, from the deceitfulness of our own hearts. Teach us the truth that hurts but makes us grow. Confront us with your stern demands in Christ until we learn the true meaning of repentance, the unspeakable gift of true faith. In these days of conflict and turmoil, of poverty and starvation, help us, your servants, enter the marketplace of life and seek changes in the name of your kingdom. We ask for the sake of those who perish without our love.—Paul D. Simmons.

EVENING SERVICE

Topic: The Angel Who Made People Cry
TEXT: Judg. 2:1–7.

Folks would be startled to attend church and discover that the angel of the Lord was standing in the pulpit to deliver a direct message from God. People would sit up and listen—no sleeping this time. When the children of Israel gathered in the promised land expecting to hear Joshua preach, God sent his own angel to preach the sermon (Judg. 2). The angel's words were direct: "I made you to go up out of Egypt, and have brought you unto the land; . . . I said, I will never break my covenant with you. . . . But ye have not obeyed my voice: why have ye done this?" (vv. 1–2). God had blessed them, but the people had broken their agreement with God. They had failed. They had intermarried with the heathen and adopted their practice of idol worship. The angel's question, "Why have ye done this?" brought guilt and grief. "The people lifted up their voice, and wept" (v. 4).

I. *There were tears of regret.* The conviction of the people's sins brought sorrow. Even the place where the experience happened was forever called Bochim, which means "a weeping place."

The results of sin are hurt and sorrow. The idol gods were a "snare" to them (v. 3). And the succeeding generation "knew not the Lord" (v. 10). The sins of the parents affected their children.

II. *There were tears of repentance.* The people "sacrificed there unto the Lord" (v. 5). They turned from idols to the living God.

God's continuing love for his people in the midst of their sins is a beautiful picture of the Father's grace. Undeserving violators of his covenant, we are sinners in need of redemption. Repentance is the first step on the road of spiritual recovery.

III. *There were tears of rejoicing.* New commitments result in new directions. "And the people served the Lord all the days of Joshua" (v. 7). The "great works of the Lord" are cause for rejoicing in any generation. Fulfillment took the place of emptiness. Life had meaning.

This parable of life was experienced by Peter. He found a Bochim after tears of failure (Luke 22:61–62). He, too, experienced repentance and rejoicing in the Lord's forgiveness. Remember, Jesus asked Peter for a confession of his love three times, the same number of times he had to declare his faith in a crisis.

The prodigal son experienced his Bochim in the form of a pigpen. Times of guilt and tears of regret brought tender repentance and overwhelming rejoicing (Luke 15:11–24).

This is the way back to God, to a Father who expresses unchanging and unending love.—Craig Skinner.

SUNDAY: APRIL FIFTH

MORNING SERVICE

Topic: A Visitor from Nazareth
TEXT: Matt. 21:11.

Riding there into Jerusalem with the crowd milling about him, shouting and singing, he seems far enough away to be comfortable. His world hardly touches our own. I am not sure that all of us would listen long; a few minutes perhaps, and we should walk away indifferently or interrupt him angrily. I wonder what his coming would be like, if it were not so utterly out of the question—where he would live, who his friends would be, how he would set about making the same deathless name for himself he made two thousand years ago; and this perhaps most of all, what there is about our modern life, if anything, that he would approve, and what there is about it that would sadden him.

I. I think most certainly he would approve the knowledge we have acquired.

(a) That long search through the musty records of the past, building up for us bit by bit the life of hidden ages; that patient delving in the earth, the laborious deciphering of strange inscriptions; the study of the rocks and the stars, of matter and life and man himself, of philosophy and mathematics—until he would be a bold Aristotle indeed who would attempt a summary and synthesis of human knowledge! And with all of it Jesus of Nazareth would find himself in deepest sympathy. No doubt that is putting it mildly. I dare say it would kindle a light in his eyes and something like the movement and rhythm of a great symphony in his soul.

(b) Only the issue of it would sadden him: the cynical, disillusioned lives that seem unable to bear the weight of much knowledge and turn back from the quest as though they had found some sad emptiness where they thought God was; others keep on, dispirited, plodding, and the shadows grow black as night because they have missed their way. I have talked with them. They told me to a man that losing their faith was like getting rid of a "heavy portmanteau full of old rags and brickbats." But they could not gaze into their own faces as I gazed into them, to see the weariness of all that fine new freedom they had won, and how loose the fibers seemed that were so taut before. They thought they were better for it, standing there staring at nothing within and without.

(c) It's ugly and weird what knowledge can do to a soul that isn't ready yet for the burden of it. Even knowing another life may take the beauty out of yours, unless this Christ is somewhere near enough to have him clutch you back desperately from the edge of an abyss like that, and change the hurt in our wide-open eyes to love again! Knowledge? Thank God for the hue and the cry and the broadening road; but the issue of it in a thousand lives, Jesus of Nazareth, pity that!

II. Or take our skill. I know it would stir him. There is no romance, except the miracle of God in a man's soul, which can compare with the impossible magic of human ingenuity.

(a) What we need is a way out, not a way back: Jesus Christ striding on, thrilled at the triumph of wheels roaring, the doubling and tripling of God's bounty; delicate fabrics pouring in glossy waves from swift, pointed fingers of steel; great towers rising; lights springing on; planes soaring; voices whispering through the air to the ends of the earth and back again; sight in the dark reaching out across the sea; the whole rolling world busy with its traffic, everywhere man conquering, and nature tamed now flashing about to do his bidding!

(b) Perhaps one might be allowed to stop long enough for the registering of a little unqualified awe at this story which has been unraveled down here on our whirling dervish of a planet during the last years of its history. Those fifty years are like the last third of an inch in a timetable two hundred and sixty miles long! About twenty inches back along that timetable the psalmist was writing, "What is man, that thou art mindful of him? Thou madest him to have dominion over the works of thy hands; thou hast put all things under his feet, all sheep and oxen"—one almost smiles!—"the fowl of the air and the fish of the sea." He was like an infant in the nursery gurgling over his toys! In two generations we have come away from sheepraising to germ culture, from the care of oxen to the study of vitamins, from fowl to zeppelins, and from fish to submarines!

(c) No curse yet, until you think of the use some of us have made of it all. That's Christ's Calvary now. We have built a world with it so deliberately and so damnably unjust that it is even sick of itself and refuses every now and then to run any more. It isn't the machine. You can't alibi this tragedy. It's the man, playing his sordid game, bent on getting what he can out of his cunning devices, pulling the petals one by one off a little blue flower called happiness. And the flower is nearly gone now! The wheels are silent and men are cold; plows are being used to destroy while children go without food. The curse is in ourselves and in what we have done with the clean glory of our genius. Skill? Magnificent skill! The only thing for God to pity is our use of it!

III. Finally, there is our energy. Back of all the knowledge and the skill, the ceaseless, pulsing drive of the human spirit.

(a) Without that hint of eternity in his soul, I think man would long since have grown tired; but the pacing goes on. Those feet, marching—just to hear the deathless sound of it might well drive you mad. God must look on men proudly; they are so much like him—pushing, striving, hurled back, and coming on again! Energy is just history in a word. I wish we could get some idea of the sweep and tide of it, never tired and never appeased, driving up out of savagery into civilization, out of huts into the grandeur of a great city's skyline rising like "diamond-studded granite in the night," out of dirt and filth into medicine and art and universities and "the second movement of the Seventh Symphony dropping down into your room out of the clouds the mystic, healing beauty" of a noble spirit gone from this earth long since.

(b) I wonder if there aren't huge, stalwart, worthy tasks for anybody who will see them, tasks that will take all the knowledge and the skill and the energy you have without ever leaving a dusty taste in your mouth! I wonder what this visitor from Nazareth would have to say in our noisy, thrusting world about the moral lassitude of the human soul, looking on at a thousand wrongs and throwing up its puissant hands as though it were quite impotent! Don't tell me that we can do nothing about the kingdom of God; we have done too much about everything else! We don't have to sit down in this welter of futility. We who have built so much alone can build with him if we will. Appalling tides of energy, on the one hand, and abysmal spiritual lethargy on the other, that's the paradox you and I have to thank for our present bewilderment: tense, quick muscles, and inertia in the soul! I think nothing describes us better, as we sit, so many of us, and gaze at the world withering beyond these adventureless doors of ours, where no quest mounts its stirrups any more and doffs its hat and rides off for a Holy Grail!—Paul Scherer.

Illustrations

THE MEANING OF LIFE.   Fitz-James Stephen wrote many years ago, "The 'Great Eastern,' or some of her successors," he said, "will perhaps defy the roll of the Atlantic, and cross the seas without allowing their passengers to feel that they have left the firm land. The voyage from the cradle to the grave may come to be performed with similar facility. Progress and science may perhaps enable untold millions to live and die without a care, without a pang, without an anxiety. They will have a pleasant passage and plenty of brilliant conversation. They will wonder that men ever believed at all in clanging fights and blazing towns and sinking ships and praying hands; and, when they come to the end of their course, they will go their way, and the place thereof will know them no more."—William James.

THE ADVENTURE OF FAITH.   Noah's faith is exactly like our own—a growing faith. As the flood destroyed and buried every living thing Noah's faith grew and bore him high above the abodes of catastrophe. And this is the very miracle and wonder of faith—that the very thing that kills and buries and overwhelms is now compelled to bear him up. Anybody who has made this venture of faith and knows it from his own experience knows that this is just simple truth. Everything that comes to us like an assault of fate—dread of the future, human disappointments, embroilments in our life, trials and afflictions—all this becomes for him who has faith an element which can no longer swamp and bury him, but mysteriously bears him up, as Noah was borne up by the flood.—Helmut Thielicke.

Sermon Suggestions

GOD IN HISTORY   Text: Ezek. 37:1–14. (1) The narration: The prophet's vision. (2) The meaning: God is able to do for and with him people what they could never do themselves. (3) The application: The church may go into decline and cultural captivity, but God's Spirit will give it new, incredible life (cf. Matt. 16:18–19).

IF CHRIST IS IN YOU.   Text: Rom. 8:6–11. (1) You set your mind on the higher things. (2) You enjoy being right with God. (3) You anticipate complete and final victory over your human nature.

Worship Aids

CALL TO WORSHIP.   "He was in the world, and the world was made through him, yet the world knew him not. He came to his own home, and his own people received him not. But to all who received him, who believed in his name, he gave power to become children of God" (John 1:10–12 RSV).

INVOCATION.   O God, we call to you out of the turmoil of our world. Great forces of evil and great forces of good compete in our personal lives and in the life of the larger world. Help us to find the key to victory in the midst of it all as we look to you.

OFFERTORY SENTENCE.   "You shall receive power when the Holy Spirit has come upon you; and you shall be my witnesses in Jerusalem and in all Judea and Samaria and to the end of the earth" (Acts 1:8 RSV).

OFFERTORY PRAYER.   Our Father, let these offerings go forth into all the world with your blessing, so that your witnesses may speak the saving truth that affirms all the good and challenges all the evil. We thank you for giving us this partnership with you in what you are doing on this earth.

PRAYER.   We draw near to thee, our Heavenly Father, with gratitude and with thanksgiving. At thine hands we have experienced bounties innumerable, joys more than we can tell, mercies inexpressible. What tongue can speak of the kindnesses thou hast manifested toward us by the great realm of nature, which thou hast ordained to serve us, and which is the minister of thy bounty; by all the blessings which thou hast sent into life through society; and by all the overrulings of thy providence by which the events of every day have conspired together for our good; but, above all, by thine own precious self, by Jesus, our Master and companion, and by the power of the Holy Ghost, through which we commune with thee, and by which our life is lifted up above the flesh, and holds sacred and blessed companionship with thy life? Thus, we are indeed the sons of God, not alone by thine innumerable bounties and gifts, but by our daily habit of life. By all our thoughts, by all our affections, by every spiritual sentiment, we are brought into this companionship, and are the sons of God in very deed.

Oh! that there were in us that spirit which should make manifest more gloriously the power of God on the human soul. Oh! that, since we are sons, we might show ourselves princes. Oh! that there might be such luminousness in every thought, in all virtues, in every affection, that they should shine out, and men should behold them. We beseech of thee, O Lord our God! that we may come more and more, every day, into this blessed communion, and that, going forth, our faces may shine, and that men may know where we get our inspiration; where our comfort comes from; whence are all the gifts by which we are made strong in our combat with grief, with temptation, and with wickedness in high places.

We pray, O God! that thou wilt comfort any that are beginning this life, and that see men as trees walking. Touch their eyes again. Grant that they may see clearly. May all those that are striving to follow thee, but that see the discrepance between their ideal and their real life, and mourn over it, be comforted and encouraged to persevere.

We beseech of thee that those who are tempted and carried by gusts of passion out of the way, and find themselves disheveled and turned upside down, like men that are whirled in the tempest, may not give up in despair, but gather again their energies, and attempt once more to walk the royal way. Let none, having once put his hand to the plow, turn back. May no one count himself unworthy of eternal life.

Oh! that every one of us might behold the coming glory, and be inspired with the thought of the joy and dignity to come. May every one of us take hold of present duty. And though we are filled with weaknesses, and are conscious every day of sins; though infirmities multiply themselves without number on every side, and the carriage in us of thought and feeling and sentiment is most imperfect; though our whole life is illiterate, untaught, in things spiritual, yet may we look forward, and "press forward, toward the mark for the prize of the high calling of God in Christ Jesus."—Henry Ward Beecher.

EVENING SERVICE

Topic: Strength for Your Toughest Struggles

TEXT: Col. 1:1–14.

Surely one of your toughest struggles will be to stay on track, to remain faithful under the pressure and confusion of today's religious alternatives. It will be to avoid being fooled by the counterfeits. That is the issue that Colossians addresses.

I. First of all, begin positively. This is verse 1 of Colossians: "Paul an apostle of Christ Jesus by the will of God."

(a) That is positive! Paul knows who he is, to whom he belongs, and under whose authority he communicates. He doesn't try to hide it.

(b) Paul says in verse 2, "To the saints and faithful brethren in Christ at Colossae . . ." Paul was addressing a church with real problems. Still the picture he held in his mind was not of a problem church. It was a picture of a possibility church, a caring, faithful, dynamic congregation. It is a simple fact that negative thoughts drain energy and enthusiasm and tend inevitably to produce negative results. Positive thoughts release God's power within and release people to grow in a creative way.

(c) Paul continues in verses 3, 4, and 5, "We always thank God, the Father of our Lord Jesus Christ, when we pray for you, because we have heard of your faith in Christ Jesus and of the love which you have for all the saints, because of the hope laid up for you in heaven. . . ." That is positive and affirming. He chose to focus his attention upon the faithful members rather than upon the unfaithful ones.

(d) That positive word continues. Paul calls the gospel "the word of truth." It isn't human imagination or human invention. It is truth—that which corresponds ultimately and accurately to reality. The church of Jesus Christ is alive and well on planet earth and is at this very moment showing signs of a tremendously new and exciting awakening.

II. The second great step is to continue prayerfully.

(a) Paul says in verse 9, "And so, from the day we heard of it, we have not ceased to pray for you." There are different ways of telling people that you are praying for them. You can tell people that you are praying for them and really put them down. Paul's prayer was so constructive. That is because it was a prayer with dynamic faith that already visualized a new future.

(b) There was a tremendous sense of excitement in Paul's prayer. Paul was saying, in effect, "I pray that you will be what God wants you to be . . . that you will fulfill the exciting possibilities that he has placed within you. . . ." That is the way that we are to strengthen each other in prayer. We are to pray that each person would move to the fulfillment of that unique creation of God's grace which he has so freely given.

III. How do you find strength for your toughest struggles? You begin positively. You continue prayerfully. You proceed dynamically.

(a) Listen now to verses 11 and 12, "May you be strengthened with all power, according to his glorious might, for all endurance and patience with joy, giving thanks to the Father, who has qualified us to share in the inheritance of the saints in light." Now please understand that his verse is more than a pious wish from an ancient letter. What I am hearing this morning is an energy-releasing word, spoken over my life.

(b) God's Word is powerful to effect what it announces. When God speaks, it happens. God says, "May you be strengthened with all power." And it is happening. The word *power* is *dunamis.* Twice that word is used in verse 11. I expect you to go out of here this morning with positive self-esteem, with a new openness to spiritual wisdom and understanding, and with spiritual power and vitality surging through you.

IV. There is a fourth great step in finding strength for your toughest struggles. Accept personally the grace of God in Jesus Christ, and live victoriously by faith.

(a) The Colossians didn't need a new religion. God had already won the victory in Jesus Christ. "He has delivered us from the dominion of darkness and transferred us to the kingdom of his beloved Son, in whom we have redemption, the forgiveness of sins."

(b) You are no longer bound if you have faith in Jesus Christ. You are not a prisoner. The door is open. You are delivered from the kingdom of darkness and transferred to the kingdom of his beloved Son, Jesus!—Joe A. Harding.

SUNDAY: APRIL TWELFTH

MORNING SERVICE

Topic: The Ultimate Dilemma
TEXT: Heb. 10:4; 9:26.

The history of mankind has been the record of the endeavor to answer one stubborn question, to deal with one radical dilemma. How is man to be reconciled to life? How to make his peace with the universe? Can the human heart break through the vicious circle that remorselessly hems it in? Can any expedient be devised that will take away sins?

In the course of the centuries, three historic expedients have been devised to solve the dilemma. There have been three classic answers to the question.

I. The first is the answer of the Hebrew. "The blood of bulls and goats," that is to say, the whole elaborate sacrificial system —such was the answer. Hence, through the dim mists of antiquity you can discern the laden altars, the smoking hecatombs, the endlessly repeated ritual—all witnessing to the belief in the efficacy of religious observances for the taking away of sins.

(a) Now we all have something of the Hebrew in our constitution, and in some degree this answer has been ours. When I trust to the externals of religion to secure me in the sight of God; when I commemorate at the Communion table the sacrifice of Christ's death, but make no sacrifice myself in the region of heart and will; when I repeat daily acts of prayer, and my life remains unchanged, I am perpetuating the blunder of those in every age who have imagined that religious acts and attitudes can justify the soul before God, and that the blood of bulls and goats can take away sins.

(b) There came a time when even the Hebrew began to doubt his own solution: "Wherewith shall I come before the Lord, and bow myself before the high God? Shall I come before him with burnt offerings? Will the Lord be pleased with these?" There is no healing there.

II. The answer of the Greek. The Greek mind owes a double allegiance—to art and to philosophy. Hence the answer of the Greeks to the great dilemma had two sides to it—the one aesthetic, the other intellectual. Over against the radical evil of the world the Greek set the apprehension of beauty and the logic of thought. Why should men vex their souls about sin? The loveliness of nature would charm it away; or alternatively the wit of the philosopher would rationalize it away.

(a) Now we all have something of the Greek in us, and in some degree his answer has been ours. We have tried to deliver our souls aesthetically and intellectually.

(b) But can the beauty of nature "break the power of cancelled sin"? Will the perfumes of Arabia work the cleansing miracle? And what of our attempts to rationalize the mystery of evil away? We say that all the troubles of humanity could be solved by the application of a little logic and intelligence. Then God makes a silence in our souls, and out of the silence comes a voice: "Ye must be born again!" It is not possible that man's intellect, any more than his sense of beauty, should take away sins.

III. The answer of the Roman. This can be expressed in a single word—moralism. The Roman, with his marvellous sense of law and order, and his genius for constructing a code, believed that ultimately the only thing that mattered was disciplined conduct. And it is significant that his answer reappeared subsequently in the theology of the Church, in a doctrine of salvation by good works.

(a) Now we all have something of the Roman in us, and in some degree his answer has been ours. We have trusted to man's natural virtues, his innate decency, for the redeeming of the world. We have looked to our own moral achievements, our personal righteousness, to give us a secure standing before God.

(b) And where have they landed us? Is it not written clear on the page of history today that man cannot be his own redeemer? And as for our ingrained habit of relying on good works, can we not see that it tends inevitably toward that self-centeredness and pride which are the basic human sins—so that the more satisfaction our good works give us, the more surely is sin tightening its grip upon us, and thus the vicious circle goes on forever?

(c) The answer of the Roman fails us. It is not possible that the world should ever be saved by moralism.

IV. What then? Then rising out of the midnight of man's despair, smiting the darkness like a sudden dawn, comes the solving word: and all the classic answers fade away before the glory of it:

All for sin could not atone;
Thou must save, and Thou alone.

Every other experiment fails. Only Christ's experiment—the experiment of the cross—triumphantly succeeds. "He hath appeared to put away sin by the sacrifice of himself."

(a) Let no one suppose that this answer —the Christian answer to man's desperate dilemma—is just archaic language, doctrinal theorizing, vague and rhetorical and irrelevant. In point of fact, it is the most terrific thrust of absolutely shattering realism that the world has ever seen. Words stagger before the mystery of the cross; but that is because the cross itself is the eternal Word, dynamic and explosive, supercharged with the energies of grace. It is more than a Word—it is the supreme deed, God's deed, the dramatic breakthrough of the world beyond into this world of time and history. And when I survey the wondrous cross, I am witnessing the whole formidable array of man's once invincible foes challenged at the very seat and center of their power, trampled underfoot in the very moment when the might of evil was concentrated for its supreme decisive stroke. That is why the answer of the cross succeeds where every other answer fails. I am seeking the victory of God.

(b) But let us remember that it is only as we align ourselves with the Christ who reigns from the tree that his victory becomes valid for us. God's crowning deed demands our crowning decision. If it elicits no response in personal surrender it will mean nothing; and we shall go back to the old struggle, the old frustration, the old monotony of defeat. But if we respond with every atom of our mind and soul, it will mean everything; and we shall know the joy of being made more than conquerors, through him that loved us.—James S. Stewart.

Illustrations

THE INCLUSIVE CROSS.   How could he have called us if he had not been crucified, for it is only on the cross that a man dies with arms outstretched? Here, again, we see the fitness of his death and of those outstretched arms: it was that he might draw his ancient people with the one and the Gentiles with the other, and join both together in himself. Even so, he foretold the manner of his redeeming death, "I, if I be lifted up, will draw all men unto Myself."—St. Athanasius.

THE HEART OF HUMANITY.   The human heart is not shaped like a valentine heart, perfect and regular in contour; it is slightly irregular in shape as if a small piece of it were missing out of its side. That missing part may very well symbolize a piece that a spear tore out of the universal heart of humanity on the cross, but it probably symbolizes something more. It may very well mean that when God created each human heart, he kept a small sample of it in heaven, and sent the rest of it into the world of time where it would each day learn the lesson that it could never be really happy, never be really wholly in love, and never be really wholehearted until it went back again to the timeless to recover the sample which God had kept for it for all eternity.—Fulton J. Sheen.

Sermon Suggestions

WHEN GOD TEACHES US.   Text: Isa. 50: 4–9a. (1) We have a word to share with others. (2) Yet our most-needed message may not be welcomed. (3) Nevertheless, we can be confident of God's support and vindication.

HOW TO GET ALONG WITH YOUR FELLOW CHRISTIANS.   Text: Phil. 2:5–11. Like Jesus Christ, (1) be willing to give up your superior status; (2) be willing to suffer for the will of God and the good of others; (3) expect God to let you share his glory in the good you accomplish.

Worship Aids

CALL TO WORSHIP.   "If we walk in the light, as he is in the light, we have fellowship with one another, and the blood of Jesus Christ his Son cleanseth us from all sin" (1 John 1:7).

INVOCATION.   O God, as the light is shining in the person of our Lord Jesus Christ and in the holy Scriptures that bear witness to him, grant that we may walk in the light that he casts on our way and that your word will become increasingly a lamp to our feet. To that end, illuminate this service of worship with the brightness of heaven itself.

OFFERTORY SENTENCE.   "The earth is the Lord's and the fulness thereof; the world, and they that dwell therein" (Ps. 24:1).

OFFERTORY PRAYER.   Lord God, accept these gifts that give concrete expression to our deepest held beliefs that God is love, Christ died for all, and we must be doers of the Word and not hearers only.—E. Lee Phillips.

PRAYER.   Almighty God, thou who hast bent chaos to thy will and who hast established order in the midst of the dark deep, we turn to thee that we might know thee better; that we might in this moment share the deep within us with thee and find our selves reordered; that we might raise the chaos in us and in thy presence find our troubled wills recreated by thy hovering Spirit. We seek communion with thee because all else offers us what we seek at our expense; all else is a bargain made with the devil that demands from us payment with our lives and love, but in communion with thee there is friendship that gives what we could not demand and offers what we could not live without. It is thy gift to us. We know thy power is the power of love, which refuses to retreat and refuses to quit. We know thy will is the will that shall bring into our midst all that thou hast prepared for us despite the obstacles and rejections of our pride. We know thy future to be always pressing upon our present with the promise of making all things new, and yet we will not dismiss the past without a struggle. We know thy grace, for we have seen its face in flesh and blood, the flesh and blood of Jesus Christ as he sought to share with us the grandeur of thy glory, the flesh and blood of our common life as we have liberating experiences from the bondage and burdens of this world. We thank thee for the great multitude of thy gifts, but we do not turn to thee to speak in gratitude only for thy gifts nor even to ask for their continuance; but to speak with thee in order to be in thy company and to enjoy thy fellowship.

Where else will we find a friend who is willing to listen to our complaints and can respond, "I understand. I have endured them all myself"? Where else will we find a friend who understands and feels our sorrow and our grief, who knows the injustices and absurdities of life and can respond, "I understand. I have endured them all myself"? Where else will we find a friend who has time to receive our anger and wrath because of insults to our humanity and can answer, "I understand; I have endured them all myself, but remember this, I know that you are capable of overcoming all with love, for I love you very much"? Where else can we find a friend who knows when our complaints are rationalizations, knows when our excuses cannot explain the evil that we have done, when our sorrow is self-pity, and our declarations of love are but the veiled confessions of self-love or self-hatred; a friend who can respond, "I understand; I indeed know who you are and what you have done, but I love you very much"? A friend who is both judge and redeemer. Thou art our friend. All other friends are limited investments; there are limits to their time and concern, but thou hast set no limits to thy love. Thou art our friend even as we resist thy friendship. We pray that we might more eagerly receive thy love and that we might be more open to the communion with thee.—Richard Brand.

EVENING SERVICE

Topic: Guilty Bystanders
TEXT: Obad. 11.

This text challenges us on our tendencies to stand aloof from the sufferings of others, our inclinations to be mere bystanders. It warns us that in complacent unresponsiveness to the sufferings of others we become one with those who are responsible for that suffering.

I. *First, when you stand aloof from human suffering you are indeed like those who inflict suffering.*

(a) This is a clear lesson of the parable of the Good Samaritan. A priest and then a Levite, a religious administrator, come along the road—and each in turn passes by without stopping to help the injured man. They are guilty bystanders. So the priest and the Levite stand aloof and make themselves of one mind with the robbers who had beaten the man.

(b) Traditional Christian thought distinguishes between sins of commission and sins of omission. The first are sins that go counter to moral law or convention; the second are failures to do something that duty or moral principle demands. Jesus' strongest condemnations were for certain sins of omission, failures in compassion and mercy, aloofness towards the needs and sufferings of others.

(c) Many of us good men and women seem inclined to do nothing—or not very much, anyway—about the hunger that afflicts so many millions throughout the world. Some of us good people are mere bystanders with respect to the poverty in our society. Some of us good people stand aloof and do nothing about environmental pollution and about the menace of nuclear weapons, excusing ourselves by thinking that these issues are in the hands of the powerful and that we ordinary citizens have little influence. When we stand aloof from human suffering, like the priest and the Levite, we are indeed of one mind with those who inflict suffering.

II. *Second, when you stand aloof you may be deceiving yourself and depriving yourself of much that makes life meaningful and good.*

(a) Jesus made that point very strongly in his parable about the rich man and Lazarus. For that rich man every meal was a banquet. But he ignored Lazarus, the sick beggar who lay at his gate. Of course, he didn't go out of his way to make things more difficult for him. He simply ignored him.

(b) Jesus finishes the parable by picturing the rich man agonizing in hell, and he makes it very clear that it was his indifference that got him into hell. Should you find the notion of a person being consigned to a place called "hell" inconsistent with our modern modes of thought, you can get the message Jesus intended by seeing the rich man as deprived by his indifference of those things that make life meaningful and good.

(c) And we need to be warned, in these days of intense discussion of big problems and the proliferation of good causes, with elaborate organizations to go with them, that it is possible to become so desperately concerned for suffering humankind-in-general that one has no time or inclination for dealing with the suffering person-in-particular who lies at one's own gate. We sometimes deceive ourselves by thinking that noble and inspirational talk somehow gets us off the moral hook.

Yes, when you stand aloof you may be deceiving yourself and depriving yourself of much that makes life meaningful and good.

III. *Third, when you stand aloof from human suffering you repudiate the fundamental Christian principle of love.*

(a) Love, as the New Testament understands love, is the active, sometimes sacrificial willing of the real good of other persons. Love requires that the Christian be involved with the needs and sufferings of others. Compassion means, literally, "suffering with."

(b) The message of Jesus' parable about the final judgment comes through loud and clear. In the last section of it we see a great king sitting in final judgment on certain of his subjects. "The curse is upon you," the king says to them. "Go from my sight to the eternal fire that is ready for the devil and his angels." He then explains to these unfortunate people why they are being punished in that way: "For when I was hungry you gave me nothing to eat; when thirsty nothing to drink; when I was a stranger you gave me no home; when naked you did not clothe me; when I was ill and in prison you did not come to my help." This puzzles the condemned, and they say to the king: "Lord, when was it that we saw you hungry or thirsty or a stranger or naked or ill or in prison and did nothing for you?" The king answers straightforwardly, "I tell you this: anything you did not do for one of these, however humble, you did not do for me."

(c) I wish I could explain away the discomforting challenge of those words. But there is no ambiguity in them. They are Jesus' judgment on guilty bystanders, on those who stand aloof from the needs and sufferings of others.—J. A. Davidson.

SUNDAY: APRIL NINETEENTH

MORNING SERVICE

Topic: How Real Is Easter to You?
TEXT: Mark 16:1–8.

I. It was early in the morning. The roosters were crowing, and here and there a donkey lifted its ivory trumpet to the dawn and brayed for its breakfast. The women were astounded to find the tomb open, the stone rolled away. That was a new experience. In all their visits to the tombs of loved ones, it had never happened before. Then an angel appeared to them. That too was a new experience.

They had heard about angels all their lives, but they never expected to see one. And the angel told them that Jesus was not there, that he had risen from the dead. They were to go back to the disciples and tell them that he would meet them in Galilee, which was the scene of most of his earlier ministry. Of all their experiences, this was the most incredible. The Master risen from the dead! That tortured, broken body that hung so lifelessly on the cross, now vibrant again, going to Galilee. They were overwhelmed. They had never known anything like it. They had no formula for dealing with it. It was too new, too startling, too far beyond their experiences. Seized by terror, says the Gospel, they ran away and said nothing to anyone about what had happened—not even to the disciples to whom they were supposed to carry the message!

II. It has been almost twenty centuries since that first Easter morning. My question is this: Are we any more capable of hearing the news of the resurrection of Jesus than they were?

(a) It has been preached from every pulpit in the world for nearly two thousand years. It has been read billions, perhaps trillions, of times. It has been witnessed to in homes and offices, on street corners, in factories and resorts, on university campuses, and military bases—wherever people are. The news is no longer new. We have heard it again and again. But are we any closer to believing it, to acting on it, to making it the heart and center of our lives, than those poor, frightened women who came to the tomb on the first Easter Day and found it empty?

(b) Our problem is that the reality of the resurrection—if indeed we are even convinced it is a reality—is different from the reality of our experience. It is not what we are familiar with in everyday life. Our world is a world of breakfast cereals and luncheon salads, carpooling and ballgames, drinks at six and dinner at seven, with clubs and church on the weekend. It is a world of motorcars and business deals and TV programs and trips to the seashore. It is not a world of empty graves and visiting angels. It is not a world of resurrection and messages from God.

III. Or is it? There was the trouble with the women in the Gospel, you see. They didn't think their world was that kind either. They didn't know that there is a world of transcendent reality just beyond this one, waiting to break into it.

(a) This is the point Mark has made all the way through his little Gospel, that people must be prepared to see the other reality if it is ever to have real meaning in their lives. We must learn to watch and pray and be open to the incursions of this other reality, or we will pass through life and never know it exists. "You have eyes," said Jesus, "can't you see? You have ears; can't you hear?" (Mark 8:18)

(b) Think what it might mean: that the world is not merely a random concatenation of atoms; that there is eternal purpose and meaning in human life; that there is a just intelligence behind everything, which will one day tip the scales in favor of those who are today broken and despised and neglected; that all human wars are only the prelude to God's everlasting peace, when the lion shall lie down with the lamb and the ox eat straw with the bear; that a cup of cold water given in the Master's name shall have the Master's reward; that love is indeed the greatest gift in the universe, and that we need never be depressed or disheartened, for it is ours in abundance from our heavenly Father; that Christ, the risen Lord, is with us at this very moment and has been with us all along, though we could not see and did not know it; and that his promises are true, that we shall live with him forever, caught up in a glory beyond any we have ever known.

III. Do you have that trouble with Christian experience? I mean, you're never quite sure which reality is the true one, the one about the risen Christ or the one about the everyday, secular culture you live in? Have you ever thought about letting the Christ-reality transform the other one, so that they are no longer two realities but one? "Don't be conformed to this world," said the Apostle; "be transformed"—so that Christ becomes the key to everything!

IV. How about you? Are you beginning to glimpse a reality you have never fully experienced before? If you are, don't fight it. Let God bring the picture in more clearly. That reality may be the one that will sweep you out of yourself and into the arms of the Father.—John Killinger.

Illustrations

GOD'S YES AND NO.   What does it mean to celebrate Easter? It means to see this light of Good Friday. It is there, it is shining, it is waiting only for our eyes to see it. We may, we must, we want to open our eyes, to see it. To celebrate Easter means to hear the yes and the no which God has spoken in what he did on Good Friday: the yes to all of us and the no to our estrangement from him, which is our misery.—Karl Barth.

REAL EASTER FAITH.   Many say, How can I believe in the Easter message of the resurrection? I cannot know for certain whether that is true which the Gospels record; I cannot go back and prove it. And if I would simply force myself to believe it because it is recorded in the Bible—assuming that I could so force myself—how would that help me? That would not give me a joyful, living hope. They are entirely right. Such a faith whose authority is merely history has no worth. The real Easter faith does not come from the fact that one is reconciled to God through Jesus Christ. This reconciliation is not a mere belief but a rebirth, a new life. Through this reconciliation, godlessness and anxiety are rooted out and one becomes a new person. From this reconciliation through Jesus Christ faith in his resurrection from the dead arises of itself. —Emil Brunner.

Sermon Suggestions

GOD'S EVERLASTING LOVE.   Text: Jer. 31:1–6. (1) It is a love demonstrated at a point in time. (2) It is a love that persists through many difficulties. (3) It is a love that at last brings great rejoicing.

THE UNIVERSAL GOSPEL.   Text: Acts 10:34–43. (1) For all nations. (2) By Jesus Christ. (3) Through chosen witnesses. (4) To be received by faith. (5) For the forgiveness of sins.

Worship Aids

CALL TO WORSHIP.   "Blessed are they that have not seen, and yet have believed" (John 20:29b).

INVOCATION.   Almighty God, gently move us, wisely urge us, mercifully forgive us, deftly guide us, and generously grant us to worship thee in spirit and in truth, through Christ who died for us.—E. Lee Phillips.

OFFERTORY SENTENCE.   "God is able to make all grace abound toward you; that ye, always having all sufficiency in all things, may abound to every good work" (2 Cor. 9:8).

OFFERTORY PRAYER.   We thank thee, our Father, that we now, because of the risen Christ, can do things that without his power we could never do. Let the glory of his resurrection be seen both in our living and in our giving.

PRAYER.   Eternal God, before whom the morning stars first sang together, and who holdest in thy hands the destiny of every living thing, we worship thee. Thanks be to thee for the note of victory that fills our souls today! Thanks to thee for our living Lord over whom death had no dominion! For the rich heritage of faith that life is ever lord of death, and that love can never lose its own, we thank thee. Strengthen our believing. Confirm our confidence in thee and life eternal.

We thank thee for all things excellent and beautiful that make faith in immortality more sure. For our friends who have loved us, our homes that have nourished us, for the heights and depths of the human spirit, full of promise and prophecy, for all victories of right over wrong, and above all for Christ, who has brought life and immortality to light, we thank thee. Join to our company today those whom we have loved and who live with thee in the house not made with hands. Gather us into the fellowship of the Church, both militant and triumphant, as we sing praise to thee.

We pray for those defeated souls to whom the note of victory sounds distant and unreal. Thou seest them here, known to thee though not to us, spirits frustrated by circumstance, overwhelmed by temptation, facing griefs too heavy for their unaided strength. O thou, who canst make the barren place rejoice and the desert to blossom like the rose, redeem some stricken souls here from defeat to victory.

Replenish with new hope all who are discouraged about the world, who find faith in the ultimate victory of righteousness difficult. So often might triumphs over right, and the good is undone by evil that, like our Master on his cross we cry, "My God, my God, why hast thou forsaken me?" O thou to whom a thousand years are but as yesterday when it is past, and as a watch in the night, speak to us and refresh our souls with a new hope. Lift our vision above the immediate; illumine for us that eternal purpose which thou didst purpose in Christ. Say to us this Easter day that no Calvary can finally defeat Christ.

We lay before thee our concern for thy Church. For the great tradition of her strong and saving faith, thanks be to thee. Draw her members together into increasing unity. Grant that in these days of danger and opportunity her Gospel of deathless hope, or unconquerable faith, or invincible courage, may inspire thy people. Send us out from this high hour of worship to be fearless and faithful citizens of thy kingdom.

To that end may the living Christ be not only in our creed but in our experience. Let not Easter day represent to us only an historic victory; may it mean a present triumph in our souls—the living Christ our inspiration and our strength, so that we live, and yet not we, but Christ lives in us, the hope of glory. In that sustaining faith may we, too, like our Master, overcome the world.—Harry Emerson Fosdick.

EVENING SERVICE

Topic: Death Did Not Win!
TEXT: 1 Cor. 15:55, 58.
I. This is a strong and conclusive word. It closes out a lengthy message from Paul about what the resurrection of Christ means and foretells. It is his doctrinal statement about how Jesus triumphed over death and what that victory means for our experience as persons who must die.

After reminding the Corinthians about the fact of Jesus' resurrection, and after explaining the effects of that event upon life and death, Paul ended with an encouraging word to strengthen his readers for their daily tasks. As he summed up his message, Paul was saying that death did not win against Jesus and that it cannot win against those who belong to Jesus. Death was not Jesus' undoing, and death will not undo his people.

II. Much like the people of our time, the Corinthians had been badgered by clashing notions about life and death. They knew the teaching of the Epicureans: "There is nothing after this life!" They had heard the word of the Stoics: "There is nothing personal after this life!" And they had heard the words of the Platonists: "There is nothing but the soul after this life!" Paul countered all three notions in his message and labeled them false. Then he declared that there is something after this life, namely a full existence, and that we will be individual, personal, and in bodily form.

(a) It is always heartening to remind ourselves that the grave is not the final scene of our existence, and that death does not have the last word about life. The resurrection of Christ reassures us. We humans die, but we will live again. The resurrection of Christ reassures us of this.

(b) The resurrection of Jesus also reminds us that our work is not lost when we die. Just as we have a future beyond death, so does the work we have done while on earth.

Death will not defeat us. The grave will not undo what we have done for God. We are therefore encouraged by Paul to "be steadfast" in our living and in our labors. Life has meaning and a future that death cannot defeat. God will give us that future "through our Lord Jesus Christ."

(c) It is not easy to see that future during our troublesome moods. Our faith in it all is severely tested in precarious moments and when we fall victim to some disabling disease. It is not easy to see beyond death when we stand at the graveside of a friend or loved one whose life was cut short by an incurable sickness or taken in a fatal accident. At such times we are tempted to accept the view before us and the feelings within us as the last word of life about itself. So often we are left with this incomplete word about life, which is a word about death, brokenness, sorrow, loss, and the indescribable horror of knowing that life is that way.

(c) No, it is not easy to see the truth of our coming triumph when we feel at our lowest in mind and spirit. But the truth is still the truth, and moods have nothing to do with it. What is true remains true, and the scenes of life cannot change it. The sorriest scene of human loss cannot long hinder the light that streams from the shining face of our resurrected Lord. Paul knew this! He had seen that shining face and was thus converted to preach the message he once tried to debunk and destroy. No wonder Paul became the man he was! No wonder he wrote so fully about the resurrection truth! Paul had experienced the impact of that truth and knew its power to keep him steady in his life and labors.

(d) The Christian message was given to help us handle our past, rightly shape the present, and keep us related to the future God has willed for us in Christ. This faith has a sure return because Christian life is an investment.

Death did not defeat Jesus. Death will not defeat us. Death could not win over Jesus. Death cannot win against those who love and serve him. As Christians, we do not live in vain, nor do we work in vain.

III. Christian service is no vain or unpaid labor. We are saying this to ourselves and others every time we have an epitaph carved on a tombstone, every time we prepare a eulogy or condolence honoring someone for his or her work. We know that labors have meaning that should last and multiply. We know that labors should be rewarded.

(a) The New Testament has promised that they will be. There is a history of harvests here on this side of death, and there is a harvest on the other side as well. We need not fear being discouraged by having what we have done rejected as of no worth, and consequently gaining no pay. The test promises returns from our work for God; it promises wages to match services rendered. With this kind of future in view, Paul has encouraged us to "keep on keeping on." History here must not daunt us, and death must not frighten us. Death will not be our undoing, and we shall not be disappointed by God.

(b) The text therefore helps to increase our steadiness in faith and faithfulness in work for God. Every Christian is reminded that there is a future to what we are and returns from what we do. It is a good future, a future with eternal returns shared with us by a loving and gracious God. No Christian's life is lived in vain. No effort for Christ will fall flat in defeat.—James Earl Massey.

SUNDAY: APRIL TWENTY-SIXTH

MORNING SERVICE

Topic: Shadows

Text: Acts 5:15.

Simon Peter is one of the most interesting men in religious history. More conspicuously than any other, he illustrates the possibility of the growth of a human life into the image of God.

At no time during his career did the common people pay him a finer tribute than is revealed in the incident of our text. Some of the people of Jerusalem brought sick folk into the streets so that the shadow of Peter might fall upon them.

I. The most potent influence is characterized by silence. What a silent thing a shadow is! Noiselessly it falls, not a word does it speak, not a sound does it make. But so are all great healing ministries. The mightiest forces in nature as well as in human life are always silent in their operations.

(a) The most potent of all the forces that move our human nature is the power of love. How silent are its mighty conquests! You know what it does but you never hear its movements; you know that it gives luster to the eye, adds music to the voice, transfigures the commonest things, but no one ever heard the movement of love. When Elijah stood in the cave of Horeb he learned that God was not in the wind, nor the fire, nor the earthquake, but in the still small voice. For a voice which is a whisper you have to listen.

(b) And so did the Master teach concerning his kingdom. "The kingdom of heaven is like unto leaven which a woman took and hid in three measures of meal," and the leaven works silently. "The kingdom of heaven is like unto seed which a man took and cast into the ground," and the seed grows noiselessly, "Ye are the light of the world." The Christian life by its own innermost nature, by a sort of inevitable necessity, is to give light to all around. The Christian is not to nurse his religious life in solitude and retirement. That would be putting out the light. Shine, says Jesus, like the unselfish sun. Don't be stingy with your light. Remember, your light is needed. Shine, says Jesus, like the unselfish sun; only don't make a great noise about it. The sun does not blow a horn to let the world know it is about to rise. It just rises and shines.

(c) "Ye are the salt of the earth." The Christian is to act as salt. He is to be a savour of sweetness. The character of every follower of Jesus should be contagious. It should affect positively every other character with which it comes in contact. It should be true of disciples as of the Master that as many as touch us will be made whole. Even the physical life will be strengthened. Christly character has not wholly lost its power over bodily disease. Is it not easy to understand why certain sick folk in Jerusalem felt they could be healed by Peter's shadow? "Ye are the salt of the earth." And remember, salt does not require any publicity to do its work. It does its work silently, by simply being in contact with that which needs its conserving powers, and all that is required of it is that it should keep its own peculiar saltness and should remain in contact with what it preserves.

II. The most potent form of influence is not only silent but also unconscious. Just as we are rarely conscious of our shadow, so it is true that we are rarely conscious of our influence.

(a) If we say, "I want my influence to be so and so," it does not follow that our influence will be just like that. Conscious influence is but the smallest part of influence. We read in a certain narrative how Moses went up to the mountaintop with God, and when he came down again his face manifested some mysterious spiritual exaltation. Then the sacred writer adds this significant comment, "And Moses wist not that his face was shining." Of course not. Had Moses been conscious of himself his face would not have been transfigured with the divine light that was shining in his soul. But the world knew that here was a man that had been with God.

(b) I wish this feature were more prominent in our religion. We are all far too self-conscious in our faith. When a man is living a real Christian life he does not need to stand at a street corner and tell men so. Those with whom he lives, those with whom he has intercourse, know that here is a man who has secret sources of support and comfort. There they find the one unanswerable argument for the faith.

(c) We can weigh sugar but we cannot weigh sweetness. We can register heat, but the beam of light which can transform the world may fall across the most delicate balance and not move it a hair's breadth. And real influence cannot be tabulated. It never rises into consciousness at all. It is invisible and intangible. What one is speaks louder than what one does. Influence is the steady, persistent, irrepressible power of what one is. If we think too much about the effect of our actions upon others, the nerve of action will be cut. If we want to increase our influence we must grow inwardly. As a man grows in purity, in sincerity, in unselfishness, in devotion, he develops outward power that moves the lives of others.

III. The most potent form of influence is conditioned by a man's relationship to Christ.

(a) A man's shadow is the result of his position with regard to the sun. The form of it and the size of it and the intensity of it depend upon the man's attitude towards the light. Let him crouch in the shade, and his shadow cannot be seen; let him stand in the sunlight at noonday, and his shadow is small, sharply outlined, intense; let him turn his back on the sun, and his shadow lies along before him; let him walk toward the light, and his shadow lies behind him. It is our attitude to the light that determines our shadow. And so with influence.

The soul's attitude toward the Light of the world determines what that influence is to be—its form, its size, its intensity. If we would have our influence to be healing and helpful we must walk in the light until we become children of the light. If we walk with Christ those who are overshadowed by our influence will be helped and quickened by a spiritual power.

(b) Perhaps the most eloquent preacher Israel produced was Isaiah, and nowhere, I venture to assert, did he soar to such heights of imagery as when he said, "A man shall be as the shadow of a great rock in a weary land." He has the desert in mind. He sees a company of pilgrims in the glare of the Syrian sun with eyes smarting and lips burning and tongue and throat parched and dry, and then he sees a mighty rock in the midst of the desert, and the pilgrims nestling in the shade. Then breaks out his figure in the richness of its imagery. "A man shall be as the shadow of a great rock in a weary land." There have been such men in the world. The past bears clear witness to this truth. They whose lives have been as the shadow of a great rock in a weary land have linked themselves by their influence to times gone by and therefore go forward into times to come, the true kings of humanity. They hold as their heritage the gratitude of the ages and all hearts are their empire. They rise before us as we speak—statesmen, missionaries, philanthropists, martyrs; until passing over the paths strewn with heroic ashes and saintly blood we stand in the presence and beneath the cross of him who fulfilled the prophet's vision of a man as no other could possibly do.

(c) This word applies to parents whose shadow is always falling upon their children; to masters whose shadow is always falling upon the servants of the household; to teachers whose shadow is always falling upon their scholars; to preachers whose shadow is always falling upon their people; to all of us with the innumerable opportunities with which our lives are full for the exercise of saving influence upon others. Standing in the light we shall be able to cast a shadow of which in the day of Christ none of us shall be ashamed. —W. A. Cameron.

Illustrations

UNCONSCIOUS INFLUENCE. When Charles Dickens was passing one day through the streets of York an unknown woman accosted him saying, "Mr. Dickens, will you let me touch the hand that has filled my house with many friends?" Such, then, are the beneficent results of the shadow of a good life or a good work, or a good word, even when the doer or the speaker thereof is unconscious of it.—Clarence E. Macartney.

INFLUENTIAL, THOUGH HANDICAPPED. There is no handicap which cannot be turned into a medium of fruit bearing if the Christian wants with all his heart to bear fruit, and if he dedicates the handicap with the prayer that God will use even that limitation to his glory. So, take another look at your physical handicap, or your difficult family background, or your lack of anything which you have mistakenly thought to be imperative to significant fruit bearing. Looked at through the eyes of the world, the ignominious cross was regarded to be a sure and fatal stigma to the name and message of Christ. Looked at through the eyes of God, that same cross became the medium through which the incomparable fruit of salvation was provided for a lost world. Look at your handicap this time through the eyes of God!—Chester E. Swor.

Sermon Suggestions

GOD'S PLAN WINS THROUGH. Text: Acts 2:14a, 22–32. (1) From eternity, God intended that Jesus should be his means of salvation for humankind. (2) The acts of lawless people who crucified Jesus appeared to cancel the good he had undertaken. (3) However, God raised Jesus from the dead and caused the world to know him as both Lord and Christ.

WHAT CHRIST'S RESURRECTION MEANS TO YOU. Text: 1 Pet. 1:3–9. (1) A living hope. (2) A glorious inheritance. (3) A safe passage through testing. (4) A loving and joyous relationship to Jesus Christ. (5) Each step of it means "the salvation of your souls."

Worship Aids

CALL TO WORSHIP. "The Lord reigneth; let the earth rejoice" (Ps. 97:1a).

INVOCATION. Today, O God, we sit together in heavenly places in Christ Jesus, rejoicing in the power of the resurrection. Let nothing dim that vision. Teach us what it means in everyday life—in our homes, at school, at work, wherever we are. May your Spirit during this hour of worship guide us into the personal truth and realization of our being raised with Christ to walk in newness of life.

OFFERTORY SENTENCE. "He that taketh not his cross, and followeth after me, is not worthy of me" (Matt. 10:38).

OFFERTORY PRAYER. Our Father, we realize that the resurrection and the cross are bound together and cannot be separated. Even as we rejoice in Christ's victory we are still committed to that which gained victory for him. Help us so to participate in cross bearing, in our giving as well as otherwise, that we may know the fullness of the joy that was set before him.

PRAYER. Dear Heavenly Father! We are thankful for thy permission and commandment to come together in this hour to adore thee, to proclaim thy word, to listen to it, and to receive it in our hearts.

Yet we are not wont to come before thee in a way pleasing to thee and salutary for ourselves. Therefore we sincerely and humbly beseech thee to be with us and to take thy cause in thine own hands! Cleanse our speaking and our listening! Open and enlighten our hearts and our minds! Awaken and strengthen our willingness to acknowledge thee and our readiness to let thee establish thy right among us! Let us breathe the fresh air of thy Spirit, enabling us to return to our work tomorrow with forbearance, love, and joy renewed!

To thy presence and guidance we commend, together with ourselves, all the people of our neighborhood, of our town and country and everywhere. Thou hast ways and means to speak to each one of them and to comfort and admonish them.

Do not abandon them nor us, we beseech thee, but let there be light where darkness now reigns, let there be peace where there is now strife, let there be courage and confidence where now sorrow and anxiety hold men in their grip. Hearken to our supplications, not because we deserve thy mercy, but for Jesus Christ's sake in whom in thy incomprehensible mercy thou hast deemed us from all eternity to be thy children.—Karl Barth.

EVENING SERVICE

Topic: The Problem of Suffering (I)

Lest we be too quick to blame God for all the suffering that is in the world, let us hasten to admit that a great portion of the world's suffering is with us because we bring it upon ourselves.

(a) Accidents cause suffering. Well, I'm not certain that God wills for us to have accidents. I think God wills for us to be responsible in all of the situations of life, accepting the fact that sometimes accidents will happen which, in turn, produce suffering. But let's be careful not to blame God for the accidents that we have which, in turn, bring suffering to us.

(b) Likewise, evil brings suffering. It is not God's will that people are victimized by evil. Evil is real, and evil is powerful. And there are people in our society whose minds and hearts are so possessed by evil that they do not value persons or property. It is God's will that we love each other, that we respect each other, and that we treat one another with dignity. It is not God's will that we be victimized by the forces of evil.

(c) Likewise, some suffering is among us because of our impulsive, thoughtless behavior. God does not will impulsive, thoughtless behavior that harms and damages other people. God's will is that we face our problems and that we work to solve them one by one and in the very finest way possible.

(d) Likewise, fear brings to us tremendous suffering. The great monk and thinker, Thomas Merton, said that all war is rooted in fear. It's rooted in the fact that people don't know each other, so therefore they fear each other. And because we don't know each other, because we assume things about each other and because we fear each other, those kinds of feelings erupt in war.

God doesn't love one nation more than he loves another nation. God loves all his children the same, and he sends the rain to fall upon the just and upon the unjust. War is not God's will. God's will is that people know and trust one another.

(e) Likewise, we have experienced great suffering because of hatred in the world. God does not will for us to hate each other. God wills for us to love each other, and when we do not love each other, it is at that point that we violate the will of God.

(f) Sometimes we are sick because we have not taken care of ourselves. I really have to accent the fact that sometimes I don't take care of myself. I don't rest properly. I don't recreate myself. I don't eat properly. I treat my body like a garbage can. I don't get enough sleep. And when all of that comes together, compounded with the pressures of life, sometimes our bodies give in by being sick. It is not God's will that we be sick, it is God's will that we respect our bodies and take care of them

just as we take care of our children or another part of our life.

Yes, a lot of the suffering that we have in the world is here because of selfishness, greed, sloth, gluttony, exploitation, and poor values. All of these things bring suffering to us and also to those whom we love.

II. What then does this say about God? It says to me that God loved us enough to create us free. God, you see, didn't create us puppets. So God calls upon us to be responsible in all areas of our lives. It seems to me that God often allows that which he does not will. Life, after all, is a problem-solving process. We solve this problem only to go to the next one. The Christ of the Gospels did not say to us, "I will save you from all of these things." He did not say to us, "If you follow me, you'll have a problem-free life." No, Jesus said to us, "Lo, I am with you even until the end of time." God does not save us from our suffering, but God enters into the suffering and uses it in order that we might become more loving and more human people, even as he used the crucifixion, worked it, and brought from it a resurrection.—Joe E. Pennel, Jr.

SUNDAY: MAY THIRD

MORNING SERVICE

Topic: For the Living of These Days
TEXT: Dan. 10:12.

I. We all need God's help for the living of these days. What fools we are to imagine anything else. We talk about our sufficiency and our independence, and about our being self-made men as if we owed nothing to God, as if we were not dependent upon him, and as if we will not have to give an account unto him at the last. The assumption of our self-sufficiency is foolish because, as the book of Daniel makes clear, we need God's help in at least three ways.

(a) We all need his forgiveness. If we stand in the presence of God—if we are confronted by the holiness which is God— then our immediate reaction will be a devastating sense of our own unworthiness

and of our need for divine grace. Daniel is a case in point. "To thee, O Lord, belongs righteousness but to us confusion of face, as at this day!" (9:7) Daniel is an example of a man standing in the presence of God who recognized his need of forgiveness.

(b) We all need God's forgiveness and we all need God's guidance. We are all dressed up with our vast resources and our modern technology, but we lack a sense of direction and any great single, integrating purpose. Our generation has everything to live with but nothing to live for! What is that but to say that we all need not only God's forgiveness but also his guidance. Without that guidance Daniel would have been lost. Without it the prophet would have been nothing. Without it Saul of Tarsus wandered about in a fog of confusion. And without it we are like blind people groping in the dark.

(c) We all need God's forgiveness, and we all need God's guidance, and we all need God's power—his inner reinforcement and spiritual quickening. We all need to realize that there are experiences that break down the strongest will and that shatter the finest courage. You see that in the life of Daniel who tells us that when he was left alone and saw the vision there was no strength left in him (Dan. 19:8).

We all need God's help and the truth of the matter is that we never outgrow that need of him. We need that help to the very end of our days. Thus at the time when this chapter was written, Daniel must have been an old man of 86, assuming that he was a youth of sixteen when he was taken away captive from Jerusalem. And at 86 he still needed God's help though his situation and circumstances were vastly different from what they had been when he was a boy. That is equally true of us. We all need and will need God's help to the very end of our days.

II. We all need God's help and we need to realize on the other hand that God wants to help us. Is God both indifferent to our need and powerless to help? The answer of the Book of Daniel is an emphatic no! It makes it clear that God both waits and wants to help us.

(a) That is apparent from this story of Daniel. Thus the angel makes it crystal clear that as soon as Daniel's request was made he set out to minister to Daniel and was only prevented by opposition he met on the way. "Fear not, Daniel," he says, "for from the first day you set your mind to understand and humbled yourself before your God, your words have been heard, and I have come because of your words" (Dan. 10:12).

(b) God wants to help us. That is the second great truth which we can learn from this book of Daniel. We are not alone in the living of these days.

III. The third lesson which we can learn from this chapter is if we want God's help we must ask for it.

That is what Daniel did. He "turned his face to the Lord God, seeking him by prayer and supplications with fasting and sackcloth and ashes" (9:3). "I ate no delicacies" says Daniel, "no meat or wine entered my mouth, nor did I anoint myself for three full weeks" (10:3).

Daniel sought God's help and so did Peter as he began to sink on the storm tossed sea of Galilee. "Lord," he cried, "Lord save me" (Matt. 14:30). Whereupon Jesus reached out his hand and caught him!—S. Robert Weaver.

Illustrations

FOR MERCIES PROMISED.   True son of Abraham and Isaac and Jacob was this Daniel. My Father, my Shepherd, my Friend, my Lord, and my God! Yes, here lies power in prayer, when a man can talk with God as his covenant God. That man cannot miss; every arrow sticks in the center of the target when he pleads "before his God." That man must conquer the angel at Jabbok's brook who grips him with both hands by a faith which knows its heaven-wrought claims. It is not winning mercies from another's God, nor pleading outside the covenant, but the believer feels that he is asking of his own God mercies already promised and made sure to him by oaths and covenant and blood. —Charles Haddon Spurgeon.

OUR NEED FOR GOD.   What separates us most decisively from God is self-righteousness, self-certainty, self-praise, self-satisfaction—that disposition to approach God with a claim: "God, you will surely acknowledge me, for you know who I am. . . . I have, of course . . ." Whosoever thinks on these lines does not need God at all. He is justified by and in himself, he needs no Savior, no Deliverer; he has already saved himself. Hence, Jesus suggests the same truth as Paul in his doctrine of salvation not by works but by faith in Jesus Christ alone: salvation solely because Jesus, without our having any claim to recognition, acknowledges us as his own, with the result that we ask in astonishment: "Why ever should I be among the saved?"—Emil Brunner.

Sermon Suggestions

HOW TO BE SAVED.   Text: Acts 2:14a, 36–41. (1) Recognize your guilt before

God and your need. (2) Take a new attitude toward God and his Christ. (3) Seal and declare your change of heart through baptism. (4) Live by the values of your new life. (5) Let the church enrich, strengthen, and guide you.

IF YOU SAY YOU ARE BORN AGAIN, . . .
Text: 1 Pet. 1:17–23. (1) Live as one answerable to your heavenly Father. (2) Consider the cost of your redemption. (3) Trust God completely. (4) Love your fellow Christians "earnestly with all your heart" (TEV).

Worship Aids

CALL TO WORSHIP.   "He shall call upon me, and I will answer him: I will be with him in trouble; I will deliver him, and honor him" (Ps. 91:15).

INVOCATION.   We are here today, gracious Lord, not only to praise you, but also to call on your name. Some among us may at this very moment feel the pain and loneliness of deep trouble. Let this service of worship bring reassurance of your promised help.

OFFERTORY SENTENCE.   "All the law is fulfilled in one word, even in this; Thou shalt love thy neighbor as thyself" (Gal. 5:14).

OFFERTORY PRAYER.   O God, as we see what we can do for one another and for others outside our church by our giving, we rejoice that our offerings do not have to be a matter of law and demand, but an expression of love and caring. Deepen our love for neighbor and help us to find practical ways of expressing that love.

PRAYER.   Accept, O Lord, our thanks and praise for all that you have done for us. We thank you for the splendor of the whole creation, for the beauty of this world, for the wonder of life, and for the mystery of love.

We thank you for the blessing of family and friends, and for the loving care which surrounds us on every side.

We thank you for setting us at tasks which demand our best efforts, and for leading us to accomplishments which satisfy and delight us.

We thank you also for those disappointments and failures that lead us to acknowledge our dependence on you alone.

Above all, we thank you for your Son Jesus Christ; for the truth of his Word and the example of his life; for his steadfast obedience, by which he overcame temptation; for his dying, through which he overcame death; and for his rising to life again, in which we are raised to the life of your kingdom.

Grant us the gift of your Spirit, that we may know him and make him known; and through him, at all times and in all places, may give thanks to you in all things. *Book of Common Prayer.*

EVENING SERVICE

Topic: The Problem of Suffering (II)
TEXT: 1 Pet. 2:18–25.

I. How does one believe in a good God in a world like this? That's really the question, isn't it?

(a) History does not give us an answer to that question because history is filled with both good and evil. Throughout history good people have gone forth to do good and good people have gone forth to fight holy wars.

(b) Nor does nature answer our question. Nature is filled with both pain and beauty, sunset and hurricane.

(c) Thinkers have not really answered our question. In the Old Testament, people believed that all suffering came from sin. Jesus, however, did not hold to that position, nor did Jesus give us an explanation to our question that really answers it sufficiently.

(d) If then, we do not find our answer in history, in nature, or in great thinkers, possibly the best we can do is to find a clue that might point us in the direction of an answer.

II. I believe that the question of suffering is related to how God uses his power.

(a) God does not use power the way we use it. We use power to straighten things out. We use power to make things right. We use power to fix and adjust things. In the New Testament, God came to human-kind not in a powerful way, but through weakness, pain, suffering, and love. In the New Testament, God came as a vulnerable baby. He grew as a suffering servant and he died upon a cross. Those are not symbols of power as we understand power. Those are symbols of weakness and vulnerability that contain within them a stranger, and yet stronger power than we understand.

(b) If I understand the New Testament correctly, the God of the Christian faith often clothes himself in suffering and in pain. Every temptation that Jesus faced was a temptation to use power in human ways. In the New Testament, every single time that Jesus was tempted to use power in human ways, he refused. In his refusing he was saying, "If you want to see the divine at work, you look for him in the simple things like sacrifice, love, suffering, and pain."

In another place Jesus said, "If you want to see the divine at work, you look for the divine in the hungry, the thirsty, the stranger, the naked, and in the prisoner."

III. God is present in the suffering of the world. God is present in every refugee camp this morning. Christ is present by every fevered bedside in the world this morning. Christ is present in all of the distortions, absurdities, and mysteries of humankind.

(a) Christianity says that God is often dressed in the agony, the pain, and in the heartbreak of suffering. It's a strange answer that the New Testament gives us to this problem and it's not the answer that we always want to hear. The New Testament never does say, "I will save you from these things." The New Testament simply says, "Lo, I am with you always, even until the end of time." The New Testament does not give us an explanation that answers all of our questions, but the New Testament does give us an assurance that God is with us in the sufferings of our life and society.

(b) For me, suffering does not cancel out the goodness of God, because I believe that the good God takes up residence in the sufferings of our life, meets us there, identifies with us there, and provides us the strength that we need to cope wisely and well.

(c) In our Scripture lesson, so beautifully read this morning, Christ, who was sinless, suffered. And God entered into that suffering and brought from it the redemption of humankind. Thanks be to God.—Joe E. Pennel, Jr.

SUNDAY: MAY TENTH

MORNING SERVICE

Topic: When You Come to Your Wit's End

Text: Col. 3:15–24.

Today is Mother's Day; and I want to talk about what to do when you come to your wit's end. The Bible is full of pictures of mothers who have literally come to their wits' end.

I. *Biblical mothers.*

(a) We meet the first mother in the third chapter of Genesis. Her name was Eve, which resembles the Hebrew word for life or living. Can you imagine what it would have been like to overhear Adam's speech to the Lord after he and Eve had rebelled against the Lord's authority and sovereignty? Adam blamed Eve for the whole problem. Eve was listening. Imagine how that kind of statement builds self-esteem and warm feelings toward your husband! Now think what it would be like to have had two sons. She loved both of them. Then one, Cain, killed his brother, Abel. What a tragedy for the first mother! How could she deal with the sorrow? How could she forgive one son who had killed the other? The Bible makes it clear that this murder is the result of the sin that has entered the world through human pride, rebellion, and greed. From chapter 3 we learned that mothers give birth to their children in an imperfect, flawed, and tragic world, which threatens children and in which children grow up to threaten and destroy each other.

(b) You turn over a few pages to chapter

21, and you see another mother who is at her wits' end. She was in the middle of a burning desert south of Beersheba in the wilderness of Judea. She was trying to get home, back to Egypt; but she wasn't going to make it. She had a little boy whose name was Ishmael. The bread was gone. The water skin was empty. She had put the child under a bush so as not to have to see his agony. Her words in the wilderness have been told or read for three thousand years. Hagar said, "Let me not look upon the death of the child" (Gen. 21:16). Hagar sat down at a distance and waited for death. Then there is this powerful word of hope, "for God heard the voice of the lad . . ." (Gen. 21:17). There is a God who cares. God sent a messenger who said, "Arise, lift up the lad, and hold him fast with your hand; for I will make him a great nation" (Gen. 21:18).

I am convinced that God is calling us to be that messenger of hope, to be that angel, to say to mothers, "God has heard the cry of your babies. Don't give up. Don't abandon him. Look! There is a well! There is food!" That is what missions is all about.

(c) Turn over a few more pages and you get a picture of another mother who is at her wits' end. Deep concern and anxiety are written across her face. She has a tremendous problem. The children of her people are being killed—being thrown into the Nile by a cruel and oppressive government. She has a child that is now three months old who can no longer be hidden. She is working on a little basket made of bulrushes. She daubs it with bitumen and pitch. She puts it down among the reeds early in the morning at the river's edge. The baby's sister watches over him at a distance. You know the story. You know how the daughter of Pharaoh came down to bathe in the river, and she saw that little basket floating in the reeds. She had one of her maids bring it to her.

Moses grew up in Pharaoh's palace. He grew up with the luxury and splendor of the greatest empire of the ancient world. He learned faith and true identity from his mother, however. When the time came for his decision, he turned his back upon the wealth, power, and ease of Egypt and cast his lot with the oppressed people of the Hebrews. You cannot explain Moses or understand the contribution of his life apart from the story of his mother, who, when she had come to her wits' end, refused to give up. She kept her faith. She used her creative imagination. She taught her child—and even got paid for doing it!

(d) The New Testament begins with a story of a mother who had come to her wit's end. How do you think Mary felt when she saw Joseph coming back shaking his head and saying, "There is no more room in the inn?" How do you think she felt being led back to that little cave where the animals were kept—where she knew that her first child would be born? How do you think she felt when they had to flee to escape the mad fury and wrath of Herod? How do you think she felt when she and Joseph each traveled all day long, thinking that Jesus was with them—only to discover that he was with neither of them?

Mary was there at the foot of the cross. She saw her son die. She was a witness to the resurrection and was present in the little gathering in the upper room in Jerusalem on the day of Pentecost. Mary knew what it was to weep and to rejoice, to have her heart torn and then healed, also to be filled with praise and joy.

(e) When you come to your wits' end, what do you do? Paul speaks to this theme in the third chapter of Colossians. You will remember that this letter was written from a prison setting. In chapter 3 he is dealing with the practical application of the great truths that he has taught in chapters 1 and 2.

II. *A word to mothers.*

(a) First, "And let the peace of Christ rule in your hearts. . . ." (Col. 3:15). That is Paul's word. Let the peace of Christ give you inner guidance in keeping priorities straight and in giving you the wisdom you need. Hold on to your faith. Trust the Lord who upholds and sustains you and let his inner peace give you strength and inspiration. Let the power of Christ give you strength. Let the patience of Christ give you serenity.

(b) Second, "Let the word of Christ dwell in you richly. . . ." (Col. 3:16). Each day hear the word of Jesus Christ. What kind of word? Words like these: "Your sins are forgiven"; "I am with you always"; "Be not afraid, only believe"; "According to your faith be it done unto you"; "In the world you have tribulation, but be of good cheer; I have overcome the world"; "Come unto me all who labor and are heavy laden and I will give you rest"; and, "Do not be anxious about your life"; "Let the word of Christ dwell in you richly . . . and sing psalms and hymns and spiritual songs with thankfulness in your hearts to God." Learn to praise him in the midst of all of the frustrations, and you will find that there is a flow of joy from inner depths that is absolutely amazing and beautiful. "Let the word of Christ dwell in you richly."

(c) The third step is to dedicate your life to Jesus Christ and understand that your life is incredibly important. Don't put yourself down. Don't say that what you are doing doesn't matter. Paul says in verse 17, "And whatever you do, in word or deed, do everything in the name of the Lord Jesus, giving thanks to God the Father through him." Let your life be an offering in expression of gratitude and praise. Your work as a mother, your role as a friend or encourager of a child or of young people is far more important than you realize.

III. *A word to husbands and children.*

(a) "Husbands, love your wives, and do not be harsh with them" (Col. 3:19). The word for love here is *agape*, unconditional, nonjudgmental, sacrificial love. There is a specific warning about harshness, which means not just physical brutality but also a cold, judgmental attitude. So often highly paid professionals think that a home should be run like the plant or lab. Kindness and understanding and acceptance are to be given, not harshness.

The New Testament is really calling husbands to take responsibilities in the home. Too many of the husbands have abdicated all spiritual responsibility to their wives. They are saying in effect, "If you want to go to church, that's OK. If you want to take the children to Sunday school, that's OK." The biblical expectation is that the husband will assume leadership.

(b) Now a word to children. "Children,

obey your parents in everything, for this pleases the Lord" (Col. 3:20). Give simple respect and obedience.

(c) Let us as a church recommit ourselves to the support of our families. The affirmation, the appreciation, and the encouragement of mothers should occur, not just in the families that are represented here today, but also to the mothers and parents of this hurting world!—Joe A. Harding.

Illustrations

RESPECT AND OBEDIENCE.   I remember a particular time when, as a child, I disobeyed my mother. Not only did I refuse to obey her; but when she asked again for my cooperation and explained that she was tired, I snarled in a biting sort of way and said, "And that's too bad for poor, old mother." I turned and walked away, trying to congratulate myself for my independence, but inwardly feeling rotten and terrible because of the harsh, cruel words that had rushed from my mouth. I tried to avoid her. She said nothing. Later, as she was doing the work that I was supposed to have done, our eyes met for a moment. I saw that her eyes were red. There were tears that had fallen from her cheeks. I knew that I had caused them. I suddenly was confronted by the terrible thing that I had done. I rushed into her arms and sobbed, "Oh Mother, forgive me! I didn't mean it!" She took me in her arms, and we wept for joy together.—Joe A. Harding.

HONORING   WOMANHOOD.   On this Mother's Day, let us pledge ourselves to resent and resist every cheapening of womanhood in current fads and fashions. Let us demand of publishers that books and papers and magazines stop flooding filth in the name of literary realism. Let us stay away in droves from plays and pictures that portray crass or criminal plots. Let us refuse to have our homes invaded by radio and television programs that destroy the very values of household holiness. Yes, let us cry havoc, make a tumult, raise a clamor for cleanliness! The time has come for the Church to cease its silence.—William Frederick Dunkle, Jr.

Sermon Suggestions

TRUTH AND CONSEQUENCES.   Text: Acts 2:42–47. (1) The truth: the apostles' teaching; new fellowship in Christ; the Lord's Supper; private and public prayer. The solid facts and disciplines of Christian faith and life. (2) The consequences: signs of God at work; a special warmth of feeling for one another; a generous response to human need; attendance at public worship; the winning of people to Christ and the church.

HONORABLE SUFFERING.   Text: 1 Pet. 2:19–25. (1) Suffering is not honorable if it is the fruit of wrongdoing. (2) Suffering is an honor borne in obedience to Christ and for him. (3) Christian suffering has a redemptive quality that benefits even the oppressor.

Worship Aids

CALL TO WORSHIP.   "Whatsoever ye do in word or deed, do all in the name of the Lord Jesus, giving thanks to God and the Father by him" (Col. 3:17).

INVOCATION.   O God, open our hearts to thee, that we may be led by thy Spirit to render to thee true worship. Receive, we pray, the words from our voices, the gifts from our hands, and the service from our daily living.

OFFERTORY SENTENCE.   "Where your treasure is, there will your heart be also" (Matt. 6:21).

OFFERTORY PRAYER.   Lord, we have professed to have surrendered our all to you. Help us to know if it is really true or if there are still miles to travel in our stewardship, and then strengthen our true desires to make what we are and what we have available for your service.

PRAYER.   Gracious Lord, our heavenly Father, we pray for our homes, those most precious and important of all human institutions. In them are fashioned the health of society, the hope of the future. Give us the joy of shared forgiveness, the mercy and life of shared love. Help us learn the fine art of disagreeing without bitterness; of being angry without destructiveness and hurt; of forgiving without vengeance. Then our love shall be like that of Christ and our homes a fitting place for your spirit to dwell. We ask this in Christ's name but for the sake of us all.—Paul D. Simmons.

EVENING SERVICE

Topic: The Problem of Suffering (III)
    TEXT: Matt. 26:36–46.
    I. Today we conclude a three-part series on the question of suffering. I want to look with you at the third kind of suffering which is, in many ways, the noblest of all suffering.

(a) Maybe we could understand it if we looked at it like this: A teenage girl put a note under her mother's dinner plate. When her mother cleared away the dishes that night to wash them, she saw the note. The note said, "Dear Mother: You owe me $3.00 for cleaning up the bathroom; $2.00 for ironing; $1.00 an hour for babysitting with my baby brother; and 50¢ for taking out the garbage." The mother read the note very thoughtfully. Late that night she sat down to answer it. She answered it, put the note under the little girl's breakfast plate the next morning and it said this: "For all the nights I had my sleep interrupted, no charge. For that time I bought you a dress when I really needed one, no charge. For all of the days that I have built my schedule around your needs, no charge. For all of the afternoons that I ran a taxi so you could be where you wanted to be, no charge."

(b) Or maybe we could understand it if we thought about it like this: Handel, I am told, took 24 days to write "The Messiah." He went away to an apartment. For 24 days, without leaving that apartment, he worked on *The Messiah*. He had very little sleep. And he got so excited about what he was doing that when he wrote the last words to the "Hallelujah Chorus," the person who lived under him said, "I heard him banging the piano and singing at the top of his voice."

(c) Or maybe, just maybe, we can understand this kind of suffering if we think of a man like Leslie Weatherhead who preached in the heart of London before, during, and after World War II. From that pulpit, Leslie Weatherhead took his stand about war, peace, capitalism, contraception, eugenics, euthanasia, adultery, and capital punishment. Because Leslie Weatherhead took his position on those very vital issues, he experienced great rejection from members of his congregation and from the press.

(d) Or maybe, we can understand this kind of suffering if we can think of a woman by the name of Rosa Parks who refused to go to the back of the bus. Her action became the match stick which ignited the civil rights movement as we have experienced it in our lifetime.

(e) All of these people have something in common. All of these people suffered voluntarily for a higher and a greater good. Love, you see, is always the parent of voluntary suffering.

II. Jesus is our model for voluntary suffering. In the text we see Jesus in Gethsemane praying, "God, let this cup pass from me." Even God's Son did not want voluntarily to give himself up to suffer.

(a) But if I understand it correctly, many humans suffer when good people do not speak out. In Germany, when millions of Jews were being incinerated, Europe had 300 million people within its borders. Out of those 300 million people, only 3,500 people gave succor to Jews who needed a place of safety and hiding. Because good people have not suffered voluntarily, we still have problems with housing, race, nuclear war, capital punishment, public schools, and world hunger. Because, you see, silence has a strange way of being a partner with that which is evil.

(b) One Sunday morning after church a woman said to me, "I wish I could do something about the problems of the world, but I am just one person." It's my conviction that every person here can be a part of God's answer to the problems of the world. Even one person can be a part of the answer.

(c) Harry Haines likes to tell the story about the time he had a visit with Mother Teresa. In that visit, Harry Haines talked with her about the great humanitarian work that she has done. And he complimented her for it over and over again. And Mother Teresa, as Harry Haines tells the story, said back to him in a very quiet voice, "Dr. Haines, we all have a chance to do something for God." And we do.

(d) A person who is now deceased once told a beautiful story about the stained glass windows of a congregation. She said, "At the time when the sanctuary was built, a little boy came into the church with his mother one day. The little boy looked around at all the stained glass windows. The little boy said to his mother, 'Mother, who are all of those people up in those stained glass windows?' His mother did not quite know how to answer him. She really didn't recognize Jesus at the temple when he was 12 in the window over there. And she really didn't recognize the Ascension window over here. So she said to the little boy, 'Son, those people are saints.' And the little boy walked up and down the center aisle, looked at the windows all over again, and then he said to his mother, 'Mother, a saint must be a person who lets the light shine through.' "

Jesus said it still another way when he said: "Every man must take up his cross and follow me."

(e) There are times in life when life calls upon us and challenges us to suffer for the greater good, for the larger cause, and for the greater purpose. And when we do that, the light shines through.—Joe E. Pennel, Jr.

SUNDAY: MAY SEVENTEENTH

MORNING SERVICE

Topic: The Great Banquet

TEXT: Luke 14:15–21.

"A man once gave a great banquet and invited many." Notice that he gave the banquet. He did not sell tickets. He didn't run specials. It was a free gift. He invited many. The banquet was a free gift to enable him to share some special joy in his life. Perhaps it was the wedding of his oldest son. Perhaps it was the visit of a very important dignitary to his home. Perhaps it was the healing of a disease for his wife. Perhaps it was some particular victory that he had won. But behind the great banquet, there was a tremendous sense of joy in the life of the host and a great desire to share that joy.

I. *Old Testament context of the banquet.*

(a) You see, this is THE GREAT BANQUET. We don't understand the power of the story Jesus told until we begin to visualize the fulfillment of a prophecy in Isaiah, which the people carried in their hearts. Through the long years they kept saying, "Someday . . . someday . . . someday . . ." Then Jesus told the story with an incredible announcement, "Come, for all is now ready!" ALL IS NOW READY. The focus is upon all is "now ready." Now is the time!

(b) When a banquet invitation went out it really went out in two stages. There was an initial invitation. Servants would go out and say something like this, "My master is giving a great banquet, and he would be honored by your presence." People would answer, "It is a great honor to be invited to the master's house. I would be pleased and honored to attend." So depending on the number of acceptances, the animal would be killed and the banquet would be prepared. When you accept an invitation that day to attend a banquet that night, you are expected to be there. The animal has been killed; the host has made preparations; everything depends, then, on the acceptance of that second invitation. It was an unthinkable insult, a cruel indignity to accept the first invitation and then reject the second one. That is what is happening. That is the real horror that is described in the story. Servants go out for the second time saying, "Come, for all is now ready." People knew that they would have an incredibly delicious meal. They would wear special garments to the banquet—a garment of white cloth, actually called a "garment of praise" (Isa. 61:3). The guests would be greeted at the door and have their heads adorned with flowers. Their feet would be washed. Their hands and feet would be anointed with oil. They knew that. They would be royally received and entertained with the most beautiful music—the most glorious

entertainment available. To reject that was shocking and devastating.

II. *"But they all alike began to make excuses."*

(a) That is why the response of the people is so utterly devastating. The excuses themselves were ridiculous and absurd. The people who listened to the story would have seen that and would have cried out, "Oh no!" Some of them would have burst out laughing because the whole excuse would have been so utterly humorous. The first man said, "I have bought a field, and I must go and see it; I pray you have me excused." The man who bought the field was saying that the field was more important to him than his relationship with the host. That is really the message that is given to God by our excuses.

(b) Notice that there is a pattern to each excuse. The person who has received the invitation said, "I did this. Now I must do this. Please excuse me." The second man expressed an even more absurd excuse. This would have caused the listeners to laugh at such ridiculous words. "I have bought five yoke of oxen, and I go to examine them. I pray you have me excused." No one does that. The idea of purchasing five yoke of oxen and then going out to inspect them was utterly ridiculous and absurd. It would be like a man calling his wife on their anniversary, when she had gone to tremendous trouble to prepare a delicious meal, saying to her, "I have just talked to this wonderful salesman over the phone; and I won't be able to make it home for dinner tonight for our anniversary banquet, because I have just purchased five used cars. It is a chance-of-a-lifetime offer, and I have got to go down right now to determine their age, color, model, and be sure they will start."

(c) The third man's excuse sounds more reasonable; he says, "I've married a wife, and therefore I cannot come." Now we have such respect for family life and are so concerned about keeping families together we would say to him, "Good for you, we are glad you put your wife above that invitation." The point is, however, that it is an excuse. He probably wouldn't have been home anyway. If he had gone to the banquet, he would have been home by eight or nine o'clock because banquets did not last that long. Still, it was a rejection of the hospitality of his host to offer that kind of excuse. Everyone knew it, and they would have laughed at that excuse as well.

(d) Jesus told the story in the home of a ruler of the Jews who belonged to the Pharisees. They were trying to trap him and to trick him. He was telling the parable to enable them to see themselves in those excuses. They had accepted the invitation to be God's people. They had rejected the invitation that God has given in Jesus Christ. What was the result of the rejection?

III. *The result of the rejection.*

(a) Notice that the banquet was not canceled. The host did not say, "Well, if no one is going to come, I am just going to cancel it and forget the whole thing." The master gathered his servants together and said, "Go quickly to the streets and lanes of the city, and bring in the poor and the maimed and the blind and the lame." These are the people who would never get invited to a banquet. The maimed could never be married, so they would never have the excuse of having to stay home with a wife. The blind could never buy a field. The lame could not plow with an oxen. This group represents the outcasts of Israel. There were the very people who responded to Jesus, those whom Jesus healed and touched. Pharisees were constantly criticizing Jesus because of his association with sinners and with the outcasts. The report comes back, "Sir, what you have commanded has been done, and still there is room." And the master said to the servant, "Go out to the highways and hedges and compel people to come in, that my house may be filled."

(b) It is very important for us to understand the phrase, "Go into the highways and hedges and compel the people to come in." There is a strong custom that when an unexpected invitation from a high-ranking person was received, it must be refused. The guests of lower social rank —even if they were half starving—would feel an enormous cultural pressure to refuse. The poor people must be convinced that their presence was actually desired— that the host really meant the invitation. The servant would talk and talk and would insist. Then the poor people would be gently taken by the arm and actually led into the great banquet. They would be assured again and again. "My master really wants you. He asked me to bring you into the banquet. There is a place for you. You will not be rejected."

(c) The story closes with the surprising note, "For I tell you that none of those men who have been invited shall taste my banquet." That is indeed a sobering note. It is a reminder that God takes our freedom seriously. When we reject Jesus Christ, God allows that rejection to work its natural consequences. That is why it is so imperative to take seriously God's "Behold, all is now ready." The gospel of grace also talks about time running out, about the closed door and the outer darkness. There is an unexpected grace! Yes, there is an amazing invitation. Grace is free—but it is never cheap. If it is rejected, it is of no benefit to us. It has no meaning in our lives. There will be a time when our excuses are held up into the light of God's judgment and their real nature will be revealed to us and to others. There are no drive through windows or take out orders in the Great Banquet! You come in—or you miss out!—Joe A. Harding.

Illustrations

OUR GRACIOUS GUIDES. A Providence watches over each man's wandering through life. It provides him with two guides. The one calls him forward. The other calls him back. They are, however, not in opposition to each other, these two guides, nor do they leave the wanderer standing there in doubt, confused by the double call. Rather the two are in eternal understanding with each other. For the one beckons forward to the good, the other calls man back from evil.—Søren Kierkegaard.

THE GOD WHO WAITS. This is not a Faust-like search for meaning that carries you down endless unknown roads; what is at stake is the joy of homecoming.

You understand and catch the secret of the Christian life only in so far as you understand and catch its joy. And it is not at all as if it were only you who were always waiting and longing. There is another who is waiting for you, and he is already standing at the door, ready to come to meet you.

The deepest mystery of the world is that God is waiting for us, for the near and the far, for the homeless waif and the settled townsman. The person who understands this and takes it in is near to the blessedness of the royal wedding feast. Already there shines about him the flooding light of the festal hall even though he still walks in the midst of the valley of the shadow. He may be sorrowful, and yet he is always rejoicing; he may be poor, and yet he makes many rich; he may have nothing, and yet he possesses all things.—Helmut Thielicke.

Sermon Suggestions

STEPHEN—A MAN LIKE HIS SAVIOR. Text: Acts 7:55–60. (1) God gave him a glimpse of the better and higher world. (2) The unbelieving world refused to share his vision and faith and killed him. (3) He prayed for his persecutors, that they might be forgiven.

WHAT GOD MAKES OF NOBODIES. Text: 1 Pet. 2:2–10. (1) He gives them undeserved opportunity. (2) He gives them special standing. (3) He gives them a holy mission.

Worship Aids

CALL TO WORSHIP. "The Spirit and the bride say, Come. And let him that heareth say, Come. And let him that is athirst come. And whosoever will, let him take the water of life freely" (Rev. 22:17).

INVOCATION. Today, O Lord, as we hear you calling us, may we not harden our hearts and stop our ears. You call us in love; you call us to life. Help us to listen, as we have never listened before, and obey as we hear the saving word.

OFFERTORY SENTENCE. "No man can serve two masters: for either he will hate the one, and love the other; or else he will hold to the one, and despise the other. Ye cannot serve God and mammon" (Matt. 6:24).

OFFERTORY PRAYER. O God, our Creator and our Father, we know that we can be pulled apart by competing loves. May we know "the expulsive power of a new affection," to which we give ourselves without reservation, so that our living and our giving may be joyful and productive.

PRAYER. Heavenly Father, you have created us with the field of the world in which to test and enjoy our freedom. When one door has closed you have opened another. When temptations have come you have made a way of escape. When companions have deserted us you have given us new friends. When suffering has struck you have taught us what we could never have learned otherwise. When sorrow has visited our homes and hearts you have opened our eyes on a home eternal in the heavens. How easy it is to acknowledge these truths, but how hard it is to assimilate them. You are patient with us, and we are learning, even when we are scarcely aware that anything redemptive is happening. We trust in you, that you will never fail us or forsake us. Grant that we may rejoice in what you have done for us and in what you have promised to do for us yet. Help us in the telling moments of decision always to go your way.—James W. Cox.

EVENING SERVICE

Topic: How Do We Know the Way of the Lord?

TEXT: Isa. 40:1–5; Heb. 2:1–9; John 14:1–7.

What Jesus says about himself and what Hebrews say about Jesus is not what bothers me or concerns me today. What other people and other preachers are saying about Jesus today, who he was, who he is, how we know him, how we follow him, how we know the way of Jesus does concern me and concerns me very much.

I know of no more important task that you and I face within the church today, no more important responsibility you and I have to the church, no more important obligation that rests on you and me, than to find some responsible, intelligent, honest ways of discerning the way of the Lord in the midst of all the so-called Christian preaching around us today.

I. How, then, do you and I come to know the way of the Lord?

(a) There are many things that I think we can do. I think when we hear one opinion expressed we can read something opposite that opinion. When we hear somebody say something we don't understand then we can turn to somebody else whose judgment and whose opinions we trust and ask them for advice and counsel. I think we can pray. I think we can ask for the guidance of the Holy Spirit. I think there are many things that you and I can do today. Because when you and I try to understand what is going on, there is for all of us some process or some processes through which we decide what we will listen to and what we will not, what we will believe and what we will not, what we will follow and what we will not, what is truth and what is not. It is not enough to say, "The Bible says . . ." Or, simply to say, "I believe. . . ." There must be ways we can be responsible and know the way of the Lord.

(b) What are the filters through which you run ideas about the Christian faith? Let's look at some church history and at some of the ideas passed on to us by John Wesley, the eighteenth-century preacher who sparked an amazing revival in England and America. John Wesley had four tests for the truth. Those four tests for the truth may be as helpful as anything as we seek to know the way of the Lord. The four tests are the Bible, reason, tradition, experience.

II. How do you and I come to understand and know the way of the Lord? How do we discern God's truth in the midst of all the preaching and proclaiming we hear? We put all we hear and read up against these four tests: Is it scriptural? Does it make sense, does it stand the test of reason? Is it compatible with the tradition of the Church? Does my experience validate it?

(a) The Bible is the authoritative word for the Christian. We have every right, indeed, it is our responsibility to take every word we hear, any preaching we seek to understand, to the Bible and see if what is being proclaimed is consistent with the truth we find in Scripture. We may ask: Does it fit? Is there scriptural base for it? Wesley saw the Bible as the fundamental source of all truth for the Christian, and it surely can be for you and me.

Like that early reformer, Martin Luther, we have to be careful when we turn to Scripture for authority. Luther used to remind his people, "The Bible is not the Word of God. Jesus Christ is the Word of God. The Bible is the manger. And, like that first manger, there is some straw in it." But, for us as for all Christians, the Bible is authoritative. The test of Scripture is one test for the truth for us today.

(b) The test of reason was Wesley's second test. Does what we hear make sense? Is it reasonable? Is there coherence to it? Is it understandable to me, to others? To use the test of reason is to use the classical test for understanding and making sense out of life and living, out of faith and believing. The use of reason is another way of saying that God has given us mind, intellect, and reason, and God expects us to be responsible in using our mind, indeed, in using our whole selves to come to the truth.

It's like one of Dr. William Barclay's guides for the study of Scripture. Barclay says we are to take the whole of our selves to the study of Scripture. Do not leave your mind behind when you try to read the Bible, or when you try to know the way of the Lord. The truth of Christ is to thought and feeling, heart and mind, spirit and intellect, the head as well as the soul.

(c) The test of tradition is the third test for truth proposed by Wesley. This may be one of our greatest failures in the Church today: We do not know well our traditions as Christians. Thus it is easy, if we do not know our roots and our heritage, to be "tossed to and fro with every wind of doctrine," to be enticed and seduced by every attractive word that comes our way. When you and I read of the lives and faith of the heroes of the church, when we read the words of the hymns written by church men and women of earlier days and this day, when we read the prayers and pray the prayers of the saints of the church and of the common folk of the church, we cannot help but be moved and inspired by the tradition they pass on to us. Tradition is that experience of others that has proved the way of the Lord in the heat and fire of trial and tragedy; tradition is that liturgy that has taken shape in the workaday world of sweat and struggle, of joy and celebration; tradition is that validating word that comes to us from those who have gone before that says, as did St. Teresa when crossing a raging stream on a trembling little walkway, "Fear not. I have touched the bottom and it is sound." Tradition tells us others have touched the bottom of God's way and Word, and have found it sound.

(d) The test of experience is the fourth test, and is the one new and distinctive test John Wesley added to the other three classical tests. One's own personal experience with God is the most authoritative and is the final test. One can know God. God can and will respond if we seek to know God in our prayer life and spiritual life. Here, surely, is one way you and I can know the one who is "the way, the truth, and the life," through our own experience. The test of experience is authoritative. If you say to me, "I know in my own personal life that Jesus Christ is Lord, Lord of all, and Lord of my life," that is valid and that is authentic.

The real question, for Wesley and for you and me, with regard to experience is, "Does it work, is it true, for me?" If so, then I must believe it, must follow it, must live it!

III. All four tests are to go together: The Bible, reason, tradition, experience. We are to use all of these to help us know the way of the Lord. I don't know where you are in your pilgrimage. And I don't know how confusing any of what is going on in the world today it is to you, but if I allow myself to listen and hear and see I become very confused. So I say to you that for me and perhaps for you this morning one of the most important things you and I can do for our own spiritual well-being and then for the spiritual well-being for others is to figure out some way of understanding what is the truth, of discerning the truth and thus of knowing the way of the Lord. So we do seek the way of the Lord.—Robert T. Young.

SUNDAY: MAY TWENTY-FOURTH

MORNING SERVICE

Topic: The Reality of the Unseen

Text: 2 Kings 6:17.

I. Our story is of Elisha. It gathers around the romantic period in the history of Israel.

(a) The Syrians had invaded the land of Israel, but they failed to make further progress there. Their designs were so often anticipated that the king of Syria concluded that some one in his army must be acting as spy for the king of Israel. His servants protested that this was not the case, that the betrayal of the king's designs was due to the keen sight of God's prophet Elisha. Hearing this, the king sent horses and chariots and a great host to fetch the prophet. He was then in Dothan, a town an hour or two away from the capital of the country. This great host came by night, and in the morning Elisha's servant rose up and saw the city compassed on all sides by the Syrian forces, and he fell into a great fear. But Elisha remains full of confidence, because he sees more than his servant; he sees and knows the power of Jehovah.

(b) Not only has Elisha himself this great power of sight; he is able to impart it to his servant. How does he do it? He reawakens at the needful moment a latent belief. The ancient Hebrews believed that Jehovah was surrounded by a mighty host. "I saw the Lord sitting on his throne, and all the host of heaven standing by him, on his right hand and on his left." Now it is to the chariots and horsemen of this great host that Elisha refers. It is to this belief that he makes his appeal. "And Elisha prayed, and said, Lord, I pray thee, open his eyes that he may see. And the Lord opened the eyes of the young man; and he saw: and behold, the mountain was full of horses and chariots of fire round about Elisha."

II. Our story teaches us the reality and the importance of the unseen. In nature as in religion, it is the invisible that is most important and real. It must have been a great day for this young man when the scales fell from his eyes and he saw the glory of God in the mountains. For him that day the world was transfigured and every common bush afire with God.

(a) We live in a world that appeals at once to our senses—a world of light, of sound, of touch; a world of sun and sky, of the sweeping horizons and flowing rivers, of the rich luxuriance of fertile valleys and the rugged grandeur of the everlasting hills, of the merry dance of the rivulet and the majestic tides of the ocean; a world of hunger and disease and death. But the most important things in all this natural world are not the things that we can see.

(b) Thus our story reminds us that we live in two worlds, or rather in one world that has two aspects. How the material world forces itself upon us, floods the eye with sight, the ear with its insistent call! How it seeks to persuade us that no other world is real and that to live for its rewards is to be practical, sane, and wise! But there is another world and the great souls have always known it. It is above this world, and greater than this world; but it is in this world, and it is in us. Someone has called it "the beyond that is within." It has its goods, but they do not appear on the market. It has its forces, but they are not physical, though the tides of history have been turned by them. Truth, mercy, love, justice, freedom, righteousness, peace; these go to make up this invisible world, and back of these is he in whom these and all good things have their being, the Spirit we call God.

(c) I covet for all this vision of the invisible. It means the annexation of a new universe which eye hath not seen and ear hath not heard. It does not narrow life but broadens it. It is to the soul what the telescope is to the eye. It suggests to the ear the sound of heavenly movements and sets the mind dreaming of an infinite progress and a new earth and a new heaven that are yet to be. To all who receive this vision the show of things will lose its power; they will know the heart of life, the world that is real. They will know the importance of the invisible because the invisible centers in God. When they look out upon the universe they will see more than the round of earth and sea and sky; when they are called upon to suffer they will feel more than the agony and the sting; when they enter their church they will be aware of more than eloquence and finance; they will be conscious of the presence of the infinite, the horses and chariots of fire around Elisha.

III. Consider next the fruits of this belief.

(a) For one thing it gave courage. "Fear not," said the prophet to his dismayed and affrighted companion. There you have courage of the right sort, explain it how you will. That confidence and courage were seen, I cannot doubt, in look, in tone of voice, as well as in words which, even at this distant point of time, carry with them the sterling ring of a brave person's heart.

This courage is the need of all humankind. Rightly understood it is an unobtrusive thing. There may be moments when it reveals itself in dramatic splendor on the battlefield. These are the manifestations of courage that people see and applaud. For this very reason they are not its highest manifestations. And whether people would admit it or not, it is the result of communion with the unseen. It is the vision of the invisible that makes the difference between hope and despair.

(b) A final result of this vision splendid is an unconquerable spirit. The prophet's servant cried, "We are lost. Alas, my master, what shall we do?" But the prophet replied, "Fear not, for they that be with us are more than they that be with them." Because the children of the unseen can say this they can never be defeated. Faith in this unseen environment, faith in love, righteousness, and truth, faith in the all-conquering spirit of the living God lifts people above circumstances. It shows them the mightier powers at work around them. It kindles the souls of Christians to claim and hold the mastery that they feel in their hearts ought to be theirs and thus they are invincible.—W. A. Cameron.

Illustrations

HEAVEN AND EARTH.   It will obviously not do at all to say that our zeal for the improvement of terrestrial conditions is to be limited by the recollection that here we have no continuing city; nor again will it do to say that our longing for the heavenly Jerusalem is to be limited by the discovery that we can make things moderately comfortable for ourselves even here. The result, surely, must be all the other way: our works intensifying our faith and our faith in its turn lending power to our works.—John Baillie.

WHERE GOD IS.   A Mohammedan legend puts the matter picturesquely. A dervish was tempted by the devil to stop calling on Allah because Allah did not answer "Here am I." The prophet Khadir appeared to the dervish in a vision with a message from Allah: "Was it not I who summoned thee to my service? Did I not make thee busy with My name? Thy calling 'Allah' was My 'Here am I.' "—Gordon W. Allport.

Sermon Suggestions

THE ANSWER TO OUR QUESTING SPIRIT. Text: Acts 17:22–31. (1) God's provisional revelation in nature. (2) God's special and final revelation in Jesus Christ.

GUIDELINES FOR EMBATTLED BELIEVERS. Text: 1 Pet. 3:13–22. (1) Do not be afraid of those who would do you harm. (2) Be prepared in all circumstances to give your Christian witness. (3) Conduct your behavior and guard your speech, so as always to honor Christ.

Worship Aids

CALL TO WORSHIP.   "In the year that king Uzziah died I saw also the Lord sitting upon a throne, high and lifted up, and his train filled the temple. Above it stood the seraphims: each one had six wings; with twain he covered his face, and with twain he covered his feet, and with twain he did fly. And one cried unto another, and said, Holy, holy, holy, is the Lord of hosts: the whole earth is full of his glory" (Isa. 6:1–3).

INVOCATION.   Lord of all being, enthroned afar, thou are yet present with thy people here. Out of thy infinite wisdom speak to our finite foolishness. Out of thy marvelous grace minister to our common needs. Out of thy fatherhood understand our childhood.—J. Estill Jones.

OFFERTORY SENTENCE.   "If I give away all I have, and if I deliver my body to be burned, but have not love, I gain nothing" (1 Cor. 13.3 RSV).

OFFERTORY PRAYER.   God of love and grace, our love is pale and fitful compared to thine, yet we come to thee to say with our lips and with our gifts as well, "Thou knowest that I love thee." Accept these offerings, we pray, as mere tokens of a larger love.

PRAYER.   O eternal God, whose hand rules the wind and waves and who has set the planets in their courses, we come now reverently and yearningly into your presence.

We revere the mighty works of your hands and the wondrous wisdom and saving power of your words.

We yearn for your guiding power for our nation that we may pursue paths of peace and justice for all.

Grant, we pray, that our honored dead may not have died in vain and that we may help the nations of the world move toward a new birth of freedom.

We ask your kind compassion for all victims of war—for the maimed, the imprisoned, the dispossessed, the widowed, the orphaned, and all whose suffering has hallowed our struggle for peace among the nations.

Keep before us the vision of world peace, and the hope of nuclear disarmament. Enable our national leaders to be good and faithful peacemakers.

O holy God, let your spirit descend on us who are worshiping here, and help us bring your peace to our homes and our communities. Let us be healers and helpers and heralds of your good tidings.

Even if championing the cause of peace means bearing a cross, let us do it courageously as we follow in the footsteps of our Master, Jesus Christ, whose cross marks the graves of so many whom we gratefully remember this day and in whose name we fervently pray. Amen.—Harold A. Brack.

EVENING SERVICE

Topic: Is There Life Beyond Our Mistakes?

TEXT: Acts 1:15–26.

I. *Some case studies.*

(a) Judas. For a long time, Judas looked good on paper. Peter tells us that he was "numbered with us and obtained a part in this ministry" (Acts 1:17). Judas had a good position as far as the arithmetic of the matter was concerned. But something went terribly wrong where Judas was concerned, and he closed out his life by betraying Christ. We are not certain just why Judas made the mistake of betraying Christ. Perhaps Judas knew his inner doubts, his lack of faith, and was driven at last by a conscience that was tormented so that he sought to destroy what he had felt to be that which troubled his conscience.

(b) Simon Peter. But look for a moment at the mistakes of Simon Peter. He, along with the rest of the disciples, deserted Christ the night of the arrest. His hands were not exactly lily white when he stood up, mentioned the mistakes of Judas, and suggested that a successor must be named.

(c) The church. The early church joined Peter in making mistakes, and the church since that time has made mistakes. One way of writing the history of the church could be in terms of the mistakes it has made. Although many would justly disagree, I tend to agree with G. Campbell Morgan that the early church began by electing the wrong person as the twelfth apostle! His belief is that God had Paul in mind all along as the one to replace Judas. As I read Acts, I'm not at all sure that the

Lord intended the church to immediately fill the vacancy left by Judas.

But impulsive Peter quoted the Old Testament passage that indicated there would be one whose position needed to be filled, and immediately Peter set forth the qualifications he felt were necessary. Although the church prayed, asking the Lord's leadership, they only gave him two people from which to choose, a man named Joseph and another named Matthias. Then they made their decision by casting lots. Whether or not the church made a mistake in that instance, the history of the church is filled with mistakes. Even in the early days of the apostles, they made the mistake of supposing that God was interested only in saving the Jews, not the rest of the world. And after the first few centuries, the church gave up the missionary process as the Lord commanded it to be carried out until in recent centuries that has been regained again. In the meantime the church has condoned slavery and used Scripture to justify prejudice. Yet the church goes on, accomplishes nothing less than the miraculous work of God, proving that there is life beyond mistakes.

II. *Critical areas.* Even people trying their best to follow Christ in faith and obedience will make mistakes, natural mistakes. But some mistakes are "terminal" if allowed to run their course because they concern the total direction of life. There are two key words used in the account of Judas that point out these critical areas.

(a) The direction of life. Peter said of Judas that he had "become a guide to those who arrested Jesus" (1:16). The word translated "guide" literally means one who follows a certain path or way. One of the basic mistakes of Judas was that although he walked with Christ physically, apparently he did not do so in spirit. He walked along the same road but was quietly pursuing his own way. To let Christ determine the direction of your life is to be on the way he set forth.

(b) Estate. Quoting Ps. 69:25, Simon Peter applied it to Judas: "Let his habitation be desolate, and let no one live in it." The word *habitation* is literally the word which means "estate." Christ offered

Judas an eternal estate, but Judas chose to do his own estate planning. Your estate in the eyes of God has to do with the treasure you decide to build up in this brief life on earth. Jesus indicated we should make certain we are building up treasures in heaven where nothing can touch them. In contrast, Judas apparently saw only earthly position and power and treasures. Therefore he misused the office which Christ offered him, the position he had as one of the Twelve, and someone else would have to be chosen who wanted such an estate.

III. *Going beyond mistakes to life.* As we note how Judas made mistakes about the way he faced his mistakes, we will notice that Simon Peter responded in a different manner and found life beyond his mistakes.

(a) Confess them to Christ. When we make mistakes, we should not hide from God, not drop out of church, but take our mistakes to Christ in honest confession. Though Peter denied Christ, he returned to stand at the foot of the cross. Later, though he had thrown it all in to go back to his fishing business, he ultimately fell at the feet of Christ and affirmed his unworthiness. Judas also was filled with regret, but he did not tell Christ, he did not confess his regret. He told the people who had bribed him, even attempting to return the money. But he made no attempt at confession.

(b) Don't give up on Christ. Judas tried to manipulate Christ, to force his hand, and he failed. At that point he gave up on Christ. He saw only the pain, the death, and the blood. He didn't bother to wait for a possible resurrection. As far as he was concerned, Christ had let him down!

In contrast, Peter and the other apostles waited. They did not understand, but they did not give up on Christ. As long as God is alive, there is hope. We dare not give up on him. And in their waiting, the disciples beheld the resurrection.

(c) Don't give up on yourself. Judas not only gave up on Christ, but he gave up on himself and on life as a whole. He saw no future. And so he took his own life. The world is filled with people who arrive at the same conclusion as Judas. Many do not take their own life but choose to go on in a kind of living death wherein they entomb themselves in an effort to keep out all other people, all risks, all love, and all responsibility. They determine never to make a mistake again by never doing anything again, never caring again, never risking again.

(d) Allow God's grace to redeem your mistakes. Christ is in the business of redeeming our mistakes. He transforms them. He overcomes them. He adds later chapters to them that allow us to go on and leave them behind. He brings us to life beyond our mistakes.—Bob Woods.

SUNDAY: MAY THIRTY-FIRST

SUNDAY: MAY THIRTY-FIRST

MORNING SERVICE

Topic: What God Does When We Botch It

TEXT: 1 Pet. 3:18.

Why is depression such a problem today? Why are we so depressed? We wake up each morning and go to bed each night with a feeling that we have failed, that we have botched it, that we have let other people down—more significantly, that we have let God down.

So what does God do when we have botched it? How does God react to our failure? Peter gives us an answer to that question in our text which if understood could be the foundation for a new life of hope and joy and victory.

I. *God's purpose.* Why did God put us on this earth? The answer to that question is found in the story of creation. The key verse is Gen. 1:26, which explains the purpose of God. God made us in his image!

(a) Much debate has ensued over the exact meaning of that phrase, "the image of God." Some identify it with our rationality. Others point to our emotional capacity. We can feel. Still others point to our morality. The fact that we can discern right from wrong is what testifies to the image of God in our life. Others suggest that the idea of responsibility is the key. Humanity was given authority over the earth. That is what is involved in the image of God in human life.

(b) Each of these suggestions has some merit. All are necessary to explain the idea completely. Because we were created in the image of God we do have the ability to think, and we do have the capacity to feel, and we do have the capability to discern between right and wrong, and we do have the responsibility to administrate in God's stead. Say all of that, however, and you have still not come to the heart of what the image of God in humanity means. The fact that we were created in the image of God means that we have the capacity to have fellowship with God.

II. *Humanity's perversion.* Let's take it a step further and consider humanity's perversion. Look closely at the world and you will quickly discover that something happened to God's plan. We are not living in obedience to God. We are not administering the universe on his behalf. We are not living in fellowship with God. Something has happened to God's world.

(a) Read Genesis 3 and you will discover that we have perverted God's world. Instead of obedience, we chose disobedience. Instead of working for God, we chose to work against God. Instead of walking with God, we chose to go our own way.

That's not just the story of Adam and Eve. That is the story of every person of every generation. We have perverted God's plan. As a result, we who were created to live in fellowship with God are separated from God, estranged from God.

(b) Every moment of despair that stabs the human heart, every wave of depression that sweeps against the shoreline of our soul, every ounce of discouragement that weighs down upon our shoulder comes from that inescapable insinuation that weaves its way through all the centuries of time—we have failed. We have let God down. We have perverted his plan. We have botched it.

III. *Christ's provision.* That leads to the third foundational fact that I want us to understand today: Christ's provision.

(a) What does God do when we botch it? Peter answers that question. Listen to this remarkable revelation. Peter says that when we failed, when we perverted God's plan and fell out of fellowship with him, he sent his son Jesus to die for our sins. Because of his death on the cross, Jesus is able to bring us back into fellowship with God.

(b) The Greek word translated "bring us to God" in our text comes out of two distinct backgrounds.

(1) The word has a Jewish background. The word was used in the Old Testament to speak of the bringing to God those who are to be priests (Exod. 29:4). In the Jewish religion, all but the high priest were limited in their access to God. In the temple, a Jewish layman could pass through the Court of the Gentiles, and the Court of Women, and the Court of Israelites—but there he had to stop. Only the priests could go into the Court of the Priests. And of the priests, only the high priest could enter into the very presence of God in the Holy of Holies. But Peter says that what only the high priests could do, now every Christian can do. Through Jesus, we can be brought into the very presence of God.

(2) The word in our text also has a Greek background. In the Greek courts of the king, there was an official called the *prosagogues,* an introducer, one who could give you access to the king. It was his function to decide who should be admitted to the king's presence and who should be kept out. He had the keys of access to the king. Peter uses that same term of Jesus. He is our introducer, the one who has the keys of access that will enable us to come into the very presence of God.

(c) The Bible declares that through Jesus Christ every person can be returned to the fellowship with God for which we were originally created. When we fail God, he does not count us out. Instead, he calls us to come back to him. When we botch it, and remove ourselves from fellowship with God, he does not slam the door shut and lock it. Instead, he opens the door and bids us to come back in.

That is the message I want us to hear. That is the clarion call that comes to us in the midst of our despair and depression.

You have botched it. And so have I. But God is ready to give us a second chance. And he will, if you'll let him.—Brian L. Harbour.

Illustrations

THROUGH JESUS TO GOD.   There was a brilliant schoolteacher in one of the higher institutions, who had been reared a non-Christian and then as a student had joined the Ethical Culture Society. In a single winter she lost by death the man to whom she was engaged and her mother, and in her bleak loneliness the Ethical Culture Society seemed chill and comfortless. Through a Christian fellow teacher she started attending a church, and after some months she came one day, under great emotion, to speak with one of its ministers. She said, "I see it now." "What do you see?" the minister asked. "I see that all I adore as divine is there in Jesus; and all I need a God for he does for me."— Henry Sloane Coffin.

PRAYERS FOR US.   You are aware that December 25 is Christmas Day. Do you know what day in the Christian year December 26 is? It is the feast of Stephen, the first Christian martyr. His death is remembered within twenty-four hours of the birth of our Lord. Do you know what Stephen's last words were as he was stoned to death? "Lord, lay not this sin to their charge" (Acts 7:60). Isn't that "Father, forgive them" in other words? A young Pharisee named Saul heard that prayer. Do you know what Augustine said about Saul hearing that prayer? It was the beginning of the conversion of Paul: "If Stephen had not prayed, the church would not have had Paul."

And the prayer goes on down the centuries, because the followers of Christ, strengthened by his spirit, have prayed it. —James T. Cleland.

Sermon Suggestions

LESSONS FROM CHRIST'S ASCENSION. Text: Acts 1:6–14. (1) The ascended Christ promises us power to proclaim his truth. (2) The ascended Christ stirs us from our pious paralysis. (3) The ascended Christ awaits our prayers concerning our universal task.

DON'T BE SURPRISED!   Text: 1 Pet. 4: 12–14; 5:6–11. (1) You will be called on to share the sufferings of Christ in one way or another. (2) But you can handle the situation: by surrendering to God; by resisting the devil, conscious of your solidarity with all Christians in doing so; by patiently expecting from God the strength to see you through.

Worship Aids

CALL TO WORSHIP.   "For God so loved the world, that he gave his only begotten Son, that whosoever believeth in him should not perish, but have everlasting life" (John 3:16).

INVOCATION.   O God, how could we be more assured of your love than by knowing that you gave your beloved Son to save us from all that would destroy us and to share your very life with us? Give us eyes to see this saving truth this hour and hearts to rejoice in your goodness.

OFFERTORY SENTENCE.   "Set your mind on God's kingdom and his justice before everything else, and all the rest will come to you as well" (Matt. 6:33 NEB).

OFFERTORY PRAYER.   Move in our hearts, Lord, that as we search our pocketbooks and billfolds we might also search our souls and find the grace to give as we ought, through him who laid down his life for many.—E. Lee Phillips.

PRAYER.   Eternal God, it is good to remember the dead; it is good amid the peace of stones and flags and flowers to pause by them, for a moment undistracted, unhurried; to pray not so much in words but as the clouds above them pray, by slowly taking time to unfurl; to pray as the wind prays upon the flags and through the pines. It is good to pause by the beloved dead and to pray, for a moment undistracted, unhurried. To pray as markers pray, by remembering a name.

To place flowers. To drink from our own deepest springs of thanks and pain and shaping memory. And creatures of the dust and of the particular that we are, to confess without shame with the psalmist that we miss a closeness not even resurrection can altogether assuage, that we miss the simple things—and so for a moment, with sun and shadow, with grass and wildflowers and the wind through the trees, with the names above their remains, to hold them close before again we yield them up to you in whom alone is our hope. —Peter Fribley.

EVENING SERVICE

Topic: Knowing Our Place.
Text: Ps. 8; Heb. 2:5–10.

Where are you in your awareness and acknowledgment of your place in relationship to God? Already God has acknowledged who we are and what we mean to him. Today I invite you to consider three crucial acknowledgments which the Bible leads us to make regarding our place in God's providence. Our rightful place is that we are under God, over creation, and in Christ.

I. We are under God.

(a) The outward reach of a telescope and the inward reach of a microscope both portray the same phenomenon—the wonder of God's activity in the world he has created. We are in the midst of a universe so delicately balanced that an eclipse of the sun can be predicted hundreds of years in advance. We live in bodies so delicately regulated that the thermostat is set on 98.6 degrees whether we are in the tropics or at the North Pole.

(b) As you read the Bible's account of creation, you realize a wonderful thing. When God created humankind, for the first time God addressed something he created as "you." He created the sun, moon, and stars, and all of the plants and animals, but to none of these did God say, "you"! Only with man and woman does God initiate what Martin Buber called the "I-thou" relationship. Only human beings are addressed as persons in relationship with God.

(c) But we need to make sure that we understand the nature of this relationship. The Bible teaches that we are "under God." He is the creator. He is the owner. He is the Lord. We are his partners. But we are junior partners. Everything we have and everything we are belong ultimately to him.

II. Not only are we under God, we also are over creation.

(a) What a high calling God has for humankind. He thinks more highly of us than we may think of ourselves. Here is God's greatest purpose for his highest creation: We are to manage the rest of creation to bring it to its fulfillment.

(b) But perhaps we should stress that God said, "Have dominion over it." Don't let it have dominion over you. You know the problem. Instead of mastering and managing material things, too often we let them master and manage us. When this happens, we are no longer conscious of God as he truly is. We worship the creation instead of the Creator. And unless I'm badly mistaken, this is the essence of sin. We take the good things of God's creation and misuse them, allowing them to dominate us.

There are expressions of this on every hand. A person may become dominated by a job, by responsibilities, by leisure pursuits, or even by church activities. Almost any material object or human activity, if allowed to do so, can become an obsession.

(c) All of this is to say that the world and all the things of the world that God has created are good. They are to be enjoyed and received with thanksgiving. But when they begin to exercise control over us, the same good things become a curse. We are called to be over creation. Creation is not to be over us.

III. And if we are to realize God's full destiny for us, we must not only acknowledge we are under God and over creation, we must also be in Christ. God tells us to exercise dominion over the earth and subdue it. But the truth is, we have not yet subdued creation! The things which God has created yield only stubbornly to our human attempts to have dominion over them.

(a) It's obvious that since the dawn of

creation, something has happened to affect God's original purpose. We all are aware of the incompleteness, the disharmony, the frequent antagonism among human beings and between human beings and the rest of creation.

(b) It is through Jesus that we fulfill our original destiny. What all person fail to do, Jesus Christ has done. He has been the person God wants us to be. He has set forth perfectly what it means to live under God and over creation. The Gospels show how Jesus created harmony with God and with creation. It is as we acknowledge the Lordship of Jesus Christ that we find our rightful place. We ultimately and perfectly find what God intends for our fulfillment. —J. Altus Newell.

SUNDAY: JUNE SEVENTH

MORNING SERVICE

Topic: Filled with the Holy Spirit
Text: Acts 4:5–12.

One of the things that bother some of us is the fact that there are two people inside us instead of one. There is the person we know we are. We are basically selfish. We often make extravagant gestures of unselfishness but, especially in times of crisis, we know that our lives revolve around our own interests. We believe in God honestly and sincerely, and yet, when we look at the future, we are filled with anxiety. When we approach the darkness of the night, we are frightened.

Then there is the person we would like to be, single as the shining of the sun without the slightest trace of duplicity, willing one will, to do one thing in the world; steady like the stars, unshaken by any of the confusion or tumult of the world; and selfless as Jesus was selfless in the sense of handling a situation without reference to his own interests.

The difficulty for many of us is that these two persons seem to be poles apart, and as the years pass they seem to grow not much closer together. Is there any chance of our ever becoming the person we would like to be, or shall we give up and settle down to keep house with the person that we know we are?

I. We can say at the outset that it has been done. It has happened. Let me give you a classic example. According to the story in the Acts of the Apostles, Peter and his friend John had spent a night in jail. We would say that they had been thrown into jail without any hearing or trial. The powers that represented the status quo wanted to squelch that resurrection movement, so they put them in jail.

(a) The next day the two men were brought before an investigating committee of the top ranking officials of the church, the high priest, his father-in-law, and all his family, all the church lawyers and officials. The cards were against them from the very start, and the question was swiftly put before them, "By what power, or by what name, have you done this?" Then Peter, "filled with the Holy Spirit," began to speak.

(b) Notice the transformation that had taken place in Peter. Peter was by nature a hot-tempered person, impulsive, impatient, blustering, impetuous. Normally a situation like this which was filled with unfairness and injustice would have irritated him to the point where he would have lost complete control of himself and his passions. Yet when he spoke, he spoke quietly, all his passions completely mastered and in perfect control. Again, he was an uneducated and untrained man who had spent his early life as a fisherman and had no formal education at all, and yet when he spoke, he spoke with the eloquence of simplicity that is the sure sign of reality. In his earlier days he had been a very self-protecting sort of person. He had even gone to the extent of denying his Lord in order to save his own skin. Yet here before all the authorities he freely and completely exposed himself and stood there in their presence without any self-defense whatsoever.

So it can be done. It has been done. The Peter that was, the vacillating, hot-tempered, restless, irritable, self-centered Peter, became the Peter that was to be.

That is the first clue to the answer of our question.

II. We want, however, to explore the matter a little further. Granted that it can be done, that it has been done, not only of course in this case but in thousands of others in its train, we want to know how it can be done, if it is possible to know that. The clue to it in this particular case is in the phrase, "then Peter, filled with the Holy Spirit."

(a) You notice that the story does not say that Peter mustered every ounce of energy that he could muster; it does not say that Peter, taking a deep breath and gritting his teeth, set about to defend himself; it does not say that Peter drew deeply on his own reserves and resources and brought up from unknown depths strength he did not know he had in himself. It says, "Peter, filled with the Holy Spirit," which means, of course, that Peter himself did nothing. It means that Peter had the human capacity to receive powers outside himself, and that into him were poured energies from beyond himself, and he was filled with a power not his own that enabled him to rise to heights that neither he nor any of his friends ever dreamed he could reach.

(b) In Peter's case, that spirit was the spirit of Jesus, I am quite convinced of that. And the power that filled him was the influence of Jesus. Peter had been exposed to Jesus day after day for at least a year or two, probably longer. And without any doubt Jesus was the greatest single influence in the life of Peter. He changed his career.

(c) But now, in a case of extreme emergency, when Peter found himself in a situation that taxed his own strength beyond its resources, Peter remembered Jesus, how he too stood before a humiliating investigating committee, how he too had questions that were unfair and unjust flung at him, and how he had stood there, quiet, self-possessed, protesting nothing, not defending himself at all and answering the questions in a single word, sometimes by complete silence. And as he stood before that mocking group of investigators, nothing that he did made him a different man, but he was filled with the influence of Jesus, and the spirit of his Lord took possession of him, and he became for a moment at least the Peter that he longed to be.

III. Now we may begin to see the answer to our question.

(a) If we do find ourselves in a state of dissatisfaction about ourselves, we must recognize at the outset that we cannot make ourselves any better. The only thing that we do by trying to make ourselves better is to make ourselves self-righteous and unbearable to those who live with us. We may end in the valley of despair and depression.

(b) But—and this is the good news that I wish I could make more real than words can make—on one side we lie open to eternity. We are like an electric light bulb that cannot create light but that can be filled with light. We too lie open to forces and energies from beyond ourselves. What we cannot create in and by ourselves, we can catch. We have the capacity to take in powers, energies, vitalities and by them be enabled to do the things that otherwise we could not do.

(c) And the greatest spiritual power to which you and I can expose ourselves is the influence of Jesus. It is in the air we breathe. Take it in today. It is in the nooks and crannies of our memories, no matter how they may be clogged with all other bits and scraps of information. The influence of Jesus is pushing itself through the blocks of our memory to make itself felt upon our immediate perception. Let it make its way.

(d) The thing that I want for myself more than anything else is that I may grow up more and more into him, that I may carry myself a share of his reconciling life in the world today. I know that I cannot do that by myself, only as I expose myself to his influence can he do it in me. Next to that I want you to be more and more like him, more charitable, more understanding, slower to speak, less ready to bear grudges, greater in your understanding, and more sure in your confidence of God. You cannot do that yourself, but he, like a mighty rushing wind, can fill you with his spirit, if you will let him.—Theodore Parker Ferris.

Illustrations

PENTECOST AND PAUL. As the story of the Syrophoenician woman so dramatically illustrates, it is no mark of perfect holiness or of the filling of the Holy Spirit to be able easily and lightheartedly to go over the dividing walls of partition, whatever they may be, in a constructive and positive manner. J. A. Findlay has well said that "in the parable of the Pharisee and the publican the Pharisee was perhaps repeating aloud the familiar Jewish prayer. 'My God, I thank Thee that I was not born a Gentile, but a Jew: not a slave, but a free man: not a woman, but a man.' When St. Paul wrote, 'There is neither Jew nor Greek, there is neither slave nor free, there is neither male nor female,' he is contradicting his earliest prayer clause by clause: something has happened to a man who can do this."—J. E. Fison.

JOY IN GOD. The second in Paul's list of fruits of the Spirit is joy. This is splendid! There are so many people, Christians and non-Christians, who regard Christianity and joy as irreconcilable opposites. Out of the whole gospel the only test they know is: "Woe to you that laugh now. . . ."
Let us be quite clear about it: there are many Christians who consider it their most urgent duty to suppress joy and to turn it sour wherever they come across it. One has only to look at their austere faces for joy to vanish; but it is even worse if they are preaching the gospel, which for them has more to do with Sodom and Gomorrah than with Jesus and the Sermon on the Mount. These are the "preachers of death," of whom Nietzsche spoke, "who have no choice save between lust and self-torment. And even their lusts are still self-torment. . . . They cling to life as to a straw, and then deride themselves because it is a straw they cling. . . . Better songs than these must they sing, if I am to learn to believe in their Redeemer; his disciples must look as though they were redeemed!"—Theodor Bovet.

Sermon Suggestions

THE GIFT OF THE SPIRIT. Text: Acts 2: 1–21. (1) The ancient phenomenon: The young church experienced the presence of God in a new and powerful way. (2) The timeless meaning: God's purpose is to fill the lives of all his people in a creative and unifying experience in Christ. (3) The timely application: All believers are potential witnesses; the Spirit draws us all toward each other at the deepest level; the Spirit gives courage and power to do what we could never do without the Spirit.

UNITY AND VARIETY IN THE CHURCH. Text: 1 Cor. 12:3b–13. The Holy Spirit: (1) leads us to faith in Jesus as Lord; (2) assigns a variety of gifts for the good of the entire church; (3) gives dignity and importance to each person's task.

Worship Aids

CALL TO WORSHIP. "Then said Jesus to them again, Peace be unto you: as my Father hath sent me, even so send I you. And when he had said this, he breathed on them, and saith unto them, Receive ye the Holy Ghost" (John 20:21–22).

INVOCATION. Holy God, who alone knowest what this hour of worship might begin, what hearts lift, what hopes engender, what visions bring; make us open and available and honest before the leading of the Holy Spirit.—E. Lee Phillips.

OFFERTORY SENTENCE. "If a brother or sister be naked, and destitute of daily food, and one of you say unto them, Depart in peace, be ye warmed and filled; notwithstanding ye give them not those things which are needful to the body; what doth it profit? Even so faith, if it hath not works, is dead, being alone" (Jas. 2:15–17).

OFFERTORY PRAYER. Send thy Holy Spirit upon this offering, Lord: surround it, touch it, use it, and multiply it, so that a thousand tongues may newly proclaim that Christ is Lord.—E. Lee Phillips.

PRAYER.   Grant, we beseech of thee, thy blessing to rest upon thy servants that gather together this morning to worship. Bless, according to their several necessities, all that are here. For thou knowest the secrets of every heart. Cares and troubles are familiar to thee. Sorrow and anguish are knowledge which thou hast had since men lived. Thou knowest how to make the crooked way straight, and the rough way smooth. Thou knowest how to subdue unruly passions, and to teach men so. Thou knowest how to interpret thine own providences, and to teach thy servants how to see the end. Thou knowest how to inspire faith, and teach thy servants how to see the end. Thou knowest how to inspire faith, and by that faith to give fortitude. Grant to all thy servants, according to their need, these various blessings of thy providence. And grant, not by the wisdom of their calling and asking, but by the wisdom of thine interpretation. And still keep the burdens upon those who must needs bear them for their good, though they ask that they may be removed. Still say to those that would have the thorns removed from their side, My grace is sufficient for thee. Still say to those that are bowed down in tears and in darkness, The morning shall come: bear with the night. Grant, we pray thee, that those who are tempted may find thee near to them, strengthening them, and giving them victory over temptations. We pray that thou wilt point to the path of duty those who are bewildered and uncertain. May none be afraid to follow their feelings, that lead to purity, and love to God, and all that is good. Take away the selfishness which superstition hath imposed in all the world. Grant that those blinding fears, and those grinding doubts, and those oppressive misconceptions, which do so cloud the glory of God from so many minds, may be altogether taken away by the bright teaching of thy Holy Spirit. —Henry Ward Beecher.

EVENING SERVICE

Topic: Nailing Down the Holy Spirit.
TEXT: 1 Sam. 10:12.

"Is Saul among the prophets?" That question suggests an enquiry, the answer to which is desperately needed today. Actually, it is an enquiry in two parts. First of all, how can we nail down the Holy Spirit? How can we be sure that what people claim to be the work or leading of the Holy Spirit is really that, and not human enthusiasm or exhibitionism or exploitation? This is the second: How can we be nailed down by the Holy Spirit? How can we appropriate and enter into this new life which the Spirit brings? Let us consider these two questions in turn.

I. First of all, then, how can we nail down the Holy Spirit? If that means how can we control the Holy Spirit the answer is that we cannot. On the other hand, if it means how can we identify the presence and work of the Holy Spirit, then there are some very definite things that can be said.

(a) The first is the test of light. It is the business of the Holy Spirit to open our eyes and ears to Jesus so that we are convicted of our sin and led to put our whole trust and confidence in him. Thus John says: "By this you know the Spirit of God: every spirit which confesses that Jesus Christ has come in the flesh is of God, and every spirit which does not confess Jesus is not of God" (1 John 4:2–3). He means that the spirit which leads us to see that Jesus is the Christ—the Messiah, the Promised One of God, the Savior of the world —that spirit is the Spirit of God! If the spirit brings me to the realization of my need, then that spirit is the Holy Spirit.

(b) The test of life. The Scriptures tell us that whenever we see a life that is fully committed to Jesus Christ, a life in which he reigns supreme, we can be sure that the Holy Spirit has been at work there. That is what Paul has in mind when he says: "No man can say 'Jesus is Lord' except by the Holy Spirit" (1 Cor. 12:3). He means that it is the Holy Spirit that causes us to bow in surrender before the lordship of Christ and that it is the Holy Spirit that sends us out to serve him as Master and Lord.

(c) The test of love. That is the supreme test of the Spirit's presence. According to the Scriptures, when a spirit ceases to create and foster community and fellowship it is no longer the Spirit of God. Thus Paul reminds us that the gifts of the Spirit are not given to us for our personal exaltation but rather for the welfare of all. "To each," he says, "is given the manifestation of the Spirit for the common good" (1 Cor. 12:7). Where the Spirit is there is light and life and love—"and the greatest of these is love" (1 Cor. 12:13).

II. That brings me to our second question. How can we be nailed down by the Holy Spirit? How can we enter into and appropriate this new life of the Spirit?

(a) The first thing we need to realize is that, if we are Christians, we already possess the Holy Spirit. Paul makes that crystal clear when, in writing to the church at Rome, he says: "If anyone does not have the Spirit of Christ, he is none of his" (Rom. 8:9). To be a Christian is to be born of the Spirit and to be born of the Spirit is to have the Spirit of God abiding in us.

(b) If that is the case we can stop looking for the Spirit. We can give up seeking him in some second blessing, in some new experience and we can begin letting him take full possession of our lives as we commune with him, as we surrender to him, and as we seek to show our love for him. One thing is clear. The measure of our fullness —the extent to which we will be filled with the Spirit—is the measure of our obedience.—S. Robert Weaver.

SUNDAY: JUNE FOURTEENTH

MORNING SERVICE

Topic: A New Kind of Community
Text: Acts 1:10–12.

I. Jesus introduced to the world not only a stunning new message. He also created a new kind of community, one not seen before. When I read the book of Acts in the New Testament, I find myself reading it primarily from the perspective of a fledgling sect discovering what it means to be church. The book of Acts conveys the story of the emerging of a new kind of community in history.

(a) Surprisingly, the text in Acts rather matter-of-factly ticks off the names one by one of all the remaining disciples. We go down the list name by name. The names are mostly familiar: Matthew, Simon the Patriot, Andrew, James, John, Peter. In the new context of an emerging church just prior to Pentecost, the list of names becomes more than a perfunctory reiteration. Personalities come to mind, particular personalities so distinctive and so different that they must have clanged against each other threatening community.

(b) The group had a good number of natural reasons for human friction among these particular disciples. Recall that Zebedee owned his own boats; indeed he owned a fleet of boats, and he had hired fishing assistants who had shared in his enterprise. His sons, James and John, appear to have regarded themselves as a so-cial class above such proletarians as Peter and Andrew. Think about Philip. He was called by a Greek name and seems to have been of a speculative turn of mind. He was like a college sophomore who always asks the pesky kind of questions. And Nathaniel, mentioned in the same breath in the record with Philip, is characterized as "a guileless Israelite," the sort of individual who accepted faith easily. I wonder to what degree these individuals ever understood each other. I wonder to what degree a Philip and a Nathaniel ever really comprehended where the other was coming from.

(c) And surely a classic philosophical, political clash must have existed between Matthew and Simon. Simon the Patriot, as the Good News translation has it, or Zealot, as in the King James, probably belonged to a violently nationalistic society. Now Matthew, on the other hand, was a tax collector who had been an employee of the Roman empire. They were called into the same disciple band. There had to have been some collision, their political philosophies light-years apart.

(d) It must have been quite a struggle for these disciples to live together in community. The ambitions of James and John to sit at the right and left hand of Christ in glory would have done much to dampen, even destroy, the community that was trying to come into existence. There were many human causes for friction. There were doubters, there were dogmatists. There were conservatives, there were radicals. There were passionate personalities, there were temperamental moods. There was marginal subsistence and there was mild affluence. Yet they were invited to love one another, just as Jesus had loved them. The Christian church owes its modern existence today to the fact that they learned to live with one another in community.

II. Now I am leading up to an important assertion. The church was, has been, and sometimes is a sociological miracle. The first disciples managed a miracle of koinonia, a trembling transcendence of ordinary sociology. A new kind of community was a-borning. A new kind of community we call the church was on its way, and it was a sociological miracle. Isn't that one thing we discover about what church is and ought to be—a sociological miracle? It is nothing less than a recreation of humanity around Christ into a community of love—a new kind of community.

(a) Langdon Gilkey, following the lead of the Apostle Paul, has pointed out that the created difference among people has in fact been the cause of a good deal of human friction, even a source of hate. Then he brightens as he thinks about the church and as he thinks about what it is called into being to be. "But now," he says, "in Christ a new age has arrived. The old humanity is to be cast off and men have in Christ become new creatures who are to serve rather than oppress one another, and love rather than hate. In the church," he said, "these amazing powers of the kingdom are manifested. In its life, this final purpose of God for a new humanity has, through Christ, at last become a reality." This is good news, that ours is a new kind of community, a sociological miracle.

(b) But I hear someone saying within our congregation that sometimes the sociological miracle flounders. The tough sociological realities stubbornly stick around. There is no shortage of acute criticism of the American church, some of it valid and painful to admit. Yet with all of the church's failures, now and again, in a quivering way, we see a trembling transcendence of ordinary sociology. Just look around you. In this sanctuary there are children and senior citizens. There are men and there are women. There are single people and there are married people. As you think about other groups you know and as you think about the congregation that is the church you take notice of a quivering, trembling transcendence of ordinary sociology. The church now and again is a sociological miracle.

III. We return to the description in our text. We pick up a couple of other vital details that will contribute further to our understanding of this kind of community that Christ is calling into being. The names of the disciples are enumerated in verse 13, but in verse 14 it appears that there were actually nineteen people or more in that room. There were not just eleven, but nineteen. And the thing I propose is to pay more attention to the other eight people, bearing in mind that they are the charter members of the first church that ever existed.

(a) By all means, then, pay attention to the composition of the other eight. Two groups are distinguishable and both are important. There were women there and there were brothers present. The names of those women ought to be as familiar and as respected as those of the eleven disciples. Those women present in addition to the mother of Jesus were Mary Magdalene and Joanna and Susanna. These women in a real sense had earned a right to inclusion in the inner circle because they remained faithful. They stood by faithfully at the crucifixion of Jesus (Luke 23:49). They attended the tomb on Easter morning and were the first to discover the Easter truth (Luke 24:1–10). They are disciples. They have a right to be present. They belong. They, if you please, are a constitutive part of what it means to be church. Women were members of the church from the first day forward. It is important for us to pay particular attention to their presence. The group fervently praying in one spirit extended beyond the male disciples. The resurrection called into being a new reality not even existing during the historical ministry of Jesus.

(b) Another harmless detail is also important, that the brothers of Jesus were also present. Let us remember the four brothers: James, Joses, Judas, and Simon. Recall that they were not the most enthusiastic followers of Jesus throughout his lifetime. They apparently stood apart. They were unpersuaded. Indeed on occasion the whole family came to take Jesus away in protective fashion. The brothers were not believers. However, when the Apostle Paul described the appearances of the risen Christ to the disciples, he mentions not only that Christ appeared to Peter and to the Twelve, but he also says that Christ appeared to James (1 Cor. 15:7). James was not a believer. For him the resurrection was a victory over unbelief. So the sheer presence of the brothers of Jesus in the Upper Room is highly significant, for we discover that the church includes some individuals who found belief difficult but who enjoyed a victory over unbelief. I can identify with James in his experience of a victory over unbelief.

IV. Not only is the church a sociological miracle, but at its best the church is a community of the resurrection. I am finding it increasingly helpful to think of the church in this manner, as a community of the resurrection, created by and empowered by the resurrected Christ. It is an Easter society. Jesus was the firstborn from the dead who leads many sons and daughters to glory. The risen Christ has inaugurated a new race. Our community was called into being by the resurrection and is sustained and continued by the risen Christ. The resurrection is the fountain from which flows the stream of power. The church owes its existence and its continuation to the resurrection.

(a) Now we put the test of reality. Is it possible for our congregation to be a community of the resurrection? I would point out that when we have a baptism we become a community of the resurrection. When a person is baptized and we gather around and participate in that experience, then we are the community of the resurrection. The church is risen with Christ because its members have been raised to newness in life. An invitation at the end of our service is to become a part of the community of the resurrection. You may be a part of the community of the resurrection. And when we gather in the sanctuary to celebrate the Lord's Supper we are a community of the resurrection. We gather around Christ living and present at the Supper. When someone within our congregation has fallen in serious error, and there are those who care enough to keep loving, then we are the community of the resurrection.

(b) I invite our congregation to dare to be a sociological miracle, dare to be a community of the resurrection. Let us be a new kind of community. Let us be the church. Our experience may be broken, struggling, almost in process of happening. At best it will be a trembling transcendence of ordinary sociology, but let it happen. Let God make it happen.—Peter Rhea Jones.

Illustrations

IMAGINING THE TRINITY.   In God's dimension, so to speak, you find a being who is three persons while remaining one being, just as a cube is six squares while remaining one cube. Of course we can't fully conceive a being like that: just as, if we were so made that we perceived only two dimensions in space we could never properly imagine a cube. But we can get a sort of faint notion of it. And when we do we are then, for the first time in our lives, getting some positive idea, however faint, of something super-personal—something more than a person. It is something we could never have guessed, and yet, once we have been told, one almost feels one ought to have been able to guess it because it fits in so well with all the things we know already.—C. S. Lewis.

EXPERIENCING THE TRINITY.   God the Father lives in the heart of the Christian through Christ, the objective revelation of himself, and through the Spirit, who subjectively reveals and quickens love for him in the believer's heart. And, just as in looking at that great picture, a man might be conscious now of the genius of the artist, or again of the beauty of the picture, or again of his own appreciation of the picture, so the believer may sometimes be distinctly conscious of God the Father, again of God the Son, and yet again of God the Spirit. But all three persons of the triune God live ever in and through him. —C. Norman Bartlett.

Sermon Suggestions

THE ONE GOD. Text: Deut. 4:32–40. (1) Focusing on one nation. (2) Achieving incredible victories. (3) Requiring grateful obedience.

A PRESCRIPTION FOR PREVENTIVE RELIGION. Text: 2 Cor. 13:5–14. (1) Examine your faith and life. (2) Mend your ways. (3) Rely on the multifaceted help of the triune God.

Worship Aids

CALL TO WORSHIP. "And Jesus came and spake unto them, saying, All power is given unto me in heaven and in earth. Go ye therefore, and teach all nations, baptizing them in the name of the Father, and of the Son, and of the Holy Ghost: teaching them to observe all things whatsoever I have commanded you: and, lo, I am with you always, even unto the end of the world" (Matt. 28:18–20).

INVOCATION. Father, as we gather in your presence, it is not the promise of a brief rest nor the beauty of the day, nor the beauty of the sanctuary, which turns our hearts to you. It is rather the wonder of your love in Christ Jesus, the marvel of your call to us, the surprising relationships here in this hallowed place. These make us conscious of your majesty and of our insignificance apart from your purpose. It is enough. . . . we worship you in Spirit and in truth.—J. Estill Jones.

OFFERTORY SENTENCE. "Lay up for yourselves treasures in heaven, where neither moth nor rust doth corrupt, and where thieves do not break through nor steal" (Matt. 6:20).

OFFERTORY PRAYER. Help us, our Father, to bolt the door against the thieves that would steal our compassion for the poor, our concern for the lost, and our generosity toward needy causes of all sorts. Help us to open the door toward those who would teach us Christian love, responsible stewardship, and joy in giving. Help us to stay alive and human as we keep in touch with the work of the living Christ in the world.

PRAYER. Our Father, our God, you have made a place for us where we are safe. You are our refuge, and we have put our trust in you. Many forces that threaten us are at work in the world. In many ways they do us harm. Sorrow comes to all. Accidents happen; suffering lays us low; temptation beguiles—yet in your secret place we are safe.

Grant, O God, that we may always depend on you to help us in times of danger and weakness, but may we never presume on your goodness and grace by foolish and willful acts. We need your gift of friends to encourage us, your Spirit to guide us and make us brave, your word to temper our excesses and prod us to daily obedience.

While we receive your good gifts, let us be helpful friends, praying for one another and speaking your words of grace in the precious moment of opportunity or necessity.—James W. Cox.

EVENING SERVICE

Topic: The Relevance of the Doctrine of the Trinity for Faith Today

TEXT: Mark 1:16–20.

I. The experiences that gave rise to the doctrine of the Trinity were experiences in New Testament faith. I would illustrate this for you from the life of Simon Peter, the rugged, matter-of-fact fisherman who became preeminent among the followers of Jesus. Peter became aware of God in three ways.

(a) When Peter was asked by Jesus to leave his boat and nets and become a "fisher of men" he was an ordinary religious Jew of his time. He was aware of the reality of God as the Creator of all things and as giving the Hebrew people the task of making known to all peoples his nature and his will and his purposes. It is likely that Peter thought of God as the heavenly

Father, for that was one of the great metaphors of Hebrew devotion.

(b) One day Peter and the other disciples were walking with Jesus along a highway in the region of Caesarea Philippi, in the far north of Galilee, when Jesus turned and asked them, "Who do people say I am?" One of them said, "John the Baptist." "Elijah," said another. Another offered, "One of the prophets." "And you," Jesus then asked, "who do you say I am?" After a pregnant silence, Peter gasped, "You are the Messiah." That day Peter got a glimpse of the truth that the Messiah of God had come in a different form and with a different mission. Perhaps the idea that Jesus was the Messiah had been simmering for some time in Peter's mind below the level of conscious thought—and then that day he saw in a flash that Jesus is the Messiah, the Christ sent by God, God himself coming into history in a unique way.

(c) At the time of the crucifixion the disciples and other followers of Jesus scattered in fear and bewilderment. But gradually they came to know that Jesus was not a dead friend to be mourned but the living Lord with whom they could have a creative and redeeming relationship. And on the day of Pentecost, seven weeks after Easter, they had an intense emotional experience when they had gathered in a house in Jerusalem. They knew that they were being dealt with by a power that came from beyond them. This experience caused them to behave in a conspicuously emotional manner, and the Jerusalem crowd asked questions about them. Peter told the crowd about what God had done for humankind in coming into history in a special way in Jesus. Some of those present asked, "What are we to do?" Peter answered, "Repent and be baptized, every one of you, in the name of Jesus the Messiah for the forgiveness of your sins; and you will receive the gift of the Holy Spirit."

Peter spoke out of his own experience and out of the experience of the followers of Jesus as a group. When he used the expression, "the gift of the Holy Spirit," he was referring to a presence and a power in the hearts and minds of individuals and within the community of faith.

II. Peter, you see, had come to be aware of the reality of God in three ways—and in this we see the pattern that became the special Christian awareness of God as Father, Son, and Holy Spirit.

(a) The doctrine of the trinity, then, did not come out of the speculations of theologians who had nothing better to do than to try to make things more difficult for simple believers. This doctrine came out of the experiences of the early Christians. The doctrine of the trinity is essentially a description, not of God's reality, but of our awareness of God.

(b) The doctrine of the trinity, despite the abuse it has had from within the church and from outside it, remains a key doctrine of our faith. It is not an exotic something added to New Testament Christianity by later generations. It is a doctrine demanded by New Testament faith. It is a summing-up of New Testament experience in faith.

III. Look again at the experience of Peter. He was aware of God as the heavenly Father. He was aware of God, so to speak, focusing himself uniquely and decisively and redeemingly in Jesus Christ. He was aware of God as Holy Spirit, creatively impinging on the hearts and minds of the faithful in the community of faith that is the church. Peter was aware of the one God making himself known to us in three ways.

(a) The doctrine of the trinity, like all our doctrines, was developed as an instrument and support of our faith. In the early church the formulation of the doctrine was in part a defense measure to protect faith and worship against assault from outside the church and against distortion and subversion within.

(b) God known merely as the Creator is in danger of becoming for us simply a distant deity who somehow created the universe and got it going and now sits idly by as it runs down. God known merely in the Son can lead us to a misleading sentimentalism about Jesus, in which faith becomes primarily a matter of paying pious homage to the splendid life and the sublime teaching. And God known merely as indwelling Spirit very easily leads us to a vague and flabby mysticism, an emotional thing with little or no moral force.

(c) The doctrine of the trinity is—I hope you see—intensely relevant in our faith today, for it helps sustain the necessary balance in our awareness of God. It supports our faith and helps us understand and express it.—J. A. Davidson.

SUNDAY: JUNE TWENTY-FIRST

MORNING SERVICE

Topic: Things Are Not as They Appear!
TEXT: Rev. 4:1.

In this fourth chapter of Revelation John tells us that things are not as they appear. In compliance with the command of Jesus, given in chapter 1, he sets out to tell his readers both "what is, and what is to take place hereafter" (1:20). Up to this point he has been showing them what is here upon the earth—the spiritual condition of the churches and the threatening power of Rome (Rev. 2–3). Now, before setting before them what is to take place hereafter, which he begins to do in chapter 6, he tells them what is—in heaven! (Rev. 4)

I. *The first picture is the picture of a throne in heaven.* Thus John says: "At once I was in the Spirit, and lo, a throne stood in heaven" (4:2). He is telling his readers that in that world in which they live, a world dominated by the power of the emperor, the last word is not with Rome but with heaven!

(a) We can understand that in terms of John's day but what does it mean in our day and generation? It means, to begin with, that we are not in the hands of fate. We are not at the mercy of blind, impersonal forces. Life is more than "a tale, told by an idiot, full of sound and fury, signifying nothing." It has meaning and purpose and direction!

(b) It also means that life's meaning and direction are something more than what we give to it. Human decisions are important and significant. There is no refuting that. But what John is saying by this picture of the throne in heaven is that the last word—the final, authoritative word—is not with fate and it is not with humanity.

II. *He goes on to show us one sitting upon that throne.*

It is good to know that we are not in the hands of blind fate, nor in the hands of fallible humanity, but whether it is good that we are in the hands of the one who sits upon the throne depends upon the character of the one sitting there. What is he like? John meets that fundamental inquiry by telling us that he who sat upon the throne appeared like jasper and carnelian and round the throne was a rainbow that looked like an emerald. What are those things meant to signify? They are meant to quiet our fears and confirm our confidence in the character of God.

(a) Thus the jasper, probably our diamond, with its white, pure brilliance, suggests the holiness of God. The God who is seated upon the throne of the universe is the God of Isaiah and Habakkuk, a God of infinite holiness and therefore a God who is of purer eyes than to behold evil. He is a God of righteousness and justice.

(b) And as such, says John, he will bring judgment upon the wicked. That is the message of the carnelian or sardian, which was a blood-red stone coming from near Sardis. The God who is seated upon the throne, John is saying, is not only holy in himself, he also demands holiness of others. As such he will cast the wicked from their thrones and he will avenge the injustice of the oppressor.

(c) If God is the God of holiness and justice, how can anyone escape his judgment? John answers that by telling us that "all around the throne shone a halo like an emerald rainbow." That rainbow speaks of God's covenant with his people, while the emerald with its green color of the freshness that follows after rain, speaks of "the times of refreshing which will come from the presence of the Lord" (Acts 3: 19). The God who sits upon the throne is a God of grace and therefore a God of hope.

III. What a pillow of assurance that is for the anxious and troubled soul! Yes, but what will that love avail if God is only God in heaven and we are people upon the earth? What good will it do if there is no commerce, no communication, between heaven and earth? But that is not the case, for *round about the throne are four and twenty elders and four living creatures.*

(a) What do they signify? Most commentators agree that the four and twenty elders are angels—messengers of God who bring help to God's people from beyond—and that the four living creatures are the cherubim—God's agents, the symbols or representatives of God's power in the world.

You see what John is saying. He is telling us that heaven and earth are one, that there is commerce between them, that God is not shut off from his creation but that he is active and present in his world and able to do exceeding abundantly above all that we can ask or think.

(b) Men and women, things are not as they appear! We are not alone wrestling with the hosts of wickedness in high places! There is a throne in heaven, and there is one who sits upon that throne who loves us with an everlasting love, and there are those round about the throne that await his command. Thus there is at this very moment a power in the world, not our own, that makes for righteousness, and even now there is help available for each and every situation. There is a throne in heaven and God is on that throne—the God revealed to us in Jesus Christ! And that God worketh hitherto and will work until his perfect will is established. And until then, his power and grace are available to us in every time of need.—S. Robert Weaver.

Illustrations

HIGHER MEANING. Is it not conceivable that there is still another dimension possible, a world beyond man's world; a world in which the question of an ultimate meaning of human suffering would find an answer? This ultimate meaning necessarily exceeds and surpasses the finite intellectual capacities of man. What is demanded of man is not, as some existential philosophers teach, to endure the meaninglessness of life; but rather to bear his incapacity to grasp its unconditional meaningfulness in rational terms.

A psychiatrist who goes beyond the concept of the supra-meaning, would sooner or later be embarrassed by his patients just as I was when my daughter at about six years of age asked me the question, "Why do we speak of the good Lord?" Whereupon I said, "Some weeks ago, you were suffering from measles, and then, the good Lord sent you full recovery." However, the little girl was not content but she retorted, "Well, but please, Daddy, do not forget in the first place, he had sent me the measles."—Viktor E. Frankl.

DIMENSION OF DEPTH. In order to express who God is and where man encounters him, Tillich replaces the familiar concept of height with that of depth. This signifies more than merely a change in a spatial conception. Depth does not refer to a level of reality, in such a way that God, instead of being understood, as before as the highest being, is now regarded as the deepest being. Depth refers to a dimension of reality. The changed image is intended to express the fact that the reality of God is not to be sought above all the reality of the world as its highest level, nor beneath all the reality of the world, but as the " 'really real' among all the things and events that offer themselves as reality." Thus anyone who asks about God must not turn away from the world and look upwards into the heights, into an imaginary heaven, but must in fact turn towards the world, exploring more deeply the world, his own existence, and its relationship to the existence of other men. Then he will encounter in the depth the reality of God as the ground and meaning of all being.—Heinz Zahrnt.

Sermon Suggestions

WHEN YOU LEAST EXPECT IT. Text: Gen. 28:10–17. (1) God may visit you. (2) God may change the direction of your life. (3) God may give you a new sense of meaning and purpose for your life.

THE TWO AGES. Text: Rom. 5:12–19. (1) The reign of death in the age of Adam. (2) The triumph of life in the age of Christ.

Worship Aids

CALL TO WORSHIP.   "As it is written, Eye hath not seen, nor ear heard, neither have entered into the heart of man, the things which God hath prepared for them that love him" (1 Cor. 2:9).

INVOCATION.   As we come before thee in worship, our Father, remove the scales from our eyes, that we may behold thee in thy majesty, wisdom, and love. Let our songs, our prayers, and our thoughts honor and glorify thy holy name.

OFFERTORY SENTENCE.   "These words Moses spoke to all the community of Israelites: This is the command the Lord has given: Each of you set aside a contribution to the Lord. Let all who wish, bring a contribution to the Lord" (Exod. 34:4b–51 NEB).

OFFERTORY PRAYER.   Sometimes, Lord, our willingness to give outruns our ability; sometimes our ability is greater than our willingness. Make us generous givers, but better than that, make us cheerful givers.

PRAYER.   We thank thee, our Father, that thou hast quickened our knowledge of thee, and that thou art in the center of our homes, by the voice of our little ones, teaching us to say to thee, as they say to us, Our Father. We know something of the meaning of that in them; and as we interpret their confidence and faith in the simplicity of love, so may we know how to draw near to thee with a corresponding experience. Though they are dependent and ignorant, and constantly erring, we feel that our love is large enough to forgive them, and that our wisdom is large enough for their need, and that all our life is a sacrifice—a living one—for them. For them we toil; for them we suffer inconvenience; for them we give up our time and our rights; for them we willingly take on weariness and pain; for them we live; and we pour our life into their souls, that they may grow up in a self-sustaining and fruitful life. And hast thou not herein taught us what thou art? What is the wonder of thy living sacrifice, set forth and manifested in Jesus Christ, and more gloriously effulging in the everlasting life of God in heaven, forever bearing the sorrow, the inexperience, the suffering the sin and the wickedness of the world, teaching, restraining, punishing, all in love, to rear up generations that shall serve thee!

Blessed be thy name, O Lord God! that we need not go up into the heaven, nor down into the deep, nor far away on the wings of philosophy, to know who thou art, and what thou art. Thou hast written thy nature upon our souls. Thou hast interpreted thyself in our own best feelings. Thou art no longer reminding us of thee by the thunder of Sinai, or by the suffering of Calvary; but thou art by the teachings of both giving us to understand what secret things were hidden from the foundations of the world in those whom thou hast made in thine own image. Thou art bringing forth; thou art teaching; and behold all things reveal thee to those that seek thee. For thou art in the heaven and on the earth, the night and in the day, and in the uttermost parts of the earth. Where shall we go that we may flee from thy presence? Thou art everywhere; and on all things which thou hast made thou hast left thine impress. We rejoice in the fullness of the knowledge which thou hast given to the world of thee. And we pray that the blindness of our own hearts, and the misinterpretations of our passions, and our mistakes, may no longer hinder our seeing the bright and glorious face of God, or of Jesus. Grant that we may see and rejoice in him as our soul's best Friend, our beloved Savior, our appointed Head. May we clasp by faith and love, Jesus our Forerunner and Intercessor, and, following humbly in his footsteps and in his spirit, wait for the clearer and more blessed revelation of the fullness of his nature, and by the divine nature in him be led to the land of knowledge and of perpetual light.—Henry Ward Beecher.

EVENING SERVICE

Topic: Principles of Positive Parenting
TEXT: Pss. 127–128.
From God's word and from the findings of those who have studied family life

today, I have drawn several principles for positive parenting that I want us to consider together.

I. *The first principle is to be authentic.*

(a) If there is anything children can discern it is a fake. You can fool all of the people some of the time and you can fool some of the people all of the time, but you can't fool your children for long. That is why the foundation for a happy home is parents who are genuine and sincere.

(b) We parents often mask our feelings and hide our true self and present a fascade of perfection and sainthood because we are afraid true self-disclosure will drive our children away. The findings of family researchers and counselors alike has been exactly the opposite. Self-disclosure does not drive people away. It draws people to us. The best thing you can do for your children is to let them know you are for real. Be authentic.

II. *The second principle is to be attentive.*

(a) Ross Campbell in his book *How To Really Love Your Child* lists as one of the most vital ingredients of successful parenting what he calls "focused attention," that is, giving children our full, undivided attention in such a way that they feel without a doubt that they are completely loved.

(b) There are two reasons why such attention is important. First, attention is important because of what it will enable us to communicate to our children. It is not our words but our actions which will make the most lasting impressions on our children.

(c) Second, attention is important because of what it will enable us to teach our children. Teaching occurs best when there is an openness in the lives of our children. This openness is called "the teachable moment." The mind of a child has doors like those to a building. A teachable moment occurs when that door, through some circumstance, has been thrown open. These teachable moments cannot be created. They can only be sensed. Through attention to our children, these teachable moments can be discerned, and learning can occur.

III. *The third principle of positive parenting is to be affirmative.*

(a) Acceptance creates a climate in which personal growth occurs, and it is therefore one of the most important ingredients for a healthy home.

(b) Every child is packed full of potentiality that is released by someone who believes in them, confirms their worth, and helps them to realize their possibilities. So, be affirmative.

IV. *The fourth principle of positive parenting is to be affectionate.*

(a) Affection is important because of what it will do for your children. There is a direct relationship between parental love as perceived by the child in the home and a feeling of self-assurance in the child when she or he grows up. If children find a place of acceptance and love in the home, they will be more likely to find a place in later life. Security comes from a feeling of being loved. The primary source of such love is parents who dare to declare and express their affection.

(b) Affection is also important because of what it will do for you as a parent. We are drawn to those who love us. When people care for us and show that appreciation with their eyes, their attention, and their declarations of affection, they create a field of emotion that draws us in. By truly loving them, we create an emotional field that will draw them to us.

V. *The fifth principle is to be available.*

(a) The cry of youth, sometimes vocalized in anger and at other times internalized in silent rage, is "Where were you when I needed you?" The greatest tragedy of today's family is children who have been orphaned by parents unwilling to change their agendas to spend time with their children.

(b) Sometimes it is not our busyness but our attitude that makes us unavailable to our children. Your children have feelings. They have questions. They have things they need to talk about. They need you, so be available.

VI. *A sixth principle of positive parenthood is to be aspiring.*

(a) Everyone needs goals, for goals give both meaning and motivation to life.

(b) What aspirations do you have for your children? What do you pray for? If you daily go before the Father with this prayer on your lips, "God make a man out of him. Lord, make a Christian woman out of her," then you have taken a key step toward positive, productive parenting.— Brian L. Harbour.

SUNDAY: JUNE TWENTY-EIGHTH

MORNING SERVICE

Topic: Matthew: The Man of Business
TEXT: Matt. 9:9.

How broad-minded the Master was! His ideals were the highest the world has ever seen and his insistence upon them clear and firm, yet he stood at a long remove from the narrow, one-eyed partisan. He had a place in the treasure-house of his interest for the widow's mite. He has also a place for the generous means of the well-to-do business man.

His eyes of sympathy swept the whole social scale from the top to the bottom and from the bottom clear up to the top. He called fishermen and made prophets of them. He also called a man profitably engaged in the revenue service of the Roman empire and made an apostle of him. "He saw a man named Matthew, sitting at the receipt of custom, and said to him, "Follow me!"

I. We will notice four things about this man of business who was called to be an apostle. He was a publican, that is to say a tax collector.

(a) In Palestine, where the taxes were farmed out by the Roman government, the tax collector, socially speaking, was a leper. He stood about where gamblers and bootleggers stand with us. Some man would pay the Roman government a fixed sum for the right to collect taxes in a given district. Then he took all he could get. He had but one rule, "Pile on all the traffic will bear."

(b) "He saw a man named Matthew sitting at the receipt of custom." It was a venture of faith for Jesus to call such a man to be an apostle. Matthew was a government official, suspected and hated by the common people. He was a publican, that is, a tax collector. One could hardly go to church in those days without hearing some Pharisee say, "Thank God, I am not as other men are, unjust, extortioners, adulterers, or even as this publican." Matthew was a publican, yet here stands his name as one of the Twelve. It was indeed a venture of faith.

(c) Most of these tax collectors were Romans—the patriotic Jew refused to hold office under the hated Roman rule. Now and then a Jew with an eye to opportunity did accept the office of a publican. He was then regarded as an apostate Jew, a man who had sacrificed race pride and national loyalty to his desire to make money.

These tax collectors were regarded by all upright Jews as traitors to their country. Their money was tainted money and was not to be accepted in the synagogue. They were no longer "the salt of the earth"—they had lost their Hebrew savor and were to be trodden under foot by the fathers of Israel.

(d) Matthew was one of those men. He was sitting at the receipt of custom, collecting revenue for the Roman government when Jesus first saw him. The Master did not come to call the righteous, but sinners, to repentance. He had a mission to "the lost sheep of the house of Israel." He saw beneath the hard exterior of this tax collector the making of a splendid apostle.

II. It is interesting, in the second place, to notice this publican's method of doing Christian work.

(a) When Matthew became a follower of Christ, he made a feast at his own house. He invited his friends to meet the Master. "There were many publicans and sinners among them," the record says. It had to be so—they were the only friends Matthew had. He was bearing his testimony as a Christian in the presence of his former associates. Had he invited pious Jews, they would not have come.

But when Matthew invited Jesus, he went. He sat down and ate with publicans and sinners. It stirred the social circles of Jerusalem to the depths. "He eateth with publicans and sinners!"

The Master ate with publicans and sinners because he was a physician. He told the Jews who criticized him that a physician's main business was not with those who were well, but with those who were sick. They needed him the most.

(b) Jesus was interested in Matthew's method of doing Christian work. When this tax collector wanted to bring people into contact with Christ, he did not invite them to a prayer meeting, he invited them to a dinner. He did not say, "Come around to the synagogue next Sabbath and sit in my pew." He invited them to come to his home the next night and sit at his table. That interested the Master; he had not always seen it done after that fashion.

The religion of Jesus is intensely social in its whole spirit and method. "The Son of Man came eating and drinking"—he was a diner-out. He was criticized for it. Some of the people said that he was "a winebibber and a gluttonous man." This was untrue, but it indicated his social habits.

III. The main emphasis that Matthew reveals in reporting the work of Christ is also significant. Here was a man who had not talked much about religion in the past —it was not a common topic of conversation among tax collectors. He had never been caught up into the third heaven of spiritual ecstasy as Paul was. He did not know as much about heaven as he did about this common earth, where people buy and sell and make gain and pay their taxes or get out of them when they can. He never had seen the heavens open and the angels of God ascending and descending. He lived close to the ground. He had, however, seen many a soul go down in defeat because of that love of money which lies at the root of so much that is evil. His religion, therefore, was very practical—it was the religion of a business man.

(a) His years of service in the Department of Internal Revenue had made him familiar with the Roman regard for order and precedent. His Gospel stands first in the New Testament because it forms a connecting link between the old dispensation and new. It links up the best there was in the Old Testament with the finer teachings of the New, showing how Jesus came

"not to destroy one jot or one tittle" of that which was good, but "that all should be fulfilled" in a more complete manifestation of God's moral interest in humanity.

(b) Matthew joins with Luke, whose Gospel most nearly resembles his own, in exalting the plain teachings of the Sermon on the Mount. He regarded it as a kind of moral platform for the world of action. The final solution of all industrial and social problems would, in his judgment, have to be made upon the basis of the principles and ideals there contained. He made clear the binding obligation of the Golden Rule.

(c) In his Gospel, Matthew particularly emphasizes those principles which impel people to fair dealing, to kindly speech, to unselfish action. He would have them pay what they owed regularly and promptly, so that others might not suffer hurt and loss by their careless delay. He would have people uniformly kind and courteous, even to the thankless and thoughtless. He would have people like God who sendeth rain upon the just and the unjust, who causeth the sun to shine upon the evil and the good, that they might be the children of the highest. His main emphasis was upon the doing of the Father's will in the round of daily life.

(d) Here in Matthew, we find certain splendid teachings of Christ which are not contained in the other Gospels. He alone tells us about the man who found a treasure hid in the field and sold all that he had in order to purchase that field and secure the treasure. The man knew that "the price of the best" is always all that one has; it cannot be had on any easier terms.

Matthew alone tells us about the merchant who dealt in goodly pearls, finding one pearl of great price that was worth more than all the rest put together. He too sold all that he had in order to purchase that pearl. The kingdom of heaven is like that.

(e) His Gospel emphasizes more strongly than either of the others those great words of the Master: "No man can serve two masters. He will either hate the one and love the other, or he will hold to the one and despise the other. You cannot serve God and mammon." One of them must be put first. Is God first or is gold first? When two people ride the same horse at the same time, one of them must ride behind, leaving the task of directing the movements of that horse to the other. Matthew was a man with a past—he had seen the power of greed—and he used that past to make his service to Christ more effective. He would have every person put first that which is first.

IV. In the fourth place, notice the main value of this man's work for the kingdom.

(a) His acceptance of Christ's call meant sacrifice. Here was a government official, a man with a good position and an assured income, for the Roman government gave good pay! He was able, if he had chosen, to build big barns and fill them to the eaves with good things. He too might have said to himself: "Take thine ease! Eat, drink and be merry! You have a sure thing for all the years to come."

Now he was asked to leave all that and follow one who had nowhere to lay his head. He was called to a life of uncertainty and sacrifice. He had the moral courage to accept and make the venture. People like that will always add up large on the balance sheet of any religious movement.

(b) Matthew had learned the lesson of attending strictly to business, whether he felt like it or not. It is a quality which has abiding worth. It was one who spake as never another spake who said, touching his own philosophy of life, "Wist ye not that I must be about my Father's business?"

(c) I wonder if we have not had about enough of careless contempt heaped upon people of affairs? A lot of it has been altogether undeserved. Business people are not all mean, sordid, and grasping. Some of the very finest Christians I have ever known were people who were not clergy nor teachers, not professionals of any kind —they were business men and women.

The Master showed that he knew what was in human nature when he chose as one of the Twelve a man who had been successfully engaged in business.

(d) "Six days shalt thou labor and do all thy work"—it is a divine command! It was handed down from the top of Sinai. It is an essential part of that commandment which says, "Remember the Sabbath day to keep it holy." The person who fails to use the seventh day of worship and aspiration for the high ends of character building breaks the Sabbath. The person who fails to perform some useful and necessary kind of work breaks all the other six days. No matter what particular form that work may take in those six secular days which lie between Sundays, high purpose, fidelity, an honest regard for the rights of others will make of it a spiritual exercise no less sacred and helpful than those worshipful exercises that are held apart for the seventh day.

(e) Your field of action may lie in a store, in a factory, in an office. Your main task may be the baking of loaves of bread which people can eat with comfort, or driving nails straight without splitting the board, or making useful articles which will serve the needs for which they were designed. I care not what form your action may take. Whatsoever your hand or your head finds to do, if you do it thoroughly and well, it becomes straightway a vital part of your own religious development.

(f) Here it is then in modern phrase. The Master sees people sitting in their places of business, and he says to them all, "Follow me." They may be surrounded with ledgers and letter files, with wage-scales and price lists. They may be handling materials that feed and clothe, house and warm the race. They are called to follow Christ, not always nor commonly, by leaving all that. They are called as people of business to follow him by devoting and consecrating all that material and ability and the whole economic process that they are helping to direct to those high ends, human and divine, for which it was designed. When people of business, here and there and everywhere undertake to do just that, we shall see the kingdom of God coming upon earth evenly and steadily, with all that consequent human betterment which will make glad the heart of the Lord.—Charles Reynolds Brown.

Illustrations

WHAT CHRIST SEES IN US.   There is a legend which has come down from some unknown source. Some boys were standing one day around the body of a dead dog as it lay in the gutter on the streets of Jerusalem. They were showing their contempt for the poor brute. "He has had one of his eyes gouged out," one boy remarked. "He has lost an ear in some dog fight," said another. "What an ugly brute he is," added a third, "his hair all matted with dirt and blood!"

"But look at his teeth!" a stranger said, who was looking over their shoulders at the body of the poor dog. "Look at his teeth—they are as white and as fine as pearls!"

"Who is that?" one boy said as he looked up. An older boy, who knew the man by sight, replied, "It is Jesus, the Galilean."

The Master had a clear eye for those better qualities sometimes overlooked in dogs and in people. He looked for the best, saw the best, and was forever bringing it out. He saw the tax collector whom the people despised, and by a venture of faith he called him to be an apostle. —Charles Reynolds Brown.

GOD'S BUSINESS. If we begin to follow Jesus, we slowly learn to let this and that go, perhaps even sometimes to let our own self go.

Here is a master carpenter who runs his trade as a fellowship. He does not run it as if everyone were a Christian. However, he tries at least to be serious about it. He counsels with his workers. He shares his earnings with them. He gives them some of the responsibility. Many times a person must give up a few hundred dollars in order to be granted a few human hearts.

Take young people who are choosing their vocation. Some of them give up their career and a substantial salary to travel a road on which they are repeatedly showered with gifts, namely with people they serve. I know persons who care for the chronically ill. They are very simple people; no newspaper writes about them. Their work is very unromantic, but day after day they are richly blessed with the persons whose existence depends upon them. And even today some people literally follow Jesus into death, for the sake of those entrusted to them. Death is not easy; and it is not promised that the way will be easy. But it is indeed true that only the person who is where Jesus is sees the glory of God in Jesus.—Eduard Schweizer.

Sermon Suggestions

AN UNEVEN MATCH. Text: Gen. 32:22–32. (1) *Situation:* Jacob unwittingly wrestled with God. (2) *Complication:* Though Jacob was strong, he was no match for his opponent. (3) *Resolution:* Jacob lost the bout but won a new name, a high mission, and the blessing of God.

WHAT YOUR BAPTISM MEANS. Text: Rom. 6:3–11. It signifies and seals: (1) your union with Christ; (2) your putting away of a life dominated by sin. (3) your aliveness to God and his will for your life.

Worship Aids

CALL TO WORSHIP. "Because of God's great mercy to us I appeal to you: Offer yourselves as a living sacrifice to God, dedicated to his service and pleasing to him. This is the true worship that you should offer" (Rom. 12:1 TEV).

INVOCATION. God of grace, Father of mercies, we come to you to be taught again how to worship you in spirit and in truth and how to serve you in the world. Guide our thoughts, capture our hearts, and strengthen our wills, so that all that we are and can become shall be pleasing in your sight.

OFFERTORY SENTENCE. "The poor shall never cease out of the land: therefore I command thee, saying, Thou shalt open thine hand wide unto thy brother, to thy poor, and to thy needy, in thy land" (Deut. 15:11).

OFFERTORY PRAYER. Gracious Father, thou hast blessed us already; therefore we can bring an offering today. Now bless, we pray thee, this offering and those causes and persons that benefit from it.

PRAYER. Almighty God, whose Son Jesus Christ in his earthly life shared our toil and hallowed our labor: Be present with your people where they work; make those who carry on the industries and commerce of this land responsive to your will; and give to us all a pride in what we do, and a just return for our labor; through Jesus Christ our Lord, who lives and reigns with you, in the unity of the Holy Spirit, one God, now and forever. —*Book of Common Prayer.*

EVENING SERVICE

Topic: The Waste Basket—Paul
TEXT: Phil. 3:13–14.

I. This text lets us into the secret of one of the most majestic and useful lives that was ever lived on this planet.

(a) From this text we learn that Paul was a specialist. Paul was not bent upon a dozen different enterprises. He was not even engaged in two. He was giving all his time, all his attention, all his vast abilities to one single task.

(b) Not only was Paul a man of one single purpose, but that purpose was one that was altogether worthy. If Paul staked everything upon one single adventure, it was an adventure that was genuinely worthwhile.

(c) Not only did Paul set himself to one high purpose, but he went about the achieving of that purpose in a most wise and intelligent fashion.

II. "Forgetting those things which are behind." This does not mean that Paul forgot everything that was behind. There are some things that you dare not throw away.

(a) Do not forget that bill that you owe the grocery store owner just because you have eaten the groceries. Do not forget the pledge that you made to the church just because you made it last year. Do not forget the vow that you made to God, the pledge of a new service and of a new loyalty. It is exceedingly easy to forget these things. But they must not be forgotten. To forget them is to deal a death blow to our honesty.

(b) Do not forget the wrongs that you inflicted, wrongs you might right if you desired. Do not forget the wound you made that it is your duty to heal.

(c) Paul is not asking us to forget the kindnesses that have been shown us.

(d) Do not forget the mercy of God that came to you. Paul was the last one who would have urged upon us that we forget the blessings that are behind us. And if we would not fling away real treasure, let us carry the memory of God's mercies with us.

III. But there are some things that we can afford to throw away. We must part with these things or the chances are we shall make no progress at all.

(a) I would advise that you throw away whatever wrongs you may have suffered. Why keep them? They do not help you in the least. It is worthwhile to cultivate roses. But why give your time to the cultivation of nettles?

Has someone injured you, deceived you, cheated you, done you a great wrong? Forget it. For if you remember it the memory of it will harden into hate. Hate will be changed into cynicism. You will become bitter, antagonistic, disillusioned.

(b) As you enter into tomorrow you can afford to throw away the record of your past failures and blunders and mistakes. You made a mistake that you feel will cast a shadow over all your tomorrows. What are you doing about it? I can tell you what not to do. Do not keep your eyes fixed upon it. Do not allow it so to unnerve you and discourage you as to keep you from doing anything with the present.

(c) Then there is your old sin. Yesterday you sinned. What are you going to do about that grim fact? The answer to this question may startle you. Forget it. Turn your back upon it through faith in Christ. For God himself forgets it. If you are trusting in Jesus this morning he has forgotten that you ever sinned. Every sin that you have ever committed he has blotted out of the book of his remembrance. And what God forgets you have a right to forget.

(d) Paul forgot himself. Is not the biggest tragedy of our lives just this: that we are self-centered rather than God-centered? We live within our own wills instead of within his will. Is it not true that this has been the source of our loss of opportunities? But if we are trusting Christ today, the old life of self is to be forgotten.

IV. And why does Paul forget the things that are behind? Why does he urge us to forget? For the simple reason that he knows we will never run forward when our eyes are turned backward. If you are constantly looking in the past, looking at past sins and failures, you will never go forward. People walk in the direction in which they look. And if you have the backward look this morning, you also have the backward step. It is only as we turn our eyes to the future, to the things that are before that we will make progress.

V. But you say, "That is all well enough. But how can I forget?" And let me tell you frankly that you will not forget by simply trying to do so. You will never succeed in this great undertaking by simply saying, "Now, go to. I am going to forget."

(a) How can I forget the things that are behind? There is only one way and that is by becoming absorbed in the things that are before. That is the way Paul forgot his yesterday. He became absorbed in the things of today and tomorrow.

(b) Do you remember the Jackal in *The Tale of Two Cities?* What an unlovely and self-centered and repellent personality was Sydney Carton! But one day he forgot himself. And in that noble forgetfulness he slipped into a prison cell. He took another man's place at the guillotine. And those who saw him die said his face was the most peaceful face upon which they had ever looked. He lost his self-love in the love of another. And so we are to forget self by giving our heart's love to Christ and to our brothers and sisters for Christ's sake.

VI. "Forgetting the things which are behind and reaching forth unto those things which are before"—that is the only way we can become emancipated from the past. But what are some of the things that are ahead of us this morning that still make life worth living, that make the hilltops ahead golden with blessed possibilities?

(a) Jesus Christ is still ahead of us. You rejected him last year maybe. But you have not run past him yet. He was in yesterday, but, thank God, he is in today and will be in tomorrow. So you have him to look forward to as you turn your back upon the past. And he says to you just what he said to his disciples who failed him as you failed him: "Rise up; let us be going."

(b) Eternity is ahead of you. You have a whole eternity yet on your hands. And what a wonderful man you may become among the tall sons of the morning if you will only begin! If you have only one more minute to live in this world, still I say, eternity is ahead of you. Lay hold of this heartening fact and you will start even yet to press toward the mark for the prize.

(c) If you will dare to begin, perfection is ahead of you. However warped and bent and broken and unsightly you are at the moment, however stained and tarnished, however eaten and disfigured by the leprosy of sin, yet perfection is ahead of you if you will only claim it.

(d) Home is ahead of us. Our real home is ahead. "Let not your heart be troubled. Ye believe in God, believe also in me. In my father's house are many mansions. If it were not so I would have told you. I go to prepare a place for you; and if I go and prepare a place for you, I will come again and receive you unto myself, that where I am there ye may be also." Thank God that blessed experience is not behind us. It is in this home that we shall find our finest friendships. It is in this home that we shall lock arms with those whom we "have loved long since and lost awhile."—Clovis G. Chappell.

SUNDAY: JULY FIFTH

MORNING SERVICE

Topic: The Lost Secret of Great Religion
TEXT: Ps. 118:1–9, 19–24, 29.

I. It is an old secret—one of the oldest in religion—that people should trust in God, and in that trust find strength sufficient for the trials of any day. It is plain to even the most casual student that the fundamental strength in religion is confidence in God, in his mercy, in his providence, in his redemptive love.

(a) "Trust in God?" you ask, "What is that anyway?" Is it an emotional state of peace and serenity that we reach by continuous repetition of the words, "I trust God, I trust God, I trust God"? Is it a state of peace and serenity that we reach by stifling or ignoring or neglecting honest doubts until it appears that everything falls into line and fits into a pattern of ideas in terms of which we find peace of mind and peace of soul? Or is trust in God simply a state of social conformity in the life of a religious group—a willingness to let our doubts rest, our anxieties cease, and our life find its peace through subordination of mind and life to the will and way of the group?

Trust in God, as used in prophetic religion, as demonstrated by the life and teachings of Jesus Christ, has not meant any one of these possible perversions of it. What it has meant, to try to put it in three closely related words, is this:

(b) Trust in God means (1) Belief in God—a consciously sought, clearly faced, factually grounded, intellectually trustworthy conviction that God is the supreme Fact and Factor in human life and history.

Trust in God means (2) Faith in God— a belief in him so strong, so vital, so certain that you are willing to let it guide your life.

Trust in God means (3) Confidence in God—a confident knowledge, born of your own experience that he can be depended upon, that he knows and cares, that he is sufficient for all things, that you can put the hand of your life in his outstretched hand and go where he leads.

II. Read it any way you will, the Bible is one long document of trust in God no matter what may befall a person or a people in life.

(a) When Job cried, "Though he slay me, yet will I trust him," he was putting the secret of vital religion in an immortal phrase. Read again that breathtaking section on anxiety in the Sermon on the Mount. To disciples who were about to be arrested for preaching the gospel and haled before magistrates who held the power of life and death in their hands, he counsels, "Do not be anxious how you are to speak or what you are to say; for what you are to say will be given to you in that hour; for it is not you who speak, but the Spirit of your Father speaking through you."

Jesus' trust in God was so patent a fact about, and so potent a force within, his life that his enemies at the cross chose to articulate what they regarded as their triumph in terms of it. "He trusts in God," they screamed one to another. "Let God deliver him now, if he desires him; for he said, 'I am the Son of God.' " Yet even this ridicule could neither dampen his spirit nor drown out his final testament of trust: "Father, into thy hands I commit my spirit!"

(b) The great figures in Christian history discovered the serenity and the strength of trust in God: Paul could emerge from many years of doubt, anguish, and spiritual tragedy with this word of trust on his lips, "I know whom I have believed, and am persuaded that he is able to keep that which I have committed unto him against the day"; St. Augustine could bring his long and fretful journey through the philosophies and theologies of his day to complete peace of mind and spirit in his assurance. Luther, Wesley, and a whole host of others share in the great tradition of trust in God.

(c) Yet this selfsame secret of trust in God comes close to being the lost secret of our generation. This better than anything else explains the spiritual tragedy that has overtaken us and our civilization. We have trusted everyone and everything but God. We have rejected the disciplines of prophetic religion only to discover to our immeasurable sorrow that the pleasures of paganism come terribly high. One would think that the tragic sacrifices which we have been forced to make in the name of these man-made and man-centered religions would label them once and for all as the charnal houses of destruction which they are and close them forever in the minds of thoughtful people.

III. The writer of the 118th Psalm saw something like that happening in his day. Thereupon he drew a sharp line between his faith and that of his pagan contemporaries. To the humanist he said, "It is better to trust in the Lord than to put confidence in man." To the totalitarian he said, "It is better to trust in the Lord than to put confidence in princes." There we have it: the eternal difference between man-made and man-centered religion and divinely inspired and divinely centered religion! Great religion does not begin with man and trust in man; it begins with God and trust in God.

(a) This kind of trust in God deserves our undivided attention in this day of confusion. We are living at a time when high ideals are hard to maintain; when high hopes daily grow dimmer; when people once more are preparing to rebuild the altars of humanism and totalitarianism and put their whole confidence in man-made devices. Before we start once more on what has always been a one-way trip to disaster, it surely is the part of wisdom to investigate more carefully the survival and redemptive value of placing our whole trust in God. Trust in God is not divorced from ordinary living. Like all great religious declarations, it is rooted and grounded in daily living. You simply cannot live without trust.

(b) What I am saying amounts to this: the only known way of redeeming a trust betrayed in human relationships begins with an affirmation of a vital trust in God. Among the many things that trust in God may mean, certain ones stand out: it means a forgiving spirit, an understanding spirit, a sacrificial spirit. When a breach occurs in human relations, the person who trusts God reaches out at once and seeks by every known way to span the gap. That is the spirit that eventually bridges chasms between and among people. When we are estranged from one another, there rests upon us an infinite obligation to take it seriously and seek to heal the misunderstanding.

IV. Consider why it is important to increase trust among people. Psychologists tell us that there are two ways in general of viewing and approaching life: the contractive and the expansive. In the contractive view of life we take our stand at the center of self; we try steadily to draw in the horizons of our responsibility. In the expansive view we stand at the center of self —where obviously one must stand—and move outward, eager to meet and to understand other people, glad to work with

them with a certain degree of trustfulness. We welcome new experiences.

(a) The difference between these two kinds of living is enormous. It is all the difference between a cooperative and a combative type of life; all the difference between going through life with a chip on the shoulder, looking for trouble and always finding it; and going through life with the confident assurance that, by and large, one can count on other people at least as much as they can count upon you.

(b) One of the most urgent tasks before us today is to rescue the home from the clutches of disintegration. Our divorce rate is overtaking our marriage rate. If a cure is to be effected, the healing must begin at the source of the infection. We must master the art of living together with trust and confidence in each other, not simply when things are going well with us, but more especially when it seems as if all the demons in hell have interposed themselves between us. Misunderstandings come between even the most devoted lovers, but need such misunderstandings grow into mistrust and solidify themselves in separations? They will, unless they are redeemed by the kind of trust in God with which we have been dealing here. And when two people work at a common misunderstanding with humility and sincerity, it will not long separate them. Of this we may be sure.

(c) When we say we trust in God we are not saying that from here on out the job is his to do. Rather, we are saying that we do not have to do it all ourselves. We are saying that as we move or seek to move human life in the right direction, some of his strength and power comes flooding in and through us, and we become instruments of his holy will. We become "coworkers together with Christ." This famous phrase touches off the real meaning of trust in God. For we can have him as ally or enemy in this matter of building a new world. Move in the direction of increasing mistrust, and he is our enemy. Move in the direction of increasing community goodwill and trust, and he is our ally. One thing is sure: God is not neutral. Where these breaches exist in human relationships, God is not just on one side pushing at somebody; he is on both sides trying to bring people together. His love and purpose for all people are our deepest guarantees that our efforts for world community will finally be successful.

Trust—the kind we need—will give us both the power to let go of our fears and move ahead with our faith.—Harold A. Bosley.

Illustrations

A WORKING FAITH.   "Launch out," for if you stay in the shallow waters, if you look back with longing eyes to the placid safety of the harbor, you will find that there is nothing living left to your faith. Here is what Kierkegaard, that great Scandinavian thinker, had to say: "To be sitting quietly in a boat in calm water is not an image of faith. But when the boat has sprung a leak, to keep it afloat by enthusiastically manning the pumps, yet with no thought of returning to port—that is an image of faith. . . . While the understanding, like a desperate passenger, stretches out its arms to terra firma but in vain, faith works with all its might in the deep waters: joyfully and triumphantly it saves the soul." —Joost DeBlank.

AT HOME IN ETERNAL LIFE.   At every stage throughout life man is confronted in some manner by the living God, in the common crises of ordinary life. In each such confrontation the human soul is challenged to growth and further maturity. And at every stage he can go forward in faith or shrink back in unbelief.

Then as the human drama draws toward its close, a man is moving toward his final and most profound confrontation, which is not death but life, life in transition.

The "I am," which is the human soul, knows itself about to encounter, not a nothingness, but the "I am" who is God. And if one has been able to simplify the soul to its depths so that love is the foundation and essence of its being, that soul is at one with God. There is no need for a frantic unburdening of cargo as if preparing for a storm. That disburdening of the soul has already been done in the process of simplification.

Then it is as if the soul, already well at home in eternal life, should some day slip quietly away, "from out our bourne of time and place," and sail into the sunrise. And the going is not an hour for sorrow, but rather for gladness. For the soul knows that it is not, and will never be, alone.—Lewis Joseph Sherrill.

Sermon Suggestions

GOD NEVER FORGETS HIS PEOPLE.   Text: Exod. 1:6–14, 22–2:10. (1) He hears the cry of the oppressed. (2) He prepares a leader. (3) He calls the leader he has prepared to deliver his people.

A TRIAD OF CHRISTIAN TRUTH.   Text: Matt. 11:25–30. (1) The knowledge of Christ: It is special and exclusive. (2) The teaching of Christ: It is universal and inclusive. (3) The life of Christ: It is relevant and rewarding.

Worship Aids

CALL TO WORSHIP.   "O give thanks unto the Lord; for he is good: because his mercy endureth for ever" (Ps. 118:1).

INVOCATION.   Father of our Lord Jesus Christ, because two or three are gathered in thy name, we know thou art here. In sermon and hymn, prayer and offering, keep us alert. And between the lines, stir up the gift of faith that fills all the spaces of our lives with hope eternal.—E. Lee Phillips.

OFFERTORY SENTENCE.   "And he said unto them, Take heed, and beware of covetousness; for a man's life consisteth not in the abundance of the things which he possesseth" (Luke 12:15).

OFFERTORY PRAYER.   Our Father, we slowly learn both from life and from thee what is truly important in our earthly pilgrimage. Spare us the pain of always learning the hard way the precious lessons. As we learn, may we grow in possession of those things that truly matter.

PRAYER.   Our Eternal Friend, whose fields are everywhere, stretching throughout all eternity, whose joys are the joys and field flowers and field scents, take us this morning, we pray thee, into the larger places of the day. We would stray away this morning under thy guidance, and while we stray we have our hand in thine, looking for mercies, finding the richness of thy grace, going from pool to pool where thou dost give living water, and finding in hillside and glen and everywhere the presence of our God. Soothe those that are fevered with care. Bless those who feel they are unworthy to follow thee; give the word of comfort, we beseech thee, to those who are distraught and weary with the weight of sin, and may we be guided in our thoughts and purposes, as always, for the sake of our Lord and Savior, Jesus Christ.—Frank W. Gunsaulus.

EVENING SERVICE

Topic: Dealing With Paralysis

TEXT: Acts 3:1–21.

The followers of Christ, following the Day of Pentecost, had some important decisions to make. They had experienced the powerful presence of the Holy Spirit. They could not become a kind of charismatic subculture where they lived to themselves and where their purpose would become the enjoyment of this new presence of God which they had felt. They could develop their own kind of in-language and isolate themselves from all the pain about them. On their decision hung the future of the church, as to whether it would live or die.

Peter and John were suddenly confronted with that decision as they were about to enter the temple for the evening prayer time by means of the Beautiful Gate. There lay a beggar who was helpless. Friends carried him to that spot every day and he survived by begging for enough money to buy food. Let's focus on this experience for a moment and try to see ourselves in the picture.

I. Peter and John could have looked the other way, ignored the beggar, and made their way rapidly on to the prayer time. To their credit, they paused and took time to look at the man.

(a) When they paused to look at the man, he supposed they were about to give him money. The problem was they didn't

have any. Peter then said, "Silver and gold I do not have, but what I do have I give you." They could give him Christ. We are not told all that they said to him about Christ, or all that he responded. But the end of the conversation was that Peter took him by the hand and commanded him in the name of Christ to rise up and walk. And he did!

(b) This passage requires us to deal with the whole flood of miracles that came during the life of Christ, and immediately following his resurrection. The world has never seen anything like that before or since. God seemed to have flooded the world with his miraculous healing power at that point in time in order to give credulity to the preaching of the gospel, and to the resurrection.

(c) When this particular man was healed, and the crowd marvelled at it, Simon Peter was quick to say, "Why look so intently at us, as though by our own power or godliness we have made this man walk?" Peter wanted them to understand that it was not by their own particular power or piety that this miracle had been done. He went on to explain it was done by Jesus Christ. They had merely called upon Jesus Christ. We are not guaranteed miracles on demand, but we are guaranteed that through prayer we are in touch with him who has the power of all miracles. So we can face any problem, any paralysis, any crippling that the world has inflicted upon us, or others, in the power of him who can do all things.

II. In dealing with the paralysis so often seen in the lives of people all about us, and in our own life, we must do as the early followers of Christ did, we must see the larger issue.

(a) Simon Peter recognized the larger issue had to do with spiritual wholeness. We are all crippled in one way or another. Somehow Simon Peter must have recognized there are many areas of paralysis beyond the inability to walk. Therefore Peter did not call the crowd together to give a seminar on how to heal crippled people who could not walk. Rather he chose to deal with the larger issue, how to bring wholeness to people through a right relationship with Jesus Christ.

Peter chose to use the occasion, not to

teach some simple plan for healing crippled legs, but to point people to the ultimate wholeness, to the new life to be found in Christ. And so his message again was the same as on the Day of Pentecost: "Repent and be converted, that your sins may be blotted out, so that times of refreshing may come from the presence of the Lord, and that he may send Jesus Christ, who was preached to you before" (Acts 3:19–20).

(b) As Simon Peter preached the simple facts of the gospel, of the life and death and resurrection of Jesus Christ, he told the crowd how they had been a part of killing the author of life, how God had chosen to raise that same Christ from the dead, and how both the rulers, and the people who listened to Peter, had done all of that in ignorance (Acts 3:17). Here we have the basic ignorance that causes all the brokenness that we see about us. It is an ignorance of the reality of God in Christ. It is an ignorance that God is in our midst to bring healing and forgiveness to us.

(c) Notice carefully that Simon Peter, having spoken of the basic ignorance that caused them to crucify Christ, to try to kill life and thereby choose death, did not indicate that some educational process would suffice. His solution to that kind of ignorance of the presence of God in our midst, a presence to heal and bless, cannot be corrected by education alone. Peter told them they would have to repent!

(d) One mark of repentance and faith is obedience. Obedience becomes the simple test of whether we have turned from our sins, and whether we have dared to have faith in Christ. So as we deal with the paralysis of the world about us, and even our own areas in which we feel crippled, we have to ask if we are willing to say what Simon Peter said: "What I have, I give to you." We have to say that not only to those about us who need our help, but we have to say that to God, who alone has the power to make us whole.

III. And so every kind of paralysis comes down ultimately to personal faith. We are called to repent and turn to Christ. That's how God sends to us the time of refreshing, that's how he sends to us the living Christ present in the Holy Spirit.

(a) Simon Peter warned those who heard him that time was not unlimited. He indicated that this Christ who was not "out of sight" in the sense that he had been received now by Heaven on his resurrection, would someday return visibly, at the time of the restitution of all things. We can know the presence of this Christ now in our own hearts and lives, in a healing way, or we will stand before him some day visibly, and give an account as to why we chose to cling to our own paralysis.

(b) On an earlier occasion in the life of Christ, he had healed a crippled man at the Pool of Bethesda. But first he had asked him, "Do you want to be healed?" I think that's the question that the Lord keeps sending to us. Do we really want to be made whole? Do we really want our spirit to be healed? That's what faith is all about. And that's how we have to deal with our own paralysis. Are you ready to rise up and walk?—Bob Woods.

SUNDAY: JULY TWELFTH

MORNING SERVICE

Topic: His Jerusalem and Ours
Text: Luke 9:51.

To this day there is something sinister in the physical features of Jerusalem. For one thing, you are never out of sight of walls, grim and forbidding. You are constantly reminded by these ancient and battered ramparts of days when the city was embattled and under a devastating siege.

In Jesus' day Jerusalem was a hotbed of political and religious strife; but for the faithful the city of the Great King had not lost its glory, and as the central place of worship, with the massive temple rebuilt by Herod, attracted myriad worshipers. Under the Roman yoke at that period, the Jewish population for the most part made no effort to conceal their hatred of Roman rule. The governor of the province was Pontius Pilate, a proud pagan, who had no sympathy with the nationalistic fervor of his Jewish subjects and no understanding of their devotion to the faith of their fathers. Pilate's way out of a critical situation was to wash his hands of the matter and call it a day.

I. Jesus was in Perea on the east side of Jordan when the incident occurred which supplies the text. His public ministry was drawing to an end, and there rested upon him the responsibility of an awful decision. He had halted where the roads forked—which way should he take?

(a) Let this incident be faced squarely as we see it in perspective and as our own crucial experiences have unfolded to us the costliness of duty. Suppose Jesus had taken the road back to Galilee and bypassed the trials that awaited him in Jerusalem. Could he have found peace in Nazareth, peace of mind, serenity of conscience? The answer is no. How can anyone find peace who has taken the easier way out of a dilemma? Imagine Jesus returning to Nazareth knowing that he had chosen the wrong road, had purchased apparent peace, and saved his life at the price of cowardice. How could the process be otherwise than painful?

(b) Is it not plain the roads which Jesus faced cannot be so sharply contrasted as, say, the brightness of the road to Nazareth, and the darkness of the road to Jerusalem? Each of these roads presented problems, offered difficulties, but with this vital moral difference: To travel the road back to Nazareth was wrong; to take the road to Jerusalem was right.

Jesus made the choice. He took not the low road to Nazareth, but the high road to Jerusalem. He had counted the cost. It was great, but not too great.

II. Jesus was advised not to go to Jerusalem. Simon Peter so admonished him when in Caesarea Philippi Jesus announced that he must go to Jerusalem and suffer many things of the elders, chief priests, and scribes, be put to death, and rise again the third day.

(a) Jesus rebuked Simon sharply, saying, "Get thee behind me, Satan: thou are a stumbling-block unto me: for thou mindest not the things of God, but the things of men" (ASV).

(b) When we face our Jerusalem there will be many to advise us one way or another, but at the long last, in lonely contemplation, we must make our own decision for or against, to do or not to do, to stay or to go, to hug the shore or to put out into the deep; and the finer the character of the person who must make the choice, the lonelier the state of suspense and struggle. No, I am not forgetting divine companionship; the pure in heart are sure of that. I am speaking of well-meaning human beings who would advise us to take the road that offered less opposition and conflict. Their counsel is not to be despised, but the final decision often has to be made in utter loneliness of soul.

III. Let no one believe for a single care less moment that these decisions Jesus made, which are part of the history of his public ministry, were easily reached or that they did not cost him struggle and tense inner conflict. The facts oppose this view.

(a) Recall the incident in the Gospel narrative of his rising early in the morning and retiring into the mountains for prayer and communion. Behold him saddened by the wrongs done to the poor and the humble by the powers of church and state. See him weeping at the grave of Lazarus. Hear him exclaim in a voice choked with emotion, "O Jerusalem, Jerusalem, that killeth the prophets, and stoneth them that are sent unto her! how often would I have gathered thy children together, even as a hen gathereth her chickens under her wings, and ye would not!" (ASV)

Turn to the account of Jesus in the garden of Gethsemane and the soul struggle that took place there. Luke, who was a physician, describes his agony as he prayed beneath the olive trees through the branches of which the moonlight filtered. Here are the words the beloved physician wrote of that event, a description which he must have received from an eyewitness: "And being in an agony he prayed more earnestly: and his sweat was as it were great drops of blood falling down to the ground."

(b) Here is stark reality, no play acting; no pantomimic performance this, but awful agony, anguish, pain, and suffering.

The more sensitive a human being is, the more he or she suffers when a hurt is experienced. Contemplate the sensitivity of the stainless character of Jesus and then estimate if you can the costliness of the struggles through which he went and the rough handling he received by word and deed of his enemies.

(c) There are times when our Jerusalems exact much from us, handle us roughly, push us about ruthlessly, deflate our pride, and humble us to the earth. A disciple is not greater than his Master. If we live deeply, we cannot escape disappointment, disillusionment; but nothing that can happen to us can approach in awful poignancy what Jesus endured even before he came to his cross.

IV. One of the finest tributes ever paid Jesus fell from the lips of his enemies who milled about the foot of his cross. According to Mark, they were the church leaders of his day, the chief priests and the scribes. They mocked him and said, "He saved others; himself he cannot save." Here is the law of the cross. Here is the new commandment in action. Like a scarlet strand, this principle of losing one's life by saving others runs through the tapestry of history. If we think of this principle as a motif in a symphony, it appears both in major and minor strains. Faithful, devoted parents can save their children, but cannot save themselves. In times of depression, business people may save their businesses, but cannot save themselves. Men and women everywhere who possess ideals and follow the gleam are able to save some righteous cause, yet cannot save themselves. Unnumbered hosts have worn themselves out and died prematurely for others' sake, illustrating the law laid down by Jesus when he said, "Whosoever would save his life shall lose it; but whosoever shall lose his life for my sake, the same shall save it" (ASV).

V. No one is exempt from life's Jerusalems, not even those who stand in preeminent pulpits or serve at high altars. I recall some of the famed preachers of Christendom and pause to contemplate the Jerusalems to which they set out.

(a) There was Chrysostom, "the golden-mouthed," possibly the greatest of early Christian preachers, who swept with his eloquence the multitudes that crowded the great church to hear him, first at Antioch and then at Constantinople. Yet, in the end the court at Constantinople turned savagely against him, and a wicked empress banished him to faraway Armenia. At last, worn and weary, he begged that he be taken to a little wayside church that he might die, and his last words as he lay on the cold stone floor were "Glory to God in all things."

(b) I think of Phillips Brooks and his truly marvelous preaching genius, honored and loved by millions. Phillips Brooks preached a sermon titled "Going Up to Jerusalem." In this sermon, near the end, there occurs one of the most precious and widely quoted sayings of that noble servant of God. Seldom has so much been said in so few words:

O, do not pray for easy lives. Pray to be stronger men! Do not pray for tasks equal to your powers. Pray for powers equal to your tasks! Then the doing of your work shall not be a miracle. But you shall be a miracle. Every day you shall wonder at yourself, at the richness of life which has come in you by the grace of God.

Here endeth the lesson!—Edgar DeWitt Jones.

Illustrations

PLAYING CHURCH.   One time a Sunday school class decided to play church with minister, ushers, offertory, choir, organist, and all. After a while they tired of playing the game, as children will, and were wanting to change it. One boy said, "I know, let's play Jesus." Well, that was a new one for the group and sounded great. When the other children asked the boy to explain the game he said that one boy would play Jesus and then the rest would be mean to him, call him names, strike him, spit at him, tie him to a tree, and pretend to crucify him. That took a bit of the glow off the honor of playing Jesus, but the children went on with the game. After a few minutes of absorbing the cruelty of the other children, the boy playing the part of Jesus called a halt to it and in so doing uttered a profound statement. He said, "Let's not play Jesus anymore, let's go back to playing church."—Walter D. Wagoner.

THE SACRAMENT OF SERVICE. The humblest ministry, no less than the highest, takes on haunting meanings when done in love.

Hear now the words of Browning, a golden-hearted poet: "All service ranks the same with God." There is no high, no low; it is not what we do, but how we do it, with what faith and motive, with what spirit and healing skill.

A bishop, a baker, a candlestick maker, a wife washing dishes, a man digging a ditch, a preacher in his pulpit, a farmer plowing a field, Brother Lawrence with his pots and pans, equally with a poet with his lyrics—all serve.

Many kinds of life must be lived, many sorts of work must be done—some of it hard work, heavy work. Yet no matter what we do, whether it is writing music or making a road, "All service ranks the same with God."—Joseph Fort Newton.

Sermon Suggestions

THE LEFT HAND OF GOD.   Text: Exod. 2:11–22. (1) God sometimes permits what he does not direct. (2) God works behind the scenes to overcome and transmute the results of our wrongdoing. (3) God even brings undeserved happiness as a gracious gift of his providence.

MARKS OF OUR IDENTITY.   Text: Rom. 8:9–17. We belong to Christ (1) if we live by the Spirit, rather than by the flesh; (2) if we live as children of the Father, rather than as slaves; (3) if we are willing to suffer with Christ, rather than avoid the claim that love makes upon us.

Worship Aids

CALL TO WORSHIP.   "On the road they had been arguing among themselves about who was the greatest. Jesus sat down, called the twelve disciples, and said to them, 'Whoever wants to be first must place himself last of all and be the servant of all' " (Mark 9:34b–35 TEV).

INVOCATION.   Our Father, take us today down unaccustomed roads of thought and commitment. Grant that we may render our spiritual worship as we present ourselves to you a living sacrifice that is both holy and acceptable.

OFFERTORY SENTENCE.   "Walk in love, as Christ loved us and gave himself up for us, a fragrant offering and sacrifice to God" (Eph. 5:2 RSV).

OFFERTORY PRAYER.   Our Father, we know that through the poverty that our Lord Jesus Christ embraced we have been made rich. Not only spiritual blessings are ours, but material blessings as well. With joy we bring to you tokens of our gratitude and ask your blessing upon them as they are used to advance the good news and your kingdom.

PRAYER.   Father of all creation, we praise you for the grandeur of your creative genius. We thank you for this bright day. We rejoice in the life you have given us.

Father of tender mercies, we praise you for your grace in Jesus Christ. We thank you for your mercy in forgiving our sins. We rejoice in the love you have poured out on us.

Father of great compassion, we share with you our interest in these our fellow worshipers, and ask healing where there is illness, and ask comfort where there is grief, and ask strength where there is weakness, and rejoice with those who welcome new life.

We pray for one another. We pray for our nation this day and ask both your wisdom and your compassion.

Father of us all, we worship you in spirit and in truth through Jesus Christ our Lord.—J. Estill Jones.

EVENING SERVICE

Topic: How the Church Grows
TEXT: Acts 2:41–47.

Church growth is very much in the news

today—and it ought to be, because church growth should happen wherever right living continues and right witnessing takes place. My textual passage, Acts 2:41–47, is an instance of fulfillment. It helps us to understand the dynamics and dimensions of the church growth process.

I. First of all, the church grows through conversions.

(a) Whenever someone decides to follow Christ, turning from an ungodly life to please the Lord, conversion results. There are many other New Testament expressions for this. The descriptions are many but the result is the same: one has made a new start in life through faith in Christ as Savior from sin. This is the meaning of conversion.

(b) The true church is composed of persons who have experienced forgiveness of sins and have been converted, persons who have turned from sin to God. This is the plain meaning of Acts 2:47b, "And the Lord added to their number day by day those who were being saved." This is the Lord's way of increasing members.

II. But conversions don't just happen in a vacuum; they are always caused. Conversions occur as a response to the call of God, and that call is usually spoken through another human agent acting on God's behalf.

(a) Throughout the book of Acts we see apostles, preachers, and lay witnesses speaking for God, sharing some word about their experience with Christ and summoning their hearers to repent, turn to God, confess their sins, and believe in Christ so as to be saved. The Christian church addresses that same call to all, but it must be spoken by someone to all.

(b) Peter was obeying that mandate on the day of Pentecost as he preached with vigor about Jesus. Preaching with such drive, timeliness, and pointed approach, Peter interpreted to the people God's deed in sending the Christ they had killed. Peter did not spare his hearers the facts about their involvement in the murder of Jesus, and because he was true to their need to know the truth about themselves his preaching caused conviction in their hearts which led to conversion for their lives. As those hearers sensed the depth of their sin, as they felt the thrust of the truth Peter spoke, as they saw the way they should take in repentance, they believed that truth and took that offered way.

(c) Conversions do not just happen, they are caused. It takes solid and informed witnessing to help people be convicted, turn to God, and be converted.

III. The passage then goes on to mention some other dimensions to church growth. Acts 2:42 lists four: apostolic teaching, fellowship, breaking of bread, and prayers. All of these reflect qualitative growth within the church.

(a) The rise of new interests and the posing of new questions across the centuries have influenced many in the church to accept and embrace alternative teachings, many of which do not faithfully honor what the apostles taught under the authority given to them by Christ. Those who have responded obediently to God's call to repentance need nurture. They need sound teaching about the nature of the new life and how to live life on God's terms. There is an organic relation between right teaching, right belief, and right behavior. The apostles knew this and spent time indoctrinating new converts in what Christ taught and authorized them to teach. The teachings of the apostles were not explorations into theory, something novel to capture interest and entertain; those teachings were revelational, reasonable, and related to life as God intended it to be understood and lived. With the apostles, teaching and preaching had to be of strict content. Under their work the church grew.

(b) Along with sound teaching, earnest fellowship was nurtured in the early church. A common life was promoted because of a common Lord. The quality of a congregation's life is always enhanced when a common life is understood, valued, and shared by all. When full sharing is encouraged, fellowship is always deepened and personal worth is reaffirmed with every contact. Fellowship is such a full word because it is such a full experience.

(c) So is "the breaking of bread" together in love. This is true whether one sees in these words a reference to the

Lord's Supper or views them to mean the sacredness of the common meal, a reminding expression of God's goodness and providence. In either case the material food links us with spiritual meanings.

(d) Add group prayers to the other experiences of being taught, having fellowship, and sharing sacramentally with others at the table, and church growth deepens still more. The spirit of eternity is readily sensed when the church is at prayer, and the pull of the world is more easily resisted when our hearts and knees stay bent in submission to the God who called and saved us. The early Church grew inwardly and outwardly as the members prayed. The early church grew by praying together. Group prayers are strategic in church growth.

(e) Teaching, fellowship, breaking of bread, prayers—as the church grows in these, it also grows in contagion. And contagion is just another word for the winsomeness the Lord gives to those on mission for their Master.

That was how the church grew then. That is how the church should continue to grow now.—James Earl Massey.

SUNDAY: JULY NINETEENTH

MORNING SERVICE

Topic: The Tolerance of Christ
TEXT: Luke 9:50.
I. One of the things that strikes us about Jesus is his many-sidedness. How urgent he was, and yet how leisurely! How full of indignation against hypocrisy, and yet how tender to sinners who knew their need! As someone has said, "He is too big for our small hearts."

(a) There is perhaps nothing in him more difficult to realise than his amazing tolerance. In this case a man has been using such skill as he had to heal tormented minds, with the name of Jesus as a kind of spell. The disciples found fault with him, because as they said "he followeth not us." He was not one of their band. To their surprise, when they brought the matter to him, Christ rebuked them. "He that is not against us is for us." It is a tolerance that amazes us.

(b) God is not limited to the channels which we try to dig for him. His spirit overflows and uses any means people put at his disposal, if only they are sincere and are following the light they have. Christ does not say that it would not have been better for the man had he stood in openly with the disciples. Later he might discover his deeper need and come in. But meantime he was serving the kingdom and that was enough.

II. What wonderful charity! Our small hearts are humbled by the greatness of his. How many of us can put ourselves so completely in the background if the kingdom is being served?

(a) There are few things we need so much as tolerance. It is important, of course, to understand it. There is nothing here to encourage us to be satisfied with the second best. Christ would not have us use it for an excuse to keep us from going all the way with him. There is a false broad-mindedness which is blind and shallow. But when people are sincere and honest with themselves and with God as they know him, Christ claims them that he may lead them further on. The one big sin in his eyes is lack of love. And that shows itself when we exclude others from fellowship with us because they do not see eye to eye with us. It is his all-inclusive charity we need.

(b) We need it in the region of service. There are people today, for instance, who are keen on social service but have little touch with religion. They will not come into our churches. They do not feel much need of prayer. Human service without the faith that lets God fully in has no real power to touch the nerve of human trouble. It may be a substitute for a suppressed religious instinct. It may even be a way of escape from our own inner problem. But we shall not help such people by refusing to recognize their service. The passion for social work has often been a protest against the creed that fails in practical love. It calls us back to reality. The real test of the Christian spirit is not the fervor of our worship, but the greatness of our love. We should be grateful for the lesson. Meantime, let us accept them in fellowship and thank God for their work.

(c) The same tolerance is needed in religious belief. It is good to hold a creed and to hold it strongly. It is another matter to imagine that our particular belief is the only vision of truth. The habit of making a creed the test of discipleship is fatal to fellowship. The truth about God has many sides, and none of us sees them all.

III. It is that fellowship which Christ seeks to build up. The sin of sins is to break it by bigotry or intolerance. It is by fellowship alone that we shall find our way into the fullness of his light. The more we come together to seek him, the more we are likely to find the big things in which we can all agree.—James Reid.

Illustrations

PROBLEMS OF PLURALISM.   Christianity is not alone in facing these problems, of course. All religions face pluralism on a large scale; all must deal with hard questions of disbelief in a society immersed in rational philosophy, scientific culture, and critical historical studies. All, too, must face the issues of experiential versus externally grounded religion; each type has its own difficulties. Christians must face such issues in their own distinctive way, reflecting on their traditions, returning to their resources in the Bible, religious thought, and practice, while at the same time developing as deep an understanding of each issue as possible. In that continuing dialogue of the Christian religion with its culture, in the ongoing struggle to define Christian existence, the Christian quest for perfection will continue.—Sandra S. Frankiel.

LIBERTY AND JUSTICE.   Lincoln asked for liberty and justice not only for the black man, but for all men, regardless of race, color, or creed. He had no racial rancor, no religious bigotry. In his mind each man stood on his own feet, free to be a man, and to worship God in the way his heart loved best.

In 1863 General Grant issued an order excluding all Jews from his department, but Lincoln quickly revoked it. He was the first president to appoint a Jewish rabbi an army chaplain. To do so required an act of Congress. Up until that time it was actually illegal—and in the United States, too!

When the Know-Nothing craze came along, extending hatred not only to Negroes but to "foreigners and Catholics," Lincoln said he would "prefer emigrating to some country where they made no pretense of loving liberty—to Russia, for instance, where despotism can be taken pure without the base alloy of hypocrisy."—Joseph Fort Newton.

Sermon Suggestions

WHEN GOD CALLS.   Exod. 3:1–12. (1) It may be in ordinary, everyday circumstances. (2) However, God's presence and purpose impart extraordinary significance. (3) With the call comes God's promise of adequate resources to carry out his mission.

A HOPE TO KEEP US GOING.   Rom. 8:18–25. (1) The gospel gives us confidence that our future destiny with God outweighs our present difficulties. (2) Therefore, we can put up with persecution, physical pain, economic reverses, family problems, anxiety, and depression.

Worship Aids

CALL TO WORSHIP.   "Peter began: 'I now see how true it is that God has no favorites, but that in every nation the man who is godfearing and does what is right is acceptable to him' " (Acts 10:34–35 NEB).

INVOCATION.   God of the universe, Creator of the whole human family, enlarge our minds and open wide the doors of our hearts that we may think your thoughts after you and pattern our love after yours. So may we worship you in spirit and in truth.

OFFERTORY SENTENCE.   "Each one, as a good manager of God's different gifts, must use for the good of others the special gift he has received from God" (1 Pet. 4:10 TEV).

OFFERTORY PRAYER. Father, help us to do good not only to the household of faith, but also to all who have true need. Bless these offerings to that end.

PRAYER. O God, our heavenly Father, we do not know how to pray as we ought. We acknowledge that we often come to you so driven by our selfishness, our prejudices, and our ignorance that a direct answer to what we have asked would mean only that we would get things that would harm us, that would harm others, and that would generally frustrate your loving purposes. So we pray that you would increase our love for one another, as well as our self-regard, that you would broaden our understanding of one another, and that you would open our eyes to new ranges of truth that we have not known before. —James W. Cox.

EVENING SERVICE

Topic: What Is Vital Religion?
TEXT: Eph. 1:3–14.
Jesus often spoke of religion as power. He used it in speaking of the moral and spiritual energies of life. The kingdom would come with power, not because of legions of angels, but because it came from God and possessed a life-changing energy that worked in the moral and spiritual nature of humankind in some manner like yeast working in bread dough.

Paul also was fond of the word power. He saw powers that others overlooked. He saw God as a giving God and he speaks of Christ being in one, God working in us, and our becoming new creations.

I. No one who has ever lived was more concerned about the saving of his soul than Paul. To be saved to him meant to become a new kind of person, with a new inner nature, a new joy and triumph over life. Once he had been at the mercy of the forces about him where he could be pressured into doing things he did not want to do; now he possessed a power to become as he expressed it "more than conqueror through him—Jesus Christ."

(a) The life of Paul is plainly a life of power. He possesses a depth which becomes a sure foundation for all the trials and tribulations of life. He has the power to conquer that which might destroy one who did not possess that power.

Power is that which makes religion vital in life.

(b) And yet so many approach religion from the opposite view. To them religion is something to be saved, to be preserved, to be protected rather than it being something which gives them power. They treat religion as something they must defend rather than as something which is to save them by giving them the power to become more than conquerors.

II. God can provide the power which makes his church "more than conqueror."

(a) When people fail to seek out that power and give their lives to it and let it change them they may say, "Our religion is in danger. We have lost it. Now there is nothing to live for!" Quite the contrary is true; there is plenty to live for, God is not defeated because someone or some group turns against him. Life is rich in things to give self to. There is truth to be discovered, beauty to create, friendship to lay its claim upon us

(b) Faith is God's work within us. It transmutes us and makes for our rebirth in God. It kills the old Adam and makes us different, recreating our heart, courage, understanding, and all other forces, and it carries with it the Holy Spirit. There is a power and life about faith that makes it impossible not to do the good. "Faith does not inquire whether there are good works to be done, but even before asking questions, faith has done these works already."

(c) Thus faith enables us to rise above many things that would otherwise defeat us. It does not guarantee our prosperity. God, however, is not so much interested in our prosperity as he is in the quality of our lives and it is for that quality that he gives us the power to live out life amid turmoil.

III. To give up faith in times of misfortune is a sign of immaturity. The most influential people in the world have been those who have suffered. This is the victory of faith—this is the power of religion —to live so as to encourage those who may be about us or come after us to find and live by the power of faith.

(a) When a crisis arises there is always the tendency to want to steady the ark, to try to defend God rather than have him defend us. People are apt to say, "In this emergency we must set aside our ideals and face facts realistically." This may lead to a moratorium on their faith just when its power should be released.

The record of the Apostle Paul relates that the power of religion was not given for his sake, or for the persons who were naturally saintly. It was given for the rank and file. This powerful energy, which makes us respond to God's upward pull and which makes all of us different, Paul called faith.

(b) We have a nice system of thought that accounts for everything and explains everything and that leaves no place for faith. We know too much. We say to our-selves that only the ignorant and uncultured are led by faith. But we need to permit the power of God to work and create good where evil had previously existed. The power of religion can help raise life to new heights.

IV. Power is the vital factor in religion. Its force is greater than those tidal powers which wait for us to use in our tasks. This power has always been there. It is now present.

But the power of religion does not work, does not operate, until we lay hold of it and use it for present-day purposes.

We know that in everything God works for good with those who love him, who are called according to his purpose. God works.

We must be coworkers with God. He has called us, and if we love him we will respond and open our lives to receive his power—the vital factor of religion.—E. Paul Hovey.

SUNDAY: JULY TWENTY-SIXTH

MORNING SERVICE

Topic: The Man Who Dug Old Wells
TEXT: Gen. 26:18.

Here is a very natural and understandable act. Isaac is moving here and there in Canaan, pitching his nomadic tents where he can find sustenance for his people and for the flocks that he carries with him. Most vitally of all, of course, he needs water. He remembers how as a child he has gone that way with his father, Abraham, and he remembers how Abraham had dug wells in the valleys where the waters gathered. One by one, he does discover them, but they have been filled by the hostile Philistines who resented this intrusion into their land by the newcomers from the east. So he sets to work to dig again the former wells. He will recover what the foe has destroyed and drink once more of the waters of which his father drank.

I. The motives that moved him to seek his father's wells instead of trying to dig new ones were the simple ones that a moment's reflection will suggest.

(a) In the first place, Abraham had sunk his wells in places that had already been proven. It was no venture in the dark to go seek water there. Since water had been drawn thence before, it could be drawn thence again.

(b) In the second place, it was easier to clear the shaft of a well that had once been dug than it was to sink a new one in the unbroken earth.

(c) In the third place, there must have been a sentiment for Isaac in drinking from these wells where he had drunk beside his father. The thought of them was linked with far reflections of his childhood, which came back to him like distant music there by the familiar waters, sweet with old associations of days and faces that were gone. Who is there of us that does not recognize the values that gather round things in themselves not inherently better than something else of their same kind, but invested with the glamour of memory that lifts them up and sets them apart?

Who is there that does not think at this moment of some well that is played upon by the golden sun and the sweet still shade of childhood, the well under the great, wide tree to which the paths lead from the hot fields and the dusty roads, the clear water coming cool from the dim depths, the pure sparkle and the freshness like the morning dew? The water from wells like these is more than water. It is magic potion for the spirit. It quickens into life the romance of lovely memories, and sets to ringing again the bells of old, forgotten happiness.

II. Herein, we say, we find a most natural and simple act. Yet here is also something more. It is the parable of a spiritual truth that we may well ponder and appropriate.

(a) There is in all life the instinct to go back and dig again the wells of our fathers. Sometimes we call it conservatism. Sometimes we call it reverence.

Today we may well remember that the same motives that impelled Isaac will impel us, if we are wise. The wells of our fathers, to begin with, are proven wells. At our peril we cast aside the ripe experience of many generations. The newest things are not of necessity the truest.

(1) Apply this thought to some of the facts of today. Take, for example, the matter of our social standards. There are many who are deliberately in rebellion against old conventions which used to seem a matter of course. The liberty wherewith we have been made free becomes a cloak of license. Young people want to have their own way and resent the advice of their elders. They imagine that the freedom of their own personalities can only be expressed by repudiating the guidance of those who have learned by experience. "The former generation may have thought they knew where the wells of clearest pleasure were, but we will go make ours in other ground."

(2) Take also the matter of our religious faith. The world is full of new cults. In some of the great cities, people are deserting avowedly Christian organizations and flocking into the so-called Community Church, which meets in a theater and professes no creed. Restlessly they hunt for a place from which they can draw water for their spirit which they think will be more satisfying than their fathers' wells. They may sink their shafts of the quest for truth

into deeper and richer springs of God than they had known before. Yet always this fact remains: the wells of the fathers are proven wells. Out of the worship, out of the fellowship, out of the faith from which they drew, we know that water has come and can come again. We must be very sure that God has guided us to a better place before the Isaac of today turns his back upon the wells of Abraham.

(b) In the second place, the wells of the fathers are easier to draw from than are new wells. This, of course, is no decisive consideration, but the weight that it does have deserves to be taken into account.

(1) When Isaac went to the wells of Abraham he found that the Philistines had filled them up, but, as we have said already, it is a simpler matter to clear the old shafts than to create new ones. And here is surely a truth which the impatient temper of our time needs to recognize. The reason many people are estranged from the wells of their fathers, whether it be in the social code of pleasures, or in the deeper matters of all-embracing religious conviction, is because they are angered to find that the wells that they thought would flow with full, sweet streams of water are all but choked with rubbish. Theologians may fill the wells of truth with the lumber of their unprofitable dogmas. The sweet naturalness of the religion of Jesus may be buried beneath the drift of formalism, so that people, impatient at all the wretched accumulation that blocks the life-giving draught they hoped to drink, turn indignant and disillusioned away from the church to seek elsewhere some water for their spirit.

(2) There is a task today for all those open-eyed people who see the faults of the church and the errors of a sometimes stereotyped religion, to put their hands deliberately to the task of clearing away false things and making an outlet for the truth. There is need in the church for those who see the stodginess of accepted ideas and the inconsistencies of life that hide the deep things of God that are supposed to underlie the church, to bring such sympathetic and patient love for that which they know to be the reality of Christian experience as shall broaden the rivers through which these realities may pour.

(c) And, in the third place, there is that other motive that we ascribed to Isaac. We cannot cast out of any life, save to its infinite impoverishment, that immeasurable thing which we call sentiment.

(1) We in America are in danger of forgetting the incomparable loveliness of ancient things. We live, so many of us, in cheap houses and pretentious apartments knocked together out of shoddy stuff by speculators who built them for today's profits, regardless either of yesterday or tomorrow. The old homes in which families dwelt for generations are growing scarcer. Old churches are abandoned to build some new one convenient to the people. In the same way the thoughts, the ideals, and the principles that have been the homes of human spirits, full of strong and sweet suggestion, are lightly abandoned, that we may move into some new and gaudy-fronted thing.

(2) Yet, when we search our souls, we know that the hunger and thirst for the old loveliness of association is still there. In the midst of what we call our modern conveniences our souls may be wistful in our deep-regarding moments for the simplicities of our childhood days. And in the modern convenience of these hasty expedients which sometimes our souls set up in place of the slowly built and richly furnished convictions of our parents, we know that there is an emptiness. We must go to the brink of the old sweet wells. We must taste again the waters that are atrill with the best that our fathers knew.

III. It would be simple, and it is tempting, to leave the message here. It is always tempting to set forth truth with a simplicity that obviates those seeming contradictions which are so often a part of actual life. Yet truth is never truth when it is looked at from one side only. And so as we think of Isaac, who represents in this instance the best there is in the conservative spirit, we must turn and look also at the spirit of the man who dug those wells that he should dig again. Isaac was the conservative; yet the man whose work he was making precious by his conservatism had been a radical and a pioneer. Isaac cleared again his father's wells, but that father of his dug those wells in a land far beyond the horizon that his fathers had ever dreamed.

(a) This is a fact, and this is what we must take into account: Side by side with all that we recognize to be noble in the spirit of Isaac, if we would see the rounded truth. Life cannot be made up all of conservatism. There are times when radicals have their incomparable place. There are times when with heroic adventure they must turn their backs upon the familiar wells, and across the desert seek the mightier promised land where they shall dig new wells for the thirst of human souls.

(b) Out into Canaan Abraham went, moved by such an impulse of the spirit as has moved the pioneers in all great chapters of human change. We cannot analyze that impulse. The great creative souls themselves who feel it can never analyze it. They know only that the urge of God is within them. The compulsion of an irresistible command brings them into the path that leads ahead. By faith Abraham went out, not knowing whither he went. By faith he looked for the city which as yet had no foundation save in his dreams—the city of a new civilization, a new religious experience for the human race, a city whose builder and maker is God.

(c) Therefore, even as we value all that is beautiful in the conservative spirit, let us keep clear of the intolerant blindness of determined prejudice that makes people unable to recognize the hour when, for the reconstituting of our industrial relations, for the reinterpreting of religious truth in terms of modern science and modern scholarship, for the refashioning of the church to meet more vitally the needs of today, the signal strikes for the pioneers. The wells of the fathers are precious wells, but they who know best how precious the wells are as channels of ancient truth will be most swift to recognize when the time has come to sink shafts elsewhere, if the teachings of the fathers do not satisfy the thirst of life.

IV. Here, then, it would seem, there is a plain contradiction. First we advocated one attitude toward life, and now we seem to advocate another. First we commended Isaac who dug again the wells of his father. Now we glorify Abraham who went out from all his father's lands to dig his wells and live his life beyond the horizon of new dreamt-of days.

(a) Is there any harmony between these two seemingly opposite suggestions? I think there is. It is the sort of harmony that life often presents—the harmony that does not consist in fixed definitions laid down in advance, but in a sort of living balance which, in a soul sensitive to the touch of God, inclines according to an instinctive perception of the immediate purpose of God. For ordinary times and over great stretches of our experience, the natural act is that of Isaac. Yet we too may need to go beyond those wells, nor shall we be troubled if only we can find the principle to guide us in recognizing the moment when this larger appeal of the spirit calls. When we are moved to turn away from the wells of yesterday and dig new ones for today, do we stop to make sure that the motive that rules us is clearly and wholly the motive of the soul that looks to God for guidance and looks to God alone? Our place is by the wells of our fathers until there comes within us, as there came within Abraham, such a conviction of God's consecration for a new adventure, and such a sense of compulsion of a new truth, as lays hold upon us with a power which it would be treason to deny.

(b) Let us remember that none can dig new wells that will really flow save as they link their lives in pure intent and wholehearted plan with the unchanging facts of God. Abraham went out beyond the land of his fathers. He went on a way by which he dug new wells. Wherever he might have gone, he never could have dug those wells nor drawn water from them except in such spots of the earth as had been prepared by God before. If by some freak of willfulness he had determined to dig his wells on barren slopes, he might have dug forever and his wells would forever have been dry. He must seek the valleys where rains long since fallen and the slow accumulation of hidden springs had gathered the hidden waters for his finding. There and there alone, where God's forces had made wells possible, could he sink his shafts and find water. He could not make a well; he could only open the wells that God had made

already. So is it also with the facts of the spirit. The normal place for most human lives in most of their experience is by the wells of their fathers. When we are moved to go from these, as sometimes souls are moved so mightily that it would be spiritual betrayal to disobey, let us be sure that this desire by which we are moved is consistent with the deepest that we know of God and of his ways of revelation. When we separate from the wells of the fathers, let it be to dig new wells only where we believe that God's truth has gathered itself in a fullness that is his larger answer to our thirst.—Walter Russell Bowie.

Illustrations

THE INSTINCT OF SECURITY.   In the animal all is reflex, habit, repetition, training. Take the case of my dog: When my surgery time is ended and I am going out to visit a patient, he is there at the door waiting for me. When I appear he jumps for joy—the joy of going in the car with me, not because it is a new experience but, on the contrary, because it is a habit. What is peculiar to man is his instinct for adventure, and this is why I see it as an expression of the resemblance to God of which the Bible speaks. It is also why man feels truly man only insofar as he follows his instinct of adventure and becomes something more than a robot or a collection of conditioned reflexes.

There is in man, however, a conflict between the instinct of adventure and the instinct of fixity. Man can follow his instinct of adventure only if he represses his instinct of fixity, and he can satisfy his instinct of fixity only if he represses his instinct of adventure. The behavior of the animal is quite simple, regulated as it is by a single instinct. That of man becomes complex, problematical, even anguished, since all repression is felt as anxiety, and since he is of necessity repressing one or the other of his instinctive tendencies, to novelty or to repetition. We have come here to something characteristic of human nature and often described in connection with other internal conflicts peculiar to man—the way man is eternally torn between two worlds to which he belongs equally, the world of nature and that of the Spirit.—Paul Tournier.

FRUITLESS ADVENTURE.   I saw a story in the newspaper about a man in Kentucky who had an amazing hound. He was a fast runner, but he was a kind of pacifist. He never wanted to kill anything. He would come up behind a fox, put on an extra burst of speed, and run right on past him. The man said he had never seen so much frustration in all his life as when the fox suddenly discovered he was chasing the hound and couldn't keep up with him. People are sometimes like that hound and use all their energy to run fast, but they never capture anything. They might have achieved the goal at one time, but they ran right past it. Now it is too late to turn back. For one of the traps life lays for us is to assume that the running is an end in itself and whether we catch anything is unimportant.—Gerald Kennedy.

Sermon Suggestions

DISCOVERING WHO GOD IS.   Exod. 3:13–20. (1) We, like Moses, may have had only vague ideas, even pagan ideas, of God. (2) A time of crisis comes when we see that our unfocused notions are inadequate. (3) Then we may discover, by God's grace, that God is specifically "the God who acts"—who has acted in nature and history, who is now at work, and who will carry out his will in the future. Thus we can rely on him for his strength and support.

OUR WEAKNESS AND GOD'S HELP.   Rom. 8:26–30. (1) God's Spirit pleads for us. (2) We are strengthened by the assurance of what God is doing in our lives: shaping us into the likeness of Christ.

Worship Aids

CALL TO WORSHIP.   "Honor thy father and thy mother: that thy days may be long upon the land which the Lord thy God giveth thee" (Exod. 20:12).

INVOCATION.   Grant, O Lord, that we may be your faithful agents in carrying for-

ward all of the good that has come to us out of the past. Save us from idolatry of yesterday and fear of tomorrow. To that end, strengthen us in this service for every good work.

OFFERTORY SENTENCE.   "Let your light so shine before men, that they may see your good works, and glorify your Father which is in heaven" (Matt. 5:16).

OFFERTORY PRAYER.   O God of truth and love, let your light go forth from this place into our community and into our world through these offerings that we bring. We thank you for the privilege of being partners with you in your redeeming work in the world.

PRAYER.   Almighty God, our heavenly Father, who settest the solitary in families: We commend to thy continual care the homes in which thy people dwell. Put far from them, we beseech thee, every root of bitterness, the desire of vainglory, and the pride of life. Fill them with faith, virtue, knowledge, temperance, patience, godliness. Knit together in constant affection those who, in holy wedlock, have been made one flesh. Turn the hearts of the parents to the children, and the hearts of the children to the parents; and so enkindle fervent charity among us all, that we may evermore be kindly affectioned one to another; through Jesus Christ our Lord. —Book of Common Prayer.

EVENING SERVICE

Topic: The Thumb and Toe Specialist
TEXT: Judg. 1:4–7.

I. The account in these four short verses jumps out at us from a rough-and-tumble world full of petty tyrants and crude and cruel men. It was a time when "every man did that which was right in his own eyes" (Judg. 17:6). Unforgettably good men, like Samson and Gideon, stand in stark contrast in the time of the book of Judges against the dark background of a lawless age. Adonibezek is the first evil man mentioned here who received what he justly deserved.

Adonibezek was a thumb and toe specialist. Although an untrained surgeon, he made a specialty of amputating the thumbs and great toes of the enemy chieftains he captured. He was the king (Adoni means "lord") of Bezek, a border district in the Promised Land. He was a prince ruling in the Canaan stronghold. He remained unsubdued at the time of Joshua's death. God asked Judah and Simeon to be agents of his judgment on Adonibezek.

Within his palace Judah and Simeon found seventy warrior leaders with their thumbs and great toes cut off. Kept as slaves in the king's dining hall to boost his ego, they provided cruel entertainment. Without toes men can only hobble, not run. Without thumbs weapons have no dexterity. These were effective controls on their future enmity but also cruel afflictions in daily living. The detestable king threw them scraps of bread and meat from his table and laughed cruelly at their pathetic attempts to grab for food with hands that were only claws and to move to reach it on feet without balance. As they slipped and slithered, scratched and clawed, they provided sickening sport for their captor, while desperately struggling for survival.

But an amazing coincidence happened to Adonibezek! Judah and Simeon led a band of soldiers to his stronghold, captured him, and did to him exactly as he had done to others! It was judgment well fitted to his offenses, and its appropriateness led him to trace the connection between his sin and its results under the sovereignty of God. "Threescore and ten kings, having their thumbs and great toes cut off, gathered their meat under my table: as I have done, so God hath requited me" (v. 7).

II. This is an Old Testament illustration of Gal. 6:7: "Be not deceived; God is not mocked: for whatsoever a man soweth, that shall he also reap." You can disregard the connection between sin and judgment for a time, but you cannot ever finally escape it. This Old Testament story pictures some of the links between sowing and reaping.

(a) You will reap the seeds you sow. You cannot reap strawberries from a cucumber vine or potatoes from cucumber seed. Parents who sow neglect will reap heartache. Evil examples can return in our families to cause great pain.

In this life or the next you are always certain to reap what you sow. Bad seed means a bad harvest. Sin draws judgment. All of us shall give accounts of ourselves to God, and we must all keep the appointment of death and "after this the judgment" (Heb. 9:27).

(b) You may reap the seeds someone else sows. Everything in this story cannot be explained by the simple statement that you reap the same kind as you sow. Other insights in this Old Testament story teach us that in life you may reap more than you sow. Seventy innocent kings suffered because of the evil of one man. The innocent sometimes suffer more than the guilty.

For everyone who gets what he or she deserves, it sometimes appears there may be seventy more who unjustly get more than they deserve! This can be the kind of harvest that makes people lose their grip and balance in life and slip in their faith.

(c) You may reap good fruit from a bad harvest.

You can always gather some good seed from a bad harvest. The final word about Adonibezek is that he saw the hand of God in his bad harvest and did something about it. "As I have done, so God hath requited me. And they brought him to Jerusalem, and there he died" (v. 7).

Life's bitter experiences, deserved or undeserved, can be seen as the hand of God pointing to new understandings and new faith. Christ did not deserve his cross but was wounded for our transgressions (Isa. 53:5) and delivered for our offenses (Rom. 4:25). The discovery of God's amazing and eternal love can give new life in Jesus Christ.

Persons have found him more than sufficient down through the ages. Bernard of Clairvaux said, "Jesus is honey in the mouth, melody in the ear, a song of jubilee in the heart, which leaps to the lips." Thomas à Kempis said, "O Jesus, brightness of the eternal glory, comfort of the pilgrim soul, with thee are my lips without a voice and my silence speaks to thee. Thou my God, my hope and my eternal salvation."

He is truly the Lily of the Valley, the Bright and Morning Star.—Craig Skinner.

SUNDAY: AUGUST SECOND

MORNING SERVICE

Topic: The Great Hinges

TEXT: 1 Cor. 16:8–9; 2 Cor. 1:8–10.

In that last chapter of Paul's first letter to the church of Corinth, we come upon some interesting words: "But I will stay in Ephesus until Pentecost, for a wide door for effective work has opened to me, and there are many adversaries" (1 Cor. 16: 8–9, RSV). The *New English Bible* makes it even clearer: "A great opportunity has opened for effective work, and there is much opposition" (v. 9).

Haven't you found it true in your own life? The things that mean the most to you were purchased at a very great price. Good things never come easy.

Doesn't this verse run counter to so much religion we hear on all sides? You're in God's will if everything works out all right. It runs like this: Good people have untroubled marriages. Good people do not get divorces and do not fuss. Good people do not have doubts with the faith journey. Good people's kids never get into trouble. Good people have things work out to their advantage. Good people don't suffer or have emotional problems or financial worries. Good people find that everything works out just fine.

And down beside that subtle heresy we place today's Scripture. "A great opportunity has opened for effective work, and there is much opposition." Is there a more universal truth?

I. Paul would stay in Ephesus, he said. Piecing the record together, we find that he was there, on and off, for at least three years. Ephesus was a large seaport city in the Roman province of Asia. That city was a commercial and religious center. It was the number one city in the province. Paul recognized that if the gospel could take root in Ephesus he could see it spread like a bonfire across the whole of Asia.

(a) All of us have some Ephesus, some great challenging opportunity that would change us for the rest of our days. We all have let some opportunity slip by us that cannot be called back.

But Paul, much wiser than most of us, saw in his Ephesus an open door—and so he walked through it.

(b) Open your eyes to the doors that are open to you. What is your Ephesus? If you are a parent or spouse, it may have something to do with giving yourself to those closest to you in meaningful ways. If you are a teenager, Ephesus may mean getting to know your parents as people and not just as parents. If you are a student, what you do in the next four years may determine the rest of your life. If you are on the edge of retirement, your Ephesus may be to see life not as a finished thing but only the beginning of a new adventure.

II. We are not uncertain of the opposition at Ephesus. In 1 Cor. 15:32 Paul spoke of the "beasts" he had to battle at Ephesus. In 2 Cor. 1:8–9 he talked about how he was under the sentence of death in Asia. We do know that the silversmiths at Ephesus had a pretty good business forging their shabby little silver statues of the great goddess Artemis. They saw in Paul's words a threat to their business. When you tamper with people's pocketbooks, you usually get a rise out of them.

(a) For me at least there are two kinds of enemies:

(1) There is the enemy within. My own insides can immobilize me. Fear of the unknown, of the unsure, of making a fool of myself can be a powerful adversary. The weight of my past and the fragile little ego bequeathed to me can make it hard to walk through when the great hinges open. It is so much easier to drift, procrastinate, evade, than to walk through those challenging doors. The enemy, for me, has been within.

(2) But the enemy, for me, has also been without. Circumstance can make life more difficult. Being in the wrong place at the wrong time can make it more complicated. Not having the advantages of somebody else muddles the matter.

(b) Always there is opposition. Trouble

comes with the territory. Nothing good ever has come to any of us with a small price tag attached. When will we ever learn that the only things we ever get at bargain-basement prices are trinkets best left in the basement?

III. So what are we to say? Paul said: "I will stay at Ephesus at least until Pentecost." There is a great door and there are many adversaries. And he chose to stay.

(a) And you, what will you do? Stay or run away? It comes down to that choice at the end, doesn't it?

(b) Skip from that last chapter of 1 Corinthians to the fourth chapter of 2 Corinthians. Paul had a falling out with those at Corinth. Many in that church did not understand his motives. Some would not speak to him. Some doubted his word. But the apostle did not turn back. "Therefore, having this ministry by the mercy of God, we do not lose heart." In between all those adversities, he weaves a golden thread: "We are not crushed. . . . we are not driven to despair. . . . we are not forsaken. . . . we are not destroyed." Though our outer nature is wasting away, our inner nature is being renewed every day.

(c) I do not know what you have on your heart as you read this. There may be a myriad of opportunities you have let slip through your fingers. There may be some Ephesus toward which you have failed to walk. There may be a host of adversaries that have crippled and drained you of so much that makes life good. But remember that Paul, in writing to a fussy, troubled church, burned into their hearts: "A great opportunity has opened for effective work, and there is much opposition. But I will stay in Ephesus. . . ."—Roger Lovette.

Illustrations

GLORIOUS SUFFERING. The theme of Jesus, the Son of God, could be developed by setting the transfiguration in the center of three Son of God confessions, as Mark does. The first is the voice of God to Jesus himself at the baptism (1:9–11), in which Jesus' identity as Son of God is established. In the second, the transfiguration, that identity is confirmed to an inner circle of three disciples, offering a parallel to Peter's confession of Jesus as Christ, as counterpoint to the first passion prediction, and a foretaste of the parousia announced in the verses immediately preceding. The last in the series is the crucifixion, a sort of reverse transfiguration, in which the sight of Jesus dying in utter abandonment to the will of God wrings from the lips of a Roman army officer the confession, "Truly this man was the Son of God." For those who have eyes to see, his very suffering in steadfast obedience to the will of God is a mark of God's own glory; but that glory can only be understood by resurrection faith, and it will become evident to all only at the parousia of the Son of Man. In the transfiguration, then, Jesus is revealed as Son of God, the one in whom is manifested simultaneously the splendor and the lowliness of God. —Lamar Williamson, Jr.

THIS IS MY BELOVED SON; LISTEN TO HIM. Take these words into your imagination. Let them run freely over time and space. Consider how many occasions there are when the words "This is my beloved Son; listen to him" have been and are the supreme wisdom. When a life looks out on the world in the early years, when it is choosing its goals and its way, its ambitions and aspirations, then listen to him who rejected the proffered kingdoms of this world for the larger kingdom of God. When life goes into eclipse, when darkness covers the face of the sun, in sorrow and failure and despair, then listen to him who was a man of sorrows, and whose revelation of God brings the sustaining word of comfort and the enabling word of hope. When life waxes in might and gathers power or riches, when the siren voices of self-indulgence are sounding, then listen to him who can save life from going to pieces. So, too, at every turning point of human history, as the nations stand choosing between life and death.—Halford E. Luccock.

Sermon Suggestions

PASSOVER EVERY DAY! Exod. 12:1–14. (1) The blood of the ancient Passover sacrifice signified God's protection in the tenth plague of the Exodus (vv. 7, 13). (2) The blood of Jesus Christ, God's paschal lamb, signifies eternal salvation and is celebrated in daily life with thanksgiving and communion (1 Cor. 5:7–8).

GOD IS FOR US.   Rom. 8:31–39. (1) God justifies us. (2) Christ intercedes for us. (3) The love of God in Christ Jesus protects us against all enemies.

Worship Aids

CALL TO WORSHIP.   "You know what hour it is, how it is full time now for you to wake from sleep. For salvation is nearer to us now than when we first believed" (Rom. 13:11 RSV).

INVOCATION.   Almighty God, our heavenly Father, we come to thee in the midst of the crises of our times and of our personal lives, asking thee to give us a clear view of thy purpose for our lives, the strength to live up to that vision, and the wisdom to live as those who have already won the victory through thee.

OFFERTORY SENTENCE.   "Although the fig tree shall not blossom, neither shall fruit be in the vines; the labor of the olive shall fail, and the fields shall yield no meat; the flock shall be cut off from the fold, and there shall be no herd in the stalls: Yet I will rejoice in the Lord, I will joy in the God of my salvation" (Hab. 3:17–18).

OFFERTORY PRAYER.   Heavenly Father, help us to keep our stewardship and gratitude intact in the bad times as well as in the good. May we always find reason to rejoice, knowing that you are a faithful Father. May we rejoice in the little that we can bring as well as in the abundance.

PRAYER.   Eternal Father, because our Lord lives today, we live. But some of us have not felt the lifting power of that truth. We go about as those who know that our Lord was crucified but hardly knowing that he was raised from the dead. We have been told that thou hast caused us to sit together in heavenly places with him, yet the sights and sounds and smells of earth are still too much with us. May we hear in thy Word the trumpet blast of victory and rise up with confidence, wide awake to who we are and what we should be doing. Help us to live on this earth as those whose citizenship is in heaven, but as those who are eager to bring the life of heaven to this earth. Grant strength to those sorely tempted every day to live as if this world were all. Grant concern and tact to those who see others tempted and wish to help. And give us all a knowledge of thy comradeship with us in our pilgrimage.

EVENING SERVICE

Topic: The Transfiguration
TEXT: Mark 9:2–8.

This mysterious event took place at the turning point in Christ's ministry. It was the first clear decisive step on the road to Calvary. Jesus took Peter, James, and John, the three who were nearest to him in understanding and sympathy, and went up into the mountain to pray.

The deepest meaning of this incident is to be found when we take it not as first and foremost a sign to strengthen the faith of the disciples but rather as an encouragement to Christ's own heart, an aid to his faith and patience.

I. The transfiguration was a witness to Christ's sinless sonship.

(a) The disciples were familiar with the prayer habits of the Master and were so casual about the event that they fell asleep. They were awakened by the sound of voices or by the brightness of a light that shone even through their dreams. It was such a vision as they could never forget.

(b) When the disciples opened their drowsy eyes they saw Jesus "appareled in celestial light." What was this strange new quality in the face of Jesus? It was the light of heaven shining through. When Moses came down from Sinai we read that the skin of his face shone by reason of God speaking with him. Of Stephen, the first Christian martyr, we read, "Gazing at him, all who sat in the council saw that his face was like the face of an angel." How holiness refines the face and goodness transfigures even plain people!

(c) The voice of heaven accompanied the transfiguration and testified to the distinctive personality of Jesus. "This is my Son, my chosen, hear him." It was the seal of God's approval set upon Jesus' choice of the cross. It was the assurance that God had a mighty stake in what was happening now on the earth.

II. The transfiguration sets the seal to suffering saviorhood. The Gospels make it plain that there was in Jesus an instinctive shrinking from the thought of death. Yet clear in front of him stretched this course of misunderstanding and rejection and the cross.

(a) We have not fully appreciated the loneliness of Jesus. He had his faithful friends, but how dense and dull they were! There was no one on earth with whom he could share the secret that he was God's beloved Son, Messiah, Suffering Servant. So God sent Moses and Elijah. They had known what it was to be alone in the midst of ungrateful people who misunderstood them and they had no one to turn to for sympathy. Jesus in their company found friends who could understand him and fortify him for what lay ahead.

(b) The presence of these brave souls brought comfort to the soul of Jesus as he looked from the mountaintop down the narrow way that led to Calvary. Luke says, "They spoke of his exodus which he should accomplish at Jerusalem." The word *exodus* spoke of enemies pressing hard upon the servants of God. He too was facing the ordeal of his greatest peril. He too needed to be reminded of the glory and the peace that lay waiting on the other side.

(c) Moses and Elijah had toiled alone and in much trial. They too had endured agony and bitterness and disappointment and Jesus took their imperfect work and finished it. The vision passed and the conversation ended but the comfort it brought to the lonely heart of Jesus remained with him to the end.

III. The transfiguration was a forecast of Christ's supreme sovereignty.

(a) This was obscured for a moment by Peter's impulsiveness. He made two errors of judgment. The first was in the proposal to stay on the holy mount, living above the fever and fret of common life. Here at last is the Jesus of Peter's dreams, Jesus where he ought to be, on the throne. How natural for Peter to wish to remain in such a glowing experience, but he could not. The world was waiting for Jesus: the cross was calling.

Peter's second error was in estimating Moses, Elijah, and Jesus to be of equal importance. Peter did not understand even yet that Jesus was he of whom Moses in the Law and the Prophets did write.

(b) The foolish speech of the disciple was silenced by the voice from heaven that came as the climax of the vision. "This is my beloved Son in whom I am well pleased. Hear ye him." There is none like Jesus. He is supreme Lord. Therefore we must listen to him and do what he says.

(c) The cloud parts Peter from Jesus as he speaks, as it always did when he tried to push the picture of the cross away. When the cloud had disappeared they saw no man save Jesus only. He remained in unshared eminence. He was left supreme. It is at the name of Jesus that every knee shall bow. His dominion is undivided, his throne unshared, so that Christ may be all in all.

IV. So from the mystery of the transfiguration a clear challenge comes to us all. The one thing for which we have been created is the doing of God's will. Obedience to that will may mean sacrifice, self-denial, and the hard road of the cross, but there alone can true joy be found and peace and a life made radiant like the sun.

It must not be forgotten that although it is on the mountaintop that we may behold the beauty of Jesus and learn his will, it is down in the valley that we are to obey his commands and tread in his steps. We are permitted to gaze on his glory only in order that we may be equipped to take the Calvary road with him.—John Bishop.

SUNDAY: AUGUST NINTH

MORNING SERVICE

Topic: Shall We Be Patient with Evil?
TEXT: Matt. 13:24–30.

I. How shall we deal with evil? This question has perplexed people from the beginning of time. It has pressed in upon the Christian conscience with special intensity from the day Jesus addressed this parable to his disciples.

(a) This story, like all parables of our Lord, comes straight from the life of his own day and people. A man sowed his field with good grain and then went to sleep. As he slept, an enemy sprinkled the field with a seed that produced a weed that, in its early stages, so resembled wheat that the two could hardly be told apart. As they grew, discerning servants suspected that something was wrong and brought word of it to the farmer. After a quick look, he agreed with them that an enemy had tried to ruin the crop. What should he do? Go over the field and pull up the weeds? No, that would ruin the good grain. There was only one thing to do: "Let both grow together until the harvest," when the separation can and will be made.

(b) The early church treasured the parable and used it steadily as they tried to deal with the conflict between evildoers in their fellowship and the purists who wanted to throw them out. This controversy rumbles through Paul's letters like thunder in distant hills. Paul makes it plain that he is on the side of patience. He would subscribe to our Lord's admonition, "Let both grow together until the harvest." Evildoers are to be warned, prayed over, given every chance to mend their ways, and, only as a last resort, asked to leave the fellowship.

(c) The sheer power of this parable will come through to anyone who gives it careful examination. In a half dozen sentences it suggests almost as many fundamental truths about the proper relationship between God, people, and evil:

1. Good and evil are real facts to be encountered and dealt with.

2. Good and evil are, finally, as different as weeds and wheat; there is no ultimate confusion about which is which.

3. There is need for the wisdom and the patience of God in dealing with evil.

4. A person alone is neither capable of, nor able to, root out evil; only God can do that.

5. Hardest of all, people must accept the inevitable interval involved in the growth of good and evil to that point where they can be identified and dealt with.

(d) There is a time for planting and a time for harvesting, and stretching between the two is the inevitable interval— a time for patient waiting during which the plant grows, and the determination of its true nature is made. It is the counsel of our Lord that we should "let both grow together to the harvest," and then the separation can be made.

II. Stand on this insight of our Lord, which towers above the landscape of the way we usually do things, and we get a different perspective on people and events.

(a) Take the Civil War, for example. Everything was crystal clear then—on both sides—if we may judge by what they were saying. It was a time of black-and-white judgments. You were for or against; "perhaps" was not admitted.

But something has happened during the interval of a century since that dark day. Gone is the sharpness, the harshness of snap judgments—now, an awareness not only of the evil of slavery but also of the equally great evil of what can only be called the will to misunderstand, to misrepresent, and to misjudge people who disagree with us. If evidence were needed for the adage "Two wrongs do not make a right," I would submit this tragic chapter from the experience of our country.

(b) Why do we act this way? The answer is not easy. Sometimes because we are afraid of the changes proposed by those who differ, and fear is always a risky guide. Sometimes because we do not take the time to be sure before we make up our minds.

(c) To talk this way is not a poorly disguised plea to be soft with evil; it is an open plea that we seek to be sure that evil is actually evil before we move in on it, lest we destroy the good as well. And we have reason enough to be cautious on this matter. The policy to wait and see may not please the young Julians of the world who cry, "Let me go forth and purge the world," and launch a reign of naked persecution of all who differ, but it will commend itself to anyone who has studied the way in which the dangerous radicals of one generation become the founding fathers by the next.

III. The implications of all this will not be lost on persons in positions of responsibility in our colleges and universities as well as in our churches and other public institutions.

(a) Every wise college president with an eye to the genius of his or her school knows that he or she must always be on the lookout and guard jealously the right of the teachers to grow toward the full maturity of their thought. Even as it was the part of wisdom then to "let both grow together to the harvest," it is the part of wisdom for a great center of learning to prize criticism and differences of opinion as essential to its very soul.

(b) Every lover of civil liberties will want to take to heart this insight of our Lord into God's way of working with the world. We have seen it demonstrated a dozen times over the last half century that people can lose freedom either by overthrow from without or by betrayal of the spirit of freedom within their own country.

IV. Patience—great patience—patience akin to that of God is essential to the building of anything worthwhile—especially the greatest thing of all, the kingdom of God. How clearly Jesus saw that!

(a) We need his kind of patience if we are to be workers together with God in the building of that kingdom. His was a positive, radiant grace flowing from the awareness of the greatness and the goodness of God. Believing that God was working a mighty work of redemption through him, he gave himself to the realization and

fulfillment of that work. Lying deep beneath all that happened to him was this confidence that "I work and my Father worketh in me."

(b) The disciples, like us, wanted to get things done in a hurry. Some thought the kingdom would come right away. When it did not, many concluded that their faith had been misplaced and they left the fellowship. Others concluded that time was on God's side and that he would use whatever amount of it he needed in the building of the kingdom. Thereupon they began to do two things that belong together in Christian ethics: "wait and see" and "work and pray." This is not quietism, a folding of the hands in moral irresponsibility, rather it is a clear recognition that all great undertakings take time—and the work of the kingdom may take eternity—only God knows.

(c) Patience, so conceived, does not mean being soft with evil or sentimental about evildoers. Rather, patience requires firmness—the firmness of conviction, purpose, and loyalty. But a firmness tempered by gentleness—a gentleness born of an awareness of the need for time in which the evil can grow to the point where it may be distinguished and overcome.

(d) What a different kind of home, church, community, and world we would have if the human point of this parable could get through to our calloused consciences and hard hearts! No more snap judgments. No more hurrying from headline to headline in frantic haste. No more execution of character by hearsay and gossip when someone disagrees with us even in fundamental matters. None of these, but a willingness to let both grow together to the harvest and the infinite patience to let the truth be proved in the event itself.

V. Truly we need something of the patience of God if we are to live with each other. As well we know, it is hard to be honest with other persons—especially those who disagree with us. Yet we know from the snap judgments that people pass on us and that we have passed on other people how utterly unfair they usually are. Here, as elsewhere, Jesus shows us the way.

(a) He heard the word *sinner* applied

freely to persons round about him. And it was more than a word then. It had real bite to it. It indicated people you could not associate with or exchange greetings with, even though you knew them by name. You would deny every form of deep fellowship with them. To call people sinners was to make them outcasts—and you were supposed to separate yourself voluntarily from all relationships with them. It is a striking thing that our Lord paid little or no attention to the distinctions that were supposed to separate sinners and saints. He knew that there was much more to a person than any sin he or she might have committed. That is why Jesus lived in a different ethical world from that of the custodians of accepted religious ethics in his day.

(b) How can we escape the conviction that this is the clue to Christian ethics in personal relationships and world policies alike? We are not called upon to build a kingdom of God with rack and screw, nor even with fear and bombs. Rather we are called upon to believe and to incarnate as best we can a simple yet divinely inspired truth: "God so loved the world that he gave his only Son, that whoever believes in him should not perish but have eternal life" (John 3:16).

(c) Whatever else this may mean, it cannot be fashioned into a club for pounding people into the kingdom of God. Nor is it a mold into which we pour human beings in order to shape and form them to our own desires. It is the worst text imaginable for the heresy hunters and the grand inquisitors who seem to be springing up like poisonous mushrooms in all walks of life these days.

Rather, it puts its finger squarely on the great event that we celebrate in the gospel and in the Christian church, namely, the love of God for all people in Christ. And it gives us a message to believe, to live, and to share with others—all others.—Harold A. Bosley.

DELAYED UNDERSTANDING.   In Harrisburg, Pennsylvania, I went to the old capitol building, now a museum, to study again the huge painting of Pickett's "Charge at Gettysburg." In front of me, a mother and two small sons were seated, looking at the picture. The older boy asked, "Which are the goodies and the baddies in that picture?" His mother replied softly, "It's hard to tell." "Why are they trying to kill each other?" the boy persisted. The mother answered slowly, telling about slavery and other troubles. "Did they have to fight?" the lad asked. And I treasure her reply: "They thought so."—Harold A. Bosley.

GOD'S SURPRISES.   The last judgment is full of surprises. The separation of sheep and goats, of wheat and weeds will be made in a way completely different from that which we permit ourselves to imagine. For God is more merciful than we, more strict than we, and more knowing than we. And, in every case, God is greater than our hearts. But one thing is certain and that is that Jesus the King will come with his sickle and crown. Then our sickles will fall and all the false and illegal crowns will drop from men's heads. Then all will be changed and everything will be different, utterly different. But one thing will remain: love, the love in which we have believed and hoped and endured, the love which never let us forget that God can find and bring home and set at his table even the blasphemers, the erring, the deceivers, and the deceived.—Helmut Thielicke.

Sermon Suggestions

GOD'S ORDINARY ANGELS.   Exod. 14:19–31. (1) The history of God's dealings with his people is one long miracle. (2) Our mistake may be this: to think we are locked helpless in a steel-and-concrete universe; or, to assume that we can do everything that can be done; or, to dismiss as mere coincidence some natural phenomenon that favors us. (3) Our proper attitude is this: to accept favorable events with humble and reverent gratitude; to leave unfavorable events in faith to the mystery of God's providence; to expect God's presence in all circumstances.

STOPPING SHORT OF THE GOAL.   Rom. 9:1–5. (1) The fact that Israel, so favored of God across the centuries, had not gone on to accept Jesus as the Christ was the source of deepest anguish to Paul. (2) Everything in Israelite history and universal human need as well have pointed to Christ for fulfillment.

Worship Aids

CALL TO WORSHIP. "Love must be completely sincere. Hate what is evil, hold on to what is good" (Rom. 12:9 TEV).

INVOCATION. Eternal God, as you have raised your Son, Jesus Christ, from the dead, make our spirits alive to you and to one another, so that we may render to you the worship and service due your holy name.

OFFERTORY SENTENCE. "Keep your life free from love of money, and be content with what you have; for he has said, 'I will never fail you nor forsake you' " (Heb. 13:5 RSV).

OFFERTORY PRAYER. Our Father, help us to keep our lives, including our relationship to money, in true perspective. Grant that our decisions will always be made remembering what is right and who is faithful.

PRAYER. O thou that dwellest in the heaven, and whose heart is in the earth; thou that wert once a man of sorrows and acquainted with grief, but now art ascended on high, a Prince and a Savior, reach forth to us this morning that sovereign and reviving joy which thou hast and dost impart, and which all thine may have if they are united by faith to thee. Care, and labor, and sickness, and anxieties, and disappointments, and the whole round and turmoil of earthly experience overshadow us. As birds in deep forests forget to sing when the morning is coming, not knowing in the twilight that the whole air above the forest is full of daylight; so we are silent and voiceless, though thy glory flames above. Help us to fly into that upper air where all the beauty of thy presence is, where thou art, and where we shall be undisturbed by those sluggish thoughts that hold us down, those envious and corrupt thoughts which mar the purity of the soul. Deliver us from the power which holds us to the earth and makes us earthy. Give us more of the vital power of divine inspiration in those elements which unite us together and make us the heirs of immortality.

We beseech of thee, O Lord! that thou wilt this morning draw near to every one of us. We hate our hatreds; we hate our prejudices; we hate our selfishness; we hate all those corrupt ways, and all those compliances with the world's corrupt ways, which our weakness too often leads us to. We have, today, in thy presence, such a thought of manhood in Christ Jesus, that we look upon our real and worldly selves with shame, and can scarcely believe that men who are competent to form such ideas of themselves—bless so high and Christlike—do walk in a way so burdened; in a way so full of imperfection and sin and unloveliness. When we fain would follow thee, who dost breathe peace and give forth joy, how often do we find ourselves breathing forth anger, and seeking cruelly to hurt! Thou that didst love thine enemies, are we thy followers, who hate our fellow-men with a bitter hatred? Thous didst forgive even those that were slaughtering thee; and can not we forgive those who have reached but a little way to disturb our worldly peace and outward prosperity and interest? How shall we call ourselves thine, if we can not forgive as we are forgiven? How are we the children of the Lord Jesus Christ, if our hearts are fountains of bitterness, and are not fountains of love, with all its sweet and blessed fruit?

Grant, we beseech of thee, O Lord! that we may be changed, and be no longer carnal, nor follow the law of the beasts that rend and ravage. Grant that we may be born into thee, and that we may have that higher beneficence which becomes the sons of God. Teach us that gentleness, that deep peacefulness, which they have whose souls are staid upon thee. From all the fluctuations of our passions; from the disturbance of pride; from hungerings after the fantastic follies of vanity, deliver us. Grant unto us that subtle fidelity, that fealty to thy name, that hearty and thorough love of thee, that childlike docility, that leaning and yearning on thy bosom, which shall make us indeed thine own children.—Henry Ward Beecher.

EVENING SERVICE

Topic: Doxology: Motivation in Christian Living

TEXT: Eph. 3:20–24.

I. The word *doxology* literally expresses the thought, "a glory word, a word about glory." To write a doxology is to ascribe to God glory. Doxology is always the natural response to anything of value.

(a) When we experience anything of supreme worth we wish to comment, to praise, to give vent to the inward experience of expansion that we feel in the presence of great art, poetry, music, or architecture. Our doxology, our praise of anything, helps us complete and deepen the experience of it.

(b) This necessity of praise for a full experience of anything, above all else, applies to God and our experience of him. What makes a giant like Paul? Praise, and praise, and more praise. Praise in his preaching, praise in his singing, praise at midnight in Philippi.

(c) It is in these heavenly moments, in these transcendent experiences, in the outbursts of response to the supreme value that we find in God that we refill the inward springs of Christian motivation. Christian service and duty will deplete you and your inner person will lose its elasticity. But Christian praise has an enlarging, expanding, stretching capacity to make your heart more spacious, your soul more magnanimous, your life more resilient.

II. The great doxology begins with a word of general characterization, "Unto him that is able to do." Concerning the object of God's praise there is to be no confusion. The unadulterated praise ,of Paul in an unmixed manner belongs to God and to him alone. The grammar of the Greek statement makes this strikingly apparent. God is the sole, unique, undiluted object of God's praise.

(a) This is a warning to us. How often do we think more of the preacher than of the Christ preached? How often do we think more of the choir than of the God praised in song? How often are we more impressed with the scholar than with the Lord whose word the scholar investigates? How often are we more impressed with the architecture of the sanctuary than with the Christ who animates the living body who meets within the lifeless bricks and mortar?

(b) When we fail to praise, we betray the fact that God is not acting in our lives. The great contest of Mt. Carmel is the contest of every generation—where is the God who acts, the God who answers by fire? You'll find no First Church of Baal, anywhere. No preachers, singers, or sanctuaries of Baal. Baal is not praised because he did not act. We praise God because he is the God who acts.

III. Praise grows as we realize the absence of limitation, "exceeding abundantly above all." We praise God for there is no limit to his ability to act.

(a) This is one of the most interesting words in the New Testament. It combines three prepositions. *Huper* means above. God is able to do *huper*, above all I think or ask. That is the height of it. What is the highest aspiration of your life? God can exceed that as the heavens are high above the earth.

(b) The next part of that word is the preposition *ek*, out of. Out of you, beyond you, without calculation extending from you God can act.

(c) Then the next part of the word is *peri*, around you, in your circle, in your circumference of friends and family God can do beyond all you can imagine. The ability of God to do is above us beyond measurement, out of us beyond calculation, around us beyond our perception.

IV. For God's ability there is no prayerful limitations. Did any mortal ever dare pray like Paul? First, he was the greatest Christian. Then he was the greatest apostle. Next, he was the greatest mystic who ever lived.

(a) Most of us struggle in some valley of prayer. Paul scaled the alpine peak of prayer and cried down to us poor souls below, come up here—but look, there are higher peaks, and higher, and still higher, up and up into the light of heaven itself. And so he motions us come up.

(b) There are no intellectual limitations to this promise. Beyond all I can think, God will do for me. The word means ponder, consider in depth. Not beyond my superficial thoughts. But beyond my profoundest musings. Paul himself in this epistle has soared above all other thought in the New Testament. His thought has been cosmic, ethereal, eternal. And yet he says, "I am but a child playing at sand castles on the beach. His eternal wisdom comes and washes away my little sand castle, and I have done nothing."

V. Our praise should aspire to a perpetual presentation. The true-hearted believer longs for a time when praise shall never cease. The object of this praise shall be God himself, alone. The content of our praise will be to ascribe to him glory. That word means beauty, symmetry, dominion, personal power, all revealed perfections.

(a) The vehicle of that praise throughout eternity will eternally be the church. We are just getting tuned up here on Sundays. When all else is gone that detracts from that praise—the last sin has been sinned, the last unbelief has been silenced, the last opposition has been disarmed—then there will remain only the church as the eternal orchestra of divine praise.

(b) Paul coined an expression for the duration of this praise, "Unto all generations of the age of ages." Wrestling with the concept of eternity, he surrenders in a torrent of words and ideas of unending time.—Joel Gregory.

SUNDAY: AUGUST SIXTEENTH

MORNING SERVICE

Topic: The Christian Church a Family
TEXT: Eph. 3:14–15.

In the verses immediately before the text the Apostle Paul has been speaking of what he calls a mystery, that is, a revealed secret. And the secret was this, that the Gentiles would be "fellow-heirs and of the same body, and partakers of the promise in Christ by the gospel." It had been kept secret from the former ages and generations; it was a secret that the Jew had not suspected, had not even dreamt of. Our text today speaks of the manifestation of Jesus Christ to the Gentiles. We know that in the whole range of Scripture we could not find a passage that more distinctly and definitely than this brings before us the spirit in which it is incumbent upon us to enter upon this duty.

I. In the first place, let us consider the definition given by the Apostle Paul of the Christian Church, taken in its entirety. It is this, "the whole family in heaven and earth." But in order to understand this fully, it will be necessary for us to break it up into its different terms.

(a) First of all, it is taught by this definition that the Church of Christ is a society founded upon natural affinities—a "family." A family is built on affinities that are natural, not artificial; it is not a combination, but a society.

It is upon another principle altogether that that which we call a family, or true society, is formed. It is not built upon similarity of taste, nor identity of opinion, but upon affinities of nature. You do not choose who shall be your brother; you cannot exclude your mother or your sister; it does not depend upon choice or arbitrary opinion at all, but is founded upon the eternal nature of things. And precisely in the same way is the Christian church formed—upon natural affinity, and not upon artificial combination. That is not a church, or a family, or a society which is made up by people's choice, as when, in the upper classes of life, people of fashion unite together, selecting their associates from their own class, and form what is technically called a society; it is a combination, if you will, but a society it is not, a family it is not, a church of Christ, it cannot be.

(b) Another thing taught by this definition is that the church of Christ is a whole made up of manifold diversities. We are told here it is "the whole family," taking into it the great and good of ages past, now in heaven; and also the struggling, the humble, and the weak now existing upon earth. Here, again, the analogy holds good between the Church and the family. Never more than in the family is the true entirety of our nature seen. Observe how all the diversities of human condition and character manifest themselves in the family.

All these diversities of character and condition are necessary to constitute and complete the idea of the Christian Church.

(1) The Church of Christ takes not in one individual form of goodness merely, but every form of excellence that can adorn humanity. Nor is this wonderful when we remember who he was from whom this church was named. It was he in whom centered all excellence—a righteousness that was entire and perfect. But when we speak of the perfection of righteousness, let us remember that it is made not of one exaggerated character, but of a true harmony, a due proportion of all virtues united. In him were found, therefore, that tenderness towards sinners which had no sympathy with sin; that humility which could be dignified, and was yet united with self-respect; that simplicity which is ever to be met with side by side with true majesty; that love which could weep over Jerusalem at the very moment when he was pronouncing its doom; that truth and justice which appeared to stand as a protection to those who had been oppressed, at the same time that he scathed with indignant invective the Pharisees of the then existing Jews.

(2) There are two, only two, perfect humanities. One has existed already in the person of our Lord Jesus Christ. The other is to be found only in the collective Church. Once, only once, has God given a perfect representation of himself, "the brightness of the Father's glory, and the express image of his person." And if we ask again for a perfect humanity, the answer is, it is not in this church or in that church, or in this person or in that person, in this age or in that age, but in the collective blended graces, and beauties, and humanities which are found in every age, in all churches, but not in every separate person.

(c) The last thing taught us by this defi-nition is that the Church of Christ is a society that is forever shifting its locality and altering its forms. It is the whole Church, "the whole family in heaven and earth." So, then, those who were on earth and are now in heaven are yet members of the same family still. Those who had their home here, now have it there.

(1) Let us see what it is that we should learn from this doctrine. It is this, that the dead are not lost to us. There is a sense in which the departed are ours more than they were before. There is a sense in which the Apostles Paul or John, the good and great of ages past, belong to this age more than to that in which they lived, but in which they were not understood; in which the commonplace and everyday part of their lives hindered the brightness and glory and beauty of their character from shining forth.

(2) Once more, the Church of Christ is a society ever altering and changing its external forms. "The whole family"—the Church of the patriarchs, and of ages before them; and yet the same family. Remember, I pray you, the diversities of form through which, in so many ages and generations, this Church has passed. Consider the difference there was between the patriarchal church of the time of Abraham and Isaac, and its condition under David; or the difference between the church so existing and its state in the days of the apostles; and the marvellous difference between that and the same church four or five centuries later; or, once again, the difference between that, externally one, and the church as it exists in the present day, broken into so many fragments. Yet diversified as these states may be, they are not more so than the various stages of a family.

(3) Institutions pass, churches alter, old forms change, and high-minded and good people cling to these as if they were the only things by which God could regenerate the world. Christianity appears to some people to be effete and worn out. People who can look back upon the times of Venn and Newton and Scott—comparing the degeneracy of their descendants with the people of those days—lose heart as if all things were going wrong. "Things

are not," they say, "as they were in our younger days." No, my Christian brothers and sisters, things are not as they then were; but the Christian cause lives on—not in the successors of such people as those; the outward form is altered, but the spirit is elsewhere, is risen—risen just as truly as the spirit of the highest Judaism rose again in Christianity. And to mourn over old superstitions and effete creeds is just as unwise as is the grief of the mother mourning over the form that was once her child. The Church of God remains under fresh forms—the one, holy, entire family in heaven and earth.

II. Pass we on now, in the second place, to consider the name by which this Church is named. "Our Lord Jesus Christ," the Apostle says, "of whom the whole family in heaven and earth is named."

(a) First, the recognition of a common Father. God revealed in Christ—not the Father of the Jew only, but also of the Gentile. The Father of a "whole family." Not the partial Father loving one alone—the elder—but the younger son besides: the outcast prodigal who had spent his living with harlots and sinners, but the child still, and the child of a Father's love. Our Lord taught this in his own blessed prayer—"Our Father"; and we lose the meaning of that single word *our* as we say *my* Father—the Father of me and of my faction—of me and my fellow-believers, instead of *our* Father—the Father of the outcasts, the profligate, of all who choose to claim a Father's love.

(b) The recognition of a common humanity. He from whom the Church is named took upon himself not the nature merely of the noble, of kings, or of the intellectual philosopher but of the beggar, the slave, the outcast, the infidel, the sinner, and the nature of every one struggling in various ways. Let us learn then, that we shall have no family in God, unless we learn the deep truth of our common humanity, shared in by the servant and the sinner, as well as the sovereign. Without this we shall have no Church—no family in God.

(c) Lastly, the Church of Christ proceeds out of and rests upon the belief in a common sacrifice.

(1) There are three ways in which the human race hitherto has endeavored to construct itself into a family; first, by the sword; secondly, by an ecclesiastical system; thirdly, by trade or commerce. We who have observed the ways of God in the past are waiting in quiet but awful expectation until he shall confound this system as he has confounded those which have gone before.

(2) Therefore there is but one other system to be tried, and that is the cross of Christ—a system that is not to be built upon selfishness, nor upon blood, nor upon personal interest, but upon love. Love, not self—the cross of Christ, and not the mere working out of the ideas of individual humanity.

A love, brighter, deeper, wider, higher than the largest human heart had ever yet dreamed of. But the apostle tells us it is, after all, but a glimpse of the love of God. How should we learn it more? By sitting down to read works of theology? The Apostle Paul tells us, no. You must love in order to understand love. One act of charity will teach us more of the love of God than a thousand sermons; one act of unselfishness, of real self-denial, the putting forth of one loving feeling to the outcast and "those who are out of the way," will tell us more than whole volumes of the wisest writers on theology.—Frederick W. Robertson.

Illustrations

ALL POTENTIALLY IN THE FAMILY. Today's Christian has not only the task of commending the gospel to those whom Friedrich Schleiermacher called its "cultured despisers" and to those who Kierkegaard said "had done away with Christianity without being aware of it," but also to the many displaced persons who have no knowledge of the Christian God at all. The disposition in some circles to exhort clergy and laity to simply "preach the gospel" has hurt rather than helped the church's potential witness. Paul preached Christ crucified, but he borrowed shamelessly from Judaism and Hellenism to proclaim this glad, good news. Paul understood both cultures. Luther understood some—certainly not all—of the cultural realities of sixteenth-century Europe. Wesley had a vivid picture of displaced persons in the changing society of eighteenth-century Britain. Dietrich Bonhoeffer was a cultural realist as well as a believer. Christian witnessing has always required faith in, knowledge of, and obedience to God and his ways in his world. —Wallace E. Fisher.

SOLIDARITY. One for whom conversion means literally an about-face, a radical step in the opposite direction from what he has been traveling, would probably find a continuation of many of the old associations both difficult and undesirable. He will be expected therefore to forsake his old associates, give up his old fellowships, and leave behind him those means of enjoyment that are inconsistent with his Christian profession and purpose and that are likely to exert a back drag upon him which will endanger his continuation in the new life. But he cannot be expected to live in a social vacuum following his conversion. Consequently, if he has not already begun to build some new Christian fellowships and friendships which will support and confirm him in the new life, he is temporarily stranded and is at a very critical point in his religious experience. —Harry C. Munro.

Sermon Suggestions

THE CRY FOR BREAD. Text: Exod. 16: 2–15. (1) The need for bread is crucial. God did not ignore it. Jesus taught us to pray for it. We may be God's miracle to answer that cry. (2) Jesus Christ is the bread of life, the answer of God to the world's most crucial need (John 6:31–40). For the distribution of that bread we as Christians have, in the long range, an even more urgent responsibility.

THE MYSTERY OF GOD'S MERCY. Text: Rom. 11:13–16, 29–32. (1) Because of the disobedience of Israel, the Gentiles are blessed. (2) Because of the obedience of the Gentiles, the Jews are blessed. (3) The final truth is that all have been disobedient and all need God's mercy.

Worship Aids

CALL TO WORSHIP. "O magnify the Lord with me, and let us exalt his name together" (Ps. 34:3).

INVOCATION. O thou giver of every good gift, we rest in thy bounty this day: conscious of thy loving presence in the midst of thy people, comforted in many ways by the ministry of thy Spirit, constrained in our service by the loving example of thy Son. We thank thee for one another and for this occasion which draws us together. Sensitize us to thy truth for this hour.—J. Estill Jones.

OFFERTORY SENTENCE. "Freely ye have received, freely give" (Matt. 10:8b).

OFFERTORY PRAYER. Gracious Lord, we know that there has been no end to your giving to us. Even when much seems to have been taken away from us, we have been receiving from you all along—riches of grace and comfort and strength. Give us eyes to see what our blindness of disappointment keeps us from seeing. May our giving go beyond what we do in these moments. May love and consolation and encouragement go out from us to those about us who are having a hard time.

PRAYER. Gracious God, in Jesus Christ you are kindness incarnate, and I give you thanks for people who are kind, people for whom to smile seems as natural and easy as for the sun to rise, people who are Christ bearers, with power to melt some of my snow. I thank you for these people who leave vengeance to God, but not relief, people who are kind; I can hear it in their voices, see it in their faces, see it in their eyes, above all their eyes, these people who seem in no great hurry, seem not anxious, driven, knotted, but to have time, way inside the grace of time, perhaps the luxury. They seem to have an eternity, time to notice, time to listen, time to stop by, time to sense how it's going, time in any case to ask, and grace to hear, time to let me think my own thoughts, time to understand, time not to panic when they know, time to step inside my skin, time to pitch in on no notice at all and make it seem I'd made their day. I thank you for these people who, when they are with me, seem nowhere else, not one small part of them, making me, for that moment, the center of their entire world, watched over and doted upon, as surely as my infant Lord by angels and archangels at Bethlehem. Gracious God, in Jesus Christ you are kindness incarnate, and I thank you for people who are kind, are to me Christ bearers, with power to melt my snow; now in part, and when I shall see you face to face, with all such saints, then in full. I thank you for these people who are just plain kind. Without them even your goodness might seem as the dead of winter sun. And as you have been kind to me, may I, being kind to all that is yours, be kind to you.—Peter Fribley.

EVENING SERVICE

Topic: Duty: Demonstration of Christian Living

Text: Eph. 4:1–3.

In a moment Paul moves from creed to character, from confession to conduct. There is a continental divide in Paul's letters from which in one direction flows doctrine and another flows duty. Are we chosen in him; that reflects every choice we make. Do we sit with him in heavenly places; that affects everywhere we sit. Married in the closest possible way in the apostle are doxology and duty, doctrine and conduct.

I. This is demonstrated by a command that is definitive: "Walk worthy of the vocation wherewith you are called." The source of this command is inspirational, none other than Paul, the prisoner of the Christ. The context from which we speak always extracts from or enhances what we say. Here Paul points to his imprisonment as a motive not for sympathy but as a source of motivation. He exults in his bonds for Christ. They are to him duty, and more than duty. Let one call me into battle from the safety of the back ranks and I do not hear him. Let him stand in the heat of it like a MacArthur and I follow him to the end. But the character of this command is fraternal; the apostle

beseeches as father and founder of the church. Spiritual character cannot be commanded, forced, or coerced. Our appeal is fraternal, in the bonds of love.

II. The context of this command is exceptional, nothing less than a walk worthy of Christ. It is part of the Hebrew genius that it speaks of a man's life before God with a word of motion, progression, and intent. "Enoch walked with God. Blessed is the man that walketh not in the counsel of the ungodly. To walk even as he walked." Doxology and duty demonstrated—to walk. But the exceptional part of this statement is doing so in a way worthy of Christ. Worthy of his person, offices, and ministry. How do I do that?

III. The apostle explains with a conception that is descriptive. The worthy walk does not begin with the dramatic, the meteoric, or the electrifying deed. It begins with the passive Christian virtues. Without these all the rest cannot be called Christlike. Lowliness, esteeming ourselves small because we really are. We must always feel how miserably short we fall from our ideal. The more we advance in knowledge and grace, the higher our ideal becomes, so that it is always high above us. This is the Christian grace that allows us to regard others as more important than ourselves. This is the garment that covers all other Christlike graces. This attitude was despised by the Roman world but transformed by Christ.

Meekness. A submissiveness toward God in his dealings with us. A restraint toward people in the face of provocation. Long-suffering. Endurance and constancy in the face of illness or trouble. The abnegation of revenge in the presence of wrong. In Romans 2:4 it refers to the forebearance of God in the face of our wrongdoing. Forebearing. Not ceasing to love our neighbors because of the faults in them that offend and displease me. This is the inward character of a worthy walk. We want to move on to the showy, the dazzling, center stage, and Christ says, "Start here." Until you conquer yourself in these four battles, do not worry about going on. Perhaps it is just at this point that we most need to claim the prayer of his great benediction.

IV. From this inward character described there flows an outward behavior displayed. That behavior is a diligent effort to cherish the peace in a Christian community. The manner of this effort is one of diligence, haste, and expertise. The word ["eager" RSV] describes one making a quick departure on an important trip. The object is to cherish the unity of the Spirit. The chain that holds them together is to be peace. The worthy walk begins with peace in the Christian community. It is just here that we should claim the great premise of the doxology. Is it too much to believe that God can do above, out of, and beyond all we can expect?—Joel Gregory.

SUNDAY: AUGUST TWENTY-THIRD

MORNING SERVICE

Topic: The Silence of God
TEXT: Ps. 28:1.

Of all the moments when a man may doubt that life has meaning or that God exists, none is so common and so desolatingly personal as when he prays with pious faith only to find no answer comes. Only silence. Nor are these prayers superficial. They concern some intolerable burden too much for human shoulders to carry or when the heart is bruised or out of an unspeakable anguish of the soul. Yet nothing happens. Alone in his room, the clock on the wall ticks on the meaningless minutes of life. Outside in the city street, the world passes by unheedingly. He hears the rhythm of city traffic, the incoherent conversation of passersby, and here and there the laughter of teenagers having their evening fun and banter. He lifts his eyes heavenward but sees no heavenly vision, only light from the street lamps streaking across the ceiling, and the sound of his own husky voice framing his prayer of dereliction.

In this same mood the psalmist cried out, "Be not silent to me, lest if Thou be silent to me I become like them that go down into the pit."

The dread of God's silence is shared by all. The questions for believer and unbeliever alike are, "Does God really care? Why then this indifference to my plea? If God is truly God, why this silence?"

I. *Silence is always significant.*

(a) Whatever be the metaphysical nature of silence, everyday experience would indicate that silence is never meaningless but always significant. Music, for instance, has its silences, its crotchet and semibreve rests. And the composer uses these rests as part of the structure of his theme. Who of us has not heard "the flutes of silence" when, escaping from the din of the city streets, we find ourselves in a country cottage, the pitch-black darkness pressing upon our eyes and our ears ringing with the silence of the universe.

Indeed, silence can be eloquent. Bernard Shaw called silence the most perfect expression of scorn. And as every family knows, if at breakfast father is surprisingly quiet, his silence does not mean there is nothing wrong. Precisely the opposite. Father has something on his mind.

(b) If, then, silence plays such a variety of roles in the life of man, must we conclude that God's silences are meaningless? Always it is dangerous to seek to know the divine mind from the analogy of the human. The divine mind is so totally different from the human that even to compare the one with the other is blasphemous. Yet there surely are times when we may without too much risk deduce from our own experiences a glimmer of the radiance of God. Have we the right to assume that because it seems to our finite sinful mind that God does not hear our prayers or has not desired to answer them, that God in fact has not heard our prayers and has not already answered them?

II. *The silence of judgment.* Silence played a significant part in the life of our Lord. May not silence be equally significant with God? Thus Jesus reveals to us the silence of the judgment of God, the Judge of all the earth.

(a) Take, for instance, the scene of our Lord before Pontius Pilate in the marble judgment hall. Jesus the prisoner stands before Pilate the judge. Jesus is shackled.

The marks of the scourgings are covered by the mock royal robe. Pilate, cool, aloof, certain of his own power (if not of his own soul), hurls leading questions at the prisoner, cross-examining him with cold Roman logic. Finally he appeals to Jesus' common sense. "Answerest thou nothing to these charges?"

But no word passes the lips of the prisoner. Jesus could have denounced Pilate as he had denounced the Pharisees. Jesus could have eloquently pleaded his case before Pilate, Herod, Annas, Caiaphas, and the Sanhedrin. But the hour for words was past. This was the hour of Judgment, a judgment of burning silence.

Here is an insight into the eternal judgment of God upon evil in all its forms, upon the suffering of the innocent, the duplicity of the human heart, upon the hypocrisy of organized religion, upon the prideful ambitions of men that will not be thwarted even though a Man die for their ambitions. The silence of Jesus is the judgment of God upon blind spiritual leaders, upon a misguided mob, upon duty-fulfilling unknowing soldiers, upon a frightened procurator insecure in his position and prestige.

The silence of God still speaks through those mute lips of the Master. "Hear my prayer," we beseech the Lord. And only silence comes back. "Please, God, hear my prayer," we repeat. And only silence comes back. "God does not care," we cry. And still only silence comes back. What if this be the silence of God's judgment upon our sinful, deceitful lives?

(b) But we must be honest with God in our prayers. What is the prayer we wish God to hear, what is the plea we make? What do we expect God to answer when in a multitude of petty instances we slyly and artfully try to "make the less appear the better reason": when we sing God's praises at public worship, joining in the chorus of committed good people down the ages, and as a matter of daily fact leave to God the leftovers of our time, our interest, and not least our money? What answer can God give to a man who unctuously asks God to forgive him his sins, when deep down in his heart he is not at all sorry for his sins and is determined to

continue in precisely the same manner of life as before because he has no deep intention of forsaking his sins? What is God to answer a man who says he weeps because of his sins when in fact he weeps because he was found out? Or to a man who will spend his time in prayer and Bible reading, using these gifts of grace as manipulative devices to make life the easier and the more successful, and when such prayer and Bible reading do not give him his heart's desire, sulks or blames the minister, or whomsoever he can make a scapegoat for his own personal failures?

(c) It is an act of mercy of God that he does not answer some of our prayers, else long ago we should have died. Suppose God meted out to us our deserts for the shoddiness of our lives, the hate and revenge and the egotism that have bound our souls in slavery—who of us could stand? But God does not speak. And we hopefully think perhaps he has not noticed. Or like the dying Heine we believe it is after all God's business to forgive our sins.

What if the silence of God is the judgment of God upon our wicked ways, making the Lord of Hosts speechless at our rebellion against his love and righteousness?

III. *The silence of forgiveness.* Again, the silence of God can also be his expression of forgiving love.

(a) Silence certainly was the significant fact when the prodigal son returned to his father's house. Here was a foolish boy who had spent his inheritance on the insubstantial passing things of this life until at last he comes to himself amidst the stench of a piggery. Torn between shame at his position and a greater shame to meet his father, he prepares a speech to be delivered before his injured parent.

Then one day his waiting father, ever watching the roadway hoping his boy might come back, espies a limping figure in the distance climb the pathway that leads home. The father runs to the boy. The boy is at his feet kneeling with penitent tears. But the father does not hear his words. The end of the boys' speech is mumbled into embracing arms. It is to the servants the father speaks.

But not one word to the boy! No word, but a kiss; no rebuke but a caress. Language is superfluous at the hour of reconciliation. The most pithless, pointless expression in the language is "I'm sorry." However sincerely meant, it always sounds inadequate. Forgiveness is not a speech but a spirit; not an expression but an experience; not an affirmation of words but a confirmation of love.

(b) The parable of the prodigal son supremely illustrated the nature of Jesus' attitude to sinners. Once the scribes and Pharisees brought to the Master a woman, a sinner caught in the very act. "Teacher," they demanded, "this woman was caught in the very act of committing adultery. Now Moses has commanded us in the Law to stone such creatures; but what do you say?"

Jesus did a strange thing. He stooped and began to write upon the sand of the streets, as if he had not heard them. When they persisted in their question, he rose to his full height and thundered at them, "Let the innocent among you throw the first stone at her," and stooping down continued with his writing upon the ground.

When the accusers of the woman had edged away ("beginning with the older men," as John describes it with telling insight), Jesus looked up, and seeing himself alone with the woman, asked with some surprise, "Woman, where are they? Has no one condemned you?"

"Not one, sir," she said.

"Neither do I; be off and never sin again."

Thus comes forgiveness into the soul, imperceptible at first like the rising of the sun dispelling the dark shadows of night and shame.

IV. *The silence of fellowship.* What if the silence of apparently unanswered prayers be the silence of the fellowship of God? What if the darkness that broods upon the soul in its forsaken loneliness be no other than the cloud that covered Sinai, where Moses saw God face to face and communed of holy things no man might ever know?

(a) Returning to the analogy from human experience, the deepest personal human relationships are experienced in silence. Of course much human companionship is a wordy business. Friends speak plainly and much to one another. Friends not only tire "the sun with talking and send it down the sky" but sometimes tire the moon as well.

On the other hand, there are deep moments in the basic friendships when no word is spoken, nor is there any awkward pause or embarrassment at the silence.

(b) For the two disciples journeying together on the first Easter evening, there was silence indeed in "the hour of knowing." Bewildered by the events of this strangest of days, these two disciples had set out from Jerusalem to spend the night in the neighboring village of Emmaus. On the way a stranger overtook them and joined in conversation, noting their sad appearance and inquiring with the air of an innocent traveler what was disturbing them. When at length they reached their destination, the disciples invited the stranger to break bread with them, if not to spend the hours of darkness. The guest, given the honor of returning thanks to God, broke the bread. In the moment of fraction they suddenly saw he was the risen Jesus himself. Not during the heated discussion of biblical truth, not in the friendly conversing by the table, but now as he broke bread, they saw. Perhaps the swaying shadows against the wall recalled a similar evening with Jesus. Perhaps they saw the bread lie upon the nail-pierced palms in the breaking. Perhaps the lamp showed up the features that they had not noted on the road. This much was certain: silence was the hour of revelation.

(c) Thus it always is in the life of prayer. As we grow older our devotional life becomes less frantic, fussy, and noisy. When this happens, our prayers become more silent. Meditation upon God and his love and his ways in our lives, and upon the assurance of his great promises kept again and again down the years—these occupy our times of devotion as we grow old.

(d) So God comes to us silently and still as if we were walking with a loved one upon a night of darkness, the air still save for the distant hum of the great city, and no sound save the fall of our footsteps. No word is spoken for no word is needed. So God speaks to a man in silence and answers his prayers out of the great echoing unknown. Thus does a man brood upon God with no embarrassment if he can find no true word to express his thoughts; without fear if there seems no answering voice, nor troubled and uneasy if the hour of prayer seem long. But all is calm and still as the peace and presence of God breaks through the turmoil of the day. In silence he touches the hem of the garment of the living God.—George M. Docherty.

Illustrations

BEYOND THE PARALYSIS OF DOUBT.   For my part, I have as many doubts on all the great subjects connected with theology as probably anyone here; but they do not interfere in the very slightest with my trying, in what humble way I can, to follow out the religion of Christ. They do not even touch that region; and I don't want to lose these doubts. I don't want any man to rob me of my problem. I have no liking and little respect for the cocksure Christian—a man who can demonstrate some of the most tremendous verities of the faith, as he can the fifth book of Euclid. I want a religion and theology with some of the infinite about it, and some of the shadow as well as some of the light. Believe me that you can follow Christ without having solved any of these problems. Why, there was a skeptic among the first twelve disciples, and one of the best of them, and one of the most loyal of them. That man sat down at the first Lord's table, and Christ never said any hard words against him. He tried to teach him. That is the only attitude, it seems to me, we can take to Christ still. We can enter his school as scholars, and sit at his feet and learn what we can; and by doing his will in the practical things of life, we shall know of this and that doctrine, whether it be of God. The only use of truth is that it can do somebody some good. The only use of truth is in its sanctifying power; and that is the peculiarity of the truth of Christianity, that it has this sanctifying power and makes men better. —Henry Drummond.

PLUNGING AHEAD.   Some years ago the late Dr. John Henry Jowett was interpreting Paul's counsel to the Romans, "Walk in newness of life." Dr. Jowett began by saying that he could probably express the purpose of the remark by relating the fable of the young bear cub that was puzzled to know how to walk. "Shall I," he said to the old she-bear, "Shall I move my right paw first or my left, or my two front paws together, or the hind ones, or all four at once, or how?" In reply the old she-bear growled, "Leave off thinking and walk." The point of the simple old fable is pertinent. We get into moods of bewilderment about what to do. We keep thinking over this problem and that problem until we are paralyzed with the feeling that the problems are too much for us. The thing to do in such a predicament is to start walking. Walking settles a heap of problems. And it is significant to note how frequently the word *walk* appears in the New Testament: "Walk in love," "Walk in the light," "Walk in newness of life."—Ralph W. Sockman.

Sermon Suggestions

PUTTING THE LORD TO THE TEST.   Text: Exod. 17:1–7. (1) By complaining—as if God did not care. (2) By living loosely—as if God did not judge us. (3) By giving in to despair—as if God did not exist.

A RHAPSODY OF FAITH.   Text: Rom. 11:33–36 (NEB). We glorify God: (1) though his wisdom and knowledge are beyond us; (2) though we cannot understand all that he does or allows; (3) rather, because he is God—"the source, guide, and goal of all that is"—and we are willing to let God be God!

Worship Aids

CALL TO WORSHIP.   "Behold the days come, saith the Lord God, that I will send a famine in the land, not a famine of bread, nor a thirst for water, but of hearing the words of the Lord" (Amos 8:11).

INVOCATION.   God of life, renew in us the joy of our belonging to thee. In song and prayer, sermon and silence, revive our souls and give us a holy worship.—E. Lee Phillips.

OFFERTORY SENTENCE.   "Walk in love, as Christ also hath loved us, and hath given himself for us an offering and a sacrifice to God for a sweet-smelling savour" (Eph. 5:2).

OFFERTORY PRAYER.   Bless, O Lord, these gifts of love, a token of our devotion to thee, and a means of reaching out to those who need the message of thy love by word and deed.

PRAYER.   Almighty God, Creator of the universe, Father of our Lord Jesus Christ and our Father, we come to you out of our need and our dependence. You have shrouded so much of yourself in mystery, yet you have revealed to us as much as we need to know through Jesus Christ. We stand in awe in your presence, yet we yield our hearts to you in trust and love. We confess that we often vacillate between faith and doubt. We see the tracery of your handiwork and we rejoice. Then some experience that baffles and pains us clouds over what we have so clearly seen and felt. Give us always, we pray, such commitment of love that the night and the day will be the same to us as to our obedience, so that in even the darkest times we shall be led, as it were, by a pillar of fire. May no duty be left undone, no word of witness unsaid, because of a wavering heart. Lord, we believe. Help our unbelief.—James W. Cox.

EVENING SERVICE

Topic: Work in Christian Perspective
TEXT: Col. 3:23.

Work has become almost exclusively an economic concern. This is unfortunate. We in the church have allowed the definition and values given to work to be drawn from the wrong sources.

In reality, work is a theological concept, not an economic one. The idea of human labor was born in the creative mind of God. Thus, in order to understand the meaning of work, our attention must be focused not on the textbooks of Keynesian economics, not on the virtues of the capitalistic free enterprise system, or the management charts of corporate enterprises, but on the truths of Holy Scripture.

I. *The nature and significance of work.*

(a) While the command to work is written into the creation accounts of the Old Testament, the best insights into the nature and significance of work are to be found in the New Testament. Paul wrote to the Colossians: "Whatever you do, work at it with all your heart, as though you were working for the Lord and not for men" (3:23 TEV).

(b) In the New Testament, the only distinction between types of work is that between work done for the Lord and work done for other purposes. Notice what distinctions this understanding destroys. Gone is a comparison of different types of work on the basis of physical versus mental labor, manual skills versus supervisory abilities. Gone also is an evaluation of various types of work based upon amounts of remuneration. All that matters is how or whether the work is offered to God.

(c) The New Testament view of work makes no distinction between sacred and secular tasks. In fact, the New Testament apparently has no concept of secular employment. When work is done for the Lord, any work, it becomes sacred.

II. *The purpose of work.*

(a) As you would expect, one's understanding of the nature of work will directly affect that person's grasp of the purpose of work. Our desire is to see both the origin and the goals of work in Christian perspective. Paul wrote to the Ephesians: "The man who used to rob must stop robbing and start working, in order to earn an honest living for himself and to be able to help the poor" (4:28 TEV). We are to work in order to sustain life for ourselves and for our families and in order to be of help to others.

(b) The New Testament offers no condemnation of income. But the New Testament is harsh in its judgment on the accumulation of goods for the sake of accumulating goods. The labor of our hands is not to build monuments to ourselves but to do ministry for others. The purpose of work is income—but income over which the Christian acts as a steward to see to the sustenance of family and self and to see to the help of those in need. Quite frankly, my fear is that while intellectually we know the Bible is right, experientially we live more in response to the economic determinism of Karl Marx's *Das Kapital* than to the moral teaching of the New Testament.

(c) Again let the church model what it teaches. Let us be a community of believers dispersed to assume all kinds of employment but united in an agreement of our major business.

But through the work we do and with the products of the work we do, we can be about the central tasks of meeting human needs in Christ's name and bringing all of life into subservience under Christ's lordship.

III. *Restrictions on work.*

(a) In our society life's meaning has been too exclusively identified with employment. That is why vacation periods either are often not used or are used to do some different kind of work. That is also why retirement is frequently viewed as failure. You know the situation. All of the conditioning of early life has been work oriented. Persistent expectations have elicited punctuality in beginning work and an unconcern for time until a task is done. Then one day at a certain age, a person is required to set all of that aside, walk away from job and job-related friends, and seek to find meaning where for years he or she has been told that meaning cannot be

found. Many folks understandably have simply not been able to do it.

(b) Work is certainly an important dimension of life but life does not, must not, consist of work alone. Some things are worth far more than a particular job. Morality and personal integrity are more valuable than work. Family solidarity and healthy intrafamily relationships are worth more than any one job. A good relationship with the church is of greater significance than a particular position of employment.

(c) Work is important, but it is not so important as to demand the entirety of life. The truth is that when our total allegiance and energies are devoted to any temporal concern, this is sin. God alone is absolutely worth living for and dying for.

(d) I hope this sight can be a reminder to us about the relationship between labor and faith. To be able to view one's work from the perspective of faith and at the same time to be able to look up from one's work and see reminders of faith is the way life should be. I hope those who labor in our city will be able to understand their work not so much from within the narrow perspective of a particular job but from the broader perspective offered by that community in which the Scriptures are read, faith is nurtured, worship is offered, and ministry is performed. I believe it is from that perspective that work may be best understood. "Whatever you do, work at it with all your heart, as though you were working for the Lord and not for men."—C. Welton Gaddy.

SUNDAY: AUGUST THIRTIETH

MORNING SERVICE

Topic: The Voice in the Cave
TEXT: 1 Kings 19:1–21.

I. A schoolteacher had not returned her students' papers for over three weeks; they sat in a pile on her desk, but she could not muster the energy to look at them. An insurance adjuster listlessly prepared to go to work in the morning; he got in his car and sat there for an hour, unable to turn the key in the ignition and leave his

home. A minister who had been known as a good preacher found himself completely bereft of ideas for sermons, and wondered if he could ever preach again. A high school student who had always made top grades was suddenly overwhelmed by the thought of writing a simple essay, and thought she would not be able to graduate.

(a) You recognize the syndrome. It is called "burnout." It usually strikes the very people who have worked the hardest and been most successful, and in whom it is therefore the most unexpected. They themselves cannot understand what is happening to them. They are tired and grumpy and depressed. They feel listless and powerless and unable to think clearly or creatively. Eventually they begin to have feelings of guilt and worthlessness and wonder if they will ever be able to cope with life.

(b) This is the way it was with Elijah. No prophet of the Israelites had ever been more successful. But after all feats that made him the most popular prophet in Israel until the time of John the Baptist and Jesus, Jezebel threatened to kill Elijah and he lost his nerve and ran into the wilderness and wanted to die, saying, "Lord, take away my life, for I am no better than my father."

Elijah was experiencing burnout. He didn't know that was what it was, but it was. After a period of enormous success in his life, he was exhausted and depressed. He had a sense of worthlessness and thought he would never again be able to cope with life. He probably thought all of his achievements had been accidents, and he wasn't able to go on.

II. Fortunately, God came to his rescue. It is interesting to see how God did it.

(a) First, God gave him two nights of good sleep and two nourishing meals. Or maybe it was a night and a day of sleep, with a good meal after each. The important thing was, Elijah had rest and nourishment. Maybe he was able to sleep because he was running away from all responsibility. Sometimes it happens that way: we can rest deeply when we know we don't have to go back into the arena again.

(b) Then God took him on a retreat—a religious retreat. Elijah spent forty days and nights on Mt. Horeb, which is another name for Sinai, the most sacred mountain in Hebrew history, the one where Moses received the Law of God. Moses himself had spent forty days and nights on the mountain when he received the commandments.

(c) And God revealed himself to Elijah on the mountain. God "passed by," the Scripture says. First there was a tremendous storm outside, and rocks tumbled down the mountain; but God "was not in the wind." Then there was an earthquake; but God was not in that either. Then there was a fire; but again God was not in it. Then there was silence—a void or a lull in all the activities of nature. And God was in the silence. The Bible says God spoke to Elijah in "a still small voice." The Hebrew words actually say "a voice of gentle stillness." God was a God who spoke to his people in their hearts, who spoke out of the stillness. God listened to the litany of Elijah's complaints and worries; and then God told Elijah what to do to overcome his situation. God sent him back into the conflict with renewed energy and told him to appoint his successor, who would for a time be his servant and helper in the prophetic role.

III. Perhaps the important thing for us today is to realize that God answers our needs as he answered Elijah's. The schoolteacher who cannot look at the papers on her desk, the insurance adjuster who can't turn the ignition key of his automobile, the minister who cannot prepare another sermon, the student who can't face the writing of another essay can all learn something from the pattern of God's dealings with the ancient prophet.

(a) First, rest and nourishment are vitally important. People who are suffering from burnout often have trouble sleeping. The sleep they do get is fitful and disturbed. They wake up edgy and irritable. They may not be eating well, or they may eat too much, and they need to bring their diets under control again. If we will allow it, God will give us peace when we lie down at night, and we can sleep. And then, with a sense of God's presence and guidance, we can bring order into our dietary habits again, so that our bodies can function maximally to help us with our psychological distress.

(b) Next is the retreat—the religious retreat. It may be in the form of a vacation. But the sense of identification with some place where God has been strongly expressed in the past is also important. Elijah went to the most sacred place in Israel's entire history. For us, that might be roughly equivalent to making a trip to the Holy Land, the birthplace of our faith, or to the place where we grew up and first became aware of God, or to some religious encampment, where we know that others have become greatly sensitive to the presence of the divine mystery. We are speaking, in other words, about a sacred pilgrimage, about a real attempt in our day to find God by journeying to a special location associated with some visitation by God.

IV. Something happens to us when we get away from things that way. We slip out from under the burdens that have crushed us. We get a new perspective on ourselves and our jobs and our situations. We can hear the "voice of gentle stillness," and something inside us snaps into place. We have the energy to go back again.

(a) We may even reconceive our missions in life, and go back to do things differently. Elijah did. He saw, for one thing, that he wasn't alone in what he was doing, the way he thought he was. "I, only I, am left," he had moaned to God. That was why he was so frightened; he didn't have any partners in his great undertakings. But God told him there were still seven thousand faithful Israelites in the land—seven thousand that hadn't "bowed the knee to Baal." Moreover, God gave him the name of his successor, Elisha, and told him to anoint Elisha for the day when it would be his responsibility to be God's prophet in Israel. This gave Elijah a proper perspective on himself as one in a great line of prophets, so that he didn't feel so alone in history. He had a new friend and ally in his work. His horizons were expanded. His sense of what God was doing was enlarged. His spirit was revitalized.

(b) That is the way it can happen for all of us when we are feeling tired and discouraged and burned out. When we see that God is still at work in the world, and that we don't have to carry our burdens alone, it does something to the way we feel about everything. Our hearts are lifted, our steps are quickened, our shoulders are thrown back. New energy surges through our bodies, and we want to get back into the fray again.

(c) That's what the "voice of gentle stillness" is about, my friends. He is "the God

of beginning again," and in the stillness that is what we learn.—John Killinger.

Illustrations

GOD PRESENT AND ABSENT.   As to our duties, we ought to live as if God's all-seeing eye were ever upon us, that is, in a state of hypersensitiveness to the presence of God; as to our needs we ought to live without dependence upon God, as if, indeed, he did not exist. The atheist who lives his life with real interior courage is intrinsically better than a sniveling churchman forever crying for help from an avuncular deity. It is one thing to have the assurance Christians claim: "Ask, and it shall be given unto you; seek, and ye shall find." It is another thing to live as if one were relying on supernatural aid as a holy anesthetic against difficulties and trials.—Geddes MacGregor.

EXTRAORDINARY WORSHIP.   A poet once wrote, "The common tasks are beautiful if we have eyes to see their shining ministry." I wonder how beautiful we should find the tasks of an orderly in a hospital for aged and incurably sick people. To the average person it would be exhausting work, thankless, drab, and perhaps repulsive, just a job, an unpleasant necessity in the grim business of earning a living. One orderly, however, though a humble man with little formal education and few gifts of intellect, performs his tasks with surprising dignity and efficiency. He takes a genuine pride in his work and speaks of it as a vocation requiring special skills and aptitudes. He handles these crotchety old men with such poise and gentleness, scarcely pays attention to the work of his hands, but gets through routine tasks to his patients' personalities. He really cares for them. If one has to be moved to another hospital for surgery, this orderly will travel with him in the ambulance, even during his off-duty hours. If one is dying, the orderly will stay at his bedside. This young man—he is still comparatively young—represents security and friendship for many of these pathetic people who have no one in the world to love them. Their eyes light up when he comes into the room with his cheerful smile. It is he who makes tolerable their last days of loneliness and infirmity and pain. He is a Christian, this young orderly. He goes to church on his free Sundays, but if worship be defined as communion with the Spirit of Christ, then his whole life is an act of worship.—A. Leonard Griffith.

Sermon Suggestions

ON EAGLE'S WINGS. Text: Exod. 19:1–9. (1) God tests and proves his people (Deut. 32:11–12). (2) God claims his people in a covenant of obedience. (3) God gives his people a mission in the world.

SPIRITUAL METAMORPHOSIS. Rom. 12:1–13. (1) It is based on the mercies of God (which Paul has described in chaps. 1–11). (2) It derives its pattern from "the coming age." (3) It produces an ethic that encompasses all relationships in life.

Worship Aids

CALL TO WORSHIP. "Show me thy ways, O Lord; teach me thy paths" (Ps. 25:4).

INVOCATION. O thou who hast cried out in the wildernesses of this world and arrested the vagrant thoughts and affections of those who were far from thee and hast made the desert like the garden of the Lord when people have obeyed thee, grant us in these confusing days ears to hear thy voice, hearts to obey thy will, and tongues to repeat after thee thy truth.

OFFERTORY SENTENCE. " 'Why spend money on what does not satisfy? Why spend your wages and still be hungry? Listen to me,' says the Lord, 'and do what I say, and you will enjoy the best food of all' " (Isa. 55:2 TEV).

OFFERTORY PRAYER. We confess, O Lord, that it is difficult to understand that our faithful stewardship of time, talents, money, and influence brings greater rewards than our grasping selfishness. Enlighten us and deepen our devotion to you, so that we may find the truly abundant life.

PRAYER. Every day, O Lord, your hand of grace is upon us. We receive blessing upon blessing from you. Not a moment goes by that is not touched by your providence. We are the beneficiaries of your mercies throughout the ages. Yet we must confess that we sometimes walk about in your wonderful world as if you were not real or did not care. We let the anxieties and responsibilities of life dull our sensitivity to you. Forgive us our sin, for we *have* sinned; and open our eyes and our hearts to you once more. Give us another opportunity to walk with you, assured of your presence; to talk with you, assured that you hear us; to work with you, assured that what we do counts.—James W. Cox.

EVENING SERVICE

Topic: The Christian's Cross
TEXT: Matt. 16:21–25.

(a) In the name of relevance, contemporary churches have talked much about "applied Christianity," about being the "scattered church in the world," about "the cross in the marketplace." Such talk is not only appropriate, but it is also essential. The critical question, however, is this: Can we really carry the cross into the marketplace when we have so nearly lost it in the church?

(b) Perhaps the only thing that can save the world is also the only thing that can save the church—the cross. If Christians are not only to redeem others, but work out our own salvation as well, we must rediscover the cross. And to rediscover the cross redemptively can only mean to rediscover the indispensable morality of the cross. The burden of the remainder of this sermon is to say what this means.

(c) Now, what of the other cross? What of the cross Jesus said you must bear if you are to follow him? Back in chapter 10 of Matthew, the Christian's cross does not seem very arbitrary for the Christian. But in the 1980s, in a world where crosses are only symbols, what does it mean to "take up a cross"?

I. Some sacred cows need killing. Consider what the Christian's cross is not.

(a) First, the Christian's cross is not synonymous with poverty. Jesus and his little band were not exactly affluent, it is true.

Jesus had almost none of the earthly security we wear ourselves out to gain. He and his followers were poor as the proverbial church mice.

Jesus knew what wealth can do to people. It can so weight them down that they can't even walk across the street to get to God. But Jesus didn't require a vow of poverty from all his followers. Not the prosperous Joseph of Arimethea, who at least owned enough property to give Jesus a grave. Not Mary, Martha, and Lazarus, who apparently remained homeowners.

(b) Second, the Christian's cross is not synonymous with persecution. In the first century the cross was a terrifying instrument of death. It was considered by both Jews and Romans the most horrible way to die. One reason Jesus' cross was such a stumbling block to the Jews and such foolishness to the Greeks is that it was inconceivable to both that the Son of God would die like that!

Then Christian history began to get lined with crosses. The Christian story became endless chapters on martyrdom. Persecution has been for whole generations the normative Christian experience. But, still, the Christian's cross is not synonymous with persecution.

(c) Third, the Christian's cross is not the same as piety. Religious acts, postures, and rituals are not the same as cross bearing. As much as I like to have people present when we meet for worship, I will tell you quite candidly that you will not necessarily get any cross-bearing credit in heaven for attending church on Sunday and Wednesday nights, no matter how painful it is!

It is also interesting to remember that in his own day, and by commonly accepted standards, Jesus was not considered either pious or religious, but was charged with immorality and blasphemy. The Christian's cross is not synonymous with piety.

II. Our crosses must be moral for us in the same way Jesus' cross was moral for him if there is to be any continuity between his cross and ours. There is nothing innately moral in poverty, persecution, or piety. They can all be exercises in narcissism. Many an individual's supposed cross-bearing has been a subtle indulgence in pride.

(a) The cross was not Jesus' cross, it was our cross. He carried our cross! We have said it and sung it thousands of times; he took upon himself the sin of the world. He was under our load, by his own choice, and I know of nothing more moral than that.

If there is, then, any continuity between Christ's cross and my cross, I must come to this: my cross is someone else's burden. If I am merely bearing my own burden, so what? Pagans and animals do that. What morality is there in carrying my own load?

(b) My load is only a cross when it is the burden of someone else which I have chosen to put on my shoulder. Which I have chosen! I secretly resent other people and situations forced on me as burdens. These are not crosses. My burden is only a cross when some free, moral decision has put it there, and when it is something from the shoulder of another.

(c) Finally, consider this. Maybe some burdens which are not crosses at all are infinitely heavier and ultimately more deadly than genuine crosses. In other words, maybe there is a mysterious joy that comes from cross bearing that never comes from mere burden bearing. After all, Jesus said when we take up our crosses and follow him we find our lives by losing them (Matt. 16:25).—C. David Matthews.

SUNDAY: SEPTEMBER SIXTH

MORNING SERVICE

Topic: Accepting Yourself
Text: Matt. 15:26, 27.

I. Whatever else that means—"It is not meet to take the children's bread, and cast it to dogs"—it doesn't mean that Jesus was rude to her. Scholars who go about trying to explain it seem always to overlook the simple and, to me at least, conclusive fact that Jesus just wasn't that kind of person. If you read the Greek, into which somebody translated the Aramaic that Jesus spoke, you will find in the words themselves unmistakable indications of tenderness and affection. So that I am not at all concerned with what in English sounds like rather ordinary and boorish snobbishness. It wasn't. What concerns me is the fact that this heathen woman at once accepted the appraisal of this strange proverb and proceeded on it. "Truth, Lord: yet the dogs eat of the crumbs which fall from their master's table." She didn't go home and brood over it. It failed to induce one of our modern inferiority complexes. She didn't stop to argue that she was much better than this Jewish rabbi might suppose. She wasn't the sort that had been eating her heart out in private because she couldn't be other than she was—a Syrophoenician and an outcast. She accepted herself at her face value and persevered. "Truth, Lord: yet the dogs eat of the crumbs which fall from their master's table."

II. I wonder if you understand precisely what it means to accept yourself.

(a) It certainly doesn't mean being satisfied with what you are. She wasn't that. There is a kind of acceptance which rids the inside of you of an absolutely futile conflict and doesn't kill desire. It makes desire effective.

(b) You may very well go through life without ever really acknowledging the self that you are, dreaming of what might have been if only this or that hadn't entered in to complicate things. It began slowly to occur to you through the years that you weren't the genius you thought you'd be. The world was not as you had planned it. People didn't admire you as you hoped they would. You brushed against other shoulders stronger than yours. The figure you cut wasn't very distinguished. So you were inclined to be jealous and touchy. Without the knowledge you assumed its air. You battered the real self down and preferred appearances. Underneath all your thinking was your own condition. You set out from it and came back to it. And much that was unlovely got hold of you. And maybe you developed strange pains in your back. You didn't know why, but perhaps—it had happened—perhaps it was because most of us unconsciously argue that it's better to be something sick

than to be little or nothing well!

III. Let's see then what there is about us that needs accepting.

(a) First of all, the place we occupy in life. It would seem that that might be comparatively easy here in America, where at least theoretically we proceed on the assumption that all men are equal. But we are able by one device or another to provide as many disastrous distinctions between people as there are castes in India. In the South it's your ancestor that counts; in the North, frequently enough, it's your pocketbook; and in the West, your achievement—with plenty of nondescript hangers-on everywhere trying to climb something called the social ladder. It's a rich soil for all sorts of personal tragedies. Proud mothers send their children to schools where they associate with others who are reputed to be just a notch above them and then wonder what's happened to their discontented offspring! The absolute absurdity of it makes it pathetic, as if a fox terrier should lie awake at night trying to figure out some way of being received at the Airedale Club! It's just plain nonsense, as ninety-nine out of a hundred so-called distinctions between people always are.

(b) But it isn't so easy to accept your lot in the world if it's loneliness you are fighting, or homelessness, or childlessness. That's harder, and the devastations such things have wrought in human personality are simply beyond any kind of computing. From one end of life to the other stalks the specter of being alone. Some of us gaze at it with wide eyes and leap into marriages more tragic than any loneliness. Older people come up with it, and all their places seem desolate, their purposes unfulfilled. And the answer to it all lies in one great and final act of surrender, and the setting of one's face, if not toward the good one could do, then toward the good one can do.

(c) There is a way of accepting what you are, and instead of sitting down in it, with all the unlovely results of self-pity, beginning with it, and working out a gracious will that can outrun your own, and bring you double the poor half you aimed at! There isn't anything in this world you set your heart on so rich and full and complete as that other which God can give, if down in your soul you discover the chord you lost, and it's the "sound of a great amen."

(d) And so too with your equipment. I'm not suggesting resignation. I'm saying that what every one of us needs is a mighty, resounding, triumphant yes, deep somewhere at the very center of our being, to these selves that we are, with all their modest talents, their crippling inabilities—and I say it boldly, with all their sin!

IV. That's where I have been anxious to come out. For it's just at that point that psychology stops and religion comes fully into its own. The hands of God!

(a) I know what you'll say; you'll say, "There he goes off toward the mystic idealism into which Christianity always evaporates!" If there is anything mystic about getting this self of yours over into the hands of that God, if that isn't the most practical, straightforward bit of realism you can happen on under the sky, then you may as well burst this bubble of a Jesus myth and have it over with: it's nothing but a little iridescence in a film of soft soap around some tepid air. Go ask anybody who has said more than yes to his own soul; ask the man who has said "Yes, but—" and with that splendid addition has laid down his own bleak loneliness, his bitter memories of sin and failure, laid them all down in those other hands: go ask him if there are any mysterious margins of peace and hope and strange fulfillment when God takes up your life.

(b) That's your problem, accepting this that you are for the glory of that which he can make of you! I haven't any enthusiasm for anything that's this side of it. The wise ones of the earth talk about sublimation, which, as far as I can find out, is pulling yourself up by your bootstraps. They talk of self-analysis and the process of realization. Let them talk. A plague on all their houses. I'd rather spend one half hour in the presence of this clear-eyed Christ and let him strike my trammels off, until I stand free before him, ready for his will! He sees my worst. Let him speak. I'll hear him out. And then I shall say, "Truth,

Lord: yet . . ." and I shall lay it all down at his feet. After that I'll be going about my business preparing for the miracle!—Paul Scherer.

Illustrations

GOD AND THE ORDINARY MAN.   I am quite sure that it is a mistake to talk about the apostles and disciples as "Saint this-and-that." Because that fosters the idea that, while Christ could make something of such august souls, even he cannot be expected to do anything with our drab ordinariness. And yet the Twelve were very ordinary men—not in the least like what they look in stained-glass windows, but very human John with his temper, and Peter scared into hot oaths, and Thomas lagging so far behind that he could hardly keep our Lord in sight, wait for him how Christ might. And yet these men were very dear to Christ, and he owed very much to them, as he himself told God, looking at them the while with eyes shining with gratitude.—Arthur John Gossip.

COMPENSATION.   Fairly early in his career, Beethoven felt the darkening shadows of his inevitable deafness. At first he was in despair. Why not? "What a sorrowful life I must now live," he wrote; "How happy would I be if my hearing were completely restored . . . but as it is I must draw back from everything, and the most beautiful years of my life will take wings without accomplishing all the promise of my talent and my powers!" So it looked and, what is more, so it would have turned out, had it not been for something else inside Beethoven. "There is no greater joy for me than to pursue and produce my art," he wrote in another letter; "Oh, if I were only rid of this affliction I could embrace the world! . . . I will seize fate by the throat; most assuredly it shall not get me wholly down—oh, it is so beautiful to live life a thousandfold." Then, with awe, in Beethoven's case as in Paul's, one reads the consequence. One biographer, himself a musician, puts it thus: "We are eternal debtors to his deafness. It is doubtful if such lofty music could have been created except as self-compensation for some such affliction, and in the utter isolation which that affliction brought about."—Harry Emerson Fosdick.

Sermon Suggestions

GOD KEEPS HIS DISTANCE.   Text: Exod. 19:16–24. (1) In the mystery of his person. (2) In the reverence due his name. (3) Yet he reveals as much of himself as we need to know for our salvation, our joy, and our service (Eph. 3:8–12).

CHRISTIANS AND THE LAW.   Text: Rom. 13:1–10. (1) We citizens of the state are obligated as Christians to obey the law and its authorities. (2) We citizens of God's kingdom are obligated to live by the law of love, which surpasses and fulfills all worthy laws, rules, and regulations.

Worship Aids

CALL TO WORSHIP.   "Trust in the Lord. Have faith, do not despair. Trust in the Lord" (Ps. 27:14 TEV).

INVOCATION.   As we have assembled in your presence, O Lord, let no burden of guilt, no spirit of anger, no cloud of doubt hide your gracious face from any one of us. Come with your forgiveness, with your peace, and with your reassurance and dispel every hindrance to our true worship.

OFFERTORY SENTENCE.   "Bless the Lord, O my soul, and forget not all his benefits" (Ps. 103:2).

OFFERTORY PRAYER.   If we let memory run free and unhindered, our Father, we recall mercies too many to number. Yet we do think upon these blessings, lingering on this or that benefit, knowing that if you had not helped us we would not, we could not be here today. So we bless your name, and we bring back to you in offering a portion of what you have graciously given to us, asking you to bless it again.

PRAYER.   O Lord, we would rest in thee, for in thee alone is true rest to be found.

We would forget our disappointed hopes, our fruitless efforts, our trivial aims, and lean on thee, our comfort and our strength. When the order of this world bears cruelly upon us; when nature seems to us an awful machine, grinding out life and death, without a reason or a purpose; when our hopes perish in the grave where we lay to rest our loved dead: O what can we do but turn to thee, whose law underlieth all, and whose love, we trust, is the end of all? Thou fillest all things with thy presence, and dost press close to our souls. Still every passion, rebuke every doubt, strengthen every element of good within us, that nothing may hinder the outflow of thy life and power. In thee let the weak be full of might, and let the strong renew their strength. In thee let the tempted find succor, the sorrowing consolation, and the lonely and the neglected their supreme friend, their faithful companion.—Samuel McComb.

EVENING SERVICE

Topic: When God Chastens Us
TEXT: Heb. 12:1–15.

Most modern American people think the government, or technology, or some force ought to do something helpful about everything that is inconvenient to them. We do not accept suffering. We do not tolerate it. We eschew pain, inconvenience, heartache, all the distasteful side of life.

Why do I bring that up on a beautiful day like this? Because on a clear day with all the beauty around us and the refreshing barometric pressure of good cheer, there are still people with deep heartaches. There are people who are asking, "Why did this happen to me?" It is a universal question. The modern generation does not know how to handle it any better than the previous generation did and, perhaps, does not handle it as well.

I. Why do we suffer? How do we respond to chastening? Many people, if they do not use the way of technology to solve their problems, try to say, "Well, it is the will of God that I suffer." Everything is the will of God to them if they cannot handle it. That is an easy answer.

(a) On the other hand, chastening is a spiritual perception of meaning in something that could be just an event or accident to somebody else's viewpoint. A thing could just have happened, that is all. Some people say, "Oh, it is fate." Someone else would say, "It is nothing." But a Christian believer, a spiritual man or woman, would say, "Lord, what are you trying to show me through this event?"

(b) Most men and women who make any contribution to life get to a point sometimes when they are utterly rebuked, criticized, or even crushed. Out of that suffering comes the later fruition of their deepened lives.

I can hear someone object silently that chastening is not easy. I am not advocating pain and suffering. But do not say to yourself, young people, that it is the worst thing that could ever happen to you. Very few men and women get out of the zucchini stage of life until they do suffer. (The zucchini stage is of one season. It is soft, quick growth.)

(c) Men and women react differently. Some men and women utterly rebel. Others reject both the concept of chastening and of redemptive purpose. Some are pensive for a moment and then renege on any resolution. The true response to chastening, to reproof, to criticism, to heartache, suffering, and unreasonable pain is to repent. The proper response is to repent, to turn, to change in one's heart toward God and self and others.

Anywhere you want to look, men and women have reached their apex of fruitfulness, of personality, and of careers when they have been slammed painfully into the sideboards. "Lord," they cry, "Why me?" The answer comes, "Whom the Lord loves, he chastens." We retort, "Lord, I did not know you loved me so much!" "Whom the Lord loves, he chastens," comes the reassurance again.

II. What are the gains that come from this? First of all, you get a sense of direction in life. There is no built-in direction after you get through high school. The law compels you to go to high school. After that, you are on your own and have freedom of choice.

(a) Suffering also brings us closer to people. It is a tough job to be a human being of any substance or character. The smooth easy life is but for a short season. The beauty of life comes through the pain, and chastening drawing us closer to people.

(b) Pain also develops our character. It burns away our pride, our cowardice, our fear, our wrath. It salvages the meaning of life for us so that we can understand what St. Paul meant when he wrote out of his own pain, "What shall separate us from the love of Christ? Nothing! In all things God works together for good to those who love him and see his chastening."

(c) There are no easy nor adequate answers to pain and hardship from a natural standpoint. But from a spiritual standpoint one can perceive the gracious chastening of a loving Lord who points out deeper meaning to life through the ordinary events of our fragile human lives. He does not cause illness, unemployment, or subway accidents, but he salvages meaning out of them for our enrichment.

Weave the heartache of your life into a larger design even as a broken bone knits whole and stronger at the break. Try to discover the love and goodness of God as a constant even when you are devastated and angry at life. He will give you love, wisdom, and courage which can be a blessing to others, as you realize that whom the Lord loves he chastens in the pain and turmoil intrinsic to human existence. Chastening is a voluntary, spiritual perception of good and not an evil punishment sent upon us.

(d) You can express your love to others more warmly when you have come to terms with your own hurt and anger. You will discover other people have the same feelings. Through your chastening experience of pain and anguish you can discover a new depth to life and the assurance of the goodness of God.—Bryant M. Kirkland.

SUNDAY: SEPTEMBER THIRTEENTH

MORNING SERVICE

Topic: The Positive Life
TEXT: Eph. 5:18.

"Be not drunk with wine, but be filled with the spirit." The apostle saw the need of something to lift people out of a dull, drab existence into the sense of joyous life. Those people in Ephesus were trying to do it by drugging their bodies with alcohol. They wanted to make themselves feel joyous and well, when they were neither joyous nor well. They were teaching their nerves to lie. The poor people in the slums of a city has found that for them, the shortest road out of that depressing situation is a big drink of whisky. They have few of the comforts and none of the higher privileges in life, but by that shortcut they can feel for an hour or two that they are sitting on top of the world. It is not for those of us who live privileged lives to stand off and throw stones at them. It is rather for us to ask ourselves, in all honesty and humility, what we would probably do under similar conditions.

The apostle was offering those people in Ephesus an alternative, the substitution of something better to replace the worse. "Be not drunk with wine but be filled with the spirit." Do not rely upon alcohol for your joys but upon the development of certain qualities of mind and heart. His whole method was entirely positive. That is what I want to speak about—the value of a positive life.

I. First, in what we believe. When all is said and done, what do you think of Jesus Christ and of his influence upon the life of the world for the last nineteen hundred years? Do you like this thing called Christian life, or not? If a person has even faith enough to want to believe, that person has faith enough to seek the Lord. Be not drugged into indifference by a lot of interrogation points.

(a) Donald Hankey said, "Religion is betting your life that there is a God." Would you feel like betting your life against that claim? "The fool said in his heart, 'There is no God,' " but to establish that claim one would have to know everything, because if there was any section of the universe where his knowledge had not penetrated, God might still be there. "There is no God" is claiming a good deal for his knowledge. I would not want to stake my all upon such a wild assertion.

(b) We all bet our lives upon something by the way we order our aspirations, our purposes, our activities. Can you name a better option than this—to declare by one's whole attitude and bearing, one's confidence in these four beliefs: I believe that at the center and foundation of everything there is being, personality, intelligent purpose, a benign will. How could a universe without that at the foundation of it produce all this being, personality, intelligent purpose, benign will, which we find about us? I believe that the best use anyone can make of his or her powers is to invest them in a life of intelligent goodwill. I believe that the highest purpose anyone can cherish is to strive for the rule of the spirit of the Master in all our human affairs. I believe that to make one's approach to the highest one knows in thoughtful, reverent worship purifies and enriches the inner life beyond any other single exercise that can be named. Do you believe that much enough to act upon it? If you do, you have faith, real faith, saving faith, faith that overcomes the world.

II. Life goes on. It has to go on. Questions rise and pass, but meanwhile the doubter must live. And doubts are solved not so much by argument as by living. Where we cannot prove, we assume that which seems to have the soundest reason on its side and the finest form of experience. Where we cannot demonstrate, as we do in mathematics, we choose sides, in order to get on with the serious business of living.

(a) We have to live as if the world made sense, or else live as if it were altogether meaningless. For my part I vote with both hands up that it makes sense; and I am willing to move ahead on that working hypothesis as my philosophy of life. Be not drugged into a state of coma by a lot of doubts and denials, but be filled with the spirit of resolute faith in something that you do believe. It is the only way to live and to grow.

(b) We are to be positive in what we do. The cautious, critical weeding out of certain faults in one's nature does not develop character. It does not get the individual anywhere, nor promote social well-being. The positive determination to be good, actively, joyously, radiantly good, moves ahead like an army with banners. It moves ahead like a ship under full sail, because it has the wind and the tide and all the finer forces of earth and sky with it.

(c) Be not drugged into self-complacency by all the wretched things you might have done, but for some reason did not do. Be filled with the spirit of courage, aspiration, high resolve, touching the great, right things which we can do.

III. How much of our so-called goodness becomes feeble and futile just because it is cold, critical, negative. No heart in it! Always avoiding something rather than attempting something! Forever saying "don't" rather than "do."

(a) It is positive action that counts when the returns are all in. Positive action adds up large when the books are opened and the marks are given out. "Whatsoever things are just, true, clean, honest, reputable, likable, think on these things." Let them furnish you the steel frame and the reinforced concrete for the manhood and the womanhood you seek to rear.

(b) In these trying times, we cannot sit down and fold our hands. We cannot be satisfied with a negative or neutral attitude in the face of all the evils which confront us. We are here to put on the whole armor of God and show ourselves able to see it through as Christians. Therefore be not drunk with self-complacency over a few negative virtues and commonplace moralities, but be filled with the spirit of moral adventure. The positive attitude is life—therefore we choose life.

(c) We are to be positive in our final purposes. Heads up, eyes front, present aims! It is not what we are at this moment which marks us up or down on the books the Lord keeps, but what we want to be; and what by the grace of God, we intend to be before the sun goes down and we are gathered to the quiet west. The Lord deals with us all not according to our present attainments nor according to our immediate deserts. He deals with us according to the capacity and readiness we show for something finer. This is the meaning of that old doctrine of justification by faith. We are not saved by works but by faith, by our intentions and our willingness to cooperate with the divine purpose. The really significant fact about any life here is not what it was doing last night but the way it is headed.

IV. Now all this may seem rather simple and commonplace, as if I were merely saying that two and two make four.

(a) We have found by experience that prayer and meditation, the reading of the Bible and the practice of the presence of God renew and transform the inner life. There is nothing intricate or difficult about those exercises. They too are as simple as pure water and fresh air. But when we follow them up, we find that people are transformed by the renewing of their minds.

(b) How very simple the life of the Master was in its whole outer setting! There was no pomp nor circumstance about him. He came with no blare of trumpets or rattle of musketry, yet what a tremendous difference his coming has meant in the moral history of the world!

(c) Be not therefore carried away with those petty forms of stimulus that come and go. Be filled with the spirit of courage and aspiration, that we may share with him in building that finer social order which John saw descending out of heaven from God. "Out of heaven," to be set up in active operation here upon the earth! It is to be an everlasting kingdom, for it is destined to outlast and outshine the stars. Let's go, and give it a lift by living positive lives.—Charles Reynolds Brown.

Illustrations

FAITH AND FREEDOM.   When God gives us riches and then takes them away, it is so that he can give us more valuable riches still and bring us to true life through both of these movements. Psychology is aimed at helping men and women to follow this difficult road. Faith sees it as a divine law, and allows itself to be led by God, and relies on his support. The aim of psychology is the moral autonomy which men strive so hard to achieve, and the revelation of faith is that it is when one abandons oneself to Jesus Christ that one attains inner freedom.—Paul Tournier.

PLEASURE IN MARRIAGE. If sexual pleasure is sought so strongly for its own sake and exalted so highly it is obviously because it is being neglected in marriage and regarded as inferior what passes for Christian morality. We must start finding our pleasure in our marriages! Everyday experience shows that pleasure outside marriage is short lived and leaves a sense of dust and ashes. "Love is much more than love," says Chardonne; it always points away from itself and is only happy when it is taken up into some greater context. The problem is not how to fight impersonal isolated sexuality grown rank but how to give marriage once again, or perhaps for the first time, its fullness, its riches, its pleasure, its blessings.—Theodor Bovet.

Sermon Suggestions

A PORTRAIT OF HUMAN OBLIGATION. Exod. 20:1–20. (1) The frame: God's merciful deliverance of his people. (2) The picture: Panel One—Duty to God; Panel Two—Consideration for Man.

HONORING OUR BROTHER'S CONVICTIONS. Rom. 14:5–12. (1) Within the scope of obedience, God allows and blesses a pluralism of conviction. (2) Therefore, it illbehooves us to pass judgment on our fellow Christian or to despise that person. (3) Each of us will at last have to answer to God and give account of his or her own behavior.

Worship Aids

CALL TO WORSHIP. "Blessed are they that do his commandments, that they may have right to the tree of life, and may enter in through the gates into the city" (Rev. 22:14).

INVOCATION. Lord of life, give a naturalness to our worship, a continuity that flows from our work in the world to our love of thee. Then flood our souls with the joy of singing thy praise.—E. Lee Phillips.

OFFERTORY SENTENCE. "And he said unto them, Take heed, and beware of covetousness: for a man's life consisteth not in the abundance of the things which he possesseth" (Luke 12:15).

OFFERTORY PRAYER. God of grace, as we give let our very giving overcome some of the hold that material things have upon us. Teach us of the good we can do to others and to ourselves as your blessing rests upon our offerings.

PRAYER. Eternal God, Father of us all, you have poured out your Spirit upon all flesh, making your power available to even the weakest among us. We praise you for sharing your own life with us. We acknowledge that we often go our own way until we find ourselves in such difficulties that we cry out to you in our utter desperation. Forgive us of our blundering self-sufficiency that again and again has betrayed us, and give us, we pray, the power and joy of your Spirit working in our individual lives and in your gathered and serving people. And may we let the Spirit impart to us your greatest gift, the gift of love. Renew our lives, put them on the right track, and help us to see and pursue our true destiny with diligence.

EVENING SERVICE

Topic: The Sanctification of Time
TEXT: Eccles. 3:1.
I. In his masterful and now classic study of Christian ritual called *The Shape of the Liturgy,* Dom Gregory Dix has a chapter on what he calls "the sanctification of time," in which he discusses the development of the Christian consciousness between the second and fourth centuries as a confrontation between the Christian and the notion of time. The birth of Christianity as a

formative religious system was based upon the anticipation of a bright and glorious future, and, therefore, the repudiation of, or at least, indifference to, the present. The Lord's Prayer, for example, not only places our Father in heaven, but in its three phrases after those opening lines, seems to place an emphasis upon what is to be, the operative phrase being, "thy kingdom come."

II. Dix suggests that the maturation of the primitive Christian experience has to do with the unexpected survival of the world and the unexpected longevity of the Christian faith and the necessity, therefore, to readjust the notion of Christian time from an almost exclusive concern with the future, to a concern for the experience of the present. It is not unlike the situation in which the late great Eubie Blake was found on his ninety-fifth birthday. When asked how he felt about attaining such a great age, he replied, "If I had known I was going to last this long, I would have taken better care of myself." For St. Augustine, to whom we owe so much of the ancient Christian synthesis of time, the future—God's time—and the present—human time—lived in an intimate relationship whereby each moved toward the other, and both would meet and be redeemed when time itself ceased to be. But for the present, time was neither to be repudiated nor simply anticipated: it was to be celebrated and made holy, sanctified, as the gift of God. Time was not simply what one used to measure the distance between now and then, it was itself part of the created order, and thereby judged to be good.

III. But we might argue that time is neither good nor bad, only a neutral means of measure. Inches are not good or bad, neither are pounds, or numbers—that is unless you have too many inches, too many pounds, or the numbers are, as they say, bad. Is time neutral? We speak of good times and bad times; we say, "The times were right," or "bad timing." The early church taught us to regard time as a gift, an opportunity, not simply an instrument of measure. Perhaps we need to discover again that a sign of growth, of maturity, is how wisely and well we use that gift, for that time, this time, is in some real sense God's gift of himself among us. The time we have is the time in which we have to come to know better who God is; it is the gift of the present God to the waiting church.

IV. We know something of that gift and how wisely to use it. It is, as Dom Gregory points out, a sign of maturity on our part. But it is also a sign of grace on God's part. Thus for prayer, as for many other things, there is no time like the present; in fact it's the only time we have, for which we thank God.—Peter J. Gomes.

SUNDAY: SEPTEMBER TWENTIETH

MORNING SERVICE

Topic: Our Wants and Our Needs
TEXT: John 5:6.

I. Few of us would think of asking a man who had been a cripple for thirty-eight years if he wanted to be healed. But that was what Jesus did. A man had been paralyzed for half a lifetime. He had spent every day lying on his bed by a pool, waiting in vain for his turn to be immersed in the healing waters. It seemed a most pitiful case. But Jesus expressed no sympathy. He merely put to him this strange question: "Do you want to be made whole?"

(a) No doubt there was a reason for the question. The man was probably one of those people who make their ailments an escape from life. If he were well, he would cease to be interesting to other people. He would get no sympathy. He would no longer be the center of the picture. He would have to carry his burden like other people. So, bit by bit, he had grown used to his condition.

(b) Whether he wanted it or not, there was no doubt that he needed to be healed. But what we want and what we need may be two different things. We do not always realize this. One of the sad features of our time is the number of people who seek only what they want. Their one question about everything is, "Do I want it?" They never ask whether they need it. If they are asked to go to church, they will only consider whether they want it. If they do not want it, that ends the matter. It is supposed to be sufficient. This point of view is disastrous. We do not leave children to decide whether they want education. We insist on them going to school because they need it. A boy who goes into life seeking only what he wants instead of what he needs will make shipwreck of life.

II. But to decide about religion by our wants instead of our needs is tragic.

(a) We may not want to pray or to find God's love. It does not appeal to us. But that does not dispose of the fact that we need it. We will not seek God, of course, until we want him, until the sense of need comes home to us and becomes a cry from the heart. That is the problem with which every preacher of religion is faced. How can men and women become so conscious of their need that it becomes the thing they want?

(b) Even those who know their need of God and his grace have periods when their sense of need becomes blunted. The world is too much with us. Life moves along smoothly without anything to jolt us out of the ruts we have made for ourselves. God becomes dim and shadowy. Prayer seems unnecessary. God has his own way of awakening us. Trouble comes, or the shock of misfortune, or some stinging moral failure. We see the chasm opening before our feet where the ground had looked so solid. It is his way of awakening us to our need of him. The first meaning of trouble is to drive us to his breast. Even if we can see no more in it than that, there is a blessing in it. It has quickened our hidden need into a want. And behind that want which forces us to seek him, there is a door that opens into his love.

(c) But we need not wait for that to become conscious of the need that brings us to him. We need only think of the world around us. The big fact that stares at us is that it is very sick and cannot cure itself. There is no one to put it into the pool. The efforts made by statesmen and others to mend things are but tinkering with a house whose foundations have given way. Only the Spirit of Christ can deliver from the fear and hate that are paralyzing us.

(d) He keeps us alive to our need of him. His light shatters our self-complacency. That is one reason why he has been so deeply hated and so dearly loved. He wakens needs we never can forget. He shows up "the plague of our own heart." When we keep close to him we realize that we need his salvation every day. We know that we dare not live out of his healing grace.

III. To be open to him means more than keeping him before our minds. It means facing the tasks that he inspires. One big reason why we lose our sense of need is that we do not face things in his name that make us aware of our own insufficiency. If we are launching out on his service, we will know our own helplessness. We will find that without him we can do nothing. We will be meeting difficulties that are beyond our own strength. That is one of the ways in which he keeps us ever humble and suppliant.

IV. But there is more. For to see him is to know that he loves us and wants us. That brings the sense of need. There are some who have this power over us. They show us glimpses of a friendship that makes us forever dissatisfied. They cross our path for a moment. Ever after, life is both richer for that moment and emptier. For a longing and a need have been awakened. It is like that with Christ.

His friendship is the one thing that can fill the heart with peace. For we can rest in nothing which is not eternal. Why should we not be able to do without him? That question is sometimes asked today by those who claim to feel no need. There is only one final answer. We are made that way. But those who have seen his love never ask it. They know only one thing. "We love him, because he first loved us." —James Reid.

Illustrations

AS HELPLESS CHILDREN. It is just when we realize that it is impossible by any effort of our own to make ourselves children and thus to enter the kingdom of heaven that we become children. We are children, perhaps, at the very moment when we know that it is as children that God loves us— not because we have deserved his love and not in spite of our undeserving; not because we try and not because we recognize the futility of our trying; but simply because he has chosen to love us. We are children because he is our father; and all our efforts, fruitful and fruitless, to do good, to speak truth, to understand, are the efforts of children who, for all their precocity, are children still in that before we loved him, he loved us, as children, through Jesus Christ our Lord.—Frederick Buechner.

THE BREAKTHROUGH. A patient in a mental institution who had been a brilliant young scientist refused to talk to anyone. He was lost in his obsessions. When he would not respond to efforts by doctors, nurses, and others to get through to him, these well-meaning but busy persons left him alone. He showed no improvement. Then a staff member at the hospital began to visit him. He made no effort to force conversation. He simply sat with the young man without saying a word for long periods of time. At last caring broke through the wall, and the young man began to talk. Thus he began to take his first unsure steps on the road back to health.—James W. Cox.

Sermon Suggestions

THE GOLDEN CALF. Text: Exod. 32:1–14. (1) The temptation to idolatry is always present among the Lord's people and takes many forms. (2) Respected leaders of thought and behavior, such as Aaron, often play significant roles in apostasy. (3) Spiritual recovery may depend on the concern and action of a special leader, like Moses, who agonizes with God for his people.

NARROW PASSAGE. Text: Phil. 1:21–27. (1) Paul's dilemma. (2) Paul's desire. (3) Paul's directive.

Worship Aids

CALL TO WORSHIP. "Cast thy burden upon the Lord, and he shall sustain thee" (Ps. 55:22a).

INVOCATION. Our heavenly Father, we come to you as needy people, for blessed as we are with the gifts of your providence, we still have need of more than shelter and food and raiment. Give us, we pray, those other gifts, those blessings of the spirit, that we too easily overlook or forget or spurn. Grant that as we seek to worship you we may see clearly what we have and what we lack and may seek earnestly the better gifts.

OFFERTORY SENTENCE. "The Lord is good to all: and his tender mercies are over all his works" (Ps. 145:9).

OFFERTORY PRAYER. Father, receive and bless the offerings of our prayers, our praise, our obedience, and our material substance. You have made all of them possible. Magnify them now and in the good works of tomorrow, to the end that your name may be glorified throughout the world.

PRAYER. O God, we beseech thee to save us this day from the distractions of vanity and the false lure of inordinate desires. Grant us the grace of a quiet and humble mind, and may we learn of Jesus to be meek and lowly of heart. May we not join the throng of those who seek after things that never satisfy and who draw others after them in the fever of covetousness. Save us from adding our influence to the drag of temptation. If the fierce tide of greed beats against the breakwaters of our soil, may we rest at peace in thy higher contentment. In the press of life may we pass from duty to duty in tranquillity of heart and spread thy quietness to all who come near.—Walter Rauschenbusch.

EVENING SERVICE

Topic: Journey into Forever
TEXT: Phil. 3:1–16.
The Christian life really is like a journey. There is a beginning, the weariness of travel, and a final glorious ending. We who are Christians know well this story, for it is our own.
I. I think Paul would intend for us first to hear this word: that we who are Chris-

tians have already begun the journey.

(a) Our journey began the moment of our conversion. We began the journey with our initial confession of Christ as our Savior. At that instant we began a walk with him that will never end. For Paul the journey began on that fateful trip to Damascus. He had intended to go there to further his persecution of the Christians and to see to it that this little band of followers were stopped before their heresy spread even further. On his way he was met by the resurrected Christ. What a dramatic experience this was, but even as dramatic as it was it was still only a beginning.

(b) What does it mean to be a Christian, to have begun this journey? Paul helps us here with a word of instruction. "I've not obtained this, am not already perfect, but I press on, because Christ Jesus has made me his own." I like the American Standard Version translation of this verse even better: "I press on that I may lay hold of that which has already laid hold of me." The notion is that in conversion the hand of God has been laid on us. He has reached out to us, tapped us on the shoulder, called us by our names, and laid his hand on us. And because he has, we can never be the same persons again. We have begun the journey with Christ.

II. The second word Paul wants us to hear from this text is that the journey, once begun, never ends in this life. We are to "press on," never giving up the faith and always reaching forth to what lies ahead.

(a) Paul defined further what he meant by pressing on. Pressing on meant two things. First it meant "forgetting what lies behind." Paul had much to forget, and so do we. If ever he were to be a powerful force for the gospel, he had to forget some bad things of his past. But he had also to forget some good things that lay behind. He had to forget those things of which he could boast. But what of the things of his present life. Did he have anything here that he too would have to forget? Oh, yes. And so do we. You see, as great a man as Paul was he could not rest on his laurels. None of us are able to rest on past experiences with Jesus Christ. The church is never to be thought of as a group of peo-

ple who, at one time in their past, had a great experience with the Lord and have now signed up to live on the memories. If we are to be authentically God's children, we are to say, "I forget what is in the past, and press on to what is in the future."

(b) Secondly, pressing on means for Paul reaching forth, straining forward to the future. Paul surely had here on his mind the image of a race. He had seen the ancient games and knew the determination and discipline required to complete the long races. He had seen the runners run the many miles, their legs tired and heavy, their breathing become difficult. And if it were not for the tenacity of spirit, the discipline deep within their souls, the desire to finish the course, they would never cross the finish line. My friends, we are running the long race. Often it is difficult and demanding. Yet if we reach forth, stretch forward, and never give up eventually we will cross the finish line.

III. Our life in Christ is a journey, an exciting adventure. It has its beginning, it has its continued travel, and just as surely, it has its ending. We have a destination.

(a) What is our destination? Paul shows us. "I press on," he said, "to the prize (the goal, or destination), which is the upward calling of God in Christ Jesus." Here is our goal—to be *in* Christ Jesus. Nothing can be quite so significant for us as Christians. Our goal is a constantly developing relationship with Jesus Christ, a deepening of our faith, a growing in intimacy with God —so that we not only live with Jesus Christ, but that he actually lives in us. It's our mark. We are in Christ and Christ is in us.

(b) To attain such a relation with Christ surely is our ultimate goal. It's clear to Paul when he states his ultimate desire, the deepest concern of his heart: "That I may know him and the power of his resurrection, and may share his sufferings, becoming like him in his death, that if possible I may attain the resurrection of the dead" (10–11). Paul wants to know Christ and to be known by him. But Paul knows that such a relationship comes in only one way, through the power of the resurrection. You see, we serve not a dead Christ —one who once lived but now is only a dim memory in the shades of history. No indeed. We serve a Christ who is alive both now and forevermore. Death could not keep him down. The tomb could not contain him. His body died but on the third day, on the first Easter morn, God reached down and raised him from the dead. And from that day to this he has continued to live in the hearts of those who call him Lord. He is alive today. The power of his resurrection is still felt in every prayer we pray, in every hymn we sing, in every sermon we preach. He is alive and in us today.

(c) The goal of the journey in the world that is yet to come is but a continuation of the journey of this world. We who are in Christ today shall be in Christ forever. There is the promise that finally and forever, in just the right way, God will bring this journey of ours, and of the world's, to its right and proper end. Then and only then will the great riddles of human life be made absolutely clear. Then and only then, in the great day, in the day of resurrection, will our hope be forever filled.—Lee McGlone.

SUNDAY: SEPTEMBER TWENTY-SEVENTH

MORNING SERVICE

Topic: Your Part in God's Plan
TEXT: Rom. 12:16.

You can see from his letter that in the congregation at Rome were all sorts and conditions of folk. Some were preachers, some taught, and some liked to help at the Wednesday evening prayer meetings, if they had any. There were families that had got further along than others, had more money, were more highly respected; and there were simple, kindly souls that didn't have much but were always trying to do the most thoughtful things for the neighbors. And the apostle is all for having them stick together with their rich diversity of gifts, not fly off a tangent. "Be of the same mind," he writes. "Keep in harmony."

I. And that's where I want to lay hold of it. Will you notice, first of all, that he thinks everybody's part in this community is important? He simply assumes that they count, and that there has to be an end sometime to this silly business of supposing that we don't.

(a) And I follow him in that! Whoever knows anything about life at all knows that our judgments of what matters and what doesn't are just wrong, and wrong nine times out of ten. The Bible is forever trying to teach us some such thing.

(b) I wish we'd let it change our minds. Maybe in the face of all our modern complexity, obsessed as we are with the idea that we can do nothing—maybe all we need is another definition of trifles. The incidents we call trivial and the people we call obscure are really the incidents and the people that make almost all the difference that's made. What's a trifle? And who's obscure? Nothing, says Paul; nobody. And I'll follow him in that!

II. But will you please notice here a second thing: that everybody's part is not only important; it's essentially a creative part. At least it can be made so. The apostle takes a handful of people in Rome and assumes that they do more than matter. They are helping to fashion a world. They aren't pawns, to be shoved about by fate. There's no such thing as fate. If anything is bound sooner or later to overtake them, it's the work of their own hands; and that to a degree which very few among us are willing to admit. They aren't just counters, to be piled one on top of the other, until you get the future out of it. They are shaping that future. And the more I think of it, the more I believe I'll follow him in that too!

(a) Let's be clear about it. We think of nature as a sort of fixed routine, with laws so unalterably regular that even God himself can't do much more than twiddle his thumbs and look on helplessly at what he got started and can't stop! Someone has suggested that from such a simple thing as typhoid he has to turn away and shake his head and say, "I did my best, but the plumbing was beyond me." That's how we figure it.

(b) That may make sense to you; but it doesn't to me. It's like cutting up a corpse to see what life is: no matter how promptly you begin, it's always too late to find out. So every time you look at the world, you're just a little too late to catch sight of the flowing, creative stream. The world to every sense you have is a solid, finished article, as stiff as a corpse, just as fixed, just as regular, with every event in it already accomplished. And that's what you pick up in your hands and weigh it and measure it and draw a diagram and say, "My word, how hard and fast it all is. Where is there any room in that for God and the human will?" It wouldn't seem so in the least, if you could only get your eyes off things done, which fill the present and the past, and watch for a while the hidden forces that are responsible for the doing and shaping of the future.

(c) Don't allow anybody to fool you, not ever: we have our own creative hold on things to come. Thank God, being the kind of sinful folk we are, that transfer isn't anywhere near complete at the moment; but it does look as if history were headed that way. For there at the dawn of it, he made us souls and gave us a conscience. Then more and more he put freedom in our reach. There have been setbacks no end; but the process has gone on. He gave us knowledge and let it grow. He set our hands on power. We haven't learned to use it yet without getting hurt. There are plenty of dangers ahead, but what of that? It's a thrilling program as it unfolds year by year, with the heights yonder that we're still scaling!

III. Perhaps we are ready now for the third thing I want you to notice here: that every bit of it is going to add up to some magnificent whole that's already in the mind of God.

(a) I know it sounds like a contradiction. How can anybody be free to create, or do what he really wants to do, if that's the case? But there is no freedom without limits, and the limits that are set to ours are set by a divine and over-shadowing providence: one who sees to it that there shall be a certain total purposefulness about life; that all its varied parts shall fit somehow into a sort of stirring music, a symphony that sweeps along with a score back of it somewhere and a deep intent.

(b) Nobody is going to prove that. Any number of people will dispute it. They will tell you that there's no goal for any of us but annihilation and no purpose whatever. They'll fling scraps of learning at you. They'll point to the chaos in the world. They'll ask you about the suffering that's scattered all over the place, and the good that gets smashed into a pulp by brute force. If you try to smooth it all over with a few glib explanations, they'll slam the door in your face as they go out; and I can't say I'd blame them. Glibness is impertinent!

(c) Your conviction and mine of God's overruling providence comes as Paul's came: it comes of looking as steadily as we can at Jesus. There is something about him so "superlatively fine" that to save my soul I can't help feeling that there at least is God's plan for me. That's what life means, as far as I'm concerned! It calls to me irresistibly. I keep staring at him on his cross; and to save my soul I can't help feeling that here is a great key-word that unlocks the secret of all the suffering and defeat we know anything about; one answer anyhow, may be the full answer, to the immense enigma of pain: a love that stands so squarely in the center of things that it can afford to lose like that without ever for a single moment risking its own chances of victory. So does the mind of Christ meet me insistently at every turn of the road; until now, "as the vast sky is reflected in a shallow pool," I have come to know it at last for the shadow of the other mind that overarches the world!

IV. Paul came at it that way. Look at him. You can read the whole story here in this letter of his. Back in the seventh chapter he's writing piteously about the war that's going on inside of him. When suddenly, almost as if he had seen Jesus for the first time standing there in the middle of it, he cries out, "Thank God!" and the disjointed bits of his life begin to fall together into a pattern: the sufferings of this present time, every creature, and all things as they work together for good when a man fears God! Shimmering there in the narrow waters of his own soul he has caught sight of this huge providence spanning time and eternity.

(a) It isn't all clear. There's one problem especially that weighs on his heart. He doesn't know what's going to become of his own people, the Jews. And that troubles him. Why on earth did God choose them and then let them go? He wrestles with it for three whole chapters. Can it be that they have been cast out once and for all? Ah no! God forbid! May be this, may be something else; not that! And he goes on floundering around with the facts, trying to fit them together and not getting anywhere at all; he is forced to say he can't make it out. "O the depth of the riches both of the wisdom and the knowledge of God! How unsearchable are his judgments, and his ways past finding out! . . . For of him, and through him, and to him, are all things: to whom be glory forever. Amen." In spite of everything, because of everything, mirrored in his own life and in the eyes of Jesus, he had glimpsed the edge and border of an amazing purpose.

(b) Maybe we should be doing something about it. We think we're standing on the sidelines watching the future being thrown together: well, we aren't; we're making it. I have a good time every morning criticizing it, muttering all along that I could manage better; then I yawn and throw down the paper and go off to live my life as if my life had no reference at all to any of it. It won't do any more! And it won't do either to keep shouting about any kind of neutrality, trying to crawl off into a smug and sleek forgetfulness that shuts its eyes and stops its ears and thanks the Lord and takes its profits! There's a sweep of events, and we're more than caught in it: we're manufacturing it! And I say God help the Christian Church if others provide a leadership that we won't even follow!

(c) That's what Paul means, writing here as he does. "Be of the same mind one toward another." "Keep in harmony." There's still the music of this epic life of old Galilee, that loved and died and

leaned its great hopes on God—and on us! —Paul Scherer.

Illustrations

THE REAL SHAKERS AND MOVERS.   The incidents we call trivial, and the people we call obscure, are really the incidents and the people that make almost all the difference that's made. Earth shakers somehow don't seem to come off very well. It isn't Albertus Magnus we remember. He wrote the first five-foot shelf of books; only his took up some fifteen feet or so. It's St. Francis, his modest little contemporary, who went around playing with birds and taking care of lepers. Not long ago I found myself looking up the Crimean War, with its sabers rattling, its orders being shouted, its Charge of the Light Brigade. I wanted to find out what it settled, so that I could place against her proper background a lone woman with a lantern in her hand walking through the barracks, while wounded soldiers kissed her shadow where it fell on the wall. I knew her all right. Her name was Florence Nightingale. What's a trifle? And who's obscure? Nothing, says Paul; nobody. And I'll follow him in that!—Paul Scherer.

GOD'S WILL AND OUR LIFE.   There are two great classes of people in the world of Christians today: (1) those who have God's will in their character; (2) those who have God's will likewise in their career.

Those who belong to the first class are really outside a great part of God's will altogether. They understand the universal part, they are molded by it, and their lives as lives are in some sense noble and true. But they miss the private part, the secret whispering of God in the ear, the constant message from heaven to earth.—Henry Drummond.

Sermon Suggestions

THE PARADOX OF GOD'S PRESENCE. Text: Exod. 33:12–23. (1) God's presence with his people is real, active, and effective. (2) Yet, there is a sense in which God remains hidden precisely when he is present.

HOW TO WORK OUT YOUR SALVATION.
Text: Phil. 2:1–13. (1) Be assured that
God is at work in your effort. (2) Consider
the example of Christ as you relate to your
fellow believers. (3) Take comfort in the
significant results of going Christ's way.

Worship Aids

CALL TO WORSHIP.   "Thou wilt show me
the path of life: in thy presence is fullness
of joy; at thy right hand there are pleasures forevermore" (Ps. 16:11).

INVOCATION.   Today, O God, may we
find greater pleasure in doing your will.
Strengthen every resolve of ours to do
your will and forgive, we pray, our frequent failures to do your will.

OFFERTORY SENTENCE.   "Now as you
excel in everything—in faith, in utterance,
in knowledge, in all earnestness, and in
your love for us—see that you excel in this
gracious work also" (2 Cor. 8:7 RSV).

OFFERTORY PRAYER.   Almighty God,
whose loving hand has given us all that we
possess, grant us grace that we may honor
you with our substance, and, remembering the account which we must one day
give, may be faithful stewards of your
bounty, through Jesus Christ our Lord.
—Book of Common Prayer.

PRAYER.   O thou great companion of
our souls, do thou go with us today and
comfort us by the sense of thy presence in
the hours of spiritual isolation. Give us a
single eye for duty. Guide us by the voice
within. May we take heed of all the judgments of men and gather patiently whatever truth they hold, but teach us still to
test them by the words and the spirit of the
one who alone is our Master. May we not
be so wholly of one mind with the life that
now is that the world can fully approve us,
but may we speak the higher truth and live
the purer righteousness which thou hast
revealed to us. If men speak well of us,
may we not be puffed up; if they slight us,
may we not be cast down; remembering
the words of our Master who bade us rejoice when men speak evil against us and
tremble if all speak well, that so we may
have evidence that we are still soldiers of
God.—Walter Rauschenbusch.

EVENING SERVICE

Topic: Loving God with the Mind
TEXT: Matt. 22:37.
An ad for the United Negro College
Fund states, "A mind is a terrible thing to
waste." This slogan reflects the sentiment
that Jesus expressed when he admonished
the lawyer with whom he spoke to love
God with all his mind.

Churches sometimes designate one day
a year for special emphasis on colleges,
seminaries, and schools. Why should we
have anything to do with Christian colleges, seminaries, and schools? Here are
three reasons.

I. *We must commit to God the best we have to
offer.* God has given every person a mind as
well as a body. Like the body, the mind
must be trained, exercised, and cared for.
Colleges and seminaries exist for the purpose of training people's minds. This
training allows people to use their very
best mental efforts for God's service.

II. *We must prepare tomorrow's leaders.*
Where will churches get their leaders in
another generation if we do not train and
prepare them today? If we want the best
men and women to serve our churches,
then we must be willing to spend the time,
effort, and money in preparing these people. This requires sacrifice but is worth the
effort.

III. *We must instill Christian values in the
process of education.* Anyone who has ever
attended a secular college or university
realizes that Christian values are often absent in these schools. Some of the values
presented in these colleges are anti-Chris-
tian. Thus Christian schools are necessary
to preserve the dissemination of Christlike
ideals and morals.

Learning only facts, regardless of the
subject, is never complete education.
Facts alone are meaningless until they are
set in a context. Christian colleges and
seminaries provide a healthy context for
both the learning and the interpreting of
facts.—Don M. Aycock.

SUNDAY: OCTOBER FOURTH

MORNING SERVICE

Topic: At the Crossroads with Christ
TEXT: Mark 8:27–33.

(a) The confession at Caesarea Philippi was the central crisis in the life of Jesus, the watershed of his entire ministry, the decisive turning point in the execution of his messianic strategy.

I. *The confession of Peter (Mark 8:27–30).*

(a) The region of Caesarea Philippi was a place of fertility and beauty some twenty-five miles northeast of Galilee, a pagan territory built to splendor by Herod Philip. In such a setting Jesus sought to discover at grass-roots level the reaction of the crowd to his ministry: "Who do men say that I am?" (v. 27) Not only would that question provoke discussion, but it would prepare for a more important question soon to come.

In reply, the disciples chose what must have been representative attitudes on the part of Jesus' most enlightened followers. Three figures were singled out in particular: "Some say John the Baptist" (v. 28a). "Others say Elijah" (v. 28b). Matthew adds "Jeremiah" (Matthew 16:14).

In studying this list of responses, several very important conclusions emerge. One is that the prevailing conception of Jesus was prophetic. A second fact, however, is that these were not only representative prophets, but they were figures closely connected with the messianic age.

(b) The second question of Jesus to the disciples was much more crucial. Already they had proved their dullness in the preceding incident (Mark 8:21). Furthermore, if their understanding of Jesus did not rise above that of the crowds, it was scarcely possible for Jesus to make further progress with them. If they understood Jesus to be nothing more than a prophetic forerunner, then it would be impossible for them to see in his mission the decisive victory of God. A mere man, even a prophet, dying on a cross could offer no salvation but only a scandal. However, if the Messiah died, then there could be something redemptive about that death.

Bound up in this pivotal question, therefore, lurked a profound issue. Was there something about Jesus that could not be compared to any other person, even a prophet?

(c) It was Peter who answered, certainly on behalf of the entire disciple band. As spokesman, Peter affirmed that Jesus was the Messiah or Anointed One of God (v. 29). It is perhaps fair to say that Peter saw in Jesus the one in whom all of the hopes of Israel would be fulfilled. He recognized in Jesus the heaven-sent deliverer who would gather the people of God under the sovereignty of heaven. The answer of Peter, like the question of Jesus to which he responded, was the climax of a long and deliberate apprenticeship together. The result of that fellowship was that Peter had spoken the mind of the disciples in testifying that his Master's vocation transcended even that of the prophets.

(d) The reaction of Jesus was an immediate charge to silence (v. 30). This was due to the disciples' need for further instruction. To broadcast any idea of messiahship would have had immediate and damaging repercussions for the new strategy of ministry which he was about to announce.

II. *The confession of Jesus (Mark 8:31–33).*

(a) Now that the disciples had accepted the fact of Jesus' messiahship, it became necessary to teach them what kind of Messiah he was going to be. Thus, there followed immediately, as a natural continuation of the confession of Peter, a confession of Jesus concerning the crux of his messianic mission. Based on the disciples' express commitment to him as Messiah, Jesus now shared the staggering truth that he would suffer, be rejected, and be killed, thus revealing in what restricted sense he would be the Messiah (v. 31).

(b) Peter had confessed Jesus as "Christ," thus using the most general messianic designation available. Jesus, in turn, replied by employing the more specific term "Son of Man" (v. 31a). Nothing could have sharpened the paradox of his words more dramatically. The Son of Man was a supernatural figure depicted in Daniel 7 and in later Jewish literature who would descend from heaven to renovate the world in a catastrophic manner. "However," said Jesus, "my glory will come by suffering. I will be Son of Man in my rejection and death" (v. 31b).

(c) This paradox of a suffering and dying Messiah instantly swept Peter off of his spiritual feet. Taking Jesus under his wing, he actually began to upbraid his Christ (v. 32). In making his confession for the disciples, Peter had bargained for no rejected and slain Messiah. Thus to spare Jesus the pain of a public remonstrance, he took him aside to correct such foolish notions in no uncertain terms.

(d) The response of Jesus was instant and unmistakable. First gathering the disciples for they were just as involved in the mistake of Peter, Jesus sternly upbraided Peter with the words, "Get behind me, you Satan! Your outlook is not God's but man's" (v. 33b). Jesus saw in Peter's protest a return of the very temptation that he had met and banished in the wilderness, a temptation to take a shortcut to the messianic victory so as to bypass sin and suffering.

III. *The confession of the Christian today.*

(a) Peter affirmed, "You are the Messiah!" Jesus replied, "You are the devil!" Such is the tension in which Christian confession is born. It is clear that in Peter's faith there were elements that were both right and wrong. What was right with the disciples' faith? Notice that Jesus utilized it as the basis for a new and deeper instruction. The Master could not share his deepest secrets with uncommitted followers, but now that they had taken a stand, burned their bridges, crossed their Rubicon, there were new possibilities for growth. It is a law of the spiritual life that understanding develops as, under God (Matt. 16:17), we commit ourselves in personal faith to Jesus Christ.

(b) But what was wrong with Peter's faith? Clearly he had affirmed the fact of Jesus' messiahship while giving little thought to its nature, thus clinging to traditional Jewish notions of an earthly political messiah. His fundamental failure was his refusal to grow. Peter's faith was orthodox and unbending; for him it was the end, whereas for Jesus it was but the beginning.

(c) Even today, in a Christian rather than a Jewish background, it is easier to say the right words than to accept their true meaning. Often we are attracted to God without understanding precisely what he would have us do. Conversion usually begins with a measure of misunderstanding, since we come to Christ with our own preconceived ideas. But once we take our stand, burn our bridges, cross the point of no return, then Christ can go further with us.

(d) What, then, is the meaning of Christian commitment? Is it the end, or just the beginning? Is it a stubborn clinging to the past, or an openness to the future, to the now of the new and disturbing word that God may speak? Faith is the willingness to change, to stretch the mind toward new horizons, to keep the soul taut before one who calls, "Follow me." Faith is the availability of the total person to the savior of surprises, to the one whose new word may be the promise of a cross.—William E. Hull.

Illustrations

THEOLOGY OF THE CROSS. The true meaning of the Christian doctrine of atonement is that Christ died for our sins "according to the Scriptures," not according to later forensic or philosophical ideas that use the language of Scripture only to misuse it. Christian theology, as Luther insisted, is always theologia crucis, because the cross is the supreme manifestation of the redeeming love of God.—J. S. Whale.

FRIENDLY TEMPTATION. In *Gareth and Lynette* Tennyson tells the story of the youngest son of Lot and Bellicent. He has seen the vision and he wishes to become one of Arthur's knights. Bellicent, his mother, does not wish to let him go.

"Hast thou no pity on my loneliness?"

she asks. His father, Lot, is old and "lies like a log and all but smouldered out." Both his brothers are already at Arthur's court. "Stay, my best son," she says, "ye are yet more boy than man." If he stays she will arrange the hunt to keep him happy in the chase and find some princess to be his bride. The boy had had the vision, and, one by one the mother, who loves him dearly, produces reasons, excellent reasons, why he should stay at home. It is someone who loves him who is speaking with the tempter's voice all unaware that she is doing it. But Gareth answers,

O Mother,
How can ye keep me tethered to
you—Shame.
Man am I grown and man's work must
I do.
Follow the deer? follow the Christ,
the King,
Live pure, speak true, right wrong,
follow the King—
Else, wherefore born?

So Gareth went when the vision called.—William Barclay.

Sermon Suggestions

MOSES' MAGNANIMITY. Text: Num. 27:12–23. (1) Because of his disobedience, Moses was not permitted to lead the Israelites into the promised land. (2) Still devoted to the welfare of the people, Moses prayed for the right leader for them. (3) God heard Moses' prayer, and Moses shared his authority with Joshua and commissioned him to carry on.

WHAT IMPERFECT CHRISTIANS HAVE TO DO. Text: Phil. 3:12–21. (1) Recognize their need. (2) Remember the grace of Christ. (3) Forget the past. (4) Press forward to share God's glory.

Worship Aids

CALL TO WORSHIP. "Rejoice, inasmuch as ye are partakers of Christ's sufferings; that, when his glory shall be revealed, ye may be glad also with exceeding joy" (1 Pet. 4:13).

INVOCATION. Great God our heavenly Father, as we steal away from the din of the world, do thou fill our souls with the bliss of heaven, that in praise and prayer we might go forth in the earth renewed to proclaim the grace of undying love.—E. Lee Phillips.

OFFERTORY SENTENCE. "If he will obey my voice indeed, and keep my covenant, then ye shall be a peculiar treasure unto me above all people: for all the earth is mine: and ye shall be unto me a kingdom of priests, and an holy nation" (Exod. 19:5–6a).

OFFERTORY PRAYER. Help us as individuals and as a congregation, O Lord, to see what is in our power to be and to do for thee. Let out obedient stewardship prepare us for the good and gracious service thou hast for us.

PRAYER. Almighty and everlasting God, whom no man hath seen at any time, who art Spirit and the Father of our spirits, unto thee do we come. When we think of thee we are troubled, for we know we have not surrendered ourselves to thy service, which is our highest good; yet we are drawn to thee, and we say with one of old, "Thou hast made us for thyself, and our hearts are restless till they find rest in thee." Bring us at this time into thy banqueting house, and may thy banner over us be love. We would tell thee all our wants, our sorrows, and our sins, that out of the fullness of thy grace we may receive healing and forgiveness.

We lament our desires covetous of worldly things, the coldness of our affections, the prayerlessness of our lives, the want of relish for thy law. Forgive us all that our resolves to lead the higher life have been so easily broken, and grant us true repentance, that henceforth we may build our lives on the abiding foundation of thy holy will, as it is revealed in Jesus Christ. Cause us to walk in the paths of purity and sincerity, to renounce the hidden things of dishonesty, and to have no fellowship with the works of darkness. We pant for a purer air, a wider space. O God, lead us out of the twilight of our own dark, narrow souls into thy glorious light, that we may be the children, not of the night, but of the day. Strengthen us, that we may finish the work thou hast given us to do. Comfort us in the troubles that wait upon our earthly lot. Guide us through the shadows of time into thy blessed eternity. —Samuel McComb.

EVENING SERVICE

Topic: On Finishing the Job

TEXT: Deut. 30:15–20; Philem. 3–7; Luke 14:25–33.

I. For several years in my hometown of Columbia, South Carolina, I was a paper boy. On one of my routes there was an unfinished house. Equipment and pieces of the building trash were strewn carelessly about the yard as if someone had just walked off and left it. The scuttlebutt was that what looked to be so, was. Someone had just left it. The man building it had run out of money and left town and the house was abandoned.

(a) In Sunday School I learned the passage in the Gospel lesson today about the man who started to build a tower but ran out of money and couldn't finish it. I think I never passed that unfinished house but what that passage didn't flit across the back edge of my mind. I can still hear my Sunday School teacher: "Don't forget to count the cost of taking up the cross." That unfinished house became a symbol to me of not counting the cost, of dropping the cross in the middle of things. I understand it better now. I have plumbed it deeply in my years as minister.

(b) Juxtaposed to this Gospel lesson is Deuteronomy. Moses is taking leave of his people and these are his last discourses. He talks to them about good and evil, life and death. He says that they are to love God, obey him, and keep or persevere in his laws. You may not see the similarity between these passages at first, but it is there.

II. Both of these are talking about finishing the job. Moses: you are about ready to go across Jordan and take the land. You must persevere in his principles in order to survive in the new land. This meant to finish the job of taking the new land and to

keep the principles of God before you. Persevere.

(a) Jesus is saying the same thing. Taking the cross, being disciple, counting the cost, finishing the tower, or, in the case of the king, having enough soldiers to complete the battle plans, are all related to Moses' final instructions to his people.

(b) So, on this day in which we think about work, jobs, completion of our tasks as workers and laborers, and as we come before the table by which we are symbolically reminded of Jesus' dedication in completing the job he started, what comes to the fore? The matter of perseverance. Moses: persevere in the principles (laws) that have brought you to the lip of the promised land. Jesus: persevere in toting the cross and in finishing the tower you have begun. Both: work hard at what you have started and persevere to complete the task.

III. No, we will not all agree on everything that needs to be done, or the way it should be done.

(a) The people of God have never found total consensus on anything, I suppose. The children of Israel lost forty years before they could claim the promised land. We can learn from that. Paul had fierce debates with the early church about who should be admitted and how they were to gain entrance. Jesus had detractors in his own band, Judas, the best known and most vociferous. I'm glad Moses and Jesus did not mention unanimity in their closing remarks to their people. Perseverance and discipleship are the things that get us through, not unanimity.

(b) The more experience I have with life, the more convinced I become that perseverance is the secret of discipleship. Staying with it.

Perseverance of the Saints! Indeed!

IV. I began by telling you about that unfinished house on my paper route. It stayed unfinished for a long time. And then one day I noticed that the plywood had been taken down from the windows. The doors were open. Within a month it was finished and a new family moved in.

Before I finished my tour as a paper boy I had the pleasure of delivering papers to that house and making my collections. I remember my first collection on a cold winter's evening. I stepped into the hallway and waited for my thirty-five cents. It was a beautiful home. There was a roaring fire in the fireplace and kids were playing and it was full of warmth and life.

I received my money, pocketed the change, and left. Halfway down the walk I turned and looked back at the orange glow of life emerging from its windows. I can still remember thinking: how good it is when you finish the job.—Thomas H. Conley.

SUNDAY: OCTOBER ELEVENTH

MORNING SERVICE

Topic: Being Children of the Kingdom
TEXT: Mark 9:30–37; 10:1–16.

Jesus apparently saw children as the automatic heirs of the kingdom of God. On at least two occasions, he reminded his disciples of their place in the eyes of the Father. It is interesting to note that both of these occasions occurred at a crucial point in his ministry, just before he journeyed to Jerusalem to be killed. They seem thereby to form a necessary counterpoint to the intensity of the conflict with the scribes and Pharisees. As the evil grew stronger around him, Jesus' thoughts turned increasingly to the innocence of children.

I. That is one reason for his glorification of the childlike state, isn't it? Children are innocent. The garden of Eden still lives in the eyes of children. You cannot behold the face of a little girl making mud pies or a little boy playing with a toy car without thinking you are looking at a little bit of heaven.

(a) Notice the two occasions of our text. One is when the disciples were arguing about which of them would occupy first place in the kingdom. The jealousies and competitiveness of the adult world. People trying to get ahead of one another. People vying for first place in each other's eyes. Sales people cutting each other to get ahead in the company. And Jesus stopped it cold. Putting his arm around a child, he said, "Here—this is the secret of the kingdom. When you put a child ahead of yourself, you will be receiving me."

(b) The other occasion is when a crowd of people were putting Jesus to the test on the question of divorce. "Is it lawful?" they asked. "What did Moses say?" Jesus replied. "Moses gave a way out," they said. And Jesus chided them. People are always looking for a way out. Loopholes, fine print, escape clauses. The world of intrigue and deception. "You have to be like the children," he said, "—innocent; that's what the kingdom is like."

II. This is the secret of the gospel. We don't enter the kingdom by keeping laws. Laws can be manipulated. Laws become complicated and reflect the deviousness of adult societies. We enter the kingdom by being innocent, by being like the children.

(a) A child can understand this, for a child is alive to mystery, to the miracle of grace. Haven't you noticed that? Children are naturally curious, and want answers to many things, but they are often satisfied with the simplest of explanations. "What makes the leaves turn red and gold in the autumn?" they want to know. "A little fellow named Jack Frost paints them," we say. "When does he paint them?" they ask. "Before you get up in the morning," we reply. And they are delighted. It isn't that they fully accept the answer; their young minds are already questioning such fanciful responses. But they like it. They see the universe as music and poetry. Jack Frost or photosynthesis, it is the same. A world of wonder.

(b) It isn't that they don't understand the real world. They do. They understand it better than grownups, because they see it whole, with the ego and the id together. They haven't compartmentalized it and rationalized it and turned it into a spare parts factory. They accept their environment as miraculous and don't relegate God to a book and an ancient history. For them, Jesus can still turn water into wine and make a blind man see and raise the dead to life. For them, the world is still mystery and life is grace. They can see

God in a puddle of water or the glow of a firefly. They have the vision that was envied by Blake and Wordsworth. They are the true seers, the ones who have it all together. Not we. They.

III. Oh, they would have a difficult time organizing the world without us, it is true. They need the adults to keep a roof over their heads and cut their meat and make them eat their spinach. But how much poorer we would be without their vision, their way of seeing things. We need their point of view, said Jesus, to enter the kingdom.

(a) They are so trusting, you see. They alone know how to have faith. We live in the world so long that we forget how. We become cynical and distrustful and disbelieving. Like these people Jesus was talking to about divorce, we know all about the fine print in contracts. We keep wanting to trust and believe, we long to trust and believe, but we don't know if we can do it.

It is the children who know how to believe in the kingdom. They have no history of disappointment. They can still believe with a whole heart.

(b) Innocence, a sense of mystery, a trusting nature. You can see, can't you, why Jesus said we must become as little children to enter the kingdom of heaven? Our problem is that these qualities become repressed as we grow older. They are buried deeper and deeper inside us, covered by the debris of life and experience. We need to get in touch with them again, to exhume them, to give them new life in our adult existence.

(c) That's what the experience of Christ is all about. "If any person is in Christ," said the Apostle Paul, "he or she is a new person." Innocence, mystery, trust are renewed. As tired and guilty as we are, we get in touch with innocence again. As rational and matter-of-fact as we have become, we have a new sense of miracle. As abused and burned out as we feel, we discover a new kind of belief and trust.—John Killinger.

Illustrations

DIFFICULTY OF BELIEVING.   Are you worried because you find it so hard to believe? No one should be surprised at the difficulty of faith, if there is some part of his life where he is consciously resisting or disobeying the commandment of Jesus. Is there some part of your life which you are refusing to surrender at his behest, some sinful passion, maybe, or some animosity, some hope, perhaps your ambition or your reason? If so, you must not be surprised that you have not received the Holy Spirit, that prayer is difficult, or that your request for faith remains unanswered. Go rather and be reconciled with your brother, renounce the sin which holds you fast—and then you will recover your faith! If you dismiss the word of God's command, you will not receive his word of grace. How can you hope to enter into communion with him when at some point in your life you are running away from him? The man who disobeys cannot believe, for only he who obeys can believe. —Dietrich Bonhoeffer.

EXPERIENCING TRUTH.   It is one's own inner experience that tips the scales of decision. It is a mistake to rely on what is often termed blind faith, though this might better be called credulity. Christian faith is not belief in the absurd; it is commitment in trust to what one's living experience validates. The "will to believe" of which another famous philosopher, William James, wrote so persuasively is not wishful thinking; it is decision based on the convergence of external evidence with the intuitions of the soul.

So let us not try to "prove" the resurrection, or to say just what may have happened in it. But let us rest upon it in faith and hope, and know that because of it the living Christ is with us, right here, right now.—Georgia Harkness.

Sermon Suggestions

THE BURIAL OF MOSES.   Text: Deut. 34: 1–12. (a) Moses' burial was a secret. (2) On the other hand, Moses' mighty words and deeds have been declared for all to know. (3) Nevertheless, one greater than Moses has come (Heb. 3:1–6).

A PLEA FOR PEACE.   Text: Phil. 4:1– 9. (1) Peace in the Christian fellowship.

(2) Inner peace that passes understanding. (3) Peace with God, the source of all true peace.

Worship Aids

CALL TO WORSHIP. "Whosoever exalteth himself shall be abased; and he that humbleth himself shall be exalted" (Luke 14:11).

INVOCATION. Lord, how we prepare in order to have a party! How we prepare so we can enjoy a delicious dinner! How we prepare so we can be presentable to the eyes of the world! How we prepare so we can do well on a test or a report or a job interview! How we prepare so we'll be all set to go on a trip or on a vacation!

We know that preparation is a necessary and vital part of being able to perform and participate well in life's activities and relationships.

How did we do with our preparation to worship you, Lord? Did we release any sins from our lives? Did we ask you to forgive us for anything? Did we ask whether we're ready, willing, and able to see ourselves, and others, from your point of view? Did we prepare ourselves to feed and clothe our souls with the same kind of care we take to feed and clothe our bodies? Did we throw away any attitude that will keep us from giving you the attention you are worthy of because you are our God? Did we consider how true worship changes things and people, how it challenges as well as comforts, convicts as well as cleanses? Did we say in advance a prayer of commitment telling you we are prepared to come into your presence, that we'll go where you want us to go, do what you want us to do, be what you want us to be: just give us your Word?

Lord, make this Sunday a very good preparation for the tomorrows of our lives. May we prepare for tomorrow by living wisely and well today: for this reason do we dare and care to worship you, right now.—Gordon H. Reif.

OFFERTORY SENTENCE. "For God so loved the world, that he gave his only begotten Son, that whosoever believeth in

him, should not perish, but have everlasting life" (John 3:16).

OFFERTORY PRAYER. Receive now our offerings, O Lord, however large, however small, and bless them. Bless those who will know more of your love and caring through what we do. And bless us as our hearts open wider to the needs of others.

PRAYER. Eternal God, we thank thee for the promise of thy kingdom and its challenge for our future. Forbid that we should ever settle for the rags of earthly riches and miss the true rewards of thy kingdom. Fashion our lives in the image of thy Son until we incarnate thy truth for our time. Teach us the stern lessons of suffering, the bright discipline of learning; enable us to speak words of comfort to the lonely and disheartened, and words of prophetic judgment where there is injustice, arrogance, and vice. Help us to love thee with our whole being: with our minds to know thee more clearly; with our hearts to love thee more devotedly; with our spirits to seek thee more diligently; with our strength to serve thee more constantly. —Paul D. Simmons.

EVENING SERVICE

Topic: The Gift of Life
TEXT: Ps. 90:1–12; 1 Cor. 6:19–20; James 4:13–15.

I. Life is a gift of divine grace. Life should be received with gratitude and respect. Helmut Thielicke reflects on an illustration from German literature that pictures a group of frivolous passengers on a swaying, lamp-lighted boat, floating down a small stream. In the darkness along the shores are the sinister eyes of beasts waiting for the boat to come within reach. Thielicke commented: "At bottom almost all of us go floating along in this way, enjoying life 'as long as the little lamp glows.'" We get serious about life when someone calls attention to the dangers which lurk in the darkness or when the beasts crawl into the boat with us. The rest of the time we spend accepting our lives as they come with little thought for either our origin or our destiny. Certainly we should not go through life with the fearful curse of Coleridge's Ancient Mariner. I would not suggest that you should be so serious about your existence that you carry a sign about your neck announcing that the end is coming. The God who has given us life has also given us laughter and joy. To be sure, life is a gift worthy of our highest celebration. Yet, life is not all laughter and joy, and I suspect that the folks who have the most to celebrate are folks who are receiving the gift of life with the utmost seriousness and respect.

II. The points at which our lives touch the shore are the moments of reflection on our meaning and worth—when someone close to you dies, when you pass through a crisis stage or a crisis event in life, when you have a near miss in an auto or airplane. These are the times when we are prone to ask with Pascal, "Who has put me here?" Is there a Creator who has given me life and thus given my life a purpose? The sobering events of life can be revealing, and in some of our tragic experiences the only good that we can see is the revelation of the brevity and value of life. I would suggest a better way to live. If the crises of life bring a healthy pause to our existence, why not pause ahead of the crisis and begin to ask now why we are here and where we are going. This is really the theme of the Bible. Out of a thousand years of lived experience with God, we can discover who we are and why we are here.

III. The psalmist was sobered by the thought that God is our dwelling place in all generations. Beyond the brief span of a human life or even the vast span of the formation of the earth stands the eternal God, Creator of all that is. Or consider the counsel of Paul to new Christians torn between the practices of a pagan society and the call of the gospel. Anchor your personal ethics in the firm knowledge that you belong to the God who has made you and dwells in you. Or consider the wisdom of James who suggests that we cannot presume that we possess our lives so as to be certain of all of our future plans. We are bounded by the will of God. Karl Barth describes the Bible's view of human life as "a divine loan unmerited by man. It must always be regarded as a divine act of trust that man may live. And the basic ethical question in this respect is how man will respond to the trust shown him in the fact that he may do so."

The most basic question of our stewardship as Christians concerns who we are rather than what we have. We live in a world which tends to rate and classify people by what they have, but long before we can say "net worth," God has already set upon us a value beyond anything which money can buy. The most precious gift in all of the world is the gift of life itself, and the ultimate question of our stewardship is the seriousness with which we receive the gift and the purpose in which we invest ourselves.—Larry Dipboye.

SUNDAY: OCTOBER EIGHTEENTH

MORNING SERVICE

Topic: The Parable of the Importunate Widow

Text: Luke 18:1–8.

(a) In the parable the praying church is presented in the figure of a widow to whom injustice has been done and who is completely helpless against her adversary. Even in the judge she runs into a stone wall of cold indifference. A widow is a woman who has lost the protection of a man and therefore may often be victimized. For most people are pitiless and cold enough to be impressed only by someone who has power behind him and can defend himself. A widow is often a negligible quantity, a nonentity that can be brushed aside.

(b) If we take the time to study the surrounding texts in which our parable is embedded, we shall note that they all refer to this last moment of history and that we cannot understand this story of the petitioning widow unless we see it in the light of this last day. The church of Christ is bidden to pray, "Thy kingdom come." And this means that it has influence upon this last day.

For the widow stands at the strategic key-point of world history. She rests in the heart of God, and God has promised her that his heart will not be deaf to her pleadings. He who has influence upon the heart of God rules the world. The poor widow is truly a world power.

I. The first thing that strikes us about the praying of this woman is the incredible intensity with which she presents her petition. She is beset by people who are perhaps bent upon driving her from her house and home and threatening the life and welfare of her children. And now in this utmost distress she knows that nothing will do her any good, no appeal to her enemies, no clever move, nor even her own energy and ability by which she might hope to prevail against malicious fortune. She knows that there is only one thing—actually, only one single thing!—that can help her, and that is to get this one man on her side. And this one man on his part needs to speak a single word and all her troubles will be over.

(a) And this is precisely what our Lord is saying to us: If you were to take seriously, if *you* were to take seriously the fact that God reigns, that he holds in his hand your personal destiny as well as peace and war among the nations, and if you were also to take seriously the assurance that you have a voice in all this and that God will listen to you; if therefore you were to take seriously the fact that everything depends on this one thing and this one Man, then you too would keep dinning your prayers in the ears of God with this same persistence, this same stubbornness, this same intensity.

(b) I know very well what some of you may be thinking as I venture objection to express all this in terms so gross and almost offensively blunt. You may think that this dinning of our prayers into the ears of God is simply lack of respect. After all, we see this kind of thing in the pure human realm. When a petitioner keeps hounding us and sticking to us like a bur, he becomes a nuisance. We find this repulsive, and finally even our good-naturedness begins to go on strike.

But with God it is quite different. Here the parallels on the parable let us down. In other words, when we keep pestering him this is not at all a sign of lack of respect, but rather a sign that we are taking him and his promises seriously, that we are tak-

ing him at his word. And God rejoices when we do this, because then he knows that we understand his heart and that now we are no longer pious and superior but dare to come to him as helpless children.

(c) The petition "Thy will be done" must never be the first petition in our prayers. So here we must be careful. First I must boldly, heartily, and quite ingenuously speak out what I want to receive from my Father. This and nothing else is what he desires of us, for he no longer wants to be "God" at all (as we conceive of him), but rather our Father, with whom his children may speak freely and frankly, even foolishly. For is not what we so often ask for in our prayers actually the merest stuff and rubbish? In order to be able to present serious, worthy petitions I would really have to know what I need. And to know what I need I would have to be capable of correctly interpreting my own life and the lives of other people, indeed the life of the world itself. But can I do this? So, for example, I pray that I may get well, but in reality my most bitter need is to remain longer in the school of suffering. I pray that I may have a successful career or that I may win the sweepstakes, whereas God needs me in some altogether different place, and he knows that success and money would be poison to my character. In the midst of a war I pray for the gift of peace; but God knows that we must drink the cup to its dregs. Thus in my prayers I make all kinds of false diagnoses, false estimates, and false interpretations of the real situation. And therefore our prayers are often merely foolish talk.

(d) So, after we have spoken frankly and openly in our prayer, we should draw a clear line at the end and then (but only then!) say, "Thy will be done; thou wilt do what is right and good; thou wilt choose what is right from all our foolish prayers. Thou knowest best what we really need."

II. Secondly, the intensity with which the widow pleads with the judge—she "kept coming to him" repeatedly—is also related to the fact that the judge is an unjust judge, a man with a heart of stone. At any rate he is a man whose justice—to put it mildly—is not immediately apparent and not to be had at the first asking.

(a) But it is precisely this bidden justice,

this justice that is not immediately apparent, that spurs her on to go all out. And here again our Lord is giving us a hint; for God often seems to us to be just as dour, hard-hearted, and uninterested as this judge was in fact. Is he not constantly ignoring our wishes? Time and time again is not our praying like telephoning—when nobody answers at the other end or the other party suddenly hangs up just as we are about to state our business?

When we have such experiences, we either resign ourselves, or we crack up, or we shake our fist in defiance of this leaden, taciturn heaven. But this very silence of the judge only prompts the widow to press her demands upon him even more vehemently.

(b) May it not be that very often God remains silent in order that we shall not submit in fatalistic resignation and content ourselves with the cheap snap judgment that says, "Whatever happens must happen"; but rather in order that we may learn to remain in communication, in constant contact with him? God's grace is not cheap; it is not handed out for a mere song. God loves those who take the kingdom of heaven by force (Matt. 11:12). They are the only ones who then have their experiences with God and know what they have in having him.

(c) Moreover, in life, too, it is often true that the people who mean the most to us are not the amiable charmers, with whom we establish contact at first sight; rather it is with the very people who make it hard for us and whom we learn to know only after repeated painful attempts that the deepest and most fruitful relationships result. But then we know, too, what we really have in them. Even in God's silence and his refusing to give himself easily there is a hidden goodness. He only wants us to seek him more passionately; and all the while he has long since found us.

(d) But as soon as we put it in this way it becomes apparent how completely and utterly different is our heavenly Father from this judge. The judge is in actuality what God only appears to be to our feeble faith. The judge finally relented only because the widow kept hammering at him until he was literally softened up and because he was afraid that she might even begin raving at him.

"How much more," says the Lord, "will not your Father in heaven, who is really just, vindicate his elect, who cry to him day and night?" And he says this not without a grain of irony: You so-called believers, you immediately give up if God isn't on the spot to comply at once to the first whisper of your prayers, when all the while, if he tarries a while with his comfort, he is only waiting to see whether we shall continue to be faithful to him.

III. Thirdly, we must consider one final essential feature in our parable. The whole parable is directed toward the day of judgment and closes with the question, "Will the Son of Man, when he returns, find faith on earth?" Or will all the people have fallen asleep?

(a) Here we people of today will have to change our ideas considerably if we are going to understand this. We think that the only person who is awake and watchful is the one who is "alive," who keeps his eyes open on the job, watches his chances, is constantly on the go and always a nose ahead of his competition, and is therefore exhibiting incessant activity. But this is just the kind of person who, in a very deep sense, may be sleeping and dreaming.

(b) And because we are made miserable by this question and the possibility that despite all our success we may have missed the meaning of our life, we plunge all the more madly into our business in order to anesthetize ourselves, which means, put ourselves to sleep. So people go on dreaming, though outwardly they may look like wide-awake realists and executives whom nobody could easily bamboozle.

(c) And now the Lord says to us: The man who prays is the man who stays awake, who does not dream and confuse the big things with the small things, but retains a wide-awake and realistic sense of the real proportions of life. The man who prays knows that there is only one thing that really counts and that is getting straight with God. The man who prays also loses the anxiety of life because he knows that, despite all the tricks and whims of fortune, history will end according to plan, and that nothing can happen to us except what he has foreseen and what is for our good. The man who prays is recalled from his anxiety-dream into reality, for he has the measure of eternity and the day of judgment and that gives him his sense of proportion.

(d) We understand then why Jesus' parable concludes with this question of whether there will be those who pray here on earth when he comes again. One thing is sure: our prayers are heard above. But are there petitioners here below? That is the problem, not whether our prayers are heard, but whether there are any who pray. We men keep asking, "Where is there a God who hears me?" Which of the two is right? In any case, he will come again when days and hours are done. But what will things look like then? Will the lamps of the virgins be extinguished; will a great darkness lie upon the face of the earth with only the skeletons of deserted cathedrals rising above it? Or will God find here and there in this darksome world a gleam of shining light? Will he find the burning lamps by which he recognizes those who pray, by which he sees that there is one who has been waiting and has not fallen asleep as he stood still, or as he kept running about?

(e) The Lord concludes his parable with a question. And this meditation, too, shall end with a question: "Am I one of those points of light to which God can come? Do I bear that fireproof Name?" He who has ears to hear, let him hear!—Helmut Thielicke.

Illustrations

GROUNDED IN PRAYER. As to the evidence in experience of the effects of intercessory prayer, it is necessary to proceed both with assurance and with caution. Hosts of people have prayed for the recovery of loved ones from sickness, have seen the tide turn and flow upward when physicians saw no hope, and are therefore convinced beyond all argument that prayer was the only decisive factor. One may well believe this conclusion to be right, and nothing is to be gained by scoffing at their assurance. On the other hand, others have been prayed for with equal earnestness and faith, and they have died. What is important is not to decide in each case just how much effect prayer had, for lacking divine wisdom we cannot estimate the delicate balance of forces involved. What is vital is to live the life so grounded in prayer that, whatever the outcome, we will still go on trusting God and praying for spiritual victory for ourselves and others.—Georgia Harkness.

GOD'S ANSWERS. A God without concealings or rigor, who always kept pace with our pedestrian minds, would not be God. His worship would be trivial, and the worshiper merely flippant. We see God as a sailor might see a promontory—now in sunshine, now in storm, the tiny visible only a sign of a vast Unknown. Some petitions are not answered, and if they were we could not worship him, for his ways are higher than our ways. But some petitions are answered: he is surprise of mercy, outgoing gladness, rescue, healing, and life.—George A. Buttrick.

Sermon Suggestions

ONE WOMAN'S COURAGE AND ITS CONSEQUENCES. Text: Ruth 1:1–19a. (1) The story of Naomi and Ruth. (2) The significance: Naomi clearly had borne a winsome witness to her faith. Ruth nevertheless showed remarkable personal courage to cross the boundaries of race and religion. God in his providence thus made Ruth an ancestor of King David and of Jesus the Christ.

THE GOSPEL IS MORE THAN WORDS. Text: 1 Thess. 1:1–10. (1) It *is* expressed in words. (2) It is expressed in the mighty working of God within and among his people—which provides an example, inspires joy, wins affirmation from fellow believers, produces obedient service, and brings ultimate assurance.

Worship Aids

CALL TO WORSHIP. "Seek the Lord and his strength, seek his face continually" (1 Chron. 16:11).

INVOCATION.   Lord, we are here today because you have called us together. We need the strength you can give and the strength of one another. Grant that we worship in this place and serve wherever we go, in the power of your Spirit.

OFFERTORY SENTENCE.   "He that spared not his own Son, but delivered him up for us all, how shall he not with him freely give us all things" (Rom. 8:32).

OFFERTORY PRAYER.   Grant, O Lord, that we may see and know by experience that the most important things are always available to us and that we may trust you to give us such other things as accord with your purpose. From what we have received we give back to you a portion with our prayer that others may be blessed by what we give.

PRAYER.   O searcher of hearts, thou knowest us better than we know ourselves, and seest the sins which our sinfulness hides from us. Yet even our own conscience beareth witness against us, that we often slumber on our appointed watch; that we walk not always lovingly with each other, and humbly with thee; and we withhold that entire sacrifice of ourselves to thy perfect will, without which we are not crucified with Christ, or sharers in his redemption. Oh, look upon our contrition, and lift up our weakness, and let the dayspring yet arise within our hearts, and bring us healing, strength, and joy. Day by day may we grow in faith, in self-denial, in charity, in heavenly-mindedness. And then, mingle us at last with the mighty host of thy redeemed for evermore. Amen.—James Martineau.

EVENING SERVICE

Topic: Twenty Other Commandments
TEXT: Ps. 15 and Pauline writings.
I. This is a didactic psalm. Its purpose is to instruct people in religious faith and practice. It arose from the ancient custom of repairing to a seat of worship, seeking through a priest an oracle that would give the suppliant guidance in decision and action—perhaps throwing light on some affliction or calamity that had overtaken a nation or a person. Again the ancient Hebrew might seek from the temple priest an interpretation of law in a particular or a fresh definition of duty. With this much as background, there comes the pilgrim asking—"Who shall sojourn in thy tent? Who shall dwell on thy holy hill?" The seeker has no inherited rights in the community but is permitted to enjoy permanent privileges of membership. To be accorded such a status brought in its wake the riches of divine protection and favor. What kind of person must we be to enjoy this hospitality? Here is the answer. A scholar named Peters sees "a temple Decalogue" maintaining that nowhere else in The Old Testament do we have so full a statement of the obligations of holiness.

(a) "(1) Be righteous in life; (2) Be truthful to the core; (3) Refrain from gossip; (4) Do no harm to a friend; (5) Do not insult a neighbor; (6) God despises the persons who make themselves odious; (7) God honors those who fear God; (8) Keep the oaths you take though you suffer for them; (9) Do not loan money at interest because you are in the covenant community where borrowing takes place only in the case of dire need. (10) Do not take a bribe against an innocent person."

(b) When these standards are satisfied, there is reward. The reward is security in God. Compare Jesus' parable of the wise and foolish builders, the head of household who built upon rock and the other who erected a home upon sand. When the rains came the floods rose, the winds blew and beat upon both—you can imagine what happened!

II. The psalmist passed over the ceremonial requirements of religion to speak only of the ethical. However primitive some elements appear, the prophetic influence on the priestly is marked; and that is a great gain! However, little is said of duty to God, nor is there a warning against such sins as murder, theft and adultery. For the most part Psalm 15 deals only with sins we can describe as antisocial since they destroy goodwill and brotherhood. Evidently the singer lived in an age not unlike our own when the need was for integrity. His was a tract for the times! Even these injunctions are based on love— that we are not to be lovers of money, but persons of principle who adhere to the greater importance of life beyond things.

(a) Now to pass from that psalm to smorgasbord with the Apostle Paul, texts drawn from many contexts: "(1) Abstain from doing anything which causes your brother or sister's downfall; (2) Make the most of every opportunity you have for doing good; (3) Don't tire of doing what is right; (4) Remember that a person will always reap the kind of crop they sow; (5) Don't let the sun go down with you still angry; (6) Test all things to see if they are true, and if they are, hold onto them; (7) Pray about everything; (8) Follow the Holy Spirit's leading; (9) Serve the Lord Jesus Christ enthusiastically; (10) Give thanks no matter what happens!"

(b) The fact that Paul is known to us mainly through his occasional letters gives us insight into his powerful personality with a wide range of conditions and sensibilities surrounding him and within him. What were Paul's assets? There was his Jewish upbringing and his Roman citizenship; there was the gospel of the historic Jesus; there was the gospel of the older apostles; and there was Paul's own conversion and his reflection upon that gigantic experience. This made Paul confront the law with reflection upon that gigantic experience. This made Paul confront the law with Christ crucified. This made the Savior and salvation available. The sphere of salvation was the body of Christ which is the Church. That made for his three missionary journeys, his arrest and trial and appeal and journey to Rome and imprisonment and martyr's death. Not a limited life at all!

III. It is obvious that I could spend some fruitful minutes on each of those subtopics, but it should be equally obvious that I perceive that the apostle's ten additional commandments are more dramatic and that their totality is more dynamic for our lives than, perhaps, the original ten or those deduced from the psalm as commandments.

(a) Of course that's debatable; of course I stated my preference; of course Paul could have advanced a negative principle—how it is wrong to exercise freedom when someone suffers as a consequence, but self-restraint as an axiom of Christian conduct could be turned into something health-giving and positive! The Christian faith is both a sanctuary and a battle station, ours is a call to the strenuous life; and this is not lessened by a pessimistic view of our age. Withdrawal is not the Christianity of the New Testament! Consider the role of the emotions—they may be dwarfed by birth or dulled through drink and drugs or weakened by false stimulation, but they are to be used, and their best use is to respond to God's craving Spirit! A Christian is like a doctor who respects the diagnosis of the previous physician when coming on a case, but needs to make his own inasmuch as some time has lapsed; trailing that is this, having made your own diagnosis, stick with it until other symptoms develop.

(b) Our happiness is that when we have been sufficiently into the Holy Spirit and often enough, we know the identification of the still small voice speaking loud and clear. We are able to judge the passing from the permanent, pointing out and cooperatively correcting faults in persons and society, upholding what is right and good, yet not feeling that we are being used!

And the bottom line on all bottom lines is that we have to give thanksgiving to God other than only on the last Thursday each November "for our creation, preservation, and all the blessings of this life."

(c) We all need some spoken commandments in life—either directly from God via Moses, or by the temple priest when a pilgrim approached asking for entrance, or as Christians when the Apostle Paul wrote to first century churches. And thus, in each instance, commandments to each of us!—Al Eliason.

SUNDAY: OCTOBER TWENTY-FIFTH

MORNING SERVICE

Topic: There Came One Running
TEXT: Mark 10:17.

The story of the rich young ruler has always been one of my favorites. It has a constant sense of freshness and reality, and it speaks to me with directness and authority. It begins with great promise, for Jesus did not make the first approach, but the young man came to him running.

Yet in spite of this good beginning, the story comes to a tragic ending. When the conditions are placed before him, the young man cannot accept them. What started off with such promise ends with such great disappointment. I am convinced that the incident has within it important insights for us.

I. For one thing, he was rich, and that of course impressed his contemporaries. Here is no middle-aged or elderly man coming to repent for wasted years. Everything is before him, and the right word will start him on a great career.

The New Testament says he was a ruler, which must have meant that he was a man of importance and standing in the community. He had status and he commanded respect. He was the kind of person advertisements talk about when they offer us gifts for "the man who has everything."

(a) Turn now to our situation and see how similar he was to us. Think of the riches we possess and we shall see that as this young man stood out from his society, so we stand out from the whole world.

(b) He was young and we have a great admiration for youth. We are a young nation, and with the exception of a few extremists, we are looking toward the future and not the past. Unlike some other civilizations, we have no great respect for age and its experience. The worst possible thing is for us to look old and act old, so we employ all kinds of subterfuges to cover up the marks of the passing years. The main thing is to look and act young, even if it kills us.

(c) We have great power and prestige around the world. Our decisions affect millions beyond our borders. We need enough imagination to realize what it is to be a part of a society whose very existence depends upon other people's choices. To be an American is to be where the influential decisions are made. So that altogether we would have to say as it was said of the young man, we are rich, we are young, and we are influential.

II. In the second place, this young man speaks to us because he needed a purpose for living. In spite of everything he possessed, he was poor. In spite of all his good fortune, he was miserable. A society that finds tension increasing and simple happiness harder to achieve will understand something of his state of mind.

(a) Now the rich young ruler is not a man who is down and out. Here is no moral leper shunned by decent people. He says without any embarrassment and apparently without any hypocrisy that he has kept the commandments from his youth. He is clean-cut, moral, and beyond reproach in his living.

He seems to be competent in handling his own affairs. He is not an outcast who cannot adjust himself to his station in life, but he seems to have done very well. He gives every appearance of being at home in his world and quite able to fill his position in an exemplary way. The world had treated him very well. But in spite of it all, he was unhappy and miserable. Somehow life had bogged down and somehow the future had no promise and no hope.

(b) I believe that the extremism of some people today is produced by this lack of purpose. For who are these extreme people anyway? Often they are individuals who are not very prominent, and to join a cause and oppose other folks gives them a sense of being involved in something important. People who can form a kind of conspiracy against others have the same childish joy as boys forming a secret club or girls organizing a secret sorority. The tragedy of the whole extremist movement is its witness to a way of life that has found no constructive purpose worthy of men who must give as well as receive.

III. This leads to the third point, which is that the young man recognized his personal responsibility. In this, of course, he differed markedly from us, and here he has something very important to teach us.

(a) Something that impresses me very much today is a growing lack of personal responsibility for what happens to us. If you read the contemporary novels, you must be impressed with a general spirit of blamelessness that fills most of them. Here are people portrayed living like pigs and then very much upset when they begin to feel like pigs. There is never any indication that this stale, corrupt life is any fault of the people themselves, but on the contrary, they talk about being betrayed and disappointed by life. Their lives are all mixed up and complicated by silly choices and stupid behavior but never the slightest hint of personal blame. I sometimes want to cry out to these people, "For heaven's sake, what else can you expect if you live like this? If you want to find life, then listen to Jesus and obey him." But you will read a long time before finding a modern novel picturing people in any other guise than victims.

(b) It is refreshing to look at a young man who believes there is a good life that he has missed. I am sure that he had stood in the crowds more than once and listened to the Galilean teacher. Jesus impressed him as having what he knew he wanted and must find. He had listened to this prophet from Nazareth speak, and the words carried authority and hope. So there came a time when he could wait no longer and ran to hear the secret. He knew he must do something about it, and there was no profit in bewailing the sadness of his life and wallowing in his despair. There was someone who could tell him what he needed to do and he must go to him quickly.

(c) He asked, What shall I do? There is a sense, of course, in which he was quite wrong because the good life is not mere busyness. It is being. We shall never find it by doing or by obeying the commandments. But he was quite right in recognizing that nothing could happen until he

made the choice and opened up his heart. It is true that there is always something we have to do before we can find life.

IV. The last thing to note is that Jesus said people must lose to win. It is the paradoxical nature of life that the young man could not accept. This is no general teaching that all wealth has to be sacrificed but a specific word to a specific young man who found that his possessions stood in the way of finding what he sought.

(a) The first impression of the Christian life is always sacrifice. Jesus goes out of his way to make clear that there is a cross in every life. He speaks of the joyful life but never of life that is cheap or easy. Often this frightens us away as it did the young man. We are likely to ask if it is not possible for us to make a deal with him. We are willing to give him this much but not everything. To this he makes no answer, and he will not bargain. There is no giving part of ourselves and withholding something for our own purposes.

(b) But we have to believe that what we will receive is well worth anything that it costs. If the young man could have understood how Jesus loved him and how it was out of this love that he gave his command, he could have been saved. It is for us to believe that God puts his demands upon us not because he wants to make us squirm but because he wants to help us live.—Gerald Kennedy.

Illustrations

OURS—OR WHOSE? The commuter train was clanking its way into the city terminal. A valiant effort had been made by one of two companions to read a newspaper. The obituary page had been reached at last, and suddenly there was a low whistle. "Did you see this? P. G. is dead!" "How much did he leave?" came the almost mechanical reply. "Everything!" the newspaper reader answered laconically. "Everything!"—Elam Davies.

IDENTIFYING OUR NEED.   Arthur Miller, one of our outstanding playwrights, was discussing the stage and what makes a drama great. He said that in any successful play there must be something that makes the audience say within themselves, "My God, that's me." Well, here is a great drama, and if we look at that young man and say within our hearts, "That's me," it will have done its work. Then we will know what we must do to receive eternal life which he came to give to all who are willing to ask for it and able to receive it.—Gerald Kennedy.

Sermon Suggestions

MARRIAGE AND DIVINE PROVIDENCE. Text: Ruth 2:1–13. (1) *Then*—The providence of God in bringing together Ruth and Boaz. (2) *Always*—High ethical standards from both parties should prevail in courtship. (3) *Now*—Recognize both the hand of God and personal decision and responsibility. Let love protect and not selfishly exploit the parties in this new experience.

A POSITIVE PICTURE FROM A SOMEWHAT NEGATIVE REPORT.   Text: 1 Thess. 2:1–8. Virtues needed in those who preach and teach the gospel: (1) A clear perception of the truth. (2) Purity of motive. (3) Honesty of approach. (4) Concern for God's approval. (5) Gentleness. (6) Yearning, self-giving love.

Worship Aids

CALL TO WORSHIP.   "Be not conformed to this world: but be ye transformed by the renewing of your mind, that ye may prove what is that good, and acceptable, and perfect, will of God" (Rom. 12:2).

INVOCATION.   God of renewal and reformation: you raised up brave and able men and women to reform the church. We confess we have lost our way again and need new reformation. We are content with easy religion, with too many things and too little charity; we cultivate indifference. Lord, let your word shake us up, and your spirit renew us, so that we may repent, have better faith, and never shrink from sacrifice.—E. Paul Hovey.

OFFERTORY SENTENCE.   "And he said to them, 'Go into all the world, and give the good news to everyone' " (Mark 16:15 N.T. IN BASIC ENGLISH).

OFFERTORY PRAYER.   Lord Jesus Christ, as we are partners in the proclamation of the good news of your love, so let us enjoy our participation in what we give as well as in what we live.

PRAYER.   Lord Jesus, teach us to live as they should live who have eternity to live in. Lift us more and more into the steadying exercise of an immortal bearing. Give us the courage this day to sift all that we hold here in our hands, and may we keep fast nothing but that which fits our destiny with thee. For thy name's sake we ask it.—Paul Scherer.

EVENING SERVICE

Topic: God's Inescapable Nearness
TEXT: Phil. 4:4–8.

Paul tells us, "The Lord is at hand." This is the way the Lord himself says to us, "I am at hand." It is not because we live in his nearness, but because he promises that to us. This fact has its source in him, not in us. And why? Because the Lord has a name, the name Jesus Christ.

I. How near is the Lord? As near as one born as I was born, though probably under much more primitive circumstances; as near as one who has a glass of wine with me under the disapproving eyes of the onlookers; as near as one who passes through the experience of death as I will have to do, but under more horrible conditions. This is how the Lord is at hand. Whether I think about it or not, whether I believe it or not makes no difference. He is at hand for me anyhow.

(a) Because that is true, because we live on the basis of what has already happened, we therefore live also on the basis of what is to come. We live from Jesus Christ, and we live toward Jesus Christ. Timewise, Paul placed the Lord's coming not very far ahead. Of course, he was mistaken about that detail. But what of his belief that the goal of his life and the goal of all the world signifies Jesus Christ? A person with Paul's perspective lives not only in anticipation of the meeting he will attend tomorrow evening, that book he will read this afternoon, the examination he will stand in the spring, the trip he will take next summer, his wedding this year, or the surgery he will undergo next month. He lives toward the day when God will be all in all, for then neither death nor little faith nor sins will be able to separate us from him any more. And he knows that the entire world moves on toward that day.

(b) But what does that mean? It means that God is always out ahead of us. The totality of what is out there is neither the wedding nor death nor meaninglessness, but God. However, such an argument sounds completely different from what we find in the Old Testament. In the Old Testament, when the prophets speak about the nearness of the Lord they mean the near wrath of God (see Zeph. 1:14–18). To be sure, the wrath of God came. To be sure, no one who has not come to grips with the God of the prophets understands anything about God.

(c) However, this wrath fell upon the very one who is even now near us as the Lord. He passed through this day of wrath. God now wears the face of Jesus Christ. God lets us look into his own face and heart in Jesus. What, then, is awaiting us at the end? Not darkness, nothingness, or extinction, but God! This hope stands over all the world and over every event. So nothing about that has changed, even if Paul did die before the whole world achieved this goal. For this reason, the Lord is near.

II. We may have trouble believing what Paul says to us in our text. But we can practice it. And that is far more important. In four sentences, Paul tells us how to practice it today, tomorrow, and the next day, whether we can grasp its full significance yet or not.

(a) Look at the first of Paul's four sentences: "Rejoice in the Lord always; again I will say, rejoice." The most important thing for us to do is to rejoice. Paul is well aware that we need to be told to do it. Why? A person can, surprisingly, will to rejoice. One can work at the problem of seeing what our Lord who is near us gives us day by day.

(b) Consider Paul's second sentence:

"Let all men know your forbearance!" Again, we can live by the nearness of the Lord if we take special pains to observe others and their needs and questions— even if it hurts us. We need very much to do that, at least until we can get free from ourselves at a few points and actually see other persons.

Hundreds of our decisions, decisions we have arrived at with wisdom and common sense, would have been different if we had made every effort to see their possible effect on other persons. As wise and sensible as they were, our decisions were wrong after all. How remarkable it is that God's love for us becomes real to individuals only when they begin actually to practice love and make themselves open their eyes and become aware of other persons.

(c) Consider Paul's third sentence: "Have no anxiety about anything, but in everything by prayer and supplication with thanksgiving let your requests be made known to God." Once more are summoned to practice something. If we refused to pray until prayer welled up spontaneously within us, we would never learn to pray at all. We have to practice even that. As to anxiety—of course, we do worry. And we do not help matters by pushing it down into the subconscious.

(1) What did Paul have in mind? Certainly not precaution or provision, so that we would give no thought to having something to put on the table for breakfast! He had in mind solicitude, worry, dread. "What might happen next?" Paul had in mind the sort of calculating and scheming that so often shuts up our heart.

(2) He had an excellent solution to the problem: Pray! But pray in such a manner that thanksgiving is already in your prayer. Then all of the nervous tension would be removed. Perhaps we might experience once again a little foretaste of how it will be sometime, when God is all in all.

(d) Now consider the last of Paul's four sentences: "And the peace of God, which passes all understanding, will keep your hearts and your minds in Christ Jesus." Those words, dear friends, sum up, of course, all that we experience with the practice that we have been talking about.

In brief, it is always God himself who becomes great and strong in us. We do not keep our own hearts fixed on Jesus Christ —his peace accomplishes that. We do not overcome the tumult and confusion and perplexity of our mind with our own peace —his peace does that again and again.

III. The nearness of the Lord consists in the fact that he takes a firm grip upon our heart and our mind a long while before we understand and grasp it. This is the nearness of the Lord: he awaits us with his kingdom, and his kingdom shines into this life of ours even if we are far from believing it.—Eduard Schweizer.

SUNDAY: NOVEMBER FIRST

MORNING SERVICE

Topic: God and Our Choices
TEXT: Luke 6:12–13.

Choices are like legs. They give us movement and help us to go places—on our own. Choices are also like doors. Through them we enter into new areas, but they also shut us off from old areas. Choices are personal, necessary, and decisive. We often need help in making them. Our text shows Jesus at a time of crucial choice in his life: the appointment of his twelve apostles. The account is more than a page from his life; it is a means of insight into decision making and how God relates to us in it when we ask his help.

The time finally came, the text suggests, when Jesus decided to single out certain persons for an assignment in his name.

It was a service time. A crucial decision was in the making. A vision of human possibilities was taking shape in his heart and mind, and Jesus felt the pressure of planning to fulfill it. The text tells us what he did as he reached the point of concern.

I. *How Jesus decided.*

(a) Under pressure to decide, Jesus withdrew to pray about the coming decision: "In these days he went out into the hills to pray."

Choices and decisions should be steeped in the flavor of prayer. Prayer lifts the spirit and heightens the consciousness. It lights up the mind, exposing the dark corners of thought. Prayer lets dialogue with God happen. "He went out into the hills to pray."

(b) Due to the nature of the concern, Jesus set himself and "prayed through": "and all night he continued in prayer to God."

All decisions of a major nature need to be bathed in prayer—open, unceasing, unhurried prayer. A set of choices was in the offing. Jesus wanted his thoughts and impressions corrected or confirmed. He wanted to explore his options in a spirit of reverence and illumined thought.

(c) Having "prayed through," Jesus seized the moment and acted upon his decision. "And when it was day, he called his disciples, and chose from them twelve, whom he named apostles."

II. *Freedom to choose.*

(a) Like us, Jesus also had to make choices. It is so easy for us to overlook this as we emphasize his commitment to the will of God. But that commitment was only the framework for making his decisions. Jesus was not caught and held in a determined schedule of events over which he had no control or in which he had no voice. He was not branded in mind and soul to use his freedom under compulsion. His freedom was like our freedom: It was true freedom. He had to handle that freedom, as the temptation accounts plainly show. Yes, Jesus lived out his life like us, making choices as he went along.

(b) Jesus kept his decision within the framework of his love for God. This fact helps us to understand the praise he received from God: "Thou art my beloved Son; with thee I am well pleased" (Luke 3:22). His right choices were worthy of praise. He was living out the constraints of his freedom and his deepest character was showing itself in his choices.

(c) No one has escaped the demand to choose between paths to follow, doors to enter, and possibilities to entertain, not even Jesus. Yes, he too had to choose his friends, his apostles, his style of ministry, his approach to handling problems. He had to choose. He too had to invest in freedom. He chose to keep himself in the pleasure of God. He used his freedom to serve God's bidding and help others find release and relief. He used his freedom wisely, assured that God would help him rightly shape his end.

III. *Making wise choices.* All of us who are serious about God and life want to be able to look back over our years with some satisfaction about the choices we made. We all want to rejoice that our decisions worked meaningfully and fruitfully for us. We want to take some pride in the fact that our lives were not shaped by accident or chance but by heavenly design, and that God was at work with us as we lived and made our choices.

How can we seek to make wise choices? How can we plan for guided and God-approved decisions? The text supplies us with a set of ready answers.

(a) Enter the decision-making process with seriousness. Make each decision knowing that all your past is invested in each act of decision.

(b) Prayerfully study the matter to be decided. Wisdom from Scripture can illumine the matter. Prayer will help steady the mind and spirit to handle the burden of deciding. A firm commitment to God will help to grant perspective. In all major decisions we need an adequate set of facts and a clear focus. Prayer and Scripture help us mightily in this regard. Both help us to see human issues from the divine side.

(c) Release all your feelings of insecurity and fears to God. Then stay open to fresh impressions and any last-minute caution or reinforcement God might give. We need God as we take the risk of a final decision about something.

(d) Make the decision in a reasonable period of time. If a decision is not made on time, time might make that decision unnecessary.

(e) Act on the decision, trusting God to oversee the full results of your action. We do decide, but that decision involves many factors beyond us. We cannot fully control our setting or circumstances. We must trust as though all depends upon God, and yet work as though all depends upon us, and let the results be as they will.

Jesus had to do that. Did he not choose Judas after praying all night? Did not God approve that choice of Judas as well as the others? The choice is understandable. The choice was fair. Jesus chose the twelve on the basis of their possibilities in grace. Judas began as did the others; he was a trusted disciple. Somewhere along the way his choices turned sinister. Judas was not chosen as a traitor; he became a traitor by his own choice. This was the risk Jesus took in choosing every one of the twelve.

Dr. Henry Sloane Coffin once asked, "Have you thought of Judas Iscariot as an answer to prayer? But among the twelve thus prayerfully chosen was one who turned out a traitor." Trust should be matched with honor, causes matched with commitment, and careers with character. But the basic factor is choosing to be and do. Judas failed in his choices, not Jesus in his. But God still controlled and used the consequences of that decision.

Be serious about making decisions. Bathe the decision-making process in prayer and reexamine it all under the searching light of Scripture. Yield all anxieties and fears about planning to God. Go ahead and make the decision. Then act on the decision with timeliness, trusting God to oversee the results. Jesus made his decisions this way. His method will surely work for us as well.—James Earl Massey.

Illustrations

PERSONAL GUIDANCE.   This is always a fearful danger. Magic gives all the answers, unravels all the difficulties, dazzles and overwhelms as the problems evaporate into thin air. But grace sends you out into the night of doubt and sorrow, and pushes you out on the road of uncertainty and fearful risk. Let a man bounce up to you and claim that he is certain of the guidance God has given him, and for the most part you can dismiss him as a pious guesser. Let him quietly come alongside of you, however, and say that he trusts the God who will lead him, and you will find a man who has unmistakably discovered the ground of personal guidance. There is no magic in God's way, no shortcut through struggle and failure, no bypass for the valley of defeat and humiliation. —Elam Davies.

INTELLIGENT DECISION.   Any decision we reach based on intelligence is a decision we have been helped to arrive at by God. Why did we get our intelligence if not for use? A comment made by Dr. Farmer will bear repetition. "We have not infrequently heard the prayer in pietistic circles, at the opening of business, 'May we have no ideas of our own,'—a prayer which, as a friend once tartly remarked, is only too often swiftly and completely answered."—Robert J. McCracken.

Sermon Suggestions

MARRIAGE AND THE FUTURE.   Text: Ruth 4:7–17. (1) The story of the marriage of Ruth and Boaz and the birth of Obed. (2) The significance: Marriage, while having current meaning in itself, points to the future. This future may be eclipsed by childlessness, early death of children, disappointing behavior of children, or problems unrelated to children. In any case, God blesses in his own ways those who invest responsibly in the future as they establish their homes.

PAUL AT WORK.   Text: 1 Thess. 2:9–13, 17–20. (1) His task. (2) His testing. (3) His triumph.

Worship Aids

CALL TO WORSHIP.   "What God the Father considers to be pure and genuine religion is this: to take care of orphans and widows in their suffering and to keep oneself from being corrupted by the world" (James. 1:27 TEV).

INVOCATION.   O Lord Jesus Christ, who art the Way, the Truth, and the Life, we pray thee suffer us not to stray from thee, who art the Way, nor to distrust thee, who art the Truth, nor to rest in any other thing than thee, who art the Life. Teach us by thy Holy Spirit what to believe, what to do, and wherein to take our rest. For thine own name's sake we ask it.—Desiderius Erasmus.

OFFERTORY SENTENCE.   "Truly, truly I tell you, unless a grain of wheat falls into the earth and dies, it remains a single grain; but if it dies, it bears rich fruit. He who loves his life loses it, and he who cares not for his life in this world will preserve it for eternal life" (John 12:24–25, MOFFATT).

OFFERTORY PRAYER.   Grant, O loving Father, that we may know in the depths of our hearts that nothing that is given to you is ever really lost. Let our lives be planted in your eternal purpose and so bear rich fruit.

EVENING SERVICE

Topic: Spiritual Greed: A Thirst For More Faith

TEXT: Ps. 37:1–9; 2 Tim. 1:1–10; Luke 17:5–10.

What were the thoughts of Jesus when the disciples came to him with the request for him to increase their helping of faith? He made a reply about faith the size of a mustard seed—very small and inconspicuous—and then told them a story about the way a servant is to be related to. Both of these are obviously strange and seemingly unrelated. Look at these passages with me a moment.

I. Jesus is not to be taken literally about the transplanting of a mulberry tree in the sea. We really don't need faith to do that, nor do we need it to move mountains.

(a) If those first-century disciples could see what we have done with some of God's world, planting a tree seaward and moving mountains would pale by comparison.

(b) What Jesus is saying in his hyperbole is not that we have enough faith to be gardeners with extraordinary power, but that we have powers of faith we haven't yet used. So, the task is not to garner more faith, or to make our faith greater, but to use what we already have. Indeed, a request for more faith before we've exhausted what we have is a kind of spiritual greed that betrays the very essence of faith, which is, at its heart, action and response to needs.

II. When I first read this passage I could not bring the part about moving the mulberry tree into line with the piece about the servant. But the more I looked at it the more evident it became. As it is the nature of a servant to serve the master, so it is the nature of belief to express itself as faith in action.

(a) So, as the servant doesn't get extra credit for doing his job, so the faith-er does not get an extra star in his or her crown for doing works of faith. Indeed, if Timothy is right, the Spirit of God does not make us timid but gives us power, love, and self-control. What that means is that all of life is then lived believing, faithing-it, taking the risk necessary to be called a person of faith.

(b) The table is an example of that. The man Christ died, believing, faithing-it. If you think he knew it all beforehand, OK, that's your prerogative. I don't think he did, frankly. He had preached the message, done his job, and exercised his faith, and in the Garden he gave it all into the flow of God. The cup says it: "If it be possible let this cup pass from me." That, to me, is not the prayer of a man who has read the script and knew the next steps and believed it was all necessary to play out some predetermined scenario. No. It is the prayer of a man who was ambivalent about taking the cup and who was not too sure about the will of the Father and its direction. "If it be your will," he said.

(c) If I am wrong about this, then his identification with us is a farce. He is not human at all, but an acting God who is going through the motions. I think he was human, knew the dilemma of human limitations and had to faith-it through not knowing all that was to transpire, but believing that God would be with him and with the entire life-and-death struggle. This faithing-it is the opposite of spiritual greed.

III. The bottom line to all this using what we already have before we ask for more, has a very practical effect. It lifts our vision.

"Give us more faith," they said. "Use what you have," he said. And that really is the better way. Then they, and we, can go back for a second helping.—Thomas H. Conley.

SUNDAY: NOVEMBER EIGHTH

MORNING SERVICE

Topic: Time, Talent, and Treasure
TEXT: Matt. 25:29.

This is a hard text: it paints a picture we would rather not see; it speaks a truth we would rather not hear. It implies an injustice and an inequality most of us find difficult to accept. It cuts across the conventional wisdom of what the teachings of Jesus are all about, and this is just the reason we should be forced to examine this text.

I. The parable is called the parable of the talents. And as a talent was a denomination of ancient money, it would appear that this is a story about money and its use. The master gave to three of his servants sums of money. The text tells us that the money was "entrusted," which means that the master expected to have it back. It was not a gift, and not even a loan, for there is no reason to believe that the servants were in need. The money was given to the servants to be held upon the master's return. The text suggests that there was an expectation as to the management of that money, for it says that he gave the sums to each "according to his ability." Not only were they not given equal sums; but their capacity to manage the sums given them was also unequal. Everyone did not start either with the same sum or the same ability.

(a) And we know what they did with the money, how their ability was put to work. And when the master returned to settle his accounts, we know that the first servant invested his five talents and got two more, thus giving his master seven back. The second servant did likewise with his two and got the same rate of return, returning to his master four talents. The third servant, however, fearing his master, and being a cautious soul, did not risk his talent and returned exactly what he had been given, one talent. He thought that his master had more confidence in the others than in him, hence the small initial investment in his abilities. And he shared his master's lack of confidence in himself; and fearing to lose what little he had, "he went and dug in the ground and hid his master's money."

(b) Now, if we were to rewrite this story according to our image of what a good master should do, assuming, of course, that the master is God, we would have the master say to the now terrified servant, "There, there; I understand your fears and your ambitions. I know you have a learning disability as far as figures are concerned, and I know that you wanted to do what was right. It could be worse: you could have lost all of my money in some foolish investment."

(c) But that is not how the text reads. The poor servant is harangued for his caution and deprived of the little money he has preserved by that caution. And "the moral" of the tale is that he who has will get more, and he who hasn't will get to hell where such men will weep and gnash their teeth: not a pretty sight.

II. As a first step toward the rehabilitation of this text, I want to suggest that despite the popular title attached to it as the parable of the talents, the story is not about money at all, but about time, and not just about any time, but the time in which we find ourselves, the time between the beginning and the end, the "time being," as W. H. Auden would put it.

(a) This story is told by St. Matthew between the story of the wise and foolish virgins and the story of the last judgment. It is the second of the three final stories Jesus tells just before he is delivered up to captivity and the death on the cross. And so this parable is among those most significant last sayings of Jesus concerning the end both of his ministry and the end of the age of which his ministry was a sure and certain sign. Jesus was always warning his followers that the end of the age would come like a thief in the night, with great suddenness, without warning or preparation, and therefore, the faithful were encouraged to be watchful.

(b) We may laugh at that silly eschatology, that sense of premature apocalypse, but is that so strange a litany? I think not. Living within the shadow of our own home-grown apocalypse, there are some who are equally quick to say that there is neither good nor need to do much of anything: the end is at hand. There is an anxiety to our times, a fear that says that time is no longer on our side. The greatest crime is that such fear has cheapened and debased our use of the present, what time we do have.

III. In these last parables about time, Jesus warns that what counts is not so much how we anticipate the future, but how we use what time, what resources we are given: how we redeem the present.

(a) The parable of the talents has nothing to do with investment, and everything to do with engagement: what we do with what we have where we are. When the master in our parable went away, he did not tell his servants how long he would be or when he would return. He left them with a splendid sense of insecurity. The burden of the text is not on "what do we do when he returns," but rather, "what is to be done in the meantime." Jesus' meaning is unmistakable; we are not simply to wait until he comes, until it all ends. As it was true for Jesus, it is true for his followers: "We must do the works of him who sent us," and, "we must not grow weary in well-doing."

(b) The third man, the subject of the parable of the talents, suffers from what we may well call a loss of nerve. He is given this opportunity and he finds himself in a state of paralysis. Filled with fear of God and fear of himself, fearful that he will not succeed and fearful of the master, he plays the safest game possible: no risk, no fault. "If I don't try great things, I get credit if I don't lose great things." Who can ask for more than that? I will give back what I was given. What might have been an example of prudence, a virtue most esteemed in the Bible, becomes in fact an example of cowardice and selfishness. Rather than trying to enhance what has been entrusted to him, the servant is more interested in protecting himself; his is a denial of the trust that has been given him.

IV. This is not the first time Jesus uses money, coin of the realm, to make a very clear point about the use of that which belongs to God. Remember in the tricky question about Caesar's coin, Jesus asks, "Whose face is on it?" "Caesar's," say his questioners. Then render to Caesar what is his, and to God what is his. And since we are created ourselves in the image of God, imprinted with his likeness even as was Caesar's coin, so we too belong to God and must give ourselves and what we are and have to God who gave them to us.

(a) Talent belongs to God: God gives us ability and opportunity that we might better do the work he has given into our hands to be done. In not using his talents to the fullest of his limited ability, the servant of our story cheated God by not giving full value. And if a talent is to grow, it must be put to use. The most gifted and profound talent, unpracticed, unemployed, never put at risk, is as good as nothing. A great talent or a modest talent—if they are to have the chance to do good things in behalf of the one who grants them, they must be practiced, used, and employed. And if the talent given by God is not used, if the gift is not practiced, you will lose it.

(b) Now, a clever exegete and a cleverer preacher can put our minds to rest about the terrible tale of the talents. We understand this to be an eschatological tale about the end of the age and an encouragement to good works in venture capital. The simple maxim, simply put, is "no risk, no gain." It is an extreme story told in extreme times; we may now better understand it, but what on earth does it have to do with us?

V. This is a story about time, about the right and good uses of time, and about the time in which we are found: the time being, now. It is a story as well about talent, not money, but the ability and the opportunity God gives us to use our time to his glory and the help of his people, here and everywhere. Jesus tells this story near the end of his own time to warn that we will be judged not on how much we have, or even how much we get or give,

but on how wisely and well we use what we have in the time that we have. God has great expectations: and so must we!

(a) This then, is a parable about stewardship, and so is this sermon. You are asked in the time that you have to use what you have been given wisely for the kingdom of God. That means that you must consider not only how you spend your time, but how you spend your money and use your talent as well. The gifts that you have do not belong to you: they are not yours to possess; they are yours to improve, and if you do not, you will lose them. The parable and life are very clear.

(b) Stewardship means returning to God what belongs to God: your self, your talent, time, and treasure. How you do that is up to you, but that you do that cannot possibly be at issue for a Christian who takes the gospel seriously. Obviously, I want all of you who care for this church and its ministry to be stewards of the resources you have in behalf of this church. You need to do much more than you have ever done before, much more than you think is your fair share, much more than you had planned to give. And why? Because the work and witness of the church of Jesus Christ require no less. That is why.—Peter J. Gomes.

Illustrations

NEEDING ONE ANOTHER.   We need others to help our search for God's will, whatever our specific circumstances of life. We need others to correct our sometimes imbalanced interpretations of the Bible. We need others to give opportunities for sharing our time and resources. We need others to provide support when we experience suffering, setbacks, and temptations. We need others to control our sinful pride and greed when all is going well and when we are successful in terms of the world's standards. "For none of us lives to himself alone and none of us dies to himself alone" (Rom. 14:7 NIV).—David O. Moberg.

OUR ALL TO GOD.   The believer who would be evangelistic in thought and action must make available to his Lord all that he is and has. All ten tenths should be acknowledged as belonging to the Lord. One tenth should be dedicated as holy to him (Lev. 27:30). After this action by faith and love, the Christian is free to ask his Lord for the leading of the Holy Spirit to ascertain how much his offerings should be to the work of the kingdom. The believer who dares to step out on faith to dedicate all that he has as belonging to the Lord, with a decision to use it to help others to come to know him, can be unusually used and blessed by the Lord.—D. Wade Armstrong.

Sermon Suggestions

IT MAY SURPRISE US. . . .   Text: Amos 5:18–26. (1) That the day of God's judgment could find us weighed and found wanting. (2) That we cannot buy God's favor with pious acts. (3) That God tests our religion by our acts and attitudes toward others.

CHILDREN OF GOD.   Text: 1 John 3:1–3. (1) Through the love of the Father. (2) For a glorious destiny. (3) With a purifying hope.

Worship Aids

CALL TO WORSHIP.   "Each one, as a good manager of God's different gifts, must use for the good of others the special gift he has received from God" (1 Pet. 4:10 TEV).

INVOCATION.   Our Father, we come before you as people with rich gifts, which we have received through your providence. Open our eyes today, and give us renewed confidence in what we can do for one another with our own special gifts.

OFFERTORY SENTENCE.   "Give, and it shall be given unto you; good measure, pressed down, and shaken together, and running over, shall men give into your bosom. For with the same measure that ye mete withal it shall be measured to you again" (Luke 6:38).

OFFERTORY PRAYER.   Lord, as long as we say there is nothing we can do, nothing

is what we likely will do. As long as we decide somebody else should do the work that needs to be done, make the sacrifices that need to be made, or carry the crosses that need to be carried, we will likely allow, and even insist, that others do what you want us to do.

As long as we decide the good we can do is too insignificant to matter one way or the other, and therefore really not worth doing at all, we will provide ourselves with a nice-sounding reason to disobey you.

As long as we are more concerned about what's in it for us than we are about what we can do for you, we'll neither believe in our hearts nor practice with our hands the words of Jesus when he said, "It is more blessed to give than to receive."

As long as we convince ourselves to go ahead and take as long as we wish before we get around to seeking first your kingdom and righteousness, we will play well the game of delay and lose badly the life of decision.

Joshua of old speaks to us still: "How long will you go limping between two gods? If Baal be god, follow him; if the Lord be God, then follow him! As for me and my house, we will serve the Lord!" —Gordon H. Reif.

PRAYER.   Eternal God, who has bared your fatherly face to us in Jesus Christ, we give you thanks for the love in which we have been created, for the mercy by which we are sustained, and the grace by which we are saved. Make us faithful stewards of the mystery of this faith, this hallowed, sacred treasure that we bear in earthen vessels. Forbid that we should only exult in mercy and forgiveness; Grant that we shall be driven to share by word of mouth and deed of life the good gift of eternal life. Deliver us from the judgment that any have perished because of our failure to share your word, your love, your truth, your life.—Paul D. Simmons.

EVENING SERVICE

Topic: Concerning Prayer
TEXT: Luke 11:1.
It is of very great significance to me that the only specific request the disciples of Jesus made of him for themselves was the

request concerning prayer. "Lord, teach us to pray." This is important because it suggests that it was in the area of his religious experience, in the area of his experience with God, that Jesus was most utterly compelling. So compelling was he that with unerring insight his disciples put their hands on this key to the meaning of his life, the accent, the flavor of his power and contagion.

I. The basic proposition underlying our need for prayer is this: We wish never to be left, literally, to our own resources. Again and again, we discover that our own resources are not equal to the demands of our living.

(a) We know that we are not self-contained. We know how utterly dependent we are upon so many things around us. Our dependence upon those we know and upon many whom we do not know is evident. How contingent our present life is upon life that has gone before!

(b) We do not often, however, apply our sense of dependence to our personal relationships to God. What is the most dramatic utterance that we make when pressure bears down upon us? We cry out something to somebody. Sometimes we do it in conventional ways, and sometimes in ways that are not quite conventional. But in dire necessity we always recognize the poverty of our little lives. We feel that we can't go on alone if left to our little resources, however powerful we may seem to be at other times.

II. Now prayer is one of the most searching, and I think one of the most comprehensive, methods for tapping resources that are beyond ourselves.

(a) It is possible to draw upon resources beyond ourselves. You will recall the man to whom Jesus said, "This can be done, if you have faith." And the man replied, "I have faith, help thou my lack of faith." It is as part of the awareness of faith itself that the sense of the lack of faith arises. The resource that is within us is the clue to the resource that is beyond ourselves, and this we tap in the experience of prayer. The thing within me is also that which is without. I tap the resource that is beyond me by making conscious contact with the resource that is within me.

(b) Now, if this presents a true picture, then some preparation is very much in order. It takes time to learn how to tap the resources that are beyond ourselves. And we are all in a hurry. Our lives are moving at a rapid rate. We cannot reach to the support we need if we do not take time to ready our spirits, to prepare ourselves. We must have time for quiet and some place where we can have an atmosphere of quiet outside, before what is outside begins to move inside our consciousness.

III. It is important to recognize that we cannot prescribe the rules by which spiritual power is available to us. Who are we, with our little conceits, with our little arrogances, with our little madnesses, to lay down the conditions upon which we will accept the resources of life that sustain and confirm the integrity of our being? No, we must learn how to be quiet; and this takes discipline. We must find, each of us for himself, the kind of rhythmic pattern that will control our stubborn and unyielding and recalcitrant nervous systems and nourish our spiritual concerns and our growth in grace.—Howard Thurman.

SUNDAY: NOVEMBER FIFTEENTH

MORNING SERVICE

Topic: Mankind's Unfailing Lamp
TEXT: Ps. 119:105.
Psalm 119 speaks of the Bible in terms of such a light. "Thy Word is a lamp unto my feet, and a light unto my path." We need that light. But we who stand in the Hebrew-Christian tradition have something more to say than that. From the Old Testament and more especially from the New Testament the divine voice calls to our hearts, Never fear! Travel on. No night is so dark but God will see that there is a light in our darkness. The glory of our faith is that no one need miss his way; God provides light in the dark to walk by.

Consider with me how this lamp gives unfailing light. We might speak of it as a three-purpose lamp.

I. For one thing, it is the book of the beautiful.

(a) Not only because as Keats said, "Truth is beauty," but because of its incomparable poetry and prose, its haunting expression of timeless insights and events, is this lamp itself beautiful and in turn the means whereby we perceive the beautiful. Renan, the French critic and man of letters, described the Gospel according to St. Luke as "the most beautiful book ever written." It is not extravagant to extend that title to the Bible as a whole. The most familiar version, the authorized King James Version, has been called "the noblest monument of English prose."

(b) How skillfully the translators chose their words from our rich vocabulary! They preferred, for the most part, short words: "Blessed are the pure in heart, for they shall see God." In Ruth, how the wording matches the setting: "The Lord do so to me, and more also, if aught but death part me and thee." Say aloud to catch the stately rhythm of the opening words: "In the beginning God created the heaven and the earth." Or the impassioned cry of the prophet Amos: "The lion hath roared, who will not fear? The Lord God hath spoken, who can but prophesy?" The more lyrical beauty of the Psalms: "The Lord is my shepherd, I shall not want." The Lord is my light and my salvation: whom shall I fear? The Lord is the strength of my life; of whom shall I be afraid?"

(c) Turning to the New Testament, who would deprive himself of idyllic loveliness of the story of the birth of Christ? The parables are significant, of course, for what they say, but also for the "luminous simplicity with which they say it." Elsewhere one comes upon sentences "that in sudden gleaming beauty shine like stars": "Let the peace of God rule in your hearts." "Be strong in the Lord, and in the power of his might." "He looked for a city which hath foundations, whose builder and maker is God." "They need no candle, neither light of the sun; for the Lord God giveth them light."

II. "Thy word is a lamp unto my feet, and a light unto my path."

(a) This unfailing lamp shines on the road we travel. Consider the Bible as a guidebook. In the New Testament Christianity is described as "the way." In the Old Testament there are frequent references to the religious life as walking the way or the path. The metaphor is a good one. Life is a pilgrimage, a journey, and we need a road map. The Bible provides it. It indicates the route, marks the road, points out the highway to God.

(b) Great indeed was the company who labored to record the Word of God, to preserve it, and to transmit it. How different they were, and yet how one they were in their conviction that life is from God, in God, and to God. So we may speak of the book they gave us as "an age-long diary recording the search of man for an understanding of God," and also as the record of God's age-long search for man. It is indeed a guide for our lives. To those who seek its wisdom and follow its truth, it is indeed an unfailing lamp casting its beams down through the days and years.

(c) The psalmist spoke of God's Word as light—"a light unto my path." Light is one of the great words of the Scriptures, and so is life. And both are closely related. Scientists have made fascinating discoveries concerning light and have shown us how the simple ray of sunlight takes to itself the wonder and mystery of the divine. We know of particular rays that stimulate our health and the growth of vegetation. On the other hand, other rays of light are successfully used to destroy disease-producing germs, bacteria. The photoelectric cell has many beneficent uses, and its basic principle is a beam of light. So the Bible is a many-colored light that releases power within the mind and soul of the person who reads it reverently, intelligently, expectantly. Light has always been associated with life. How early and how widespread has been man's worship of the sun as the source of life! In many psalms God is spoken of as the sun, whose beams carry healing. As nowhere else, we find within this book concentrated life-giving power.

III. Who does not need power? You and I need power to live decently and well, power to manage human relationships, power to do one's duty, however irksome, power to overcome temptation and to replace bad habits with wholesome ones, power to run a straight race, to keep on doggedly when the terrain is difficult and the energy flags, power to handle well adversity and prosperity, power to triumph over disaster and sorrow, moral failure and death. Here is power.

(a) The reason why so many of us are spiritually anemic is that our spiritual diet has been poor, deficient in life-giving vitamins. The central figure of the New Testament, the Word of God incarnate, declares: "The words I speak unto you they are spirit and they are life." Power for healing us of our self-despisings, for curing us of our basic fears, power for useful, outgoing living is often transmitted to us by the Spirit of God through the book of books. Too many in every age have found it there for us to be skeptical or indifferent. For within its pages we encounter the source of all power and wisdom and love, the God who has said through his Son Jesus, "All power is given unto me. . . . go ye. . . ."

(b) But the power made available through the Bible is not alone for our solitariness. It speaks to us together, in community; to the nation, to the nations. It sets moral standards. It insists on recognition of the dignity of man, of his rights as a child of God made in his image. It is through the revealing Word of this book that we encounter the power that makes for righteousness, the power which enables frail children of earth to work miracles of social transformation.

(c) That is the conclusion of the matter. Take the book off its pinnacle. When the blackout descends, you have a lamp. Use it. Before the darkness falls, become familiar with this unfailing light. Before you journey far, become bewildered or lost, study this road map. When you need strength for daily living, and before you are conscious of such need, make regular devotional reading of the book of books part of your spiritual diet.—David A. MacLennan.

Illustrations

THROUGH BIBLE TO GOD.   Imagine that you are standing in front of a solid brick wall. Only if there is a window in the wall can you see through it. Even then, if you look at the windowpane, you cannot focus on the view beyond. So you must look through the windowpane and focus your attention on what lies beyond. Similarly, the Christian does not so much look at the Bible as through the Bible to the encounters between God and man which are described on the printed page, and which we could not see at all if we did not have the printed page. If we just look at the Bible, its statements and propositions, the image beyond may be blurred; we have not come to know God as fully as we should. But if we look through the Bible, it serves as a kind of window by means of which God and Christ are brought into true focus. Thus the Bible is the means by which God can make his impact upon us today.—Robert McAfee Brown.

GOD SEEKING US.   It is not the right human thoughts about God which form the content of the Bible, but the right divine thoughts about men. The Bible tells us not how we should talk with God but what he says to us; not how we find the way to him, but how he has sought and found the way to us; not the right relation in which we must place ourselves to him, but the covenant which he has made with all who are Abraham's spiritual children and which he has sealed once and for all in Jesus Christ. It is this which is within the Bible. The Word of God is within the Bible. We have found in the Bible a new world, God, God's sovereignty, God's glory, God's incomprehensible love. Not the history of man but the history of God! Not the virtues of men but the virtues of him who hath called us out of darkness into his marvelous light! Not human standpoints but the standpoint of God! —Karl Barth.

Sermon Suggestions

THE GREAT DAY OF THE LORD.   Text: Zeph. 1:7, 12–18. (1) A serious call for silence before God. (2) A fearful warning of judgment to follow. (3) An unexpressed need for deliverance (promised in chap. 3).

FACING THE TIME OF TESTING.   Text: 1 Thess. 5:1–11. (1) The *when* is unpredictable. (2) The *how* is definite: with alertness; with faith, love, and hope; with mutual encouragement.

Worship Aids

CALL TO WORSHIP.	"Man doth not live by bread only, but by every word that proceedeth out of the mouth of the Lord doth man live" (Deut. 8:3b).

INVOCATION.	O Thou who hast spoken to human hearts in many and various ways, especially in thy Son, but also through the words of holy people of old whom thou didst inspire, grant that today we may hear thy voice as the Holy Spirit takes the words of ancient Scripture and makes them the living word of God.

OFFERTORY SENTENCE.	"He that findeth his life shall lose it: and he that loseth his life for my sake shall find it" (Matt. 10:39).

OFFERTORY PRAYER.	Lord of life, grant that we may love thee so well that we will not withhold money or time to spread the word that Jesus Christ cared enough to die for lost sinners.—E. Lee Phillips.

PRAYER.	Most loving Lord, you are our Father and we are your children. You are good, gentle, loving, merciful, patient, holy, righteous, and faithful. You have given us an example for our lives in what you are and in what you do. If we say we dwell in you, we ought to do as you do. You have not called us to uncleanness, but to holiness. The blood of your Son Jesus Christ has cleansed us from all sin, not that we should continue in darkness, but rather walk in the light, as he is in the light. You did choose us in Christ before the foundations of the world were laid, that we should be holy and without blame before you through him. We are your workmanship, created in Christ Jesus for good works, which you marked out beforehand, for us to walk in them. Grant therefore, we pray, that our life may answer to what we profess and that the light of our good works may so shine before men, that they may glorify you.—Adapted from Thomas Becon.

EVENING SERVICE

Topic: The Pharisee and the Publican
TEXT: Luke 18:9–14.

The thing that makes this particular story quiver is that Jesus allows us to overhear two persons' private prayers. Both characters etched by Jesus live on every busy street and even sit on church pews. Their prayers were as opposite as they themselves. Let's look first at the Pharisee and then at the tax collector.

I. The Pharisee was so good that he could hardly stand it. You have known some people like that. He had a personality like a stop sign. Can't you just see him swaggering up the steps of the temple like he owned the place? We overhear him pray as he catalogs his negative virtues and reminds God of his good deeds. And as we listen to them, notice at the outset that he does not ask for anything in his prayer. There is not one single petition, only self-congratulation.

(a) Listen to him as he catalogs his negative virtues, his virtues of omission. He says, "I thank God that I'm not like other men." We soon find out that he's not really grateful to God, but he is exceptionally pleased with himself. And so he begins to parade before God his virtues. But notice the root of his folly, his illusion, is "I'm not like other people." He imagines that he is somehow insulated by his religious practice from being like other human beings, an illusion that can overtake a preacher, a deacon, or any regular attender of church.

(1) He spoke of swindlers, of the unrighteous, and of adulterers. We can just imagine as he prays his prayer and he says "swindlers"—can't you just see his eye glancing off the tax collector, because after all tax collectors worked for the Romans and fleeced their fellow citizens. Can't you imagine him looking at that tax collector and saying, "What in the world is he doing in church? He's not the church type; he has no right to be in church because he's a sinner."

(2) And so we begin to sense the spirit of a Pharisee particularly emphatic to establish that he is not like the tax collector. He enjoyed the comparison. It bolstered his own ego to compare himself to an ir-

religious scalawag. It was no competition. But you know: no one who despises a neighbor can pray. He is deluding himself to take the pose and posture of prayer at the same moment he despises his neighbor. We listen as he divulges what he does not do and as he projects what the tax collector must be like.

(b) And then he goes on to list his good deeds, his virtues of commission. He said, "I fast twice a week," as though God did not know that already. "I give a tithe of all that I make." The Old Testament only required him to fast one time in a year. He found himself wanting to excel religiously, and so he fasted twice between Sabbaths. And when he tithed, he was the kind of person who figured out a tithe with a slide rule. He tithed not only his income, but his garden; and not only his garden. When he bought something at the market he tithed on the produce as well. Quite naturally, he enjoyed a good impression of himself in his own mind.

(1) How repulsively religious this character is. He was one of the weeds of ritualism. Five times he finds it necessary to use the first person pronoun "I" in some form. We find this individual so impressed with himself that he is constantly self-centered even in the midst of prayers.

(2) "Two men went up to the temple to pray." Or rather say, one man went up to brag and the other went up to pray. The Pharisee was altogether unconscious of any defects. Isn't it really true, as both Paul and Jesus have pointed out, that there is not one further away from God than someone self-righteous. It is possible for our attitudes to be a "before-people religion" rather than a "before-God religion." I wonder about this individual. Could it be that down deep inside psychologically he was trying to avoid God's presence in his life? Look at his religious activity; he is constantly involved in religious activity; he's fasting, he's tithing, he's praying, he's doing all the things he should do. But I wonder if in his case religious activity is a substitute to avoid God's presence, of which he is afraid and which he is avoiding. Could that be the case?

II. But the tax collector was so bad he could hardly stand it. We see him enter the temple, neither swaggering nor prepossessing. I dare say we are to envision an individual driven to the temple, a person who is there because he must be present, because he has a burden. He has a problem. When Jesus mentioned this figure in his story, listeners likely bristled, because Jesus now presented a man who was a tax collector. Bear in mind that society among the Jewish population had already decided about tax collectors. There was already a category for them; they already knew who all tax collectors were. They were all the same. And here comes Jesus, with that annoying kingdom-of-God point of view, and before he is done, he is going to intimate that the tax collector is nearer to God than the Pharisee. That had to be a mite shocking.

(a) In our day we have become more conscious of body language. Look at his body language. His physical actions tell the story. He does not feel worthy to stand in a prominent place, but he stands afar off. The normal posture for prayer was standing with one's hands above one's head, looking up to God. This man had taken his hands and made fists and pummeled his own chest with contrition. And we hear his prayer. His prayer is only a sentence but when the heart is stirred it speaks in telegrams. His prayer is an outburst: "O God, mercy me, the sinner." All of his body language—the tone of voice, the posture, the place in the building—everything expresses where he's coming from, how he feels. "O God, mercy me, the sinner."

(b) One of the things I like about that one-sentence prayer is that there is not an empty phrase in it. There is not a cliché to be found. Every word is from the heart. It's real prayer that comes from a person's struggle and conviction of sin and genuineness of repentance. And so he comes, with a broken, contrite spirit, to a God who will not despise him. Isn't there something downright lovable about the tax collector, despite his image and what you are supposed to think about him and all the rest? He was a sinner. There's no need sentimentalizing that. But he comes to a God that will accept him, and it's in that context that we hear the story today, so conscious that there are people who do not feel they have to stand a far ways off and pummel their chests.

III. In a grand climax Jesus delivers a punch line to his story. "The tax collector went down to his house justified and the Pharisee did not." There in a kingdom-of-God moment, when this world's understandings are set aside, and when the perspectives of God's will are put in place, we are able to see something important about the gospel, about Jesus, about God. There is a grace lurking beneath this universe that is so radical. Indeed, I am convinced that the most radical idea loose in the world is the idea of grace. There is nothing more radical. And it is a grace that reaches out to anybody, not just church types, anybody, in love and acceptance. Before Jesus is through he has turned the popular view upside down with a grace that is radical. "The gate of heaven is so low that you cannot enter it except on bended knee." The kingdom of God is an exclusive club: it is for sinners only!

(a) Let us hear the parable as we would, as we need to, in the midst of our own lives and our own development, and if there be someone who has never experienced God's love, God's acceptance, we would invite you to hear the gospel today and allow it to wash over you. Hear the divine acceptance. Feel the acceptance. Accept it.

(b) Two individuals invaded the temple precincts to pray. Actually the first thanked God that he was not a sinner. The second confessed that he was a sinner. Jesus, who knows both human secrets and the judgments of God, exposed the phoniness of the first and the authenticity of the second. His story and his verdict require an encounter of ourselves with ourselves and with a God we cannot dupe and with a grace downright amazing.—Peter Rhea Jones.

SUNDAY: NOVEMBER TWENTY-SECOND

MORNING SERVICE

Topic: Coming Up Thankful

TEXT: Luke 2:33–38 NEB.

You've probably never heard a sermon about Anna. After all, we are told little about her, except the name of her father and his tribe, and her exemplary piety, and her age of eighty-seven. But, as I was re-reading the opening of Luke recently, I noticed this delightful verse in the New English Bible. "Coming up at that very moment, she returned thanks to God." Enter Anna on cue—and she came up thankful. There, I said to myself, is my thanksgiving text and our theme this morning is "Coming up thankful."

I. It's not easy, is it? We can all dredge up a bit of gratitude to God when asked to do so in church, and perhaps a little more when an entire nation is summoned once a year to be thankful. But are we people who spontaneously come up thankful as each new experience comes our way?

(a) There are those moments in even the dullest day when something good, and often unexpected, happens. It may be a letter; it may be meeting an old friend; it may be something unusually funny; it may be what we call the human touch breaking into the routine; it may be a gorgeous sunset; it may be a remark or a paragraph in the newspaper that stops us in our tracks; it may be news of the birth of a baby or the death of a saint. Whatever it is, do we come up thankful?

(b) It's not beyond the reach of any of us to cultivate this glad and grateful response to the good things that happen. But what about the bad things? If we get really bad news about our health or our solvency, it would for most of us be hypocritical to say, "Thank you, God," but we can surely be grateful for the grace we are promised to meet it with courage and with hope. Even if the news is dreadful and soul-shattering, when the first shock has passed it is possible for us to hear somewhere the voice of Christ saying, "My grace is sufficient for you," and to be thankful.

(c) Even if it is impossible for us to summon up a spirit of thankfulness when we are agonizing in body or in mind, we can be thankful for the heroic souls in whom that miracle happened. We are surely grateful to belong to the household of faith, to a communion of saints that includes saints and martyrs who have praised God from the depth of their suffering. Such a "coming up thankful," such victorious grace, such an insight into the heart of God, leads us to say with the psalmist, "Such knowledge is too wonderful for me; it is high. I cannot attain unto it." But we can be thankful for the thankful who blaze the way for us and surround us with their love.

II. Probably all of us here have experienced the gratitude of hindsight. We are able to be thankful now for experiences that were almost intolerable for us when they happened. But that's not our theme this morning. We are thinking about thanksgiving now, thanksgiving that springs up spontaneously.

(a) It's one thing to respond to an invitation to give thanks to God in a hymn or a prayer in church and to remember special blessings for which we are grateful. We are doing that this morning. But it's another thing to be the kind of person who responds gratefully at the very moment something happens. What we read about Anna is that "coming up at that very moment, she returned thanks to God." This isn't a question of dutifully remembering what we ought to be grateful for. It's a question of being the kind of person who naturally and impulsively gives thanks at the very moment something breaks into the regular routine of our days.

(b) We are being led by Anna to ask a deeper question than "am I willing to give thanks to God for all he has done for me?" The question is rather: "Am I the kind of person who always comes up thankful?" The average congregation that hears the invitation "let us give thanks to God" is probably saying inside something like: "All right. I'll try to get into the mood." But supposing the invitation were, "From now on will you try, by the grace of God, to be a thankful person?" That's getting down to business.

(c) What comes up, what spills out in a moment of crisis depends on what we have inside. When something bumps into your life what spills out tells a lot about what you are inside. The grumbler will grumble; the cynic will shrug his shoulders; the

irritable will be irritated; the thankful will thank God. Of course, we're not all so easily labeled with our characters set in concrete. But, as we get older, we are more and more seen to be dominated by one particular characteristic, and our friends can often predict fairly accurately how we will react in almost any circumstances. I can think of nothing better for any of us here this morning than to be set on the course of becoming truly thankful people.

III. How do we do it? Let's have another look at Anna. I see her as the kind of old lady who always comes up thankful when she saw this baby in the temple. She might have said, "I wish they wouldn't disturb my prayers with these ceremonies. Yelling infants get between me and God." She had no children of her own but was thankful for those given to others. And God rewarded her with an insight into who this infant Jesus was—the promised Messiah. She was so excited she couldn't wait to spread the news. "Coming up at that very moment she gave thanks to God; and she talked about the child to all who were looking for the liberation of Jerusalem."

(a) Yes, but how did she get that way? Luke tells us. She haunted the temple that was the center of her life. With perhaps a touch of exaggeration Luke says that she "worshiped day and night, fasting and praying." Translate that into our terms, and we learn that acquiring a thankful nature has a lot to do with the habits of regular worship and prayer. We are unlikely to develop a spirit of thankfulness that is always ready to overflow when the crisis comes if we have gotten out of the habit of worship and prayer. The spontaneous "coming up thankful" is much more likely to happen if we have been willing to exercise the discipline of set times when we pray alone and when we worship with others.

(b) If there is some special thanksgiving in your heart today it is because a general thanksgiving has been implanted in your soul. May God so work in us the grace of a grateful spirit that at this very moment, and whenever in the future the unexpected happens, we may come up thankful.—David H. C. Read.

Illustrations

CAUSE FOR GRATITUDE.   I read recently of Cardinal Mercier, who was one of Belgium's heroes in World War I. When he lay dying of a torturing disease he said, "I leave my fate in God's hands, and only ask one thing of him, to draw such glory as is possible from my humble person, at whatever price it may cost. . . . I thank the good Lord for having permitted me to follow him at least part of the way to Calvary and to have suffered on the cross."—David H. C. Read.

WELLSPRINGS OF RECONCILIATION.   "We love because he first loved us" (1 John 4:19). Gratitude for God's redeeming love thaws the icicled springs of our minds and opens the streams of refreshing memories that flow out in all directions toward our fellow men. When we recall what God in Christ has done for us, we are lifted out of our bitter thoughts about what others are trying to do to us. As we stand before the altar trying to comprehend with all saints what is the breadth and length and height and depth of the love of Christ which surpasses knowledge, our love gains new dimensions and our reconciling thoughts take new directions. We remember persons and points of reconciling that would not occur to us on the street.—Ralph W. Sockman.

Sermon Suggestions

WHEN THE LORD IS SHEPHERD.   Text: Ezek. 34:11–16, 20–24. (1) He seeks his scattered flock. (2) He restores his flock to peace and health. (3) He establishes himself as the faithful guardian of his flock.

THE KINGSHIP OF CHRIST.   Text: 1 Cor. 15:20–28. Three stages: (1) He came in weakness. (2) He was raised in power. (3) He will at last yield all things to God the Father, "that God may be everything to everyone."

Worship Aids

CALL TO WORSHIP.   "It is a good thing to give thanks unto the Lord, and to sing praises unto thy name, O most High" (Ps. 92:1).

INVOCATION.   Grant, O Lord, that as we sing thy praises our hearts may be filled with the gratitude due thee, for salvation in our Lord Jesus Christ and for all the gifts and joys of life.

OFFERTORY SENTENCE.   "It is in God's power to provide you richly with every good gift; thus you will have ample means in yourselves to meet each and every situation, with enough and to spare for every good cause" (2 Cor. 9:8 NEB).

OFFERTORY PRAYER.   Lord, our Creator, some of us do not have a great deal of money to give today. We know thou knowest our hearts. Would that we had more we might share, yet, such as we have we give, praying thou wilt multiply it mightily.—E. Lee Phillips.

PRAYER.   Let us give thanks for the blessings of God. Thanks be to God. For health and strength to do our daily tasks, thanks be to God. For family and friends who support and encourage us, thanks be to God. For minds and bodies so wondrously made, thanks be to God. For the capacity to work and to earn our living, thanks be to God. For the nation in which we live—the land of freedom, abundance, and opportunity, thanks be to God. For the church, which keeps alive the hope of the world through the preaching of the gospel, thanks be to God. For the opportunity to give our offerings as an expression of our gratitude to God, thanks be to God. Most of all, let us give thanks for God's gift of his Son—Jesus Christ. Thanks be to God for his inexpressible gift! Let us pray: O God, we are a most privileged group of people. We have mentioned a few of the things for which we are thankful. To name everything would be impossible. Help us to be more generous givers because we are reflections of your generosity. Help us to be more willing givers because we have seen what your son gave for us. Help us to be more joyful givers because we have seen that giving is the key to abundant living.—Thomas L. Reynolds, Jr.

EVENING SERVICE

Topic: Living for Harvest
TEXT: Ps. 126.

I. The Bible is loaded with images from agriculture. The reason is obvious. The people lived close to the earth. They might not readily understand the deep things of God, but they knew about the cycles and processes of nature. Thus, when Isaiah sought a picture of God's relationship to Israel, he turned to the figure of a farmer tending his vineyard; or when he wished to illustrate the power of the divine word, he pictured the rain nourishing the earth, "making it bring forth and sprout." Christ turned frequently to the experiences of rural life, from the parable of the sower, the proclamation of the gospel, to the illustration of his relation to his disciples as the flow of life from the vine to the branches. We are reminded that the quality of a tree is determined by the quality of its fruit, and the people of Sychar pouring out to hear the one identified as Messiah were like fields white for harvest.

II. Paul pictured the variety of ministries done by Paul, Apollos, Cephas, and Christ for the Corinthian Christians as the various works required to make a crop: "I planted, Apollos watered, but God gave the growth." He saw in the planting and germination of seed a picture of our death, burial, and resurrection in Christ; and he took the norm of sowing and reaping as a warning from nature, "Whatever a man sows, that he will also reap." The psalmist reflected on better days in Zion, days when the surrounding nations bore witness to the blessings of God on the people, "The Lord has done great things for them." The Jewish people were unique among their neighbors in believing that God was Lord of nature rather than a fragment of life or the processes of the earth. Thus, the psalmist could pray for a change in the course of nature, like the filling of the riverbeds in the Negeb desert, or like the sowing of tears for the harvest of joy.

III. I have always felt a disadvantage in reading Scriptures for not having had a reservoir of farm experience from which to draw my understanding of God. The limit of my agricultural existence was lived out of the tiny boundaries of a "victory" garden, a cow, and a few chickens on the edge of Houston during World War II. One insight that I gained from my childhood observations as well as from the biblical illustrations from nature is that farmers live for harvest. I am sure that there are many rewards from plowing, sowing, cultivating, and spraying crops, but the absence of a harvest tends to rob the whole process of its meaning. I also learned from gardening that the harvest comes at the convenience of the crop rather than at the convenience of the farmer. A great deal of patience and informed timing go into the completion of a crop. There are few immediate rewards in the work of nature. The wage comes at the end of the labor. Finally, I learned that with all of the tedious efforts and sincere intentions in the world, the outcome of the crop is determined by forces greater than the farmer. The farmer is dependent on the ups and downs of nature.

IV. Like all metaphors, the comparisons of the growth of a crop to the people of God has its limits, but I still believe that it speaks to us in this urban setting. We live not for today but toward the harvest. While we wait for the harvest, we have a stewardship responsibility for the care and nurture of God's world. Finally, God gives the increase.—Larry Dipboye.

SUNDAY: NOVEMBER TWENTY-NINTH

MORNING SERVICE

Topic: Repentance
TEXT: Luke 19:5 NEB.

The evangelist gives us a few brisk brush strokes from which emerges a rather complete sketch, if not portrait, of Zacchaeus. We know he was a "little man," small of stature, and we know that to overcome his smallness, he climbed up into a tree. By this, we also know that he was a man of initiative. He was not content to be lost in the crowd, nor was he unwilling to take risk, not the least of which was falling down or to be seen as foolish or pushy. We also know that he was a tax collector and thus very rich. Furthermore, Jesus describes him as a son of Abraham, so we know that he is a Jew.

I. The external circumstances of this story do not give us any reason to think that Zacchaeus was agonized or tortured of spirit, a man who indulged in self-hatred and was caught in some sort of cosmic identity crisis. We have no reason to believe that he did not enjoy his tax collecting and did not enjoy the high standard of living that came from it, and we have no sense either that he longed to be accepted by his fellow Jews as just one of the guys. We don't know any of this, but we do know that he was curious and eager enough to satisfy his curiosity by pursuing this Jesus to the branches of a sycamore tree.

(a) He was a Jew behaving as a Roman lackey. If he was rich in things but poor in soul, as Harry Emerson Fosdick puts it in his great hymn, he is also living a precarious lie in which the principle of easy come easy go applies with rigorous and impartial logic. And if he appears secure and happy when he is insecure and miserable, he has to work twice as hard to stay in the same place, for he not only has to persuade others of his illusions; he has to persuade himself as well. This is hard work. Is this not why most of us fakers, and I suspect there are at least a few here this morning, run so hard and play so hard? We do not disapprove of leisure, idleness, and silence because we are Puritans. We are not work-aholics, play-aholics, and diversion-aholics because we like work, play, or diversion. We do all of this and more because in order to maintain our illusions, our facades, we must always do something, lest we stand there and confront ourselves coming around the corner.

(b) Could it be something of this dilemma that persuaded Zacchaeus to stop chasing himself for a few moments and to pursue Jesus of whom he had doubtless heard? For by whatever motivation, Zacchaeus took the initiative. The text tells us, "He was eager to see what Jesus looked like." It doesn't say that he wanted to repent of his sins, or give up his money, or

even to talk with Jesus. Unlike the many others who come to Jesus, he had nothing to ask of Jesus: no daughter to raise from the dead, no friends to heal, no wound of his own to be made clean. There is no reason to believe that he wished to encounter Jesus at all, simply to see him for himself. And so he climbed that famous tree.

(c) Now it would be fun to speculate that Zacchaeus wished to see and not be seen, that his motives were private and passive, and a brilliant sermon could be preached on how God invaded his privacy and called him out into the light. It is appealing to see Zacchaeus as the unseen observer, looking over the heads of the crowd at Jesus, hidden by the leaves of the tree, even as Nicodemus sought out Jesus hidden by the darkness of night. But then, out of curiosity I looked up "sycamore" in an old commentary, and it described a tree frequently planted by the roadside in ancient Palestine. Its growth habit is irregular and it tends to be one sided with low, long branches hanging over the roadway, and with very thin foliage. Such a tree was hardly a seat of obscurity; in fact, one seated in it would be hard to avoid. It was Zacchaeus's curiosity and his initiative in seizing the opportunity to satisfy that curiosity that put him in the vision of the Savior, and there he was, not only observing, not only seeing, but he was seen, and he was seen of him who is the light of the world.

II. It is Jesus who takes it from here. It was Jesus who saw a man who wished to be seen and to see, and Jesus gave him his opportunity. And he did this in a most remarkable way: he did so by putting himself in the hands of his drafted host. Zacchaeus did not invite Jesus to dinner, and he certainly hadn't planned on doing so today, and yet Jesus said, be quick, I wish to submit myself to your hospitality today. The action is so precipitate, so hasty, so spontaneous, it almost appears as if in some perverse sort of way it is God who planned the whole thing and that whole episode was a way of placing Zacchaeus in the presence of the Christ.

(a) For Zacchaeus the waiting was the work, waiting for the moment when he could confront himself, waiting for the moment of redemption, waiting and watching for it to come and then to pass on to some other place, some other day, some other soul. But in that great mystery of faith, redemption did not pass by. Redemption stopped and invited Zacchaeus to join in; he became part of that for which in secret and ambiguity he had waited. He was no longer the obsessed. Nor was he simply the observed. He was engaged, a participant in his own rebirth and renewal. And that is why the story of Zacchaeus is not the story of Zacchaeus, but rather the story of God's loving purposes in the redemption of the world by our Lord and Savior Jesus Christ, the engagement of the human and divine!

(b) We could go on and discuss what happened at that impromptu luncheon party to which Jesus invited himself. I could talk about how the repentent Zacchaeus gave half his possessions to charity and made fourfold restitution. And we could preach about the disapproval of the crowd who censured not Zacchaeus, but Jesus, for entering the house of a sinner and dining with him. Consider that crowd for just a moment: usually they ooohed and aaahed when Jesus performed one of his tricks, when he healed somebody's running sores or cured a cripple or gave sight to the blind or fed a hungry and curious crowd. But when Jesus opened the heart of sinful man and allowed him the freedom to repent, that is to turn from his false self to his true self—for that is what repentance is—freeing him from the need ever to fake it again, the crowd disapproved and murmured.

III. But is this not just the sort of miracle of God's coming, his Advent, for which we ought to wait in hope and joy? Is it not the fundamental miracle of our faith that God gives us the opportunity to turn from our sins, to be freed for ever from our sense of faking it? To repent is to be allowed to discover and affirm our authentic identity, our real name and character in Christ. To repent is not simply to give up, it is also to find and be found, to embrace and be embraced, it is the joy of self-discovery in Christ.

(a) At Advent, the church teaches us that we wait to catch a glimpse of the Lord. We wait for his return, and looking down the long highway of time and hope, we light candles to illumine his way and ours, that he might better see us and we him. We don't have to go on faking it, fearing exposure and censure, trying to be more than we are and less than we ought to be. Our humanity is the object of God's love, and we wait for the lovingkindness that transforms us from the fakers to the faithful. "Love is not consolation: it is light."

(b) But Advent requires that we do more than wait, more than sit on the branches of our sycamore tree in our pews and observe the passing show, interested but uninvolved. We have to engage ourselves to be engaged, to hope that by and by God will catch our eye, and we his, that in such a way he will enter into our homes, our hearts, and our lives and reign there forever. The Advent hope of the repentant is to turn from what we think we are to what God intends for us to be. We want to see the light, and in that light we too would be one with him who is the light of the world, even Jesus Christ, the Savior. —Peter J. Gomes.

Illustrations

THIS IS SIN. Two men board a train. One of them perhaps does something sensible, the other something stupid upon entering the coach. But as they look out, both notice that they have taken the wrong train and are going in the wrong direction. That one man was reasonable and the other stupid is a difference between these two men; it is a difference, however, which has no significance in relation to the fact that both, whatever their individual differences, are going in the wrong direction! This is what the Bible means by the word *sin,* the total perverse direction of our life, the tendency away from God. In this train all men are traveling, says the apostle. He himself, one of the most blameless, according to human opinion almost a saint, says of himself quite clearly, "O wretched man that I am, the evil which I would not, that I do; the good that I would, I do not." —Emil Brunner.

REPENTANCE BEFORE THE FACT. Anyone seriously tempted to get a divorce at fifty or sixty and "begin life all over again" with a young woman should consider this: That if a sixty-year-old man has a splendid old lime tree standing in his garden and suddenly decides that a nut tree would look better he can if he likes cut down the old tree and plant the young one in its place, but he will not be able to sit in the shade of it for a long time—until he is lying under it, in fact, in his grave.—Theodor Bovet.

Sermon Suggestions

FROM ANGUISH TO HOPE. Text: Isa. 63:16–64:8. (1) Like the prophet, we may mourn over the sins not only of the world, but also, and especially, of God's people. (2) Like the prophet, we may be impatient for God to act and bring an end to our grief. (3) Like the prophet, we may—and rightly!—cling to the assurance that God will finally shape us into vessels worthy to serve him.

A CAUSE FOR GRATITUDE. Text: 1 Cor. 1:3–9 (MOFFATT). (1) Full power to speak of one's faith. (2) Full insight into the meaning of this faith. (3) A rich variety of spiritual endowments.

Worship Aids

CALL TO WORSHIP. "The Lord is nigh unto them that are of a broken heart; and saveth such as be of a contrite spirit" (Ps. 34:18).

INVOCATION. O God our Father, the source of our lives and our redemption, we are often burdened by many cares that seem to gnaw away at us in our quiet moments. The demons of doubt, insecurity, and anxiety often seem to control us and to undermine our faith. We feel, O Lord, that we are alone in our struggles and problems. We most earnestly pray, O Lord, that you will grant unto us a new vision and a new purpose for life that will help us to more effectively cope with the many burdens and cares we experience. Grant us new hope, this season of Advent,

that we may truly see that our human destiny lies in the coming of your Son, Jesus Christ. Help us to realize, most gracious Father, that in Christ Jesus we are freed from preoccupation with troublesome burdens and cares.—Rodney K. Miller.

OFFERTORY PRAYER. Let us give thanks to God our Father for all his gifts so freely bestowed upon us. For the wonder of your creation, in earth and sky and sea, we thank you, Lord. For all that is gracious in the lives of men and women, revealing the image of Christ, we thank you, Lord. For our daily food and drink, our homes and families, and our friends, we thank you, Lord. For minds to think, and hearts to love, and hands to serve, we thank you, Lord. For health and strength to work and leisure to rest and play, we thank you, Lord. For the brave and courageous, who are patient in suffering and faithful in adversity, we thank you, Lord. For all valiant seekers after truth, liberty, and justice, we thank you, Lord. For the communion of saints, in all times and places, we thank you, Lord. Above all, we give you thanks for the great mercies and promises given to us in Christ Jesus our Lord; to him be praise and glory, with you, O Father, and the Holy Spirit, now and for ever. Amen. —*Book of Common Prayer.*

PRAYER. Teach us to walk humbly before thee, O God, for all that we know thee so familiarly in Christ Jesus. And may we never sit down safely in the victory thou hast so dearly won through him, lest sitting there we come to think but poorly of it. We ask it for his name's sake.

EVENING SERVICE

Topic: Redeem the Time

TEXT: Eph. 5:15–20.

I. This text contains a double attitude toward time: both the positive challenge of making the most of the time and a negative assessment of "the times," and I fear that it's this negative attitude toward time that Christians have found most congenial. In fact, every generation has said its amen to this warning, taking a perverse pride in the uniqueness of its own brand of immorality, the way a gardner takes pride in a homegrown two-headed cabbage.

(a) I happen to believe that the "evil" the writer of Ephesians had in mind was not exceptional; in fact, just the opposite: it is banal, unimaginative evil which he calls drunkenness and debauchery, activities that are not unknown among us.

(b) There is self-destructiveness all around us, but we are blinded to it. Instead, what do we lament? We lament the lost power and privilege of the past, of days when children were polite, streets were safe, America was boss, men were men and hamburger was fifty cents a pound. You shouldn't think I'm speaking of a mentality common to older people, for whether you're eighteen or seventy-eight, whenever we look over our shoulder, it is to a happier, less complicated time.

(c) But what about today? How can we let go of nostalgia for yesterday and preoccupations with tomorrow in order to make the most of today?

II. There are many ways of thinking about time: the old pagan way was to escape it by celebrating the eternally recurring cycles of nature. The new pagan way is to seize it, to seize the day and drain every drop of pleasure from it, and to discard it. The Eastern way is to empty time of all significance until one attains a blessed state of uncaring extinction; and the communist way is to destroy time by destroying current institutions so that from their ashes the phoenix of something authentically new may arise.

(a) The point is that we try most of these or entertain most of these before we are even capable of hearing the way of Jesus, which is not to condemn time, nor to escape, seize, empty or destroy it, but to redeem the time.

(b) The Revised Standard Version translates the phrase: "Making the most of the time." That I understand. It means to buy cheap and to sell dear; it means keeping the factories running twenty-four hours a day; it means to be efficient, smart, and sometimes even driven by the clock on the wall or your own intestinal clock. But the Revised Standard translation does not do justice to the religious idea lodged in the word and therefore we translate the phrase, "redeeming the time." We do so with a sense of reluctance, knowing the even greater demands this translation places upon us. "Redeem the time" is a metaphor that, in all its contradictoriness, doesn't compute. If we take the word *redeem* in its first dictionary meaning, "to buy back" or to "buy up," or in its deeper sense of "to transform by God's grace," it appears that there is nothing so unredeemable as time.

III. But our worship offers a God who was baptized by immersion into time in order to redeem it. He was in every way subject to time. He was born; he aged; he grieved at the premature death of a friend, and shortly thereafter, he died.

(a) As the days ticked by when Jesus' body lay in the tomb, time should have done its traditional job on him; it should have erased him the way the sea claims sand castles and civilizations. It should have worn him smooth. Because it did not defeat him, it does not defeat us. History is going somewhere. It is moving toward an outcome when all our yesterdays and lost moments and missed opportunities may be reclaimed in the risen Christ. For he is not only subject to time as its slave, but he rules it as its Lord. Only in the power of resurrection can Paul tell us to do the impossible: "redeem the time, Christians, because Christ already has."

(b) And how, how do you bring that redemption to bear on your cross-section of experience? You begin by getting wisdom, says Ephesians, which is a way of seeing. So what is wisdom? It is more than the analytical knowledge that carves up the world into specialties and opportunities for making money. Wisdom has to do with finding your generation, your life, your constellation of opportunities in the plan of God, so that you see yourself as a bearer of the mystery.

IV. The primary response to mystery is doxology. Doxology (the praise of God) gathers up everything we know and do and offers it to God. Making the most of the time means getting good grades, giving stimulating lectures, writing books, mastering material, and preparing for the future. Redeeming the time means taking all these activities and hours and semesters from the "time-kept city" and saying, "O God, receive these to your glory, and now that I have done them in your name, take away my anxiety about their outcome, for always and for everything I give thanks to you and praise your name."

(a) Those who redeem the time find themselves out of sync with the times, sometimes articulating words no one wants to hear, engaging in acts of faithfulness that no one understands. You can't witness to your times if you are intimidated or swallowed up by them. In the Old Testament the prophets are always out of joint with their societies. So Jeremiah walked through Jerusalem with a

homemade wooden yoke across his shoulders symbolizing the coming servitude to Babylon. As a sign to Israel, God had the prophet Hosea marry a prostitute named Gomer. After a stint with the prophet during which she bore him three children, Gomer went back to the city to ply her old trade. Do you know what Hosea did? He followed her to the city and bought up all her time.

(b) That's a perfect image of what God did for Israel and for us. He loved us with a love beyond our capacity and pursued his faithless people to the "time-kept city," and there, through the ministry, death, and resurrection of his Son, he bought up all our time.—Richard Lischer.

SUNDAY: DECEMBER SIXTH

MORNING SERVICE

Topic: I Am Sure
Text: Phil. 1:6.

Poor Paul! He must have been either very insecure or else frozen stiff in his own past! At least it is the claim of some psychologists that at whatever point we are ourselves the most insecure, we make the loudest and strongest claims in order to assure ourselves that we really do believe what we say.

So persons, churches, and civilizations can become frozen stiff in these areas. To be dogmatic is to suffer from a frozen decision. Poor Paul said, "I am sure," when perhaps he should have said, "Right now it seems to me rather likely that . . ."

I. Or perhaps he had earned the right to say, "I am sure." Perhaps he actually was sure. His certainty, in any case, to a large extent changed the course of human history. Let us grant that insecurity and dogmatism are always ready tempters to an immature and an unearned certainty. But let us consider well whether there cannot be the kind of certainty that stems precisely from security, from insight, from open-mindedness, and from obedient maturity.

(a) Such certainty, in any case, is never based on external authority, be it church, creed, or book. However much these may

guide us toward the sources of certainty, they cannot give certainty. External authority is the acceptance of someone else's say-so. This acceptance evidences immaturity. It is precritical; childish, not childlike.

There is, however, another kind of certainty that is usually not accounted as such. This is the certainty of the critical. Have you not known people to say, "I am sure that no ultimate truth can be known by man"? With what certainty those in the critical stage will argue that one can know with certainty only analytical truth and sense knowledge only as probable!

(c) But those who have passed through the precritical and the critical periods and have truly entered into postcritical maturity know far better what Paul meant when he said, "I am sure." They know because they have seen; they know because they have experienced; they know because they go from light to light within the power of the Holy Spirit.

II. Paul could say, "I am sure," because he had witnessed God's mighty acts in history. The gospel of Christ was not mere academic speculation. Though Paul knew not Jesus in the flesh, he knew him in living experience. The life of Jesus was no mere theory; it was power to heal spirit, mind, and body, a life of abounding inner peace and freedom, a new kind of community, leveling the artificiality of human barriers and creating open, adventuresome human relations. God's act in the Christdeed was the power of his own love, beyond human origination and control. Paul lived within the burst of that new power unto salvation, made real and ready in history, which made him unashamed to say, "I am sure," because of what he had seen.

III. Paul could also say, "I am sure," because he had personal insight into the meaning of God's mighty deeds. These events for Paul explained experience and the course of history.

(a) Do you recall his majestic interpretation of the drama of history in the Epistle to the Romans? Do you hear his anthem of insight into the nature of love in the first Epistle to the Corinthians? How experience is lighted up by the reading of the Epistle to the Philippians! Only they who have worshiped the Lord God with all their mind in surrender of defensive pride and with critical honesty can give a reason for their faith at their level of experience and earn the right to say, "I am sure that God . . ."

(b) How often I have walked and walked in search of a faith more real and true. After each experience I have come back even more convinced that I am sure that I see what God has done and what this means for all of us frail and sinful people, who are nevertheless sovereignly created for God and for the community of his perfecting.

(c) Much more is one struck by the force of meaning of Christian truth to solve life's problems, when one really comes to see. As A. E. Taylor has said, "Knowledge is vision." Paul had more than the vision on the Damascus road. He had the vision of what Christ meant for the world. Therefore he could say, "I am sure."

IV. Paul could also say, "I am sure," because he had himself experienced Christ.

(a) He had been freed from the power of death and died daily. How he faced stonings, flogging, persecutions—all for the love of Christ! In prison he could exclaim, "For me to live is Christ, and to die is gain." Paul lived in the present, because

his past was forgiven and the future was in the hands of God. He would not mind earthly things, thereby becoming an enemy of the cross of Christ; for his conduct was in heaven.

(b) There is no substitute for personal experience. The mind can be convinced without the whole self feeling sure. Mere intellectual vision is sterile and unsatisfying. Laypeople, clergy, missionaries, even famous professors of divinity have spoken with me, disturbed for lack of conviction in spite of the fact that their minds were convinced of the truth of the Christian faith. Paul could say, "I am sure," because his whole self had experienced the power of the gospel.

V. But when all is said and done, Paul could most readily say, "I am sure," because the Holy Spirit witnessed with his spirit that God can finish that which he has begun, and this witness was the inspired experience of going from light to light.

(a) The Holy Spirit tolerates no closed system; he keeps leading us into all truth. The infinite Creator eternally evades being exhausted by his creature. The Spirit breaks through all human finalities. Where the Spirit is, there is life as adventuresome steering and no rigid rudder. Where the Spirit is, there can be no defensive dogmatism but a humble open-mindedness. There is no frozen decision of life, but a going from light to light as we obtain light within the living Word of God.

(b) The Holy Spirit is never a pampering parent nor a sentimental nursemaid, sparing us the risk and adventure of steering. While he provides no closed external authority, he does, of course, use the fixed stars of his own revealing, and the lasting landmarks of God's mighty work in history. But certainty comes only as we go from light to light, as we keep steering toward the distant, unfolding goal.

(c) When the Holy Spirit witnesses with our spirit, and when our lives are fulfilled within the will of God, then we become possessed with a certainty that needs neither external defense nor internal justification. Though we know in part, we nevertheless know that we know and, more importantly, we are fully known.

(d) This world is looking for certainty to

make it free and secure. Certainty can be had, but only at the price of doing God's will. Within that will are quietness and confidence. Within that will are peace and power. Within that will are both rest and creative satisfaction.—Nels F. S. Ferré.

Illustrations

FROM DOUBT TO FAITH. When I started for college my junior year, I told my mother that I was going to clear God out of the universe and begin all over to see what I could find. I could not swallow the Christian faith unquestioningly. I had to fight for it. And so it's mine! Every doubt raised against it, every question asked about it, I have faced often with agony of mind. I am not afraid of atheism; of all my disbeliefs I most certainly disbelieve that! And now in my elder years what a Christian of the last generation said I understand: "Who never doubted never half believed."—Harry Emerson Fosdick.

ONE LARGE HOPE. The Christian's final hope is based on communion, a union with God that is indestructible. Even in situations where we do not tangibly experience God's support, impossible situations without a glimmer of hope, even in these dark nights of faith we believe that God is near at hand. This is what is revealed in the resurrection of Jesus; death cannot sever our bond with God. All our smaller hopes are drawn from this one large hope. Yet Christian hope will often stand in contradiction to reality as we experience it. Death remains death, and suffering is a cry of the human heart to which there is no easy answer. Jesus based his hope on the unshakable conviction that God's power was at work in the world and that the reign of God would finally appear in its fullness. He hoped sufficiently in God not to try to hasten the reign of God by changing stones into bread or becoming the kind of political Messiah the crowds expected. The Christian moves through suffering, guilt, and death where in fact they have been broken through—that is, in the raising of the crucified Jesus.—Kathleen Fischer, *Winter Grace.*

Sermon Suggestions

TAKE COURAGE! Text: Isa. 40:1–11. (1) At last, God will show his power. (2) God's word will accomplish its purpose. (3) God will deal with his people with great compassion and tenderness.

WHY GOD WAITS. Text: 2 Pet. 3:8–15a. (1) God has his own timetable. (2) God gives us space to repent.

Worship Aids

CALL TO WORSHIP. "Let us draw near with a true heart in full assurance of faith, having our hearts sprinkled from an evil conscience, and our bodies washed with pure water. Let us hold fast the profession of our faith without wavering; (for he is faithful that promised;) and let us consider one another to provoke unto love and to good works" (Heb. 10:22–24).

INVOCATION. Lord, thou hast withheld nothing we need and given us more than we could ever deserve; therefore, we do not withhold our great praise of thee and we sing of thy salvation. Great thou art and greatly to be praised, O Lord of hosts.—E. Lee Phillips.

OFFERTORY SENTENCE. "Thou art worthy, O Lord, to receive glory and honor and power: for thou hast created all things, and for thy pleasure they are and were created" (Rev. 4:11).

OFFERTORY PRAYER. To thee, creator God, heavenly Father, we bring in worship and dedication a portion of the things that thou hast created and put in our care. Bless them that they may continue to fulfill thy purpose.

PRAYER. O God, our Father, we thank thee for the revelation of thyself to us, thou who at sundry times and in divers manners didst speak unto the fathers by the prophets, but in these days hast spoken to us by thy Son. Show us thy glory, whose face we may not see save in him whom thou didst send; and in him deliver us, not just from peril, not just from pain, but out of the bondage of our narrow, selfish ways into the freedom of thy love—for his name's sake.—Paul Scherer.

EVENING SERVICE

Topic: Creation and Re-creation
Text: Rev. 4:11; 5:9–10.

This concept of God as Creator and Re-creator runs all through the Bible. The opening pages of Genesis portray God's great creative act. Yet the world he created was marred. In theological language, it "fell." Because of human sin, thorns and thistles grow competing with the crops we grow for food.

The only way we can gain peace is not only to be created by God, but to be re-created by him, too.

I. Let us reexamine the affirmation of Scripture that God created the world.

(a) There is absolutely no question in the biblical writers' minds that God had created the world. We can reaffirm this belief ourselves today. Out of nothing God created the world. He made it, and it is his. The world is his because he did create it. There can be all sorts of statements and disclaimers to the contrary, but the earth is the Lord's. All our statements denying that fact are so much shouting in the end.

(b) The Hebrews had a unique way of affirming God's ownership of the land. God had given them the land to use, but the title always remained in God's name. The Israelites held temporary ownership and were forbidden to sell the land permanently (Lev. 25:23). Although the world was made by God and belongs to God, he allows us to use his world. Not only does he allow it, he wants us to use it. But in allowing us to use it, God also lays down some guidelines for us to follow.

II. Much like a parent whose small child asks to use the scissors will set some rules for doing so, even so has God established some rules for our usage of his world.

(a) The first rule is that we recognize God's ownership. When we borrow something from a friend, we normally take better care of it than we would if it were our own. If we truly accept the fact that this is God's world, and he is letting us borrow it for a while, we will use it in a different way.

(b) A second rule God sets up for our use is that we not abuse it. God decorated the world with beautiful trees, painted the sky a brilliant blue, scattered clear, sparkling rivers across the land, and threw in some majestic mountains for scenery. One day he came back to look at his world after we had been in it just a short time, and he was aghast! He had trouble even seeing through the cloud of smog that surrounded the earth. The trees were gone. The sparkling rivers were so filled with waste they could catch fire and burn. And his majestic mountains were gutted and raped by great strip mines! And God sat down by one of the polluted rivers and watched the beer cans and dead fish float by and said, "How can people be like that?" One rule for using God's world is that we not abuse it.

(c) A third rule God has established is that we share his world with all of the people in it. Yes, one of the rules for use of this earth which God has established is to share with others what God has loaned to us.

III. As one studies the Bible it becomes increasingly clear that not only did God create the world, he also re-creates or redeems it as well. Although God set some rules for using the world, people paid no attention to them. They disregarded the rules and the Rulemaker.

(a) But in such a Godlike act, God sent his Son Jesus to buy back the wayward people, to redeem them, to re-create them. Our text declares: "Our Lord and Our God! You are worthy to receive glory, and honor, and power. For you created all things, and by your will they were given existence and life" (Rev. 4:11). God is worthy to receive honor not only because he created the world, he is also worthy because in Jesus he re-created or redeemed it.

(b) Those whom God re-creates, those whom God redeems, have even greater responsibilities to respond both to God's creation and his re-creation. We who have experienced this saving, redeeming, grave of Jesus must respond in some way. Surely we will be more careful in observing God's rules for using the earth. We will recog-nize God's ownership and our steward-ship. We will use the earth and not abuse it. We will share what we have and not hoard it.—James E. Taulman.

SUNDAY: DECEMBER THIRTEENTH

MORNING SERVICE

Topic: Is Christ About to Come Back?
TEXT: Mark 13:32–33.

I. It is not often that I raise a question in a sermon title that can be perfectly an-swered in three words on the authority of Jesus himself. Speaking about the end of the world and his own return, he said: "But of that day or that hour no one knows, not even the angels in heaven, not the Son, but only the Father." If the angels don't know, if Jesus himself while on earth didn't know, then most certainly I don't know.

(a) You have only to read the New Tes-tament to discover that the first Christian communities to come into being lived in a vivid expectation that the Savior who had been born at Bethlehem, the Word who was made flesh and dwelt among us, would very soon come back and be re-vealed as the Lord and judge of the whole human race. To describe that event they often used the language and symbolism of Jewish apocalyptic writing, which is the name for the kind of writing that talked of great upheavals on the earth and in the heavens before the appearance of the Messiah who would rescue and vindicate the servants of God. Apocalyptic writing appears when men and women begin to give up hope for a human solution to their troubles. So the early Christians in a time of distress and persecution looked for an early return of Jesus, their Messiah, to wind up history and finally establish the kingdom of God.

(b) In the modern era, when the faith was challenged and the church lost its hold on the nations of the West, the Chris-tian hope was secularized. Not only was any idea of a sudden ending to human history dismissed but the kingdom of God now became a human utopia that would be reached as human beings more and more mastered their environment and modern science and technology sought new fields to conquer.

(c) Well, where have we come into the picture? One thing is clear. We are not living in a time when people comfortably expect either the gradual triumph of the church around the world, or the gradual arrival of some secular utopia. The sense of being on an escalator steadily moving up to a better world has vanished. So within the church there is bound to be a rethinking of the doctrine of the second coming of Christ as well as an outbreak of wild speculations as the year 2000 ap-proaches.

II. This is about the point in a sermon where a congregation may want to say, "Enough of this analysis and historical background. Tell us what you believe."

(a) That's what I'm going to do. But first, to clear the air, let me tell you what I don't believe and why. That's necessary because there is an interpretation of the second coming being circulated today that is being welcomed by millions who are scared by the kind of world we are living in and the threat of nuclear war. Here, roughly, is what is being taught:

(1) Christ is about to come back. All the signs are being fulfilled. It is all foretold. The climax will be the fearful battle of Ar-mageddon. But then Jesus will visibly ap-pear and he will draw up out of the chaos all who believe in him. (This is technically known as the "Rapture of the Saints.") So the elect will be safe and forever with the Lord.

(2) That, briefly, is the story that is being told. Of course, there are many in-ternal arguments about just when all this is going to happen, just how to interpret the Scriptures that refer to such events whether Christians will be raptured before or after the great tribulation, and many more.

(b) I cannot accept this teaching for at least four reasons.

(1) Jesus clearly said that no one knows the time of his return. And there is no time in history when you could not find wars and rumors of wars, earthquakes and other such signs.

(2) If we really believe that all future events have been already determined, and that, for instance God has decided that there will be a nuclear holocaust on a certain date, then we should have no incentive to work for peace, justice, freedom, or anything else.

(3) This kind of teaching asks us to conceive of the final triumph of Christ—an event that baffles our imagination—in crude literal terms.

(4) Most important of all is the sheer unchristian selfishness of much of this teaching. The New Testament speaks of a redeemed community, of a new creation, of a glorious consummation

III. That leads me to summarize what the doctrine of the second coming means to me, how it affects my vision of things to come and therefore surely my behavior now.

(a) It means that we are not adrift on an ocean of chaos. We are called into the stream of redemptive history that began when "the Spirit of God moved on the face of the waters" and ends when "the kingdoms of this world are become the kingdoms of our Lord and of his Christ." Human history thus has meaning and direction.

(b) The powerful truth that comes to me from this neglected doctrine is this. At a time when many are wondering where this world is really going and what awaits us in the end, I hear the ringing reminder that the end is Christ. What does that mean? Let me put it this way as Christmas draws near. The first coming of Christ shows me what life can be. His second coming assures me that it is his way that will in the end prevail. The light shines on in the darkness, in spite of the darkness, till the days come when the darkness is over and "the Lord shall be unto thee an everlasting light, and thy God thy glory."

(c) To believe in the second coming is not to hold peculiar ideas about the end of the world. It is to let oneself be drawn, here and now, towards that victory day. It is to renounce all cynicism and fatalism and do what we can right now in response to the call of the kingdom of peace and the Lord of love. The Christ who came at Christmas and will come at the end of time tolerates no slackers. "Take ye heed; watch and pray, for ye know not when the time is."—David H. C. Read.

Illustrations

CHRIST AT THE DOOR. Christians refuse to surrender the image of Christ standing at the door because in his death he has already opened the door to God's forgiveness and to an indestructible freedom and has become in himself an open door. The crowing of the cock or the blast of the trumpet comes through to their ears as sounds of a new day, the Lord's Day, when he comes to judge his people.—Paul S. Minear.

THE POWER OF EXPECTATION. We can trace in the history of Christendom something like a law, that the more vitally hope is present in the ekklesia, that is, the more powerfully life in the Spirit of God is present in it, the more urgent is its expectation of the coming of Jesus Christ; so that the fullness of the possession of the Spirit and the urgency of expectation are always found together, as they were in the primitive community.—Emil Brunner.

CHRIST IS ALWAYS COMING. The Savior is coming. He is not quietly sitting somewhere in eternity, waiting for a certain moment when he will suddenly plunge in. He is on the way. We may at all times have his future before our eyes. We may expect it every day. The coming of the Savior runs through Christian history, through God's working in the world, like a thread. If this thread is not to break, the Lord Jesus must ever be coming. Often there will be times of storm and thunder, of sorrow and suffering. Yet in all such storms, in all sorrow, at all times when we think we cannot go on, there will be new ways. New revelations will enable us to continue working and watching. There will come a time when our waiting and watching, which at all times has prepared the coming of the Lord Jesus, will be consummated.—Christoph Blumhardt.

Sermon Suggestions

A SERMON YOU COULDN'T AFFORD TO MISS. Text: Isa. 61:1-4, 8-11. (1) Because it encourages the oppressed. (2) Because it promises justice for those who have been wronged. (3) Because it celebrates God's deliverance as if it had already happened.

HOW TO PREPARE FOR THE COMING OF OUR LORD JESUS CHRIST.   Text: 1 Thess. 5:16-24. (1) Attend to your private prayer life. (2) Attend to your public witnessing. (3) Attend to how you live both publicly and privately.

Worship Aids

CALL TO WORSHIP.   "When Christ, who is our life, shall appear, then shall ye also appear with him in glory" (Col. 3:4).

INVOCATION.   Lift up our hearts, O God, that we may lift up our voices in joyful praise. Lead us by your Spirit into new and challenging depths of devotion, as we now seek to worship you.

OFFERTORY SENTENCE.   "Bless the Lord, O my soul, and forget not all his benefits" (Ps. 103:2).

OFFERTORY PRAYER.   Merciful Father, help us to remember that you have forgiven us our sins seventy times seven and more, that you have brought us through sickness and danger, that you have given us our daily bread, that you have been patient with us in our foolish ways. As we recall your providences, let gratitude well up within our hearts; let stewardship of what we are and have be the lightest of our burdens, and let joy and generosity overtake and surpass our sense of duty.

PRAYER.   O God, whose throne of grace is hymned with continual praise and thanksgiving, we add our voices to those of all the saints and angels and say,

"Thank you, Lord, for your love and mercy and power that flow constantly into our universe, filling it with hope and energy and redemption!" There is nothing in us that deserves your gifts, and yet you have chosen to share yourself with the very least of us, and to send your bounty upon us even when our hearts were not turned in your direction. Help us in recognition and gratitude to turn our thoughts and lives to you, and to align ourselves with your hopes and vision for our world. Use us as instruments for loving your little ones in all the earth—for seeing that they are fed and clothed and educated, that they receive the medical and technical aid they need, and that, with all of this, they hear the good news of your kingdom in Jesus Christ. Bless with your mercy in this holiday season all children who are away from home, all students who travel on the highways, all the elderly who languish in pain or loneliness, all patients in hospitals and inmates in prisons, all ministers and teachers of the gospel, and all servants of society. Let the hope that was born at the coming of Christ continue to flower among us, leading us to new heights of commitment and new depths of love for one another. For yours are the kingdom and the power and the glory forever.—John Killinger.

EVENING SERVICE

Topic: From Problems to Possibilities
TEXT: Luke 5:24-26.

I. Luke shares a brief but unforgettable drama of a man who experiences exciting possibilities in the midst of problems and difficulties that seem to totally overwhelm him. We meet this man in chapter 5 of the Gospel of Luke. As the curtain of the text rises, Luke begins to shine four spotlights upon different centers of the stage in this small Galilean town. Our attention is drawn immediately to these circles of light.

(a) Spotlight number 1—Jesus.

He stands straight and tall. He is the center of the Gospel of Luke. We have met him earlier. We know that at the time of his baptism by John in the Jordan River, the Holy Spirit descended upon him and remained on him. We know that he struggled with real temptations. Then he began to preach the gospel of the kingdom of God. Then we saw Jesus in Capernaum as he reached out in compassion to multitudes of sick people to heal them. Toward the end of verse 17, Luke adds a very powerful phrase about Jesus. He says simply, "And the power of the Lord was with him to heal" (Luke 5:17). That is a word which immediately announces the tremendous possibilities that are before us. God's power, according to Luke, is not some vague or general force. It is personal. It is present in a human life—in Jesus.

(b) Spotlight number 2—religious leaders.

Luke tells us that Pharisees and teachers of the Law had come from every village in Judea and Jerusalem. Look closely at them. Observe with me that they had not come to listen to Jesus because they wanted to receive his teaching. They had come to find fault! They had come to attack! They remind us that it is possible to find fault even with Jesus. We really find what we are looking for. Our discoveries are so largely influenced by our expectations! Negative experts—religious leaders were there.

(c) Spotlight number 3—paralytic.

We know very little about the paralytic. We are not given his name. He is described to us by Luke in the very fewest words, as, a man who is paralyzed. As I look closely at this man, I see not just a nameless or faceless person. I begin to see people who are my friends. Paralysis is a terrible experience. There is not great pain—only numbness.

(d) Spotlight number 4—friends.

Spotlight number four shines upon the friends of the paralytic. No names are given to them in the gospel of Luke, either. They appear quite suddenly and without introduction. Somehow these people had heard Jesus or had heard about him. They had faith that he could make a difference for their friend. Then they were stopped short. They had no way to get their friend to Jesus. Every doorway was packed. When faced with difficulties, they began to dream of new possibilities. Someone saw an outside staircase. The

man could be lowered through the roof! They removed the roof tiles and lowered the man into the room. Jesus didn't condemn them because of their interruptions. Luke says, "And when Jesus saw their faith he said, 'Man, your sins are forgiven you.' " Notice that Jesus saw the faith of the friends.

II. Let's think back, for a moment, upon this inspiring picture which Luke gives us, to recall together four steps in moving from problems to possibilities.

(a) We must believe that Jesus still turns problems into possibilities. The compassionate Lord is here with us! Luke wants us to understand the scene that he gives us is not just something that happened nineteen hundred years ago. The possibility of that kind of miracle is here today.

(b) Receive the help of the caring friend. The paralytic doesn't get to Jesus by himself. He is fortunate to have some people who really care about him. The helping friends give us a great picture of the nature of the church. We are to be a people who are sensitive to the needs of others. We are to be carriers by our love, our commitment, our service, and our gifts.

(c) Receive in simple trust the word of grace that is spoken to us. Jesus Christ said, "Your sins are forgiven." The man had to believe that. He could have said, "No way, I am too guilty. I have done too many terrible things." God wants to turn our problems into possibilities. Remember—as we said earlier—Jesus went to the cross to be able to announce that word of forgiveness. That is his word to you and me today.

(d) Act in obedient faith. Jesus said to the paralytic, "Take up your bed and walk." That was the thing that the man could not do. Since he was willing to try, he put forth his maximum effort and believed it was possible. He gave it all he had. There is such encouragement in Jesus' words. He is really saying in effect, "You can do it, with my help, with my power, you can do it!"

III. You see the man walking out of the house with a great smile on his face and a rolled-up bed over his shoulder. The thrilling thing about it is that the man disappears and all attention is given to

God. Luke tells us that he went home glorifying God, and amazement seized them all and they glorified God.

(a) Notice how thrilling this is—because one obscure paralytic believes and obeys, this great multitude glorified God! That, too, is what the church is all about! As we put forth our effort and join with the grace of God, then miracles do occur.

(b) How long has it been since you have been seized by amazement? We have seen something we can't quite understand or comprehend. Here we are a great Christian congregation. The living Lord is in our midst. He has work to do in us and through us. As we join him, commit our lives to him, we catch the excitement of the power and presence of the living God at work among his people. He is forgiving our sins. He is giving us hope and courage. He is enabling us to see that our "carrying" does make a difference! And he is bringing us together in worship and praise so that the problems begin to lose their hold on us. We catch the vision of new possibilities as we give thanks and praise to the God who is so wonderful—whose compassion and grace never fails! "But that you may know that the son of man has authority on earth to forgive sins . . . I say to you 'Rise take up your bed and go home.' "—Joe A. Harding.

SUNDAY: DECEMBER TWENTIETH

MORNING SERVICE

Topic: Faith and Fulfillment
Text: Mic. 5:2–4; Heb. 10:5–10; Luke 1:39–56.

(a) What is Christmas to you? To many of us it is filled with warmth and goodness. The smells are there. The fragrance of roasting turkey, wassail, special breads and cakes and Christmas cookies made in the image of Santa, Rudolph, and Christmas trees. And real Christmas trees with that fragrance that fills the house; wreaths that hang a welcome on the front door, and stockings hung by the chimney with care. It's knowing you've passed too close to the tree when the icicles cling to your leg and a trail of tinsel winds back to the tree. Presents that, each day, seem to multiply and grow more mysterious.

(b) Is this what Christmas is to you? Memories and experiences that linger through the years and like vintage wine become richer, better, with time? That's what Christmas is to many of us. But not really. Oh, I would not try to touch those memories for anything. But the coming of the Christ child wasn't filled with memories like that.

I. There was a tremendous amount of faith, hope, fulfillment that oozes out of the cracks in that story. You almost have to read between the lines because the church wrote us a report that was really a summary. Like us, they remembered the good parts and left out some of the ragged details. Parts of the pain they put in, but what we've got in that story is a "written up" version approved for media.

(a) There was, for example, a tremendous amount of faith in this story, and it was faith that the hope held over the years would come to fruition. There's a lot riding on the shoulders of this baby boy. You just have to be sensitive to the national yearning present in Israel.

(b) The problem with this is these folk have hooked their faith and its fulfillment to the wagon of the nation. That wagon won't sustain much pulling. Nations are great and we can't do without them. They are sociologically essential. They are developmentally necessary, but the entity known as "nation"—whether ours or someone else's—has to be checked and constantly monitored. The nation develops its own vested interest that may or may not include the folks who make it up.

(c) Our faith had best not be hooked to the national wagon. "We the people"— the best governmental plan tends to get perverted to "they, the people." What we create tends to outgrow us and becomes not our child anymore, but our adversary that looks after itself or the majority or those with the loudest voices. Faith that seeks fulfillment in or through the plights and plans of national won't be rewarded. Israel is a case in point.

II. But there's something else here in the Christmas story. The faith of Mary and Joseph also went beyond their personal circumstances. If it had not, then I don't think there would be a story.

(a) Most of us have hooked our faith onto our personal circumstances, haven't we? Nothing new, this life style, exemplified in the fool and his barns, says, "I'm doing well, I have most of what I want, thus, I must be blessed by God. And if I'm blessed I must be OK in God's eyes." This is more an absorbed attitude than a conscious reflection. What's wrong with it is that when the signs of blessings disappear, the crash of '29, or the tents of prosperity fold, our faith, like with Job's wife, takes a tumble: "curse God and die."

(b) Joseph's family, angry and protective and all giving advice at the same time: "You better put her away while you can. You marry this woman and you're in for a long time of trouble."

Her family, heartbroken over a pregnancy that did not make sense. Here they almost had their daughter grown and out and well-established. Perhaps Mary and Joseph went to Bethlehem long before she was due to deliver. Perhaps they went to Bethlehem and waited for the birth. What the magnificat doesn't tell us is that these were oppressed people racially, *personae non grate* socially, and religiously they would not have been nominated for our diaconate, or Mary for the president of the young women of the church. You wonder if a rabbi ever made a house call, or if there was a baby shower.

(c) Had Mary and Joseph hooked their faith to their own personal circumstances like we are prone to do, they would have despaired. Our faith has to go beyond circumstances, or when our circumstances are bleak our faith reflects it.

III. I remember the rough times my mom had trying to keep everything together after dad died. She kept going, nurtured a faith beyond the present situation that was sometimes bleak. I'm not sure all

that sustained her, but I do know that every Sunday, regardless, we were in church and Sunday school.

(a) It was spring of 1964, final graduation from seminary. Mom had to fly to get there, and she had never flown and had vowed never to fly. But, as she reasoned, "it would kill me if I didn't see that graduation so if I'm going to die I might as well die trying to get there," so she came. The graduation was over and someone was taking our picture together on the steps of the chapel and she reached up and pulled me down to her and whispered: "You know this is the fulfillment of everything I've worked for."

(b) Years later I was home one summer and my first book was there by her bed on the reading table. "Mom, haven't you finished this by now?" I joked.

"Oh, I keep it there to remind me it was all worthwhile." And I remember when she first held each of her grandsons, her words: "I guess it's all been worth it hasn't it?" Seeing her fulfillment, I understood the faith.

(c) She was talking about fulfillment—the fulfillment of a faith that had waited and hoped, and made dozens of journeys to Bethlehem to give birth to a mystery she had never understood—but it was time, and she went. Hers was a faith that went beyond nation and circumstance. And I wish that for me and for you. For I suspect nothing much will happen in life without that faith that hopes and waits for fulfillment. For when it comes, how sweet it is.—Thomas H. Conley.

Illustrations

THE GOSPEL ACCORDING TO MARY. This Gospel according to Mary, which adumbrates the words and actions of her Son, is something more than a decorative appendage to a comforting Christmas story. It speaks to those same questions of power and arrogance, oppression and acquisitiveness that plague us today. It accounts for the brighter side in the record of the Christian church—the care for the poor and helpless, the founding of hospitals, the sharing of wealth, the support of the oppressed, the defiance of demonic powers. At its best the church has translated the inward liberation and satisfaction that Jesus brings to each one who trusts in his cleansing and nourishing love into an outgoing concern for the rescue of the oppressed, the defense of the weak, and the feeding of the hungry.—David H. C. Read.

IDENTIFYING OUR IDOLS.   In a manicured park of a foreign city stood a huge idol as the center of attraction. A despondent missionary stood nearby, trying to preach the gospel to the people who passed by; but they were indifferent to his work. In prayer for divine guidance the missionary sought some way to break the obvious coldness to gain a hearing. The answer came as a revelation. He remembered that back in his native land human curiosity could be called into play. It might be used here to lead the group to pause and look in the general direction other people were staring. He stood like a statue in total silence, pointing toward the gaunt idol before him. Curious people began to stop and stare in that direction, wondering what it was all about; soon a sizeable audience had gathered. At that point the missionary spoke loudly but slowly and dramatically.

"Look! Look at your god. He has eyes, but he cannot see. He has a mouth, but he cannot speak. He has feet, but he cannot walk. . . ."

Having caught the drift of the idea and lamenting the obvious needs of the people, a native cried: "He has hands, but he cannot help, for he has no heart with which to feel." No heart with which to feel! Thus the pagans lamented their own helplessness and hopelessness. Such hopelessness brings death and despair to a world. It is the world's cry, if we would only listen.—James L. Sullivan.

Sermon Suggestions

A GREATER KINGDOM.   Text: 2 Sam. 7: 8–16. (1) David's kingdom came to an end. (2) The kingdom of Jesus Christ— son of David, Son of God—will last forever.

GOD GIVES US STRENGTH.   Text: Rom. 16:25–27. (1) By what Jesus did and taught. (2) By the wonder of his gracious revelation. (3) By the universal significance of his coming in Christ Jesus.

Worship Aids

CALL TO WORSHIP.   "Thine eyes shall see the king in his beauty" (Isa. 33:17a).

INVOCATION.   Almighty God, we come into thy presence this day at the end of the season of Advent, and on the eve of the birth of thy Son, filled with the Spirit of the holiday. We thank thee, O Lord, that thou hast made our holiday so merry and full of cheer, so happy and full of love. Never allow us to forget, however, that the spirit of this season of Advent is much more than just a time when we are to feel happy and comfortable. This season of Advent is a time during which we remember the reasons for which thy Son was given unto us. Help us remember, O Lord, that thy Son was given to rescue us from our sinful ignorance of thee, from our sinful neglect of our fellow human beings, and from our sinful pride in ourselves. Grant unto us the courage, wisdom, and love to share our preparation for the Christ child with all of those whose lives we touch.—Rodney K. Miller.

OFFERTORY PRAYER.   God of promise, the angels sang a song of joy, the shepherds came in obedience, the wise men brought gifts, and we bring our offerings, to herald the Christ child, in whom salvation resides and prophecy is fulfilled and our joy is made full.—E. Lee Phillips.

A CHRISTMAS LITANY.
Minister: Eternal Spirit, Father of all grace and goodness, we thank thee for the children, and at this Christmas time we bless thee for Christ's revelation of the beauty and value of childhood.
Response: Alleluia. Blessed be God, eternal friend of children.
Minister: For his tender compassion toward them; for his burning indignation

against those who do them wrong; for his deep and overflowing love, drawing them toward himself; for his message of their nearness to the Father of all,

Response: Blessed be God.

Minister: For the loveliness of children; for their mirth and laughter; for the gladness and light they bring into the world,

Response: Blessed be God.

Minister: For their enthusiasm, their abounding energy, and their love of the heroic and adventurous; for their candid, generous trust in those around them; and for their quick response to calls of love and service,

Response: Blessed be God.

Minister: For the childhood of Jesus our Lord; for his birth and helpless babyhood, for his mother's gentle care and nurture; and for all unknown souls who nursed and tended him,

Response: Alleluia. Blessed be God, eternal friend of children.

Minister: For his joyful, eager, obedient boyhood, uplifting all human childhood; for the grace and love of God, which in him were revealed and which gave to us the joy of knowing the Father,

Response: Thanks be to thee, O God.

Minister: As we give thanks for the infinite value of children, so we pray for fathers and mothers, and for all of us through whom children receive their first thoughts of God, and their early ideals of character. May we have a deepened sense of the Fatherhood of God, and may we so practice his presence, that the children may be won for goodness and beauty of life.

Response: Lord, have mercy upon us and grant us this blessing.

Minister: O Heavenly Father, make our hearts burn within us for all children who go neglected or unloved; let thy Spirit breathe into us a living renewal, that with wise statesmanship and generous philanthropy may we make of this earth a more decent and kindly place into which children may be born.

Response: Lord, have mercy upon us and grant us this blessing. Amen.—Harry Emerson Fosdick.

EVENING SERVICE

Topic: Emmanuel, God with Us

TEXT: Luke 2:1–14.

I. From our earliest days of religious instruction we remember well the text, "there was no room for them in the inn." When we ask ourselves whether there is room in our lives, in the inn of our souls, in our daily schedules, we ask of ourselves, "Are these inns, are these lives overcrowded?"

(a) For most of us, we would have to answer in the affirmative, at least in some measure. How easy it is for our lives to become overcrowded, often with things we would not choose to honor.

(b) And so in the first instance, we look at the innkeeper and the inn wherein there is no room for this Christ child; and we are reminded, we the choice makers, we the animals of history, that we must make choices. We must have priorities. Who will stay in the inn of our lives? Will the Christ be welcome? Will he be central?

II. "But Mary kept all these things and pondered them in her heart." It is well observed of Mary that she welcomed her Son as the fruit of her own body.

(a) It was this same Mary who never is reflected in Holy Scripture as having any opinions about Jesus. We know that when he returned to his hometown, he was thrown out of the synagogue. There were those who had known him, who viewed him with derision, with criticism, with skepticism, with cynicism, but not Mary.

(b) Mary reminds us over and over again that if we are to know God we must first know ourselves. We must first know those around us. Mary knew her son as a human being. She rejoiced in him as a human being. And thus, in fidelity and loyalty, she came to him as the Son of God.

III. The wise men came from a very different culture, very different from our own, though not necessarily different from the culture of Jesus. What did they think of the Lord's Christ? We know not. In the great tradition of the East, then and now, those who know do not say.

(a) You may well recall that in some Eastern traditions life is divided into three seasons. The first season is the season of being a student. The second season of life is that of the householder. The last season is that of the pilgrim. And when one has discovered these secrets, one comes back to the family but does not discuss those secrets. This is best represented in our own Western tradition by grandparents, grandparents who in the main no longer attempt to correct or instruct their grandchildren. They just are. And if the grandchildren have sufficient sensitivity they will observe that witness.

(b) And so we come in the spirit of the wise men, who do not give us any report, they simply give us their witness. These are the pilgrims who found the Christ.

(c) In our search for God, easily hobbled by our anxieties about what might have been, we are leaping with our minds and souls to a world yet unborn, to a world never to be born, or we are falling back into the past—those rich memories, pretended and real. And yet, there we do not find God, either in the anxiety of the future or the yearning for the past. We find God, as did the wise men, in the eternal now, in the present, here. "Emmanuel, God with us."—Spencer Morgan Rice.

SUNDAY: DECEMBER TWENTY-SEVENTH

MORNING SERVICE

Topic: The Power to See It Through
TEXT: Philem. 24; Col. 4:14; 2 Tim. 4: 10.

(a) There is one character in the New Testament, mentioned only three times, concerning whom one suspects that many Christians have not even heard. His name was Demas, and, alas, some of us are much more like him than like the great New Testament figures we know so well. First, in Paul's letter to Philemon, we read, "Demas, Luke, my fellow-workers." So Demas, along with Luke, and named first at that, was standing by Paul in his Roman imprisonment, a devoted and promising disciple. Second, in Paul's letter to the Colossians, we read, "Luke, the beloved physician, and Demas." Reading that, one wonders why Demas and Luke, who were praised together at the first, were separated in this passage as though Luke indeed retained Paul's confidence as "the beloved physician" but Demas had become merely "Demas." Third, in the second letter to Timothy, incorporating, we suppose, one of the last messages Paul ever wrote, we read, "Demas forsook me, having loved this present age." Three points on a curve that enable us to plot its graph! For here is the story of a man who made a fine beginning and a poor ending: Demas, my fellow-worker; Demas; Demas forsook me.

(b) As one considers this familiar experience of a fine beginning and a poor ending, it is obvious, for one thing, that the qualities that make a good start possible are not identical with the qualities that see life through to the end. Starting power and staying power are not the same thing in any realm.

(c) Another general truth concerns our thought: namely, that however beautiful one's start, nothing matters much in human life without a good ending. Of course one does not mean that we may demand an outwardly successful and fortunate conclusion, as in old sentimental novels where everything had to come out all right. But without a good end, without morale and staying power and steady character to see a man through to a worthy conclusion what else in human life can be much worthwhile?

(d) Let us talk together not about starting power—there is no soul here that has not more than once made a fine beginning —but about staying power. I celebrate the qualities of faith and character that enable a man to see life through.

I. For one thing, staying power is always associated with a certain central integrity of conscience. Whatever else life may give or may deny, one thing is absolutely indispensable to a man—that he should not break faith with himself, that he should not inwardly be a failure.

(c) Now, as we see Paul and Demas in

Rome, it is obvious Paul had that. He would have liked outward good fortune and success could he have had them on honorable terms—of course he would! But whether fortune or misfortune befell, one thing was absolutely indispensable— he must not break faith with himself and the Christ within him. Demas, however, was of another sort. He soon found something else that was indispensable. "Demas forsook me," wrote Paul, "having loved this present age." So that was it! Roman civilization was brilliant like our own. It had ugly aspects, but for agile minds and grasping hands there were prizes to be gained. All around Paul's poor prison house was Rome. To be loyal to the royal in himself was not absolutely indispensable. He loved this present age.

(b) You see, I am not really talking about Demas now, but about us. One would not minimize the sacrifice that such a conscience as we are speaking of often costs in a world like this, but the great souls who have most possessed such conscience have commonly thought of it not as a burden of duty but as a gospel of liberty. Listen! No man ever needs to be a failure. Trouble, outward breakdown of hopes, may come, but a man who cares most that he should not be a failure can capitalize trouble.

That is the final difference between people. Paul faced many kinds of failure but he himself was no failure. If, however, the old legend is correct, Demas went back to Thessalonica and became a priest of idols in a pagan temple. He himself was a failure.

II. In the second place, staying power is always associated with the experience of being captured by a cause, laid hold on by something greater than oneself to which one gives one's loyalty—an art, a science, a vocation, a social reform, an object of devotion that one conceives to be more important than oneself. All staying power in character is associated with that.

(a) Christ had never gotten so deep as that into Demas. Demas had laid hold on some of the more comfortable aspects of the Christian gospel, but the Christian gospel had never laid hold on Demas. Demas had possessed himself of this or

that detail of Christ's message, but Christ had not possessed himself of Demas. So the man's Christianity was a superstructure easily put up, easily taken down—jerry-building on slim foundations. For the foundation of enduring character is always laid in something greater than oneself, which one will serve through life and death.

(b) There is a fascinating contrast between two phrases in the New Testament: the first, Paul's description of Demas— "having loved this present age"; the second, the description of a true Christian in the Epistle to the Hebrews as one who has "tasted the . . . powers of the age to come." So that is the difference, as the New Testament sees it. An apostate is a man who loves the status quo, this present age; a Christian is a man who has tasted the powers, been laid hold on by the hopes, of the age to come.

(c) When someone tries to tell you that the Christian social gospel is a modern innovation not in the New Testament, face him with that. The Christian social gospel is in the very heart of the New Testament —set, to be sure, in mental frameworks appropriate to the first century and different from ours but indubitably there. The primary emphasis on the kingdom of God in Jesus' teaching and in the first church was so dominant that they tested Christian discipleship by it. A man who loved this present age was an apostate; a man who had tasted the powers of the age to come was a Christian. Whenever we see a New Testament Christian carrying through to the finish, one fact is always apparent; he had set his devotion on a coming kingdom of God on earth for which he was willing to live or die.

(d) I suspect that this is the outstanding challenge to us in the churches—our attitude not on theological questions but on practical, ethical, social questions. We find it easy to love this present age. We make fine beginnings, especially at New Year's time, but then some comfortable corner of this present age invites us and we nestle down. So our Christian profession lapses, our faith grows formal, and we do not amount to much in the end as Christians. If I should accuse some of you of being

Judas Iscariot you would be indignant. You would never deliberately sell anybody out. But Demas—ah, my soul, how many of us have been that!

III. Finally, staying power is commonly associated with profound resources of interior strength replenished by great faiths. We do faint, peter out, go flat, lose our morale unless our interior resources are replenished by faith in something. We may be sure that Demas, before he left Paul, had lost some of his first convictions about Christ and the God whom Christ revealed.

(a) Suppose that someone should ask you what your faith in the Christian God really does for you. What would you say? For one thing, I should say that when a man believes in God he does not need to worry about the universe any more. If a man believes in God, that is off his mind. He can concentrate upon the task in hand, get on with his moral business here on earth with some high hopes about its outcome, and not be haunted by a huge, cosmic apprehension.

(b) Deeper yet, a vital faith in God means a faith in an eternal moral purpose in the light of which a thousand years are as yesterday when it is past and as a watch in the night. That gives a man wide horizons, long outlooks, steady hopes, so that when people lose heart over the disappointment of some immediate expectation, such faith still has standing ground and carries on.

(c) Deeper yet, a vital faith in God gives a man available resources of interior power. We never produce power. We always appropriate it. That is true from the harnessing of Niagara to eating a dinner or taking a walk in the fresh air. We never create power; we assimilate it. So, a man with a real faith in God senses around his spiritual life a spiritual presence as truly as the physical world is around his body, and as truly from that divine companionship he draws replenished strength. He knows the deep wells of staying power.

IV. If faith in God means such things, how do men live life through without it? How do they meet the shocks of fate, the ugliness of evil, the shame of man's inhumanity to man, the disheartenment of moral failure, the impact of personal sorrow, and still keep their morale? I celebrate the resources of Christian faith. —Harry Emerson Fosdick.

Illustrations

SURRENDER. A young woman, very much a woman of this world, wanted to find God; and when I suggested surrender as the first step, she replied, "Why, if I did that, I would be at God's mercy." She thought God was looking for a chance to make her miserable. She did not understand that God's will and her highest interest were one. God's will is love in action—perfect love in action.—E. Stanley Jones.

UNTAPPED RESERVOIRS. A faithful daughter gives herself to a stricken mother through long months of illness. When the long fight is over and the crisis is passed, she looks back at her effort and exclaims, "I did not know it was in me to go through all that." She had manifested an energy and endurance that she could not calculate in advance nor summon at will. She had tapped hitherto unknown and unused reservoirs of strength. By losing sight of herself in looking after her mother she had joined forces with "him that is able to do exceeding abundantly above all that we ask or think, according to the power that worketh in us" (Eph. 3:20). —Ralph W. Sockman.

Sermon Suggestions

A NEW NAME. Text: Isa. 61:10–62:3. A new name means: (1) a new standing with God; (2) a holier character; (3) a more glorious destiny.

FROM A SLAVE TO A SON. Text: Gal. 4: 4–7. (1) What God did: he changed our status. (2) When God did it: in the fullness of time. (3) How God did it: he sent forth his Son and put his Spirit within us.

Worship Aids

CALL TO WORSHIP. "Let us not be weary in well doing: for in due season we shall reap, if we faint not" (Gal. 6:9).

INVOCATION. Eternal God, who can make all things new, we humbly bring before you the record of our lives in the year now ending. Where life has been good to us, do not let us take more of the credit than we deserve. Where we have been good to others, help us to forget all thoughts of honor and reward. Where we have fallen short, forgive us, and free us from brooding over what is past. Cleanse us by your mercy, guide us by your truth, fill us with your love, lead us forward in your all-conquering hope.—E. Paul Hovey.

OFFERTORY SENTENCE. "No servant can be the slave of two masters; for either he will hate the first and love the second, or he will be devoted to the first and think nothing of the second. You cannot serve God and money" (Matt. 6:24 neb).

OFFERTORY PRAYER. O God, we thank you for the gift of your infant son to become our Savior. As we bring our gifts to you and ask your blessing upon them, we bring more than our money and tithes. We bring our selves—our hearts, souls, and bodies to be spent in your service and to show our gratitude for your precious gift to us of Jesus the Christ, in whose name we pray.—Harold A. Brack.

PRAYER. We thank thee, Almighty God, for all the things which thou hast made our children teach us. How much do we know of ourselves that we never should have known but for our offspring! How much do we know of thee that we never should have known but for our children! How much do we know of thy government and of thy feelings which no language could have interpreted to us, but which we have learned from those who are so much weaker than we are, and who are so far below us! How much thou hast taught us of time, and how much of eternity! Many as are the pains that we have had, carrying burdens; much as we have had of care; much as we have suffered from sorrows and bereavements, thou hast paid us back a thousandfold, for all our trouble at the hands of our dear little children. We thank thee for them; for that blessed estate into which, by them, we are brought; for all the sanctities of love in the household; for all the disclosures of truth in the affections thereof.

And now, O Lord! we thank thee for the mercy which thou hast shown each of us as have children grown up and entered into life. We thank thee for all thy great goodness to them, and to us through them.

We beseech of thee, O Lord! that thou wilt look upon the children of this church; upon all that have been brought with consecration into the sanctuary; upon all that have been offered with prayers and tears in the closet. We beseech of thee, that thou wilt inspire them with wisdom and fidelity, that they may be able to bring up their children in such a way that when they are old they shall not depart from integrity and truth and piety.—Henry Ward Beecher.

EVENING SERVICE

Topic: Face the Light and Dispel the Shadows

TEXT: Isa. 9:2–7; John 8:12–20.

My message to you is the one Jesus gave to the people when he stood tall and said, "I am the light of the world."

I. The profound first chapter of John says, "The light came into the world, and the people preferred the darkness." "But the darkness cannot overcome the light." People tend to get all mixed up in these metaphors, and, as a result, they turn off. God is light, and the light of God shines in the lives of men and women.

(a) What does this deep and profound truth say to you in the tedium and the struggle of your everyday life? It challenges you to face the light in your marriage problem, your financial problem, your health problem, your political problem. When you turn your face to the light, the tough, creative, courageous work of bringing forth your real, best self is revealed.

(b) There are a lot of men and women who are gloom and doom. They are really happiest when things are going badly. They ignore the sunshine, and they always see the rain. Now, of course, that kind of vision is what good journalism is all about, but it is very poor mental health.

II. Jesus told of this light in his historical background with the menorah, the seven-branched candlestick that we associate with Judaism. Philosophically men and women have always known that God is light. If you face the light and don't run, the shadows will fall behind you.

(a) Remember that the Jewish people had been desecrated along with their temple. Part of the temple from God's revelation to Moses had been the candlestick with the seven branches, a symbol of God's great light. Through the ages, men and women have always had light as a symbol of God. The temple desecrated by heathen forces was liberated by the Jewish people. After the liberation, they wanted to dedicate and purify it. So they lit the menorah that Moses had established. There was only enough oil for one day, whereas the ceremony required oil for eight days. According to the story, the oil for the supply of one day lasted for eight miracle days. It is a beautiful story because it tells of God's wonderful love.

(b) Biologically, the same principle exists within each of you. Your supplies are limited. Your maximum supply of oxygen is four minutes. After that, unless it is regenerated, you are out! But I am not worrying, are you? I have no guarantee of sufficient oxygen, but I have lived these years, and God has not yet failed to supply it moment by moment.

III. So this is the story when Jesus said, "I am the light of the world." He was standing in a situation where people understood what the menorah meant. The menorahs we use today are small. The one Jesus used was a great tall one. In the ancient Festival of the Lights they used to take the old linen clothes of the priests, their worn-out robes, and make great flaming wicks out of the holy rags. It was a beautiful sight like Fifth Avenue at ten o'clock on Christmas Eve. The lights went out, and in the middle of that Jesus stood up and said, "I am the light of the world." No wonder they pummeled him. "What do you mean?" they shouted. "You are the light of the world." He explained his deity, that he came to us as God where we could see him. God incandescent. God incar-nate, God made visible. My point is that light has always been the main metaphor of all religious people, Christians included.

(a) Light has always been the metaphor for the mystery of God. We do not have God all figured out in our textbooks or in our computer banks. Light is also the metaphor for the meaning of life, because light is really illusion. Do you realize that a lot of what you go by today is illusion? That is difficult to accept. Light casts meaning, and the light you put on something gives it the meaning. All of you in theatrics know that. You can change the mood of a whole scene by changing the lighting.

The light that you bring to the job makes the job. The job does not make the light. The light you put in your marriage makes the marriage. The marriage does not make the light. A lot of you are saying that you are waiting for a more directive light, a signal light as it were. The hard truth is that you will probably never get it. It is always the light you bring to the subject that is meaningful and of ultimate import.

(b) Light has always been a symbol of meaning. That is why the Bible says, "Walk in the light." Walk in the light that you have. It is enough. Light is the symbol of the assurance of our great future hope.

IV. Occasionally, I have stood at the base of the great lighthouse on Bermuda Island. It is a tremendous lighthouse that stands tall on the great coral reef that stretches out into the Atlantic. It is a symbol of hope to modern aircraft as it once was to ancient sailing ships. I discovered that the great lighthouse was all about one five-hundred-watt bulb! That is all. One five-hundred-watt bulb shining through those prisms made a beacon of hope, guidance, and assurance to men and women flying in from south Europe. It is a tremendous analogy. "You are the light of the world," said Jesus. You are the beacon on an island or a mountain. Don't put a bushel basket over your candlestick, but put it on a stand, lift it high, that it may give light, hope, and meaning to others as they wrestle in the dark.

V. Then there is the future. Do not give

up on the future. When you go out tonight, look up at the stars. Realize, men and women, that the light of the stars you see tonight started their journey centuries ago, hundreds of years before the birth of Christ. Only now do you see that light. Realize that the light that is shining from these stars now will not reach this earth for millennia! The sun, which is our central symbol, is actually a very small star of the fifth magnitude. In Orion is a star that is more than forty times larger than our sun. That is why men and women have always said as the psalmist did, "When I consider the sun and the moon and the stars, what am I that you are even mindful of me, O God." "Thou turnest the darkness into light." "Lo, I am with you always."

God is light. God is love. God is life. Keep your face to that light, and the shadows will fall behind you. Change your mental health patterns. Join a branch of the Christian church. Get into the light. Give your heart to Jesus Christ, and lift your own lantern so that others can see the path of life and walk with you.—Bryant M. Kirkland.

SECTION XII. Ideas and Suggestions for Pulpit and Parish

COMPILED BY MARY JANE ALLEN

CHILDREN'S CORNER.   Cynthia Weeks Logan, associate pastor of Oak Cliff Presbyterian Church in Dallas, Texas, set up a children's corner in her office. It is furnished with two small chairs, crayons, coloring books, puzzles, stuffed toys, a few books and a Tonka truck. The corner provides a special welcome for children while their parents talk with the minister.—*Church Teachers.*

CATERING EXCHANGE.   When the First United Church of Christ in Findlay, Ohio, was planning its stewardship dinner and program, the pastor checked with neighboring churches to see if an exchange of catering services could be arranged. This resulted in the East Mount Zion United Methodist Church preparing, serving, and cleaning up for the dinner, using the menu and food provided. They even provided child care for the evening. First United Church of Christ agreed to return the favor by providing the same service for East Mount Zion's Sweetheart Dinner. Besides allowing church members to pay full attention to the program for the evening, the two churches experienced true community in Christ.—*Leadership.*

SHOWING APPRECIATION TO VOLUNTEERS. Ross W. Marrs, senior pastor of First United Methodist Church in Bloomington, Indiana, gives the following suggestions for showing appreciation to volunteers:

1. Walk by and notice what they are doing.
2. Provide replacements when volunteers must be away.
3. Provide refreshments.
4. Have a special "thank you" event.
5. Include pictures of volunteers in church publications.
6. Introduce volunteers to the congregation periodically.
7. Send birthday cards, get-well cards, "thinking-of-you" cards.
8. Exhibit trust—don't hover.
9. Replace them when they wish to be relieved of the responsibility.—*Church Management: The Clergy Journal.*

YOUTH DIAL-A-DEVOTION.   A youth minister in Wheaton, Illinois, set up a daily youth devotional line for a 2½-minute devotional with a new message daily on the church's two phone answering machines. The youth promoted it by blitzing local schools and concerts with business-sized cards with the phone number and the message, "A dynamite call for a lift." The young people tape messages on weekends. They tell about their faith experience or give a brief devotional. They ask their friends to call, thus giving a witness. At the end of the devotional the youth minister gives details of upcoming events. —*Group.*

ASK-THE-PASTOR.   On the Sunday of Memorial Day weekend, Cottage Brook

350

Assembly in Woodinville, Washington, features Ask-the-Pastor Sunday. For several years this event has offered the opportunity for people to satisfy their curiosity about doctrinal, theological, biblical or practical questions. The special service, which replaces the Sunday morning sermon, also prevents an attendance slump over the holiday weekend. A month prior to the service, a large box is placed in the foyer to receive the questions. A casual atmosphere is created for the occasion by having a couch and chair replace the pulpit. The pastor, having done appropriate research, is "quizzed" by an associate.—*Leadership.*

SOUPER STUDY. The Sunday school leadership of Ridgedale Baptist Church in Chattanooga, Tennessee, enjoyed a unique midwinter training session called a "Souper Study." Small groups were hosted in homes where beverages were provided. Participants brought the home-made soup or chili, and the church provided other essentials. After a time of food and fellowship, the leaders received training for their Bible study responsibilities. A break provided time for dessert.—*Sunday School Leadership.*

MISSIONS CONFERENCE. On three weekends each year the Ahwahnee Chapel in Ahwahnee, California, has a missions conference in which the visiting missionaries are encouraged to relax as they share their experiences with the church. The following is a sample schedule:

Friday night—Each missionary has a display at the church. Two present brief slide presentations. The focus for everyone is on food and fellowship. The missionaries then spend the night in homes of church members.

Saturday morning—Breakfast is served for the missionaries only, giving them some time to share with each other. The pastor leads in a brief devotional time, after which church members join the group for prayer in small groups. The prayer needs mentioned by the missionaries are printed for distribution on Sunday.

Saturday afternoon—Free time for the missionaries to enjoy recreation, sightseeing, or just rest.

Saturday night—The missionaries, deacons and their families meet for two more slide presentations. A guest speaker encourages the church members and the missionaries.

Sunday morning—The missionaries attend church as worshipers, not speakers, although some may speak in Sunday school groups. Two more slide presentations are given in the morning worship service.—*Leadership 100.*

TWENTY SUGGESTIONS. William W. McDerment, III, pastor of a Christian Church (Disciples of Christ) in Indianapolis, Indiana, suggests the following tried and proven ideas to add a "spark" to your church:

1. Share ministry with another congregation. Examples: community ministry, joint project or worship service, Vacation Bible School, youth trip.

2. Allow members the opportunity to volunteer. Use your church newsletter or meetings to let needs be known.

3. Give a symbolic gift to those who worship on Christmas Eve. The worship committee can plan and implement this; it doesn't have to be costly—a Christmas cookie, a flower bulb, etc.

4. Start all events on time. The most important business in the world should not be handled lackadaisically.

5. Sponsor a refugee family. Check with your denominational offices or contact Church World Service.

6. Once a year share what you would like to see happen in the coming year. Establish some guidelines and spend some time with small groups to brainstorm and dream.

7. Encourage members to write fresh words to hymns. Include the words on an insert in the worship bulletin and use in a service.

8. Participate in the New Testament example of letter writing. Select a Sunday, preach on "Letter Writing as a Ministry." Then provide paper and envelopes and ask members to write a letter of encour-

agement, guidance, and/or hope to some-one.

9. Establish a Learning Experience Fund. Use it to fund learning experiences at a nearby college or seminary (auditing courses) or to invite a special resource person to hold a workshop or Bible study.

10. Encourage people to say amen. Lead members to affirm spoken prayers by saying amen.

11. Install a thermostat with no connections! Place it in a conspicuous place, allowing members to set it as desired.

12. Provide a "Put and Take Table." Place it in a main areaway or narthex and place a sign above it. Members may bring magazines, books, vegetables, etc.

13. Have informal sharing within the worship service. Occasionally provide time for support, sharing and caring—happy or sad events.

14. Allow for prayers from persons in the pews. Provide a time occasionally for spontaneous sentence prayers.

15. Attend a Jewish service of worship. Contact the nearest synagogue and talk with the rabbi. Set a time for the visit. Have a session before the service with someone from the synagogue who will explain the elements of worship, and meet with someone afterwards to ask questions.

16. Provide a list of disciplines for Lent. Print a list of opportunities for growth during the Lenten season, placing emphasis on positive possibilities such as:

—I will pray at least once each day.

—I will eat more simply that I usually do.

—I will spend at least fifteen minutes a day in Bible study.

—I will read one religious book.

17. Have open discussion on the sermon topic following worship. Announce the topic and discussion questions a week in advance. Select a moderator and allow members to express feelings and opinions.

18. Form a Membership-Celebration Committee. Appoint, elect, or delegate a group of six to eight to plan large and small events throughout the year to provide opportunities to affirm life—a birthday party with seating by months of birth,

a church picnic, special fellowships.

19. Have your committee in charge of welcoming visitors visit other churches. Have them experience being a visitor to gain insights that will help your church more effectively receive visitors.

20. Make an Event Banner for the year. In January unveil a large banner with only the date of the year. Encourage individuals and groups to make and attach symbols throughout the year related to the life and work of the church.—*Your Church.*

FAMILY SUNDAY SCHOOL CLASS.   First Baptist Church of White Bear Lake, Minnesota, and Salem Baptist Church in Eau Claire, Wisconsin, offer a Sunday School class for families. The class has the following characteristics:

1. It lasts for a three-month period as a special feature.

2. There is an enrollment limit of 20 to 25, with the younger age limit being a first grader.

3. The lesson is built around Scriptures that provide story and truth.

4. Discovery teaching methods are used rather than lectures. Families are given something to do together and assignments are given to do at home.

5. The setting is informal. Chairs are placed in a circle and ample space is allowed for activities.

This type of class has appealed to some who never come to the "regular" classes and has encouraged families to continue Bible study together at home.—*Leadership 100.*

AN APPLE FOR THE TEACHER.   The Oakton Church of the Brethren in Oakton, Virginia, expressed appreciation for the Christian Education ministry with a program entitled "An Apple for the Teacher." Classes and individual members were invited to show their appreciation to their teachers by using an apple in some way, shape, or form. Everyone met in the fellowship hall during Sunday School for apple cake, apple juice, and coffee, and expressed verbal appreciation to their teachers. The pastor continued the theme during the worship service. The worship bulletin cover and insert focused on Deut. 6:4–9.—Bonnie D. King, *Church Teachers.*

YOUTH GROUP GREETING CARD. In Fisher, Illinois, the youth minister helps his group send group greeting cards. Using large sheets of paper or poster-board and bright colored markers, one letter of the greeting is printed on each sheet (Get Well Soon, Happy Birthday, Have a Fun Trip, We Miss You, etc.). The young people huddle close together holding the letters for a photograph. The photo is enclosed in a card.—*Group.*

ADOPT-A-STUDENT. First Baptist Church in Lubbock, Texas, a college town, has an Adopt-a-Student program to provide "family-type" support for young people away from home. Church families "adopt" a college student for the school year. Each family decides on types of involvement with the student, but suggestions include having an occasional home-cooked meal for the student, providing a place for the student to go when campus doesn't feel like "home," being a listener, calling occasionally to keep in touch. A form is printed in the church newsletter asking church families to indicate how many students they wish to adopt and whether they have a preference for young men or young women.—*The Vary Idea.*

NEWCOMER SUPPORT. Aware that the average family moves once every four years, Christ United Methodist Church in Bethel Park, Pennsylvania, has organized a support group for women entitled "New Horizons." This nondenominational group advertises through newspapers, Welcome Wagon, and realtors' organizations. A group is formed each spring and fall for newcomers to the community and meets one morning each week from 9:30 to 11:00 for six weeks. Child care and refreshments are provided while the women discuss moving, their feelings, needs, and problems. Adjustments and goals are discussed along with what to do and where to go in the community.—Reported by Marjory Lenox in *Leadership.*

HUNGER SCAVENGER HUNT. Instead of just collecting canned goods for the poor, a youth minister in Grandville, Michigan, has a "Hunger Scavenger Hunt." He contacts a food distribution center to determine specific needs. These are made up into lists with a notation of points to be awarded (per pound, box, can, dollar, etc.). The youth group is divided into pairs and a deadline is set two weeks ahead. He encourages the young people to contact neighbors, church members, and stores explaining what they are doing. At the deadline, the items are brought to the church and the scores are tallied with the winning pair receiving a small prize. The items are then delivered to the food distribution center.—*Group.*

GIFT OF HELPS MINISTRY. First Baptist Church in Houston, Texas, has a "Gift of Helps Ministry." A card is distributed to church members on which to indicate their willingness and ability to help with home upkeep and/or repair, transportation, car repairs, visiting, babysitting, blood donation, etc. Cards are also provided to people who have need of help to indicate the specific need. The minister of pastoral care and leaders of the program review and approve requests for help. Time and labor are free—those helped provide for the cost of parts, materials, etc.—*The Vary Idea.*

FAMILIES-IN-TRAINING. Perth Bible Church near Amsterdam, New York, has a FIT (Families-in-Training) Weekend. This joint retreat for teens and parents takes place at a camp about 1½ hours from home with guest speakers providing leadership. The teens go on Friday afternoon and have session one that night, with sessions two and three on Saturday morning. The parents arrive around noon on Saturday. In the early afternoon the parents have their first session while the teens enjoy recreational activities. This is followed in midafternoon by a session for mothers and daughters while the dads join their sons in recreation. Late on Saturday afternoon this is reversed with mothers and daughters having planned recreational activities while the fathers and sons have a session. After supper together, there is a general session for teens and parents. Late that night the parents return home, leaving the teens for a night of fellowship and a final challenge on Sunday morning.—*Leadership 100.*

SHARING IN CONFIRMATION.   To include parents and sponsors more meaningfully in confirmation, the pastor of Trinity Lutheran Church in Grande Prairie, Alberta, Canada, holds a weekend retreat at the end of the two-year confirmation program and before Confirmation Day. During the retreat, the group reviews the sessions, has a final comprehensive test, writes individual confessions of faith, worships together, and enjoys fun and fellowship.

As the young people leave the church with the pastor, the parents meet with the pastor's wife for prayer. The parents are given a large candle in a glass container which has the name of their confirmand on the outside. They are asked to burn the candle throughout the weekend and to use it as a reminder to pray specifically.

Prior to the weekend, parents are asked to write notes of encouragement. These are distributed by the pastor about halfway through the retreat.—*Sharing the Practice.*

EASTER ECHOES.   To extend the joy of the resurrection, First United Methodist Church in Selma, California, has created "Easter Echoes." On the second Sunday after Easter the choirs from eight local churches meet at 4:00 P.M. for this special music program. Each choir sings one or two anthems it performed during Lent or Easter and then they join together for two or three numbers. Members of small churches without choirs are invited to join the mass choir, which meets for two practices prior to the program. This enables the choirs to share their efforts for this special season with others and to enjoy the work of other choirs.—*Leadership.*

WEDNESDAY ON TUESDAY.   The West Jackson Baptist Church in Jackson, Mississippi, moved its regular Wednesday mid-week service and activities to Tuesday during Thanksgiving week. Tuesday night visitation was moved to Monday. This proved a good way to provide for this holiday week.—*The Vary Idea.*

ADVENT CELEBRATION.   The First Presbyterian Church of Mason, Michigan, held a "Sharing the ADVENT-ure"—an intergenerational Advent Celebration. It consisted of three parts:

Sharing a Meal—The dining room tables were covered with white cloths and were decorated with streamers of purple and green. Ham was provided by the church and participants brought side dishes. The youth had made cookies for everyone. During dinner each family chose two of four interest centers to attend from a printed program which described the events of the evening.

Sharing the Word—Each of the four interest centers provided a learning activity and an area in which to make an ornament representing that center. The centers and activities included the following: (1) Light —a filmstrip was shown; (2) Star—games and a worksheet were used; (3) Wreath— a presentation and a song were used; (4) Candle—participants watched a dramatized story. All ornaments were made of white, gold, and/or silver.

Sharing the Celebration—The families moved to the sanctuary where youth and lay leaders had chosen Scripture, hymns, anthems, and readings to complement the four concepts of the interest centers. During the final hymn, "Silent Night," people hung their ornaments on a blue spruce tree, which was lighted only with white bulbs.—Jannel Glennie in *Church Teachers.*

FAMILY CHRISTMAS DINNER.   The Trinity Lutheran Church in Alton, Illinois, began several years ago to have a Family Christmas Dinner preceding the church school Christmas program. They ask all families (parents, grandparents, aunts, uncles, cousins) to come 1½ hours before the program. Each family is asked to bring enough sandwiches for their family. (These are left in the church kitchen to be cut and placed on large trays.) Christmas cookies and beverages are provided. The tables are arranged around a Christmas tree. After the light meal, the families enjoy a time of prayer, Christmas carols, and stories. Then the adults go to the sanctuary and the children prepare for their program. The event unites the families and reduces the stress and pressures before the program.—John-Herbert Jaffry in *Church Educator.*

SECTION XIII. A Little Treasury of Illustrations

THE IMPERFECT CHURCH: The study of church history is not unlike a visit to Madame Tussaud's, where you find yourself in front of the distorting mirrors. There are two in particular which hold your attention. The one makes you look like a clothes-prop; the other makes you look like a barrel. You recognize yourself in both mirrors; it is your overcoat and muffler, your walking-stick and your face; but the exaggerations are deplorable, almost painful. It is a relief to turn to a plane mirror where, in spite of obvious and admitted imperfections, you see the normal thing. You wish it were better, but are glad it is no worse.—J. S. Whale.

REVELATION. A singular instance of this openness to the spirit of Christ is found in pastor John Robinson's advice to the Pilgrims as they departed from Holland. One of the Mayflower company reported, "He charged us . . . to follow him no further than he followed Christ; and if God should reveal anything to us by any other instrument of his, to be as ready to receive it as ever we were to receive any truth by his ministry; for he was very confident the Lord had more truth and light yet to break forth out of his holy word."— Dwight E. Stevenson.

GRAMMAR OF THE CROSS. Dr. Arthur T. Pierson used to tell us that over the cross of the impenitent thief might be written the words "In and On." Sin was in him, and the guilt of sin was on him. Over the cross of the penitent thief, "In not On." Sin was still in him, but through the forgiveness of Christ the guilt of sin was no longer on him. Over the Central Cross, "On not In." Sin was not in Jesus, but he was bearing the guilt of sin which was laid on him.—Thomas J. Villers.

OUR IDENTITY WITH CHRIST. Everything that happens to Christ also happens to us. This means, among other things, that we don't all have to experience the same things at the same time. This saves us from the bullying attitude of some believers, who insist that to be a true Christian one has to duplicate their experience exactly. If they are happy, then we must be happy. If they are gloomy, we must share their gloom.

If we follow the life of Christ as set out in the Gospels, however, we find a wide range of possible experiences. There is a birth and a growing up. He is driven by the Spirit into the wilderness to be tempted. He engages in an active ministry of teaching and healing. And he sets his face towards Jerusalem to suffer and endure a shameful death. He is raised on the third day and now reigns in glory and in the hearts of his faithful people. So runs the story. And so for the believer there are Bethlehems, times of growing up, wildernesses, and bursts of compassionate activity. There are also Good Fridays and Easter Days. If we take as our maxim, "Everything that happens to Christ happens to us," the Christian life won't always take

356

away our suffering and our hurt; but it will place them within the context of meaning and hope.—Alan Jones.

TRUE WORSHIP.   Were one to indulge in paradox, it is not too much to say that the most relevant thing about worship is its irrelevance. True worship is an act of liberation because it defies every criterion of utility by which our lives are too much bound.

This does not mean we should strive for irrelevance as an end in itself. Antiquarians who defend the use of esoteric language and obscure ceremony frequently emphasize the need for a sense of mystery in worship. But we should not mistake obfuscation for the Christian mystery. The Christian mystery is the presence of Christ among his people, the reality of the kingdom's presence because the king is present where two or three are gathered in his name. Whether in a rural Methodist chapel or in a cathedral's solemn high mass, everything done and said in Christian worship should be a manifestation of, a clear response to, and a clear pointing toward this mystery of Jesus the Christ encountering and accompanying his people on the way to the kingdom. Incense, vestments, chanting, tambourines, testimonials, dancing, and "Amen corners"—all are appropriate to the extent that they illuminate the mystery. The best form becomes perverse when it is merely a contrivance to create a "worshipful atmosphere" or to run tingly sensations up and down our spiritual spines.—Richard John Neuhaus.

CHRISTIAN COMMITMENT.   A church-related university had a powerful football team being led by a renowned coach and an unusually talented player who ran well, passed accurately, and also was the punter for the team. His leadership was affirmed by an incident that occurred in his sophomore year.

The team had played poorly one Saturday afternoon but had won the game. The coach was very unhappy with the play of the young man. In the postgame session, the coach plainly stated his displeasure by telling the team he was calling them to a Sunday morning practice session (an unusual event) to prepare for their touch opponent the next Saturday.

After the coach's announcement, the talented player raised his hand. The coach gave him permission to speak. The young man said, "Coach, I can't be there for practice in the morning, for I teach a class of boys in the Sunday school of my church." The coach then changed the practice to eleven o'clock. Again the young man raised his hand. "Coach," he said, "that is the time for the worship service, and I always sit with the boys in my class." The embarrassed coach then informed the team they would not have a Sunday practice but would work harder during the week.

After thinking it over the coach apologized on Monday to the team for his Saturday behavior and commended the player.

Following that experience, that talented football player was the team leader until his graduation. His fellow athletes and students sought his advice and counsel in moral and spiritual matters as well as football. He lived by his conviction that the Christian should always be concerned about doing the thing that will bring glory to Christ in every situation, because some other person is observing the behavior of one bearing the name of Christ.—Brooks Wester.

THE ART OF LIVING.   When we are young we dream big. We are going to sing like Luciano Pavarotti, dance like Patricia McBride, write like Maya Angelou, have the courtroom career of Louis Nizer, or the fastlike left of pitcher Ron Guidry. But then, say at age thirty-five, comes the cold shower, the sharp contrast between the dream and what became of it. Suddenly we realize we are not going to sing, dance, write, orate, or pitch like anyone but ourselves. It is discouraging but also creative; it is another important crisis of faith, for the art of Christian life is to take such defeats and turn them into the occasions for the victories God always had in mind for us. It is not God who wants us to seek status; through his love he has already given us that, and to each the same. God does not want us to prove, only to express, ourselves.—William Sloane Coffin.

GROWING BY SUFFERING.   Rembrandt was the most popular painter of his day until he was about thirty-five. He had the whole of Holland, virtually the whole of Europe, applauding him, clamoring for his work. He painted everybody of any distinction at all and could command any price he wished. Then, when he was about thirty-five, another painter came along—Van Dyke—more elegant than Rembrandt, easier for the general public to grasp and understand, and Rembrandt was rejected in favor of his more elegant successor. Then years before his death, he was forced to sell everything that he had, and he lived the last years of his life in poverty. "And yet," writes an art critic, "most of his finest painting belongs to those difficult years." He was finally rejected, but the rejection was not final. Somehow or other, you cannot help but feel that the rejection had something to do with the greatness that followed, that the rejection, as it were, pierced him and struck open a new vein so that the genius was greater than before.—Theodore Parker Ferris.

NEW CREATIONS IN CHRIST.   In Oxford there was a holy club; a group of young men seeking a way of upright and holy living, ruling their lives by moral rules and concerned with works. They were members of the Anglican church. John Wesley, one of their number, went to Georgia as a missionary clergyman. During the ocean voyage, a bad storm arose. This young man, himself fearful, was impressed by the calm and courage of a group of Moravian missionaries coming to America. Indeed, so impressed was he that he commented on it to one of the missionaries. The missionary asked Wesley, "Do you know Jesus Christ?" "I know that he is the Savior of the world," replied Wesley. "Yes," stated the missionary, "but do you know him?" John Wesley was sent searching. He spent some time in Georgia and then returned to England, a morally correct clergyman, keeping his rules, but dissatisfied. He found his way to a little Moravian meeting house in London, and there he felt his heart strangely moved by the love of Jesus. He became a new being, and John Wesley,

the fiery evangelist, was set free to serve others, to found the Methodist church, and to inculcate a new era of personal values and social concern in England and later in America. He became a new creation.—Eric C. Rust.

ETERNAL LIFE.   But again, we don't know the circumstances. We know only who, not what, is beyond the grave. This side of the grave, we are like the Swiss child asked by a traveler, "Where is Kandesteg?" The child answered, "I cannot tell you where Kandesteg is, but there is the road." We are on the road to heaven if today we walk with God. Eternal life is not a possession conferred at death, it is a present endowment. We live it now, and continue it through death.—William Sloane Coffin.

A GOOD SPORTSMAN.   Not only do good sportsmen or women play the game their best, but they keep themselves fit to play their best. When an athlete becomes a member of the football squad, he is put under training rules. There are certain foods that he is permitted to eat, whereas others are forbidden. Suppose I am entertaining a member of the football team. For dessert I serve a juicy piece of mince pie. I expect my guest to go for it eagerly, but he refuses it altogether. Why? Does he think it would be a sin to eat a bit of pie? No! Does he think the pie would kill him? No! He has been told that he might play the game better if he leaves off sweets. Therefore, he refuses the pie because he feels it his duty to be in the best form possible. This is perhaps the sanest test of what we may or may not do as Christians. There is no practice that is either right or wrong in itself. Shall I take this course or not? I can find help in my decision by asking this question: Will such a course help me to play the game or will it hinder? If it will help, I ought to take it; if it will hinder, I ought to reject it.—Clovis G. Chappell.

GOD IS THERE.   I know where there is a spring at the bottom of a hill. The water there is so fresh. The water runs out from under a bluff, sparkles over some gravel and stones, then runs under another bluff.

It is cool there. There is a big flat slab rock you can step out on and dip up a cup of the best water you may have ever tasted.

Sometimes when it rains the entire spring area fills up with muddy runoff water. The clear spring water is still there. If you could reach down through several feet of the runoff water with a TV camera you could see it. Before long the fresh water takes the muddy water away.

Sometimes we relate to God that way. There is muddy water covering the fresh water. Yet, God is always there. We gather to worship to have our cups filled to the overflowing. We come expectantly. God is there like the clear fresh water.—Earl Eden.

THE BEST MEMORIAL. Christopher Wren is the name that is remembered in London in connection with St. Paul's Cathedral. He was an inventor, mathematician, astronomer, draughtsman, and eventually London's most famous architect. After the Great Fire of London he drew up plans for a new city of London, but they were turned down. Instead, he designed the new St. Paul's Cathedral and supervised the building of it, as well as building or rebuilding fifty other churches, all different from each other.

Christopher Wren is buried in the great cathedral he designed. His epitaph, written by his son, reads, "If you would seek his monument look around you."—Eugene I. Enlow.

MINISTRY/SERVICE. Dr. Daniel Poling, then editor of the *Christian Herald,* once told a group in our church a story about his son. His son Clark was one of four chaplains who gave their life jackets to others and went down with a ship sunk by a German submarine torpedo during World War II.

Dr. Poling said having ministers in the family was a long family tradition. He hoped to perpetuate the tradition, but he felt so strongly that the ministry was a divine calling that he avoided the subject with his children. He nevertheless was disappointed when one by one his children went off to college and none of them mentioned the ministry among their plans. When Clark, the youngest son, came home from college, however, he announced a change in his vocational plans. God had called him to study for the ministry. Dr. Poling could not conceal his pleasure.

After seminary training Clark enlisted in the armed forces to serve his country. The night before he was to leave for a trip overseas, Clark spent some time with his father. Dr. Poling sat at his desk as his son paced the floor.

To be reassuring, Dr. Poling said, "Son, you may be sure I will pray daily for your safe return." His son's reply was: "Dad, I would rather that you not do that. My safe return might mean someone else would die in my place. I would rather have you pray that God would make me adequate for whatever ministry he calls me to perform."

On the day Clark and three other chaplains of different faiths gave their lives for others, God made him adequate. In his sacrificial self-giving to God and to his fellow countrymen, moreover, he showed he knew what ministry was about.—E. Earl Joiner.

WAYS TO PRAY. There is a need to cultivate a sensitivity to what gift God is giving: to learn to know when it is the time for free prayer, when for liturgical prayer, when to get out a book, when to shut up and be still in the presence of God, when to do not much more than sit in front of him and twiddle our thumbs. When we do not know how to pray, says Paul, "the Holy Spirit prays in us with sighs too deep for words, with unutterable groanings." If you are utterly parched and exhausted prayer may simply mean giving the Holy Spirit your body to groan in.—Geoffrey Preston.

LIVING THE TRUTH. Again we must ask ourselves if the devil has not persuaded us that the good should usurp the best because it is more realistic. At the outset of World War II, I stood with the poet Charles Peguy: "People who insist on keeping their hands clean are likely to find themselves without hands." And forty years later, I am still fearful of putting purity above relevance. But much has passed in forty years, and in the nuclear age it may be that nothing short of the best is relevant. As God is not mocked, we shouldn't be surprised that the day is dawning when the so-called ethics of perfection are becoming ethics of survival. When we live at each other's mercy, we had better learn to be merciful. If we don't learn to be meek, who is going to inherit the earth?—William Sloane Coffin.

LASTING INFLUENCE. In 1523 two young men in Brussels were burned at the stake. Their crime was their profession of the reformed faith; they refused to recant their affirmations of faith when threatened with death, and so they were martyred in the public square. In their honor and to celebrate the faith for which they died Martin Luther wrote the hymn, "A Mighty Fortress Is Our God," which for four hundred years has itself been a never-failing bulwark to those who trusted God in the day of adversity. Suppose the two young men of Brussels had run away. What a loss it would have been to the world! Two inconspicuous lives, counting for so much. Theirs was the courage to pray, "Not my will be done, but thine."—Halford E. Luccock.

PRUNING AND PREPARATION. Once when I was in upstate New York for a conference, I took my children on a tour of a vineyard. The guide pointed out that every vine is cut back during the coldest weeks of January. If this isn't done, the more productive plants take over and smother the others, eventually reducing the quality of the overall crop. Such cutback plants have long life spans. The ones left unpruned eventually stop producing quality grapes and die prematurely. The guide also noted that until a vine is seven years old, its grapes are not made into wine; only after years of pruning and patience does a crop reach its full sugar potential. During those first seven summers and winters the roots grow deep, becoming less and less vulnerable to root diseases. They intertwine with the root systems of other plants, and together they hold onto the nourishing topsoil.

God is not in a hurry. He deemed Moses ready to lead his people only after eighty years of training. Jesus was thirty when he started his public ministry. Paul spent the first few years of his Christian life in solitude and isolation. If we walk in the light, we will be pruned by the vinekeeper. —Harold L. Bussell.

THE SUFFERING GOD. Faith calls for an experience of atonement, calls for God to deal with evil. Christians hold that in the event of Calvary, God entered the darkness of human pain and changed it, made it glorious and redemptive, made it the instrument of deliverance and transformation. But for this to be so, it is necessary to see God in the pain and the dying. There must have been a Calvary in the heart of God before it could have been planted on that hill outside the city of Jerusalem. In Luther's words, "The absolute necessity for the sacrifice of the Son is grounded in God himself." Some Christian thinkers, such as Pascal, have spoken of Jesus being in agony until the end of time: for his suffering cannot cease until human liberation and human salvation has been fulfilled. So while the physical suffering of Jesus on Calvary occurred once and for all and can never be repeated, there is a prolonged sharing by God in the pain of humankind, God remains a suffering God, a passionate God.—Kenneth Leech.

A COVENANT. On February 28, 1638, the Scottish National Covenant was signed on parchment in Greyfriar's Churchyard, Edinburgh, as Christian men and women become Covenanters. That parchment, in possession of the Edinburgh Town Council today, shows that there are signatures in blood! Out of this came the Solemn League and Covenant in 1648 whereby the Reformed faith was affirmed in Scotland. In the Upper Room our Lord signed and sealed himself to his people. We now return that at the table of Communion when we observe the rite. This is the hour of our commitment anew to show our loyalty to him. We own that in the death of the cross he made us his own. Gladly we stand at the salute and in fealty we pledge our lives in return!—Ralph G. Turnbull.

BARRIERS IN PRAYER. I once had a friend who was inclined to be overweight but always wanted to be thin. One day she confessed to me her motivation. The thought in her mind always was, "I'll fix them. I'll get fat." Fatness was her response to personal hurts and rejections. It is sometimes the same in our relationship to God.

"I'll fix him. I won't pray." But who is really the loser by this rejection of God's love? In prayer, what the Lord offers us is an intense perception of his tenderness and care. We may insist that when we pray we don't feel anything at all. But we should also be honest enough to admit that when we don't feel anything, it may be because of the walls we have built to protect ourselves against rejection, the layers, the walls, the defenses against the possibility of being hurt. To remove these barriers in prayer takes time and will not come in a moment or a day.—Emilio Griffin.

FRUITFUL SUFFERING. I say that no man or woman is fit for the highest offices of friendship and of life until he or she has had a full experience of suffering. I do not say that there are not admirable people who never have suffered; but I say that they would be more admirable, good as they are, if they had suffered more. I do say that suffering is necessary to turn the acids of life into sugar—to make the saps sweet. I do say that suffering should be to human dispositions what the early frosts of autumn are to the almost ripened leaves, which turn them into gorgeous colors and fill the whole sky with the tokens of coming death and glorious beauty.

A vine that is left to ramble till it grows all over the treetop, is not half so much a vine as one that is cut back skillfully, and laid in fair proportions on the trellis, and tied there. And a man that has his own way, and rambles just as his affections choose to go, is not half so much a man as one whom God has tenderly pruned, and cut back, and laid, and tied in. In the case of the man, as in that of the vine, the one that is wisely checked and trained becomes more fruitful, and the fruit becomes better.—Henry Ward Beecher.

FORGIVENESS. A wife and husband were having a heated conversation about something that had come between them. The husband said to his wife, "I thought you had forgiven me." She replied, "I did, but I don't want you to forget that I have forgiven and forgotten what you have done to me." It is a devillike thing to return evil for good, and it is a Godlike thing to return good for evil. It reveals you to be a spiritual child of your heavenly Father. If we are not willing to forgive those who sin against us, "neither," said Jesus, "will your Father forgive your trespasses" (Matt. 6:15).—Friedrich Rest.

GOD'S HELPERS. Recently I was told the story of a tiny child who wanted to help his father garden. The father knew that there was nothing the toddler could do to help him, but he loved to involve his little son in his activities. Loading the wheelbarrow with earth, he invited the youngster to reach up and take hold of its handles. Then, placing his own strong hands over the little one's weak ones, he "helped" him to push the barrow to the flower bed he was preparing. Although the child's fragile strength could contribute nothing to the task, he grew in spirit and in oneness with his father as he shared his activity and participated in his life.

And so it is with God's children. As we come to God in Jesus' name, praying as he prayed, our wills in submission to his, God lets us place our puny hands on his great purposes—purposes too lofty for our finite minds to comprehend—and participate in carrying out his plan. Graciously covering our feeble prayers with his sovereignty. He pushes the barrow where he will until his purpose is accomplished. —Margaret Clarkson.

SHARING CHRIST. When I was a small boy and had just become a Christian myself, I did not know the plan of salvation well enough to explain it to someone else, but I did know Jesus Christ personally. So I shared my testimony with a close friend who was ten years old. I told him my story of conversion, and to my knowledge that was the beginning of his serious interest in Christ. Soon he received Jesus as his Savior, too. I didn't know a single verse to share with him, but I had met the person whom he needed to know. That introduction is the beginning place for evangelism. We are not merely sharing facts, but a living person.—Billie Hanks, Jr.

HONEST QUESTIONS. I have a friend who often says, "Never be afraid of a person who is asking questions. Fear only those who say they have all the answers." That's sound advice. So often we are disturbed by young people who dare to challenge the most sacred ideas of our faith. Why should we be so fearful? Do we have a faith that will not withstand the honest inquiry of an intelligent mind? If the great ideas of religion are not sturdy enough to stand examination, can they survive in our kind of world? Honest questioning is often the beginning of a healthy faith. Instead of stifling such inquiries, we should encourage them.—Ernest A. Fitzgerald.

COOPERATION. Cecil Myers reports a definition of a happy home as given by a thirteen-year-old boy: "A happy home is like a baseball team, with Mom pitching, Dad catching, the kids fielding, and everyone taking a turn at bat."—Ernest A. Fitzgerald.

THE RESURRECTION. Rather than becoming disturbed over the kind of body we will have in the resurrection, Paul advised us to trust God, who has so expertly fashioned the various forms that we can know and observe in this life, to give us the kind of body we will need in the life to come. Whatever it is like, it will not be the same expendable, earthly body that we know here, but rather a spiritual body partaking of the nature of God's own heavenly glory. We get some inkling of God's ability to transform life when we study the garden caterpillar which, through the process of metamorphosis, is transformed into the beautiful butterfly. If God can work this change, then surely he can take care of our needs in the resurrection.—Batsell Barrett Baxter.

THE TRUTH. Ed Heacock was a builder of beautiful custom homes in our city. Several years before he died of cancer, he accepted Jesus Christ as his Lord and Savior, and the experience revolutionized his life. One day I asked him, "Ed, what changes have you noticed in your life since you became a Christian?" He replied, "The way I go to the telephone. In fact, I was thinking of it last night as my son called me to the phone to talk to a woman for whom I am building a house. Previously I would be racking my brain, trying to recall what I had said in our last conversation. Instead, I walked calmly to the phone, knowing that whatever she asked, I would give the same answer I did last time—the truth."—Tim LaHaye.

MEETING NEEDS. As a parent I am not responsible for meeting all the needs of my children. If my son breaks his arm, I don't set it. But I am responsible for seeing that the needs of my children are met. I will take him to a doctor and have him set the arm. The same principle applies to discipling. Others in Christ's body will help meet the needs of those whom you are seeking to influence.—Walter A. Henrichsen and William N. Garrison.

CHRISTIAN SERVICE. We come down history years and see a young man, wealthy, arrogant, richly appareled, and mounted upon a splendid horse. As he passed by, he flung a reward to the sore-covered beggar by the wayside and went on his way. Then something happened. He met Jesus Christ. He then took the road of service, stopped by the wayside to wash and bind up the beggar's wounds, and spent himself in the service of his fellows. Francis of Assissi became the joyful troubadour of God and founded a new order of Christian service. He saw the world differently and lived from a new life center.—Eric C. Rust.

SEEING LIFE WHOLE. There are stars that can be seen only in the northern sky, as the North Star itself and the constellations of the Big and the Little Dipper, and there are those that can be seen only in the southern sky, as in the constellation of the Southern Cross, and there are those that can be seen in both, as the constellation of

Orion the Hunter. Thus, when I travel to the southern hemisphere, I come to see stars and constellations I have never seen before, although I see also the continuity and the overlap of the northern and southern sky. So too, when I pass over into another's life, I see events and patterns of events I have never seen before, although I see a continuity and an overlap of my life and the other's. I come by traveling to see the whole sky over time and all the stars that are visible to the naked eye. So too, I come by passing over to see human existence as a whole and all the things that belong to a human life.—John S. Dunne

PROBLEM OF LISTENING. Despite all the assurances of how easy it is to learn Morse code, it can be exceedingly difficult. To obtain a radio operator's general license, the candidate must be able to send and receive the code at thirteen words per minute. When the Federal Communications Commission examiner tests a candidate, he simply monitors his ability to receive the code at thirteen words per minute. The assumption is that if one can receive messages at that speed he will certainly be able to transmit them at that speed. No test, therefore, is given for the ability to send messages.

The Morse code testing procedures highlight the one great principle of human-to-human communication—it is much easier to send than to receive.—John W. Drakeford.

GOD IN THE DEPTHS. How late I came to love you, O beauty so ancient and so fresh, how late I came to love you! You were within me while I had gone outside to seek you. Unlovely myself, I rushed towards all those lovely things you had made. And always you were with me, I was not with you. All these beauties kept me far from you—although they would not have existed at all unless they had their being in you. You called, you cried, you shattered my deafness. You sparkled, you blazed, you drove away my blindness. You shed your fragrance, and I drew in my breath and I pant for you. I tasted and now I hunger and thirst. You touched me and now I burn with longing for your peace. —St. Augustine.

AN UNCERTAIN FUTURE. A businessman was permitted to have any one wish come true. After some thought, he wished for a newspaper dated two years in the future. Miraculously the paper was placed in his hand. Turning to the stock reports, he made careful notes on stocks that had shown unusual growth. He would make a fortune! As he closed the paper, his eyes caught the obituary column of the paper. To his dismay, his name was there. The paper said he had suffered a heart attack, and his funeral arrangements were spelled out in detail before him.—Brian L. Harbour.

WHOLENESS AND HOLINESS. When I think of wholeness in my own life, I think of a finely tuned orchestra in which each instrument, guided by the conductor, contributes its part toward a magnificent symphony of sound. There are times—and in recent years, increasing times—when I have heard this sound and I know that I am in tune with the Spirit of God who moves within me. Sometimes the sound is discordant, even harsh, but it is nonetheless one sound. This is wholeness. It can include themes of joy and themes of pain, but there is still one sound. This is very different from what happens when the instruments that represent the many-faceted aspects of my personality are playing in opposition to each other. When this happens, I experience inner chaos and confusion—the very opposite of wholeness. The answer is not to play louder, nor to pretend we do not hear, but rather to take time to listen to the many sounds so that the message they contain can be brought to light. The inner freedom the gospel promises is experienced when our identity in Christ is honored and trusted and nourished. It is experienced when our inner lives are in tune, not in the sense of having arrived, but rather in the sense of being able to hear and respond to the themes and rhythms that the Spirit offers in calling us out of ourselves. The journey in Christ is a journey shaped by the biblical story of salvation in which is embodied a will to holiness.—James C. Fenhagen.

THE POWER OF A GOAL.   A goal stimulates excitement, energy, motivation, and effort. In fact, the capacity to grow results in part from anticipating and acting in terms of a future goal. Commitment to an idea or goal facilitates concentration of attention and efforts, helps provide the courage to take calculated risks in order to overcome inhibitions and to master fear of failure. The secret of Edison's intensity of effort, which led him to invent not only the electric light but also the phonograph, electric locomotive, microphone, electric pen, and cinematography, was in setting one goal at a time and adapting his life to it.—Ari Kiev.

THE FINALITY OF CHRIST.   This recapitulation of all things in Jesus Christ, at the end of the process of history, is already taking place in the world. It is personal experience that when the entries in the book of men's lives are brought under the heading of Jesus Christ, many a transaction which seemed at the time to be gain will be seen really to have been loss, while others that seemed at the time to have been loss will be seen to be gain. Besides, because this life and activity of Jesus Christ is his life and activity in the world, it is meaningful to speak too of human cultures being recapitulated in him and through him. Thus, when an Indian thinker speaks of "wedding the Spirit of Christ with the spirit of India," he is asking that Christ's presence in India be discerned so that that which belongs to India may be brought into his obedience and into the service of his glory. "They shall bring [unto Zion] the glory and the honor of the nations" (Rev. 21:26).—D. T. Niles.

JESUS AS VICTOR.   The light of Christ was not extinguished by the power of darkness that apparently snuffed it out; that is the good news on which the whole Christian message is fundamentally based. Christian imagination has richly embroidered this amazing story of a divine defeat and surrender that led at last to a divine victory. Christ has been represented in Christian legend as descending into hell to ransom the captives of the prince of darkness. He goes as a defeated prisoner of war, so to speak, but his grim captor presently discovers that he cannot hold this prisoner. Clad in light, Christ moves at will in Satan's dark domains. He preaches to the spirits in prison and liberates the righteous patriarchs from the limbo where they have been awaiting his advent. The devil is cheated! Mankind is ransomed by Christ's captivity to the powers of darkness, but the sinless Christ cannot long be "holden of death" and reascends to the right hand of God.

I for one value this ancient Christian legend, and I do not bracket the descent into hell when I encounter it in the Apostles' Creed. It seems to me characteristic of the real Spirit of Jesus to go to the very bottom of the evil in the world, wherever that bottom may be, and to break the power of evil in the world by suffering that power its most infernal intensity.—Walter Marshall Horton.

HIDDEN SPRINGS.   "Dick" Sheppard, greatly loved dean of Canterbury Cathedral and rector of St. Martin-in-the-Fields, London, carried during his all-too-brief life incredible burdens of unhappiness and heavy responsibility; yet he was always keenly and vibrantly alive. His exuberant faith and winsome vitality were contagious. Ellis Roberts says of him, "That stream of unceasing refreshment [which always flowed from him] depended for its powers on deep hidden springs, on its renewal from the melted snows of lonely and distant heights of the spirit." Sheppard's secret was the lonely and distant heights of the spirit to which he went for renewal.—Halford E. Luccock.

UNINTIMIDATED.   On October 20, 1743, John Wesley was busy writing in the home of Francis Ward after preaching in the streets of Wednesbury, England. Suddenly a mob appeared outside the house demanding, "Bring out the minister; we will have the minister." John Wesley went boldly out to the crowd, whereupon they seized him and after two magistrates refused to deal with him the crowd from three towns took matters into their own hands and for six hours dragged him through the streets, striking him and flinging all manner of rubbish and filth at him. During all this time Wesley was at the mercy of the hooligans who roared, "Kill him! Drown him! Throw him in the pit!" His escape was a miracle. But after an interval of a few months he was back in Staffordshire again, preaching in the streets in which he had been scourged. Methodist societies were organized and the foundations laid for the church that was to awaken all of Protestantism to new life. —Halford E. Luccock.

THE MASTERY OF TIME. Carlyle noted that "It is one of the illusions that the present hour is not the critical decisive hour. Write it on your heart that every day is the best day in the year." Each day provides opportunity for self-renewal. Today's accomplishments, not yesterday's, produce the most satisfaction. What you accomplish today can give you an immediate sense of self-mastery and direction.—Ari Kiev.

INDEX OF CONTRIBUTORS

SERMON TITLE INDEX

(Children's stories and sermons are identified cs; sermon suggestions ss)

SCRIPTURAL INDEX

INDEX OF PRAYERS

INDEX OF MATERIALS USEFUL AS CHILDREN'S STORIES AND SERMONS NOT INCLUDED IN SECTION X

INDEX OF MATERIALS USEFUL FOR SMALL GROUPS

INDEX OF SPECIAL DAYS AND SEASONS

TOPICAL INDEX

ACKNOWLEDGMENTS

Acknowledgment and gratitude are hereby expressed to the following for kind permission to reprint material from books and periodicals listed below:

ABINGDON PRESS: Excerpts from *Making Friends with Life* and *The Temple in the Heart*, by James Reid.

C. S. S. PUBLISHING COMPANY: Children's sermons, "Time to Be Quiet," "This Is My Son," "Something's in the Way." Copyright © 1985. "Now We Can See," "When to Say No," Copyright © 1986. Used by permission.

CHURCH EDUCATOR: Extract from article, "Family Christmas Dinner," by John-Herbert Jaffry, November 1985, page 11. Copyright © 1985 by Educational Ministries, Inc., Used with permission.

CHURCH MANAGEMENT: THE CLERGY JOURNAL: Extract from article, "Volunteers: Appreciation." Copyright © 1985 by Church Management, Inc., P.O. Box 1625, Austin, TX 78767. Used with permission.

CHURCH TEACHERS: Excerpted material from Volume 11, Number 3, November/December 1983, page 90; Volume 12, Number 1, June/August 1984, page 7; and Volume 13, Number 2, September/October 1985, page 7. Used by special permission. *Church Teachers,* 7214 East Granada Road, Scottsdale, Arizona 85257.

CONSULTATION ON COMMON TEXTS: Bible references from the *Common Lectionary: The Lectionary Proposed by the Consultation on Common Texts,* copyright © 1983, James M. Schellman. Used with permission.

EXPOSITORY TIMES: Excerpts from a sermon by the Rev. James S. Stewart, "The Ultimate Dilemma," *Expository Times,* Vol. LIV. No. 6, March 1943, page 160.

GROUP: Digest of articles, "Youth Dial-A-Devotion," "Hunger Scavenger Hunt," and "Youth Group Greeting Card," from January 1985, March-April 1985, and June-August 1985. Reprinted by permission from Group Magazine, copyright © 1985, Thom Schultz Publications, Inc., Box 481, Loveland, Colorado 80539.

HARPER & ROW, PUBLISHERS, INC.: Digest of sermons by Harold A. Bosley, "The Lost Secret of Great Religion," *Sermons on the Psalms,* Harper & Bros., 1956, pp. 118ff., and "Shall We Be Patient with Evil?" *He Spoke to Them in Parables,* Harper & Row, 1963, pp. 124ff. Digest of sermon by W. R. Bowie, "The Man Who Digged Old Wells," *Great Men of the Bible,* Harper & Bros, 1937, pp. 25ff. Digest of sermons by Charles R. Brown, "Matthew: The Man of Business," *Those Twelve,* Harper & Bros., 1926, pp. 115ff, and "The Positive Life," *Being Made Over,* Harper & Bros., 1939, pp. 105ff. Digest of sermons by W. A. Cameron, "The Reality of the Unseen," and "Shadows," *The Gift of God,* Geo. H. Doran Co., 1925, pp. 78–87, 178–190. Digest of sermons by Clovis G. Chappell, "The Works of the Road—Moses," *Sermons on Old Testament Characters,* Harper & Bros., 1925, pp. 70–80, and "The Waste Basket—Paul," *Sermons on N.T. Characters,* Harper & Bros., 1924, pp. 108ff. Digest of sermon by Geo. M. Docherty, "The Silence of God," *One Way of Living,* Harper & Bros., 1958, pp. 103ff. Digest of sermon by Nels F. S. Ferre, "I Am Sure," *God's New Age,* Harper & Bros., 1962, pp. 92ff. Portions of prayers by H. E. Fosdick, *A Book of Public Prayers,* Harper & Brothers, 1959, pp. 64–65, 126–127, 136–137, and 180–181. Digest of sermons by H. E. Fosdick, *The Hope of the World,* Harper & Brothers, 1933, pp. 59ff, and "The Power to See It Through," *The Power to See It Through,* Harper & Bros., 1935, pp. 28ff. Digest of sermon by Edgar DeWitt Jones, "His Jerusalem and Ours," *Sermons I Love to Preach,* Harper & Bros., 1953, pp. 105ff. Digest of sermon by Gerald Kennedy, "There Came

One Running," *Fresh Every Morning,* Harper & Row, 1966, pp. 177f. Excerpts from "Life's Indispensable Portion," *The Importance of Being Ourselves,* by Arnold H. Lowe, Harper & Brothers, 1948, pp. 32ff. Digest of sermon by David A. McLennan, "Mankind's Unfailing Lamp," *Joyous Adventure,* Harper & Bros., 1952, pp. 46ff. Digest of sermon by F. W. Robertson, *Robertson's Sermons,* Harper & Bros., n.d., pp. 555ff. Digest of sermons by Paul Scherer, "A Visitor from Nazareth," *When God Hides,* Harper & Bros., 1934, pp. 10–17, "Your Part in God's Plan," *The Place Where Thou Standest,* Harper & Bros., 1942, pp. 150ff, and "Accepting Yourself," *Facts that Undergird Life,* Harper & Bros., 1938, pp. 61ff. Digest of sermon by Helmut Thielieke, "The Parable of the Importunate Widow," *Christ and the Meaning of Life,* Harper & Bros., Harper & Bros., 1962, pp. 84ff. An essay by D. Elton Trueblood, "Forgiveness of the Unworthy," *Comforting Christ,* Harper & Bros, 1960, pp. 11–12.

LEADERSHIP: Excerpts from articles, "Help for Modern Ruths," "You Scratch My Back . . . (or Cater Our Dinner)," and "Sunday Morning Questions and Answers," copyright © 1985, *Leadership,* and "Easter Echoes," copyright © 1984, *Leadership.* Used by permission.

LEADERSHIP 100: Excerpts from articles, "A Family Sunday School Class," "Parents and Teens Throw a FIT," and "The Conference That Refreshes," copyright © 1982, *Leadership 100.* Used by Permission.

SHARING THE PRACTICE: Digest of article, "Prayer Support for Confirmands," Volume VIII, No. 1, January-February-March 1985, pp. 39–40. Published by the Academy of Parish Clergy. Used with permission.

SUNDAY SCHOOL BOARD OF THE SOUTHERN BAPTIST CONVENTION: From *Adult Life and Work Lesson Annual,* 1984–85. © Copyright 1984 The Sunday School Board of the Southern Baptist Convention. All rights reserved. Used by permission: Illustration by Brooks Wester from commentary for Sept. 1, 1985. From *Advanced Bible Study* July-Sept., 1985. © Copyright 1984 The Sunday School Board of the Southern Baptist Convention. All rights reserved. Used by permission: Illustrations by Eric C. Rust, pp. 11 and 81–82. From *Adult Bible Teacher,* July-Sept. 1985. © Copyright 1985 The Sunday School Board of the Southern Baptist Convention. All rights reserved. Used by permission: Illustration by Earl Joiner, pp. 101–102. From *Award Winning Sermons,* Vol. 1. © Copyright 1977 The Sunday School Board of the Southern Baptist Convention. All rights reserved. Used by permission: Excerpts from a sermon by Earl C. Davis, "A Portrait of God's Love," pp. 41–46. From *Award Winning Sermons,* Vol. 2. © Copyright 1978 The Sunday School Board of the Southern Baptist Convention. All rights reserved. Used by permission: Digest of sermon by C. David Matthews, "The Christian's Cross," pp. 47ff. From *Award Winning Sermons,* Vol. 3. © Copyright 1979 The Sunday School Board of the Southern Baptist Convention. All rights reserved. Used by permission: Digest of sermon by Welton Gaddy, "Work in Christian Perspective," pp. 11ff. From *Award Winning Sermons,* Vol. 4. © Copyright 1980 The Sunday School Board of the Southern Baptist Convention. All rights reserved. Used by permission: Digest of sermon by Roger Lovette, "The Great Hinges," pp. 59ff. From *Open Windows,* Vol. 50, No. 1, October-December 1985. © Copyright 1985 The Sunday School Board of the Southern Baptist Convention. All rights reserved. Used by permission: Devotionals by Harold Dye, "Goodness and Mercy," (Nov. 26, 1985), "The Great Supper" (Oct. 17, 1985), "Trust Your Guide" (Oct. 25, 1985), and "John Baptizes Jesus" (Oct. 13, 1985). From *Proclaim.* © Copyright The Sunday School Board of the Southern Baptist Convention. All rights reserved. Used by permission: Sermons by Craig Skinner, "Little Things Are Important," 1 Sam. 9–10, "The Angel Who Made Men Cry," Judges 2:1–7, "The Thumb and Toe Specialist," Judges 1:4–7; Oct. 1979, pp. 12–13, p. 13, and pp. 13–14; sermon by Roger Lovette, Oct/Nov/Dec. 1983, pp. 27–28; Sermons by Don M. Aycock, "Christian Duplications," and "Loving God with the Mind," Jan/Feb/Mar., 1984, pp. 37, 38, and 39. Sermon by David M. Jones, July/Aug./Sept., 1985, p. 26. From *Sunday*